The Religious Architecture of Islam

The Religious Architecture of Islam   Volume I
of Islam   Asia and Australia

Edited by **HASAN-UDDIN KHAN & KATHRYN BLAIR MOORE**

With contributions by
ABEER HUSSAM EDDIN ALLAHAM
NEZAR ALSAYYAD
IMDAT AS
SHEILA BLAIR
MEGAN BOOMER
KATHRYN BLAIR MOORE
FARSHID EMAMI
TAMMY GABER
MATTIA GUIDETTI
AKEL ISMAIL KAHERA
HASAN-UDDIN KHAN
MELANIE MICHAILIDIS
HEBA MOSTAFA
STEPHENNIE MULDER

KAMIL KHAN MUMTAZ
BERNARD O'KANE
ROBERT OUSTERHOUT
OYA PANCAROĞLU
LAURA E. PARODI
ALKA PATEL
ALI UZAY PEKER
D. FAIRCHILD RUGGLES
MATTHEW SABA
JAMES STEELE
NANCY S. STEINHARDT
IMRAN BIN TAJUDEEN
MICHAEL A. TOLER
İPEK TÜRELI
ZEYNEP YÜREKLI

BREPOLS

Copyright © 2021 Brepols Publishers, Turnhout, Belgium.

All rights reserved. No part of this publication may be reproduced
or transmitted in any form or by any means, electronic or
mechanical, including photocopy, recording or any other
information storage or retrieval system, without prior permission
in writing from the publisher.

ISBN 978-2-503-58935-0
D/2021/0095/264

Designed by Paul van Calster

Printed in the EU on acid-free paper.

Contents

Hasan-Uddin Khan and Kathryn Blair Moore

Introduction   7

BACKGROUND THEMES

Heba Mostafa
Locating the Sacred in Early Islamic Architecture   12

Nezar AlSayyad and İpek Türeli
The Mosque in the Urban Context   24

D. Fairchild Ruggles
Gardens as Places of Piety and Faith   34

Imdat As
*Complex Patterns and Three-Dimensional Geometry
in Islamic Religious Architecture*   48

Matthew Saba and Michael A. Toler
Archives and Archival Documents in the Study of Islamic Religious Architecture   62

WEST AND CENTRAL ASIA

Abeer Hussam Eddin Allahham
The Holy Mosque of Mecca   84

Akel Ismail Kahera
The Mosque of the Prophet at Medina   100

Kathryn Blair Moore
The Dome of the Rock through the Centuries   108

Mattia Guidetti
The Great Mosque of Damascus through the Medieval Period   124

Mattia Guidetti
Early Islam and Byzantine Churches   138

Melanie Michailidis
Early Mosques in Iran and Central Asia   148

Matthew Saba
*Funerary Architecture in Iraq under the Abbasids
and their Successors, 750–1250*   160

Megan Boomer and Robert Ousterhout
Muslims, Byzantines, and Western Christians on the Haram al-Sharif   174

Stephennie Mulder
Mosques under the Ayyubids   188

Stephennie Mulder
Shrines in the Central Islamic Lands   196

Melanie Michailidis
Shrines and Mausolea in Iran and Central Asia   214

Sheila Blair
The Ilkhanids and their Successors   226

Bernard O'Kane
Religious Architecture of Central Asia under the Timurids and their Successors   242

Farshid Emami
Religious Architecture of Safavid Iran   256

Oya Pancaroğlu
Islamic Architecture in Medieval Anatolia, 1150–1450   274

Zeynep Yürekli
Three Sufi Shrines under the Ottomans   298

Ali Uzay Peker
Seljuk and Ottoman Mosques   314

Imdat As
Kocatepe: The Unbuilt State Mosque of Turkey   328

James Steele
Regionalist Expressions of the Mosque in the Arabian Peninsula and Middle East   338

SOUTH AND EAST ASIA   Alka Patel
The Sultanates in South Asia, 700–1690   356

Laura E. Parodi
Mughal Religious Architecture   372

Kamil Khan Mumtaz
Badshahi Masjid, Lahore   392

Kamil Khan Mumtaz
The Architecture of Sufi Shrines in Pakistan   400

Imran bin Tajudeen
Pre-Islamic and Vernacular Elements in the Southeast Asian Mosques of Nusantara   408

Nancy S. Steinhardt
The Mosque in China   428

Hasan-Uddin Khan
The Great Mosque of Xi'an (Qing Zhen Si)   446

AUSTRALIA   Tammy Gaber
New Australian Mosques   456

Glossary   474
Index   477

Introduction
HASAN-UDDIN KHAN & KATHRYN BLAIR MOORE

The religious architecture of Islam is fundamental to our understanding of architectural traditions because it often expresses in physical terms the cultural aspirations of the faith. Here we present an overview of the religious built environment of Muslims across the globe and over the course of time. This work does not try to be encyclopedic, but instead aims to be comprehensive enough so to allow for an exploration of the full range, breadth, and depth of diverse Muslim cultures and their expression in architecture. We bring together the historic and contemporary aspects of Islamic religious architecture within one publication, with the aim of creating a new understanding of the links between the past and present.

Each essay gathered in these two volumes addresses the fundamental question of the relationship between architecture and the religion of Islam. There are numerous publications on mosque architecture throughout the world, but these volumes were instead conceived to address a wider range of building types, like religious schools, saints' tombs, and Sufi shrines. At the same time, we sought innovative studies that reflect the ever-expanding geographical scope of the study of Islamic architecture, particularly in regions previously considered peripheral to or completely outside of the history of Islamic architecture, like Eastern Europe, Coastal Africa, and Western China in the historical periods, and Europe, the Americas, and Australia in the modern and contemporary periods. As the project grew, we decided to divide the materials into two volumes, the first addressing Asia and Australia, and the second addressing Europe and the Americas. Each volume proceeds roughly chronologically from the earliest centuries of Islam through the contemporary period.

At the outset, we also wished to draw attention to themes that are common to the religious architecture of Islam across all regions of the world. To that end, we open Volume 1 with a series of introductory essays that address basic terms and types in the history of Islamic religious architecture, the significance of mosques in urban contexts, the dynamic relationship between gardens and architecture, the use of two- and three-dimensional geometry in Islamic societies, and the role that archives have played in researching the history of Islamic religious architecture. This final introductory subject on archival research reflects the forward-looking nature of our project.

Within each of the volumes dedicated to Asia and Australia (Volume 1) or Africa, Europe, and the Americas (Volume 2), the authors approach their subjects diachronically. Instead of a single unitary chronology charted from the beginnings of Islam in the Arabian Peninsula through the contemporary period, we have gathered studies that consider individual buildings or groups of buildings in their own relative chronologies, unique to regional histories and localized cultural dynamics. Often links are made between regional histories and the study of individual buildings, for example between the broader examination of architecture in China and the study of the Xi'an mosque, or between the religious landscape in the Balkans and the Šerefudin White Mosque in Bosnia-Herzegovina. In Volume 1, the Kaaba in Mecca and the Dome of the Rock in Jerusalem, or in Volume 2 the Great Mosque of Cordoba and Britain's first mosque at Woking, for example, are each presented in their own essays, in which the authors explore the dynamic histories of each building over time.

Other essays engage a flexible chronological and geographical scheme, by incorporating a territory of history that is not purely Islamic. These studies consider the role of architecture in complex spaces of cultural encounter and adaptation: for example, in Volume 1, the history of the role of Byzantine churches in the religious architecture of early Islam in Syria, or in Volume 2, the history of the adaptation of Balkan churches into mosques in the Ottoman period. Some essays also directly address the heterogenous conceptions of religious architecture within Islam itself, for example by exploring the role of saints' shrines and contemporary issues such as the space for women in places of worship. What emerges is a diverse and expansive conception of Islamic religious architecture, that is suggestive of potential pathways for new and ongoing research.

This project was initiated over a decade ago, with a comparative approach of worldwide scope. The larger project, which was never realized in its intended form, was to gather complementary histories of the religious architecture of the major religions of the world across time. The project was initially conceptualized by Richard Etlin and then developed with other scholars whose expertise pertained to the different religions of the world: for Islam, with Hasan-Uddin Khan and Cynthia Robinson. Although that ambitious project could not be realized, these two volumes dedicated to the religious architecture of Islam are ultimately rooted in the larger comparative approach to the religious architecture of the world. We have retained the peer-reviewed aspect of the earlier project to ensure its scholarly soundness. We ultimately hope that the studies in these two volumes lay the groundwork for future research and publications that will continue to engage with an expanding notion of Islamic religious architecture.

ACKNOWLEDGEMENTS

First and foremost, we thank all the authors who participated in what turned out to be a decade-long endeavor. The original project was conceived to include some thirty-seven authors. We are grateful to them for remaining involved in the work and in many cases revising and updating their texts and images. Unfortunately, two of our authors, Omar Khalidi and Melanie Michailidis, passed away before they could see their essays in print, but we are pleased to be able to honor their work in this publication. We are also pleased to have been able to add ten new authors who have expanded the work and added to its richness. We remain in awe of the scholarship and erudition of all of our authors.

We are grateful to our publisher Brepols, who supported the reconceived volumes. Working with Johan Van der Beke who facilitated our every move has been a pleasure; without his input this work would have been less complete. Our thanks also to the architectural historian Areli Marina, who introduced co-editor Kathryn Moore to Johan regarding this project. We commend the book designer, Paul van Calster, for his inspired and painstaking work.

Our thanks to Richard Etlin for his continuing advice even after the original publication did not materialize. Several others advised us over the years; here we mention Nezar AlSayyad, Mohammad Gharipour, Sheila Blair, and Jonathan Bloom for their support and suggestions. We are also appreciative of the Aga Khan Award for Architecture and the Aga Khan Archive at MIT for allowing us the free use of their materials and illustrations in the two volumes. As editors, we have enjoyed our collaboration.

The publication of this volume in full color was made possible by a generous grant from the University of Connecticut's School of Fine Arts.

Hasan-Uddin Khan and Kathryn Blair Moore
Providence, Rhode Island, June 2021

NOTE ON THE TEXT

When possible, we have sought to maintain consistency in the transliteration of terms from other languages; however, we have also allowed authors to use different transliterations, especially as a way of reflecting regional variations in Arabic and other languages. Throughout both volumes, we have italicized foreign terms, especially to indicate that definitions for those terms can be found in the glossaries. There are two glossaries, found at the end of each volume. Each glossary is tailored to its own volume. Here too, we used the most common spellings, but have also indicated alternatives as used by our authors. Unless otherwise indicated, all terms defined in the Glossary are Arabic. All dates, unless otherwise indicated, are in the Common Era (CE).

Background Themes

Locating the Sacred in Early Islamic Architecture HEBA MOSTAFA

1 Great Mosque of Cordoba, view of prayer hall.
Photo: Heba Mostafa

With tendencies towards abstraction and aniconism, early Islamic sacred spaces must have seemed revolutionary to a late antique audience accustomed to mediated and restricted access to the sacred in the form of inner sanctums in temples or icons in churches. Driven by nuanced and elusive notions of the sacred, Islam's earliest devotional spaces only obliquely invoke the sacred spatially and pictorially and privileged communal ritual practice in non-hierarchical spaces.[1] In the Islamic conception of the world, the "entire world is a place of prostration (*masjid*) and a place to purify,"[2] proclaiming nature, as God's creation, inherently sacralized. In this worldview the sacred and non-sacred co-exist along a continuum rather than a disjointed and opposed duality.[3] In fact, some of the earliest and most sophisticated sacred sites in terms of iconography and ritual practice venerate and derive their sanctity from objects in nature, such as Mount Moriah in Jerusalem, which over time housed the Jewish Temple and today is the site of the sacred enclosure known as the Haram al-Sharif (noble sanctuary) (Fig. 2). As a locale with a layered history dating back to creation, few coeval sites of memory compare in terms of iconographic complexity, longevity as loci of ritual practice, and richness of sacral histories as this sacred mountain. Although its sanctity has been distilled to its exposed summit, commemorated by the Umayyad Dome of the Rock completed in 692, the sanctity of the rock (*ṣakhra*), is also elusive.[4] This ambiguity around sacral mystique in early Islamic sacred space certainly problematizes the fundamental question of how and where the sacred resides in early Islamic architecture, but also offers opportunities to re-conceptualize approaches to the sacred in early Islam.

Early Islamic sacred spaces fall along a spectrum of sacrality in three categories that can be variably conceptualized. The first encompasses the exalted *loca sancta* of Islam, and includes the Masjid al-Haram in Mecca, the Haram al-Sharif in Jerusalem, and the Mosque of the Prophet in Medina.[5] As sacred enclosures housing central shrines or mosques, they are inherently sacred to Muslims and have served as the focus for pilgrimage and veneration since Islam's inception. As God's chosen houses, their sanctity was strengthened by narrative and encoded through ritual practice through time.[6] The second includes the congregational mosques and other sites of ritual practice such as the neighborhood mosque and *muṣalla* (urban outdoor prayer spaces).[7] By virtue of accommodating Friday prayer, mosques exist within the realm of the sacred, but as they also served varied functions from the time of the Prophet Muhammad, such as teaching, adjudication, and refuge, sacrality at the mosque requires an acceptance of a broader definition of the term.[8] Mosques are often associated with foundation legends and further sanctified through an association with relics or other sacred events, such as the Friday Mosque in Kufa or the Great Mosque of Damascus.[9] The third is commemorative and includes funerary shrines and other *loca sancta* identified with sacral events in Islam, including shrines dedicated to holy men and women or other sacred events.[10] These commemorative sites are closely in dialogue with and are often encompassed within the prime *loca sancta* of Islam and the early mosque, but they are set apart from the shrines at the heart of the sacred cities of Mecca, Medina, and Jerusalem by how their sanctity is constructed and supported.[11]

As spaces of mediation, sacred spaces inevitably bear the hallmarks of a faith's understanding of itself and its neighboring traditions, as is the case for Islamic Jerusalem. They also embody a faith's

2 The Haram al-Sharif in Jerusalem.
Photo: Heba Mostafa

understanding of humankind's relationship to God; this is particularly important in the case of Islamic sacred space, which encoded a radically redefined cosmology that reconstituted God's relationship to prophets and angels while stridently challenging pre-Islamic Arabian and monotheistic cosmologies even as it remained in conversation with them.[12]

This binding contract between humankind and God, known as the divine covenant (*'ahd*, *mīthāq*) elaborated the rules of engagement of parameters of belief, permissible behavior, and expected conduct.[13] In exchange for their adherence, Muslims are promised a favorable afterlife and a life free from worry and strife, if not misfortune per se.[14] As the arena for the enactment of this contract, sacred space is inextricably entangled with the parameters and nuances of this covenant. Throughout the Quran the guardianship of sacred locales is predicated upon honoring the divine covenant, understood as a prerequisite for their guardianship.[15] This is the case in the infamous *masjid aḍ-ḍirār* (the mosque of harm) which was

LIFE AND DEATH AT THE MOSQUE
AND FUNERARY SHRINE

held in opposition to the *masjid at-taqwa* (mosque of Righteousness) of the Prophet Muhammad and provides one of many Quranic precedents for this pattern.[16]

Entangling God's covenant with Islamic sacred space, understood to include sites of memory, such as shrines and funerary architecture, as well as mosques and other spaces of ritual prayer, allows us to view such space through a multiplicity of layered lenses. For example, sacred space can be framed as forming distinct functions and phases of the divine contract. Sites that commemorate the eruption of the sacred into the world, such as the Masjid al-Haram in Mecca or the Haram al-Sharif in Jerusalem, act as visceral reminders of the divine covenant, evoking as they do creation and the End of Days. Through intimate association with God, they also offer the opportunity to receive multiple blessings for ritual practice such as prayer.[17] As the terms of the contract can only be fulfilled during the lifetime of a Muslim, sites of ritual practice, such as mosques, can be seen as the location where the covenant is upheld in daily life. Funerary spaces, on the other hand, are where the terms of the divine contract are potentially negotiated after death, as the Muslim book of deeds is sealed at this time, with few options for receiving blessing post-death other than encouraging prayers for the deceased.[18] Alternatively, sacred spaces can be located at varying degrees of separation from God or the divine encounter, such as the Night Journey and Heavenly Ascent of the Prophet Muhammad. If the Kaaba is sacred because it is God's chosen House, the Mosque of the Prophet in Medina shares in this divine charisma by virtue of the Prophet's own charisma, endowed upon him by God. This sacral intimacy explains why prayer receives multiplied blessings at the prime *loca sancta* of Islam and why Mecca, Medina, and Jerusalem are popular sites of burial for Muslims, even to the present day. It is clear that uncovering a submerged relational logic governing Islam's elusive sacrality requires a profound reckoning with how early Muslims viewed themselves in relation to God and how the divine covenant shaped sacred space.

At the mosque, enacting the divine covenant mandates ritual practices with defined parameters that produce unique spatial configurations. Muslims are expected to pray five times a day, in congregation preferably and in a mosque ideally. While the early mosque's spatial egalitarianism and oblique sacral messaging is certainly a product of Islam's praxis and iconoclasm, the mosque also complicates the question of where the sacred resides in Islamic religious architecture (Fig. 1). Framing this slippage is the multi-faceted nature of caliphal identity in early Islam and its variable invocation depending on context; as both successor to the Prophet Muhammad and as God's caliphs.[19] In early Islam attendance at the mosque was not confined to prayer but included participation in governance through attendance of the Friday sermon and other public events, such as adjudication and caliphal public audience. These activities further problematize the mosque as sacred, with analogous events taking place within the palace. Neither is the palace audience hall in early Islam a strictly secular space; early caliphs from the Umayyad caliph Mu'awiya onwards ruled from domed spaces identified as heavenly, blurring the boundary between sanctities at the mosque and palace.[20]

As a simple hypostyle structure, the early mosque lacked the internal spatial hierarchies or restrictive internal boundaries so common in the religious architecture of late antiquity. Although the mosque evolved over time to include features such as the *mihrab* (marking the direction of the *qibla* or orientation of prayer), the *minbar* (the pulpit for the Friday sermon), and the *maqsura* (enclosure screens to protect the caliph or governor), suggesting an exalted status for the *qibla* space, these elements did not function restrictively to signal a sacral hierarchy, nor did they exude the sacral mystique of spaces restricted to a priesthood.[21] Rather, the mosque signaled dislocated sanctities far removed from the bounds of the mosque, such as the Kaaba in Mecca, the memory of the charisma of the Prophet Muhammad in the case of the *minbar* and *mihrab*, and the authority of the caliph in the case of the *maqsura*.[22] The absence of a distinct spatial sacral hierarchy, such as a secluded holy of holies or altar,

3 Interior mosaic decoration, the Great Mosque of Damascus.
Photo: Heba Mostafa

does not imply the absence of zones considered more exalted or sanctified than others, rather it challenges identification with conventional signs of sacred dwelling. In this sense it is possible to view the act of communal ritual prayer itself as the bearer of sanctity in Islamic sacred space, whereby the sacred is embodied ritually within the mosque through communal practice while also residing within the community through the upholding of the divine covenant.

At the heart of Islam lies an exhortation to seek knowledge of God without attempting to fully understand His nature. God in the Quran is described as "closer to humankind than the jugular," aware of humankind's "vices and virtues"[23] and responsive to supplication and prayer.[24] Yet God is also described as unknowable and beyond human comprehension.[25] Knowledge of God in Islam then is a mental recognition of the impossibility of knowing God and a set of spiritual practices to seek closeness to Him. Encoded through language and mediated through the revelations of an illiterate Prophet, Islam supported an infrastructure of belief contingent upon an ability to hold incompatible thoughts; God as unknowable, with humankind tethered to Him. It presupposes an agile mental and spiritual state, one attuned to and actively engaged in a contemplative state of being. Abstracted and naturalistic depictions of nature in the decorative programs of early mosques and shrines offered just such an opportunity.[26] The mosque and other sites of memory, such as the Dome of the Rock, can be understood then as empathic spaces of persuasion that place the onus on the individual to understand God through contemplation of his creation, the Quran, and the upholding of the divine covenant. The mystique of the sacred in this sense is transposed onto the individual, with sacred spaces offering opportunities for personal experience rather than prescribed practice or representation. These spaces offer a reminder to uphold the covenant while also reminding the faithful of their reward. It is no coincidence this reminder and promise of the afterlife is manifest in the mosaic decoration of the Great Mosque of Damascus and the Dome of the Rock (Figs. 3–4).[27]

The view of the self as intrinsically bound to God and grounded in emanation and return through creation, death, resurrection, and eternal life, was undoubtedly shared with other monotheistic religions.[28] However, it was novel in the sense that it challenged pre-Islamic Arabian fatalism and beliefs around the finality of death.[29] Belief in God's ability to restore the spirt to the body at the End of Times, in a process akin to creation in reverse, is also fundamentally a recognition of God's ability to create; one belief cannot exist without the other. In this worldview, life on earth is a temporary state of exile from the divine presence, but also an opportunity to uphold the covenant struck between God and Adam to righteously inhabit the earth in physical and finite bodies with the promise of eternal life after death and resurrection on the Day of Judgment.[30] Death constitutes a liminal state of being, on the boundary between life and death known, as the *barzakh*, as Muslims await the return of their souls to a resurrected and restored body through God's grace.[31] The mosque and funerary shrine both spring forth from this understanding of the body in Islam as a temporary state of physicality tethered to an exalted, eternal past and future state beyond the earthly realm, governed by the divine covenant.

As beings inhabiting a sacralized world of God's creation, bound in covenant with God, sacrality in early Islam is singularly informed by the finitude of mortal time and the reliance of one's eternal fate upon devotional acts and supplications to a transcendent and immanent deity, reconciled through ritual practice.[32] Yet even for the most pious, the finality of death and the loss of the physical bodies of loved ones is inherently overwhelming. This was certainly true for early Muslims, confronted with the novel conception of belief in an afterlife, best exemplified by the Hadith of the Prophet Muhammad, who prohibited the

4 Interior mosaic decoration, the Dome of the Rock, Jerusalem.
Photo: Heba Mostafa

visitation of tombs for the purpose of veneration of the dead while allowing visitation as remembrance (*tadhkira*) for the living and to pray for the souls of the deceased.[33] The parameters for grieving and remembrance motivated Islam's vehement reaction to public displays of grief, particularly lamentations of women and other conduct deemed inconsistent with belief in resurrection and eternal life.[34] Prohibitions on outbursts of grief, such as the rending of clothing and other acts of self-harm, can be aligned with the contested sanction around commemoration of the dead and the tension embedded within funerary practices in the first two centuries of Islam.[35] Viewing funerary practice in early Islam as a gradual reconciliation with the most heart-wrenching clause in the divine covenant, the finitude of earthly life and death and loss as part of the "deal," was never fully resolved, as evidenced by ongoing conflict over funerary architecture in various Islamic societies, particularly in the Middle East. Existing along a spatial and temporal spectrum, sacrality in early Islam eludes definition if we seek to understand it as formally or spatially prescribed. Rather it can be understood as a manifestation of the divine covenant, problematized by the specificity of context, responsive to the Muslim lifeworld and in close dialogue with it.

GOD'S HOUSES, THE DIVINE COVENANT, AND THE ERUPTION OF THE SACRED

Although God manifests in the world primarily through His creation of the natural world, he communicates with humankind through the mediation of His agents. These include messengers, prophets, and angels, but also inanimate natural entities such as animals, trees, or springs. This is aligned with existing beliefs around sacrality and nature from pre-Islam, where sites with an abundance of water, vegetation, fertility, and bounty were regarded as signs of the presence of deities. The goddess al-'Uzza was believed to dwell in a palm tree for example.[36] Similar to the sacred enclosures of early Islam, the sacrality of these sites ensured the prohibition of violence, guaranteeing equitable resource sharing based on inter-tribal agreements rather than brute force.[37] It thus stands to reason that the natural world would be the prime location for Islam's heirophanies. From God speaking to Moses in the sacred valley of Ṭuwa, to the divine revelations of archangel Gabriel to the Prophet

Muhammad in the cave of Ḥira', the eruption of the sacred into the natural world serves as monotheism's origin story. It is also clear, however, that such sacral eruptions serve as correctives, reasserting and reminding the faithful of the divine covenant.

Naturally, prophets and messengers served as the prime audience for such encounters. Muhammad's encounter with the archangel Gabriel in the cave of Ḥira' is a case in point.[38] This took place following a period of intense spiritual introspection and the practice of *taḥannuth* (secluded ritual prayer from pre-Islam). Although mountains and caves were common locales, the Quran curiously identifies private oratories (referred to as *maḥārīb* or *miḥrāb*) as the locus of divine communication, via angelic presence or other manifestations of divine grace.[39] Associated with Mary, Zechariah, and David, Muslims naturally located these Quranic *mihrab*s in and around the Haram al-Sharif in Jerusalem. Over time they too became sites of veneration.

In fact, every reference to a *mihrab* in the Quran is accompanied by a communication or negotiation of a facet of the divine covenant.[40] This is certainly the case with the Quranic *Miḥrāb Dā'ūd* (Quran 38:23–26) which narrates the context of David's endowment with successorship (*khilāfa*).[41]

In Islam adherence to the divine covenant is absolutely central. This includes belief in God's unity, His prophets, angels, as well as resurrection and the End of Days and both humans and angels are bound by it. The Quran likens it to "the only rope to which the faithful must cling," emphasizing adherence to the covenant as the singular path to salvation. In addition to these beliefs, upholding the covenant includes consistent ritual practice, such as daily and seasonal prayer, fasting, pilgrimage, and the paying of alms, which permeate both the day cycle and the lifecycle of Muslims. In exchange for their adherence, Muslims are promised a favorable afterlife and the possibility of earthly prosperity and serenity. There are further associations between sacred space and the divine covenant in the Quran, or in this case, breaches to the divine covenant. In fact, breaches to the divine covenant inform nearly all the criticism levelled against non-believers and People of the Book in the Quran, cited as cause for divine retribution and in some cases, total annihilation.[42] Quran 17:4–7 describes the destruction of the Jewish Temple as a direct result of such breaches by the Children of Israel;

their loss of sacred locale emblematic of their loss of sacral authority. In the Quran this episode acts as a narrative prelude to the emergence of Islam as the rightful and true faith whereby "the turning of Muhammad's face in the heavens," seeking a "pleasing" *qibla* is resolved with the proclamation that Muslims should turn their face toward the Masjid al-Haram in Mecca for prayer and Muhammad's elevation as a Prophet granted his own *qibla* and sacred locale.[43] This effectively transferred sanctity from the Temple to the Kaaba, orientating humankind away from the *qibla* of the past Jewish nation and towards the *qibla* of the new nation of Islam, a sanctity reversed with the exaltation of Jerusalem in the middle of the seventh century.[44]

Building outwards from this understanding of a community bound in covenant, ritually circumambulating a shrine, it is possible to extrapolate the societal and cultural functions of the inviolability of sacred enclosures (ḥaram) in early Islam. This inviolability was signaled by a boundary wall that would often mark these early sacred enclosures.[45] The root of the term ḥaram (sacred enclosure) itself connotes prohibition and protection, from the root ḥrm (prohibit).[46] In cities this would often take the shape of a more formal structure, with the site often evolving into a temple complex, such as the temple of Bel in Palmyra (Fig. 5).[47] The concept of the ḥaram as a zone where the shedding of blood was strictly forbidden, meant that during seasonal pilgrimage,

5 The Temple of Bel in Palmyra, view of inner shrine and enclosure.
Photo: Heba Mostafa

LOCATING THE SACRED IN EARLY ISLAM ARCHITECTURE 19

which occurred during the violence-free months, security was guaranteed both temporally and spatially. Within these months the security granted by the *ḥaram* allowed for inter-tribal interaction, the brokering of political alliances, and the negotiation of commercial partnerships, so central to the flourishing of early Islamic society. In Arabia, control of a *ḥaram,* offered political, cultural, and spiritual dominance. This slippage between the sacred and economic should come as no surprise, since the sanctity of the shrine "infused consecrating power into commercial activities," rendering economic transactions, in a certain sense, inviolably secure.[48]

The prime *ḥaram* in Islam is the Masjid al-Haram in Mecca with the Kaaba at its center, a site of ritual worship and pilgrimage since the birth of Islam. In the Quran, God is the Kaaba's eternal Lord (*rabb al-bayt*) and protector,[49] and the Kaaba was the first sanctuary placed on earth,[50] known as *al-masjid al-ḥarām* (the inviolable masjid),[51] *al-bayt al-atīq* (ancient house),[52] *al-bayt al-ḥarām* (the inviolable house) or simply *al-bayt* (the house).[53] A simple structure built of low walls of mortar-free masonry and draped in cloth,[54] it had been rebuilt in stone and wood salvaged from a shipwreck during Muhammad's life.[55] It possessed features common to other sacred spaces in pre-Islamic Arabia,[56] such as a high threshold which had to be accessed by a ladder for added protection and "door with a lock and a *kiswa* (draping)," reportedly gifted to the shrine by a Himyarite.[57] It attracted pilgrims from across the confessional spectrum of Arabia, including Christian pilgrims,[58] and is described as a "(a place of) shelter and security."[59] The reconsecration of the shrine at Mecca through *hajj* (pilgrimage) and the *'umra* was a corrective to distorted Abrahamic ritual practice, the *jāhilī* practice, known as *duwār*,[60] and later known as *ṭawāf* in Islam, seen as no more than a warped version of the Abrahamic ritual now redeemed by Islam. Ritual circumambulation thus symbolically re-enacted the upholding of divine covenant through communal devotion to God at His house, building upon existing pre-Islamic Arabian beliefs in the communal bonds represented by ritual revolution around a central sacralized axis.[61]

The Kaaba was not the only House of God ritually circumambulated by Muslims in the first century. Jerusalem was viewed as the first *qibla* (direction of prayer), and the Temple Mount, or Masjid al-Aqsa (Farthest Mosque), is described in the Quran alongside the Kaaba, as inherently blessed by God. For this reason, early Muslims believed the Haram al-Sharif to be the site to which the Prophet Muhammad was transported during his Nightly Journey and Heavenly Ascent. For this earlier period consensus has stabilized around a reading that recognizes the multilayered meanings of the Haram al-Sharif and Dome of the Rock as both commemorative and anticipatory – looking back to the Moment of Creation (the rock as God's point of arrival and departure during the act of creation) while simultaneously looking to the future (the rock as the point of God's return on the Day of Judgment and the location of his Throne).[62] Specifically it identifies the monument as responding to the eschatological anxieties of early Islam. By the twelfth century the rock itself became identified as the location of the Prophet's heavenly journey, the true commemorative associations evoked by the Umayyads lost to memory.

Operating within a ritually and symbolically competitive environment, which included memories of Abraham's foundation of God's House, the Jewish Temple, and the Church of the Holy Sepulcher, early Muslims rehabilitated ritual practices, including public oathtaking at sacred sites, invocations of relics and the sacred enclosures of pre-Islam (*ḥaram*), leveraging fear of the breach of divine covenant to guarantee oases of security within chaos. Over time, early Muslims probed the spatial, symbolic, and temporal ambiguities of sacred dwelling not only to Islamize pre-Islamic Arabian, Jewish, and Christian spaces, but to access the divine for many purposes, existential, and eschatological, but also political, to secure allegiances, alliances, and leadership of the Muslim community.

CONCLUSION

Abstracted and removed from physical representation or earthly dwelling, Islamic sacrality presents as more of a continuum than a dichotomy, responsive to Islam's unique conceptions of the sacral and its elusive nature. Through re-imagination and appropriation of ritual practice, and exaltation of *loca sancta*, Muslims strove to constitute relationships with the sacred that challenge our conventional understanding of sacrality as spatially prescribed. By taking as our starting point how Muslims viewed themselves in relation to God, we can rethink how conceptions of sacrality shaped sacred space both in the formative period of Islam and beyond. Positioning sacred spaces in early Islam in dialogue with the Muslim lifeworld allows them to manifest as products of belief infrastructures and modalities of embodiment encoded by individual experience of the divine in shared spaces. Situating sacred space within notions of divine covenant and encounter also links Muslims to non-Muslims, offering a historical context for the exploration of parameters of interfaith co-operation, if not co-existence, at moments of crisis, while also problematizing questions of governance, religious orthodoxy, dogma, and political difference. It also contributes to ongoing debates around cultural transmission and translation that transcend geographic and confessional boundaries and inform narratives of continuity, discontinuity, and rupture. In fact, such debates have emerged as central to the discipline of Islamic art and material culture, particularly in the context of late antiquity and Islam. By placing early Muslim sacral beliefs in conversation with the history of early sacred spaces, sacred geographies, as well as ritual and devotional practice, a submerged relational logic can emerge, offering new horizons of interpretive possibility for our discipline. If Islam presented itself as a blueprint for a state of being to attain salvation, sacrality and sacred spaces can be seen as the containers of that experience, mediated by the senses and experienced in a community bound in covenant with God.

HEBA MOSTAFA is Assistant Professor of Islamic Art and Architecture at the Department of Art History, University of Toronto, St George Campus. She received her doctorate from Cambridge University's Department of Architecture in 2012. Her research focuses on the formation of Islamic architecture as well as Islam's interface with late antiquity, Christianity and Judaism through commemorative architecture, pilgrimage, and ritual practice, with a particular focus on Jerusalem and Cairo.

SUGGESTIONS FOR FURTHER READING

Grabar, Oleg. "The Architecture of the Middle Eastern City: The Case of the Mosque," in Ira M. Lapidus, ed., *Middle Eastern Cities: A Symposium on Ancient, Islamic and Contemporary Middle Eastern Urbanism* (Berkeley: University of California Press, 1969), 26–46.

Guidetti, Mattia. "Sacred Spaces in Early Islam," in Finbarr Barry Flood and Gülru Necipoğlu, ed., *A Companion to Islamic Art and Architecture*, Wiley-Blackwell Companions to Art History 12 (Hoboken, NJ: John Wiley & Sons Inc, 2017), 130–150

Kister, M. J. "Sanctity Joint and Divided: On Holy Places in the Islamic Tradition." *Jerusalem Studies in Arabic and Islam* 20 (1996), 18–65.

Mostafa, Heba. "The Early Mosque Revisited: Introduction of the Minbar and Maqṣūra." *Muqarnas* 33 (2016), 1–16.

NOTES

1. Joseph Chelhod, "La notion ambiguë du sacré chez les Arabes et dans l'islam," *Revue de l'histoire des religions* 159, no. 1 (1961), 68–70 (67–79); Mattia Guidetti, "Sacred Spaces in Early Islam" in *A Companion to Islamic Art and Architecture*, ed. Finbarr Barry Flood and Gülru Necipoğlu, Wiley-Blackwell Companions to Art History 12 (Hoboken, NJ: John Wiley & Sons Inc, 2017), 130–134 (130–150). See also Joseph Chelhod, *Les Structures du Sacré chez les Arabes,* Islam d'hier et d'aujourd'hui 13 (Paris: Maisonneuve et Larose, 1965); Finbarr B. Flood, "Bodies and Becoming: Mimesis, Mediation, and the Ingestion of the Sacred in Christianity and Islam," in *Sensational Religion: Sensory Cultures in Material Practice*, ed. Sally M. Promey (New Haven: Yale University Press, 2014), 459–93; Alain George, "Paradise or Empire?" *Power, Patronage, and Memory in Early Islam: Perspectives on Umayyad Elites*, ed. Alain George and Andrew Marsham, (New York: Oxford University Press, 2018), 39–68; Avinoam Shalem, "The Body of Architecture: The Early History of the Clothing of the Sacred House of the Kaaba in Mecca," *Clothing the Sacred: Medieval Textiles as Fabric, Form, and Metaphor*, Kapustka, Mateusz, and Warren T. Woodfin, Textile Studies 8 (Emsdetten: Edition Imorde, 2015), 189–206.

2. Abd al-Azim b. Abd al Qawi b. Abdallah, *Mukhtaṣar Ṣaḥīḥ Muslim*, ed. Muḥammad Nasir al-Dīn al-Albanī, 2 vols. (Beirut, 1987), 1:75.

3. For a critique of the paradigm first proposed by Mircea Eliade, see *Mircea Eliade: A Critical Reader*, Critical Categories in the Study of Religion, Bryan S. Rennie, ed. (London: Equinox Pub, 2006). See also, Mircea Eliade, *The Sacred and the Profane: The Nature of Religion* (London: Harcourt, 1959).

4. Gülru Necipoğlu, "The Dome of the Rock as Palimpsest: Abd al-Malik's Grand Narrative and Sultan Süleyman's Glosses," *Muqarnas* 25 (2008), 17–105; Oleg Grabar, "Space and Holiness in Medieval Jerusalem," in *Jerusalem: Its Sanctity and Centrality to Judaism, Christianity, and Islam.* ed. Lee I. Levine (New York: Continuum, 1999), 275–86.

5. M. J. Kister, "Sanctity Joint and Divided: On Holy Places in the Islamic Tradition," *Jerusalem Studies in Arabic and Islam* 20 (1996), 18–65.

6. Necipoğlu, "The Dome of the Rock as Palimpsest"; Harry Munt, *The Holy City of Medina: Sacred Space in Early Islamic Arabia*, Cambridge Studies in Islamic Civilization (New York: Cambridge University Press, 2014); Peter Webb, "The Hajj before Muhammad: Journeys to Mecca in Muslim Narratives of Pre-Islamic History," in *The Hajj: Collected Essays,* ed. Venetia Porter and Liana Saif (London: British Museum, 2013), 6–14.

7. Oleg Grabar, "The Architecture of the Middle Eastern City: The Case of the Mosque," in *Middle Eastern Cities: A Symposium on Ancient, Islamic and Contemporary Middle Eastern Urbanism,* ed. Ira M. Lapidus (Berkeley: University of California Press, 1969), 26–46.

8. Andrew Marsham, "'God's Caliph' Revisited: Umayyad Political Thought in Its Late Antique Context," in *Power, Patronage, and Memory in Early Islam: Perspectives on Umayyad Elites*, ed. Alain George and Andrew Marsham (New York: Oxford University Press, 2018), 3–39; Heba Mostafa, "The Early Mosque Revisited: Introduction of the Minbar and Maqṣūra," *Muqarnas* 33 (2016), 1–16.

9. Simon O'Meara, "The Foundation Legend of Fez and Other Islamic Cities in Light of the Life of the Prophet," in *Cities in the Pre-Modern Islamic World: The Urban Impact of Religion, State and Society,* ed. Amira K. Bennison and Alison L. Gascoigne, 27–41; Nancy A. Khalek, *Damascus after the Muslim Conquest: Text and Image in Early Islam* (Oxford: Oxford University Press, 2011).

10. Necipoğlu, "The Dome of the Rock as Palimpsest"; Amikam Elad, *Medieval Jerusalem and Islamic Worship: Holy Places, Ceremonies, Pilgrimage* (Leiden: E.J. Brill, 1995); Jacob Lassner, *Medieval Jerusalem: Forging an Islamic City in Spaces Sacred to Christians and Jews* (Ann Arbor: University of Michigan Press, 2017).

11. A case in point is the construction of sanctity at the Great Mosque of Damascus, see Khalek, *Damascus after the Muslim Conquest*, 85–125.

12. Mohammad Ali Tabatabaʾi and Saida Mirsadri, "The Qurʾānic Cosmology, as an Identity in Itself," *Arabica* 63, no. 3–4 (May 26, 2016), 202–10 (201–34).

13. The covenant is founded on a set of core beliefs: the unquestionable unity and supremacy of God, the scope and exclusivity of His authority and the designated roles of his messengers, angels and apostles, see Quran, 2:285.

14. The Quran recognizes the inherent suffering of humankind and offers solace and comfort through God's grace and serenity, see Quran 90:4 and 48:4.

15. For example, the destruction of the Jewish Temple only came about as a direct result of the Children of Israel's repeated breaches of this divine covenant, see Quran 17:4–7.

16. Unrighteous control of sacred space is also invoked in the incident of *masjid aḍ-ḍirār* (the mosque of harm) that is juxtaposed with the *masjid at-taqwa* of the Prophet. See Quran, 2:114: "And who are more unjust than those who prevent the name of Allah from being mentioned in His mosques (*masājid*) and strive toward their destruction. It is not for them to enter them except in fear. For them in this world is disgrace, and they will have in the Hereafter a great punishment."

17. Although contested by scholars such as Ibn Taymiyya, these beliefs circulated throughout the Islamic period, see Kister, "Sanctity Joint and Divided," 23.

18. Amila Buturovic, "Funerary Culture in Islam," in *The Routledge Companion to Death and Dying*, Routledge Religion Companions, ed. Christopher M Moreman (New York: Taylor and Francis, 2018), 76–77 (74–85).

19. Marsham, "God's Caliph Revisited," 8–9 and 19–25.

20. Oleg Grabar, "From Dome of Heaven to Pleasure Dome," *The Journal of the Society of Architectural Historians* 49.1 (1990), 15–21; Charles Wendell, "Baghdad: Imago Mundi, and Other Foundation-Lore," *International Journal of Middle East Studies* 2.2 (1971), 119–120 (99–128); Jonathan Bloom, "Qubbat al-Khadra' and the Iconography of Height in Islamic Architecture," *Ars Orientalis* 23 (1993), 136 (135–141).

21. Mostafa, "Early Mosque Revisited," 11–13.

22. Ibid., 6–8; 9–11.

23. Quran, 91:7–8.

24. Quran, 50:16.

25. Quran, 24:35.

26. See Finbarr B. Flood, *The Great Mosque of Damascus: Studies on the Makings of an Umayyad Visual Culture* (Leiden: Brill, 2001), 35–56; Nasser Rabbat, "The Dialogic Dimension of Umayyad Art," *Res: Anthropology and Aesthetics* 43 (2003), 91–94 (78–94).

27. George, "Paradise or Empire?" 60–68; Adam Bursi, "Scents of Space: Early Islamic Pilgrimage, Perfume, and Paradise," *Arabica* 67.2–3 (2020), 229–234 (200–234).

28. Quran 2:156. "To say when afflicted with calamity: To God we belong and to Him is our return."

29. Buturovic, "Funerary Culture in Islam," 80–81.

30. Quran, 2:30.

31. Buturovic, "Funerary Culture in Islam," 77 and 84.

32. Quran 2:285.

33 Buturovic, "Funerary Culture in Islam," 81–84.

34 Leor Halevi, "Wailing for the Dead: The Role of Women in Early Islamic Funerals," *Past & Present* 183 (2004), 3–39.

35 In Islam, the body, ritually washed and wrapped in a simple white shroud, then is left to decay in the earth. On the tension between orthodox views of burial and funerary practice, see Thomas Leisten, "Between Orthodoxy and Exegesis: Some Aspects of Attitudes in the Shari'a toward Funerary Architecture," *Muqarnas* 7 (1990), 13, and 17–19 (12–22).

36 Yasmine Zahran and Robert Hoyland, *The Lakhmids of Hira* (Stacey International: 2009), 69. See also Yasmine Zahran, *Ghassan Resurrected* (London: Stacey International, 2006).

37 Robert Hoyland, *Arabia and the Arabs: From the Bronze Age to the Coming of Islam* (New York: Routledge, 2001), 158.

38 Accounts of this encounter capture the shocking nature of this divine eruption. The archangel Gabriel demanded that Muhammad recite multiple times, and each time Muhammad pled his illiteracy until finally Gabriel reveals that his recitation, is in fact the revelation of the Quran, Quran, 96:1–5.

39 These include not only the *Miḥrāb Dāʾūd* (Quran 38:23–26) but also the Miḥrāb of Mary (*Miḥrāb Maryam*) (Quran 3:37–8) and the Mihrab of Zachariah (*Miḥrāb Zakariyyā*) (Quran 3:38–39).

40 Heba Mostafa, "From the Dome of the Chain to *Miḥrāb Dāʾūd*: The Transformation of an Umayyad Commemorative Site at the Haram al-Sharif in Jerusalem," *Muqarnas* 34 (2017), 4–9 (1–22).

41 This took place after his violation of the covenant through an unspecified sinful act and set in motion events which culminated in his endowment with successorship, Mostafa, "From the Dome of the Chain to *Miḥrāb Dāʾūd*," 4–9.

42 See Quran, 3:77–79: "Indeed, those who exchange the covenant of Allah and their [own] oaths for a small price will have no share in the Hereafter, and Allah will not speak to them or look at them on the Day of Resurrection, nor will He purify them; and they will have a painful punishment." See also Quran 2:199–203.

43 The term *masjid* in the Quran alludes to the other *masājid* of God that predate Muhammad's revelation, almost certainly pre-Islamic sanctuaries, see Jeremy Johns, "The 'House of the Prophet' and the Concept of the Mosque," in *Bayt al-Maqdis. Jerusalem and Early Islam*, ed. Jeremy Johns (Oxford: Oxford University Press, 1999), 93 (59–112).

44 Quran, 2:140–145. The foolish among the people will say, "What has turned them away from their qiblah, which they used to face?" Say, "To Allah belongs the east and the west. He guides whom He wills to a straight path. And thus we have made you a just community that you will be witnesses over the people and the Messenger will be a witness over you. And We did not make the qiblah which you used to face except that We might make evident who would follow the Messenger from who would turn back on his heels. And indeed, it is difficult except for those whom Allah has guided. And never would Allah have caused you to lose your faith. Indeed Allah is, to the people, Kind and Merciful. We have certainly seen the turning of your face, [O Muhammad], toward the heaven, and We will surely turn you to a qiblah with which you will be pleased. So turn your face toward al-Masjid al-Haram. And wherever you [believers] are, turn your faces toward it [in prayer]. Indeed, those who have been given the Scripture well know that it is the truth from their Lord. And Allah is not unaware of what they do. And if you brought to those who were given the Scripture every sign, they would not follow your qibla. Nor will you be a follower of their qibla. Nor would they be followers of one another's qibla. So if you were to follow their desires after what has come to you of knowledge, indeed, you would then be among the wrongdoers."

45 Harry Munt, *The Holy City of Medina: Sacred Space in Early Islamic Arabia*, Cambridge Studies in Islamic Civilization (New York: Cambridge University Press, 2014), 19–28.

46 Hoyland, *Arabia and the Arabs*, 157.

47 Ibid., 158.

48 Hamid Dabashi, *Authority in Islam: From the Rise of Muhammad to the Establishment of the Umayyads* (New Brunswick: Transaction Publishers: 1989), 29. This is in fact is not unlike contemporary networks of trust which form part of the cryptocurrency global economy, with the community and the digital world acting as a guarantor of financial transactions.

49 Quran, 105:1–5.

50 Quran, 3:96.

51 Quran, 22:25–29.

52 Quran, 22:25–29.

53 Quran, 2:125, 2:127 and 2:158. See also Quran, 5:97, 22:25–29.

54 Hoyland, *Arabia and the Arabs*, 180.

55 S. D. Goitein, *Encyclopaedia of Islam, New Edition* (hence- forth EI2) (Leiden, 1954–2002), s.v. "Ka'ba."

56 Nuha N. N. Khoury, "The Dome of the Rock, the Ka'ba, and Ghumdan: Arab Myths and Umayyad Monuments," *Muqarnas* 10 (1993), 57–60 (57–65).

57 EI2, Ka'ba.

58 The presence of Christians at the shrine is illustrated by the presence of images of Jesus and Mary painted on the interior of the Kaaba, the record of which survives due to the account of the Prophet Muhammad reportedly protecting them with his hand during the demolition of the idols and images in the sanctuary, see G. R. D. King, "The Paintings of the Pre-Islamic Kaaba," *Muqarnas* 21 (2004), 219–20 (219–29).

59 M. J. Kister, "Some Reports concerning Mecca from Jahiliyya to Islam," *Journal of the Economic and Social History of the Orient* 15.1/2 (1972), 65 (61–93).

60 Dabashi, *Authority in Islam,* 29.

61 Nadia Jamil, "Caliph and Qutb: Poetry as a Source for Interpreting the Transformation of the Byzantine Cross on Steps on Umayyad Coinage," *Bayt al-Maqdis, Jerusalem and Early Islam*, ed. J Johns, Oxford Studies in Islamic Art, IX. Part Two (Oxford: Oxford University Press, 1999), 11–57.

62 Necipoğlu, "The Dome of the Rock as Palimpsest," 29–30.

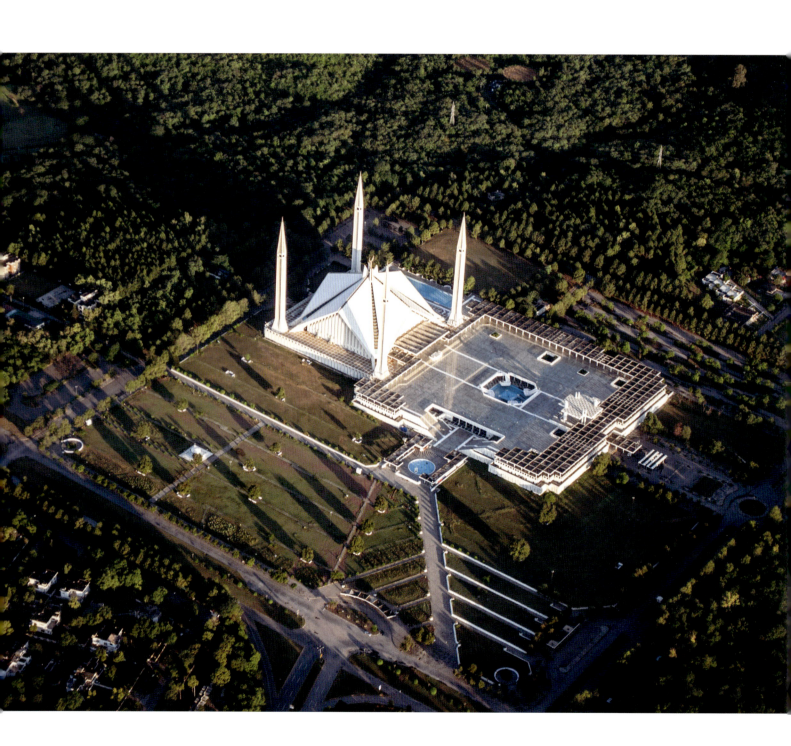

The Mosque in the Urban Context

NEZAR ALSAYYAD AND İPEK TÜRELI

1 King Faisal Mosque, Islamabad, aerial view.
Photo: Aga Khan Documentation Center at MIT

From the earliest days of Islam, the mosque, or *masjid,* meaning place for prostration, emerged as the site where the *umma,* or community of believers, could come together and discuss matters of state and religion. Thus, it became the social and political center of early Muslim urban settings. In the planned settlements or garrison towns built by the Arabs as they spread the new religion across the Middle East and North Africa, the mosque was centrally located; but in cities they conquered that predated Islam, the mosque had no specific location. At first, Arab Muslim domination did not bring significant modification to the architecture of occupied regions. But, as with any prospering civilization, it did create a variety of new demands that required architectural solutions.

The diversity of conditions within Muslim regions has led many researchers to question the existence of an Islamic architecture with common characteristics.[1] Indeed, the Islamic empire was never a monolithic entity; it encompassed people with different cultures, economic systems, and national heritages; and it included lands with different geographies and climatic conditions. Some have argued against the universality of Islamic architecture in general.[2] However, few would disagree about the commonality of mosque architecture in particular. The mosque's function and role within the community has been fairly consistent through time and space.

In spite of their social and political importance, early mosques during the Prophet Muhammad's as well as the first four caliphs' time (632–661) were not landmarks. Their locations, external shapes, and material treatments were not meant to herald them as cultural symbols. Although there were exceptions, early mosques did not enjoy the visual emphasis of the sacred structures of other religions.

For instance, the importance of the mosque within the towns of the Muslim world was muted compared to that of the church within the towns of medieval Europe. The absence in Islam of an institutionalized clergy may explain the difference. The mosque as a physical structure was not an essential part of the hierarchy of governance, and as an institution it did not possess independent power. Instead, it was intended to serve as a place where power could be transmitted and shared, where the supposed equality between ruler and ruled was manifested.[3] Therefore, the symbolic significance of the early mosque was not represented in its physical qualities; rather, its importance lay in the role it played within the community, a role deeply rooted in the structure of Islamic society.

HISTORY AND DEVELOPMENT

Early Islam did not require a specific place for prayer, for this obligation could be fulfilled anywhere, provided the times and the direction of prayer were correct. Although prayer was an individual communication with God, group prayer on Fridays (the Muslim Sabbath) was considered an essential community obligation. The *masjid jami,* or the congregational mosque, sometimes referred to as the Friday mosque, was thus established during the Umayyad period as the principal site for community prayer in larger cities. It was usually large enough to accommodate the entire adult male population of the city. As the city then expanded, the congregational mosque was enlarged and neighborhood mosques were added. Many of these smaller mosques developed certain specialties and served social, political, and educational functions.

With the expansion of Islam into new regions, existing buildings were used as the first mosques.

2 The Great Mosque, Damascus, 705–15, aerial view showing the mosque in urban context.
Photo: Yves Gelle/Corbis, 2015

Starting during the lifetime of the prophet, Arabs did not impose any architectural forms on conquered countries. Instead, they converted existing sanctuaries of other religions to serve the simple requirements of their religion. The most well known is Kaaba, originally a pagan pilgrimage site claimed by the prophet for his new religion and named as Masjid al-Haram or Sacred Mosque. Following this, the first mosques were often temples and churches, altered to serve the needs of the new Muslim rulers.

In Syria, where the direction of the *qibla* is south, Byzantine churches were converted into mosques by turning their western doors into windows and cutting new entrances into their northern walls.[4] In the city of Damascus, at first, the grounds of a previous pagan *temenos* (holy precinct) was used for communal prayer. This site had been originally built for the Temple of Jupiter, and then built over for the Cathedral of St. John during the Byzantine era (395–634). The open space outside the church was initially shared between Christians and Muslims. This initial preference suggests the colonizing Arabs were not intent on imposing a brand-new image on the city. Upon the orders of Umayyad caliph al-Walid (r. 705–15), however, the church was demolished and a congregational mosque was built to the south of the *temenos* using some of the structure, columns, of the church, signaling the power of the Umayyads (Fig. 2).[5]

In Persia, Arabs converted many fire temples and existing buildings into mosques and sometimes used their parts as spolia. The Friday mosque in Istakhr, dating from about 660 and considered to be the earliest mosque in Persia, had round columns with Achaemenid capitals featuring bullheads.[6] Most famously, and much later, in Constantinople, the famous Byzantine church of Hagia Sophia was converted into a mosque by the Ottoman Turks following their takeover of the city in 1453; indeed, it became the prototype for many later Ottoman mosques.[7]

The situation was different, however, in cities founded by the Arabs, where new religious structures had to be built. The Great Mosque of Kufa (670), for example, one of the earliest in Iraq, was originally defined only by a ditch. Its *qibla* portico was an unwalled space of reused marble columns, covered perhaps by a gabled wooden roof. Not far away, the Mosque of Basra was marked only by a fence of reed. In Egypt, the Mosque of Amr (641–2) was a small space containing a structure made of mud brick, with palm-trunk columns supporting a roof of palm fronds and mud. The floor was covered simply with pebbles.

By the time Persian Muslims reached India in the twelfth century, however, Islamic building traditions were better established. The Muslims had absorbed and modified many of the building practices of previously conquered places. The first mosques in India thus appear to reflect a more mature building tradition; although conversion of Hindu temples to mosques also occurred.[8]

The first three centuries of the Arab era witnessed the development of the highly flexible hypostyle mosque, with columns or piers as the main unit of construction. Hypostyle mosques could expand and contract according to the needs of the community. Cordoba's Great Mosque was first laid out in 784 on the site of a Christian church; it was enlarged several times (in 833–48, 965–6, and 987–8), each phase following the original design, thus achieving stylistic unity in an asymmetrical composition.[9]

MOSQUES AND THE URBAN CONTEXT

Over the past thirteen centuries the general requirements of the mosque have not changed significantly, but its location in relation to other public functions has. Minor changes have occurred in plan form, external appearance, and accommodated activities. Mosques in cities can be classified in different ways according to their relative locations. They have been responsive to existing urban contexts in accretive cities (Cordoba, Damascus), generative of urban contexts in planned cities such as Cairo, Kufa, Basra, and served as the central nodes of the sacred cities of Mecca, Medina, and Jerusalem (Fig. 3).

In the early years of Islam, the house of the Prophet in Medina provided a simple model. It combined the home of the ruler, the seat of the government, and a space of collective prayer. The following two centuries, however, witnessed the rise of the residential palace as a seat of government (Dar al-Imara, or Qasr al-Khalifa). In the Abbasid caliph al-Mansur's circular, planned city of Baghdad (762), the palace and the mosque were joined at the center of the city. Shop-lined streets led from the four perimeter gates to the center, with the areas between these radial streets reserved as the residential quarters for different groups. Over time, however, the palace and mosque complex became detached from one another, and a visit by the caliph to the mosque became a carefully crafted ceremony. As new mosques were added to the cityscape, they acquired specialization. In Fatimid Cairo, the Mosque of Amr accommodated the Sunni *khutba*, while the Shi'ite *khutba* was held in the Mosque of al-Hakim (990–1003).[10] Meanwhile, the Mosque of al-Azhar (972) emerged as an institute to teach the Ismaili doctrine. Such great mosques frequently evolved into socio-cultural complexes, combined with centers of learning, hospices, soup kitchens, and shrines.

The design of new mosques inserted into established urban fabrics responded to their dense contexts in a variety of ways. The small al-Aqmar Mosque, built in 1125 in late-Fatimid-era Cairo, negotiated the different orientation of local streets and *qibla* by means of a façade aligned with the street and, behind it, an intermediate triangular space that led to a small courtyard surrounded by an arcade one bay deep on three sides and three bays deep on the *qibla* side (Fig. 4).

In contrast, the Fatih Mosque Complex (1463–70) in Istanbul, commissioned by Sultan Mehmed II, was placed on Divanyolu, the main thoroughfare of Constantinople, which roughly corresponded to the Byzantium *mese*, and which linked the Grand Bazaar (Kapalıçarşı) to the Topkapı Palace

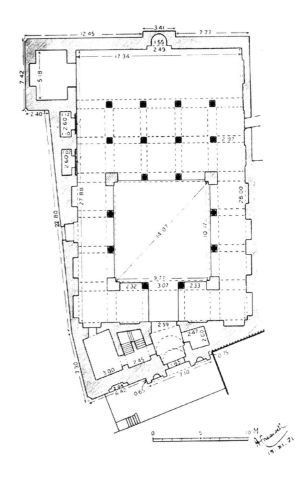

4 al-Aqmar Mosque, Cairo, 1125. Plan. After K.A.C. Creswell, *The Muslim Architecture of Egypt*. 1978.2.fig.141. Photo: Fine Arts Library, Harvard University

3 Kaaba and Masjid al-Haram during haj, Mecca, aerial showing the mosque in urban context. Photo: Bettmann/Corbis, 1975

to the east.[11] The complex was built on a hilltop site previously occupied by a Byzantine church, on vaults incorporating the cisterns of the former church. The mosque itself occupied the center of an enclosed precinct that featured the mausoleums of Mehmed II and his wife Gülbahar Sultan and that also included a formal garden, *madrasa*s, a hospital, a guesthouse, a caravanserai, a hospice, an elementary school, and a library (Fig. 5).

Almost a century later, the Süleymaniye Mosque Complex (1550–7) was likewise inserted into the existing fabric of Constantinople, but in this case more attention was paid to its affect on the overall city silhouette than its immediate surroundings. Resting on an artificial platform on top of a hill some distance from Divanyolu, it overlooked the Golden Horn and the Bosphorus (Fig. 6).[12] In addition to the grand mosque, this complex

5 Fatih Külliyesi, Istanbul. Reconstruction plan of the complex, and hypothetical section of the mosque. Source: Gülru Necipoğlu, *The Age of Sinan: Architectural Culture in the Ottoman Empire.* London: Reaktion Books, 2005, 85

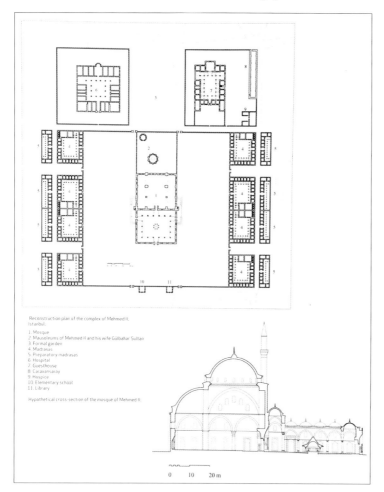

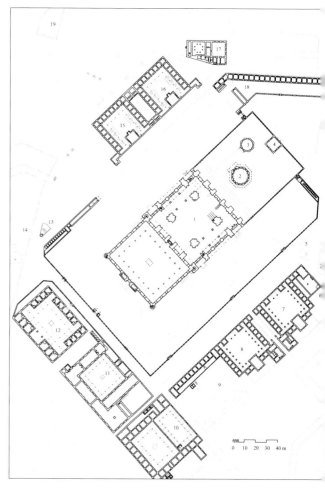

contained a hospital, a medical school, a hospice, a soup kitchen, a primary school, *madrasa*s, shops, and coffee houses.

The mosque complex, as it evolved in Ottoman times, was the culmination of a long process, as a number of functions were added in response to the needs of the community. In different parts of the world, the *madrasa* (school), *khanqah* (monastery), and mausoleum also evolved as new categories of sacred buildings.[13] Other religious structures included the *zawiya* (chapel), a prayer hall along the side streets of busy neighborhoods, and the *kutab*, which was a nursery school where children were taught the fundamentals of religion. In many cases *kutab*s were adjoined by a water fountain.

6 Süleymaniye Külliyesi, Istanbul.
Floor plan of the complex, showing:
(1) mosque, (2) mausoleum of Süleyman, (3) mausoleum of Hürrem, (4) Koran recitation school, (5) public fountain, (6) elementary school, (7) first *madrasa*, (8) second *madrasa*, (9) remains of medical school,
(10) hospital, (11) hospice, (12) guesthouse, (13) Sinan's tomb with domed *sabil* and empty plot of his endowed school and residence, (14) the janissary agha's residence, (15) third *madrasa*, (16) fourth *madrasa*, (17) bathhouse, (18) hadith college, (19) *madrasa* near the palace of Fatma Sultan and Siyavus Pasa
Arben N. Arapi, 2005, source: Gülru Necipoğlu, *The Age of Sinan: Architectural Culture in the Ottoman Empire.* (London: Reaktion Books, 2005, p. 205).
Photo: Gülru Necipoğlu

THE MOSQUE IN THE ERA OF
THE MODERN NATION-STATE

In the modern era, as many of their former functions have been assumed by state authorities, mosques have restricted their work to religious activities, leading to the "secularization" of public services and spaces, or, alternatively, to the "sacralization of the mosque."[14] While government authorities now routinely make provision for mosques, schools, hospitals, etc., when planning new communities, the locations of these institutions have become more marginal. Their administration has also become connected, respectively, to directorates of religious affairs, ministries of education, or ministries of health or social welfare.

New types of mosques have also emerged during the twentieth century, in association with new political, demographic, and economic developments. Some of these are more associated with the new unit of the nation-state than with the city. One example is the large state or national mosque, often built in the capital of a newly independent country. In some ways, these state mosques hark back to the great congregational mosques of early Muslim cities or to the subsequent great imperial mosques of Islam. An early example is the National Mosque (1965) of Malaysia, one of the most prominent buildings in Kuala Lumpur, situated among gardens across from the old Kuala Lumpur railway station and surrounded by motorways. Another national mosque from the same period and region is the Independence Mosque (1961–78) in Jakarta, Indonesia. Since the 1970s, such mosques have proliferated throughout the Islamic world, notably in Morocco, Jordan, Saudi Arabia, Kuwait, Iraq, and Pakistan.

The national mosque of Pakistan – King Faisal Mosque (Fig. 1, 1966–86) named after the king of Saudi Arabia who partially sponsored it – was designed by the Turkish architect Vedad Dalokay. It was given a particularly prominent place in the country's new capital, Islamabad. The city itself was planned (1959–60) by Constantinos Doxiadis on a prominent ancient route connecting capitals in the region. Adjacent to Rawalpindi and away from the "cosmopolitan" port city of Karachi, it was intended to catalyze the "imagined community" formed after the 1947 partition of British India

into Muslim Pakistan and Hindu India.[15] Doxiadis's design involved a 2,200-yard grid of self-contained communities, separated by motorways. It had two main axes: one (northeast-southwest) terminating in the Capitol complex, and the other terminating with the King Faisal Mosque at the foot of the Margalla Hills at the city's northwest border.[16]

It is worth mentioning that Dalokay had earlier teamed with another Turkish architect, Nejat Tekelioğlu, to win a competition to design a grand mosque for Ankara. However, after ground was broken for this project in 1967, its modernist aesthetic was shelved, to be replaced by a historicist design by Hüsrev Tayla and Fatin Uluengin that harkened back to sixteenth-century imperial Ottoman mosques. But this decision created enduring controversy, because the new mosque, Kocatepe (1967–87), visually and symbolically competes with Atatürk's Mausoleum (Anıtkabir, 1944–53), the secular national emblem that crowns the city's highest hill.[17]

The incorporation of mosques into the state apparatus has been paralleled by a rise in the building of privately funded mosques. Some of these have been sponsored by local communities; others have been affiliated with regional or transnational Islamic organizations. In addition, the 1990s witnessed the rise of political Islam across the Muslim world, particularly in places like Egypt, Iraq, and Iran. Even in secular countries like Turkey, local groups have now become key players in the production of built environments with overt formal references to Islamic heritage, so much so that it is possible to talk about a mosque building boom.

Contemporary mosques occupy a new range of sites in the urban context. They can define the urban edge, as in Jeddah's Corniche, with regularly spaced small mosques – one of them, the Island Mosque (1986) by Egyptian Architect Abdel Wahid El-Wakil (Fig. 6).[18] Or they can appear in places such as university campuses and airports that cater to large numbers of people. One example is the mosque in the middle of the lake at the King Fahd University of Petroleum and Minerals (KFUPM) in Dhahran; another is the mosque at King Khaled Airport in Riyadh.[19]

The strengthening of religious alliances in the past decades has altered how the cityscape is

7 Island Mosque, Jeddah, Saudi Arabia, 1990, designed by Abdel Wahid El-Wakil. View across the harbour. Photo: IAA2020, courtesy of Aga Khan Trust for Culture-Aga Khan Award for Architecture and Christopher Abel

appropriated and transformed by the general public for demonstrations of piety.[20] Thus, in many Muslim cities, public squares, and even sidewalks, may today be taken over as a Friday mosque accommodating hundreds of thousands of people. Alternatively, Muslims continue to adopt existing buildings as mosques, as is the case with shop-front mosques in the United States (Fig. 8).[21] Garages or other small spaces in cities such as Cairo and Beirut have also been turned into small mosques. All of these appropriations enable what may be called the distributed mosque.

Mosques continue to be places mainly for male congregation, although in some countries, such as Egypt, women-only *zawiya*s (chapels) have started to appear. In most contexts, women may only go to mosques that have separate, secondary spaces. One exception involves women in Western Europe and North America, who frequent mosques with their children more often than their counterparts in Muslim-majority countries. The increased involvement of women has potential implications for mosque design.

Whereas elite women have been patrons of mosques through the history of Islam, they have not been involved as designers. One notable exception involved the commission by the Semiha Şakir Foundation of a small charitable mosque, the Şakirin Mosque in Istanbul, commissioned and designd by Hüsrev Tayla, which was opened close to the entrance of Karacaahmet Cemetery, the oldest and largest Muslim cemetery in the city. It made international news, because Zeynep Fadıllıoğlu, who was also a great-niece of Semiha Şakir, was part of the interior design team.[22]

Despite rising Islamaphobia in countries in the West, especially following the September 11, 2001, attacks, more and more mosques are being purpose-designed and built by architects.[23] This may indicate more confidence on the part of Muslim diaspora communities and more acceptance by their Christian-majority countries, controversies notwithstanding.[24] Thus, while Swiss voters in 2009 approved a ban on the construction of new minarets in that country,[25] more recently, a New York City board approved plans for a mosque near Ground Zero.[26]

THE MINARET AND THE DOME IN THE CITYSCAPE

Perhaps the visual elements of the mosque that stand out most prominently in the cityscape are the minaret and, to a lesser extent, the dome. Although neither was used during the Prophet's lifetime, they have today become the most distinctive symbols

8 Ar Rahman Mosque, New York, entrance.
Photo: Maryam Eskandari, 2010, courtesy of the Aga Khan Documentation Center at MIT

of Islam; and their outlines are frequently used in political illustrations. For example, the ban on new minarets in Switzerland was the result of a referendum advocated by a far-right group, the campaign for which featured a striking poster that showed minarets on a Swiss flag, standing erect like missiles, and a woman wearing a *burqa*. In a country with 150 mosques, of which only four have minarets, the ban came after only two more minarets were proposed. This is not the first instance of minarets being opposed in European countries. In Cologne, Germany – a city whose main landmark is a medieval cathedral – another mosque project was opposed by right-wing activists largely because it included two, fifty-five-meter minarets.[27]

The new intolerance against multiculturalism and Islam in Europe has emerged out of fear of the spread of Muslim fundamentalism, but it seems to confuse the spatial forms of Islam with ideological extremism. The competition brief for the Cologne Mosque had required the two minarets, and the winning architect, Paul Böhm, reportedly said in an interview: "This is a mosque, and it should clearly and consciously present itself as such. Muslims should not try to hide."[28] This statement confirms the power of historic visual symbols as a source of community association and pride.

This case also shows how the slender, tall Ottoman minaret and its accompanying broad dome have evolved into the typical marker of the mosque in cityscapes across the world. This has especially been a condition of the modern era. However, the minaret's significance has been defined culturally, not religiously.[29] Its significance lies not in its shape but in the fact that it serves an Islamic function and identity. By contrast, using ideas from Islamic philosophy, some scholars have introduced broader interpretations of different elements of the mosque. The minaret is thus seen as connecting the sky to the earth. Its verticality represents the Muslim desire to reach the upper skies, where God is sitting. The dome is seen as simulating the universe. Its geometry establishes a greater contact with the earth, a symbolism that serves to remind Muslims of their earthly duties.[30]

Functionally, the minaret is no longer needed as a place to make the call for prayer. This is instead done with loudspeakers and, in many cases, a recorded call to prayer, the *azzan*. In spite of this change, most clients for mosques today still insist that architects include minarets in their designs. Apparently, their acquired symbolic value has

9 Dome of the Rock, Jerusalem.
Photo: Kathryn Blair Moore

THE MOSQUE IN THE URBAN CONTEXT 31

become inseparable from the traditional image of the mosque. However, in cultures with no tradition of minarets, other important elements have acquired symbolic significance, and these alternative forms have often been privileged in the design process. Building within contemporary societies challenges architects to identify and create forms that are new but still familiar in the sense of conveying a specific Muslim identity. The designer of a mosque has a responsibility to provide a building that is identifiable for what it is. The design should display an understanding of the mosque's role, history, and symbolic significance. The major task of the architect thus seems to be the creation of a building that is representative of both the spiritual aspirations and social reality of Muslim society.

Domes have had a considerable presence in Islamic architecture. The Dome of the Rock (c. 691–2) was the first monumental construction of Islam (Fig. 9).[31] In early instances, the dome was often added in the middle or at the end of the transept of a mosque in order to emphasize the *mihrab* and accentuate the orientation toward Mecca. In other words, it was used for ceremonial purposes as part of a larger architectural composition. Only later did the dome transform into a unifying and constructional element with a presence in the cityscape, especially as it developed in Ottoman architecture based on the prototype of Hagia Sophia. Although the dome is no longer necessary to span large spaces, and although the function of the minaret may have been superseded in an age of recordings and loudspeakers, both of these elements recur in contemporary mosque design around the world.

REFLECTIONS

A comparative survey of major mosques indicates the existence of a definite language of Islamic visual expression that possesses both a vocabulary and a grammar. The vocabulary deals with the aesthetic models underlying the different components of the mosque. It concerns such issues as constituent forms, surface patterns, colors, and materials. The grammar relates the various systems of organizing these parts into a coherent whole.

While this is true for most examples, scholars have debated the validity of this generalization, arguing that many aspects of this visual language exist in a multiplicity of dialects and are bound to specific cultural regions within the Muslim world. The dome, for instance, received important visual emphasis in the Persian and Turkish regions but was rather unimportant in Africa and the Arabian Peninsula.

The absence of an element in a particular region does not nullify the existence of a language of visual expression. Whether this language can be considered uniquely Islamic or a product of an Islamic identity will always remain debatable. What is important is that the vocabulary and grammar of mosque architecture appear to have achieved certain symbolic meanings upon which there are general societal agreements within the Muslim world.

NEZAR ALSAYYAD is Emeritus Professor of Architecture, Planning, Urban Design and Urban History at the University of California, Berkeley, where he also served as Chair of the Center for Middle Eastern Studies (CMES). He was founder and past President of the International Association for the Study of Traditional Environments (IASTE). Among his numerous books are: *Nile: Urban Histories on the Banks of a River* (2020); *Traditions* (2014); *Cairo: Histories of a City* (2011); *Cinematic Urbanism* (2006); *Making Cairo Medieval* (2005); and *The End of Tradition* (2004).

İPEK TÜRELI is Canada Research Chair in Architectures of Spatial Justice and Associate Professor at McGill University's School of Architecture. She is the author of *Istanbul, Open City: Exhibition Anxieties of Urban Modernity* (2018), and co-editor of *Orienting Istanbul: Cultural Capital of Europe?* (2010). More recent publications are on histories of social engagement in architecture as they intersect with spaces of education, housing, and civil protest events.

SUGGESTIONS FOR FURTHER READING

AlSayyad, Nezar. *Cities and Caliphs: On the Genesis of Arab Muslim Urbanism.* Contributions to the Study of World History (New York: Greenwood Press, 1991).

Erkoçu, Ergün, Cihan Buğdacı, and F. Bolkestein, eds. *The Mosque: Political, Architectural and Social Transformations* (Rotterdam, New York: NAi Publishers, 2009).

Flood, Finbarr Barry. *The Great Mosque of Damascus: Studies on the Makings of an Umayyad Visual Culture,* Islamic History and Civilization, Studies and Texts (Leiden and Boston: Brill, 2001).

Frishman, Martin, and Hasan-Uddin Khan, eds. *The Mosque: History, Architectural Development and Regional Diversity* (London: Thames & Hudson, 2002).

Grabar, Oleg. *The Formation of Islamic Art* (New Haven and London: Yale University Press, 1987).

Serageldin, Ismail and James Steele. *Architecture of the Contemporary Mosque* (London: Academy Editions, 1996).

NOTES

1   Ernst J. Grube, "What Is Islamic Architecture," in *Architecture of the Islamic World: Its History and Social Meaning*, eds. Ernst J. Grube and George Michell (New York: Morrow, 1978), 10–14.

2   John D. Hoag, *Islamic Architecture* (New York: H. N. Abrams, 1977); Doğan Kuban, "The Geographical and Historical Basis for the Diversity of Islamic Architectural Styles," in *Islamic Architecture and Urbanism*, ed. Aydın Germen (Dammam, Saudi Arabia, 1983), 1–5.

3   Albert Habib Hourani and S. M. Stern, eds., *The Islamic City* (Philadelphia: Cassirer; University of Pennsylvania Press, 1970); Ira M. Lapidus, ed. *Middle Eastern Cities* (Berkeley: University of California Press, 1969); L. Carl Brown, ed. *From Madina to Metropolis: Heritage and Change in the Near Eastern City* (Princeton, N.J.: Darwin Press, 1973).

4   K.A.C. Creswell, "Primitive Islam," *A Short Account of Early Muslim Architecture*, revised and supplemented by James W. Allan (Aldersot: Scholar Press, 1989), 6.

5   Nezar AlSayyad, *Cities and Caliphs: On the Genesis of Arab Muslim Urbanism*, Contributions to the Study of World History (New York: Greenwood Press, 1991), 88–90; Finbarr Barry Flood, *The Great Mosque of Damascus: Studies on the Makings of an Umayyad Visual Culture* (Leiden; Boston: Brill, 2001).

6   Creswell, Ibid, 7; Donald Whitcomb, "The City of Istakhr and the Marvdasht Plain," *Akten des VII. Internationalen Kongresses für Iranische Kunst und Archäologie, München 7.–10. September 1976* (Berlin : D. Reimer, 1979), 363–70.

7   Rowland J. Mainstone, *Hagia Sophia: Architecture, Structure, and Liturgy of Justinian's Great Church* (London: Thames & Hudson), 1998; Metin Ahunbay and Zeynep Ahunbay, "Structural Influence of Hagia Sophia on Ottoman Mosque Architecture," in *Hagia Sophia: From the Age of Justinian to the Present*, eds. Robert Mark and Ahmet S. Çakmak (Cambridge: Cambridge University Press, 1992), 179–94; Gülru Necipoğlu, "The Life of an Imperial Monument: Hagia Sophia after Byzantium," ibid., 195–225.

8   Percy Brown, *Indian Architecture: The Islamic Period* (Bombay: D.B. Taraporevala Sons, 1968).

9   Oleg Grabar, "Islamic Religious Art: The Mosque," in *The Formation of Islamic Art* (New Haven, Conn.: Yale University Press, 1973), 108.

10   AlSayyad, *Cities and Caliphs,* 114.

11   Maurice Cerasi, Emiliano Bugatti, and Sabrina D'Agostino, *The Istanbul Divanyolu: A Case Study in Ottoman Urbanity and Architecture* (Würzburg: Ergon Verlag in Kommission, 2004); Çiğdem Kafescioğlu, *Constantinopolis/Istanbul: Cultural Encounter, Imperial Vision, and the Construction of the Ottoman Capital* (University Park: Pennsylvania State University Press, 2009).

12   Gülru Necipoğlu, *The Age of Sinan: Architectural Culture in the Ottoman Empire* (London: Reaktion Books, 2005).

13   Doğan Kuban, "Religious Architecture other than Mosques," in *Muslim Religious Architecture, Part II* (Leiden: Brill, 1985), 27–40.

14   Hasan-Uddin Khan, "An Overview of Contemporary Mosques," in Martin Frishman and Hasan-Uddin Khan, eds., *The Mosque: History, Architectural Development and Regional Diversity* (London: Thames & Hudson, 2002), 247–67.

15   Constantinos A. Doxiadis, "Islamabad: The Creation of a New Capital," in Alexandros-Andreas Kyrtsis, ed., *Constantinos A. Doxiadis: Texts, Design Drawings, Settlements* (Athens: Ikaros, 2006), 168–89 (originally printed in *The Town Planning Review*, 36, 1 (1965): 1–28); and Ahmed Zaib K. Mahsud, "Representing the State: Symbolism and Ideology in Doxiadis' Plan for Islamabad," in Mark Swenarton, ed., *The Politics of Making: Theory, Practice, Product* (London, New York: Routledge, 2007), 61–75.

16   Ibid.

17   Michael E. Meeker, "Once There Was, Once There Wasn't: National Monuments and Interpersonal Exchange," in *Rethinking Modernity and National Identity in Turkey*, eds. Sibel Bozdoğan and Reşat Kasaba (Seattle: University of Washington Press, 1997), 157–91.

18   Khan, "An Overview of Contemporary Mosques," 250.

19   Ibid.

20   Nezar AlSayyad, "The Fundementalist City?" in *The Fundementalist City*, eds. Nezar AlSayyad and Mejgan Massoumi (London and New York: Routledge, 2010), 3–26.

21   Ibid.

22   "Interview with Zeynep Fadillioglu, first woman to design a mosque in Turkey," *Designboom* (December 3, 2014). Available on http://www.designboom.com/architecture/ interview-zeynep-fadillioglu-female-architect-turkey-mosque-12-03-2014/

23   On the United States, see Omar Khalidi, "Approaches to Mosque Design in North America," in *Muslims on the Americanization Path?*, eds. Yvonne Yazbeck Haddad and John L. Esposito (New York: Oxford University Press, 1998), 317–34; and Omar Khalidi, "Mosque Design in the United States," *Saudi Aramco World* (November/December 2001): 24–33.

24   For debates in the Netherlands, see Ergün Erkoçu, Cihan Buğdacı, and F. Bolkestein, eds. *The Mosque: Political, Architectural and Social Transformations* (Rotterdam, New York: NAi Publishers, 2009).

25   Nick Cumming-Bruce and Steven Erlanger, "Swiss Ban Building of Minarets on Mosques," *New York Times*, November 29, 2009.

26   Javier C. Hernandez, "Vote Endorses Muslim Center Near Ground Zero," *New York Times*, May 25, 2010.

27   Mark Landler, "Germans Split over a Mosque and the Role of Islam," *New York Times*, July 5, 2007; and Paul Böhm, interviewed by Thilo Guschas, "German Architect To Build Mosque: 'Muslims Should Not Try to Hide'," translated by John Bergeron, available at http://www.qantara.de/webcom/show_article. php/_c-478/_nr-446/i.html.

28   Nebahat Avcioğlu, "The Contemporary Mosque: 'In What Style Should We Build?'" in *The Mosque: Political, Architectural and Social Transformations*, eds. Ergün Erkoçu, Cihan Buğdacı, and F. Bolkestein (Rotterdam, New York: NAi Publishers, 2009), 61–78.

29   Oleg Grabar, "Islamic Religious Art: The Mosque," in *The Formation of Islamic Art* (New Haven: Yale University Press, 1987), 99–131.

30   Nader Ardalan, "The Visual Language of Symbolic Form," in *Architecture as Symbol and Self-Identity*, ed. Jonathan G. Katz (Philadelphia: Aga Khan Award for Architecture, 1980), 18–22.

31   Oleg Grabar, "The Islamic Dome, Some Considerations," in *Constructing the Study of Islamic Art* (Hampshire: Ashgate, 2006), 87–102.

Gardens as Places of Piety and Faith
D. FAIRCHILD RUGGLES

1 Great Mosque of Cordoba, courtyard, 8th through 21st centuries.
Photo: D.F. Ruggles

The Islamic garden is so closely associated with paradise in modern thought that there often seems to be no distinction between them. Historians, archaeologists, and literary scholars frequently elide the two, referring to built gardens as "earthly paradises" and treating them as reflections of the Paradise that awaits the faithful. Thus, in the first and second editions of the *Encyclopaedia of Islam* Georges Marçais wrote, "The part played by gardens in the past and present life of the Muslim peoples appears to stem from the conception of Paradise, the ideal garden, as portrayed in the Quran, which paints so detailed a picture of the state (of blessedness) reserved exclusively for Believers that it might have served as a model for the creators of gardens in both East and West."[1] In literature and the visual arts, this association between gardens and paradise begins well before the modern period, as poets and chroniclers lauded beautiful places for their resemblance to paradise, and artists adorned the *mihrab* niches of mosques with floral and tree imagery. Even the very terms used for gardens – *jannat* and *firdaus* – are synonyms for paradise, a linguistic relationship that precedes the advent of Islam. For this reason, among others, there is a long history of intertwining gardens as earthly places and as literary, ideal, or religious concepts.

Written sources tell of gardens that no longer exist or that may exist but cannot be known. In these texts, gardens are as much an idea as an actual surviving built form. The most important source is the Quran which is rich with references to paradise, described as a place of rest and delight for the reward of believers, and also to landscape, described as an earthly place of fertility and abundance produced through labor. Since the same word – *jannat* – is used for both the garden of the afterlife and the agricultural gardens of earth, the words

must be read in context to gain their full meaning.[2] The Quran describes the gardens of paradise as shady, luxuriant, fruitful, and watered by four running rivers:

> Announce to those who believe and have done good deeds, glad tidings of gardens under which rivers flow, and where, when they eat the fruits that grow, they will say: "Indeed they are the same as we were given before," so like in semblance the food would be (2:25).

Other verses of the Quran mention not one but two gardens with overhanging branches bearing fruit suspended within easy reach and hanging in pairs, two flowing springs, the ground laid with brocaded carpets (55:46–54). There are precisely four rivers and they flow with not only water, but milk, honey, and wine:

> The semblance of Paradise promised
> the pious and devout (is that of a garden) with streams of water that will not go rank, and rivers of milk
> whose taste will not undergo a change, and rivers of wine delectable to drinkers, and streams of purified honey, and fruits of every kind in them,
> and forgiveness of their Lord (47:15).

This quadrupling of the rivers has been interpreted by modern readers as a description of a cross-axial garden layout, with the channels dividing the garden into four equal quadrants, forming the classic *chahar bagh* type such as that of Taj Mahal and other Mughal gardens (Fig. 2). However, such strictly laid out gardens are rare in the early Islamic world. (The classic *chahar bagh* type to which I refer is not to be confused with the many references to *chahar bagh*s in historical texts which, as Robert McChesney has shown, did not always refer to a cross-axial layout or a garden with four parts.)[3] When they do appear, it is not in the settings of mosques, despite the fact that allusions to paradise abound in the architectural ornament wall decoration and inscriptions. Instead, the *chahar bagh* type appears first in residential palaces, where the focus is demonstrably on the sensory pleasures of worldly life, and subsequently in tombs, which provide the eternal residence for the body whose soul has gone to paradise.[4]

The Quran does not focus exclusively on the gardens of paradise. It describes other, earthly, gardens as well. Thus, verse 27:60 reminds the faithful about God's generosity: "Who created the heavens and the earth, who sends down water from the sky for you, with which He causes graceful gardens to grow?" The gardens that are described here and in verses 6:99 and 6:141 belong to the earth, not the heavens. The fecund landscape thus produced – trees laden with dates, olives, and pomegranates, fields of grain, arbors of grapes – is a sign for the believers (6:99) of God's power and stewardship over all living things, but it is the real, cultivated, agricultural landscape of earth that is portrayed, not the afterlife.

This distinction in the Quran between heavenly and earthly gardens provides a complex set of references. On the one hand, the garden is presented as an actual thing, made of tangible materials with formal qualities, but this is juxtaposed with a garden that is a future promise and thus can only be conceived in metaphorical terms as being like the finest of earthly gardens. Many built Islamic gardens – such as the Taj Mahal – deliberately superimpose the conceptual upon the built, so that the body reposes amidst a garden that deliberately evokes that of heaven. However, as semiotic references, the two are not the same. The Quran's descriptions of the gardens of paradise provide a sensuous evocation of a leisurely setting of shade, honey, fruit, and four running streams. But despite these specific details, the text does not offer anything like an architectural plan for either the ideal or the real garden and thus cannot be used to interpret the form of actual

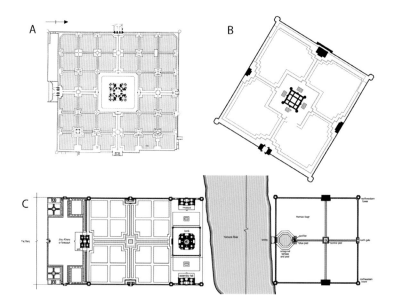

gardens realized by living patrons, architects, and gardeners. Modern historians who conflate gardens with paradise overlook the deliberate and conscious play between the real and the ideal that was present in the minds of the patron and designer as well as the audience that enjoyed the spaces.

Because the garden is an ephemeral art form, earthly gardens planted with specific shrubs and flowers in a formal scheme seldom remain. In the face of this lack of tangible evidence, historians and garden enthusiasts have imaginatively supplied for lost gardens a variety of forms and meanings that reflect more the values of the modern reader than of the gardens in the time they were built and used. Texts are an important source for understanding the way that Islamic gardens were viewed and understood. But, similarly, they reveal far more about the values and expectations of the viewer than they do about the gardens themselves. The viewer is a shifting entity that starts with the patron who surveys the garden that his wealth has produced, and may include many later viewers, including the eighteenth-century painter and nineteenth-century archaeologist imbued with Orientalist fantasies of what the garden does or ought to mean. It also includes contemporary readers who receive not only their own vision of the garden but also the layered history of garden-viewing.

2 Gardens following a *chahr bagh* plan: (A) Tomb of Humayun in New Delhi; (B) Tomb of I'tmad ud-Dawla in Agra; (C) Taj Mahal in Agra. L. Chodon after ASI (A); D. F. Ruggles and B. Variava (B); L. Chodon after Elizabeth Moynihan (C)

While historical texts tell us little about garden form, they do explain function, revealing that the preponderance of gardens were built for pleasure, relaxation, and display. With respect to built gardens with a discernibly religious meaning (as distinct from the spiritual or Islamic, which are terms that permeate Muslim life and therefore cannot be used as distinct categories), there are relatively few examples. Thus, a complete history of gardens has many more palaces and residential gardens in its timeline than mosque or tomb gardens.[5]

MOSQUE COURTYARD GARDENS

The earliest gardens with a specifically religious function were those attached to mosques. However, the evidence regarding the form of these is sketchy at best. These early sites were built in areas with strong Byzantine cultural foundations, and indeed many of the early mosques were converted from churches or built on the site where previously there had been a church. The Great Mosque of Damascus, erected on the site of the Church of St. John, which itself stood over a Roman temple, used the foundations of that church for its own plan. Byzantine churches were sometimes set within gardens with trees, flowers, and fountains.[6] (It should be noted, as so often with Byzantine-Muslim relations, that it is not clear whether the penchant for garden settings emerged first in one context or the other.) If the mosque itself was strongly guided by the preceding church, other vestiges may have clung to the site as well, such as adjacent gardens, trees, and wells. With no liturgical or symbolic significance, there would have been no reason to remove them and every practical reason to keep them.

Whether a mosque was gardened or not, it may have offered images of gardens and orchards that represented paradise to the viewer. Such pictorial programs are very much in evidence at the Dome of the Rock in Jerusalem (690–2) and the Great Mosque of Damascus (begun 705 or 706 and finished in 715). The interior of the Dome of the Rock retains much of its extensive mosaic ornament, displaying sparkling images of trees with generous canopies, some laden with dates, and pots from which scrolling vines emerge. While trees and vines had specific iconographic significance to Muslim viewers, a general interpretation reads both as referring to a paradisiac idea of vegetation and fecundity.[7]

At the Great Mosque of Damascus, mosaics wrap around the inner facade of the courtyard, the encircling arcades, and the interior of the prayer hall. Many of the mosaics represent abstract floral and geometrical ornament. However, there are also scenes of landscaped cities such as that on the façade of the central nave that leads from the courtyard to the *mihrab* (Fig. 3), and the image of the Kaaba over the *mihrab* itself. One panel in the arcades, known as the Barada panel, shows a river flowing through a city of tall buildings amidst trees with lush foliage.

3 Great Mosque of Damascus, nave façade, finished 715.
Photo: D.F. Ruggles

4 Ottoman carpet from Bursa or Istanbul, c. 1580.
Photo: Metropolitan Museum of Art. The James F. Ballard Collection, Gift of James F. Ballard, 1922

Are these intended to represent real cities of the expanding Islamic empire? Or an ideal vision of the afterlife?[8] A partial answer is provided by a mosaicist who worked on the expansions made to the Mosque of the Prophet in Medina, during this same period. He remarked that the mosaic images of gardens were "according to the picture of the Tree of Paradise and its Palace."[9]

Similarly, the innumerable representations of flowers and vines rendered in tile, stucco, paint, and mosaic on the interiors of mosques and tombs throughout the Islamic world represent Paradise. This is particularly true in the case of flower imagery adorning *mihrab*s and prayer rugs, where the act of prayer – signified by the *mihrab*'s form – was visually linked to its ultimate goal through the allusion of a few flowers to represent the celestial garden in its entirety. For example, an Ottoman carpet from Bursa or Istanbul, dated c. 1580, depicts a *mihrab* comprised of three niches, framed by a blue border whose field is filled with diverse flowers (Fig. 4). At the base of the columns, clusters of carnations and tulips emerge, not from vases, but from the ground itself, as if from a garden.

In addition to adornment with floral imagery, some mosques had actual gardens. The practice of planting mosque courtyards with trees was common in Syria and the Iberian Peninsula.[10] While the practice seems to have derived from Byzantine churches in the eastern Mediterranean, it carried over into those churches in Spain that were either converted from mosques at various stages of the reconquest or replanted in imitation of them. Hence, in Cordoba, Guadix, Carmona and other cities, even small church courtyards had a cluster of palm trees, as noted by observers in the fifteenth century as well as today. Of these, the Great Mosque of Cordoba has the oldest continuously planted courtyard, dating from the early ninth century (Fig. 1). It was planted with fruit trees at least as early as 806–8, according to a recorded legal opinion that advocated the removal of the trees, and the plantings may have been in place from the time of the mosque's foundation in 785–6.[11] While the legal judgment forbade the cultivation of trees in a mosque setting, citing them as a distraction from prayer, they nonetheless remained. The practical benefits of shade, dust reduction, and the provision of salary, in the form of harvested fruit, to the mosque guardian, must have outweighed the judge's disapproval. The mosque – now a Catholic cathedral – is still planted with rows of palm trees and oranges that bear fragrant blooms in the early spring and bright fruit in the following seasons. The juridical account's evidence for the presence of trees in the ninth, tenth, and eleventh centuries is confirmed by the visual evidence of Cordoba's city seals which, beginning in 1262, show the Mosque-Cathedral's walls enclosing tall palm trees.[12]

5 Torre del Mihrab in the Partal, Alhambra, 1333–54.
Photo: D.F. Ruggles

The Mosque of Cordoba was by no means unique: the twelfth-century traveler Ibn Jubayr saw palm trees growing in the Medina Mosque's *rawda* (funerary enclosure), and the Mosque of ʿAmr in Cairo may have had a cultivated courtyard, according to the early fifteenth-century writer al-Maqrizi.[13] In the fourteenth century, the Alhambra had a small oratory that had windows on its side walls, offering views to the verdant valley at its feet (Fig. 5).[14] While we have seen that Paradise could be envisioned through the representation of plants and trees in wall mosaics and prayer carpets, did living plants and trees provoke the same association? Was the cultivated mosque courtyard interpreted as making symbolic reference to Paradise, or even as enhancing the worldly act of prayer? There is no evidence to support a paradisiac association and – if we recall the Cordoba jurist's denouncement – firm evidence to suggest that gardens, even when planted within the mosque's enclosure, were instead regarded as distractions from prayer.

TOMB GARDENS

Mosque courtyards are public spaces and, particularly in large congregational mosques, they often reflect the normative architectural values of the surrounding community. But cemeteries and tombs, although often endowed with *mihrab*s and intended for prayer and commemoration, serve the needs of individuals and families and as such, can express personal taste and serve as vehicles for architectural experimentation. Tomb gardens vary considerably; the various kinds do not form a chronological typology. Rather, they seem to be the result of regional preferences and complexity.

The earliest and simplest is the ordinary cemetery, typically a grassy area of graves marked by simple stones. Early Muslim cemeteries were located outside the walls and controlled spaces of the city, although some cities gradually expanded beyond their original perimeters, ultimately penetrating into the cemeteries that once marked their borders. Cairo, for example, is surrounded by the vast Northern and Southern Cemeteries that, almost as soon as they began to be used for the placement of tombs, were also inhabited by caretakers and family members (often in residence temporarily to celebrate religious holidays). As these needed shops, bakeries, and bath houses for the periods when they were there, another residential community of service providers took root alongside. With houses squeezed among the tombs, these neighborhoods have become densely populated.

In some cities, cemeteries attracted loiterers and flirts because the graveyard's suburban location made it easy to avoid being seen by captious eyes. The Iberian *hisba* (city management) writer Ibn ʿAbdun (fl. late eleventh or early twelfth century) deplored the wine drinking and debauchery that transpired there.[15] But some cemeteries were more respectable and were formally designed. For example, the Hayr al-Zajjali (late tenth-eleventh century), was created as a public park by a vizier in the Zajjali family, for the enjoyment of the people of Cordoba. But when its owner died, it became an endowed funerary complex, holding first his tomb and soon thereafter the tomb of his companion, the poet Ibn Shuhayd (992–1035). The garden no longer exists, but a description remains:

> Its courtyard is of pure white marble; a stream traverses it, wriggling like a snake. There is [also] a basin into which all waters fall. The roof [of the pavilion] is decorated with gold and blue and in these colors also are decorated the sides and various parts. The garden has files of trees symmetrically aligned and its flowers smile from open buds. The foliage of the garden prevents the sun seeing the ground; and the breeze, blowing day and night over the garden, is loaded with scents.[16]

The insertion of graves into the already planted pleasure garden marked an important turning point in garden history because it united the explicitly worldly garden, associated with lover's trysts, drinking bouts, and indolence, with the implied garden of paradise, the ultimate reward for prayer and faith.

While the symbolism of gardens for expressions of eternal rest and the rewards of the afterlife seems obvious – so much so that many writers assume that *all* Islamic gardens are earthly reflections of paradise – it was not made explicitly until tombs were either gardened or placed in gardens. Prior to this, paradisiac symbolism might occur in the depiction of the divine garden, as seen at the Great Mosque of Damascus, and actual living trees might grace the courtyard of a mosque, as seen in Cordoba, but there is no evidence that the actual plantings were read in the same semiotic terms as the mosaic representations of trees and vines.

Many Muslim funerary complexes sprang up around the freestanding tomb of a prominent individual – a sultan or a venerated religious figure.

6 Cemetery at Ahlat, Lake Van, twelfth–fifteenth centuries.
Photo: Dick Osseman, Creative Commons License

The architectural tomb acted as a magnet, attracting the burials of those who were associated with the deceased in life, such as his or her children or followers. Even in succeeding generations, when the personal tie was no longer present, graves continued to be situated in close proximity to a tomb that emanated an aura of sanctity, or *baraka* (literally, "blessing"). Generally, these gravestones took the form of simple oblong slabs. Examples of such graves occurred in the fourteenth century among the Merinids of Morocco, as for example in the Chella funerary complex (1310–34) in Rabat where narrow slabs are laid horizontally on the ground, and the Seljuqs of Anatolia as at Ahlat (twelfth-fifteenth century) on the shores of Lake Van, where the horizontal stones are set against vertical slabs with *muqarnas* cornices and other forms of adornment (Fig. 6).

Some of the most beautiful funerary gardens are those in Ottoman Turkey. In Istanbul, for example, there were large cemeteries for ordinary people situated at the city's periphery, but the Ottoman rulers also endowed large complexes (*kulliye*s) that were centered on a mosque with a variety of other institutional buildings, such as *madrasa*s, a Quran school, library, soup kitchen, hospital, and baths. Attached to the mosque, either on the side of the prayer hall or, where space allowed, in a separate cemetery enclosure at the *qibla* end, the founder often placed his own tomb. Around this tomb, the intervening spaces were gradually used for smaller graves, marked by a vertical slab – adorned with a sculpted turban or fez for men, or flowers for women – inscribed with Quranic verses and the name of the deceased. The Suleymaniye and the Yeni Valide complex, both in Istanbul, have large tombs with surrounding funerary areas that are densely filled with graves.

The tomb of Sultan Suleyman (died 1566) was a large, freestanding octagonal chamber surmounted by a double-shell dome, with a porch on its eastern façade. The mausoleum is located in a courtyard attached to the *qibla* wall of the mosque. Nearby in the same enclosure, his wife Hurrem (d. 1558) was interred in a similar but smaller tomb (Fig. 7).[17] However, the construction of such funerary precincts was not the privilege of the sultan alone. The mosque built for Selim II's Grand Admiral and son-in-law, Piyale Pasha (1573), included the patron's tomb, surrounded by the graves of dervishes from the adjacent dervish lodge.[18] The Yeni Valide Mosque complex (begun 1597; fin. 1663) was built

7 Tomb of Hurrem, Suleymaniye, Istanbul, finished 1557.
Photo: D.F. Ruggles

in Eminönü, Istanbul, by the valide-sultan (queen mother) Hatice Turhan Sultan (on foundations begun by her predecessor, Safiye Sultan) with a majestic tomb in which the patron herself was interred.[19] The tomb, a magnificent domed square measuring 15 by 15 m., was built between 1661 and 1665, but this structure was expanded in the following century to accommodate the many female members of the Ottoman house who sought burial at her side. Eventually her son Mehmed IV, grandsons Mustafa II and Ahmed III, and great grandsons Mahmud I and Osman III were buried here as well.[20] The overflow was buried in an adjoining garden where vertical headstones marked

GARDENS AS PLACES OF PIETY AND FAITH 41

8 Hatice Turbe gravestones, at the Yeni Valide Mosque in Eminönü, Istanbul, second half of the seventeenth century.
Photo: D.F. Ruggles

horizontal slabs or a frame forming a box, within which grew a rose, irises or other colorful flowers (Fig. 8). The paradisiac theme of the deceased buried amidst living flowers was extended to the tomb interior in the nineteenth century when murals were painted in the spandrels of the recessed arches of the tomb added for the ladies: the scenes show Mecca and landscapes of palm trees.

The symbolism of the flowers to signify rebirth after the fading of life is a nearly universal image, not only across the Islamic world but in other religions and cultures, too (Fig. 9). The garden realized for these cemeteries was both real and metaphorical, realized through the medium of actual flowers and shrubs as well as vegetal representations in relief sculpture, murals, and tile that reminded the viewer of the promise of paradise. The present-day state of the funerary precincts described here may differ from that of the sixteenth and seventeenth centuries, but the floral imagery of the gravestones (an element that became more common in later periods) and apertures for planting actual flowers are unmistakable signs that they were gardened. Moreover, scenic prints from the Ottoman period show mosques and tombs in verdant settings. For example Selim II's large, octagonal, domed tomb (built 1574–7) was the first Ottoman sultan's royal tomb to be placed in the precinct of the Hagia Sophia, by then converted to a mosque. The tomb was placed in courtyard on south side of the complex. An engraving from the following century shows that the setting for this tomb, and others added subsequently, was thickly planted with tall trees.[21]

The Timurids of Iran and Afghanistan patronized monumental tomb complexes as well as exurban cemeteries. The Shah-i Zinda was a particularly lovely Timurid funerary complex on the outskirts of Samarkand that grew gradually from the mid-fourteenth to the mid-fifteenth century. It was patronized primarily (although not exclusively) by the princesses of Timurid house, who chose to situate their tombs in the vicinity of the remains of a Muslim saint, Qutham ibn Abbas, the Prophet's cousin.[22] Innovative, brilliant blue tilework adorns their facades and interiors, but in other respects the structure of the tombs is that of a classic Timurid dome-on-square type. If the form of the mausolea was standard, the setting was remarkable. The diminutive structures were not organized in a straight line or a courtyard but along an avenue adapted to natural terrain. Thus the avenue not only turns but rises as it reaches the summit and endpoint: the saint's tomb. All around on the hillside, persons of lesser wealth and distinction were buried to benefit from the same saintly *baraka* (blessedness) that the royal Timurid patrons enjoyed. By this point in history, a conscious correlation between earthly gardens and heavenly paradise had been made, and hence the appropriateness of the landscape setting.

When Babur, the founder of the Mughal dynasty, died in 1530 in Hindustan (India), he was temporarily interred in Agra until his remains could be transferred to Kabul sometime between 1539 and 1544. While his own tomb no longer exists, it was described in the nineteenth century as an enclosure of carved white marble in a garden setting. The Mughals made a practice of visiting the graves of their forebears to mark death anniversaries, and these ceremonies were often quite lavish. Shah Jahan's biographer noted that on the first anniversary of the death of the emperor's queen, Mumtaz, the emperor assembled with his nobles, officers, and learned sheikhs in her tomb complex – the Taj Mahal – where his staff had "erected gorgeous pavilions in the gardens around her grave, spread magnificent carpets and laid out a lavish array of foods." In addition to the feast

9 Tomb of Ali ibn Hamzeh, Shiraz, floral tribute, 2011.
Photo: D.F. Ruggles

served to the dignitaries, alms were disbursed to the poor.[23] Perhaps because of the need for such observances (known as '*urs*), Babur's tomb, by the mid-sixteenth century, had been elaborated with a mosque, caravanserai, pools, and an additional tomb arrayed on fifteen stepped terraces.[24] The garden today is one of Kabul's most frequented public parks (Fig. 10).

From India, there are many surviving tomb gardens. In the sultanate period, the *madrasa*-tomb-mosque complex known as Hauz Khas in Delhi was built by the Tughluq ruler Firoz Shah in 1352 on foundations that dated fifty years earlier. The buildings neatly border two sides of a large reservoir that filled seasonally with monsoon rains, attracting animals and waterfowl (Fig. 11). As in the Hayr al-Zajjali of Cordoba, this patron's tomb was added upon his death in 1388, after the site had already been developed as a *madrasa*. The tomb stands in a dominant position at the corner of the reservoir, while several lesser tombs fill the adjacent precinct, which was adorned with flowers and fruit trees.

While the sultans of Hindustan understood the symbol of enduring piety and presence conveyed by a mausoleum, the Mughals who succeeded them recognized the power of imperial tombs to convey not only pious presence but dynastic legitimacy. Thus the tomb built for the Mughal emperor Humayun, by his son and or wife, cast the present as an inevitable outcome of the past, and projected it forward into the future.[25] The tomb (finished in 1571) stands in an enormous cross-axial garden (almost 30 acres in area) from the center of which the great mausoleum emerges like a mountain (Fig. 12). The garden is divided by broad walkways with narrow water channels running down the center that further divide the quadrants into nine plots. Where the channels cross, they swell into pools with waterjets, and where they drop even slightly from one level to another, their waters tumble down textured waterchutes (called *chadar*s) that animate the water, and in so doing, clean it.

Humayun's son Akbar was likewise buried in a tomb set within gardens (fin. 1612–13). Although the architecture of the five-storied mausoleum has little in common with that of Humayun, the

10 Bagh-e Babur, Kabul, contemporary restoration of a sixteenth-century site.
Photo: Jim Kelly, Creative Commons license

GARDENS AS PLACES OF PIETY AND FAITH 43

11 Haus Khaz, New Delhi, fourteenth century.
Drawing after Antony Welch

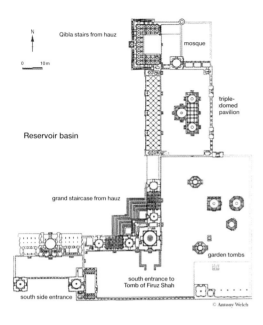

garden layout is similar: a cross-axial plan with the tomb rising from a platform at the center.[26] As in Humayun's Tomb, the quadrants are defined by wide paths with central water channels that are aligned with the monumental *pishtaq* (framed *iwan* niche) on each face of the mausoleum. The garden as seen today appears plainer, with fewer quadrants, pools, jets, and *chadar*s, but the site is poorly studied and the apparent simplicity may be the result of changes made during the colonial period.

The Tomb of I'tmad ud-Dawla (1622–8) was built by the empress Nur Jahan for her mother and father, the prime minister to Jahangir, called I'tmad ud-Dawla ("Pillar of the Empire"). Although considerably smaller than the tomb complexes of Humayun and Akbar, like them the mausoleum stands in a rectangular enclosure at the intersection of the garden's cardinal axes (Figs. 2 and 13). As in previous tombs, a grand gate marks the entry into the complex and the beginning of the primary axis, but in other respects the tomb is unique. It is positioned on the banks of the Yamuna River and the main garden axis culminates in a riverfront pavilion that served as a point of entry for visitors arriving by boat.[27] In addition to serving as a portal, the pavilion provides an elevated, airy place from which to observe the river landscape, a leisurely enjoyment further emphasized by the incised wall ornament displaying images of vases with flowers and trays with cups. The garden that surrounds the central tomb is echoed in the wall ornament of the tomb itself where the arched doorways into the tomb contain images of narcissus bouquets and cypress trees (a symbol of immortality) entwined with sinuous vines, and the inner walls are painted with images of trees, flowering vines, and flowers such as tulips, chrysanthemum, and fritillaria (Fig. 14). This theme does not contradict the complex's pious function, for paradise itself is described in the Quran (and later commentary) as a place of pleasure and relaxation. Indeed, Quran sura 89 (The Dawn), inscribed on the main gate, alludes to the tomb's verdant setting and paradise itself, inviting the visitor: "O you tranquil soul, Return to your Lord, well-pleased and well-pleasing Him. 'Enter then among My votaries, Enter then My garden.'"

The innovations developed by Nur Jahan at this tomb for her parents (who were in-laws but not members of the Mughal line), inspired the much larger, imperial Taj Mahal, likewise located on the river's edge in Agra. The Taj (1632–43) was built by the emperor Shah Jahan, for his wife, Mumtaz Mahal, although Shah Jahan was ultimately buried there as well. The tomb proper echoes the great domed Tomb of Humayun, but in a departure from that model it stands at the far end of a huge enclosure, on a raised platform that anchors the end of the main axis. It is flanked on either side by a mosque and an assembly hall (whose presence is owed purely to the desire for architectural symmetry). Unlike in previous tombs where the sepulcher interrupted the progress of the axis and firmly possessed the center, the displacement here lengthens the axis, heightening the drama of the approach. As in the tomb of I'timad al-Daula, the theme of paradise is everywhere evident. The gleaming white marble walls of the mausoleum are carved with low relief panels at floor level that represent tulips and lilies in a naturalistic (albeit often botanically inventive) manner (Fig. 15).[28] The spandrels of the

12 Tomb of Humayun, New Delhi, 1565 or 1569.
Photo: D.F. Ruggles

13 Tomb of I'timad al-Daula, Agra, finished 1628.
Photo: D.F. Ruggles

GARDENS AS PLACES OF PIETY AND FAITH

14 Tomb of I'tmad ud-Dawla, interior with (retouched) wall paintings.
Photo: D.F. Ruggles

arches of the *iwan*s on the mausoleum's façade are adorned with scrolling floral vines in incised stone that recall the *pietra dura* inlay at I'timad al-Daula. The naturalism reaches its zenith in the cenotaphs and the enclosing screen, where the *pietra dura* columbines, fritillaria, poppies, tulips, and lilies erupt in blossoms of brilliant red, a color associated with blood and death and "the mystical quest of the soul for God."[29]

Paradise was also evoked in the inscriptions that adorned the gate, mausoleum, and mosque. However, unlike the fresh beauty of the garden and floral imagery, which suggest leisure and reward, the Quranic verses that enframe the *iwan*s of the three buildings refer ominously to the Day of Judgment, insisting that the viewer ponder and prepare for the afterlife, rather than merely indulging in the fleeting pleasures of the surrounding garden.[30] In fact, tomb gardens encourage people to view them in both lights: as a site for formal commemoration and pious contemplation of the afterlife, and also as a foretaste of the paradise that will exceed the pleasure experienced on earth. At its simplest, a tomb asks the present viewer to remember the dead. But these magnificent complexes had a more ambitious political purpose: in addition to their commemorative function, they planted their deceased occupants in a dominant position in space and, more broadly, in human society.

A garden is an ephemeral form, its blooms opening in a single day to embrace the sun and then falling, spent, to the ground. Yet in these tomb complexes, the garden is joined with the mausoleum, an architectural form that unites past and present in a statement of enduring dynastic authority and pious faith calculated to project into the future. One is utterly of the moment, the other a powerful statement of permanence, exquisitely balanced in the tomb garden.

15 Taj Mahal wall relief, finished 1643.
Photo: D.F. Ruggles

D. FAIRCHILD RUGGLES is the Debra Mitchell Chair in Landscape Architecture at the University of Illinois, Urbana-Champaign. She is the art and architecture field editor for the *Encyclopedia of Islam*, and is the author of two award-winning books on Islamic landscape history, as well as eleven other authored, edited and co-edited volumes on Islamic art, cultural heritage, landscape history and theory, and the arts patronage of women in the Islamic world and South Asia.

SUGGESTIONS FOR FURTHER READING

Brookes, John. *Gardens of Paradise* (London: Weidenfeld and Nicolson, c.1987).

Conan, Michel, ed. *The Middle East Garden Traditions: Unity and Diversity* (Washington, D.C.: Dumbarton Oaks, 2007).

Koch, Ebba. *The Complete Taj Mahal and the Riverfront Gardens of Agra* (London: Thames and Hudson, 2006).

Ruggles, D. Fairchild. *Gardens, Landscape, and Vision in the Palaces of Islamic Spain* (University Park: Penn State University Press, 2000).

Ruggles, D. Fairchild. *Islamic Gardens and Landscapes* (Philadelphia: University of Pennsylvania Press, 2008).

NOTES

[1] Georges Marçais, "Bustan," *Encyclopaedia of Islam*, 2nd ed. (2004), I: 1345–6.

[2] D. F. Ruggles, *Gardens, Landscape, and Vision in the Palaces of Islamic Spain* (University Park: Pennsylvania State University Press, 2000), 217–20. All Quran excerpts are from the Ahmed Ali translation, *Al-Qur'an: A Contemporary Translation* (Princeton: Princeton University Press, 1984).

[3] See Robert McChesney, "Some Observations on 'Garden' and Its Meaning in the Property Transactions of the Juybari Family in Bukhara, 1544–77," in *Gardens in the Time of the Great Muslim Empires*, ed. Attilio Petruccioli (Leiden: Brill, 1997), 97–109.

[4] D. F. Ruggles, "Il giardino con planta a croce nel Mediterraneo islamico," in *Il giardino islamico: Architettura, natura, paesaggio*, ed. Attilio Petruccioli (Milan: Electa, 1993), 143–54.

[5] Thus for example, of the nearly 100 gardens and landscape sites listed in D. F. Ruggles, *Islamic Gardens and Landscapes* (Philadelphia: University of Pennsylvania Press, 2008), 75% pertain to residences or palaces.

[6] A. Littlewood, "Gardens of the Palaces," in *Byzantine Court Culture from 829–1204*, ed. Henry Maguire (Washington, D.C.: Dumbarton Oaks, 1997), 13–38.

[7] Myriam Rosen-Ayalon, *The Early Islamic Monuments of al-Haram al-Sharif: An Iconographic Study* (Jerusalem: Hebrew University, 1989), 46–69.

[8] Richard Ettinghausen and Oleg Grabar, *The Art and Architecture of Islam 650–1250* (Harmondsworth: Penguin Books, 1987), 42–44.

[9] Ibn Zabbala (fl. second century A. H.), cited in J. Sauvaget, *La Mosquée Omeyyade de Médine* (Paris: Vanoest, 1947), 26, 81. Translated in Rosen-Ayalon, *The Early Islamic Monuments of al-Haram al-Sharif*, 49.

[10] Ruggles, *Islamic Gardens and Landscapes*, 93.

[11] The jurist was Ibn Sahl (d. 1093). The Arabic text is published by Thami Azemmouri, "Les Nawazil d'Ibn Sahl: section relative à l'Ihtisab," *Hespéris-Tamuda* 14 (1973): 7–108; and an English translation appears in Ruggles, *Islamic Gardens and Landscapes*, 92–3. For a discussion of this courtyard garden, see also D. F. Ruggles, "From the Heavens and Hills: The Flow of Water to the Fruited Trees and Ablution Fountains in the Great Mosque of Cordoba," in *Rivers of Paradise: Water in Islamic Art*, ed. Sheila Blair and Jonathan Bloom (London: Yale University Press, 2009), 81–103.

[12] Leopoldo Torres Balbás, "El ŷāmūr de alcolea y otros de varios alminares," *Al-Andalus* 23 (1958): 192–202, in which he reproduces drawings made of the seals by J. Caro Baroja. One of the seals is also reproduced in Ruggles, "From the Heavens and Hills," 92.

[13] J. Pedersen, "Masdjid, I. In the central Islamic lands, D. The component parts and furnishings, 2. Details," in *Encyclopaedia of Islam*, rev. ed. (electronic), citing al-Maqrizi, *Kitab al-khitat*; Ibn Jubayr, *The travels of Ibn Jubayr (Rihla)*, ed. William Wright, 2nd ed. revised by M.J. De Goeje (Leiden: E. J. Brill, 1907), 194.

[14] Ruggles, *Gardens, Landscape, and Vision*, 177–9.

[15] Ibn 'Abdūn, translated in E. Lévi-Provençal, *Séville Musulmane au Début du XIIe siècle* (Paris: Maisonneuve, 1947), 57–60.

[16] Ibn Khaqan, *Qala'id*, trans. by James Dickie, "The Islamic Garden in Spain," in *The Islamic Garden*, ed. Elizabeth Macdougall and Richard Ettinghausen (Washington, D.C.: Dumbarton Oaks, 1976), 92–3 (89–105). For a full discussion of this garden and its implications for garden symbolism, see Ruggles, *Gardens, Landscape, and Vision*, 130–2.

[17] In the Suleymaniye mosque, the stones were cleaned and reerected in the 1980s according to Godfrey Goodwin, "Gardens of the Dead in Ottoman Times," *Muqarnas* 5 (1988), 62 (61–69).

[18] Godfrey Goodwin, *A History of Ottoman Architecture* (New York: Thames and Hudson, 1971), 277–9.

[19] All of the following information on Turhan's tomb is provided by Lucienne Thys-Şenocak, *Ottoman Women Builders* (Aldershot: Ashgate, 2006), 237–44.

[20] Thys-Şenocak, *Ottoman Women Builders*, 243, citing Hafiz Hüseyin al-Ayvansarayî, *Hadikat ül-Cevami* (Istanbul, H. 1281), I: 20.

[21] The image is from G. J. Grelot, *Relation nouvelle d'un voyage de Constantinople* (Paris, 1680), reproduced in Goodwin, *History of Ottoman Architecture*, 280.

[22] Roya Marefat, "Timurid Women: Patronage and Power," *Asian Art* 6/2 (1993), 28–49.

[23] 'Inayat Khan, *The Shah Jahan Nama*, ed. and trans. W. E. Begley and Z. A. Desai (Delhi: Oxford University Press, 1990), 84.

[24] Ute Frank-Vogt, K. Bartle, and Th. Urban, "Bagh-e Babur, Kabul: Excavating a Mughal Garden," in Ute Frank-Vogt and Hans-Joachim Weisshaar, eds. *South Asian Archaeology*. Proceedings of the Seventeenth International Conference of the European Association of South Asian Archaeologists, 7–11 July 2003, Bonn (Aachen: Linden Soft, 2005), 541–57; Jolyon Leslie, "Recovery and restoration: two projects in Kabul," in *Art and Archaeology of Afghanistan: Its Fall and Survival* (Handbook of Oriental Studies. Handbuch der Orientalistik. VIII: Central Asia, 14), ed. Juliette van Krieken-Pieters (Leiden: Brill, 2006), 169–85; and Salome Zajadacz-Hastenrath, "A Note on Babur's Lost Funerary Enclosure at Kabul," *Muqarnas* 14 (1997): 135–42.

[25] Ruggles, "Humayun's Tomb and Garden: Typologies and Visual Order," in *Gardens in the Time of the Great Muslim Empires*, 173–86.

[26] E. W. Smith, *Akbar's Tomb, Sikandra near Agra, Described and Illustrated* (Allahabad: Superintendent of Government Printing Office 35, 1909).

[27] See Amine Okada (text) and Jean-Louis Nou (extraordinary photography), *Un Joyau de l'Inde Moghole* (Milan: 5 Continents Editions, 2003); also Ebba Koch, *The Complete Taj Mahal* (London: Thames and Hudson, 2006), 48–53.

[28] Koch, *Complete Taj*, 158–9.

[29] Ibid., 140, 170.

[30] Wayne Begley, "The Myth of the Taj Mahal and a New Theory of Its Symbolic Meaning," *Art Bulletin* 61 (1979): 7–37, and Begley and Z. A. Desai, *Taj Mahal: The Illumined Tomb: An Anthology* (Seattle: University of Washington Press, 1990).

Complex Patterns and Three-Dimensional Geometry in Islamic Religious Architecture

IMDAT AS

1 Michel Abboud, Park51, New York City, 2010, a design proposal for an Islamic community center in downtown Manhattan.
Computer Rendering: SOMA Architects

In recent years, there has been a growing interest in the study and use of complex geometric patterns found in Islamic art and architecture. When we talk about ornament in the Muslim world, many people think about endlessly repeating intricate geometric patterns, found on a wide range of manmade artifacts, from household objects to entire monuments. Two seminal publications have spearheaded this interest: Gülru Necipoğlu's revelation of a medieval pattern book, in *The Topkapi Scroll: Geometry and Ornament in Islamic Art and Architecture* (1995) and more recently Peter Lu and Paul Steinhardt's paper "Decagonal and quasicrystalline tilings in medieval Islamic architecture" (2007) in *Science*. Necipoğlu, uncovered a late fifteenth-century Turkmen-Timurid medieval scroll found at the archives of the Topkapi Palace in Istanbul, known as the Topkapi scroll. This scroll contains two- and three-dimensional geometric patterns and inscriptions, star and polygon patterns, projections of *muqarnas* vaults, and details of architectural ornaments that medieval artisans used as templates in their projects. Lu and Steinhardt's paper, on the other hand, demonstrates how medieval artisans may have built their complex patterns using a novel tiling method. This new method resulted in unprecedented non-repeating patterns, which they argue modern science has only come to understand in the second half of the twentieth century.

Because of the recent construction boom in the Middle East, these two publications have received great interest from contemporary architects. In fact, many newer projects display traces of age-old Islamic ornaments, such as Zaha Hadid's Marsa Residential Tower project (2005) in Dubai; Farshid Moussavi's College of Design and Communication

(2010) in London; or Michel Abboud's Park51, a design proposal for an Islamic community center in lower Manhattan (2010), New York City (Fig. 1). In these and similar projects, the hallmarks of ornamentation, like repetition, serialization, and standardization reappear in new organic figures, pixel-based screens, structural elements, printed glass facades, and the like.

In this essay, I will shed light on geometric patterns as they relate to the Islamic world. I will first describe various types of two-dimensional geometric patterns; second, discuss how they may have been used by artisans in three-dimensional architecture; third, elaborate on their use in contemporary architectural practice; and finally, discuss meanings attributed to them by various schools of thought. Although geometric patterns constitute the majority of ornamentation in Islamic art and architecture, there are also floral, calligraphic, and to a certain degree figural ornaments. However, the scope of discussion is limited to geometrically constructed ornamentation.

TWO-DIMENSIONAL GEOMETRY

Geometric patterns start appearing on Islamic artifacts in the tenth century, at the same time that there were major developments in geometry and mathematics. They are made through a complex system of tightly-knit unit cells that do not leave any gap on a given surface and are interchangeably labeled as lattices, tiles, mosaics, grids, or more commonly arabesques. I will use the term *girih* (knotted) patterns throughout the essay, when referring to these geometric patterns.

Girih patterns were mainly drawn with a straightedge and compass, and two medieval

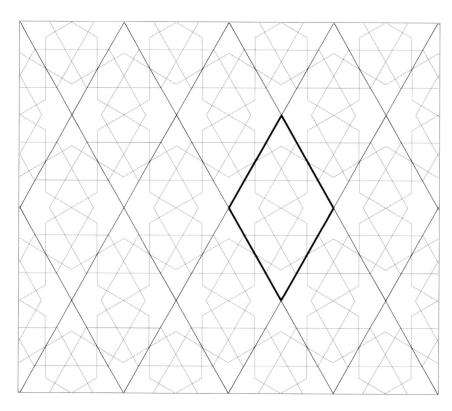

2 Periodic patterns, repetition of a unit cell to cover a surface. Drawing: Imdat As

sources describe their mathematical underpinnings: Abu'l Wafa al-Buzjani's (940–998) treatise *On Geometric Constructions Necessary for the Artisan* and an anonymous addendum on al-Buzjani's work dating to the thirteenth century, *On Interlocks of Similar or Corresponding Figures*. These manuscripts illustrate geometrical topics, such as methods of bisection, division of a circle into five equal parts, and the cutting and arranging of paper tiles to form various patterns.[1]

Mathematicians classify geometric patterns into periodic and non-periodic patterns. Periodic patterns can be infinitely repeated without any change in their coherency. That is, one can draw a polygon around a unit cell and juxtapose the cell infinitely, like using identical sheets of wallpaper in covering a wall (Fig. 2). Periodic patterns are additionally grouped according to their type of rotational symmetries. A pattern has a rotational symmetry if it can be rotated around a pivot at a particular angle and maintains its shape. Periodic patterns can only have one-fold, two-fold, three-fold, four-fold, and six-fold rotational symmetries; that is, one-fold rotational symmetries can only be rotated by 360/1=360°, two-fold rotational symmetries can be rotated by 360/2=180°, three-fold rotational symmetries by 360/3=120°, four-fold rotational symmetries by 360/4=90°, and six-fold rotational symmetries by 360/6=60°. Even though many *girih* patterns contain pentagons, decagons, and many other equilateral polygons, which in themselves have, for example, five-fold or ten-fold symmetries, they do not dictate the overall rotational symmetry of the larger pattern. Artisans were using various colors, and were applying additional rules, such as moving the unit cell along an axis, mirroring it, rotating it, or mirroring and moving it concurrently, in order to create a richer variety in pattern compositions. Nevertheless, the limited number of rotational symmetries in combination with additional translational rules produces only seventeen different types of patterns, which is also known as the wallpaper group (Fig. 3).

Non-periodic patterns, on the other hand, were only recently discovered in Islamic architecture. Lu and Steinhardt revealed five distinctive *girih*

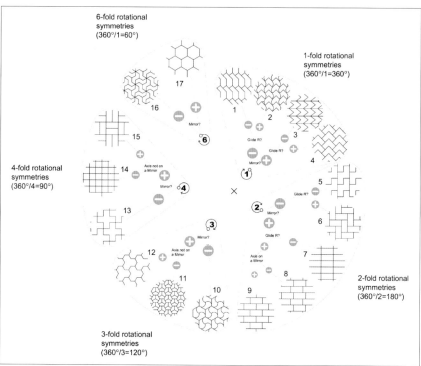

3 Seventeen periodic patterns and their rotational symmetries. Drawing: Imdat As

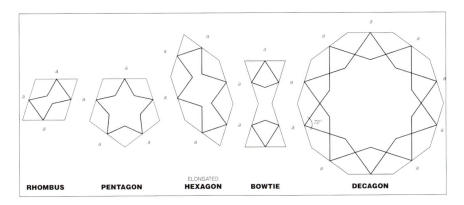

4 Five *girih* tiles of nonperiodic patterns: a decagon, an elongated hexagon, a bowtie, a pentagon, and a rhombus.

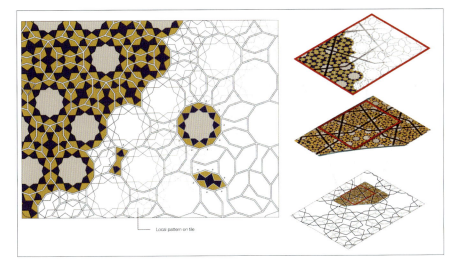

5 The construction of a nonperiodic pattern with three tiles: a decagon, an elongated hexagon, and a bowtie (right); self-similarity at different scales (left).
Drawing: Imdat As

tiles drawn with red ink on select *girih* patterns in the Topkapi scroll, and argued that a wide range of decagonal *girih* patterns were assembled by juxtaposing a combination of five *girih* tiles: a decagon, an elongated hexagon, a bowtie, a pentagon, and a rhombus (Fig. 4). The introduction of a new tiling method made it easier, faster, and more accurate for artisans to compose *girih* patterns and led them to innovate unprecedented non-periodic surface patterns with five-fold symmetries (Fig. 5).

A pattern is identified as non-periodic when it satisfies decagonal geometry and self-similar subdivisions. Decagonal geometry was achieved by two conditions: first, each tile possessed equal edge lengths; and second, each tile was engraved with a local pattern that produced internal matching rules guiding artisans in juxtaposing the tiles into uninterrupted larger patterns. The engravings were made of straight lines intersecting at the midpoints by multiples of 36°. Therefore, the pattern composition always followed a decagonal geometry (360°/36°=10). Self-similarity, on the other hand, was accomplished by the fact that each tile was able to be infinitely subdivided into identical smaller tiles. This condition produced fractal geometries that generated identical patterns at infinitely different scales.

The most well-known non-periodic patterns were discovered by English mathematician Roger Penrose in the 1970s. In its simplest form, the Penrose tiling is built by two basic shapes, the kite and the dart (Fig. 6). The ratio of kites to darts is always an irrational number that gets closer to the value of 1.618 (the Golden ratio) the more tiles are used. Lu and Steinhardt demonstrated that Penrose patterns astonishingly appear on some Seljuk monuments, such as the spandrel of the Darb-i Imam Shrine (1453) in Isfahan (Fig. 7). This groundbreaking finding vividly illustrates the ingenuity of medieval artisans and mathematicians, who perhaps collaborated and produced these complex patterns five centuries before their discovery in the modern world.[2]

THREE-DIMENSIONAL GEOMETRY

Girih patterns are mostly planar two-dimensional surface applications, but are there any geometric rules and methods that allowed medieval architects to transform these two-dimensional projections into three-dimensional artifacts? The question is not about projecting patterns onto non-planar surfaces, such as domes, squinches and the like, but about their translation into three-dimensional architecture. The answer is elusive; however, there are commonalities between two- and three-dimensional artwork in terms of construction processes, periodicity, and proportional systems. I will briefly describe the construction of *muqarnas* vaults, the use of modular units in mosque design, and the employment of common proportional systems that may have guided both two-dimensional *girih* patterns and three-dimensional architecture.

Girih patterns are possibly best reflected in three-dimensional *muqarnas* vaults, also commonly known as stalactite vaults or honeycombs. The *muqarnas* vault is the most revered invention of Islamic art and architecture and, although its origins are still debated, its widespread use in Islamic architecture dates back to the twelfth century.[3] *Muqarnas* vaults were used as decorative elements to hide odd edges and intersections of volumetric compositions; for example, most commonly at the intersection of domes and their square or octagonal bases, but also at cornices, entrance portals, minaret balconies, staircases, and so on (Fig. 8).

Despite the popularity of *muqarnas* vaults in the Islamic world, there are no historical sources describing their construction methods. For example, the Topkapi scroll only shows plain ceiling plans and do not reveal their rules of construction. Therefore, it is commonly argued that medieval artisans have empirically translated drawings of *girih* patterns into the third dimension.[4] However, one major medieval source, *Miftah al-Hisab* (Key of Arithmetic), by the Persian mathematician Jamshid al-Kashi (1427) discusses individual *muqarnas* blocks, and elaborates on how to calculate their cubic volumes. According to al-Kashi, *muqarnas* blocks are based on four elementary shapes: the square, the rhombus, the kite, and the dart. He defines the height of a unit as being roughly two times its width, but leaves the actual height to be determined by the spatial constraints of the project; for example, the height of a block would be defined by the overall height of the area to be covered, divided by the number of tiers (Fig. 9).[5] Artisans would sculpt these blocks with particular

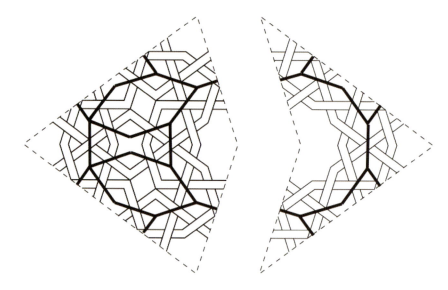

6 The kite and the dart tile in a Penrose pattern. Note the elongated hexagon, bowtie and decagon on the tiles.
Drawing: Imdat As

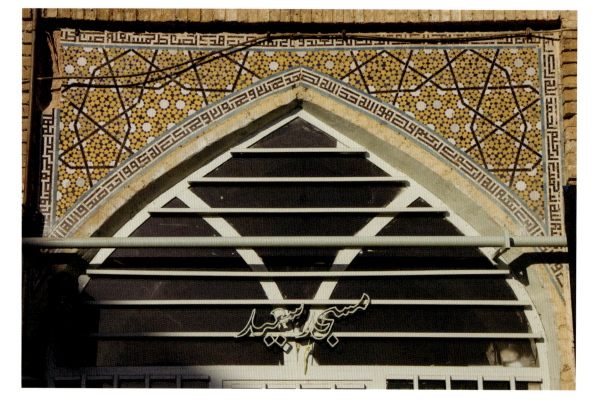

7 Darb-i Imam Shrine, Isfahan, 1453, view of spandrel.
Photo: Simon & Andrew

52 AS

8 Friday Mosque, Isfahan, eighth–eighteenth century, *muqarnas* vault at the southern *iwan*.
Photo: Rob & Ale

curvatures and create corbel-like units. Figure 10 shows a composition of a half *muqarnas* vault that consists of three tiers and is made of seven basic units. In this example, the artisan creates three tier plates according to the tier lines in the ceiling plan and arrays them vertically at equal heights on top of each other. Individual blocks are then aligned along the edge of the tier plates. If the ceiling plan in Figure 10 were to be mirrored it would produce a *muqarnas* dome, as in the spectacular Nur al-Din tomb in Damascus (1167) (Fig. 11); or, if cut in half it would produce a quarter *muqarnas* vault. Al-Kashi's detailed geometrical descriptions on *muqarnas* blocks possibly served also financial purposes. His computations may have guided clients in assessing the construction cost and estimating the wages of workers, since workers were paid by the cubit volume of work they completed.[6]

Other three-dimensional artifacts that have commonalities with *girih* patterns are modular building components. They follow the periodic principles and translational rules of *girih* patterns. In early hypostyle hall mosques, architects developed identical three-dimensional modules that could repeat infinitely. Modularity allowed architects to enlarge prayer spaces, without compromising the coherency of the mosque. For example, the prayer space of the Great of Mosque of Cordoba has been extended four times in its history (Fig. 12); each time

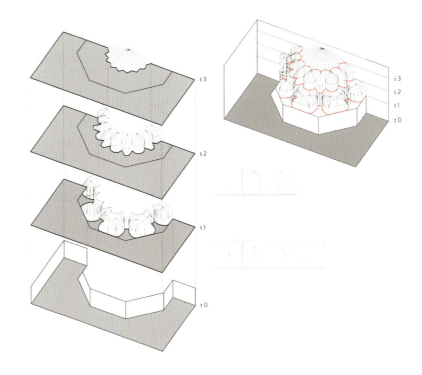

9 A craftsman working on a *muqarnas* vault.
Photo: Parsee

10 A view of a three-tiered *muqarnas* vault.
Drawing: Imdat As

COMPLEX PATTERNS AND THREE-DIMENSIONAL GEOMETRY   53

11 Nur al-Din tomb, Damascus, 1167, *muqarnas* dome. Photo: Teki

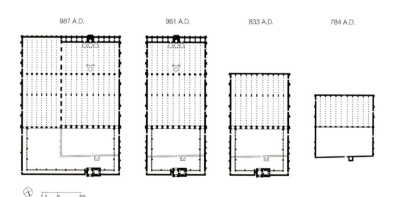

12 Great Mosque, Cordoba, eighth–tenth century, modular space extensions. Drawing: courtesy Nasser Rabbat

seven-meter deep and three-meter wide modules were added to the existing structure. The mosque was initially built of 108 modules in 784, has been extended to 180 modules in 833, then to 288 modules in 961, and finally to 512 modules in 987.

Three-dimensional modules were also used in the layout of classical Ottoman mosques. The unit cells were mostly square-shaped, ranging from three- to-four meter square units in smaller mosques to five-to-seven meter square units in larger imperial mosques. They were composed on a regular square grid system forming predetermined rectangular or square building layouts. The modules were typically generated with a straightedge and compass. Some drawings dating back to the sixteenth century illustrate the use of rigid grid paper during that period.[7] These tools and techniques produced mostly square-based (1/1) prayer halls. Mimar Sinan (1490–1588), chief architect of the Ottoman court, used additional proportional systems, such as the square root (1.41/1), and golden ratio (1.618/1). Typical square-based mosques are the Beyazit Mosque (1484); the Sehzade Mosque (1543); the Suleymaniye Mosque (1548); and the later Sultanahmet Mosque (1609), all in Istanbul. An example for a square root proportional system is the atypical prayer hall of the Kilic Ali Pasa Mosque (1578) in Istanbul (Fig. 13). The golden ratio, on the other hand, has been most famously used at the overall layout of the Selimiye Mosque (1568) in Edirne. Here, the golden ratio applies when measuring the open courtyard and enclosed prayer spaces together as one building outline. Moreover, the golden ratio can often be observed on smaller scale building components, like the portal of the Ince Minareli Madrasa (1264) in Konya (Fig. 14). The same proportions of the square, square root, and the golden ratio can be found in various *girih* patterns. For example, the commonly used rosette pattern and other periodic patterns display square based ratios; whereas the surface patterns at the Darb-i Imam shrine prove the golden ratio.

However, because of the wide range of monuments in the Islamic world both chronologically and geographically, it is hard to derive a set of standard geometrical principles for architectural projects. The associations made between two-dimensional *girih* patterns and three-dimensional artifacts like *muqarnas* vaults, modular building components, and common proportional systems derive from a limited number of projects. They certainly do not involve a direct referential link in terms of meaning and symbolism, nor do they define *girih* patterns as an essential kernel in all visual arts of the Islamic world. Nevertheless, these associations may hint to a common set of production tools, like the straightedge and compass, tiling method, grid paper, and the like. In other words, they may mirror the immanent logic of their common fabrication methods.

In the contemporary age, the link between *girih* patterns and architecture has been sometimes not

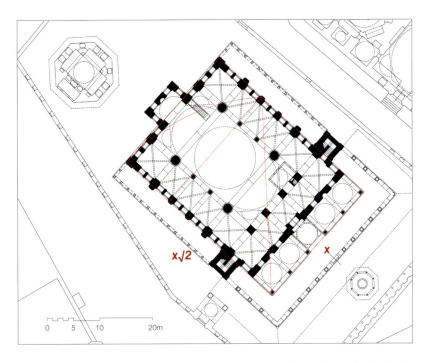

13 Kilic Ali Pasa Mosque, Istanbul, 1578, prayer hall with square root proportions.
Drawing: courtesy Gülru Necipoğlu

14 Ince Minareli Madrasa, Konya, 1264, golden section at the portal.
Drawing: Imdat As, Photo: Mehmet Günce Akkoyun; photo: Wikimedia Commons, © Bernard Gagnon

as subtle. In fact, a few larger-scale projects were literally extruded from *girih* patterns, such as the octagonal Ar-Rahman Grand Mosque in Baghdad (1999–2015). In this project, architect Jacques Barriere attributed a symbolic importance to the eight-rayed rosette pattern, which dictates the spatial disposition of the program. His mosque was envisioned as the largest mosque in the world with a dome of 120 meters in diameter and a capacity to house 100,000 worshippers at a time. It possessed eight colossal minarets, each 280 meter high, which were programmed as residential towers (Fig. 15).[8]

However, most contemporary architects use *girih* patterns as decorative surface treatments or integrate them with building systems. Developments in computer aided design (CAD) tools gave architects the possibility to easily map patterns over straight, single-, or double-curved surfaces. First generation CAD tools utilized the technique of texture mapping; that is, one would simply map identical images of a unit cell over any given surface. Texture mapping has been now

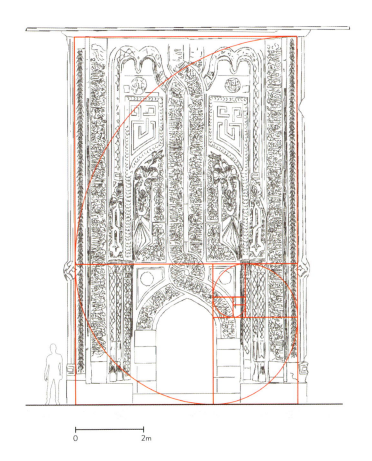

COMPLEX PATTERNS AND THREE-DIMENSIONAL GEOMETRY   55

replaced by associative and self-adapting surface tessellations with the aid of third generation CAD tools. The patterns produced in this way are referred to as parametric patterns, because they fit a unique position on a host surface and are associated to a wide range of variables. These variables can consist of mere geometric surface parameters, or can include structural, optical, or environmental parameters. For example, variables can relate to structural stress distribution, to the disposition of interior design elements, to occupational patterns of space, or to strategic viewpoints. The environmental variables can consist of contextual wind flow patterns or the intensity of sunlight hitting the surface at a particular angle. For example, Zaha Hadid in her project for the Civil Courts (2007) in Madrid, divided curved surfaces of the building envelope into adaptive unit cells that are parametrically related to the variation of sunlight intensity. As a result, the unit cells gradually change in form and create a gradient surface texture (Fig. 16). Thus, with the help of state-of-the-art CAD tools, *girih* patterns can morph from ornamental decorations to performative tessellations; that is, they can go beyond a mere surface application and respond to various structural, optical, or environmental factors to improve the overall building performance.

The free use of *girih* patterns in the twenty-first century has also raised important questions of authenticity. For example, Hanif Kara, who developed engineering solutions for Zaha Hadid, Farshid Moussavi, and Norman Foster, says: "I think that the recent explosion (due to the market in the [Middle] East) in the use of such patterns among designers can be dangerous. The patterns are often stretched, misused and ubiquitously proliferated to take away their original meanings and intentions".[9] But what are the original meanings and intentions of *girih* patterns?

MEANING

The discourse on the meaning of *girih* patterns is deeply convoluted. Opinions are manifold. I will briefly describe the main arguments put forth by diverse scholars and schools of thought: first, the Orientalist discourse arguing that *girih* patterns are timeless, ahistoric works with no iconographic significance and are pertinent to particular ethnographic traditions; second, the mystical reading of patterns, whose followers see deep symbolic meaning in *girih* patterns; and, third, the universal reading of ornament in general, and how it relates specifically to *girih* patterns in our contemporary age.

The widespread discourse on *girih* patterns in the Western world is partly shaped by the systematic work of nineteenth-century Orientalists. *Girih* patterns were presented as a common thread, spirit, or essence of Islamic art and architecture. Even though they were admired as possessing an "incomparable seductive elegance," they were nevertheless portrayed as part of a timeless Oriental tradition with no historical evolution.[10] The argument of timelessness constituted the fault-line between Western art and so-called Eastern tradition; the former was regarded as signifying progress and change, the latter stagnation and stasis. "One should not expect to recover in the history of the art of the Orient the equivalent of that rigorous chain of different phases characteristic of the art of the Occident".[11] Therefore, topics of Islamic art and architecture were treated as part of ethnographic

15 Jacques Barriere, Ar-Rahman Grand Mosque, Baghdad, 1999–2015.
Drawing: Imdat As;
Photo: Tamara Mann

studies, and not art history.[12] For example, nineteenth-century Austrian art historian Alois Riegl claimed that the ambiguity in figure-ground relationships in interlacing *girih* patterns reflects the Oriental spirit, that is, an Islamic world view with one unifying God and no hierarchies among its terrestrial subjects. He saw these patterns as a reflection of an artistic intention peculiar to the people of the Orient.[13] More stereotypically, art historian Richard Ettinghausen saw in *girih* patterns a special state of mind of the people of the Orient, who have a "tendency towards exaggeration and lavishness".[14]

Two-dimensionality was often accentuated in the representation of Islamic art and architecture in the West. Visual representations are inevitably two-dimensional projections of three-dimensional reality. However, one can further emphasize two-dimensionality by removing shade, shadow, lighting and textural articulations in drawings. Orientalists often deliberately gave their drawings an extremely flat character, devoid of any depth and contextual qualities. These characteristics also shaped the perception of the Orient in the eye of the Western world: "The Orient viewed as an object 'out there' is reduced in representation to a picture - a picture of the Orient and not the Orient".[15] Thus, the argument goes that the representation of the Orient was taken literally, whereas in contrast two-dimensional representations of Western art and architecture was always conceived as abstractions of reality, and not reality per se. Therefore, Viollet-le-Duc, French architect and protagonist of the nineteenth-century Gothic Revival, could easily argue that the people of the Orient did not change the Roman system of structure; they only modified its envelope; the geometry to which they had recourse did not cause them to discover a new system of construction; its functions were limited to giving novel curves to the arches and controlling all ornamental design; it afforded an intellectual pastime, and engaged the eye by wonderful combinations. In the Arab building, geometry adorns the dress; in the Western medieval edifice it sustains the body.[16]

Orientalists also claimed that *girih* patterns had no iconographic significance, which ultimately made it possible to consume them freely in the West. For this purpose, publications such as Jules Bourgoin's *Théorie de l'ornement* (1883) dissected Islamic art and architecture into individual components, patterns, domes, and ornamental panels, and ripped them out of their cultural and regional associations.[17]

The argument of a lack of symbolic meaning has been also shared by contemporary art historian Oleg Grabar, who claimed that *girih* patterns are repetitive abstract patterns that do not have any meaning assigned to them. According to him, they function as intermediaries between artifact and observer and mediate a certain sensual pleasure. As such, they have a universal appeal that makes them accessible to everyone and everywhere. "Humble triangles on a dress or in the weaving of a basket or the very sophisticated brick walls of Iranian towers share an ability to make us wonder what they mean, because, like moths or butterflies, we are attracted to an abstraction which seems to be devoid of cultural specificity. It is only meant to be beautiful".[18]

In contrast, Nader Ardalan and Laleh Bakhtiar in *The Sense of Unity: The Sufi Tradition in Persian Architecture* (1973) present *girih* patterns as mystical expressions that were highly symbolic. For them, the repetition of infinite patterns correlated to *dhikr*, that is, the endless oral repetitions of litanies by followers of Sufi traditions.[19] Another analogy often made is that repetitions of *girih* patterns symbolize the rich diversity of people and cultures within Islam, and the basic unit cell symbolizes the essence, which unifies all variety into a single denominator: unity in variety. Thus, infinitely extendable geometric patterns symbolize the inner esoteric dimension of Islam and the Sufi concept of the "inexhaustible multiplicity of creation, the effusion of being that emanates from the One: multiplicity within unity".[20] This role of *girih* patterns in Islamic visual culture was emphasized by Seyyid Hossein Nasr, a protagonist of the mystical reading of *girih* patterns. In his foreword to Ardalan and Bakhtiar's book, he claims that Islamic art and architecture is indeed timeless and "echoes transcendent archetypes." He relates *girih* patterns to cosmology and *tawhid*, the concept of God's unity: "Islamic art is gradually becoming to be understood for what it is, namely a means of relating multiplicity to unity by means of mathematical forms which are seen, not as mental abstractions, but as reflections of the celestial archetypes within both the cosmos and the minds and souls of men."[21] However, these claims are difficult to verify since in their work they do not show how historically *girih* patterns relate to types of theological concepts that manifest themselves in material culture.

The search for deeper meaning of *girih* patterns may be partly due to the threat of the disappearance of architectural heritage through the pervasiveness of the international style of the 1950–60s. The use of *girih* patterns, ornaments, or for that matter any type of decoration, was questioned with the advent of modernism in the early twentieth century. In "Ornament and Crime" (1909) Austrian architect Adolf Loos criticized the lavish decorations in buildings of the pre-modern Secession movement.[22] Loos's theory of ornament was complex and his arguments were based on sociological, economical, theoretical, psychological, and historical grounds. However, his main claim was based on psychoanalysis and the concept of urges or drives in

16 Zaha Hadid, Civil Courts of Justice, Madrid, 2007, parametric façade detail.
Photo: Zaha Hadid Architects

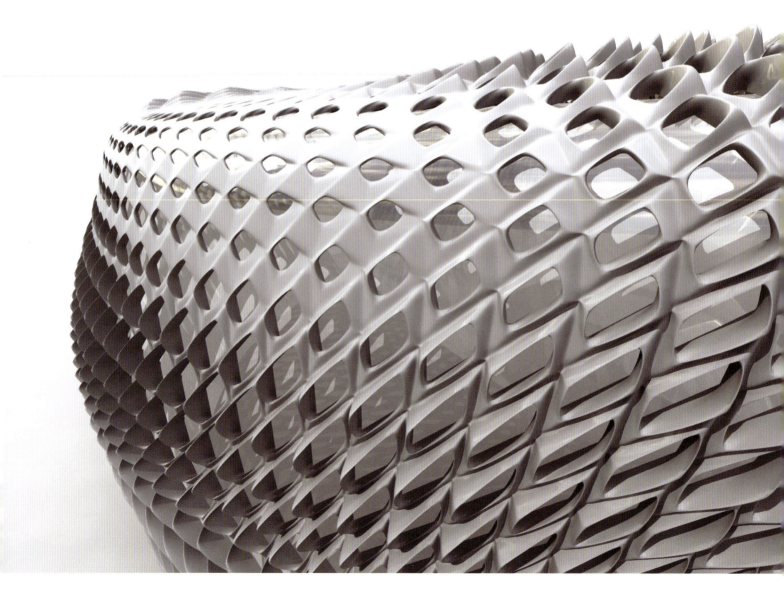

motivational psychology. According to Loos, the use of ornaments is a result of the artisan's emotional excesses. Ornamentation serves the sublimation of the artisan's urges and therefore performs functions beyond its apparent use. Thus, he argues, that since technologies do not have human urges, they should not produce ornaments. Loos considers technologically produced ornaments as non-economical nostalgic excesses.[23] For modernists, ornament was seen as a mask, a veil, a cloth, as incidental or framing, or more negatively as something slapped on or applied, or simply as unnecessary decoration. Shortly, ornaments were not regarded as a thing in themselves, but as something that hides something else.

However, modernism created an existential vacuum for the Muslim population. It lacked the narrative background and enigma that Islamic art and architecture once provided. This void in orthodox modernism was generally shared in the Western world, which led to postmodern methods and the free use of historic styles. Thus, ornament became a catalyst for the reconceptualization of architecture in the 1960s. Ornament in general, and *girih* patterns, in particular, re-entered the vocabulary of architectural projects.

Moreover, the Middle East was going through a concurrent building boom, which fostered the search for deeper meanings and justifications of the use of historic patterns. Many books from nineteenth-century Orientalists were repackaged and sold to a primarily Muslim audience, such as Jules Bourgoin's book *Arabic Geometric Pattern and Design* (1973).[24] One perhaps has to see Ardalan and Bakhtiyar's work within this framework. The irony is, of course, that these publications, once written by Orientalists to classify the "other" architectural traditions, now became inspirational sources for Muslim architects to differentiate themselves from the rest of the world, while claiming a distinctive national and cultural identity in their architectural work.

Nonetheless, *girih* patterns are apprehended semiconsciously, and it is perhaps possible to argue that particular patterns, especially the ones interlaced with calligraphy, inevitably claim certain iconographic qualities. For example, highly revered calligraphic signs of God and the prophet's name are often tightly interwoven with *girih* patterns. Therefore, the line between pattern and calligraphy is often blurred. Nasr's claim that the mystical reading of *girih* patterns "crystallized through the arts, embodied in traditional societies and available today for those who would see, presents concepts that are primordial and eternally valid" may be true for some Muslims who comprehend these patterns in this particular way.[25]

Today, the debates around ornamentation are less heated, partly because of the "theoretical meltdown" in architectural discourse where literally "anything goes."[26] Digitally produced ornaments are no longer defined as the deviant, the immoral, the forbidden, or simply the bad taste of the nineteenth century. However, when arbitrarily used, *girih* patterns can often appear as a pastiche of their historic past. Therefore, their relevance in contemporary religious architecture will largely depend on their capacity to interlace design and meaning in more creative ways.

IMDAT AS is an international research fellow at Istanbul Technical University (ITU). He received the prestigious TUBITAK 2232 grant to head the City Development through Design Intelligence lab at ITU to research the impact of emerging technologies on the future of the city. Imdat co-authored *Dynamic Digital Representations in Architecture: Visions in Motion* (Taylor & Francis, 2008), and is currently working on two upcoming books on Artificial Intelligence in Architecture and Urban Planning for Routledge and Elsevier.

SUGGESTIONS FOR FURTHER READING

Ardalan, Nader and Laleh Bakhtiar. *The Sense of Unity: The Sufi Tradition in Persian Architecture* (Chicago: Chicago University Press, 1973).

Bozdogan, Sibel. "Journey to the East: Ways of Looking at the Orient and the Question of Representation," *Journal of Architectural Education* 41 (1988), 38–45.

Frishman, Martin and Hasan-Uddin Khan. *The Mosque*: *History, Architectural Development and Regional Diversity* (London: Thames & Hudson, 2002).

Grabar, Oleg. *The Mediation of Ornament* (Princeton: Princeton University Press, 1992).

Lu, Peter J. and Paul J. Steinhardt. "Decagonal and Quasicrystalline Tilings in Medieval Islamic Architecture," *Science* 315 (2007), 1106–10.

Necipoğlu, Gülru. *The Topkapı Scroll: Geometry and Ornament in Islamic Architecture* (Santa Monica: Getty Center for the History of Art and the Humanities, 1995).

NOTES

[1] Peter J. Lu and Paul J. Steinhardt, "Decagonal and quasicrystalline tilings in medieval Islamic architecture," *Science* 315 (2007), 1109 (1106–10).

[2] Alpay Ozdural, "Omar Khayyam, Mathematicians, and 'Conversazioni' with Artisans," *Journal of the Society of Architectural Historians* 54 (1995), 55 (54–71).

[3] Mohammad Al-Asad, "Applications of Geometry," in *The Mosque: History, Architectural Development and Regional Diversity,* eds. Martin Frishman and Hasan-Uddin Khan (London: Thames & Hudson, 2002), 65 (55–71).

[4] I. I. Notkin, "Decoding Sixteenth-Century Muqarnas Drawings," *Muqarnas,* 12 (1995), 149 (148–71).

[5] Mohammad Al-Asad, "The Muqarnas: A Geometric Analysis," in Gülru Necipoğlu-Kafadar, *The Topkapı Scroll: Geometry and Ornament in Islamic Architecture: Topkapi Palace Museum Library MS H.1956* (Santa Monica: Getty Center for the History of Art and the Humanities, 1995), 354 (349–59).

[6] Gülru Necipoğlu-Kafadar, "Plans and Models in 15th- and 16th-Century Ottoman Architectural Practice," *Journal of the Society of Architectural Historians* 45 (1986), 231 (224–43).

[7] Renata Holod, "Text, Plan, and Building: On the Transmission of Architectural Knowledge," in *Theories and Principles of Design in the Architecture of Islamic Societies,* ed. Margaret Sevcenko (Cambridge: Aga Khan Program for Islamic Architecture, 1988), 5 (1–12).

[8] Patrick Cockburn, "Starving Iraq plans biggest mosque," *The Independent* October 10, 1995, accessed August 22, 2011, http://www.independent.co.uk/news/world/starving-iraq-plans-biggest-mosque-1576869.html.

[9] Hanif Kara and Mark Garcia, "Reductive Engineering Patterns: An Interview with Hanif Kara," *Architectural Design* 79 (2009), 73 (66–73).

[10] Jules Bourgoin, *Arabic Geometric Pattern and Design* (New York: Dover, 1973), 5–11.

[11] Donal M. Reid, *Whose Pharaohs? Archaeology, Museums, and Egyptian National Identity from Napoleon to World War I* (Berkeley: University of California Press, 2002), 223.

[12] Necipoğlu-Kafadar, *The Topkapı Scroll*, 62.

[13] Alois Riegl, *Stilfragen: Grundlegungen zu einer Geschichte der Ornamentik* (Berlin: Georg Siemens, 1893), 315.

[14] Richard Ettinghausen, "The Taming of the Horror Vacui in Islamic Art," *Proceedings of the American Philosophical Society*, 123 (1979): 19 (15–28).

[15] Sibel Bozdogan, "Journey to the East: Ways of Looking at the Orient and the Question of Representation," *Journal of Architectural Education*, 41 (1988), 41 (38–45).

[16] Eugene-Emmanuel Viollet-le-Duc, *Lectures on Architecture,* trans. Benjamin Bucknall, vol.1 (New York: Dover Publications, 1987), 432–3.

[17] Necipoğlu-Kafadar, *The Topkapı Scroll*, 66.

[18] Oleg Grabar, *The Mediation of Ornament* (Princeton: Princeton University Press, 1992), 154.

[19] Necipoğlu-Kafadar, *The Topkapı Scroll,* 76.

[20] Nader Ardalan and Laleh Bakhtiar, *The Sense of Unity: The Sufi Tradition in Persian Architecture* (Chicago: Chicago University Press, 1973), 3.

[21] Ibid., ix–xii.

[22] Adolf Loos, "Ornament and Crime," in *Ornament and Crime: Selected Essays,* trans. Michael Mitchell (Riverside: Ariadne Press, 1998), 171 (167–76).

[23] Jorg H. Gleiter, "Das Neue Ornament: Zur Genealogie des neuen Ornaments im Digitalen Zeitalter," *Arch plus* 189 (2008), 81 (76–83).

[24] Necipoğlu-Kafadar, *The Topkapı Scroll*, 82.

[25] Ardalan and Bakhtiar, *The Sense of Unity,* 129.

[26] Luigi P. Puglisi, "Anything goes," *Architectural Design* 79 (2009), 6 (6–12).

Archives and Archival Documents in the Study of Islamic Religious Architecture

MATTHEW SABA & MICHAEL A. TOLER

1 Interior view of the Bait Ur Rouf Mosque in Dhaka, Bangladesh, recipient of the Aga Khan Award for Architecture, 13th cycle (2013–2016).
Photo: Rajesh Vora, Aga Khan Award for Architecture (AKAA) Archive, courtesy of Aga Khan Trust for Culture

This essay is an overview of some archives and archival sources useful for the study of Islamic religious architecture. The Society of American Archivists has three definitions of the word "archives," but the most relevant is perhaps "permanently valuable records – such as letters, reports, accounts, minute books, draft and final manuscripts, and photographs – of people, businesses, and government. These records are kept because they have continuing value to the creating agency and to other potential users".[1] This definition will serve our purposes, with one important caveat. The definition only mentions various forms of written records and photographs, but archives have included sound recordings and motion pictures since they were invented. In the twenty-first century, the definition is even more limiting, as archives can include datasets, computer programs, and the like. In lieu of the term "archives," we use the terms "archival documents," "documents," and "documentary sources" in reference to sources of archival value that have not been preserved within their original archival context, as is often (but not always) the case for materials that survive from the pre-Modern period. This essay does not claim to provide an exhaustive survey of archival resources, nor does it grapple with the larger, epistemic problems with the notion of the archive in our field, though this is a question that has received increased attention.[2] Rather, it is intended to indicate the types of archives and archival documents that have been useful to researchers, along with some specific examples of each, and some suggestions for finding others.

One final clarification should be made here. In this essay, we neither discuss written documents that are parts of buildings themselves (architectural inscriptions), nor works of literature that describe buildings, such as travelogues or historical chronicles.[3] One must note, however, that the line between the literary and non-literary can be called into question. An illustrative example is the *Ṣarīḥ al-milk*, a register of properties belonging to the Shrine of Shaykh Ṣafī al-Dīn at Ardabil, compiled for the Safavid Shah Ṭahmāsp in 1570 by the court poet and secretary 'Abdī Shīrāzī. The register contains both a topographic description of the shrine of Ardabil, encomiastic descriptive poetry, and abstracts of documents detailing endowments made to the shrine. It is at once a work of poetry and a register of events and transactions not available elsewhere.[4] The nature of these sources will sometimes challenge the paradigms we follow today, and keeping this point in mind will aid the student of Islamic architecture who seeks information from them.

ARCHIVAL SOURCES FROM THE EARLIER ISLAMIC PERIODS C. 700–1500

The scholar of monumental religious architecture of the early Islamic periods will be most immediately interested in documents related to the activities of the imperial courts and their provincial governments or vassal states, as the construction of congregational mosques, and later of *madrasa*s and shrines, was a prerogative of the wealthiest and most powerful patrons. While imperial documents dating before the sixteenth century have been elusive to modern researchers, institutions whose core function was to produce official documents existed and played an important role in Islamic society. The chancery, or the department responsible for the production of official documents, was a fundamental part of the courts of all large Islamic polities from the Umayyads on.[5]

Recent studies have put to rest the notion that documents produced by the early Islamic chanceries were never archived, or that few of these documents survive today relative to what we possess for coeval periods in Europe. Plentiful references to archives or archival practices in literary sources, and a substantial amount of surviving official documentation have been enough to demonstrate this point.[6] It is more accurate to say that imperial archives in the early periods may have been more decentralized than their modern counterparts, and that a wealth of documents issued by these governments does exist, but in dispersal. Paradoxically, as Marina Rustow has argued, it may have been their dispersal from state archives in the early Islamic period to which we owe their accessibility today: due to the sheer volume of document production, some documents were pruned from court archives, and these were very frequently recycled as writing surfaces and placed in repositories that outlasted the courts and their archives themselves.[7] The relatively more common survival of documents issued by Muslim authorities in the archives of non-Muslim institutions such as monasteries is partly explained by a similar paradox. Because of their marginal position in society, these communities relied on the careful preservation of documents issued from central authorities (e.g. the legal system) for their survival, and the tucked-away archives in which such documents were stored were less frequently the targets of intentional, performative destruction, such as the overthrow of a dynastic regime.[8] In sum, one can say that there exist many documents and evidence of archival practices dating from the early periods, but few intact archives to which one can turn, and most of these outside "state" contexts.[9] Identifying the relevant items and putting them together is therefore a formidable task that falls on the researcher.

While we have few systematic and virtually no centralized government archives dating from the period between 700 and 1500 that remain intact, important groups of documents of archival value have been preserved together.[10] In some cases, legal documents dating to the periods before 1500 were deposited in government archives that developed in Ottoman territories in the nineteenth century, forming a pre-Modern archive of sorts. In Cairo, hundreds of charitable endowment deeds (waqf or waqfiyya) from the Mamluk period survive in the

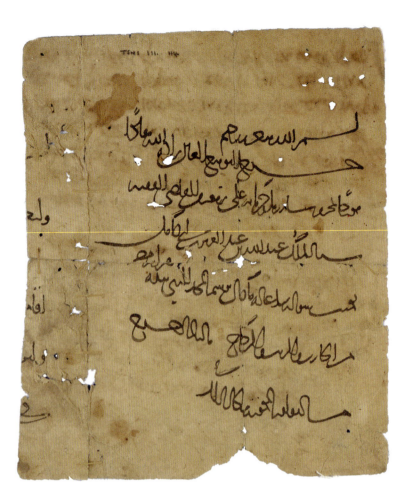

National Archives (Dār al-Wathāʾiq al-Qawmiyya) and Ministry of Awqāf (Wizārat al-Awqāf).[11] Elsewhere, disparate treasure troves of material have occasionally surfaced, shedding brilliant light on a period of time or a specific place. One example is cache of over 800 fourteenth-century documents, mostly legal, found in the Ḥaram al-Sharīf.[12] A second is a group of several hundred documents related to the activities of traders and merchants unearthed during the University of Chicago excavations at the port of Quṣayr on the Red Sea.[13] The most famous is the cache of over 10,000 documents found in the Geniza (store room) of the Ben Ezra Synagogue in Cairo: a mass of discarded papers left in an attic to decay over time rather than be burned by virtue of their containing the name of God or, in some cases, merely containing the Hebrew script. The Cairo Geniza contained a wide variety of documents accumulated by the congregation of the synagogue, providing an unparalleled view into the world outside the court from the eleventh through the thirteenth centuries.[14] The papers also included fragments of imperial

2 Part of a decree dated 1137/532 AH issued from the chancery of Fatimid caliph al-Ḥāfiẓ li-Dīn Allāh, the back of which was re-used for a legal document in Hebrew. Cambridge University Library, T-S NS 111.114, 1V. Photo: Syndics of Cambridge University Library

decrees reused as writing surfaces, demonstrating the process of pruning and accidental preservation outlined by Rustow mentioned above (Fig. 2). The question that follows is whether there is material in this massive but dispersed and inconsistent corpus relevant to the work of architectural historians. The answer is certainly yes, but the connections between monument and documentation are often indirect and require expansive thinking about what the history of architecture looks like. For example, Donald Little characterized the aforementioned Ḥaram documents as having a "residual" interest to the history of architecture.[15] By this, he meant that there was little in the cache that directly documented the foundation, construction, or architectural details of buildings in fourteenth-century Jerusalem. Rather, such material sheds light on what one might call the social life of buildings: their use, economic support, and connections to politics. This observation is particularly true of *waqf* deeds, the most abundant type of document related to religious architecture to survive.[16] Indeed, in the last three decades, *waqf* deeds have played a particularly important role in the study of architectural patronage as political process toward the end of this timeframe – the Mamluk period in Egypt and Syria, and the Mongol and Timurid Periods in greater Iran – when the *waqf* system became a pervasive instrument of urban development and political power.[17] Questions of aesthetics and the significance of form have been more difficult to address. As Sheila Blair has observed, the language of *waqf* deeds, frustrating from the standpoint of formal description, may be revealing in itself of an architectural aesthetic that prized function over form.[18] Alternately, the indirectness or vagueness of documentary sources from an art-historical point of view may have to do with a separation in early Islamic society of those who built and those who wrote about buildings, a point that applies not only to *waqf* but to other types of verbal sources as well.[19]

The broader landscape of the Cairo Geniza documents suggests similarly far-reaching possibilities for a social history of Islamic religious architecture that utilizes other, less official types of documentary sources. Combing the index to S. D. Goitein's *A Mediterranean Society*, a monumental study based on the Cairo Geniza, turns up numerous subjects of potential interest to the architectural historian. Under the letter "C,"

these include carpenters; coppersmiths; carpets; chandeliers; curtains; and columns in synagogues.[20] While the documents surveyed did not speak much to the design or construction of imperial mosques or shrines, one might glean a wealth of information regarding the materials and craftsmen who made them.

Yet, even these thought exercises may be misleading. According to one calculation, the number of documents that survive from the first six Islamic centuries is in the hundreds of thousands, and a mere one percent of the Islamic papyri and paper documents that are housed in museums, libraries, and state archives have been edited and published.[21] It would therefore be unreasonable based on the knowledge we have to draw conclusions about what we can and cannot learn about religious architecture from these sources. Rather, it should be part of our ongoing work as a discipline to discover what exists and how it connects. The Checklist of Arabic Documents, a bibliography of edited and published Arabic documents on papyrus, paper, parchment, leather, wood, ostraca, stone, and bone produced by members of the International Society of Arabic Papyrology, is one attempt to facilitate the use of these early Islamic documents by bringing a comprehensive bibliography together.[22] Historians of early Islamic architecture should watch the development of such lists and online databases closely, and communicate with their colleagues in the fields of social history, papyrology, and diplomatics to find resonances.

ARCHIVAL SOURCES AND ARCHIVES FROM LATER PERIODS 1500–1900

While documentary sources dating from after the year 1500 are more numerous and easily accessible in comparison to the material available from previous eras, the extent and nature of these sources varies substantially as a result of both historical differences in documentation practices between imperial courts, and the later histories of these governments themselves.[23]

The Ottoman Empire, a highly centralized, bureaucratic, and long-lived state whose Anatolian heartland remained under imperial control until World War I, has left a vast legacy of documents, preserved in a number of archives.[24] Greatly facilitating the accessibility of these documents is the fact that during the nineteenth century, a sweeping series of reforms (*tanzimat*) led to the centralization of archival collections and the beginning of their organization. Turkey possesses the majority of Ottoman archives. The Başbakanlık Osmanlı Arşivi (or BOA), housed in Istanbul, contains over 150 million documents, covering both the pre- and post-Tanzimat periods, much still unedited. In addition to the BOA, two other archives housing Ottoman documents in Turkey have proven vital for research on Ottoman architecture. These are the Topkapı Palace Museum Archive (Topkapı Sarayı Müzesi Arşivi or TSMA), which houses documents related to the Ottoman imperial palace and its inhabitants, and the Vakıflar Genel Müdürlüğü Arşivi (VGMA), the repository for endowment deeds. Studies in architectural history utilizing these archives have yielded fantastic results, ranging from the reconstruction of the interiors and design of now-lost buildings commissioned by individual imperial patrons, to glimpses of the lives of architects (their salaries, education, and social status), to comprehensive studies on the codification of imperial mosque architecture under the Ottoman court architect Sinan.[25] The types of documents marshalled as evidence in these and other studies include imperial decrees, land surveys, registers of expenses, endowment deeds, and private correspondence. A number of architectural plans has also been discovered, though in low numbers before the nineteenth century, yielding information regarding the architectural design processes.[26]

Outside of the imperial court, legal records have been a productive source of information on the everyday lives of both architects and craftsmen in the Ottoman empire, whose identities are often elusive. Legal decisions (*fetva*, Ar. *fatwā*) preserved in judges' registers or *siciller* (Ar. *sijillāt*), allow us to see even further into the lives of these men. Within these documents, members of artisan guilds had a more public profile than individuals, as craft guilds might issue complaints against other guilds, and customers might issue complaints against a craftsman or guild, allowing us a glimpse on practices and problems encountered in the field.

Such information is more prevalent from later periods, however, and is not uniform in depth across the provinces.[27] In Turkey, many of these *siciller* have been brought together in the Milli Kütüphane or National Library in Ankara, and other repositories exist in Damascus at the Markaz al-Wathā'iq al-Tārīkhiyya and in Cairo at the Maḥkama li'l-Aḥwāl al-Shakhṣiyya.[28] Archives formed during the Ottoman period and incorporated into national archives in Cairo also house *waqf* documents that have proven extremely valuable in reconstructing the urban history of these and other regional centers during the Ottoman period.[29]

Scholars of architecture in later Islamic Iran do not have the luxury of an intact centralized archive as deep as that which exists for Ottoman Turkey, although centralized archives for *awqāf* exist at a national and regional level in Iran.[30] The archives of various scattered institutions are equally important, and secondary sources exploiting these documents and their bibliographies of lists or publications are one method of entry into the subject.[31] The libraries of shrines are a critical source of Safavid documents related to the foundation and administration of what was arguably the most important form of religious architecture in later Islamic Iran. The aforementioned Shrine of Ṣafī al-Dīn at Ardabil is one example where hundreds of documents were uncovered, some very pertinent to the history and form of the shrine itself.[32] These included a substantial number of pre-Safavid decrees, dating back to the twelfth century, showing that the shrine became a repository for documents more broadly relevant to the history of the region. We can also assume that many documents once belonging to the shrine were dispersed before their initial cataloging in the 1970s.[33] A second example are the documents from the library of the Shrine of Imām Riżā at Mashhad (Fig. 3).[34] Among the Safavid documents in this archive are ledgers recording the payment of salaries to the shrine's many employees, as well as other expenses incurred by the shrine to continue operations; documentation of the staging of religious festivals and holidays; documents related to the agricultural activities that supported the shrine financially; records of contemporary battles and skirmishes; and records of gifts made to and from the shrine. The collections only become more informative as time goes on, and also include thousands of historical photographs of the building itself and other historical structures.[35] In 1899, a project to catalog and confirm all of the endowments deeded to the shrine, dating back to the sixteenth century, resulted in a lithographed digest of 170 documents related to the shrine's properties titled *Ās̱ār al-Rażavīyah*, a monumentally important document in the history of the shrine recently edited and published with a critical introduction.[36]

A second important but underexploited source for Safavid documents are albums (*majmūʿah* or *jung*). This genre of book is well-known to art historians, as many examples contain specimens of painting and calligraphy, and constitute in themselves an endemic form of art history.[37] Further extending their potential importance to the history of architecture, however, is that among the specimens of writing in these albums are *waqf* documents, royal and private correspondence, and decrees, including in at least one case material regarding the administration of holy shrines.[38]

3 Aerial view of the Shrine of Imām Riżā at Mashhad, Iran
Photo: Michel Écochard Archive, courtesy of Aga Khan Documentation Center, MIT Libraries (AKDC@MIT)

Albums are of course found in national, university, and specialized libraries as well as fine art museums around the world.

As is the case for greater Iran, the location of documents for the study of later Islamic architecture in South Asia requires looking in a number of institutions. The case of the Mughal archives is an example. While some important series of papers related to military and taxation do exist in national and state institutions, relying on the notion of centralized archives for this period may be misleading.[39] As Nandini Chatterjee has recently argued in a study on imperial law in Mughal India, a significant archive can be constructed from the collections of landed families. Her reconstruction of a family archive dating back to the seventeenth century, whose contents had been divided between several institutions, pointed to "the household rather than the state as the location par excellence of Mughal archives," and "the family [as] the locale for the actuation of the pre-colonial state, activation of law and storing of its records".[40] Architectural historians might do well to take note of this conclusion. For example, an important series of decrees related to the construction of the Taj Mahal was not found in the remains of a centralized imperial archive, but rather in a series of papers related to Raja Jai Singh, a Rajput prince, deposited in the Rajasthan State Archives at Bikaner.[41]

Archives and documentary sources for the Islamic countries of North Africa west of Egypt and in sub-Saharan Africa prior to the twentieth century are also widely distributed. The historical overview on the website of the National Archives of Tunisia speculates that the "successive political regimes" that have marked Tunisian history over two millennia must have created "important archival fonds," lamenting the fact that these are not available through the national archives today. It attributes this to "frequent wars and political instability" prior to 1705.[42] Nonetheless, there do exist important archival collections that cover the period prior to 1705. There are certainly archival collections for earlier periods that exist in private homes and in the libraries of religious institutions which have not yet been brought to the attention of researchers or the central authorities. We can only speculate about the nature and extent of these collections until they are made known, either through accidental discovery like the documents in the Cairo Geniza mentioned above, or through the systematic surveys and contributions made by post-colonial states, examples of which appear in the section dealing with national archives. Moreover, because Algeria and Tunisia fell under Ottoman rule, some material relating to the period of Ottoman rule can be found in the centralized archives of the Ottoman Empire that are discussed above.

Archival fonds in Morocco are certainly the most useful to researchers of architecture prior to the modern era. The largest archival repository in the country is the Ḥasaniyya Library, also known as La Bibliothèque Royal or Al-Khizāna al-Ḥasaniyya, in Rabat. This library has served as the repository for the Alawite Dynasty since Sultan Mawlāy Rashīd (r. 1666–1672), but also includes manuscripts from the Sa'dī rulers. The collection "includes manuscripts of Maghribī, Andalusī, West African, and eastern provenance," most of which date from the fifteenth century or later, and, covers a wide variety of subjects.[43] The Moroccan National Library, in the Agdal section of Rabat, holds a handful of manuscripts dating to the Almoravid era, as well as rare manuscripts from the Nāṣiriyya and Ḥamzāwiyya orders. The General Library and Archives of Tetouan the Qarawiyyīn Library in Fes, and the Ibn Yūsuf Library in Marrakech are among the other archives that contain material that dates from the eighteenth century and earlier.

In Spain, one should also take note of the Royal Library of the Monastery of San Lorenzo del Escorial and its rich collection of manuscripts in Arabic, Greek, and Hebrew. The library was established by Philip II of Spain, but the majority of Arabic manuscripts come from the library of the Sa'dī Sultan Mawlāy Zaydān (r. 1603–1627). When the Sultan was forced out of power by a rival, his books were placed on a ship for transport further south. How they ended up in the monastery is not clear.

The early Modern period changed the nature of archives in many ways, including expanding a concern for archiving beyond the ecclesiastical and political elites. These changes can be attributed to a confluence of interrelated trends that began in the early Modern period and continued through the eighteenth century. Alexandra Walsham attributes the rising of archival culture to various social and cultural changes such as expanding literacy, urbanization, "new conventions of self-expression," upheaval in political structures, and mechanized printing.[44] Lithograph printing also begins in the eighteenth century, allowing for the mass production of illustrations, maps, and other sorts of visual documentation, as the printing press had done for the written word. Mass production increases the likelihood that visual documentation will survive the ravages of time, simply because multiple copies exist in multiple places. As a result, new kinds of archival material dating from this period become available to us, and the number of archival institutions grows exponentially.

COLONIAL ARCHIVES

The European colonization of territories in Islamic West Africa, North Africa, the Levant, Central Asia, and South Asia means that it is critical to consult European archives when researching Islamic architecture. These archives are not only relevant for monuments constructed during the period of colonial rule, but also for historical monuments that the colonial governments took interest in and documented. The most important archive for the study of regions colonized by the French is certainly the Archives Nationales d'Outre-Mer in Aix-en-Provence (ANOM). The archive contains the records of the Ministry of the Colonies, as well as the archives retrieved from colonial territories. The utility of the official records for research into Islamic architecture varies depending on the extent, nature, and duration of French rule, but in addition to the records, the archive holds approximately 60,000 maps, plans, and other printed works, the oldest of which date to the seventeenth century. Depending on the region, the archives can be an excellent source of visual material, as it also holds a collection of 20,000 postcards, 150,000 photographs, and 955 albums. Much of the documentation is military in nature, but these may, nonetheless, be useful to researchers to the extent that exploratory missions often took note of possible centers of resistance that might spring from Sufi religious movements and their networks, including the study of their centers of power. There is visual documentation associated with these campaigns, but the visual fonds of the ANOM includes photographs of mosques, *madrasas*, and other religious structures from postcards and travel albums, as well as lithographs and engravings. Holdings can be searched online, but much of the material has not been digitized.[45]

While the collections of ANOM are likely to be useful to anyone researching architecture in any

territory that was a French colony, as well as many that were not (Greece Macedonia, Tanzania, Libya, Saudi Arabia), they are indispensable to researchers interested in religious architecture in Algeria. Not only was Algeria occupied by the French a long time, but it was considered an integral part of France. Indeed, there is a long running dispute between Algeria and France over the return of certain archives and artifacts.[46] However, the situation is not the same with neighboring countries. Tunisia and Morocco were both considered Protectorates, so more of the colonial archives remained in these countries. The archives from Tunisia and Morocco that are now in France mostly pertain to military affairs or the colonial administration, as well as to foreign affairs during the protectorate. This material can be found in the ANOM, as well as in the Diplomatic Archives in Nantes, selections of which have been digitized and are available online.[47]

Similar archives exist in all nations that had colonies, though some are more complete than others. The office of Italy's colonial administration in Libya were looted during World War II, and other documentation was lost when the archives were transferred to Rome.[48] The holdings of UK National Archives are predictably vast, but do not contain internal administrative records of the colonies. For example, the archives of the British Library hold the records and private papers, as well as photographs, prints, drawings and paintings from the India Office.[49] Similarly, a wealth of material on the majority-Muslim territories of the Russian Federation and the USSR exist in Russian archives.[50]

SCHOLARLY ARCHIVES

In addition to the archives of colonial governments and organizations, students of Islamic religious architecture can exploit the archives of a number of individual scholars active in the late nineteenth and early twentieth centuries. These archives, which document buildings from a scholarly vantage point, have been made accessible through digitization efforts that began in the 1990s and continue today. A few examples serve here to point to a broader landscape that is still unfolding.[51]

Among the most impactful scholarly archives related to Islamic religious architecture is that of K. A. C. Creswell (1879–1974), the British engineer turned architectural historian who authored *Early Muslim Architecture* and *The Muslim Architecture of Egypt*, both still standard references for plans, elevations, views, and basic information on the Islamic religious monuments of Egypt, the Levant, and Mesopotamia dating before 1300. Creswell donated his negatives (over 8,000) to the Ashmolean Museum.[52] Related material is dispersed between six institutions, including the library of the American University of Cairo and the Victoria and Albert Museum in London which both hold photographic prints made by Creswell.[53] Creswell's images mostly date to the second quarter of the twentieth century, and are not limited to what he published: the largest concentration of photographs documents monuments dating to the twelfth to fifteenth centuries in Egypt and the Levant.[54] A second example of a scholarly archive that has received much attention from historians of Islamic architecture in recent decades is that of Ernst Herzfeld, the German archaeologist and historian of the Near East who excavated at Samarra, Persepolis, and Pasargadae.[55] While Creswell's archive is best known for its photographs, Herzfeld's is known for its drawings: Herzfeld trained as an architect and was extremely talented at drawing both plans and details of architectural ornament. His papers are housed in the Archives of the Freer and Sackler Galleries in Washington, D.C., the libraries of the Islamic and Ancient Near Eastern Departments at the Metropolitan Museum in New York, and at the Museum für Islamische Kunst in Berlin.[56] A substantial portion of Freer and Sackler papers are digitized and available online, as are the papers in the Islamic department at the Metropolitan Museum.[57] Herzfeld's collections are important for the study of Islamic architecture in Syria, Iraq, and Iran, and pre-Islamic architecture in Iran, and include original drawings and measurements of buildings (Fig. 4).

For the Western portion of the Islamic world, Georges Marçais plays a similar role. Marçais was a professor of archeology at the University of Algiers from 1919–1944, and Director of the Musée des Antiquités Algériennes et d'Art Musulman from 1920–1961. His study, *L'architecture musulmane d'occident: Tunisie, Algérie, Maroc, Espagne et Sicile*, spans the period from the ninth to the nineteenth century, and is still the most comprehensive study on the subject. The volumes are extensively illustrated with photographs, plans, elevations, and detailed studies of architectural features. In addition to this broad, transnational survey, he is the author of numerous other books and articles that deal with specific cities, structures and artifacts. His archives are located at Aix Marseille Université.[58] More recently, the Bibliotheca Orientalis Attilio Petruccioli, founded and directed by the renowned Italian scholar on Islamic architecture and planning, holds over 12,000 books and 65,000 images, as well as maps and other documentation from Petruccioli's collection, as well as numerous other donors.[59]

The political hegemony of European colonial powers resulted in the elevation of European

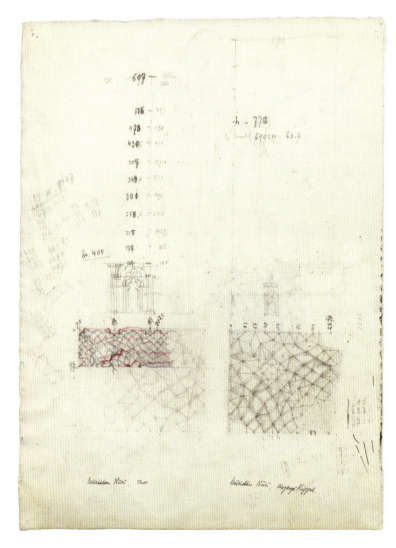

4 Drawings and measurements of *muqarnas* vaults in the Bīmāristān of Nūr al-Dīn, Damascus. Photo: Ernst Herzfeld Papers, Department of Islamic Art, The Metropolitan Museum of Art, eeh1456

scholars and their works above the scholarship of would-be colleagues from the colonies, even if these scholars contributed crucial information to the foundational surveys and preservation initiatives of the nineteenth century (e.g. translations of texts, drawings, measurements, regional and historical knowledge). The relative obscurity of early scholars such as Sayyid Ahmad Khan, who surveyed the Islamic monuments of Delhi, in comparison to contemporary British authors is one case in point.[60] It follows that the early systematic surveys and the archival material they generated are as telling for what they leave out as much as for what they include. Contemporary scholarship will only be strengthened when it considers collections of documents created from non-European perspectives alongside archives created by European scholars.[61]

NATIONAL ARCHIVES

National libraries and archives can be remarkably useful to researchers seeking information on Islamic architecture, though the quantity and quality of records available will vary according to when the national archives were established, strategies employed to acquire materials and develop the collection, and the nation's capacity to preserve its collection. National archives are a good source for archival material relating to Islamic architecture within the nation's borders, but also for material relating structures relevant to overseas diplomatic, humanitarian, or military action. The National Archives of the United States, for example, contain video, photographs, and reports on the presidential visits to the Washington Mosque, and FBI dossiers on Nation of Islam mosques in the United States and the potential for "civil unrest".[62] In addition, they include numerous images of the Paris Mosque from the archives of the Marshall Plan to rebuild Europe after World War II, and photographs of mosques, shrines, and other religious institutions in Iraq from the archive of Combined Military Service Digital Photographic Files.[63]

Egypt's National Archives (Dār al-Wathā'iq al-Qawmiyya), mentioned above in connection with Mamluk documents preserved in Egyptian national collections, were established by Gamal Abdel Nasser in 1954, and are intended to be the repository of documentation from all ministries except those of Defense and the Interior. However, there is no mechanism to compel the ministries to turn over documentation, so archives are incomplete.[64] A second institution, the Dār al-Maḥfūẓāt al-ʿUmūmiyya, houses the archives of the Ministry of Finance and is located in the Cairo Citadel. No catalog has been published, but Adam Mestyan identifies three collections, two of which may be useful to researchers on religious architecture: tax registers of buildings in Cairo and possibly other cities from the turn of the century to the 1950s, and tax registers of agricultural lands.[65]

In 2007, the National Archives of Morocco were established based on recommendations of the Truth and Reconciliation Committee convened to look into human rights abuses during the reign of Hassan II. It is intended to facilitate research and to encourage government transparency. Its largest collection is an archive of Protectorate-era materials.[66] The National Archives are housed in what was once the National Library, and some archival resources still exist in the library's collection, previously the National Library and Archives of the Kingdom of Morocco. Moreover, a small selection of the library's holdings is available online, including two magazines that are useful in the study of architecture and urban planning, *Terre d'Afrique illustrée Algérie, Tunisie et Maroc* (1920–1933) and *Batir: revue marocaine d'architecture* (1932–1933).[67]

The story of Iraq's national archives is particularly tragic. Iraq and the Ba'ath party maintained extensive archives, some of which were brought to the United States after the 1991 Gulf War. The fate of these archives has been controversial.[68] The 2003 report of the Library of Congress and the US State Department Mission to Baghdad details damage done to the National Library and the House of Manuscripts during the 2003 War to remove Saddam Hussein from power. The latter was part of the National Museum, but both contained extensive archival collections.[69] In 2018, a New York Times reporter removed a large cache of documents from Mosul, prompting statements of condemnation from the Society of American Archivists and the Middle East Studies Association Committee on Academic Freedom, among others.[70]

It is also important to remember that national archives are often curated to defend the interests of the regime of ruling class. An example of particular interest to scholars of architectural history is the Al-Saoud regime's efforts to establish modern national archives during a period of approximately twenty years following the 1991 Gulf War. Rosie Bsheer has examined these efforts within the context of institutional and political rivalries, and draws parallels between the "archive wars" and the transformation of both sacred and secular spaces of the built environment. In both contexts, constructing the national narrative necessitates the suppression of rival narratives.[71]

ARCHIVES OF NONGOVERNMENTAL ORGANIZATIONS

The archives of nongovernmental organizations may be particularly useful for research on monuments that have been restored under international initiatives. Two of the most important for the study of Islamic religious architecture are UNESCO and the Aga Khan Development Network, both of which have funded numerous restoration and preservation campaigns related to historic Islamic buildings. The UNESCO archives contains publications, documents and other materials either produced by UNESCO or pertaining to UNESCO's fields of competence. These collections are accessible at the UNESCO library or archives room.[72] A great deal of material is also available in the UNESCO Digital Library (UNESDOC). UNESDOC contains publications and documents produced by UNESCO, as well as resources shared by other institutions. Of particular interest are the collections titled "Programme and Meeting Documents" and "Mission Reports," which contain valuable observations about materials, notes on state of preservation, inventories of portable objects, and other documentation related to cultural heritage preservation projects.[73] The Aga Khan Development Network (AKDN) keeps extensive documentation on its work, some of which is made available on the AKDN website. Further information on the archives of the Aga Khan Historic Cities Programme and the Aga Khan Award for Architecture are available on Archnet.org, an online resource discussed in greater detail below.

LOCAL, CORPORATE, AND ARCHITECTS' ARCHIVES

Thus far, our discussion of archives since the beginning of the twentieth century has focused on large, centralized institutions, but there are many other sources to consult. Consider the Islamic Society of Boston Cultural Center (ISBCC), a mosque and community center in the Roxbury neighborhood of Boston. In 1970, the property on which the mosque sits was set aside for urban renewal projects by the city of Boston, so the mosque project is discussed in city records, particularly those of the Boston Redevelopment Authority. Moreover, city and state archives will contain construction permits and tax records. In 1988, the project was entrusted to the Islamic Society of Boston (ISB), the organization that raised funds for and constructed the mosque. That organization, which already existed, will have records. The architects on the project were Sami Agnawi, based in Saudi Arabia, and the Boston-based firm Steffian Bradley Associates, both of which have plans and other material relating to the project. There was some controversy around the establishment of the mosque, and it is the first purpose-built mosque in Boston, so there is reporting in the archives of local media. The ISBCC is Energy Star certified, so the federal archives of this program will also have the application and relevant documentation. Finally, there are archives of both the mosque itself, and of members of the community. These are sources of information on how the structure is actually used, adaptations to meet unexpected needs, and even of wear and tear or renovations.

Needless to say, no researcher with an interest in the ISBCC will need to consult all of this material, but the example is illustrative of the plethora of material available from diverse sources. Indeed, in a large country, local and community-based archives are much more likely to be of use to researchers than are national archives. In an era in which virtually everyone carries a digital camera and small computer in their pocket, the challenge for the archivist is sorting the wheat from the chaff. For the researcher, the challenge is discerning which archives are most likely to be useful. Most religious communities will have some sort of archives relevant to their specific community or the larger network to which it belongs. Members of the community may also have personal archives. A visit to the structures one is researching is generally

5 Great Mosque of Damascus.
Photo: Maison Bonfils, Michel Écochard Archive, courtesy of Aga Khan Documentation Center, MIT Libraries (AKDC@MIT)

de rigueur for scholars to fully understand the magnitude and nature of the structures they are studying, but researchers would do well to also seize the opportunity to locate such archives by establishing relationships with members of the community, as well as local agencies.

VISUAL AND MULTIMEDIA COLLECTIONS

For as long as scholars have been studying architectural history, they have relied heavily on collections consisting of visual documentation of Islamic monuments. These include drawings, photographs, sketches, and, more recently, video or even multimedia documentation drawn from various sources, both professional studios and amateur photographers, often for the purposes of creating a teaching or research collection. Such collections may exist as part of the personal archives of architects and scholars (Fig. 5), but are often more extensively preserved in the libraries of institutions like museums and universities which had a public-facing element (Fig. 6). Two early attempts to make such institutional collections available to a broader audience include the Mashreq-Maghreb project, a joint initiative between the Université de Paris-Sorbonne and the Institut für Orientalistik in Bamberg formed in the late 1980s, and the Aga Khan Visual Archive, an initiative of the Aga Khan Documentation Centers at the Massachusetts Institute of Technology and Harvard. The Mashreq-Maghreb project sought to catalog the slide collections held by each institution and put them in a publicly-accessible and searchable database, so that interested researchers could request copies of the images.[74] The Aga Khan Visual Archive grew from slides deposited by recipients of summer travel grants awarded by the Aga Khan Program in Islamic Architecture beginning in the early 1980s, and was supplemented by images donated by faculty, from scholars at other institutions, or purchased by the libraries. In 1985, a team of scholars, librarians, and technologists created a videodisc that contained over 30,000 images of Islamic architecture, representing an early attempt at digitization.[75] Today, AKDC@MIT houses multiple collections of images pertinent to the

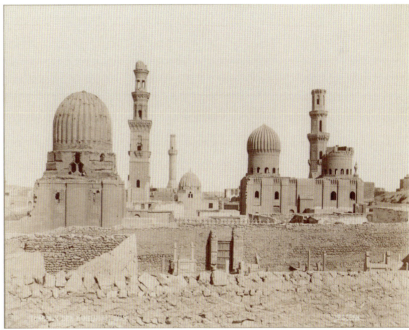

study of Islamic religious architecture, including the teaching and research collections of Yasser Tabbaa, Lisa Golombek, John and Caroline Williams, Marilyn Jenkins-Madina, and the archives of the architects Michel Écochard (Figs. 3 and 5), Rifat Chadirji (Figs. 7–8), Mohamed Makiya (Fig. 9), Hisham Munir, and Besim Hakim, all of which document historic Islamic architecture in addition to modern architectural projects, built and unbuilt, in Africa, the Levant, Iraq, Iran, Pakistan, and Europe.[76] In the

6 View of Mamluk monuments in Cairo's Southern Cemetery.
Photo: Jean Pascal Sébah, courtesy of The Metropolitan Museum of Art, Department of Islamic Art and Aga Khan Documentation Center, MIT Libraries (AKDC@MIT)

last two decades, the amount of visual documentation related to Islamic religious architecture has grown enormously, with far too many initiatives to detail here, but several helpful lists of databases are available online.[77] A project of particular note is the Arab Image Foundation in Beirut, which has united over 500,000 photographic objects from professional studios, amateur photographers, and family collections in the Arab world and its global diaspora, offering an unrivaled glimpse into the history of photography in the region.[78] These initiatives not only include the digitization of photographs, but encompass a range of analog resources, video, 3D scanning, and even virtual reality.

Aside from these specialized collections, mass media archives can be a valuable source of material for the study of Islamic architecture. While one should consult the archives of global press agencies such as the Associated Press (AP), Reuters, and Agence France Press (AFP), those of regional and local media may be more useful, as they have a social and financial interest in celebrating local architecture. To return to the example of the Islamic Society of Boston Cultural Center, one can find coverage from CBS Boston or the New England Cable Network.[79]

Of course, complete broadcast archives are not possible, as live broadcasts were often not recorded at all. Moreover, in order to economize, less well funded outlets tended to reuse tapes, recording over video or audio used in earlier stories. That said, often recordings of broadcasts are in the possession of the subjects of reporting, or even in the collections of interested third parties. A recent article by Flora Losch surveys efforts to preserve recordings of public broadcasting using new technologies.[80]

DIGITIZATION AND ONLINE AGGREGATION OF ARCHIVAL RESOURCES

In recent decades, the task of researchers looking for archival material has been greatly facilitated by the

7 Activity in the courtyard of the Kazimiyya shrine in Baghdad, taken in 1978. Photo: Kamil and Rifat Chadirji Photographic Archive, Aga Khan Documentation Center, MIT Libraries (AKDC@MIT)

8 Proposal (unbuilt) for the London Central Mosque by Rifat Chadirji, c. 1969. Photo: Kamil and Rifat Chadirji Photographic Archive, courtesy of Aga Khan Documentation Center, MIT Libraries (AKDC@MIT)

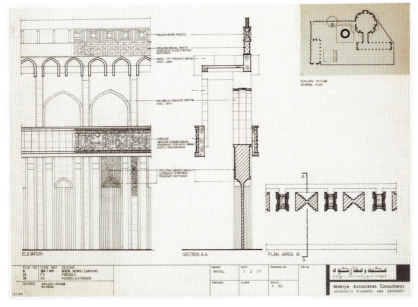

9 Khulafa Mosque, Baghdad, Iraq: northeast elevation, showing exterior niches and friezes of brickwork and carving. Photo: Mohamed Makiya Archive, courtesy of Aga Khan Documentation Center, MIT Libraries (AKDC@MIT)

trend toward online search tools that aggregate digitized resources from multiple institutions. These aggregators often allow for direct access to the digitized files, but even when this is not the case, the task of the researcher is greatly facilitated. For example, the archives portal of Europe provides access to more than 283 million descriptive units from over 7,000 archival institutions. While this is not a panacea due to the persistent digital divide, it does make the resources of a variety of institutions available without an in-person visit.

Researchers whose subjects connect to French scholarship or entail research in French archives will be familiar with Gallica, the database of France's Bibliothèque Nationale established in 1997. Gallica contains digitized material from the Bibliothèque Nationale as well as dozens of universities, scholarly societies, libraries, and other institutions throughout France.[81] The collection is also useful for visual documentation. A simple search on "mosquée" yields more than 45,000 resources that are available online, and records for another 3,775 that can be consulted in their respective repositories. Many countries and multinational organizations have provisions that research they fund must be made publicly available. In Spain, the Spanish Agency for International Development Cooperation (AECID) has an extensive collection of Arabic manuscripts, as well as material produced by or relating to overseas cooperation projects. The catalog of the AECID archives is available online, and many materials can be accessed directly.[82] An often-overlooked source for digitized archival material is the Internet Archive. The Internet Archive is best known for the Wayback Machine, which allows researchers to see older version of existing websites, or even sites that are no longer extant. However, the Internet Archive attempts to archive all online content, including digitized or born-digital publications, videos, books, software, and more.[83] *La cité de l'architecture et du patrimoine*, established in 2004, has an archive and specialized library exclusively devoted to architects and architecture related to France and its cultural heritage. Nonetheless, its holdings include a significant body of material on Islamic architecture, particularly architecture and urban planning in former French colonies or protectorates and projects involving French agencies or architects with French nationality. For example, the holdings relating to Georges Candilis (1913–1995) include numerous development projects in Saudi Arabia[84] and those of Auguste Cadet (1881–1956) include documentation of Quartier Habous in Casablanca and of at least six other mosques across Morocco.[85]

One of the earliest aggregation initiatives to focus specifically on Islamic architecture was Archnet.org, a curated online library focusing on communities in which Muslims are or have been a significant cultural presence. Developed by the Aga Khan Trust for Culture (AKTC) and the MIT School of Architecture and Urban Planning, it launched in 2003, and is

ARCHIVES AND ARCHIVAL DOCUMENTS   75

10 Section illustrating airflows for the Prince Sadruddin Aga Khan House in Aswan, Egypt, designed by Hassan Fathy, c. 1969. Fathy was recipient of the Chairman's Award for the Aga Khan Award for Architecture in 1980.
Photo: Hassan Fathy Archive, Aga Khan Trust for Culture

Archnet makes available resources from the Aga Khan Development Network, including documentation from projects related to the Aga Khan Award for Architecture (Figs. 1, 10), conservation efforts and regional surveys (Fig. 11), the Aga Khan Historic Cities Programme (Fig. 12), and the Aga Khan Trust for Cultural Education Programme.[86] Material from the collections of AKDC@MIT and other units of the MIT Libraries; and material developed by the Aga Khan Program for Islamic Architecture at Harvard and MIT (AKPIA).

Given the recent history of political and economic stability in the Middle East, digitization is often seen as essential for conservation of archives, especially in locations where the archives are vulnerable due to political or social instability. Some examples include the Manuscripts of Mali in the Library of Congress and the Yemeni Manuscripts Digitization Initiative.[87] The digitization of the glass negatives held in the Tangier American Legation Institute for Moroccan Studies is an example of a conservation effort undertaken for purposes of preservation and to make the contents of a small but highly specialized collection better known, although there is no immediate threat to the collection in Tangier, Morocco (Fig. 13).[88] In response to the issue of stability, the Digital Library of the Middle East (DLME) is a nascent project of the Council of Library and Information Resources to "create an internationally shared digital inventory of cultural artifacts, to include detailed and culturally nuanced descriptions, and confirm objects' appearance and provenance".[89] The project holds promise, but there are considerable obstacles to be overcome. DLME launched a proof concept site in 2019.

now a partnership between the AKTC and the Aga Khan Documentation Center in the MIT Libraries (AKDC@MIT), whose collections were discussed above. Organized around built structures and name authorities, the Archnet database currently hosts nearly 125,000 images and videos and 2,400 publications and other files, including CAD files. Each of these records is associated with one or more of 7,500 name authorities or 8,500 sites. Archnet's ambitious goal of providing users with authoritative resources on the built environment of Muslim societies around the world and throughout the course of history requires the support of numerous content providers who either gift their materials or provide Archnet with non-exclusive license to make the material available for unlimited educational and non-profit uses. In addition,

11 Mosque in Dougouba, Mali, from a survey of mud mosques undertaken for the Aga Khan Trust for Culture. The photographs from the survey are available on Archnet.
Photo: Sebastian Schutyser, 2001, Aga Khan Trust for Culture (AKTC)

CONCLUSION

The initiatives mentioned above are but a small sampling of a growing trend. Archives are proliferating, search engines are becoming more powerful, and the world is becoming more connected, particularly since the rise of mobile internet technologies. For this reason, libraries seek to implement comprehensive search portals, aggregating available information beyond their own catalog, and archival institutions seek to make their finding aids or catalogs available with machine-readable interfaces or APIs. Such changes have already radically altered access to information and the way that research on Islamic religious architecture is conducted, and present new sets of challenges that are still unfolding. From the perspective of librarians and archivists, the move toward digital scholarship raises questions related to digital preservation, not just of digital images and documents, but of data sets such as the point cloud generated by 3D scanning and computer-generated models. From the perspective of the researcher, the ever-expanding deluge of information available requires sharper attention to what counts as a reputable source. The concentration of digitization and documentation efforts at institutions in Europe and North America also raises a number of ethical questions. If we are not careful, the same imbalances of resources that have led to unequal access to information in the past may result in a digital divide that is just as wide.[90] These questions are critical, but must be the subject of future studies.

MATTHEW SABA is Visual Resources Librarian for Islamic Architecture at the Aga Khan Documentation Center, MIT Libraries. Before joining MIT, Matthew was as a postdoctoral curatorial fellow at the Metropolitan Museum of Art, where he worked on a project to digitize the papers of Ernst Herzfeld. His research interests include the history of early Islamic architecture, and questions related to the digitization and description of Islamic art and architecture in libraries and databases.

MICHAEL A. TOLER has been the Content Manager of Archnet.org in the Aga Khan Documentation Center, MIT Libraries, in Cambridge, Massachusetts, since 2012. Prior to that, he was Director of the NITLE Al-Musharaka Initiative, a collaborative of faculty, librarians, archivists, and instructional technologists working to enhance and expand teaching about the Islamic world in participating institutions of a national consortium of liberal arts colleges in the United States. He holds a PhD in comparative literature and translation studies from Binghamton University (SUNY Binghamton).

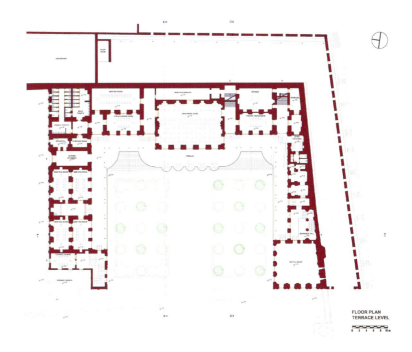

12 Ground floor plan of Bāgh-i Bābur and Queen's Palace in Kabul, Afghanistan, 2007, from documentation related to renovations sponsored by the Aga Khan Trust for Culture Historic Cities Programme.
Photo: courtesy of Aga Khan Trust for Culture Historic Cities Programme (AKTC)

13 View of market square just outside city wall in Tangier, Morocco, before the area was developed. The tomb of Sidi Bouabib is visible at left, and is now a large mosque.
Photo: Courtesy of TALIM/ Aga Khan Documentation Center, MIT Libraries (AKDC@MIT)

SUGGESTIONS FOR FURTHER READING

Hillenbrand, Robert. "Studying Islamic Architecture: Challenges and Perspectives," *Architectural History* 46 (2003), 1–18.

El Leithy, Tamer. "Living Documents, Dying Archives: Towards a Historical Anthropology of Medieval Arabic Archives," *Al-Qantara* 32.2 (2011), 389–434.

Jansen, Jan, Michael R. Doortmont, John H. Hanson, and Dmitri van den Bersselaar, eds. *Enduring Methods. History in Africa* 47 (2020).

Çaylı, Eray, ed. *Field as Archive / Archive as Field. International Journal of Islamic Architecture* 9.2 (2020).

Smith, Sharon C. "Documenting Islamic Architecture: Objectives and Outcomes in a Time of War," *International Journal of Islamic Architecture* 10.1 (2021), 159–170.

NOTES

1. "What Are Archives?" Society of American Archivists, last updated September 12, 2016, https://www2.archivists.org/about-archives.

2. For extended reflections on the practice and experience of archival research in the study of Islamic and Middle Eastern architecture, see the essays in *International Journal of Islamic Architecture* 9.2 (2020), a special issue dedicated to the topic. See especially the introductory essay by Eray Çaylı, "Field as Archive / Archive as Field," 251–261.

3. For some examples of types of literary sources relevant to the field and their potential uses, see D. Fairchild Ruggles, ed., *Islamic Art and Visual Culture: An Anthology of Sources* (Hoboken, NJ: Wiley Blackwell, 2011). For a recent statement of the use of literary sources in writing about Islamic art and architecture, see Finbarr Barry Flood and Gülru Necipoğlu, "Frameworks of Islamic Art and Architectural History: Concepts, Approaches, and Historiographies," in *A Companion to Islamic Art and Architecture*, ed. Finbarr Barry Flood and Gülru Necipoğlu (Hoboken, NJ: Wiley Blackwell, 2017), 2–56.

4. Kishwar Rizvi, *The Safavid Dynastic Shrine: Architecture, Religion and Power in Early Modern Iran* (London: I. B. Tauris, 2010), 59. For a translation of the topographic introduction to the list of deed abstracts, see 187–97. Descriptive (non-verse) sections and deed abstracts are translated in A. H. Morton, "The Ardabīl Shrine in the Reign of Shāh Ṭahmāsp I," *Iran* 12 (1974), 31–64, which also introduces the *Ṣarīḥ al-milk* genre (32–3 and footnote 13).

5. Maaike van Berkel, "Archives and Chanceries: pre-1500, in Arabic," E13, Brill Online, 2013.

6. Tamer El Leithy, "Living Documents, Dying Archives: Towards a Historical Anthropology of Medieval Arabic Archives," *Al-Qantara* 32.3 (2011), 389–434; Maaike van Berkel, "Reconstructing Archival Practices in Baghdad," *Journal of Abbasid Studies* 1 (2014), 7–22; Marina Rustow, *The Lost Archive: Traces of a Caliphate in a Cairo Synagogue* (Princeton: Princeton University Press, 2020), 1–19.

7. Rustow, *Lost Archive*, 66–82

8. El Leithy, "Living Documents," 411 and 418–21.

9. Recent scholarship on pre-Modern Islamic documents has adopted the idea of "archival practices" as an alternative to the more constricting idea of "archives." While "archives" implies a centralized institution, "archival practices" allows for the possibility of personal and familial as well as state and institutional archives. See El Leithy, "Living Documents," especially Konrad Hischler, "From Archive to Archival Practices: Rethinking the Preservation of Mamlūk Administrative Documents," *Journal of the American Oriental Society* 136.1 (2016), 1–28. For an excellent example of applying this idea to the study of one group of documents, see Daisy Livingston, "The Paperwork of a Mamluk *Muqṭā'*: Documentary Life-Cycles, Archival Spaces, and the Importance of Documents Lying Around," *'Uṣūr al-Wusṭā* 28 (2020), 346–375, https://www.middleeastmedievalists.com/wp-content/uploads/2021/01/UW-28-Livingston.pdf.

10. R. Stephen Humphreys, *Islamic History: A Framework for Enquiry*, (Princeton, NJ: Princeton University Press, 1991), 40–49.

11. Muḥammad Amīn, *Catalogue des documents d'archives du Caire de 239/853 à 922/1516* (Cairo: Institut Français d'Archéologie Orientale, 1981). For a study of urban apartment blocks (*rab'*) in Cairo making extensive use of these collections, see Hazem I. Sayed, "The *Rab'* in Cairo: A Window on Mamluk Architecture and Urbanism," PhD Diss. Massachusetts Institute of Technology, 1987. Available online at https://dspace.mit.edu/handle/1721.1/75720.

12. Donald P. Little, *A Catalogue of the Islamic Documents from al-Ḥaram aš-Šarif in Jerusalem* (Beirut: Orient-Institut der Deutschen Morgenländischen Gesellschaft, 1984).

13. Li Guo, *Commerce, Culture, and Community in a Red Sea Port in the Thirteenth Century: The Arabic Documents from Quseir* (Leiden and Boston: Brill, 2004).

14. S. D. Goitein, *A Mediterranean Society: the Jewish Communities of the Arab World as Portrayed in the Documents of the Cairo Geniza*, 5 vols. (Berkeley and Los Angeles: University of California Press, 1967–1988), 1:1–128.

15. Donald P. Little, "The Ḥaram Documents as Sources for the Arts and Architecture of the Mamluk Period," *Muqarnas* 2 (1984), 61–72.

16. Nasser Rabbat, *Mamluk History through Architecture: Monuments, Culture, and Politics in Medieval Egypt and Syria* (London: I. B. Tauris, 2010), 24–5.

17. For the Egyptian context, see Sylvie Denoix, "A Mamluk Institution for Urbanization: The *Waqf*," in *The Cairo Heritage: Essays in Honor of Laila Ali Ibrahim*, ed. Doris Behrens-Abouseif, 191–202 (Cairo: AUC Press, 2000), and cf. the methodological remarks on the corpus of catalogued Mamluk *waqfiyyas* from Cairo in idem, "Pour un exploitation

d'ensemble d'un corpus: les waqfs mamelouks du Caire," in *Le waqf dans l'espace Islamique outil de pouvoir socio-politique*, edited by Randi Deguilhem (Damascus: Institut Français d'études Arabes, 1995), 29–44. For the Iranian context, Christoph Werner, *Vaqf en Iran: Aspects culturels, religieux et sociaux* (Paris and Leuven: Peeters, 2015), chapter 2. For the roots of this development before Mamluk times, see Stefan Heidemann, "Charity and Piety for the Transformation of Cities. The New Direction in Taxation and Waqf Policy in Mid-Twelfth-Century Syria and Northern Mesopotamia," in *Charity and Giving in Monotheistic Religions*, ed. Miriam Frenkel and Yaacov Lev (Berlin and New York: Walter de Gruyter, 2009), 153–174.

[18] Sheila Blair, "Ilkhanid Architecture and Society: An Analysis of the Endowment Deed of the Rabʻ-i Rashīdī," *Iran* 22 (1984), 67 (67–90).

[19] Rabbat, *Mamluk History through Architecture*, 101–3.

[20] Goitein, *Mediterranean Society*, 6: 1–126.

[21] Rustow, *Lost Archive*, 3, 42, and fn. 9.

[22] Petra M. Sijpestein, John F. Oates and Andreas Kaplony, "Checklist of Arabic Papyri (Beta Version) [Last Updated April 2006]," *Bulletin of the American Society of Papyrologists* 42 (2005): 127–166. The checklist, including an introduction to the project, is updated regularly and is available in its last updated form (23 July 2019 at the time of writing) at http://www.naher-osten.lmu.de/isapchecklist.

[23] For a general introduction to this vast field of research, one should consult the relevant articles in various specialist encyclopedias. For example: Astrid Meier, "Archives and Chanceries: Arab World," EI3, Brill Online, 2012; Alexander Morrison, "Archives: Central Asia, EI3, Brill Online, 2016;" Sievert Henning, "Archives and Chanceries: Ottoman Empire and Turkey," EI3, Brill Online, 2012; Osman G. Özgüdenli, "Archives i. Turkish archives concerning Iran," *Encyclopaedia Iranica*, last updated August 11, 2011, https://www.iranicaonline.org/articles/archives-i-turkish.

[24] For an overview of archives relevant to Ottoman history, see Suraiya Faroqhi, *Approaching Ottoman History: An Introduction to the Sources* (Cambridge: Cambridge University Press, 2009), 49–69 and the list of collections outside Ottoman lands 76–79. Further bibliography of catalogs, hand-lists, and resources related to Ottoman archives are available in Henning, "Archives and Chanceries."

[25] Some examples include Gülru Necipoğlu, "The Account Book of a Fifteenth-Century Ottoman Royal Kiosk," *Journal of Turkish Studies* 11 (1987), 31–44; Ülkü Bates, "Two Ottoman Documents on Architects in Egypt," *Muqarnas* 3 (1985), 121–7; and Muzaffer Özgüleş, "A Missing Royal Mosque in Istanbul that Islamized a Catholic Space: The Galata New Mosque," *Muqarnas* 34 (2017), 157–195.

[26] Gülru Necipoğlu, "Plans and Models in 15th- and 16th-Century Ottoman Architectural Practice," *Journal of the Society of Architectural Historians* 45.3 (September 1986), 224–243.

[27] Suraiya Faroqhi, *Artisans of Empire: Crafts and Craftspeople Under the Ottomans* (London: I. B. Tauris, 2009), xix–xxi and 1–23.

[28] Faroqhi, *Approaching Ottoman History*, 55–57 and 59–61.

[29] Doris Behrens-Abouseif, *Egypt's Adjustment to Ottoman Rule: Institutions, Waqf and Architecture in Cairo (16th and 17th Centuries)* (Leiden: Brill, 1994).

[30] The national archives for *awqāf* in Iran is called the *Sāzmān-i Avqāf va Umūr-i Khayrīyah*.

[31] A list of published decrees to 1980 is offered in Bert G. Fragner, *Repertorium persischer Herrschererkunden: publizierte Orig.-Urkunden (bis 1858)* (Freiberg im Bresgau: Schwarz, 1982). For documents related to the Safavid Period specifically, see Renate Schimkoreit, *Regesten publizierter safawidischer Herrscherurkunden* (Berlin: Klaus Schwarz, 1982). For an entry point to scholarship up to the year 2000, including many studies by scholars in Iran, see the bibliographies of the articles in Kondo, Nobuaki ed., *Persian Documents: Social History of Iran and Turan in the Fifteenth to Nineteenth Centuries* (London: Routledge, 2011). For studies of *waqf* in particular, the journal *Vaqf: Mīrāṣ-i Jāvīdān* is a vital source. Asnad.org, an online database initiated in 2003 by Christoph Werner, attempts to bring together information on published documents from Iran: http://www.asnad.org/en/ (Accessed October 27, 2020).

[32] General remarks on an extended inventory of the documents made by A. H. Morton are available in Martin E. Weaver, "The Conservation of the Shrine of Shaikh Safi at Ardebil: Iran, Second Preliminary Study – Mission (July-August 1971)," UNESCO Serial Number 2560/RMO.RD/CLP (Paris, 1971), 3–9. Available online at <https://unesdoc.unesco.org/ark:/48223/pf0000001333.locale=en>. For an annotated bibliography of the publication of archival material related to the shrine, see Bert Fragner, "Das Ardabīler Heiligtum in den Urkunden," *Wiener Zeitschrift für die Kunde des Morgenlandes* 67 (1975), 169–174 (169–215).

[33] The Mongol decrees in the Iran National Museum are examples. See Paul Pelliot, "Les Documents mongols du Musée de Teheran," *Athar-e Iran* 1 (1936): 37–44 and F. W. Cleaves, "The Mongolian Documents in the Musée de Teheran." *Harvard Journal of Asiatic Studies* 16.1–2 (1953), 1–107.

[34] Abol Fazl Hasanbadi and Elaheh Mahbub, "Introducing the Safavid Documents of the Directorate of Documents and Publications of the Central Library of the Holy Shrine at Mashhad (Iran)," *Iranian Studies* 42.2 (April, 2009), 311–27.

[35] Hasanbadi and Mahbub, "Introducing the Safavid Documents," 313.

[36] Morikawa, Tomoko and Christoph Werner, eds., *Vestiges of the Razavi Shrine: Āthār al-Rażavīya, A Catalogue of Endowments and Deeds to the Shrine of Imam Riza in Mashhad* (Tokyo: Toyo Bunko, 2017).

[37] David Roxburgh, *Prefacing the Image: The Writing of Art History in Sixteenth-Century Iran* (Leiden and Boston: Brill, 2001) and idem., *The Persian Album, 1400–1600: From Dispersal to Collection* (New Haven: Yale, 2005).

[38] Mansur Sefatgol, "Majmūʻah'hā: Important and Unknown Sources of Historiography of Iran during the Last Safavids. The Case of *Majmūʻah-i Mīrzā Muʻīnā*," in Kondo, ed., *Persian Documents*, 73–83.

[39] For examples of archival material housed in state institutions, see the items in Mohammed Ziauddin Ahmed and S. Venkataramaiah, *Mughal Archives: A Descriptive Catalogue of the Documents Pertaining to the Reign of Shah Jahan*, 1628–1658 (Hyderabad: State Archives, 1977). See also the documents in the National Archives of India described under the heading Oriental Records: "Oriental Records," National Archives of India, Accessed October 28, 2020, <http://nationalarchives.nic.in/content/oriental-records-0>. A study using *farmāns* dating to the Bahmanid period in the Deccan to shed light on the history of the religious architecture of the Niʻmat Allāhī order is found in Peyvand Firouzeh, "Between the Spiritual and Material: The Niʻmat Allāhī Order's Institutionalization and Architectural Patronage in the 9th/15th Century," in *Shiʻi Islam and Sufism: Classical Views and Modern Perspectives*, edited by Dennis Herrmann and Matheiu Terrier (London: I. B. Tauris, 2020), 123–55.

[40] Nandini Chatterjee, *Negotiating Mughal Law: A Family of Landlords Across Three Indian Empires* (Cambridge: Cambridge University Press, 2020), 228 and 234.

[41] W. E. Begley and Z. A. Desai, *Taj Mahal: The Illuminated Tomb. An Anthology of Seventeenth-Century Mughal and European Documentary Sources* (Cambridge, MA: Aga Khan Program for Islamic Architecture, 1989), 163–184.

42 "The National Archives : Historical Overview," Les Archives Nationales de Tunisie (Republic of Tunisia), accessed January 14, 2021, http://www.archives.nat.tn/index.php?id=23&L=2.

43 Jocelyn Hendrickson, "A Guide to Arabic Manuscript Libraries in Morocco, with Notes on Tunisia, Algeria, Egypt, and Spain," MELA Notes 81 (2008), 32–34 (15–88).

44 Alexandra Walsham, "The Social History of the Archive: Record-Keeping in Early Modern Europe," Past & Present 230.11 (2016): 9–48, https://doi.org/10.1093/pastj/gtw033.

45 The catalog of the ANOM is online at http://anom.archivesnationales.culture.gouv.fr/.

46 TV5 MONDE and AFP, "L'Algérie Exige 'La Totalité' Des Archives Sur La Colonisation à La France," TV5 MONDE, December 22, 2020, https://information.tv5monde.com/afrique/l-algerie-exige-la-totalite-des-archives-sur-la-colonisation-la-france-388859.

47 "Une Bibliothèque Numérique Pour Les Affaires Étrangères," Bibliotheque Diplomatique Numerique, Ministère de l'Europe et des Affaires étrangères, accessed January 22, 2021, https://bibliotheque-numerique.diplomatie.gouv.fr/.

48 Alexandra Kolega, "Direzione di colonizzazione di Tripoli," Sistema Informative Unificato per le Soprintendenze Archivistiche, 2005, https://siusa.archivi.beniculturali.it/cgi-bin/pagina.pl?TipoPag=comparc&Chiave=209969.

49 The India Office "was responsible for the administration of British India to independence in 1947, as well as Burma and some Middle Eastern territories during the colonial period." See "Colonies and Dependencies from 1782," The National Archives-UK, September 15, 2020, https://www.nationalarchives.gov.uk/help-with-your-research/research-guides/colonies-dependencies-further-research/. For a list of guides to India Office Records in the British Library, see "Resources for the Study of South Asia, past and present," British Library, accessed January 19, 2021, https://www.bl.uk/subjects/south-asia.

50 Samantha Sherry, Jonathan Waterlow, and Andy Willimott, "Using Archives and Libraries in the Former Soviet Union, Version 2" (London: Arts & Humanities Research Council, 2013).

51 A number of studies utilizing scholarly archives for the study of Islamic architecture appear in the proceedings of the conference Islamic Heritage through the Lens of Scholarly Archives: New Perspectives in Islamic Art and Archaeology, held at the Musée du Louvre and Sorbonne Université on 3–4 October, 2019 (forthcoming 2022).

52 Teresa Fitzherbert, "The Creswell Photographic Archive at the Ashmolean Museum, Oxford," Muqarnas 8 (1991): 125–127. Digitized negatives from the Ashmolean collection can be browsed online at crewell.ashmolean.org and at http://www.archnet.org/collections/12.

53 The AUC material is described at http://schools.aucegypt.edu/library/Pages/rbscl/collections/creswell.aspx and a portion is available at http://digitalcollections.aucegypt.edu/digital/collection/p15795coll14. For the material in the V&A, see Erika Lederman, "K. A. C. Creswell's Middle East Views at the V&A," V&A Blog, Victoria and Albert Museum, June 17, 2015, https://www.vam.ac.uk/blog/caring-for-our-collections/k-a-c-creswell-and-the-victoria-and-albert-museum and Omniya Abdel Barr, "K. A. C. Creswell's Photographs of the Middle East," Victoria and Albert Museum, accessed November 2, 2020, https://www.vam.ac.uk/articles/creswells-egypt-syria-and-palestine-photographs.

54 "K. A. C. Creswell," Eastern Art Online. Ashmolean Museum, accessed November 2, 2020. http://jameelcentre.ashmolean.org/collection/6/6245/6246.

55 Examples of studies utilizing Herzfeld's papers include Trudy S. Kawami, "Kuh-e Khwaja, Iran, and its Wall Paintings: The Records of Ernst Herzfeld," Metropolitan Museum Journal 22 (1987), 13–52; Thomas Leisten, Excavation of Samarra, Volume 1: Final Report on the First Campaign, 1910–1912 (Mainz am Rhein: Philipp von Zabern, 2003).

56 For the Freer and Sackler papers, see Joseph M. Upton, Catalogue of the Herzfeld Archive (Washington, D.C.: Freer Gallery of Art and Arthur M. Sackler Gallery, 1978), and Alexander Nagel and Rachael Woody, "Excavations in the Archive. An Update on the Ernst Herzfeld Online Resources at the Freer/Sackler in Washington D.C.," in Beiträge zur Islamischen Kunst und Archäologie 4, edited by Julia Gonnella, Rania Abdellatif and Simone Struth (Wiesbaden: Ludwig Reichert, 2014), 18–27. For the Metropolitan Museum's Herzfeld papers, see Margaret Cool Root, "The Herzfeld Archive of the Metropolitan Museum of Art," Metropolitan Museum Journal 11 (1976), 119–124.

57 The Freer and Sackler's portion is available at https://asia.si.edu/research/archives/herzfeld/. The Metropolitan Museum's portion is available at https://www.metmuseum.org/art/libraries-and-research-centers/watson-digital-collections/manuscript-collections/ernst-herzfeld-papers.

58 Evelyne Disdier, "Fonds FRMMSH013_MED_019 - Documents Georges Marçais," Archives du Moyen-Orient et des mondes musulmans à partir des fonds documentaires orientalistes conservés en France, March 17, 2017, http://defter.fr/index.php/documents-georges-marcais?sf_culture=fr.

59 Bibliotheca Orientalis Attilio Petruccioli, July 13, 2020, https://bibliothecaorientalis.org/.

60 On his work, see Fatima Quraishi, "Asar-ul-Sanadid: A Nineteenth-Century History of Delhi," Journal of Art Historiography 6 (2012), https://arthistoriography.files.wordpress.com/2012/05/quraishi.pdf, and Mrinalini Rajagopalan, "A Nineteenth-Century Architectural Archive: Syed Ahmed Khan's Aṣar-us-Ṣanādid," International Journal of Islamic Architecture 6.1 (2017), 27–58.

61 A point developed in Mrinalini Rajagopalan, Building Histories: The Archival and Affective Lives of Five Monuments in Modern Delhi (Chicago: University of Chicago Press, 2018). See especially the introduction and, for an application, the study of the Rasul Numa Dargah on 61–85.

62 For presidential visits to the Washington Mosque, see for example, National Archives and Records Administration, Record Group 306: Records of the U.S. Information Agency, 1900–2003, Series: "Today" Monthly News Reports, 1957–1968, "Today" No. 1, 1957, https://catalog.archives.gov/id/131065175. For FBI Dossiers, see National Archives and Records Administration, Record Group 65: Records of the Federal Bureau of Investigation, 1896–2008, Series: Classification 157 (Civil Unrest) Case Files, 1957–1978. https://catalog.archives.gov/id/1513558.

63 For Paris Mosque, see National Archives and Records Administration, Record Group 286: Records of the Agency for International Development, 1948–2003," Series: Photographs of Marshall Plan Programs, Exhibits, and Personnel, 1948–1967, [Paris Mosque], https://catalog.archives.gov/id/18462288. For mosques in Iraq, see National Archives and Records Administration, Record Group 330: Records of the Office of the Secretary of Defense, 1921–2008, Series: Combined Military Service Digital Photographic Files, 1982–2007, https://catalog.archives.gov/id/6274097.

64 Kian Byrne, "A Survey of Middle East Archives: Egypt," Sources and Methods, Wilson Center, April 20, 2020, https://www.wilsoncenter.org/blog-post/survey-middle-east-archives-egypt.

65 Adam Meystan and Rudolph Peters, "Dar Al-Mahfuzat Al-'Umumiyya (Cairo)," HAZINE, August 20, 2020, http://hazine.info/daralmahfuzat/.

66 "Inauguration of 'Archives of Morocco': To Write Rational and Pluralistic History," Conseil National Des Droits De L'Homme, Royaume Du Maroc, June 2013, www.cndh.org.ma/an/bulletin-d-information/inauguration-archives-morocco-write-rational-and-pluralistic-history.

67 "Revues," Bibliothèque Numérique Marocaine, accessed January 22, 2021, http://bnm.bnrm.ma:86/listerevues.aspx.

68 Katelyn Tietzen, "Recording Conflict: the CRRC and Ba'th Party Archives," Sources and Methods, Wilson Center, July 13, 2020, https://www.wilsoncenter.org/blog-post/recording-conflict-crrc-and-bath-party-archives.

69 Library of Congress and the U.S. Department of State Mission To Baghdad, "Report on the National Library and House of Manuscripts," African & Middle Eastern Reading Room, Library of Congress, November 2003, https://www.loc.gov/rr/amed/iraqreport/iraqreport.html.

70 Callimachi, Rukmini, "The ISIS Files: When Terrorists Run City Hall," The New York Times, April 5, 2018, https://www.nytimes.com/interactive/2018/04/04/world/middleeast/isis-documents-mosul-iraq.html. For critical responses, see "Statement on Removal of ISIS Records from Iraq by New York Times Reporter," Society of American Archivists, June 13, 2018, https://www2.archivists.org/statements/statement-on-removal-of-isis-records-from-iraq-by-new-york-times-reporter, and "Acquisition and Unethical Use of Documents Removed from Iraq by New York Times Journalist Rukmini Callimachi," Committee on Academic Freedom, Middle East Studies Association, October 23, 2020, https://mesana.org/advocacy/committee-on-academic-freedom/2018/05/02/acquisition-and-unethical-use-of-documents-removed-from-iraq-by-rukmini-callimachi.

71 Rosie Bsheer, Archive Wars: The Politics of History in Saudi Arabia (Stanford, CA: Stanford University Press, 2020).

72 "UNESCO Archives," UNESCO, accessed January 18, 2021. https://unesdoc.unesco.org/archives.

73 "About UNESDOC," UNESCO, accessed January 18, 2021. https://unesdoc.unesco.org/about.

74 Marianne Barrucand, "Mashreq-Maghreb: Archives Photographiques du Monde Islamique," Middle East Studies Association Bulletin 24.2 (1990): 169–178. Today, the database comprises 9711 digitized and cataloged photographs (5837 architecture, 2039 manuscripts, and 1835 objects). The project's Website is http://www.mashreq-maghreb.paris-sorbonne.fr/.

75 Activities related to this project are documented in the Massachusetts Institute of Technology, Aga Khan Program for Islamic Architecture records, MIT Libraries, Department of Distinctive Collections. An overview and finding aid for these records is available at https://archivesspace.mit.edu/repositories/2/resources/206. The Aga Khan Visual Archive currently houses over 120,000 slides and is partly digitized. Digitized images are available via Archnet.org (see http://archnet.org/collections/1786 for a selection).

76 For more information on the collections of the Aga Khan Documentation Center at MIT, see "Collections," Aga Khan Documentation Center, MIT Libraries, accessed January 11, 2021, https://libraries.mit.edu/akdc/collections/.

77 Amanda Hannoosh Steinberg, "A Guide to Online Visual Sources in Middle East, North Africa, and Islamic Studies," Hazine: A Guide to Researching the Middle East and Beyond, August 22, 2019, http://hazine.info/visual-sources-middle-east-north-africa-islamic-studies-online/. One particularly important resource for the early Islamic period that has developed since 2010 is Manar al-Athar, an open-access photo archive of late antique and early Islamic architecture based at the University of Oxford and initiated by Judith McKenzie. See "Welcome," Manar al-Athar, University of Oxford, accessed January 11, 2021, http://www.manar-al-athar.ox.ac.uk/. A second project important to mention is the Syrian Heritage Archive Project, which seeks to document Syria's cultural heritage in response to the damage inflicted in the Syria Civil War. See "About Us," Syrian Heritage Archive Project, accessed January 11, 2021, https://project.syrian-heritage.org/en/about-us/.

78 Portions of this collection are online in a searchable database. For more information, see "About the Collection," Arab Image Foundation, accessed January 20, 2021, http://arabimagefoundation.com/Collection.

79 "Islamic Society of Boston Cultural Center," CBS Boston, accessed January 22, 2021, https://boston.cbslocal.com/tag/islamic-society-of-boston-cultural-center/. Searching "Islamic Society of Boston Cultural Center" on New England Cable News Network's website (https://www.necn.com) yields a number of results.

80 Losch, Flora. "Preserving Public Broadcasting Archives in the Digital Era: Circulatory Stories and Technologies, the Digital Turn, and the Return of the Past in West Africa." History in Africa 47 (2020): 219–41. https://doi.org/10.1017/hia.2020.2.

81 "A Propos: Gallica," Gallica, accessed January 18, 2021, https://gallica.bnf.fr/edit/und/a-propos.

82 "Presentación. Biblioteca AECID," Biblioteca Digital AECID (BIDA), accessed January 18, 2021, http://bibliotecadigital.aecid.es/bibliodig/es/estaticos/contenido.cmd?pagina=estaticos%2Fpresentacion.

83 "About IA," Internet Archive, accessed January 18, 2021. https://archive.org/about/.

84 "Fiche Descriptive-Fonds Candilis, Georges (1913–1995). 236 Ifa." Archiwebture. Cité de l'Architecture et du Patrimoine. Accessed January 23, 2021. https://archiwebture.citedelarchitecture.fr/fonds/FRAPNO2_CANGE.

85 "Objet CADET-A. Nouvelle Ville Des Habous, Casablanca (Maroc). 1921–1930." Archiwebture. Cité de l'Architecture et du Patrimoine. Accessed January 23, 2021. https://archiwebture.citedelarchitecture.fr/fonds/FRAPNO2_CADET/inventaire/objet-14285.

86 The Aga Khan Award for Architecture is awarded every three years. The extensive documentation accumulated as part of the submission and evaluation process is maintained by the Aga Khan Trust for Culture and is an important record of contemporary architecture in the Islamic world.

87 "Islamic Manuscripts from Mali Collection: Home," Library of Congress, accessed January 18, 2021, https://memory.loc.gov/intldl/malihtml/malihome.html, and "Yemeni Manuscript Initiative," Princeton University Library Special Collections, accessed January 18, 2021, https://library.princeton.edu/special-collections/collections/yemeni-manuscript-initiative.

88 "The International Tangier Glass Negatives Collection," Archnet, accessed January 18, 2021, http://archnet.org/pages/TALIM-negatives.

89 "About DLME," Digital Library of the Middle East, Council on Library and Information Resources (CLIR), November 13, 2019, https://dlme.clir.org/about/.

90 For these and other ethical considerations, see Sharon C. Smith, "Documenting Islamic Architecture: Objectives and Outcomes in a Time of War," International Journal of Islamic Architecture 10.1 (2021), 159–170.

West and Central Asia

The Holy Mosque of Mecca

ABEER HUSSAM EDDIN ALLAHHAM

1 The Holy Mosque of Mecca, al-Mataf with the Holy Kaaba at its center, surrounded by the Ottoman arcade of 1630, and the first Saudi expansion in 1976.
Photo: Ministry of Higher Education, Saudi Arabia, 2010

The Holy Mosque, known in the Quran as al-Masjid al-Haram is the largest mosque in the world. Located in the city of Mecca, Saudi Arabia, it surrounds the Holy Kaaba (the cube building at the center of the Holy Mosque), the direction of Muslims' daily prayer worldwide. For Muslims, it is the most important holy site, to which millions of Muslim pilgrims perform Hajj every year; it is, as Muslims believe, the first house of worship established for people on earth.

Al-Masjid al-Haram is known by many other names such as al-Bayt al-'Ateeq (the earliest and ancient house), al-Bayt al-Haram (the holy house), al-Haram al-Makki (which indicates its location in Mecca), and al-Bayt or Bayt Allah (the House of God). Some of these names relate to the Holy Kaaba, as al-Masjid al-Haram is al-Haram itself, which constitutes the Holy Kaaba and the restricted precinct (*haram*) surrounding it. It is attributed as restricted due to its inviolability and prohibition of fighting within its boundaries since the entry of Prophet Muhammad – peace be upon Him (pbuH) – to Mecca. The Haram precinct, which is exclusive to Muslims only, is estimated to cover a circle of about 127 km in diameter, with a total area of about 550.30 square kilometers.[1]

ERECTION OF THE KAABA

The Quran incontrovertibly states that the Holy Kaaba is the first house of worship ever erected on earth: "The first House [of worship] to be established for people was the one at Bakka. It is a blessed place; a source of guidance for all people" (3:96).[2] However, sources vary regarding its construction. Some date its construction before Adam (pbuH) and hold that the Kaaba was ordained by God in the shape of the House in the upper heaven, or al-Bayt

al-Ma'mour before the creation of humankind. According to this view, the Kaaba was first erected by the angels who conducted, after its completion, *tawaf* (circumambulation) around it as pilgrims do around al-Bayt al-Ma'mour. Others contend that it was first built by Adam, as commanded by God. Some scholars, basing their argument upon several traditions of the Prophet Muhammad (pbuH), instead assert that these narratives are about the demarcation of the Old House only and not about its complete building.[3] It is indisputable that the Kaaba was erected by Ibrahim (Abraham) and his son Isma'il (peace be upon them (pbuT)) (Quran 2:127, 128). As the Old House was destroyed by the Great Flood during the era of the Prophet Noah (pbuH), when its foundation and location became lost, it is narrated that God directed Ibrahim to the original location of the Kaaba; there he, with the help of his son, kept digging until he uncovered the original foundations of the Kaaba and built them up.[4]

SIGNIFICANCE AND VIRTUES OF THE HOLY MOSQUE

At the dawn of Islam, the *qibla* or direction of Muslim prayers was toward al-Aqsa mosque in Jerusalem. In the second year of the Prophet's migration or Hijra from Mecca to Medina, God commanded the Prophet Muhammad (pbuH) to reorient the *qibla* to be towards the Kaaba or the Holy Mosque in Mecca. This made the Holy Mosque the most important building for Muslims. The Mosque also obtains its significance from being the main location for Muslim pilgrimage or Hajj. As mentioned in the Quran, "Pilgrimage to the Holy Mosque is a duty owed to God by people who are able to undertake it" (Quran, 3:97). Moreover, millions of Muslims every year visit the Mosque to perform Umra, or minor Hajj, especially in the month of Ramadan, which is the ninth month of the Islamic calendar.

The Holy Mosque holds many special virtues for Muslims. It is a blessed and secure place: "Whoever enters it is safe" (3:97), protected by God, Almighty. God has related it to Himself, calling it "My House" (22:26), thus granting it honor and nobility. Also, as narrated by the Prophet, a prayer in the Holy Mosque is equivalent to one hundred thousand prayers in any other mosque. Invocation, or *do'a*, is acceptable and answerable in many places in the Holy Mosque.

ELEMENTS OF THE HOLY MOSQUE

The Holy Mosque contains some unique elements and relics that attract worshippers. Their specific locations have been assigned according to religious commands; they are fixed elements that cannot be removed from their original places. Several rituals and activities performed in the mosque have a special association with these elements, a matter that gives the Holy Mosque a great significance and distinction. These elements are:

- The Cube, or the Kaaba, is the large black masonry structure at the center of the circumambulation area (Fig. 1). It was called Kaaba because of its cubic shape, although it is not perfectly a cube. In its eastern corner lies the Black Stone, or al-Hajar al-Aswad, and at the south lies al-Rukn al-Yamani, or the corner facing Yemen. The other corners are al-Rukn al-Iraqi at the north, facing Iraq, and al-Rukn al-Shami or the Levantine corner at the west, facing al-Sham (today Syria). The foundation at the base of Kaaba is called Shadhrwan, which surrounds its sides, except for the northern side of Hijr Isma'il (described below) and constitutes part of the Holy Kaaba. It is believed to be part of the original foundation of Prophet Ibrahim (pbuH)'s Kaaba. The Shadhrawan was first built by Abdullah ibn Azzubair to protect the Kaaba walls from water leaks. It is made of white marble, with forty-one metal rings attached

to it to which the ropes of the Kaaba covering (*kiswa*) are fastened.

As constructed by Prophet Ibrahim (pbuh), the Holy Kaaba was a small roofless enclosure, built of stone from the hills surrounding Mecca, with two opposing doors at ground level, one on the eastern side near the Black Stone and the other on the western side near al-Rukn al-Yamani. It was oblong in shape, about nine cubits high (or a little higher than a human figure), where its sides were 32 (NE), 22 (NW), 31 (SW), 20 (SE) cubits long, and has a proportion of about 3:2.[5] In 608 (before Islam), the Kaaba went under a reconstruction process by the Quraish tribe, during which its dimensions were changed. Due to shortage of money, the area towards Hijr Isma'il was left unconstructed, decreasing the Kaaba's length by about three meters. Its height was increased to eighteen cubits with only one door near the Black Stone, and a roof with waterspouts was added.

During Islamic history, the Holy Kaaba went through several reconstruction and restoration processes. The present-day Kaaba is smaller than the original one. Its sides are the same as those of the Quraish reconstruction, measuring 11.68 (NE), 9.9 (NW), 12.04 (SW), and 10.18 meters (SE), with a height of 12.95 meters.[6] It has one door made of gold, 1.68 meters wide and 3.06 meters in height, and about two meters high from the level of al-Mataf, or the circumambulation area. The interior walls of the Kaaba are clad with marble halfway to the roof with Quranic inscriptions. The Kaaba is covered with an annually replaced black silk curtain, *kiswa*, decorated on its upper part with a gold embroidered band covered with Quranic text.

- The Black Stone (al-Hajar al-Aswad) is located at the eastern corner of the Holy Kaaba. This was the first original corner of the Kaaba and is where Muslims should start and end their *tawaf*. Muslims believe that the Black Stone is a sacred stone from Heaven, placed in its corner by Ibrahim and Isma'il (pbuT). However, it has never been worshipped and has no special sanctity or power. The stone is dark and oval shaped with an undulating surface, composed of a number of fragments held together by a silver frame; it is located at a height of 1.5 meters above ground level (Fig. 2). The Black Stone's current diameter is about twenty centimeters, but its original size is not clear, since its dimensions have changed considerably over time. If possible, pilgrims are to kiss or touch the Black Stone during their *tawaf*, emulating Prophet Muhammad (pbuH). If they cannot, it is adequate to point to it on each circuit of *tawaf*.

- The Yemeni Corner, or al-Rukn al-Yamani is the second original corner of the Holy Kaaba. It is named "Yemeni" because it is facing the southern direction towards Yemen.

- The Wall of Ismail, or Hijr Isma'il, is the place where Prophet Ibrahim settled his family, Hajer and his infant son Isma'il (pbuT), near the sacred Kaaba. It is the semi-circular wall on the northwestern side, within which it is recommended to pray. One of its sides faces the western corner and the second side faces the northern corner of the Kaaba. Part of Hijr Isma'il (six cubes and a hand span) constitutes a part of the Kaaba since it was left out during the Quraish tribe's reconstruction due to lack of funds. Some believe that the graves of Prophet Isma'il and his mother Hajer (pbuT) are located in this space.

- The Place of Clinging, or al-Multazam is the part of the Holy Kaaba wall that is between the Black Stone and the Kaaba door. It is about two meters long. Its name is derived from the Arabic word *iltizam* that means clinging, since Muslims cling to al-Multazam to make *do'a*. *Do'a* or invocation is answerable at al-Multazam, as Muslims believe.

- The Station of Abraham, or Maqam Ibrahim, is the stone on which it is believed that Prophet Ibrahim (pbuH) stood while building the Kaaba and when he called people for Hajj.

2 The Holy Mosque of Mecca, the Black Stone, Kaaba.
Photo: Ministry of Higher Education, Saudi Arabia, 2010

Miraculously, the prints of Prophet Ibrahim's feet are still preserved on the stone. It is located close to the eastern wall of the Kaaba where Ibrahim offered up his prayers. As part of Hajj or Umra (pilgrimage to Mecca performed outside of Ramadan) rituals, Muslims pray behind Maqam Ibrahim after finishing their *tawaf*. Today the stone is covered with silver plate except for the footprint encased inside a protective clear crystal dome.

- The Zamzam well is a sacred water well. It dates back to Hajer's time, when Prophet Ibrahim left his wife Hajer (pbuT) and his infant son in a desolate valley in Western Arabia. While Hajer was running between as-Safa and al-Marwa hills looking desperately for water for her son, Zamzam water miraculously burst forth at the feet of Isma'il (pbuH). When Hajer (pbuH) saw the water she said, attempting to contain the spring water, *zam zam* or don't spread, don't go away. The well took its name after Hajer's words. Arab tribes settled around the well, with her permission, and so was born the city of Mecca.

Many years after the death of Hajer and her son, the Zamzam spring stopped flowing. Over time, because of various floods and wars in the area, its location became lost and unknown. Abdul Muttalib (Prophet Muhammad's grandfather) saw it in a dream while sleeping in Hijr Isma'il. He dug a hole in the place that he dreamed of and found Zamzam spring, ever since then it has never stopped flowing.

Zamzam well is located approximately 20 meters east of the Holy Kaaba. The well originally was a simple well surrounded by a fence of stone. Later, in 771 the Abbasid caliph al-Mansur built a dome above the well, which afterwards underwent several repairs and restorations. In 1963, the building housing Zamzam well was moved away from its original location to facilitate crowd movement in performing *tawaf*. Currently, its entrance is 1.56 meters below al-Mataf, where its springs are located about 15 meters below the well hole. The water level is about four meters below the hole. The well depth is about 30.5 meters, with an internal diameter of about 1.0–2.6 meters. It is now housed in a basement room, protected by glass panels that allow a clear view of the well. In 2003, the entrance to the area was removed from al-Mataf, thus the well area is no longer accessible for visitors.

Muslims believe that Zamzam water, due to its unique components and properties, and because of its blessings, has healing power. Today Zamzam water constitutes the prime source of water for pilgrims. It is available throughout al-Masjid al-Haram from water fountains and containers.

- The Circumambulation area, or al-Mataf, is the flat area surrounding the Holy Kaaba, used by pilgrims to perform *tawaf*, a cornerstone of Hajj and Umra rituals. It is the circumambulation of the Kaaba seven times in a counterclockwise direction, starting and ending by the Black Stone. *Tawaf* can be performed in all floors of the Holy Mosque.

Originally, houses surrounded the Kaaba from all sides, defining the boundaries of al-Mataf, with spaces between them acting as entry points to the area. The first wall bordering al-Mataf was erected by the second caliph Umar ibn al-Khattab. Al-Mataf was limited to a circle defined by the distance between the Kaaba and Maqam Ibrahim (pbuH) and outlined by

3 The Holy Mosque of Mecca, the new al-Mas'a, 2008.
Photo: Ministry of Higher Education, Saudi Arabia, 2010

the pillars of oil lamps introduced later. In the bordering area several buildings existed such as the four settings of Islamic rites called al-Maqamat, and the building of Zamzam well. The old Mataf was 11.50 meters from the eastern Kaaba wall, 16.65 meters from the western Kaaba wall, 22.3 meters from the northern wall, including Hijr Isma'il, and 15.2 meters from the southern wall of Kaaba. In 1957, during the first Saudi Expansion of the Holy Mosque, al-Mataf was expanded about 15.3 meters from the east, 10.75 meters from the west, 4.65 from the north, and 11.5 meters from the south, transforming it into a circular shape. In 1968 it was of a diameter of 64.8 meters, with a total area of 3,085 m², surrounded by two paths of 2.5 meters wide each and 20 cm high from al-Mataf level, and in 1978 its diameter was 95.2 meters with an area of 8,500 m².

Today, al-Mataf is clear of any buildings except for Maqam Ibrahim. In 1957-78 all other buildings were demolished, and the surrounding pebbled area was paved with white marble and included in al-Mataf. Al-Mataf is currently bound by the internal walls of the Holy Mosque measuring about 155 meters east-west and 105 meters north-south, with an area of about 16,700 m², and a capacity of 30,000 pilgrims per hour.

- The Path, or al-Mas'a is the area located at the eastern side of the Holy Mosque, between the hill of as-Safa at the bottom of Abu Qubais mountain, facing the Black Stone, and al-Marwa hill linked to the mountain of Qoaiqean, where pilgrims perform Sa'i during Hajj and Umra. As-Sa'i is the devotional act of walking back and forth seven times between as-Safa and al-Marwa, as Hajer (pbuH) did while searching for water for her son. As-Safa from which Sa'i begins is located 0.8 kilometers (approximately half a mile) from the Holy Kaaba on its southern side, whereas al-Marwa is located about 91 meters from the Kaaba, on its north-eastern side.

During Prophet Muhammad's time (pbuH), al-Mas'a was wide, about 35 cubits. Later, some houses and a market were built in some parts of the old al-Mas'a, narrowing its path. When successive expansions occurred at the Holy Mosque, those houses were demolished, and their area was added to the Mosque. Throughout Islamic history, al-Mas'a was set apart from the Holy Mosque, unpaved and uncovered, and exposed to the distractions of the city marketplace. During the era of the Abbasid

caliph al-Mansur, a few steps were added to as-Safa and al-Marwa hills to facilitate climbing them. In 1922 most of al-Mas'a area was covered, and four years later it was paved with rocks.

During the first Saudi Expansion of the Holy Mosque (1955-61) al-Mas'a was enclosed and incorporated into the mosque complex for the first time in history. The two hills and the path between them were enclosed inside a long gallery that forms part of the mosque, with an area of about 16,700 m². Two additional floors were built in al-Mas'a with a length of 394.5 meters and a width of 20 meters divided by a low partition into two lanes. The first floor was 12 meters high with sixteen doors in its eastern side, and the second floor was nine meters high with two doors, one at as-Safa and the other at al-Marwa. Two elevators were installed, one on each side of al-Mas'a, as well as a dome over as-Safa hill. In 2008, al-Mas'a underwent a major expansion which significantly increased its capacity for Sa'i (Fig. 3). The new al-Mas'a building consists of five floors in which Sa'i can be performed, in addition to mezzanine levels for the disabled, with a total area of about 87,000 m², a length of 394 meters, and a width of about 33.5 meters on the ground floor. The width of al-Mas'a is divided equally into two lanes, one for each direction, separated by two narrow lanes assigned for wheelchairs. al-Mas'a can enclose in its five floors about 218,760 pilgrims and 9,793 impaired pilgrims. The basement floor and the mezzanines of the first and second floors are designed for the Sa'i of the disabled. Its maximum capacity is about 118,000 pilgrim/hour or 115,600 praying worshippers. It has 190 exits that connect its different floors with the Holy Mosque and surrounding plazas.

HISTORY OF RECONSTRUCTION

Throughout Islamic history, successive Islamic regimes have spared no cost or effort to dignify and honor al-Masjid al-Haram. It experienced several reconstruction processes that ranged from repair and restoration works exclusive to the Holy Kaaba, to area expansions. The focus in this essay is only on the expansions of the Holy Mosque that included increase in its area, as well as on the reconstruction of the Kaaba.

Reconstruction of the Holy Kaaba

At the time of Prophet Muhammad (pbuH), the Holy Kaaba maintained its shape as reconstructed by the Quraish tribe. Its size was smaller than that of the original building of Prophet Ibrahim (pbuH). In the year 683, as a result of the conflict between the Umayyad caliph Yazid Bin Muawiyah and Abdullah ibn al-Zubair in Mecca, the Kaaba was significantly damaged. Ibn al-Zubair decided to demolish the Holy Kaaba and rebuild it on the foundations of Prophet Ibrahim. However, he increased its height to twenty-seven cubits. He built three pillars inside the Kaaba in one row from north to south to support its ceiling which was covered with translucent marble brought from Yemen. He set two doors for the Kaaba on the level of al-Mataf, one in the eastern side and the other in the western side, each consisting of two eleven-cubit-high leaves. He also built a wooden zigzagged staircase inside the Kaaba at its northern corner.

In 693 Abd al-Malik ibn Marwan, the Umayyad caliph, commanded his army leader, al-Hajjaj, to return the Holy Kaaba to its shape during Prophet Muhammad's time. He closed the western door that was added by ibn al-Zubair and raised the eastern door to its former position. al-Hajjaj also pulled down six cubits and a hand span on the side of Hijr Isma'il and rebuilt it on the Quraish foundation.

Due to the collapse of the Holy Kaaba walls caused by the torrential flooding that hit Mecca, the Ottoman Sultan Murad IV reconstructed the Kaaba in 1630. Its dimensions were not changed. Since then the Kaaba did not experience any major repair or reconstruction works until 1994, when King Fahad of Saudi Arabia issued his order to repair the external walls of the Kaaba as they were in bad condition due to weathering. The stone works of the Kaaba were repaired using advanced technologies. In 1996, comprehensive restoration works took place in the Kaaba, as commanded by King Fahad. The ceiling was replaced using teak wood, the old rock bases of interior pillars were replaced with reinforced concrete, the old marble of the Shadhrwan was replaced by new similar marble, the oldest waterspout was replaced with a new one of the same dimensions, and the old marble of the wall and floor in Hijr Isma'il was removed. It was the largest ever reconstruction of the Holy Kaaba.

Reconstruction of the Holy Mosque

Although there are inconsistencies in the modern historical accounts of the successive expansions of the Holy Mosque, a general history of the reconstruction can be established (Fig. 4).[7] Most historians described the Mosque during Prophet Muhammad's time (pbuH) as an open space surrounding the Kaaba and surrounded by secular buildings with no bordering walls. Its area is estimated to be 1490-2000 m² with a capacity for about 3,300 pilgrims. The first expansion of the Holy Mosque took place in 638 by Umar ibn al-Khattab, the second caliph, who bought some of the houses adjacent to the Holy Mosque, demolished them, and added their area to the Mosque. He was the first to build an encircling wall around the mosque to delineate al-Mataf. It was less than two meters high with doors in it. He also covered al-Mataf area with gravel and illuminated it with lamps installed on the wall. The mosque area was increased by 70 percent, to be about 2,350 m². When the Holy Mosque could not accommodate all worshippers, Uthman ibn Affan, the third caliph, expanded the mosque a further 87 percent in 646. He bought some of the adjacent houses and added their area to the Mosque, increasing its area to 4,390 m². Many narratives contend that he was the first to set up arcades, sheltering worshippers from the sun.

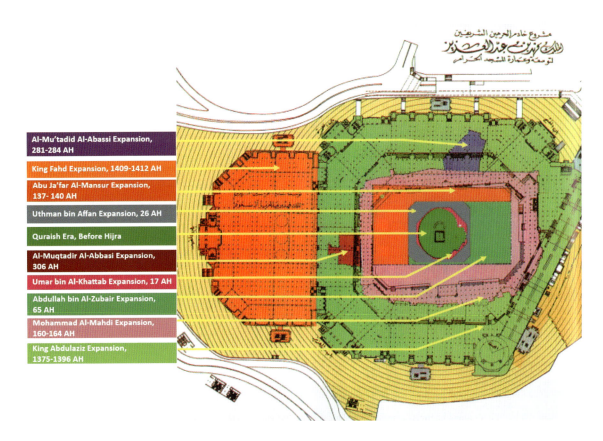

4 The Holy Mosque of Mecca, the successive expansions.
Photo: Ministry of Higher Education, Saudi Arabia, 2010, translated by the author

THE HOLY MOSQUE OF MECCA 91

5 The old Holy Mosque, with al-Mataf area marked out, showing the four Maqamat and the building of Zamzam well, 1953.
Photo: Creative Common License

In 684, after completing his reconstruction of the Holy Kaaba, Ibn al-Zubair decided to expand the Holy Mosque as its area was not sufficient for all worshippers. The mosque area was significantly expanded by some 92 percent, to be about 8,440 m², from its eastern, southern, and northern sides, with some parts covered.

In 694, al-Hajjaj, commanded by Abd al-Malik ibn Marwan, repaired the Holy Mosque with no expansion. In 709, al-Walid ibn Abd al-Malik expanded the eastern side of the mosque. He roofed the mosque with decorated teak wood and built a one-row arcade around al-Mataf, supported by marble columns brought from Egypt and al-Sham (Syria) with gold-coated capitals and arches covered in their upper parts with mosaic decorations, most likely similar to those found in other Umayyad architecture. The area of the Holy Mosque after this expansion was about 10,740 m².

In 754, the Holy Mosque was expanded from its northern and western sides by the Abbasid caliph, Abu Ja'far al-Mansur. This expansion was similar in its architecture and decorations to that of al-Walid ibn Abd al-Malik. The mosque was surrounded by a one-row arcade decorated with gold and mosaic, and Hijr Isma'il and Zamzam well area were overlaid with marble. In 756, al-Mansur added the first minaret to the Holy Mosque in its northwest corner at Bab al-Umra (Umra Gate). It had a square shape base with a cylindrical body and a semi-sphere crown. The Mosque area after expansion was about 15,440 m².

The great expansion of the Abbasid caliph, al-Mahdi was executed in two stages: the first was in 776, when houses in the area were demolished and their area incorporated in the mosque. The second stage was accomplished in 780 when al-Mahdi ordered the engineers and skilled builders to make the mosque of a square shape so as to have the Holy Kaaba in its center. The Holy Mosque was expanded from its southern side. This expansion was the greatest up to that time where the increase in area was about sixty-seven percent and the total area of the mosque was about 25,750 square meters, with a capacity of about 40,270 worshippers. By the end of al-Mahdi expansion, al-Mataf was centered on the Kaaba and surrounded by a three-row arcade of marble columns decorated with teak wood, measuring 194 × 146 meters. The arcades consisted of 498 arches, supported by 484 marble columns 4.8 meters high, 321 of them with gold-coated capitals. Together with its old gates, the mosque had twenty four doors in all, five in al-Mas'a side, seven in the southern side, six in the western side, and six in the northern side,[8] some of which were decorated with teak wooden works (*rawshan*) and colored marble walls. Furthermore, the mosque had four minarets above its corners, one by al-Mansur, and

6 The Holy Mosque of Mecca, the First Saudi Expansion, 1955–76.
Photo: Creative Common License

7 The Holy Mosque of Mecca, after the second Saudi Expansion, 1982–92. Photo: Ministry of Higher Education, Saudi Arabia, 2010

the other three added by al-Mahdi, crowned with crenellations.

In 894 al-Mu'tadid al-'Abbasi expanded the Holy Mosque by about five percent, increasing its total area to about 27,000 square meters.[9] He constructed the expansion with pillars and four arcades roofed with ornamental teak wood, with a new minaret added to the mosque. Twelve internal doors were set up in the expansion with six big arches and six smaller ones between them, and three main doors that open onto the surrounding streets. In 918, the caliph al-Muqtdir al-'Abbasi expanded the Mosque from its southern-western side by only three percent, increasing its area to 27,850 m². A new minaret was added in the western side of the mosque, which was later (date unknown) demolished. The latter two expansions did not substantially affect the planning of the Mosque as they were placed outside its squared configuration. According to several historical accounts, praying pavilions, or Maqamat, were built in al-Mataf in the eleventh or twelfth century, each relating to one Islamic school of law: al-Maqam al-Maliki in the western side, al-Hanafi in the northern side, and al-Hanbali in the southern side, and al-Shafi'i in the eastern side.

During the following centuries, the Holy Mosque did not experience any expansions except for a few repair and reconstruction works. A new minaret was added to the mosque during the Mamluk period. However, the greatest reconstruction work took place in 1570 by the Ottoman Sultan Selim II who executed a complete reconstruction of the Holy Mosque. It included the replacement of the wooden flat roof with domes decorated with calligraphy, and the placement of new supporting marble and stone columns. The Ottoman three-row colonnade of the Holy Mosque comprised of 589 pillars, supporting 881 arches, 152 domes, and 232 shallow domes, with 26 doors. The Ottoman reconstruction added an aesthetic value to the mosque with its decorative art works.

During the Ottoman era, the mosque consisted of a large courtyard surrounded by a one-floor arcade, with seven minarets, one of them added by Sultan Suleyman, and twenty-six doors. Its area was about 29,127 m². The *minbar* (pulpit for imam's sermons), the four Islamic rites Maqamat, and other buildings existed in al-Mataf. This remained the state of the Holy Mosque for nearly three centuries (Fig. 5).

SAUDI EXPANSIONS

The most significant architectural and structural changes of the Holy Mosque took place during the Saudi era with three grand expansions that have led to its present form. The first was carried out by King Abdul Aziz and completed by his sons between 1955 and 1976, to increase the area of the mosque by 450 percent (131,041 m²), to become 160,168 m², with a capacity of more than 300,000 worshippers, and 400,000 worshippers at peak times (Fig. 6). The second expansion was performed by King Fahad between 1988–92 (Fig. 7).[10] The area of the Mosque after this spectacular expansion was about 366,000 square meters, accommodating more than half a million worshippers on normal days and about 820,000 worshippers at peak times. The third expansion, currently underway, was initiated by King Abdullah. Due to their grand scale and significance, the three Saudi expansions of the Holy Mosque reconfigured its setting within its context and its relationship with the surrounding topography and enhanced its impact on visitors.

THE HOLY MOSQUE OF MECCA 93

THE HOLY MOSQUE'S STATUS AFTER THE SECOND SAUDI EXPANSION

With the Second Saudi Expansion, the Holy Mosque consisted of a central quadrangle area (al-Mataf) with the Holy Kaaba situated at its center, paved with heat resistant white marble. During the second Saudi expansion al-Mataf was cleared of some old pavilions, including the four Maqamat and the building over the Zamzam well, to ease pilgrims' *tawaf*, except for Maqam Ibrahim. Al-Mataf is delineated by the three-row Ottoman domed arcade, surrounded by the two-storey (ground and first floor, and partial basement floor) building of the first Saudi expansion. The first extension is accessed through three main elaborate gates at its corners, each consisting of three decorated arches, flanked with two minarets, and accentuated by a dome on the roof. On the western side of the Mosque lies the three-storey air-conditioned building of the second Saudi expansion, with three domes on its roof. The second extension is accessed through the monumental King Fahad Gate, at its center.

The mosque has a total of 138 doors, where the minor gates have green-tiled sloped canopies. It has nine minarets, eight of which positioned to accentuate the mosque's main four gates, whereas the ninth minaret is located at as-Safa gate. Three of the minarets were old and were refashioned, four

8 The Holy Mosque of Mecca, the interior of the second Saudi Expansion, 1982–92.
Photo: Ministry of Higher Education, Saudi Arabia, 2010

new ones were added during the first expansion, and two were added during the second expansion at King Fahad Gate, all soaring 89 meters, sitting on a square base seven meters high attached to and blending into the building structure. All minarets are marble-clad with two octagonal balconies decorated with eight slender colonettes and covered with green tiles; the first located almost at the height of the mosque roof while the second was at the top end of the shaft. The minarets are crowned with a bronze pedestal of 1.6 meters high topped with a gold-plated crescent of 6.4 meters high.

The area around the Holy Mosque has also been developed. The mosque today is separated from the surrounding buildings by wide streets and pedestrian routes to ensure the smooth flow of traffic and pilgrims from and to the area. Moreover, grand marble paved praying plazas with a total area of about 85,000 square meters surround the mosque from its three sides, increasing its capacity by around 190,000 worshippers.

During the second Saudi expansion, the roof of the first Saudi expansion was rebuilt and linked with that of the second extension to accommodate overflow. The roof is tiled with specially developed heat-resistance marble and has three ceramic-clad domes at the center of the second extension, on alignment of the main axis of King Fahad Gate. Its area is around 61,000 m^2 with a capacity of about 90,000 worshippers.

The two first Saudi expansions of the Holy Mosque demonstrate a harmonious and unified configuration. The exterior façade of the two expansions blends together, using gray marble inlaid with carved white marble bands. The window modules along the façade are covered with brass *mashrabiyya* (wooden or metal latticework) and framed with carved bands of white marble. The exterior façade is 22.5 meters high. The first expansion has marble-coated arcades and a ceiling decorated with molded plaster. The structure of the second Saudi expansion contains 1453 columns of fifteen-meter spans in prayer halls, and five-meters spans in circulation areas, and at a height of 9.8 meters on the ground floor, and 9.64 meters in the first floor. The arcade is roofed with simple square coffers decorated with plaster molding, and its columns are clad with marble panels and have ornamented capitals made of white marble and golden band, crowned by arches covered with ornamented artificial stone and plaster moldings (Fig. 8). The floor is laid with geometrically patterned white marble penetrated with black marble lines. The air-conditioning system employed is technologically advanced; it is integrated within the decorative elements of the mosque, as it circulates air below the tiled floors and is supplied and returned through ventilation grids located at the base and capital of each column.

Along the axis linking King Fahad Gate to the Kaaba, three grid modules parallel to the gate structure, overlooking the ground and first floors, are covered with seventeen-meter-high domes supported on four marble columns with special ornamentations to accentuate their setting among the other columns. The domes are decorated with artificial granite *muqarnas* pendentives that support drums perforated by thirty-two teak arched windows framed by artificial granite. Dome interiors are clad with decorated artificial granite and colored ceramic tiles arranged following a geometric pattern. The dome space is illuminated with colored glass chandeliers and a backlit stained glass panel at the apex. The use of soft brown, green, white, and other colors of artificial granite in the walls and arches helps in creating an inspiring, relaxed atmosphere conducive to meditation and prayers.

THE THIRD SAUDI EXPANSION – DEVELOPMENT IN PROGRESS

In light of the accelerating increase in the number of worshippers, the Custodian of the Two Holy Mosques, King Abdullah bin Abdul Aziz, initiated a development program in 2005, including erecting a new expansion at the northern side of the existing building of the Holy Mosque. The new expansion extends over 400 meters long in the northern side of the existing Holy Mosque, in al-Shamiya area. It consists of a main seven-storey building containing praying spaces, a gradient-terrace building, and service facilities, in addition to open courtyards and plazas.[11]

The main objectives of the project were to achieve the highest levels of functional and operational efficiency, and to ensure the safety and comfort of worshippers, considering the Mosque's unique spiritual and symbolic value for all Muslims.

The planning concept of the new expansion is founded on principles of respecting the centrality of the Holy Kaaba, lines of prayer, fragmentation of crowds, and maintaining efficiency and flexibility in operation. The design emanates from creating radial axes originating from the Kaaba and dividing the project into segments that intersect with circular rings centered on the Kaaba, forming radial segments. The project's radial segments embrace the main building, which encloses three main parts located between four radial axes, outdoor courtyards between the four radial axes to the southern and northern sides of the main building, gradient praying-terraces containing service facilities to the north of the courtyards, and surrounding plazas in the eastern and western sides of the expansion. The radial axes divide the project into defined manageable sectors that can accommodate a controllable number of people, enabling a smooth and safe flow of the crowds (Fig. 9). They function as corridors of vertical and horizontal circulation and contain service facilities. The project's radial circulation corridors connect the different parts and components of the project together, as well as connecting it with the existing building of the Holy Mosque in the south, and with areas of urban development to the north.

The design composition is generated by the replication of a functional unit called "Robust Cell." It is a self-integrated and manageable construction unit designed in the direction of the radial axes and the radial segments, vertically and horizontally (Fig. 10). This replication produces a functional and flexible composition of high standards, coherent spatial configuration, and distinct architectural and aesthetic quality (Fig. 11). Functional units are arranged in the main building to form spatial clusters of varying layouts across its seven floors, with different heights

9 The Holy Mosque of Mecca, the design concept of the third Saudi Expansion, showing the radial axes.
Photo: Ministry of Higher Education, Saudi Arabia, 2010

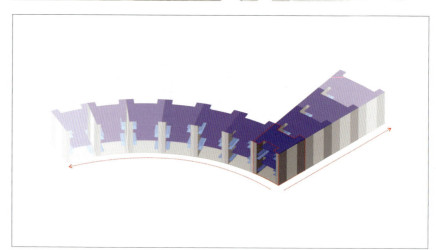

10 The Holy Mosque of Mecca, the "Robust Cell" duplicated in the direction of the radial axes and the radial segments.
Photo: Ministry of Higher Education, Saudi Arabia, 2010

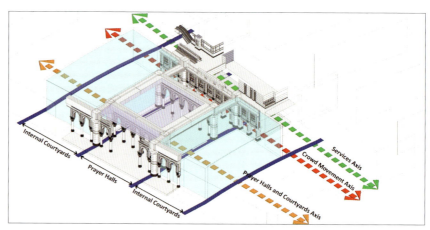

11 The Holy Mosque of Mecca, the design concept of the "Robust Cell."
Photo: Ministry of Higher Education, Saudi Arabia, 2010

between 30-42 meters in the central spaces along the main axis, 18 meters in the main praying halls, and 12 meters in the secondary praying halls, penetrated by six-meters high radial circulation corridors. This composition provides transparency and visual connectivity within the building as well as enhancing its spatial configuration and enriching its visitors' experience.

The new expansion took into consideration the architectural unity of the complex. The facades of the new expansion match up with the existing building of the Holy Mosque, with its gray marble and window frames. Corresponding to the existing building of the mosque, and as a symbol of respect, the main building of the expansion descends in height from its southern side, in the direction of the Holy Kaaba. The magnificent King Abdullah Gate, which gives access to the existing Mosque from the northern side of the new expansion, consists of three arches, carved with marble decorations. The gate is flanked by two minarets matching the nine existing ones, as well as two other minarets at the eastern and western ends of the building. Also, included in the new expansion is one main movable dome at a height of 63 meters, in the central space of the main building, along its main axis, as well as six other fixed domes, two in each of the three parts of the main building. Moreover, in addition to the King Abdullah main gate, six minor doors and another 44 secondary emergency doors are added in the new expansion. At a later stage, two 420-meter-heigh minarets were added to the expansion.[12]

The third Saudi expansion in al-Shamiya area has increased the Holy Mosque area by 331,400 m², in addition to 71,200 m² of internal courtyards, and 68,750 square meters in the external courtyards located between the four axial bridges, with a capacity of over 723,100 worshippers.

12 The Holy Mosque of Mecca, the third Saudi Expansion of the Holy Mosque.
Photo: Creative Common License

THE HOLY MOSQUE OF MECCA 97

To match up with the new capacity of the Holy Mosque, and to achieve fluent crowd movement during *tawaf*, in 1432 (2011), a new project was commenced as part of the third Saudi expansion to increase the capacity of al-Mataf. The project included reconstructing the old Mosque and the first Saudi expansion, demolishing the Ottoman arcade surrounding al-Mataf, and expanding the width of al-Mataf at the roof floor level, adjacent to al-Mas'a, from 20 m to 50 m (Fig. 12). The new arcade surrounding al-Mataf was rebuilt using the same stones and elements of the old Abbasid and Ottoman arcade, however, in a manner that corresponds to the new expansion. The project also included adding one floor to the Mosque to be of four floors, as well as adding a few bridges to the ground and roof levels of the northern expansion at al-Shamiya area to connect it with the Mosque. Moreover, the first floor level of the old Mosque was leveled to be at the same level of al-Mataf, thus creating a direct physical and visual connection between al-Mataf and the ground and basement floors of the first Saudi expansion and al-Mas'a.[13] This project will increase the capacity of al-Mataf area in all floors from 48,000 to 107,000 worshippers per hour and increase its area from 150,000 m^2 to 210,000 m^2.[14]

With the completion of the Mataf project, the total area of the third Saudi expansion will be 1,470,000 m^2, with a total capacity of the Holy Mosque reaching 1,850,000 worshippers. The project has future plans to add another two floors to the mosque to be six floors in total.

The Third Saudi Expansion of the Holy Mosque is considered the largest expansion of the Holy Mosque ever. Once complete, it will change the face of the mosque and its surrounding area. However, as the Muslim population worldwide is increasing, the expansions of the Holy Mosque will continue to accommodate more and more worshippers.

ABEER ALLAHHAM, PhD, is an Associate Professor at the College of Design, Imam Abdulrahman Bin Faisal University, Saudi Arabia. She was the coordinator of the Scientific Documentation and Editing team in the project of the Third Expansion of the Holy Mosque in Mecca. She is the author of several articles. Her research interest revolves around criticizing the rationale of contemporary capitalist built environments as compared to Islamic built environments. She was awarded the King Hussein Award for distinguished students in Jordan. She earned five international awards on the printing of two books on the project of the Holy Mosque Expansion, Mecca.

SUGGESTIONS FOR FURTHER READING

Abbas, Hamed. *Qissat al-Tawsi'a Al-Kubra* (Story of the Great Expansion) (Jeddah: Saudi bin Laden Group, 1996), (in Arabic).

Akkach, Samer. *Cosmology and Architecture in Premodern Islam: an Architectural Reading of Mystical Ideas* (Albany: State University of New York Press, 2005).

Al-Kurdi, Muhammad Taher. *Al-Tarikh Al-Qawim li Mecca wa Bayt Allah Al-Karim* (The History of Mecca and Holy Mosque) (Beirut: Dar Khader, 2000) (in Arabic).

Basalamah, Husein. *Tarikh Amarat Al-Masjid Al-Haram* (The History of the Holy Mosque Architecture), third edition (Jeddah: Tuhamah, 1400 AH. (1980) (in Arabic).

Damluji, Salma Samar, ed. *The Architecture of the Holy Mosque Mecca* (London: Hazar Publishing Limited, 1998).

Documentary series of the Third Saudi Expansion, Project- Holy Mosque, Makka. https://www.youtube.com/watch?v=fAoKP9qANq8.

Documentary series of the Third Saudi Expansion, the Largest Expansion in History. https://www.youtube.com/watch?v=49Ij5scYO9I, accessed 30 July, 2020. (in Arabic)

Documentary video on "In the service of two Holy Mosques." https://www.youtube.com/watch?v=4ZrfTATH2UI, accessed 30 July, 2020. (in Arabic).

[1] Abdul Malek Bin Dehaish, *Alharam Almakki Alsharif wa Alalam Almuhaita bih* (The Holy Mosque of Mecca and the borders surrounding it) (Mecca: n.p., 1995) (in Arabic).

[2] The Holy Quran. English translation by Abdel Haleem M.A.S. (Oxford: Oxford University Press, 2010).

[3] Mohammad Al-Bukhari, *Sahih Al-Bukhari*, tradition no. 3364, in Sunnah.com, https://sunnah.com/bukhari/60/43, accessed on 30 July 2020. See also, The Gate of the Two Holy Mosques, The Two Holy Mosques in Quran and Prophet's Tradition. http://www.alharamain.gov.sa/index.cfm?do=cms.conarticle&contentid=5935&categoryid=1021; http://www.alharamain.gov.sa/index.cfm?do=cms.conarticle&contentid=5939&categoryid=1022, accessed on 30 July 2020.

[4] Mohammad Al-Azraqi, *Akhbar Mecca wa Ma ja'a fiha min Athar* (Mecca news and its archeology), ed. by Abdul Malik bin Dehaish (Saudi Arabia: Al-Asadi bookstore, 2003) (in Arabic).

[5] K.A. Creswell, *Early Muslim Architecture* 2 vols. (New York: Hacker Art Books, 2nd ed., 1979).

[6] Yahya Waziri, *Al-Ka'aba Al-Musharrafah: Dirsah Tahliliyah lilkhasa'is al-Tasmimyah* (The Holy Kaaba: An analytical study of its design characteristics), a paper delivered in the fourteen "Inter-build" conference in Cairo-Egypt, June 2007 (in Arabic).

[7] All areas and percentages of the Holy Mosque's successive expansions differ in various historical manuscripts; this essay relies on the relevant data by Mohammad bin Abdullah in his book *Alziyadat fi Alharam Almakki Alsharif* (Extensions of the Sharif Makki Haram). (Publisher unknown, 1995) (in Arabic)

[8] Mohammad Al-Azraqi, *Akhbar Mecca*.

[9] Al-Hafidh Al-Maliki, *Shifa' Al-Gharam bi Akhbar Albalad Alharam* (Mecca: Maktabat An-Nahdha Al-Haditha, 1956), vol. 1, 253. The renovation works were completed in 894.

[10] Ministry of Higher Education, *The project of the Custodian of the Two Holy Mosques King Abdullah Bin Abdul Aziz for the Expansion of The Holy Mosque, Book Three: The Evaluation of the Proposed Project- the Local Evaluation* (Ministry of Higher Education: Saudi Arabia, 2010).

[11] All the data regarding the Third Saudi Expansion of the Holy Mosque stated in this essay is derived from: Ministry of Higher Education, *The project of the Custodian of the Two Holy Mosques King Abdullah Bin Abdul Aziz for the Expansion of The Holy Mosque, The General Summary, Book One* (Ministry of Higher Education: Saudi Arabia, 2010).

[12] Al Haramaien Channel. Documentary on the expansion of the Holy Mosque, 1436. https://www.youtube.com/watch?v=Ls44SRq2Dtk, accessed on 30 July 2020.

[13] Ministry of Foreign Affairs of Kingdom of Saudi Arabia. Documentary on the project of increasing the capacity of the Mataf at the Holy Mosque of Mecca. https://www.youtube.com/watch?v=wefl6oEjRoA, accessed on 30 July 2020.

[14] The General Presidency for the Affairs of the Grand Mosque and the Prophet's Mosque. https://bit.ly/3fmVOVI, accessed on 30 July 2020.

The Mosque of the Prophet at Medina   AKEL ISMAIL KAHERA

1 Mosque of the Prophet –
night view of the open space
to the west.
Photo: Akel Kahera

Writing in the fifteenth century, Abu al-Hassan Abdallah al-Samhudi (d. 1505), the historian of the city of Medina, relates the history of the *Masjid al-Nabawi al-Sharif*, or Mosque of the Prophet, in *Wafa al-Wafa bi Akhbar Dar al-Mustafa*, or *The Fulfillment of Faithfulness on the Reports of the City of the Chosen One*. Referring to numerous literary and oral sources, al-Samhudi first describes the Prophet's participation in the construction of the original edifice, built at Medina in the year 622, then provides a detailed discussion of the edifice itself. We are informed that the plan of the original edifice measured approximately seventy by sixty cubits.[1] al-Samhudi also mentions that the size of the edifice was one hundred cubits square and that this was perhaps the first extension of the building during the Prophet's time around 628, following the battle of Khaybar.[2] According to al-Samhudi's history, the foundation was made of stone, while the walls of the unassuming structure were built from mud brick held together with workable clay mortar paste used to bind bricks together and fill the gaps between them – a kind of building assembly commonly known as adobe construction. The roof was made from the branches of the date palm tree; and the columns – originally 2.9 meters high but later increased to 4 meters during the first expansion – were made from the trunks of the date palm tree. The edifice had two attached domestic chambers (later increased to nine) and an empty space in the center like a courtyard, with three doors: the Door of Mercy (*Bab ar-Rahmah*) to the west; the Door of Gabriel (*Bab Gibreel*) and the Women's Door (*Bab al-Nisa*) to the east, and a shaded portico (*zullah*) to the north. The courtyard of the edifice was often used as a civic space and on one occasion a group of Abyssinians performed a sword and lances dance for the audience that included the Prophet and his

wife Aisha. The thatched roof of the shaded portico, like that of the sanctuary, was supported by regular spaced palm trunks. The Prophet's companions and the devotees who frequented the portico were known as *ahl al-Suffah* or *ashab al-Suffah,* or people of the portico. The destitute could also find shelter in the mosque under the portico.

Sixteen or seventeen months after the Prophet's migration to Medina, the axis of prayer (*qibla*) was changed from Jerusalem to Mecca following a Quranic revelation (2:137–47), resulting in the alteration of the southern wall. This became the permanent sanctuary (*musalla*) three aisles deep parallel to the *qibla* wall, where the *mihrab* is typically located; this is where the *imam* stands to lead the faithful in the daily performance of the prayer. The Prophet's mosque functioned as a place for the daily performance of congregational worship. On Friday, the day of assembly, people came to hear the Prophet deliver the sermon (*khutba*). As the crowds grew, a *minbar* in the form of a raised platform of three steps was introduced to make it easier for the Prophet to be heard and seen. The call to prayer (*adhan*) was pronounced from the roof of the mosque since there was no minaret.

In the original structure, the private domestic quarters were contiguous with the prayer sanctuary. It is in this regard that the Quranic chapter *surah al-Hujurat* (The Inner Apartments) cautions people that they should lower their voices in the presence of the Prophet and refrain from shouting to the Prophet from outside of the inner apartments (49:3–6).[3] Sometime after the death of the Prophet in 632 and during the second expansion, the nine adjacent private chambers were demolished to make room for expansion of the mosque. Many historians have described the original edifice as a house rather than a mosque (*masjid*). In fact, the elements that make up the building's compositional arrangement in function and form suggest it was built primarily for communal worship. The following Hadith describes the primary spatial characteristics of the edifice:

> In the lifetime of Allah's Apostle [The Prophet] [his] mosque was built of adobe; the roof of the leaves of date palms. Abu Bakr did not alter it, Umar expanded it on the same pattern as it was in the lifetime of the Prophet, by using adobe, leaves of date palms and changing the palm-trunk pillars into wooden ones. Uthman changed it by expanding it to a great extent and built its walls with engraved stones and lime and made its pillars with engraved stones and its roof of teak-wood. (*Sahih Muslim* 1.195.1068)[4]

While al-Samhudi's account and the foregoing Hadith support the view that the original building was indeed a mosque, a contemporary of the Prophet, Hassan ibn Thabit (d. 674), the paradigmatic poet of the era, describes the spiritual sense of the Prophet's mosque with emphasis on the valorization of memory. When the Prophet died in 632 he was buried within the building and two of his successors (*caliphs*) Abu Bakr and Umar were later buried beside him. Hassan ibn Thabit's lyrics characteristically fuse the architectural and the spiritual element when he speaks of the memory of the Prophet, his *maqam* (place of standing), the *minbar*, and his *maqad* (place of sitting):

> In Medina there are still traces of the luminous abode of the Prophet although elsewhere traces disappear.
> The marks of the sacred abode that holds the *minbar* which the Prophet used to ascend will never be obliterated.
> Plain are the traces and lasting the marks of an abode in which he had a *musalla* and a mosque.
> And the mosque which longs for his presence became desolate with only his *maqam* (station) and *maqad* (seat) remaining as memorials
> In it are enclosures (*hujurat*) wherein would descend God's light brilliant and bright.[5]

The architectural elements described in the poem would later serve as a liturgical precedent and succeeding mosques built outside of Arabia would demonstrate how these elements were adopted. Undoubtedly the Prophet's Mosque was considered by later generations of builders, patrons, and the Muslim community to be a religious archetype. Successive functional and aesthetic changes were

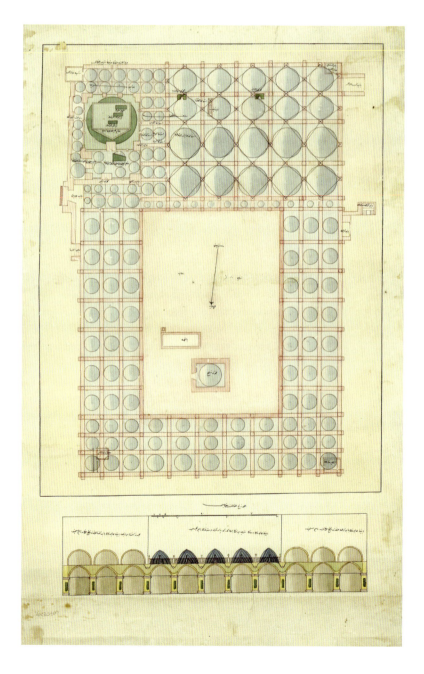

2 Plan of the Prophet's Mosque (Masjid al-Nabawi) in Medina, drawn in the second half of the nineteenth century, recording the 1849–1861 renovations commissioned by the Ottoman Sultan Abdülmecid.
Drawing: Special Collections, Fine Arts Library, Harvard College Library/President and Fellows of Harvard University

3 Mosque of the Prophet, minaret built in 1483, beside the green dome built in 1840, Medina, Saudi Arabia.
Photo: Library of Congress

made to the seminal structure in a short period of time and many layers of aesthetic treatment were added to the archetypal structure through human intervention in the first forty years after the death of the Prophet. From the year 628, when the first expansion occurred, there were eight major expansions. The last expansion occurred in 1988–95 during the reign of the Saudi monarch King Fahad ibn Abd al-Aziz, commonly referred to as the custodian of the two Holy Sanctuaries. The two caliphs and companions of the Prophet, Umar (d. 644) and Uthman (d. 656), each extended the original mosque in 638 and 649–50 respectively. This was followed by the expansion of the Umayyad caliph al-Walid (r. 705–15), who added minarets to the edifice in 706–9, as well as a *mihrab*, while expanding the sanctuary. Under the Abassid ruler al-Mahdi al-Abbasi further expansion occurred in the period c. 777–781.

After a fire in 1481, the Mamluk sultan al-Ashraf Qaitbey extensively restored the building and added the emblematic green dome over the burial chamber of the Prophet around 1486. In 1849 the Ottoman sultan Abd al-Majeed completed an extensive renovation of the mosque, which lasted thirteen years (Figs. 2–3). This was the most extensive renovation completed thus far until the twentieth century. King Abd al-Aziz expanded the mosque in 1952; this was followed by an expansion in 1973 by King Faisal ibn Abd al-Aziz who added 35,000 square meters of open area to the west of the mosque for the overflowing worshippers.[6] Perhaps the most ambitious expansion in the history of the Prophet's mosque occurred during the reign of King Fahd ibn Abd al-Aziz (r.1982–2005): six new *minarets* rising to a height of 105 meters were added, bringing the total to ten; twenty-seven electronically operable domes, each measuring fifteen meters in diameter; air conditioning for the entire mosque; and twelve giant umbrellas to provide shade in the summer months to the courtyard spaces. The current capacity of the edifice is six hundred thousand worshippers with room to accommodate up to one million worshippers during the annual Hajj season (Figs. 1, 4).

During the annual Hajj season pilgrims flock to Medina and its environs *en masse*. Among the popular sites they visit is the Quba Mosque, Medina's oldest mosque. In 1984–7, a number of large sunshades (*toldo*) were added to the two courtyards of the newly renovated Quba Mosque to provide additional comfort for the worshippers. The *toldo* took its name from the movable textile structures in the streets of Andalusia. The mosque was renovated with new additions and a capacity for one million worshippers, constituting the largest expansion of the mosque; the sunshades

THE MOSQUE OF THE PROPHET AT MEDINA 103

were designed by the German company Sonderkonstrruktionen und Leichtbau GmbH (SL) and BuroHappold Engineering under the leadership of architect Bodo Rasch (Fig. 5).[7] The temperature in Medina averages between 101–106 degrees Fahrenheit in the summer months; the shades alter the microclimate, in other words, a local atmospheric zone where the climate differs from the ambient temperature. As described by SL:

> [T]he supports consist of a tubular truss construction running along both of the longitudinal sides of the courtyard. The hinged bearings of the trusses allow the necessary deflections under wind loading with counterweights providing the required pre-tensioning. The translucent membrane consists of two layers of a net-like shading fabric, held in line, one above the other, by aluminum tubes running along their length. These are suspended from cable pulleys, which are moved by electric motors.[8]

We can take SL's Quba project as a starting point for the innovative development of the umbrella solution for the Mosque of the Prophet. The umbrellas are made of woven Teflon fabric that is similar to the fabric used in the SOM's Hajj terminal at Jeddah. The twelve retractable umbrellas are designed to withstand wind loads up to 155 kilometers per hour (96 miles per hour) measuring 17 × 18 meters (51 × 54 feet) grouped in two units of six each to fit the proportions of the courtyard.[9] "Each arm is driven by a hydraulic cylinder incorporated into the umbrella mast, with oil pressure maintained by an electric pump, making it possible to open them to in less than a minute."[10] Unlike the *toldo*, these umbrellas are intended to work in conjunction with mechanical cooling and are connected to the computerized climate control system of the mosque.[11]

Inside the Mosque of the Prophet, arabesque motifs extend across the interiors of the 27 sliding domes of the mosque. Jay Bonner, principal of the Bonner Design Consultancy, executed the designs for the domes' interiors; the sliding domes effectively transform the vaulted chamber into an open courtyard. Each dome has an approximate diameter of 20 meters. Many contemporary artists working in the Middle East have developed art in the service of religious worship, using technology as a vehicle for design action and the reclamation of culture in the aesthetic sphere.

THE MOSQUE OF THE PROPHET AS PARADIGM

It is widely agreed that mosques owe their origin to the archetypal Mosque of the Prophet at Medina. The Mosque can be considered both a spatial and spiritual paradigm for all mosque architecture; the most obvious relationship has to do with the spatial inference and function. Hence it proved

4 Mosque of the Prophet, view from the south, with the minaret of Bab al-Baqi and the Green Dome to the right (foreground) and minaret of Bab as-Salam to the left (foreground).
Photo: Muhammad Mahdi Karim, distributed under GFDL 1.2 license

5 Mosque of the Prophet, interior courtyard with *toldo* or sunshades.
Photo: Akel Kahera

acceptable as a precedent in the first instance following the importance of the Prophet's *Sunna* (practice, custom, tradition, model, law, habit, convention, and personal mannerisms). Despite the many regional variations, the Mosque of the Prophet at Medina may be understood as a spatial paradigm, with a distinct type of functional and spatial order. On the other hand, the edifice operated on several functional levels, as a civic center, a place for the destitute, a place of spiritual repose, a seat of government, a place for communal worship, and so forth. Mosques built in the first two to three centuries after the death of the Prophet were undoubtedly reminiscent of his mosque. They adhered to the spatial paradigm of a hypostyle plan and enclosure with a central courtyard open to the sky. The Great Mosque of Cordoba, Spain (eighth-eleventh centuries) serves as an example of the flexibility of the system; the building has been expanded four successive times without altering the underlying spatial order of the plan. This spatial order has also produced a number of vernacular variations, since the system of the hypostyle plan allowed for the regional adaptation even within a short period of time. Extant examples can be found throughout the Muslim world from Iraq to North Africa, such as the Mosque of 'Uqba ibn Nafi at Kairouan (seventh century), or even in the sub-Saharan mosques at Djenne, Mopti, and Timbuktu (eleventh-sixteenth centuries).[12] Because the Prophet's Mosque laid the foundation for the elements of the space and function, it can be regarded as an archetype.

AKEL ISMAIL KAHERA, PhD, Professor of Architecture and Urbanism at Hamad Bin Khalifa University Doha, Qatar, is an architect/practitioner with over twenty-five years of experience in the international arena. He is the author of over thirty peer-reviewed papers, book chapters, encyclopedia entries and three books: *Deconstructing the American Mosque: Space Gender and Aesthetics* (2002); *Reading the Islamic City: Discursive Practices and Legal Judgment* (2012); and *Design Criteria for Mosques: Art, Architecture and Worship* (2011).

6 Mosque of the Prophet, al-Rawdah, the Precinct known as the Garden.
Photo: Uleke, distributed under CC BY-SA 3.0 license

SUGGESTIONS FOR FURTHER READING

al-Amhudi, Abu al-Hassan Abdallah. *Wafa al-Wafa bi Akhbar Dar al-Mustafa* (Cairo: n.p., 1955).

Bisheh, Ghazi Isseddin. "The Mosque of the Prophet at Madinah throughout the First-Century A.H. with Special Emphasis on the Umayyad Mosque" (PhD Dissertation, University of Michigan, 1976).

Burckhardt, Titus. *The Art of Islam: Language and Meaning* (London: World of Islam Festival Publishing Company Ltd., 1976).

Damjuli, Salma Samar. *The Architecture of the Prophet's Holy Mosque, Al Madinah* (London: Hazar Publishing Limited, 1998).

Kahera, Akel Ismail. *Deconstructing the American Mosque: Space, Gender and Aesthetics* (Austin: The University of Texas Press, 2002).

Kuban, Dogan. *Muslim Religious Architecture* (Leiden: E.J. Brill, 1974).

NOTES

[1] The conventional measurement of the cubit is about 50 cm/20 inches or the length of the forearm; however it should be noted that the cubit varied among builders in Arabia and from country to country.

[2] Abu al -Hassan Abdallah al-Amhudi, *Wafa al-Wafa bi Akhbar Dar al- Mustafa* (Cairo: n.p., 1955). 334–6.

[3] Muhammad Marmaduke Pickthall, *Translation of the Holy Qur'an.* (New York: Muslim World League, 1977).

[4] *Sahih Muslim*, trans. Abdul Hamid Siddiqi. 4 vols.(Lahore Pakistan: S.H. Muhammad Asraf, 1973).

[5] See Akel Ismail Kahera, *Deconstructing the American Mosque: Space, Gender and Aesthetics* (Austin: The University of Texas Press, 2002), 25–46. This poem was first cited in Ibn Ishaq, *Sirat*, 3–4:666–9. The English version appears in the translation rendered by A. Guillaume, *The Life of Muhammad: A Translation of Ibn Ishaq's Sirat Rasul-Allah* (Oxford: Oxford University Press, 1960), 795–98. The version cited here is from Juan Eduardo Campo, *The Other Side of Paradise* (Columbia, S.C.: The University of South Carolina Press, 1991), 56.

I have included the second-to-last line as it appears in Ghazi Isseddin Bisheh, "The Mosque of the Prophet at Madinah throughout the First-Century A.H. with Special Emphasis on the Umayyad Mosque" (PhD Dissertation, University of Michigan, 1976). The line does not appear in Campo.

[6] The development has been discussed extensively in Salma Samar Damjuli, *The Architecture of the Prophet's Holy Mosque, Al Madinah* (London: Hazar Publishing Limited, 1998).

[7] Ismail Serageldin and James Steele, *Architecture of the Contemporary Mosque* (London: Academy Editions 1996), 24–7.

[8] Ibid., 25.

[9] Ibid., 28.

[10] Ibid.

[11] Ibid., 35.

[12] See Titus Burckhardt. *The Art of Islam: Language and Meaning* (London: World of Islam Festival Publishing Company, 1976). For further discussion, see Labelle Prussin, *Hatumere-Islamic Designs in West Africa* (Berkeley: University of California Press, 1986).

The Dome of the Rock through the Centuries KATHRYN BLAIR MOORE

1 Dome of the Rock, Jerusalem, c. 691–2.
Photo: Kathryn Blair Moore

In the history of the religious architecture of the world, the Qubbat al-Sakhra (Fig. 1), or Dome of the Rock, in Jerusalem has come to stand as a preeminent architectural symbol of Islam. Its construction by the Umayyad caliph 'Abd al-Malik c. 691–2 has been perceived as a fundamental expression of the triumph of Islam over Christianity and Judaism.[1] Yet the Dome of the Rock's complex history over the centuries involves violent ruptures and modifications in the basic religious function and identity of the building.[2] Rather than purely a symbol of Islam, the Dome of the Rock might be viewed as a unique religious building negotiating the interrelation of the "People of the Book" (*'Ahl al-Kitāb*), that is Jews and Christians, to Islam. The sacred mount inscribed by the building is of foundational importance to the three religions, particularly as the site of the creation of the first Temple and as the future site of God's abode on earth at the end of time. At the same time, the contested nature of the building's history is a testament to the sometimes antagonistic relations of the religions. The building, from its construction over the ruins of the Jewish Temple to its conversion into a Christian church during the Crusades and final emergence as a primary architectural symbol of Islam, has been subject to a negotiation of the extremes of identity and alterity that typifies the interrelations of Judaism, Christianity, and Islam.

INITIAL CONSTRUCTION c. 691–2

The Dome of the Rock is the first to survive intact of the religious monuments created in the Islamic Era, dated from 622. In contrast to the mosques constructed in the previous decades, the Umayyad monument in Jerusalem was not made for prayer; the essential features of the building in Jerusalem

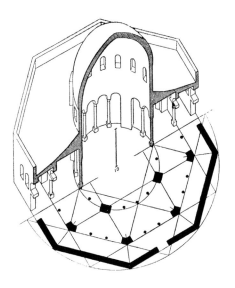

2 Dome of the Rock, Jerusalem. Sectional axonometric view through dome.
Photo: Creswell Archive, Ashmolean Museum, neg. image courtesy of Fine Arts Library, Harvard College Library

more resemble the Kaaba in Mecca, a pre-Islamic shrine at the center of Islamic worship. Both buildings commemorate God's creation of the world by sheltering a stone associated with paradise.[3] The Kaaba is believed to have been created by Abraham as the first religious shrine, while the Dome of the Rock was constructed on the site of the first Temple created by Solomon c. 961 BC.[4] The Kaaba and the Dome of the Rock both exhibit elemental geometry: the circle (*qubbat* means dome) and square (*kaaba* means cube), and each marks an axis perceived as connecting heaven and earth (Fig. 2).[5] Unlike the Kaaba in Mecca, whose refurbishment during and after the life of Muhammad primarily responded to the idolatry of the polytheistic religions of the Arabian peninsula, the Dome of the Rock's creation instead articulated the relation of Islam to Judaism and Christianity.

The construction of the Dome of the Rock was not due to necessity: a congregational mosque already existed in Jerusalem, founded some time after the Islamic conquest of the city in 637 (Fig. 3).[6] The site chosen was just north of the mosque, both located on the raised platform associated with Solomon's Temple.[7] The Rock now sheltered by the Dome (Fig. 4) was at the time of the Islamic conquest in open air, and the raised platform (Fig. 5) – referred to as the Temple Mount or the Noble Sanctuary (Haram al-Sharif) – was reportedly littered with ruins of the Jewish Temple, most recently destroyed during the siege of Jerusalem by the Roman Emperor Titus in 70. The natural outcropping of the Rock had a foundational significance within both Judaism and Christianity: here Abraham almost sacrificed his son, until God directly intervened; here David was instructed to construct the Temple to house the Ark of the Covenant, a task completed by his son Solomon; and here God would return at the end of time to judge a resurrected humanity.[8] The Rock was, in other words, the summit of a sacred mountain where God had and would again reveal himself and intervene in the history of the world. The Rock represented a fundamental physical link between heaven and earth and was for the People of the Book an origin point for religious architecture, that is, for the construction of a trans-generational monument intended to manifest in lasting form the covenant between God and man.

In the context of the early formation of Islam, the Dome of the Rock did two primary things: it demonstrated the physical and theological relations of the relatively new religion to the ancient traditions of Judaism, while at the same time articulating Islam's divergences from contemporary Christian worship in Jerusalem. The latter was primarily accomplished through the display of Quranic passages. Golden Arabic script materializes the word of God, that is, the revelations received by Muhammad beginning around 609 that would constitute the Quran. Their very existence and form, encircling the foundation stone of the Jewish Temple – the place of past and future revelations of God on earth – re-inscribed Jerusalem's sacred history in

terms of the revelation to Muhammad as the final prophet. The selected Quranic passages address the unity of the one God, denying Jesus's identity as the son of God. The inscriptions also directly address the People of the Book, with the exhortation to "not go beyond the bounds of your religion," reiterating that Jesus was another prophet, and to "not say three... For indeed God is one God...."[9] The inscriptions echoed the words revealed to God's messenger on another sacred mountain, Mount Hira (north of Mecca), and presented these revelations to Muhammad as superseding the sacred scripture of Christianity. Interspersed among the Quranic passages are repeated professions of faith, which invoke the absolute unity of God, forming a visual litany that suggests how moving around the Rock may have been perceived as a fundamental enactment of submission (islam) to the one God.[10]

While the inscriptions inside the Dome of the Rock literally articulated the theological relation of Islam and Christianity, the forms of the Umayyad building, which visually dominated the city then as it does now, broadcasted a message to the Christians of Jerusalem in a different way. The hemispherical double-shell dome is elevated by a cylindrical drum with sixteen windows; an octagonal substructure has four portals facing the cardinal directions. On the interior, two concentric ambulatories, traced out by arcades composed of slightly pointed arches of striped masonry, raised on columns with Corinthian capitals, inscribe the circular core containing the natural outcropping of the Rock. These basic forms must have been perceived as competitively emulating the religious architecture of the Byzantine Empire, specifically nearby churches relating to the divine status of Jesus and Mary. The two churches most directly linked with the divinity of Jesus were the Anastasis Rotunda (Fig. 6) and the Church of the Ascension (Fig. 7). Both were associated with sacred mountains, one Mount Calvary where Christ was crucified; the adjacent Rotunda enclosed the cave and empty tomb where Christ had been buried and from which he rose.[11] The other church was on the Mount of Olives, from which the risen Christ ascended into heaven, leaving footprints embedded in the rock at the summit of the mountain.[12] Both churches, originally built in the fourth century, were completely

3 Southeast corner of the Temple Mount with the Aqsa Mosque, Jerusalem, c. 705.
Photo: Kathryn Blair Moore

4 Dome of the Rock, Jerusalem, c. 691–2, interior.
Photo: Matson Photo Service, created/published between 1940 and 1946, Library of Congress Prints and Photographs Division, Washington, D.C.

reconstructed in the twelfth century.[13] At the time of the construction of the Dome of the Rock, they were round chapels with ambulatories covered by domical vaults, each with an *oculus* open to the heavens, commemorating Christ's Resurrection and Ascension, respectively.[14] The Quran denied the Crucifixion and Resurrection of Jesus, establishing that he was instead raised up to heaven from the Mount of Olives and would only die when resurrected with the rest of humanity at the end of time.[15]

Early traditions suggest that some Muslims made pilgrimage to the site of Christ's Ascension on the Mount of Olives, as well as the church associated with the Tomb of Mary, located in the valley below.[16] The latter was one of the centralized churches especially associated with Mary's status as the mother of God, in existence by the fifth or sixth century.[17] The other in the area of Jerusalem was the fifth-century Church of the Kathisma, located midway on the route to Bethlehem and dedicated to Mary as the mother of God (*Theotokos*).[18] Both Marian churches are no longer extant.[19]

The Kathisma presented the most striking parallels with the Dome of the Rock, with its double octagonal ambulatory enshrining an exposed sacred rock at its center, identified as the "seat" (*Kathisma*) where Mary rested on her way to Bethlehem.[20]

The churches in and around Jerusalem that were the most important architectural precedents for the Dome of the Rock were directly associated with the divine status of Christ and Mary. The competitive appropriation of the related architectural forms and the visual primacy of the new Umayyad building within the center of the city, combined with inscriptions denying their divinity, demonstrated the subordination of Christ and Mary to the one true God.[21] The denial of the divinity of Jesus and Mary was complemented by the eschewal of related figural imagery, which also registered a fundamental difference vis-à-vis Christian worship and the many churches in Jerusalem and elsewhere. The absence of figural imagery in the Dome of the Rock also aligned the Islamic place of worship with the Jewish history of its site. Here had stood the Jewish Temple, in

5 The Temple Mount, Jerusalem.
Photo: Kathryn Blair Moore

6 Church of the Holy Sepulcher, Jerusalem, consecrated 1149.
Photo: Kathryn Blair Moore

7 Church of the Ascension, Jerusalem, early twelfth century.
Photo: Kathryn Blair Moore

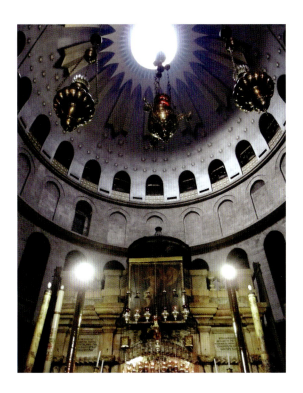

which – in accordance with the Mosaic prohibition of idolatry – no figural image of God had been instituted. Instead, the Temple and its ornamentation manifested the Divine Presence, as if a throne for an ineffable God.[22] By restoring this primary aspect of Solomon's Temple, 'Abd al-Malik could claim to belong to a line of prophet-kings, including David and Solomon, and to have restored Jerusalem to its former sovereignty.[23] The restoration of the Temple was a task neglected by the previous Christian custodians of the site, who reportedly wished to leave the area in ruins as a confirmation of Jesus's prophecy of the destruction of the Temple (Mark 13.2 and Matthew 24.2).[24] In this respect, the idea of restoring Solomon's Temple could be viewed as another way in which the construction of the Dome of the Rock articulated a point of difference with Christianity.[25]

The visual relationship of the Dome of the Rock to the idea of the Jewish Temple has been obscured due to the significant alterations made after the Umayyad period. During the reign of the Ottoman Sultan Süleyman (r. 1520–66), the exterior gold-ground mosaics were replaced with blue, white, and yellow tiles (which have since been replaced by modern reproductions in 1960–2) (Fig. 1). Until this point, the exterior surfaces would have presented a shimmering vision of glass mosaics comparable to the interior, which displays luminous jewels, iridescent pearls, winged vases, and eternally flowering trees and vines hovering in a golden field. The mosaics are raised above a level of marble panels, whose aqueous patterns evoke a moving sea of color.[26] Although the basic elements and materials of the ornamentation commissioned by the Umayyad caliph pertained to established Byzantine craftsmanship – and were most likely created by the hands of Byzantine craftsmen – the motifs were particular to the idea of Solomon's Temple and related legends about the Jewish king's famed wealth, his legendary Throne, and its garden of golden fruit trees.[27] Although Solomon's Temple had been destroyed for centuries, descriptions of its rich materials and splendor circulated in the early years of Islam and for centuries thereafter.[28]

8 Dome of the Ascension, Jerusalem, 1200–1.
Photo: Kathryn Blair Moore

Features of the Dome of the Rock apparently relating to the Jewish Temple can also be seen in light of the eschatological associations of the site, particularly the interrelated concepts of the Throne of God, heavenly temple, and paradise.[29] Solomon's Temple and Throne were generally understood to be the earthly counterparts of the Heavenly Temple and Throne of God, sharing an aesthetic of brilliantly-hued jewels and iridescent pearls, perpetually flowering gardens, and luminosity.[30] Early Islamic traditions refer to the pavement of the Dome of the Rock as one of the roofs of paradise and compare the surrounding area to one of its gardens.[31] It was widely believed that at the end of time God would return to earth – and specifically to the Rock – to inhabit his Throne and restore the Temple. The resurrected would gather to the east of the Dome of the Rock on the Mount of Olives; the intervening "Valley of Hell" would separate the believers from disbelievers.[32] The inscriptions inside the Dome of the Rock allude to the Resurrection and Judgment, found above the East Door facing in the direction of the Mount of Olives.[33] The Dome of the Rock could have been viewed not only as a restoration of the first Temple, but also a foreshadowing of the future restoration of the final Temple, open only to God's elect. The recurring theme of crowns and other jewels that resemble necklaces and earrings evoke the victory of Islam and the ultimate sovereignty of the One God, whose throne would be manifested here at the end of time, and whose chosen agents on earth – the prophet-kings David, Solomon, and now 'Abd al-Malik – in the meantime honored this location in anticipation of future events.[34]

An interest in emphasizing the eschatological associations of the Dome of the Rock is also suggested by the larger building program for the Temple Mount initiated by 'Abd al-Malik. The chronology of the buildings on the Temple Mount remains unclear, but it is known that by the eighth century the construction of two small domes was ascribed to 'Abd al-Malik. The Dome of the Ascension (Qubbat al-Miraj) (Fig. 8), to the north of the Dome of the Rock, is associated with the Prophet's Ascension into Heaven, while the Dome of the Chain (Qubbat al-Silsila) (Fig. 9), to the east at the exact center of the Haram al-Sharif, marks the place where a chain of light was suspended between heaven and earth.[35] Both buildings commemorate events perceived as signs of the future role of the Temple Mount and the Rock during the end of days. The chain had been used by King David to judge the Children of Israel, and the same chain would be used by God to judge all of humanity. The Prophet's Ascension was also a past event that proved the special relation of Jerusalem to heaven; from here Muhammad began his journey which culminated with a vision of the Throne of God, foreshadowing the revelation of God in Jerusalem at the end of time. The gates through which one entered into the Temple Mount area also acquired names associated with the Resurrection and Judgment, including the Gate of Repentance (Bab al-Tawba) and the Gate of Mercy (Bab al-Rahma).[36]

9 Dome of the Chain, Jerusalem, 1199–1200.
Photo: Kathryn Blair Moore

Either in the reign of 'Abd al-Malik or that of his son, al-Walid (r. 705–15), reconstruction of the congregational mosque of Jerusalem was initiated.[37] Throughout this and future expansions of the building, the alignment of the *mihrab*, indicating the direction of prayer to the Kaaba in Mecca, and the Rock was maintained.[38] Muhammad reportedly first prayed to Jerusalem before Mecca, and for this reason the Rock is also known as "the first *qibla*."[39] The alignment of the Rock and Kaaba also points to future events, when Mecca and Medina will be brought to Jerusalem on the Day of Resurrection.[40] This trajectory was also followed by the Prophet Muhammad, when he made his miraculous Night Journey (*'isra*) from Mecca to Jerusalem, which by the eighth century was understood to have immediately preceded his Ascension into heaven. According to the Quran (17.1), Muhammad was carried by the will of God from the Sacred Place of Prayer (al-masjid al-Haram) to the Farthest Place of Prayer (al-masjid al-Aqsa), where he was shown "some of Our signs." In 1035, the Fatimids added a mosaic inscription adapted from this Quranic passage to a new triumphal arch within the congregational mosque of Jerusalem.[41] The current name for the mosque, al-Aqsa, refers to this Quranic passage, and reflects the continual expansion of the importance of the story of the Night Journey to the sanctity of Jerusalem in Islam.

There is no evidence that the Rock was particularly associated with the Prophet's Night Journey or Ascension in the time of 'Abd al-Malik. Muslim writers first mention a footprint inside the Dome of the Rock, left by Muhammad as he began his journey into heaven, in the eleventh century.[42] Even if the Rock was not originally identified as the launching point – so to speak – for his ascent, the account of Muhammad's experience as he

THE DOME OF THE ROCK THROUGH THE CENTURIES 115

progressed through the seven heavens shares significant features with other concepts known to have been directly linked to the Dome of the Rock, its architecture, and ornamentation.[43] During the Ascension, Muhammad sees the "lote tree of the farthest boundary," marking the limit of God's presence, and the "garden of refuge," where the blessed will find shelter after the Resurrection. Both concepts could be interpreted as corresponding to the paradisical garden exhibited in the Dome of the Rock's mosaics. Muhammad's Ascension culminates with a vision of the Throne of God (Quran 17.60, 53.1–18).[44] These "signs" revealed to Muhammad will be revealed in the future to the elect.

The special resonance of the Dome of the Rock over the centuries, especially as seen from the Mount of Olives, is in offering simultaneously a vision of Jerusalem's past and future. The insistence upon maintaining the forms of the Dome of the Rock after the Umayyad period has contributed to the building's special aura, at the intersection of past and present, heaven and earth. Renovations undertaken by successive Islamic dynasties with authority over Jerusalem did not significantly alter any aspect of the Dome of the Rock's structural features, including during extensive renovations following earthquakes of 1015 and 1033.[45] The first significant alterations to the Dome of the Rock and the Haram al-Sharif were undertaken by the Christian Crusaders, who conquered the city in 1099.

THE LATIN KINGDOM OF JERUSALEM 1099–1187

The apocalyptic associations of the Dome of the Rock and the larger area of the Temple Mount set the stage for the violent confrontations between Islam and Christianity in the period of the Crusades. Following the destruction of the Church of the Holy Sepulcher in 1009 – ordered by the Fatimid caliph al-Hakim (d. 1021) – European Christians increasingly characterized Islamic rulers as agents of the anti-Christ, identified by many Christians with Muhammad. Legends about the apocalypse foretold that the anti-Christ would inhabit the Temple in Jerusalem, initiating the end of days.[46] In preaching aimed at protecting the Holy Sepulcher against further desecration by Muslims, the Dome of the Rock was characterized not as an Islamic building, but as the ancient Temple of Solomon perversely transgressed by Muslims.[47] The Crusade launched in 1095 had as a primary goal the restoration of

the Temple, purged of the pollution of Islamic worship.[48] Accounts of the conquest in 1099 describe the ancient Temple being cleansed by the blood of Muslims, who had "blasphemed God there for many years."[49] Several writers, including those who claimed to be eyewitnesses, reported the discovery and destruction of an idol of Muhammad on the Temple Mount in 1099, in some instances said to be installed specifically on the Rock – an invention which confirmed previous accounts of the idolatrous nature of Islam.[50]

Up until the Crusader conquest of Jerusalem in 1099, Christian pilgrims could not enter the Dome of the Rock or step foot on the surrounding esplanade. Once in possession of the building, the Arabic name was effaced as the building became known as the *Templum Domini,* or Temple of the Lord.[51] The name rendered in Latin the Hebrew notion of *Bethel*, the "House of God," and thereby identified the octagonal building with the inner sanctum of the Jewish Temple.[52] Opinion appears to have been split between whether the building was in fact the original Solomonic construction or Byzantine reconstruction. Some pilgrims in the Latin Kingdom of Jerusalem asserted that the Ark still existed and was hidden within the Rock inside the *Templum Domini*. As a result, the Dome of the Rock was also sometimes referred to as the "modern tabernacle."[53] Undoubtedly some of the Crusaders would have been told by locals about the true history of the Dome of the Rock, and yet it is remarkable how seldom doubts about its historical identification were expressed (at least in written records). A rare example is provided by a description of Jerusalem composed in the 1130s, in which Fretellus – a canon of the cathedral of Nazareth – indicates disagreement about the historical origins of the building, some reportedly saying that the Temple was built in the time of Constantine, others in the time of Justinian, while still others "by a certain sultan of Memphis, in Egypt, in honor of Allah Akbar, that is the supreme God, as is clearly demonstrated by the inscription in the Saracen language."[54]

The physical transformations made to the *Templum Domini* over the course of the Latin Kingdom of Jerusalem may have been intended to address doubts regarding the Christian identity of the building. The decision to install Latin inscriptions on both the exterior and interior suggests an interest in countering the Arabic inscriptions and masking the building's Islamic identity.[55] The physical transformation also involved the installation of an altar over the Rock, images of Christ and Mary, and a golden cross on the dome.[56] Nothing survives from the period of the Dome of the Rock's life as a church, except an intricate ironwork grille originally installed around the Rock, in the Haram Museum since the 1960s.[57] Two Germanic monks probably writing in the 1170s provide detailed accounts of the ornamentation of the *Templum Domini*, citing the content of the inscriptions. Those on the exterior emphasized the fundamental identity of the building as the *Templum Domini* described in the Bible, including "The house of the Lord is well built upon a firm rock" (Mathew 7.25).[58]

Inside the Dome of the Rock, inscriptions identified locations with Biblical events, like Jacob's vision and Christ's presentation to the Temple, presumably also visualized in the lost paintings. The assertion of the Rock inside the *Templum Domini* as the site of these events, especially Jacob's vision of a ladder climbing to heaven, confirmed that this was the site of both the ancient Jewish Temple and the future heavenly Temple.[59] Another inscription identified the building as the residence of the Virgin Mary, where she lived from age 3 to 14 until her marriage to Joseph. This particular inscription is not based upon a Biblical passage, but instead the *Protogospel of James*, the apocryphal account of the early life of Mary first composed in Syria or Egypt by 150.[60] Mary is said to weave the veil of the Temple along with seven other virgins and to receive angelic sustenance, details to which the pilgrim John of Würzburg alludes in his account of the inscription in the Dome of the Rock.[61] The Islamic building, originally intended to deny Mary's status as the mother of God (especially as expressed in its Arabic inscriptions), was reimagined by the Crusaders as the primary setting for Mary's early life, through which she became the architectural vessel for the Incarnation of God on earth.[62]

Additional modifications made to surrounding buildings on the Temple Mount during the period of the Latin Kingdom of Jerusalem have not survived. The Dome of the Chain was dedicated to St. James the Less and had a related tomb and Latin inscriptions.[63] An abbey was constructed for the Augustinians who had been installed in the *Templum Domini* in 1112.[64] The Aqsa Mosque was appropriated and renamed *Templum Salamonis* (Temple or Palace of Solomon).[65] The portico constructed on the main façade (Fig. 10) is one of the few Crusader structures that was not dismantled after the Islamic reconquest of 1187. The mosque was primarily used as a palatial residence for the kings of Jerusalem.[66] The entire Temple Mount became the stage for rituals in the Latin Kingdom of Jerusalem, through which the earthly sovereignty of the Latin Kings was linked to both the life of Christ and Solomonic history. During the coronation ceremony for the King of Jerusalem, a procession from the Holy Sepulcher culminated with the king placing his crown on the altar above the Rock, echoing Christ's presentation at the same altar centuries before.[67]

AYYUBID AND MAMLUK PERIODS 1187–1517

The Crusader take-over of Jerusalem witnessed the first violent inversion in the function and identity of the Dome of the Rock. The Islamic building was reimagined as the setting for events in the lives of Christ and Mary fundamental to the story of the Incarnation refuted in the Quranic passages originally inscribed within the Dome of the Rock. In efforts to rouse support for a counter-Crusade among the Muslim populations of the region, new emphasis was placed upon the significance of Jerusalem, drawing attention to the unique facets of the Rock's sanctity in Islam, especially in connection to Muhammad's Night Journey and Ascension.[68] Salah al-Din (d. 1193) awaited the anniversary of the Prophet's Ascension, on Friday the second of October 1187, to formally take possession of Jerusalem.[69] In a sermon delivered in the Aqsa Mosque during the first Friday prayer after the reconquest, Ibn al-Zaki proclaimed Salah al-Din's victory in restoring the Rock and drew attention to its significance as "the spot from which your blessed Prophet Muhammad mounted to Heaven."[70] After 1187, more and more Muslim pilgrims make note of Muhammad's footprints impressed into the Rock. The emphasis upon the place of the Dome of the Rock in the life of Muhammad effectively represented an Islamization of the building, countering its Christianization during the Latin Kingdom of Jerusalem.

The formal changes made to re-establish the Dome of the Rock as an Islamic building following the reconquest of 1187 represent the second inversion within the history of the building. In addition to demolishing the accouterments associated with

10 Al-Aqsa Mosque, Jerusalem, twelfth-century Crusader portico.
Photo: Kathryn Blair Moore

Christian worship, Salah al-Din had the Dome of the Rock and surrounding areas cleansed with rosewater.[71] The architectural activities of the Ayyubids on the Temple Mount more generally reflect an interest in returning to the pre-Crusades state, with no significant new construction. The Dome of the Chain was refurbished in 1199–1200, and the Dome of the Ascension was rebuilt in 1200–1201 using Crusader elements, apparently with a similar intent of restoration.[72] Christians were denied access to the Temple Mount, and in the region around Jerusalem warfare continued between Crusaders who sought to retain a foothold in the region and the armies of the Ayyubid sultans. In 1239, a treaty signed by Sultan al-Kamil (d. 1238) and the Holy Roman Emperor Frederick II (d. 1250) established a compromise, according to which Christians would repossess Jerusalem but the Dome of the Rock would still be accessible to Muslims. The arrangement and related truce ended in 1239, and in 1244 the city was briefly taken by armies of Khwarezmian Turks. In 1260 the Mamluk sultanate based in Cairo took control of Jerusalem and proceeded to evict the last of the Crusaders from the Holy Land, a task completed in 1291 with the conquest of Acre. In this context the original triumphal symbolism of Islam over Christianity manifested in the Dome of the Rock, now reasserted through its restoration, had a new relevance in the region-wide victory over the Crusaders who had once violently possessed the building.

Like the Ayyubids, the Mamluks focused upon maintaining the existing architectural forms of the Dome of the Rock and the surrounding Temple Mount, undertaking restorations of the Umayyad mosaics, especially in the reign of sultan Baybars (r. 1260–77).[73] The Mamluks focused their architectural patronage along the periphery of the Temple Mount. Most significant among the new buildings was the sultanic Madrasa al-Ashrafiyya, founded by Sultan al-Ashraf Qaytbay (1468–96), along the western border of the Haram al-Sharif.[74] The Mamluk *madrasa*s formed a literal and metaphorical barrier against non-orthodoxy and apostasy, and created a boundary between the Islamic Haram al-Sharif and the parts of Jerusalem accessible to Christian pilgrims. While other mosques and churches throughout and around Jerusalem accommodated both Christian and Muslim pilgrims in the post-Crusade period, including at the sites of Christ's Ascension and Nativity, the Dome of the Rock stood isolated as an exclusively Islamic monument, visually dominating the city but inaccessible to those who had not rejected the divinity of Christ and submitted to the will of the one God.

OTTOMAN PERIOD 1517–1917

By 1517 the Ottoman sultanate based in Istanbul had ended Mamluk rule and established authority over Jerusalem. The reign of Süleyman (r. 1520–66) witnessed an aggressive expansion of Islam into Christian territories of eastern Europe. Through these victories, and custodianship of not only Jerusalem but also Mecca and Medina, the Ottoman sultan could claim a status within the history of Islam equal to his Umayyad predecessors. Sources of the period suggest that Süleyman, whose name is a Turkish version of Solomon, imagined that his reign marked the final stage in world history, and that the Haram al-Sharif would imminently become the stage for the events associated with the end of days.[75]

The Ottoman transformation of the Dome of the Rock under sultan Süleyman commenced with the creation of new stained glass windows for the octagonal walls in 1528–9. The windows exhibited Quranic inscriptions that sought to align the sultan's conquests with God's will and emphasized the absolute sovereignty of God at the end of time.[76] In 1530, renovations were made to Jerusalem's water supply system, which benefited public fountains throughout the city, including on the Haram.[77] In addition to improving the city's sanitation, the renewed water system bolstered the fundamental image of Jerusalem as a mirror of paradise, as a walled city with flowing streams feeding abundant gardens. Süleyman also had new walls created, which probably had a similar combined functional – in this case defensive – and symbolic role. The new walls were constructed 1537–41, in the same years that the gilded finial of the Dome of the Rock was restored.[78] The tile revetments (Fig. 11) – the most significant physical modification of the Dome of the Rock since its original construction nine centuries earlier – replaced the exterior mosaics with panels exhibiting images of a flowering garden. The tiles incorporated an extensive program of inscriptions, which include dates indicating the time frame for their creation, 1545–6 to 1551–2.[79]

The tile revetments constitute Süleyman's personal stamp on the Dome of the Rock, with which he claimed the building as his own, in a gesture surpassing all other caliphs since 'Abd al-Malik. The motifs and epigraphic program of the tiles also suggest an interest in amplifying the original Umayyad meaning of the Dome of the Rock, confirming Süleyman's place in the distinguished lineage of Solomon and David.[80] Distinctive panels framing the north and south gates of the building depict blossoming prunus trees, associated with paradise. The Quranic inscriptions on the north gate emphasize God's forgiveness for believers, who will be accepted into the eternal gardens of paradise.[81] Verses on the south gate refer to the Prophet changing the direction of prayer from Mecca, drawing attention to the Rock's status as the first *qibla* and the physical alignment with Mecca through the north-south axis to the *mihrab* of the Aqsa Mosque. Other tilework inscriptions on the exterior of the Dome of the Rock emphasize the historic importance of the building, especially in connection to the Jewish Temple and the Prophet's Night Journey.[82] The completion of the new tile revetments in 1551–2 coincided with Süleyman's efforts to diminish Christian claims upon the sacred territory of Jerusalem, especially through the expulsion of Franciscan friars from their residence on Mount Sion in 1551.[83]

The Dome of the Chain adjacent to the Dome of the Rock was also clad with new revetment tiles, dated by inscription to 1561–2. Inscriptions above the *mihrab* refer to the justice of King David, the divine sanction for Süleyman's caliphate, and the hope that his life might extend until the end of days.[84] The image of Süleyman as a new King David was an essential aspect of the sultan's identity as a lawgiver, whose temporal authority was a prelude to God's role on Judgment Day. During his reign, the ancient role of the Dome of the Chain in determining the guilt of the people of Israel was revived in a new way, as the building became the setting for legal proceedings, through which the sultan's representatives enacted his divinely given laws. In 1564–5, the final physical modifications to the Dome of the Rock were made, with the installation of bronze-plated wooden doors in its four gates, with additional inscriptions.[85] After the reign of Süleyman, Ottoman sultans maintained the forms of the Dome of the Rock, with only minor alterations.[86]

CONCLUSION

400 years of Ottoman rule of Jerusalem came to an end in 1917; with the collapse of the Empire, the British Mandate of Palestine was formed, as Jerusalem became an annex to the British Empire.[87] The first architectural history of the Dome of the Rock was the product of the researches of K. A. C. Creswell, appointed as Inspector of Monuments in Palestine and Syria in 1919.[88] In the resulting publications the place of the Dome of the Rock in the formation of Islamic architecture was first established. Since then, the writing of the history of the Dome of the Rock has been as deeply impacted by the same interests in delimiting religious identities which have motivated the building's original construction and subsequent transformations. The dominant tendency of the

11 Dome of the Rock, Jerusalem, c. 691–2.
Photo: Kathryn Blair Moore

twentieth and twenty-first centuries of viewing the building exclusively as a foundational monument within the history of Islamic architecture has obscured the larger role of the Dome of the Rock in shaping the development of Christian and Jewish architecture, including in relation to churches of Europe and the New World as well as synagogues of eighteenth- and nineteenth-century Europe.[89] In contrast, the impact upon religious architecture in the Islamic world has been relatively well studied.[90] The contested nature of the relationship of the Dome of the Rock to the Jewish Temple in studies written since the formation of the state of Israel in 1948 should also be seen in light of competing claims to exclusive ownership of the Haram-al Sharif. The history of the building also continues to be tied up with expectations for its future role in an apocalyptic scheme.[91] Perhaps no other religious building's history is as deeply implicated in the future of entire nations as the Dome of the Rock; the combined deep history and apocalyptic expectations have and will undoubtedly continue to shape the history of the building, its use, and material existence.

KATHRYN BLAIR MOORE, Assistant Professor of Art History at the University of Connecticut, researches in the medieval and Renaissance periods in Europe and the Mediterranean region. Her book, *The Architecture of the Christian Holy Land: Reception from Late Antiquity through the Renaissance* (Cambridge University Press, 2017), focused upon the architectural legacy of Jerusalem and the Holy Land more generally. She has been a fellow of Harvard University's Villa I Tatti and the American Academy in Rome.

SUGGESTIONS FOR FURTHER READING

Avner, Rina. "The Dome of the Rock in the Light of Development of Concentric Martyria in Jerusalem: Architecture and Architectural Iconography," *Muqarnas* 27 (2010), 31–50.

Folda, Jaroslav. *The Art of the Crusaders in the Holy Land, 1098–1187* (Cambridge: Cambridge University Press, 1995).

Grabar, Oleg. *The Dome of the Rock* (Cambridge: Harvard University Press, 2006).

Grabar, Oleg, and Benjamin Z. Kedar, eds. *Where Heaven and Earth Meet: Jerusalem's Sacred Esplanade* (Jerusalem: Yad Ben-Zvi Press, 2009).

Necipoğlu, Gülru. "The Dome of the Rock as Palimpsest: Abd al-Malik's Grand Narrative and Sultan Süleyman's Glosses," *Muqarnas* 25 (2008), 17–105.

Rosen-Ayalon, Myriam. *The Early Islamic Monuments of Al-Haram Al-Sharīf: An Iconographic Study* (Jerusalem: Institute of Archaeology, Hebrew University of Jerusalem, 1989).

NOTES

1. Oleg Grabar, "The Umayyad Dome of the Rock in Jerusalem," *Ars Orientalis* 3 (1959), 33–62; Nasser Rabbat, "The Meaning of the Umayyad Dome of the Rock," *Muqarnas* 6 (1989), 45 (12–21).

2. Gülru Necipoğlu, "The Dome of the Rock as Palimpsest: Abd al-Malik's Grand Narrative and Sultan Süleyman's Glosses," *Muqarnas* 25 (2008), 22–3 (17–105).

3. Josef van Ess, "'Abd al-Malik and the Dome of the Rock: An Analysis of Some Texts," in *Bayt-al-Maqdis: 'Abd al-Malik's Jerusalem*, eds. Julian Raby and Jeremy Johns (Oxford: Oxford University Press, 1992); Oleg Grabar, *The Dome of the Rock* (Cambridge: Harvard University Press, 2006), 52.

4. Necipoğlu, "The Dome of the Rock as Palimpsest," 27; Rabbat, "The Meaning of the Umayyad Dome of the Rock," 14.

5. Rabbat, "The Meaning of the Umayyad Dome of the Rock," 13; Amikam Elad, *Medieval Jerusalem and Islamic Worship: Holy Places, Ceremonies, Pilgrimage* (Leiden: E.J. Brill, 1995), 89–91; Nuha N. N. Khoury, "The Dome of the Rock, the Ka'ba, and the Ghumdan: Arab Myths and Umayyad Monuments," *Muqarnas* 10 (1993), 57–65.

6. Myriam Rosen-Ayalon, *The Early Islamic Monuments of Al-Haram Al-Sharīf: An Iconographic Study* (Jerusalem: Institute of Archaeology, Hebrew University of Jerusalem, 1989), 4.

7. Joseph Patrich, "538 BCE–70 CE: The Temple (*Beyt Ha-Miqdash*) and its Mount," in *Where Heaven and Earth Meet: Jerusalem's Sacred Esplanade*, eds. Oleg Grabar and B. Z. Kedar (Jerusalem: Yad Ben-Zvi Press, 2009), 36–71.

8. Rabbat, "The Meaning of the Umayyad Dome of the Rock," 14.

9. Necipoğlu, "The Dome of the Rock as Palimpsest," 52.

10. Ibid., 50; Grabar, "The Umayyad Dome of the Rock," 93. See also Marcus Milwright, *The Dome of the Rock and its Umayyad Mosaic Inscriptions* (Edinburgh: Edinburgh University Press, 2016).

11. Virgilio Corbo, *Il Santo Sepolcro di Gerusalemme 1. Testo: con riassunto in inglese* (Jerusalem: Franciscan Printing Press, 1981), 51.

12. Rodney Aist, *The Christian Topography of Early Islamic Jerusalem: The Evidence of Willibald of Eichstätt, 700–787 CE* (Turnhout, Belgium: Brepols, 2009), 206.

13. Denys Pringle, *The City of Jerusalem. The Churches of the Crusader Kingdom of Jerusalem: a Corpus. With Drawings by Peter E. Leach* (Cambridge: Cambridge University Press, 2007), 6–7.

14. Ibid., 6–7, 72; Virgilio C. Corbo, *Ricerche archeologiche al Monte degli Ulivi* (Jerusalem: Tip. Dei Padri Francescani, 1965).

15. Necipoğlu, "The Dome of the Rock as Palimpsest," 48.

16. Elad, *Medieval Jerusalem and Islamic Worship*, 140.

17. Pringle, *The City of Jerusalem*, 287–8; Denys Pringle and Peter E. Leach, *The Churches of the Crusader Kingdom of Jerusalem: A Corpus. Vol. 1, A–K (excluding Acre and Jerusalem)* (Cambridge: Cambridge University Press, 1993), 137–8.

18. Rina Avner, "The Initial Tradition of the Theotokos at the Kathisma: Earliest Celebrations and the Calendar," in *The Cult of the Mother of God in Byzantium*, eds. Leslie Brubaker and Mary B. Cunningham (Farmingham: Ashgate, 2011), 9–14 (9–30); Rina Avner, "The Dome of the Rock in the Light of Development of Concentric Martyria in Jerusalem: Architecture and Architectural Iconography," *Muqarnas* 27 (2010), 31–50.

19. B. Bagatti, Piccirillo, M. and Prodomo, *New Discoveries at the Tomb of the Virgin Mary in Gethsemane*, trans. L. Scriberras, Studium Biblicum Franciscanum, Collectio Minor 17 (Jerusalem: Franciscan Printing Press, 1975); Bellarmino Bagatti, *Gli Antichi Edifici Sacri di Betlemme in Seguito Agli Scavi e Restauri Practicati dalla Custodia di Terra Santa 1948–51* (Jerusalem: Franciscan Printing Press, 1983).

20. Avner, "The Initial Tradition of the Theotokos," 13.

21. Avner, "The Dome of the Rock," 41.

22. Van Ess, "'Abd al-Malik and the Dome of the Rock," 89–104.

23. Ibid., 97.

24. Yoram Tsafrir, "70–638: The Temple-less Mountain," in *Where Heaven and Earth Meet*, 83 (73–99).

25. Van Ess, "'Abd al-Malik and the Dome of the Rock," 90.

26. Rosen-Ayalon, *The Early Islamic Monuments*, 55.

27. Finbarr B. Flood, *The Great Mosque of Damascus: Studies on the Makings of an Umayyad Visual Culture* (Leiden: Brill, 2001), 82–90.

28. Priscilla Soucek, "The Temple of Solomon in Islamic Legend and Art," in *The Temple of Solomon in Christian, Islamic, and Jewish Art*, ed. Joseph Gutmann (Ann Arbor: University of Michigan Press, 1976), 73–123.

29. Van Ess, "'Abd al-Malik and the Dome of the Rock," 90, 103.

30. Flood, *The Great Mosque of Damascus*, 91; Rosen-Ayalon, *The Early Islamic Monuments*, 46–69.

31. Necipoğlu, "The Dome of the Rock as Palimpsest," 33.

32. Ibid., 19, 162–3.

33. Ibid., 49.

34. Necipoğlu, "The Dome of the Rock as Palimpsest," 39.

35. Ibid., 24; Elad, *Medieval Jerusalem and Islamic Worship*, 49. On the central position of the Dome of the Chain, see Rosen-Ayalon, *The Early Islamic Monuments*, 27.

36. Rosen-Ayalon, *The Early Islamic Monuments*, 45; Necipoğlu, "The Dome of the Rock as Palimpsest," 26.

37. Rosen-Ayalon, *The Early Islamic Monuments*, 5–6.

38. Van Ess, "'Abd al-Malik and the Dome of the Rock, 91'.

39. Necipoğlu, "The Dome of the Rock as Palimpsest," 37; Grabar, *The Dome of the Rock*, 48.

40. Necipoğlu, "The Dome of the Rock as Palimpsest," 30.

41. Grabar, "The Umayyad Dome of the Rock," 157–59.

42. Necipoğlu, "The Dome of the Rock as Palimpsest," 29; Elad, *Medieval Jerusalem and Islamic Worship*, 72.

43. Necipoğlu, "The Dome of the Rock as Palimpsest," 43.

44. Ibid., 44, 55.

45. Ibid., 31.

46. Sylvia Schein, *Gateway to the Heavenly City: Crusader Jerusalem and the Catholic West (1099–1187)* (Aldershot: Ashgate, 2005), 147.

47. Suzanne Akbari, *Idols in the East: European Representations of Islam and the Orient, 1100–1450* (Ithaca: Cornell University Press, 2009), 200–47.

48. Jonathan S. C. Riley-Smith, *The First Crusade and the Idea of Crusading* (Philadelphia: University of Pennsylvania Press, 1986), 23.

49. Jaroslav Folda, *The Art of the Crusaders*, 32–3.

50. Michael Camille, *The Gothic Idol: Ideology and Image-making in Medieval Art* (New York: Cambridge University Press, 1989), 87; Folda, *The Art of the Crusaders*, 90–1.

51. Kathryn Blair Moore, "Textual Transmission and Pictorial Transformations: the Post-Crusade Image of the Dome of the Rock in Italy," *Muqarnas* 27 (2011), 55 (51–78).

52. Yona Pinson, "The Iconography of the Temple in Northern Renaissance Art," *Assaph* 2 (1996), 158 (147–74).

53 Albert of Aachen, and Susan Edgington, *Historia Ierosolimitana: History of the Journey to Jerusalem* (Oxford: Clarendon Press, 2007), 432-5.

54 Benjamin Z. Kedar and Denys Pringle, "1099-1187: The Lord's Temple (*Templum Domini*) and Solomon's Palace (*Palatium Salomonis*)," in *Where Heaven and Earth Meet*, 137 (133-49).

55 Necipoğlu, "The Dome of the Rock as Palimpsest," 46; Rosen-Ayalon, "Jewish Substratum, Christian History and Muslim Symbolism," in *The Real and Ideal Jerusalem in Jewish, Christian, and Islamic art: Studies in Honor of Bezalel Narkiss on the Occasion of his Seventieth Birthday*, ed. Bianca Kühnel (Jerusalem: Hebrew University of Jerusalem, Journal for the Centre for Jewish Art, 1998), 463-6.

56 Folda, *The Art of the Crusaders*, 249-53.

57 Grabar, *The Dome of the Rock*, 165; Folda, *The Art of the Crusaders*, 251.

58 Folda, *The Art of the Crusaders*, 251-2.

59 Sabine MacCormack, "Loca Sancta: The Organization of Sacred Topography in Late Antiquity," in *The Blessings of Pilgrimage* (Urbana: University of Illinois Press, 1990), 23-4 (7-40).

60 Miri Rubin, *Mother of God: A History of the Virgin Mary* (New Haven: Yale University Press, 2009), 9.

61 Folda, *The Art of the Crusaders*, 251-2.

62 Herbert Busse, "Vom Felsendom zum Templum Domini," in *Das Heilige Land im Mittelalter. Begegnungsraum zwischen Orient und Okzident*, eds. Wolfdietrich Fischer and Jürgen Schneider (Neustadt an der Aisch: Degener, 1982).

63 Pringle, *The City of Jerusalem*, 182-3.

64 Folda, *The Art of the Crusaders*, 251.

65 John Wilkinson, Joyce Hill, and William F. Ryan, *Jerusalem Pilgrimage, 1099-1185*. Works issued by the Hakluyt Society, 2nd ser., no. 167 (London: Hakluyt Society, 1988), 28; Moore, "Textual Transmission and Pictorial Transformations," 73.

66 Wayne Dynes, "The Medieval Cloister as Portico of Solomon," *Gesta* 12.1/2 (1973), 61-9; Walter Cahn, "Solomonic Elements in Romanesque Art," *The Temple of Solomon: Archaeological Fact and Medieval Tradition*, 45-72. The subterranean areas were used as stables, known as *stabula Salomonis*, or Solomon's stables.

67 Schein, *Gateway to the Heavenly City*, 101-3; Sylvia Schein, "Between Mount Moriah and the Holy Sepulcher: The Changing Traditions of the Temple Mount in the Central Middle Ages," *Traditio* 40 (1984), 184-5 (175-196).

68 Carole Hillenbrand, *The Crusades: Islamic Perspectives* (New York: Routledge, 2000), 137-41, 162-74, 184-5.

69 Ibid., 189.

70 Ibid., 189-90; Necipoğlu, "The Dome of the Rock as Palimpsest," 56.

71 Grabar, *Shape of the Holy*, 171-2; Necipoğlu, "The Dome of the Rock as Palimpsest," 56.

72 Myriam Rosen-Ayalon, "Art and Architecture in Ayyubid Jerusalem," *Israel Exploration Journal* 40 (1990), 305-14; Pringle, *The City of Jerusalem*, 183, 413.

73 Finbarr Barry Flood, "Umayyad Survivals and Mamluk Revivals: Qalawunid Architecture and the Great Mosque of Damascus," *Muqarnas* 14 (1997), 57-79.

74 Michael H. Burgoyne *Mamluk Jerusalem: An Architectural Study* (London: Scorpion Publishing, 1987), 243-5.

75 Necipoğlu, "The Dome of the Rock as Palimpsest," 57-61.

76 Finbarr Barry Flood, "The Ottoman windows in the Dome of the Rock," in *Ottoman Jerusalem: The Living City*, eds. Sylvia Aud and Robert Hillenbrand (London: Altajir World of Islam Trust, 2000), 1: 431-63; Necipoğlu, "The Dome of the Rock as Palimpsest," 60, 70.

77 Robert Hillenbrand, *The Architecture of Ottoman Jerusalem: An Introduction* (London: Altajir World of Islam Trust, 2002), 17; Necipoğlu, "The Dome of the Rock as Palimpsest," 61.

78 Hillenbrand, *The Architecture of Ottoman Jerusalem*, 19.

79 Necipoğlu, "The Dome of the Rock as Palimpsest," 62-5.

80 Ibid., 62-4.

81 Ibid., 69-71.

82 Ibid., 71-2.

83 Colin Morris, *The Sepulcher of Christ and the Medieval West: From the Beginning to 1600* (Oxford: Oxford University Press, 2005), 366.

84 Necipoğlu, "The Dome of the Rock as Palimpsest," 68.

85 Ibid., 57-60, 68.

86 Grabar, *The Dome of the Rock*, 200.

87 Daniel B. Monk, *An Aesthetic Occupation: The Immediacy of Architecture and the Palestine Conflict* (Durham, NC: Duke University Press, 2002); Grabar, *The Dome of the Rock*, 72,192-3.

88 K. A. C. Creswell, *The Origin of the Plan of the Dome of the Rock* (London: Issued by the Council, 1924), idem, *Early Muslim Architecture* (Oxford: Clarendon Press, 1969).

89 Vared Shalev-Hurvitz, *Holy Sites Encircled: The Early Byzantine Concentric Churches of Jerusalem* (Oxford: Oxford University Press, 2015); Kathryn Blair Moore, *The Architecture of the Christian Holy Land: Repetion from Late Antiquity through the Renaissance* (Cambridge, UK: Cambridge University Press, 2017); Robin Griffith-Jones and Eric Fernie, *Tomb and Temple: Reimagining the Sacred Buildings of Jerusalem* (Woodbridge: Boydell Press, 2018); Jame Lara, *City, Temple, Stage: Eschatological Architecture and Liturgical Theatrics in New Spain* (Notre Dame: University of Notre Dame Press, 2004); Bianca Kühnel, "Migrations of a Building: The Dome of the Rock in Jewish Synagogue Architecture," in *Synergies in Visual Culture = Bildkulturen Im Dialog: Festschrift Für Gerhard Wolf*, eds. Gerhard Wolf, Manuela De Giorgi, Annette Hoffmann, and Nicola Suthor (Munich: Wilhelm Fink Verlag, 2013), 123-38.

90 Hana Taragan, "The Image of the Dome of the Rock in Cairene Mamluk Architecture," in *The Real and Ideal Jerusalem*, 453-9; Gülru Necipoğlu, *The Age of Sinan: Architectural Culture in the Ottoman Empire, 1539-1588* (London: Reaktion, 2005); Ebba Koch, *The Complete Taj Mahal: And the Riverfront Gardens of Agra* (London: Thames & Hudson, 2006).

91 Christiane Gruber, "Jerusalem in the visual propaganda of post-revolutionary Iran," in *Jerusalem: Idea and Reality*, eds. Tamar Mayer and Suleiman Ali Mourad (London: Routledge, 2008), 177-82 (168-97); "Haram al-Sharif," in *The Encyclopedia of the Arab-Israeli conflict: a political, social, and military history*, ed. Spencer C. Tucker (Santa Barbara, CA: ABC-CLIO, 2008), 423 (423-4).

The Great Mosque of Damascus through the Medieval Period

MATTIA GUIDETTI

1 Great Mosque, Damascus, 705/6–715, the late medieval south-eastern minaret (called "Minaret of Jesus").
Photo: Mattia Guidetti

Established in the early eighth century, under the Umayyad caliph al-Walid (r. 705–15), the congregational mosque of Damascus was one of the most monumental places of prayer first built by Islam. The mosque, lavishly decorated with marble and wall mosaics, replaced an earlier church and became at the time of its construction the mosque of the capital of the Umayyad caliphate, an empire stretching from the Indus River to southern Spain. In medieval literature the Great Mosque of Damascus was often listed amongst the holiest sites of Islam together with the mosques of Mecca and Medina and the religious cluster in Jerusalem consisting of the Dome of the Rock and the Aqsa Mosque. Despite several transformations the Great Mosque of Damascus still maintains certain features of the original building, such as the organization of the prayer hall and a portion of the mosaics.

The mosque soon became an *exemplum*: many new constructions were modeled on the Great Mosque of Damascus, such as the great mosques in Aleppo and Harran, the eleventh-century mosque in Diyarbakir built by the same Seljuk restorer of the mosque in Damascus, and the great mosque of Derbent located in the Caucasian region of Dagestan. Outside the eastern Mediterranean region its influence reached late-eighth-century Umayyad Cordoba, inspiring both the two-tiered elevation and the alternation of piers and columns in the courtyard added in the tenth century.[1]

DESCRIPTION OF THE MOSQUE: ARCHITECTURE

The mosque adhered to and adapted a pre-existing hypostyle model and was composed of a courtyard (*sahn*) and a prayer hall (*masjid*). The percentage occupied by the prayer hall is around 35% of the total area, which represents about the average ratio of courtyard to prayer hall found in early mosques (Fig. 2).[2] The prayer hall is a three-aisled basilica divided into two halves by the central transept. The aisles run parallel to the *qibla* wall on an east-to-west axis and are composed of a

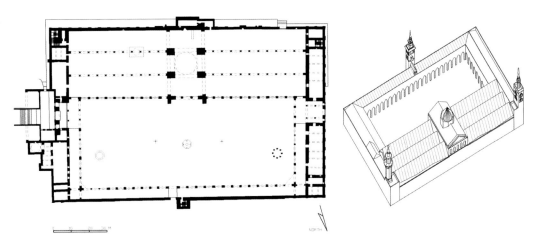

2 Great Mosque, Damascus, 705/6–715, plan and axonometric.
Drawing: © Nasser Rabbat / Aga Khan Program for Islamic Architecture, MIT.

succession of arcades resting on columns but springing from piers at the extremities. Each aisle is today covered by a gable roof resting on the upper tier of the arcades, which presents two small arches for each arcade below. These small arches correspond to windows on both outer walls, allowing the light to penetrate the prayer hall (Fig. 3). The transept, running north to south, is composed of three higher and larger arcades supported by pillars. The arcades are surmounted by three corresponding arched windows. The central bay is covered by a dome, known as the Dome of the Eagle; although the current dome is modern, in the very early period its position was probably occupied by a wooden one; it is also possible that all three bays were domed (Fig. 4).[3]

Because the three bays were rectangular in shape in order to be covered by a dome they had to be made square. During the first phase of construction the square was probably obtained through the use of crossbeams. When, following a fire (1069), a new stone dome on squinches was rebuilt (c. 1082), in order to accommodate the rectangularity of the bay four T-shaped central pillars were added to the four piers, which thereby squared the space to be covered by the dome and carried new stone transverse arches.[4]

The most detailed description of the medieval dome is given by twelfth-century traveler Ibn Jubayr, in an eyewitness account of his visit to the mosque in August 1184:

3 Great Mosque, Damascus, 705/6–715, interior of the prayer hall (view from the eastern side).
Photo: Mattia Guidetti

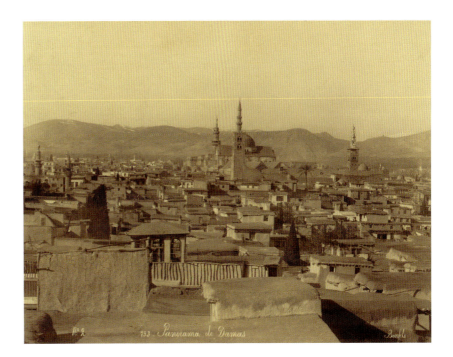

4 Great Mosque, Damascus, 705/6–715, view from south-east, c. 1870.
Photo: Maison Bonfils. Library of Congress

We ascended thereto, with a number of friends, at early dawn.... Then we hastened on to the entrance into the interior of the dome, passing through one of the grated windows which open in the lead-work; and before us was a wondrous sight. We passed on over the planking of great wood beams which go all round the inner and smaller dome, which is inside the outer leaden dome, as aforesaid, and there are here two arched windows, through which you look down into the mosque below. From here the men who are down in the mosque look as though they were small children."[5]

Notable components of the mosque's architecture were the *mihrab*s found on the southern, or *qibla*, wall. The most important of these was the *mihrab* located on the eastern side of the *qibla* wall, because it occupied the exact site of the very first Muslim foundation on the same site. A second *mihrab* was added at the end of the transept, emphasizing its longitudinal axis. Another *mihrab* was later carved into the western side of the *qibla* wall to provide symmetry. In approximately 715, a *maqsura* (a small enclosure) was constructed in front of the *mihrab* in the transept for the specific use of the caliph and his most elite courtiers during prayers. Slightly east of the *maqsura*, between two aisles, stood a column marking the spot where relics of St. John were buried after their discovery. This column was distinguished by a capital carved in the shape of a basket.[6]

The courtyard is composed of porticoes on three sides (Fig. 5). The portico façades display a refined symmetry and are composed of arcades in two tiers, surmounted by a timber ceiling roofed with sheets of lead. On the southern side of the courtyard are the entrances to the prayer hall. Because in the medieval period each arcade was not closed with a wooden door (as it is today) but only with curtains of cloth, it is easy to imagine the original coherence of all four sides of the courtyard.[7] The southern courtyard face is also characterized by the outer façade of the transept, entered through three arcades divided by two columns surmounted by three windows, which illuminate the interior of the prayer hall. This composition, framed by an arch, is flanked by two projecting buttresses that brace the transept. A triangular gable, pierced by a central arched window flanked by two circular bull's-eye openings, covers the transept (Fig. 6).

According to textual sources, since the early Abbasid time (late eighth century), the large rectangular courtyard has contained an octagonal domed structure known as the "dome of the treasure" (see Fig. 5). Located on the western side, this is an octagonal chamber supported by eight

5 Great Mosque, Damascus, 705/6–715, the Dome of the Treasure and the north-western portico of the courtyard.
Photo: Mattia Guidetti

THE GREAT MOSQUE OF DAMASCUS 127

6 Great Mosque, Damascus, 705/6–715, the façade of the transept (mid-twentieth century).
Photo: Matson Photo Service. Library of Congress

columns topped by Corinthian capitals and a classical entablature, most probably recycled from the Pagan temple which stood earlier on the same site. It was used in order to preserve the valuable objects belonging to the mosque, including precious manuscripts.[8] It is likely that a simple basin was once accommodated beneath the chamber, which was perhaps used for ablutions before a new fountain was built. Another domed structure, a type of pavilion, was erected in modern times on the opposite side of the courtyard, while the modern fountain for the ablutions was added in the late Ottoman period.

On the same site where the Great Mosque was established in 705-6, once stood the Semitic temple of the city. Under the Romans the temple was refurbished and rededicated from the Semitic god Hadad to the Latin cognate Jupiter Dolichenus. The cella was surrounded by two precincts; the inner one became the perimeter of the area of a church during the Byzantine period and of the mosque later under Islam.[9]

Before building the Great Mosque, the area within the inner *temenos* was emptied and only the walls of the precinct were maintained, with minimal changes. The Roman tripartite southern gate, once the entrance to the *temenos* and the access to the great church complex, was blocked so that it could serve as the center of the *qibla* wall (Fig. 7). A new door, called Bab al-Ziyada (meaning door of the "addition," because it gave access to a space separating the mosque from the profane surrounding city) was constructed near the southwestern corner. The existing Roman doors remained in use on the other three sides. The walls of the precinct, punctuated by a tower at each of the four corners, were built in fine masonry and were originally enlivened by a series of slightly projecting pilasters spaced around 3.5 meters apart.[10] In al-Walid's time only the western towers were preserved, while the northern ones were demolished because of their poor condition. Sometime before the tenth century, a minaret was erected over the entrance in the center of the northern wall, which was replaced with a second minaret at the end of the twelfth century.

7 Great Mosque, Damascus, 705/6–715, Roman gate to *temenos* incorporated into southern *qibla* wall.
Photo: Mattia Guidetti

8 View of the Mausoleum of Salah al-Din, Damascus, late twelfth century (late nineteenth century view).
Photo: Félix Bonfils. Library of Congress

With regard to the plan of the mosque, the medieval Damascene historian Ibn 'Asakir relates that the Great Mosque did not have a preliminary model.[11] Indeed, whereas elements such as the courtyard and the aisled prayer hall directed toward Mecca were directly inspired by the very first architectural traditions emerging after the Prophet Muhammad's house / mosque in Medina, the mosque in Damascus was inserted into a pre-existing precinct consisting of the massive walls of the Roman inner *temenos*. This is the reason for having the prayer hall made of three long aisles parallel to the *qibla* wall: it was the most logical expedient to exploit the long southern wall standing on the site.[12]

From its earliest days, the Great Mosque was linked to its architectural surroundings. In the eighth century the most important connection was to the caliph's residence, known as "the green dome," a palace located to the south of the *qibla* wall. Through a monumental path, partially arranged according to pre-existing structures (such as colonnades and a tetrapylon), mosque and palace were connected to facilitate and emphasize the movement of the caliph from his residence to the *maqsura* within the mosque where he led the prayers.[13] The dialogue between the mosque and its surroundings (and between the religious aura of the mosque and the secular elite ruling the city) would be further emphasized in

the medieval period through the construction of the Ayyubid ruler Salah al-Dın's tomb (late twelfth century) outside of the northern entrance to the mosque, and later through the placement of Mamluk Sultan Baybars' tomb (late thirteenth century) within the nearby Madrasa al-Zahiriyya (Fig. 8). The latter was decorated with a stylized band of mosaics reminiscent of those within the Umayyad foundation (Fig. 9). Also present since the eighth century was a mechanical clock mounted on the southern door of the mosque, which was substituted with a new one on the western door under the Ayyubid sultan Nur al-Din (d. 1174). These clocks, besides keeping the time of prayer, served as symbols of the technological knowledge of the rulers, and, in combination with other elements of the mosque, also alluded to other secular powers, mainly the Byzantine Empire, which likewise had access to and displayed extremely expensive courtly features.[14]

Other features of the Great Mosque have been linked to specific non-Islamic models. For example, Creswell argued that the façade of the transept intentionally evoked the late-antique palatial Byzantine tradition, best expressed in the Chalke façade at Constantinople, and later copied in the Palace of Theodoric at Ravenna, where it also

9 Madrasa al-Zahiriyya, Damascus, late thirteenth century, detail of the mosaic frieze in Baybars' tomb within the *madrasa*.
Photo: Mattia Guidetti

THE GREAT MOSQUE OF DAMASCUS 129

appears depicted in the mosaics of Sant'Apollinare Nuovo (Fig. 10).[15] Flood has convincingly emphasized the similarities between the "palace plus mosque" complex in Damascus and the "palace plus church" complex in Constantinople built in the sixth century. The disposition of the two buildings and the creation of a processional path between them similarly composed of colonnades, tetrapylon, monumental gates, and technological devices such as the horologia, made the two complexes intriguingly resembling one to the other.[16]

During the medieval period the mosque was damaged and underwent a series of alterations. One of the most significant events was a fire in the year 1069, followed by extensive reconstructions overseen by the Seljuk prince Tutush in the name of the sultan Malik-Shah. In 1270 Baybars ordered a further restoration: the mosaics and several marble slabs were repaired, the columns cleaned, and the capitals re-gilded.[17] More recently, in 1893 a great fire almost ruined the entire prayer hall, which was rebuilt in the following years, under the patronage of the sultan 'Abd al-Hamid by the French architect Paul Apéry.[18]

Successive phases of restoration also had an impact on the minarets. The northern one, known as the "Minaret of the Bride," was the only existing minaret before the Middle Ages and was destroyed and rebuilt into its current form between 1174 and 1184. The ancient towers of the *temenos* on the southern side of the building remained in place throughout the majority of the medieval period and were only crowned by minarets later. The southeastern minaret, known as the Minaret of Jesus, was burnt and reconstructed several times until the current structure was built around 1340 (Fig. 1). The southwestern one, simply called the Western Minaret, was affected by a similar series of fires and reconstructions and was finally built in its current form around 1488 under the Mamluks.[19]

THE MOSQUE'S FOUNDATION

An inscription, first reported in the tenth-century by al-Mas'udi,[20] included the date 705–6, connecting the foundation to the Umayyad caliph al-Walid. This inscription, located in the prayer hall, stated that the mosque's construction followed the destruction of a church that had previously occupied the same site. Various sources reveal that workers were brought to Damascus from as far as Egypt, clarify the amount of revenues used to finance the building and state that the construction process took 7–10 years. For this reason, it is likely that the initial construction of the mosque occurred between 705–6 and 715.[21]

These references to the mosque's foundation are particularly important in order to establish the relationship between al-Walid's mosque and pre-existing buildings on the same site. At the time of the conquest, in 634, the area of the *temenos* was occupied by the church consecrated to St. John the Baptist. The church was either a new building or the

10 Church of Sant'Apollinare Nuovo, Ravenna, sixth century, mosaic panel depicting the palace of Theodoric.
Photo: Richard Etlin

cella of the Roman temple converted to a Christian use. Soon after the conquest, the Muslims used a small portion of the vast enclosure as the place for their first place of prayer. This is probably the building described by the Latin Christian pilgrim Arculf (c. 670) as the "the church of the infidels belonging to the Saracens."[22]

It follows that from 634 to 705–6, when the new mosque was constructed, the first mosque was a separate place, distinct from the church of the Christians yet located directly next to it, suggesting a cohabitation of the two communities within the same urban area (Fig. 5).[23] The best description of this early period is offered by the late medieval historian Ibn Shakir (d. 1363), who, relying on the authority of the earlier Ibn 'Asakir (d. 1176), states that after the conquest:

> Muslims and Christians entered the building by the same doorway, which was that of the original temple placed on the south side where now stands the great *mihrab*. The Christians then turned to the West, towards their church, and the Muslims to the right to reach their mosque.[24]

In time, with the growth of Muslim population in Damascus and the consolidation of the Muslim authority in the area, the new rulers began to pressure the local Christian community in order to obtain the property of the whole precinct, offering money or the use of other former Christian properties now under Muslim control. Once he obtained the site, al-Walid opted for a *tabula rasa*: he destroyed the church and the early mosque and ordered the construction of the Great Mosque of Damascus.[25]

THE DECORATIVE PROGRAM OF THE GREAT MOSQUE

Throughout the mosque, the decorative apparatus of the walls was organized according to a tripartite pattern. In the courtyard from the level of the pavement to a height of approximately five meters, the walls were covered with book-matched quartered marble (Fig. 11). The thin slabs were juxtaposed in an

11 Great Mosque, Damascus, 705/6–715, marble veneers decoration, eastern portico of the courtyard.
Photo: Mattia Guidetti

12 Great Mosque, Damascus, 705/6–715, Roman capital reused in the early Abbasid Dome of the Treasure.
Photo: Mattia Guidetti

attempt to achieve a uniformly symmetrical effect, much appreciated in the enthusiastic tenth-century description by al-Muqaddasi: "but one of the most wonderful sights worthy of remark is verily the setting of the various colored marbles, and how the veining in each follows from that of its neighbor".[26] The middle band, approximately two meters high, is composed of other marble slabs, alternating with small pilasters and windows enclosed by marble grilles that were decorated with geometrical patterns. Above this band and extending to the roof stretched an expanse of mosaic decoration depicting non-figurative subjects such as nature-derived and architectural elements. In certain locations throughout the courtyard, a narrow epigraphic frieze was added at the top of the first band. This pattern was also followed within the prayer hall, with the difference that the intermediary band was composed of a narrow carved marble frieze decorated with gilded vine and acanthus scrolls bearing grapes. Described as the vine (*al-karma*) by several medieval authors, this was among the most precious decorative elements of the mosque. Because of the severe fire of 1893, the decoration of the prayer hall is known only through descriptions, paintings, and photographs taken prior to this date.[27]

Marble was also used extensively in the choice of columns, capitals, and in the paved courtyard, renovated many times after the foundation of the mosque. Descriptions dating from before 1893 show how the re-used Corinthian capitals chosen for the prayer hall often did not match the supporting circular columns. Capitals were also frequently gilded. As for the provenance of columns and capitals, most of them were likely found in situ among the remains of Roman and Byzantine buildings. It has been noted, for instance, that the smaller capitals used in the second tier of the western side of the courtyard are of Byzantine origins, whereas those of the first tier are Roman (Fig. 12).[28] The textual sources claim that specific columns were also transported from the Rotunda of St. Mary in Antioch at the time of the construction sponsored by al-Walid,[29] and stress the value of the two green marble columns added to the pillars supporting the transept dome, bought by al-Walid from Harb b. Khalid b. Yazid b. Mu'awiya for 1500 dinars each.[30]

The mosaic decoration of the Great Mosque has received the most attention from scholars. A rough estimate calculates that the area covered by the mosaics was originally approximately 4000 m². They formed the upper band of the decoration in the open galleries of the courtyard and in the prayer hall. Furthermore, mosaics described by al-Muqaddasi also decorated the façades of the northern minaret, the walls of the octagonal Dome of the Treasure, and the large outer façade of the transept. The largest surviving portion, located in the western gallery of the courtyard, depicts a succession of building clusters alternating with tall cypresses overlooking a rushing river. Geometrical frames surround the mosaics; they do not present any animated subject and carry a few inscriptions, mostly recalling the subsequent interventions of restoration (Fig. 13).

Modern scholars have interpreted the mosaics in two principal ways, based on selected passages by medieval authors. The first interpretation considers the mosaics to be representative of Paradise,[31] while the second proposes that they reflect the earthly possessions of the caliph.[32] Arguing that the mosaics and the vine in the prayer hall contain references both to this world and the next, Flood introduces a ninth-century eschatological text with a description of Paradise that has many similarities to the the still-visible portion of the mosaics.[33]

Parallels between single elements of the mosaic program and those of other significant

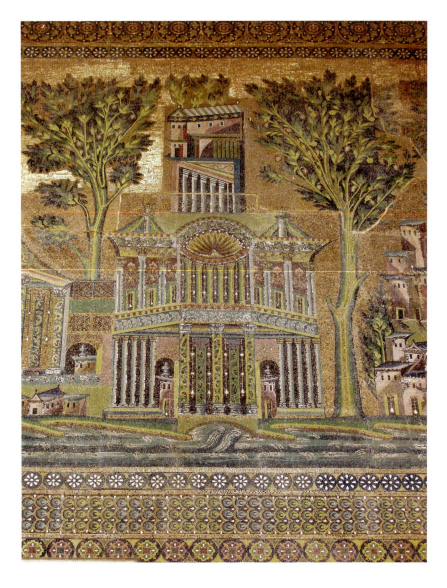

13 Great Mosque, Damascus, 705/6–715, detail of the so-called "Barada panel" mosaic, western side of the courtyard.
Photo: Mattia Guidetti

monuments have been suggested by many scholars. The strongest aesthetic parallels involve the representation of cities and architecture in various late antique church mosaics, and the similar location of vine friezes in some Constantinopolitan and Byzantine Syrian churches.[34] Yet, it is also possible to find compelling similarities to the decorative program as a whole. See, for instance, the late antique monastic church of Mar Gabriel in the Tur 'Abdin, founded by Anastasios in 512. The polychrome *opus sectile* pavement, marble slabs on the lower walls and the aniconic mosaic band on the upper walls, extending to the ceilings and the vaults, demonstrate how the artistic language typifying the local late antique churches was still employed under the Umayyads.[35]

Analysis carried out by De Lorey and Van Berchem allow us to discern the techniques used to produce the mosaics. First a thin layer of mortar made of lime and dry straw was applied to the surface of the masonry to mask any irregularities; this was followed by the application of a thinner and softer mortar layer composed of lime and sand. Prior to the insertion of the glass tesserae, a draft of the composition was drawn on the wall surface with black and red ink. The tesserae included a wide range of colors and relative shades: gold enamel, blue, green, black, silver enamel, and red. In some spots the tesserae were retouched in paint. Some of the gold tesserae used for the background were inserted at an angle so to reflect light creating a glittering effect. It appears that many different mosaicists were at work in the Great Mosque. All these were well-established features in the late antique Mediterranean region, especially in those areas where Byzantine elites devoted resources to religious buildings (Fig. 14).[36]

Within the prayer hall, owing principally to the destruction caused by the fire of 1893, only small portions of the original mosaic decorations are visible: these can be seen on the inner façade of the transept and on the northern sides of the two northern pillars supporting the transept dome.[37] An important element noticeable in the overall organization of the decoration is the desire to collect heterogeneous material from different

14 Great Mosque, Damascus, 705/6–715, mosaic decoration on the *intrados* of one arcade of the portico.
Photo: Mattia Guidetti

sources. What, at first glance, might be considered a fortuitous assemblage of diverse and unconnected elements, more likely reflects an international aesthetic strategy privileging the concept of variety over unity. Notions such as polychromatism and polymateriality consitute the main criteria in the aesthetic choices during the early Middle Ages throughout all the Mediterranean world as part of the development of late antique artistic traditions.[38] Though common during late antiquity, such an aesthetic approach privileging glittering materials and variform decorative surfaces was expanded by early Muslims. One of the most innovative features is the use of wall mosaics also on exterior surfaces, something occurring both in the Great Mosque of Damascus and the Dome of the Rock in Jerusalem. The addition of glass and gold tesserae on areas directly hit by the sun created resplendent surfaces reflecting and amplifying the light around and within these buildings.

THE GREAT MOSQUE AS A SOCIAL AND RELIGIOUS SPACE

The Great Mosque should be understood as an institution equipped with economic resources that was intended for religious and political purposes. Economic resources were necessary for the additions to the mosque and its preservation, as well as for the funding of the majority of the employees who, according to a well-established hierarchy, were in charge of carrying out religious tasks within it. These economic resources were guaranteed by a permanent endowment (*waqf*) and eventually augmented by later donations. The endowment and the donations were partly monetary and partly composed of commercial and tax incomes, such as shops and entire villages, legally defined as properties of the "*waqf* of the mosque."

Some medieval sources provide glimpses on the religious and social life of the mosque. One example can be found in the autobiography of 'Abd al-Latif (d. 1232) in which he notes that Sultan Salah al-Din allocated thirty dinars per month to allow him to teach in the Great Mosque of Damascus; this was then raised to one hundred

dinars by the ruler's sons.[39] A later source describes the establishment of a new *waqf* for the mosque, involving the donation of a Quran made by a famous calligrapher, coupled with a reader and a servant.[40] Al-'Ilmawi's *Description of Damascus* (early sixteenth century) contains an account of a budget revision of the mosque by a delegate of the Mamluk sultan. Each employee falls within a category listed in a register, among which are included: the superintendent, land agents (those in charge of the maintenance of the mosque as a building), the readers of the Quran, the *muezzins*, the readers of the Hadiths, watchmen, and the men in charge of preparing the rugs for prayers.[41]

Similarly, the organization of the mosque as a place of prayer was also carefully structured. By the ninth century, all four of the principal Islamic theological schools – Hanafi, Maliki, Shafi'i, and Hanbali – were operative within the mosque, and each of these was assigned a *mihrab*, either on the *qibla* wall or between the arcades, along with the surrounding area, which was employed for pedagogical purposes. In addition to a preacher for congregational prayers, each theological school also had its own *imam*, and this was also true of the different shrines (*mashhad*s) and sanctuaries (*zawiya*s) located throughout the mosque. In fact, like Christian great churches, the Great Mosque is a polycentric sacred building, housing a plurality of religious sites of interest.

Indeed, the Islamization of the ancient *temenos* started as soon as the mosque was built, with both the updating of the Biblical heritage associated with the site and the affiliation of early Muslim characters with the mosque, so that in several medieval texts listing the "virtues" and "excellences" of Syria, the Great Mosque of Damascus plays a prominent role.[42] According to al-Harawi (d. 1215), within the Great Mosque were located the sanctuary of the Quranic figure al-Khidr (said to have been located in front of the central *mihrab* in the prayer hall); the tomb of the Quranic prophet Hud (along the *qibla* wall); the underground site where the head of St. John the Baptist, son of Zachariah, was preserved (probably where the modern aedicule stands today) (see the cenotaph in Fig. 3). Also historical figures of early Islam were commemorated within the mosque: this is the case of the place where 'Umar b. al-Khattab, companion of the Prophet and second caliph of Islam after Abu Bakr (r. 634–644), was said to have performed a prayer (close to Bab Jayrun); the shrine of 'Ali, Muhammad's cousin and son-in-law (in the eastern section of the prayer hall); the shrine of 'Ali's son al-Husayn and Muhammad's great-grandson Zayn al-'Abidin (located in the rectangular hall between the eastern open gallery and the outer wall and marking the place where the head of al-Husayn was possibly deposited); and, among several others things, a piece of the Muslim conqueror Khalid b. al-Walid's lance (mounted on the Bab al-Ziyada). All these places were marked by fixed or movable furniture and were provided with custodians, servants, and men of religion charged with facilitating the execution of religious duties by worshipers and pilgrims.[43]

Not only cenotaphs, relics, and memorials attracted pilgrims and worshippers, but also the presence of pious men working in or even inhabiting the mosque. Indeed, while describing the minarets, Ibn Jubayr in 1184 mentions the presence of ascetics living in dwellings on the upper floors of the towers.[44] This is reminiscent of the account of the destruction of the church in 705–6 under al-Walid, when the caliph supposedly quarreled with a hermit monk who was living in one of the corner-towers of the ancient *temenos*.[45] More broadly, this correspondence underlines the intricate levels of continuity and discontinuity, already noted in the act of foundation, the preservation of John the Baptist's shrine, and the architectural and decorative features, that characterize the Great Mosque of Damascus as part of the process of transformation and Islamization of the sacred landscape in Syria between Late Antiquity and the Middle Ages.

MATTIA GUIDETTI is an assistant professor in the history of Islamic art at the University of Bologna. He held research and teaching positions at Harvard University, the Kunsthistorisches Institut of Florence, the University of Edinburgh, and Vienna University. He published the volume *In the shadow of the church: the building of mosques in early medieval Syria* (Brill, 2017). Current research projects include the reception of Ottoman artefacts in early modern Italy and Islamic objects in Bologna collections.

SUGGESTIONS FOR FURTHER READING

Creswell, Keppel A.C. *Early Muslim Architecture*, 2 vols (1932; Oxford: Clarendon Press, 1969 rev. ed.).

Flood, Finbarr B. *The Great Mosque of Damascus. Studies on the Makings of an Umayyad Visual Culture* (Boston: Brill, 2001).

Grabar, Oleg. "La grande mosquée de Damas et les origines architecturales de la mosque," in *Synthronon: art et archéologie de la fin de l'antiquité et du Moyen Age*, ed. A. Grabar, (Paris: Klincksieck, 1968), 107–14.

Lohuizen-Mulder, Mab van. "The Mosaics in the Great Mosque at Damascus: a Vision of Beauty," *BABesch* 70 (1995), 193–213.

Rabbat, Nasser. "The Dialogic Dimension of Umayyad Art," *Res: Anthropology and Aesthetics* 43 (2003), 79–94.

NOTES

1 Keppel A.C. Creswell, *A Short Account of Early Muslim Architecture* (Aldershot: Scholar Press, 1989), 72–3; Finbarr B. Flood, "Umayyad Survivals and Mamluk Revivals: Qalawunid Architecture and the Great Mosque of Damascus," *Muqarnas* 14 (1997), 57–79.

2 Alan Walmsley and Kristoffer Damgaard, "The Umayyad Congregational Mosque of Jarash in Jordan and its Relationship to Early Mosques," *Antiquity* 79 (2005), 375–6 and fig. 9.

3 For the description of the three domes by Ibn Jubayr, see Guy Le Strange, *Palestine under the Moslems. A Description of Syria and the Holy Land. From A.D. 650 to 1500* (Cambridge, Mass.: The Riverside Press, 1907), 244.

4 Keppel A.C. Creswell, *Early Muslim Architecture*, 2 vols. (1932; Oxford: Clarendon Press, 1969 2nd ed.), 1: 166–7.

5 Ibn Jubayr's *Rihla* as translated in Guy Le Strange, *Palestine under the Moslems*, 256–7.

6 Nancy A. Khalek, *Damascus after the Muslim Conquest: Text and Image in Early Islam* (Oxford: Oxford University Press, 2011), 111–6.

7 For the description of the curtains hung in the mosque of Damascus in al-ʿIlmawi's treatise, see Henri Sauvaire, "Description de Damas," *Journal Asiatique* 7 (1896), 423 (409–484).

8 Arianna D'Ottone and Paolo Radiciotti, "I frammenti della Qubbat al-khazna di Damasco. Storia di una scoperta sottovalutata," *Nea Rhome. Rivista di ricerche bizantinistiche* 5 (2008), 45–74.

9 René Dussaud, "Le temple de Jupiter Damascénien et ses transformations aux époques chrétienne et musulmane," *Syria* 3 (1922), 219–50.

10 Carl Watzinger and Karl Wulzinger, *Damaskus, die antike Stadt* (Berlin: Vereinigung Wissenschaftlicher Verleger, 1921); Dussaud, "Le temple de Jupiter Damascénien."

11 Ibn ʿAsakir, *La description de Damas d'Ibn ʿAsakir*, trans. Nikita Elisséeff (Damas: Institut Français de Damas, 1959), 21, 23.

12 The most complete and up-to-date essay on the creation of the mosque as an architectural notion is Jeremy Johns, "The 'House of the Prophet' and the Concept of the Mosque," in *Bayt al-Maqdis. Jerusalem and Early Islam*, ed. Jeremy Johns (Oxford: Oxford University Press, 1999), 59–112.

13 The reconstruction of such a relation between the palace and the mosque in early Islamic time is offered by Finbarr B. Flood, *The Great Mosque of Damascus. Studies on the Makings of an Umayyad Visual Culture* (Boston: Brill, 2001), 139–83.

14 Flood, *The Great Mosque of Damascus*, 114–38.

15 Creswell, *Early Muslim Architecture*, 1:197–8.

16 Flood, *The Great Mosque of Damascus*, 147–72.

17 Marguerite van Berchem, "The Mosaics of the Great Mosque of the Umayyads in Damascus," in Creswell, *Early Muslim Architecture*, 1:331, 346, 348–52 (323–72).

18 The most detailed list of changes to the structure of the mosque that occurred between 705 and 1930 appears in Jean Sauvaget, *Les monuments historiques de Damas* (Beirut: Imprimerie catholique, 1932), 15–8. On the fire of 1893 and the reopening of the mosque in 1902 as part of a general process of refurbishment of the old town and modernization of Damascus, see Leila Hudson, *Transforming Damascus. Space and Modernity in an Islamic City* (London: Tauris Academic Studies, 2008), 104, 122–6. Details on the archaeological survey carried out in the 40's and early 60's appear in Adnan Bounni, "Du temple païen à la mosque. Note préliminaire sur le cas de la mosque omeyyade de Damas," in *Antigüedad y cristianismo: monografías históricas sobre la Antigüedad tardía* 21 (2004), 595–605. On the most recent refurbishment, see Hassan Z. al-Sawwaf, *al-JamʿI al-Umawi: Durrat Dimashq*, 2 vols. (Damascus: Dar Ghar Hira', 2008), 2:935–60.

19 Sauvaget, *Les monuments historiques de Damas*, 15–8.

20 Al-Masʿudi, *Kitab muruj al-dhahab wa-maʿadin al-jawhar*, ed. Barbier de Meynard and Pavet de Courteille, 5 vols. (Beirut: al-Jamiʿa al-lubnaniya, 1966–79), 5: 362–3.

21 Harold I. Bell, "Translations of the Greek Aphrodito Papyri in the British Museum," *Der Islam* 2 (1911): 269–83, 372–84; 3 (1912): 132–40, 369–73; Creswell, *Early Muslim Architecture*, 1:153–4.

22 Adamnanus, "Arculfi relatio de locis sanctis scripta ab adamnano," in *Itinera Hierosomolytana et Descriptiones Terrae Sanctae Bellis Sacris Anteriora*, eds. Titus Tobler and Augustus Molinier (Geneva: J.-G. Fick, 1879), 186.

23 Creswell, *Early Muslim Architecture*, 1:187–91, fig. 99.

24 As quoted in ibid., 1:194.

25 The whole process is extensively described by al-Baladhuri: *Kitab futuh al-buldan*, ed. M. J. De Goeje (Leiden: Brill, 1968), 125–6.

26 As quoted in Le Strange, *Palestine under the Moslems*, 228.

27 Flood, *The Great Mosque of Damascus*, 57–113.

28 Marina Falla Castelfranchi, "Alcune osservazioni sulle relazioni artistiche tra Omayyadi e Bisanzio," in *Medioevo. Il tempo degli antichi*, ed. A. C. Quintavalle (Milan: Electa, 2006), 167–79.

29 al-Masʿudi, *Kitab muruj al-dhahab*, 3: 339.

30 Ibn Kathir, *Al-bidaya wa-l-nihaya*, eds. 'A. M. Mu'awwad et al., 15 vols. (Beirut: Dar al-Kutub al-'Ilmiyya, 1994), 9:148. On the purchase of material for the Great Mosque, see Ibn Sasra, *Al-durra al-mukhtiy'a fi al-dawla al-Zahiriya*, ed. and trans. W.M. Brinner, 2 vols. (Berkeley: University of California Press, 1963), 2:119.

31 Barbara Finster, "Die Mosaiken in der Umayyadenmoschee von Damaskus," *Kunst des Orients* 7.2 (1970), 118–21 (83–141); Klaus Brisch, "Observations on the Iconography of the Mosaics in the Great Mosque at Damascus," in *Content and Context of Visual Arts in the Islamic World*, ed. Priscilla Soucek (University Park, Pa.: Pennsylvania State University Press, 1988), 131–37; Mab van Lohuizen-Mulder, "The Mosaics in the Great Mosque at Damascus: a Vision of Beauty," *Babesch* 70 (1995), 207–9 (193–213).

32 Richard Ettinghausen Richard and Oleg Grabar, *The Art and Architecture of Islam: 650-1250* (Harmondsworth: Penguin Books, 1987), 44; Robert Hillenbrand, *Islamic Architecture: Form, Function and Meaning* (Edinburgh: Edinburgh University Press, 1994), 72; Nasser Rabbat, "The Dialogic Dimension in Umayyad art," *Res: Anthropology and Aesthetics* 43 (2003), 90 (78–94).

33 Flood, *The Great Mosque of Damascus*, 28–42, 57; Alain George has also shown how in the mosaic program of both the Dome of the Rock and the Great Mosque of Damascus the themes of paradise and empire are deeply intertwined; "Paradise or Empire? On a Paradox of Umayyad Art," in *Power, Patronage and Memory in Early Islam: Perspectives on Umayyad Elites*, eds. Alain George and Andrew Marsham (Oxford: Oxford University Press, 2018, 52–60).

34 See Glenn W. Bowersock, *Mosaics as History: The Near East from Late Antiquity to Islam* (Cambridge: The Belknap Press of Harvard University Press, 2006), 80–1; Flood, *The Great Mosque of Damascus*, 15–47, 68–87.

35 Gertrude Bell, *The Churches and Monasteries of the Tur 'Abdin*, ed. Marlia Mundell Mango (London: The Pindar Press, 1982), viii–x.

36 Eustache De Lorey, "Les mosaïques de la mosquée des Omeyyades à Damas," *Syria* 12 (1931), 326–49 ; Van Berchem, "The Mosaics of the Great Mosque," 364–6.

37 Eustache De Lorey, "Les mosaïques de la mosquée."

38 Beat Brenk, "Spolia from Constantine to Charlemagne: Aesthetics versus Ideology," *Dumbarton Oaks Papers* 41 (1987), 103–9; Michelangelo Cagiano de Azevedo, "Policromia e polimateria nelle opere d'arte della tarda antichità e dell'alto medioevo," *Felix Ravenna* 1 (1970), 19–56; see also: Judith S. McKenzie, "Alexandria on the Barada: the Mosaics of the Great Mosque in Damascus," in *New Light on Old Glass: Recent Research on Byzantine Mosaics and Glass*, eds. Liz James and Christopher Entwistle (London: British Museum, 2013), 291–309.

39 *Recueil des historiens des croisades (orientaux)*, 5 vols. (Paris: Imprimerie nationale, 1884), 3: 438.

40 Sauvaire, "Description de Damas," 211–12.

41 Ibid., 220–2. An inventory of the *waqf* of the Great Mosque of Damascus dated to the year 1413 is published by: Mathieu Eychenne, Sarab Atassi, and Élodie Vigouroux, *Damas et la Mosquée des Omeyyades à l'époque mamelouke: édition et étude de l'inventaire des biens waqfs de 816/1413* (Beirut and Damascus: Presses de l'Ifpo, 2014).

42 Paul Cobb, "Virtual Sacrality: Making Muslim Syria Sacred Before the Crusades," *Medieval Encounters* 8 (2002), 35–55.

43 Al-Harawi, *Guide de Lieux de Pèlerinage*, trans. J. Sourdel-Thomine (Damas, Institut français de Damas, 1953), 37–40; see also Janine Sourdel-Thomine, "Les anciens lieux de pèlerinage damascain," *Bulletin d'Études Orientales* 14 (1952–4), 80 (65–85).

44 Le Strange, *Palestine under the Moslems*, 246; al-Harawi, *Guide de Lieux de Pèlerinage*, 39.

45 The event is presented and thoroughly analyzed by Khalek, *Damascus after the Muslim Conquest*, 46–52.

Early Islam and Byzantine Churches   MATTIA GUIDETTI

1 View of the mosaic of the *bema*, 756, church of St Stephen, Umm al-Rasas, Jordan.
Photo: © Michele Piccirillo

The territories conquered at Byzantium's expense by the Muslim armies in the seventh century were largely inhabited by Christians. During the three centuries before the arrival of the Muslims, the sacred landscape of the regions overlooking the Mediterranean was radically transformed through a dense construction of Christian architectural complexes.[1] The nature of the seventh-century Islamic conquest affected, but did not obliterate, these late antique constructions.[2] The corpus of churches in use during the early Islamic period was composed of late antique churches and several new constructions (Fig. 1).[3] Because Islamic jurisprudence did not canonize rules and dispositions toward the places of worship of the minorities until two centuries after the conquest,[4] the long period before these norms were established and the successive frequency of their re-enforcement suggest a certain discrepancy between theory and practice. In the strictest periods for *dhimmi* peoples, an essential distinction was made between churches built after the seventh-century Islamic conquest (which should be destroyed or, at the very least, considered illegal) and churches built before it (for which maintenance and restoration within the limits of the original structure were granted by legislation). It was not until centuries later, in the Mamluk period, that some jurisconsults enacted more stringent restrictions, prohibiting the restoration of non-Muslim religious buildings.[5]

In the early period, the attitude of the new rulers toward minorities and their worship practices and traditions differed according to the local communities' relations, the personal convictions of each Muslim ruler, and other contingencies. The survival of several late antique churches into early and medieval Islam is attested by later accounts of the conquest presented by both

conquerors and conquered.[6] Archaeological and epigraphic evidence confirms a certain degree of continuity in many late antique centers, although the analysis is narrowed to sites later abandoned, and the precise dates of use of the buildings in question are particularly difficult to establish.[7] Due to the political and religious primacy of the area, interactions between late antique and early Islamic architecture in the Syrian-Palestinian region might be considered paradigmatic. The Muslim attitude toward Christian foundations, such as churches, cathedrals, monastic complexes, and burial sites varied widely. One phenomenon involving Christian and Muslim architecture was the special interest developed by early Muslims toward monastic foundations. Traditionally this concern has been investigated in light of the pleasures early Muslims took in the monasteries as described in literary sources.[8] But the attraction of the monasteries, originally planned as a network for serving and controlling vast territories, also had some architectural implications. Pursuing an ideal and practical continuity with late antiquity, the Umayyad rulers attempted to adopt and adapt for themselves several monastic complexes, either by building new structures where monasteries once stood or by juxtaposing new Islamic buildings with the extant structures (Fig. 2).[9] Such an approach was not always taken. Several Christian sources minutely describe the destruction and looting of a number of monastic foundations during the relentless Muslim advance out of Arabia.[10]

As regards the cities, the search for a pivotal position within the urban fabric led early Muslims to devote attention to the great churches often located in the centers of the towns. Very schematically, the pattern observable in many cities includes a shift from coexistence between Muslim mosques and

2 Aerial view of the early Islamic settlement of Qasr al-Hayr al-Gharbi erected nearby a late antique monastery.
Photo: © Photothèque de l'Institut français du Proche-Orient

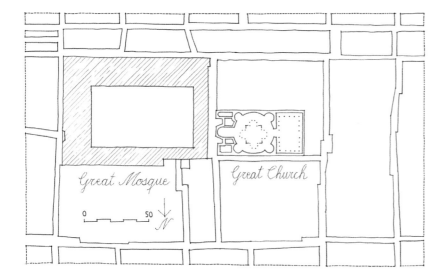

3 The great church and the great mosque of Aleppo between 715 and 1124.
Plan: Mattia Guidetti

Christian churches to the successful overwhelming of the latter by the former. The chronological frame moves from the seventh-century Islamic conquest up to the late medieval Mamluk period, which saw the definitive Islamization of Syria and Palestine. Within this general pattern there were, of course, many variations.

In Aleppo, the Great Mosque was founded around 715 by taking possession of the garden and burial area of the late antique/Byzantine cathedral complex. At the same time, the nearby tetraconch cathedral, erected in the sixth century, was kept in use by the Chalcedonian community, remaining among the places of worship attended by the Christians. The contiguous location of the two places of worship is also confirmed by the medieval author Ibn al-Shihna. This was the situation from c. 715, the date of the foundation of the mosque, up to 1124, when the great church, along with three other churches, most probably founded during late antiquity, was transformed into a mosque as a result of a violent encounter with the Frankish army (Fig. 3).[11] In 1148, the building was finally transformed into a *madrasa*, known as the al-Halawiyya. Its prayer hall preserved – as it still does today – several marble elements of the original Byzantine building, among which are columns, richly decorated Corinthian capitals, and entablatures stylistically datable to the sixth century (Fig. 4).[12]

The long coexistence in the center of Aleppo of Muslim and Christian "cathedrals" appears to have been a pattern also followed elsewhere (for example, Diyarbakir, Urfa, Mosul, Homs, as well as the center of Amman, Damascus between 634 and 705–6, and perhaps Cordoba between 711 and 756). The notion of partition, often vaguely evoked by several scholars, is therefore not exhaustive in describing the relation early mosques had with late antique urban cathedrals. It is more likely that the two communities shared the same urban area rather than the place of worship itself.[13]

In al-Rusafa, a city located east of Aleppo and deserted in the thirteenth century, the juxtaposition of the Friday Mosque with the main church of the monastic complex dedicated to St. Sergius, presents

4 A sixth-century capital in the medieval Madrasa al-Halawiyya, Aleppo.
Photo: Mattia Guidetti

a distinctive feature. The mosque was built in the second quarter of the eighth century by occupying with its *qibla* wall the northern third of a courtyard to which the church had also access (Fig. 5). During the early middle ages, the circulation of people through the courtyard, the mosque and the church, including the monumental room where the much-venerated relics of St. Sergius were displayed, made the contact between Christians and Muslims and their respective architectures much more intimate than elsewhere (Fig. 6).[14]

This pragmatic (most of the population was still Christian) and respectful (several Christian places of worship appear to have also been held sacred by Muslims) attitude shown by Muslim rulers in many cities was not followed in Damascus. In 705–6 the caliph al-Walid I decided to take the Christian complex dedicated to St. John by force, in order to destroy it and to build in its place a new structure consecrated to Muslim worship.[15] Among the possible explanations for this decision are the growth of the Muslim population and Damascus'

5 The *qibla* wall of the Great Mosque of al-Rusafa with the adjacent complex of St Sergius in the background.
Photo: Mattia Guidetti

status as capital of the Umayyad caliphate.[16] In Hama the situation was different even from the two models previously described, because it is generally acknowledged that St. John's cathedral in Hama was transformed into a mosque by simply changing the direction of worship from east to south (Fig. 7).[17] In addition to the material evidence observable in the mosque (which, however, is not exactly datable), one has the account by the local historian Abu al-Fida (1321) which dates the transformation back to the time of the seventh-century Islamic conquest (c. 636–8).[18] The opening of a *mihrab* on the southern longitudinal wall and the preservation of the three-aisled east-west axis in the Muslim building surely are part of a reorientation of a late antique/ Byzantine structure, but all these elements do not make clear whether this occurred in the very early Islamic period or later in the Middle Ages, when it appears this practice was more often enforced (see, for instance, the medieval mosque of Qara, located between Damascus and Homs).

Among the late antique buildings preserved in early Islamic Syria and Palestine, the Christian heritage of Jerusalem played an important role. The process leading Muslim rulers to choose the Temple Mount as the site for their own religious complex located the Muslim architecture at some distance from Christian sanctuaries, but nonetheless placed it in dialogue with them (Fig. 8). It has also been suggested that the articulation between the

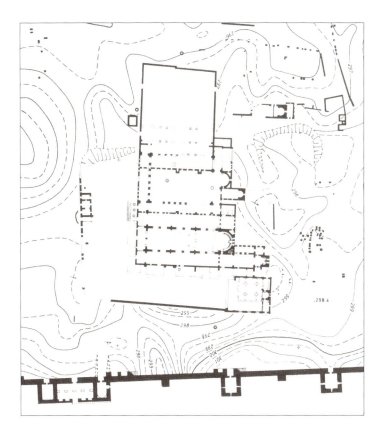

6 Plan of the great mosque and the church of St. Sergius at al-Rusafa in the Umayyad period.
Plan: © Thilo Ulbert

7 The great mosque of Hama, formerly the great church of the town, viewed from the courtyard.
Photo: Mattia Guidetti

EARLY ISLAM AND BYZANTINE CHURCHES 143

Aqsa Mosque and the Dome of the Rock might have reflected the dialogue existing between the Constantinian basilica and the rotunda of the Anastasis at the Church of the Holy Sepulcher.[19] Several texts also mention the existence of a mosque in the courtyard of the Holy Sepulcher, built to pay honor to the prayer the caliph 'Umar is said to have performed immediately after the conquest of Jerusalem. However, the references to this structure are late and the only material evidence is a Fatimid inscription later reused in a wall in the Holy Sepulcher area mentioning a mosque.[20] The case of Jerusalem shows the construction of an Islamic religious complex within the conquered city, but one which avoided any close physical relationship with the sacred buildings used by Christian communities. This is also the case with cities such as Palmyra, Bosra, and Jerash. In all of these towns, conquered and settled by early Muslims, the new mosque was built emphasizing the contact either with the *cardo* or the *decumanus* and with the related commercial areas, but without establishing a close relation with the late antique Christian religious complexes.[21]

Finally, the description by several medieval authors of the attitude exhibited by Muslims toward the performance of prayers within churches is worthy of attention.[22] The majority of the churches mentioned in the texts were connected with the worship of Jesus and Mary, the two most important Christian figures adopted, although with differences, by early Islam. To these one might add some Biblical prophets such as St. John the Baptist, and most likely popular local saints such as St. Sergius and St. George, worshiped particularly by the Arab Christian population. The veneration of such figures was surely shared by the bulk of Muslims converted from Christianity, but it is also possible that in the very early period members of the Muslim elite were accustomed to honoring them. The Nestorian patriarch Isho'yahb III (649–659), for instance, mentions some Muslims who praise the Christian faith, honor Christian saints, and give aid to churches and monasteries.[23] The only archaeological evidence suggesting a possible adoption of a Christian pilgrimage site by Muslims that has been brought to light is located between Jerusalem and Bethlehem, in the so-called Kathisma church. Within this fifth-century octagonal structure built around a rock where Mary was said to have rested during the journey to Bethlehem, a round niche identified as a *mihrab* was added to the threshold stone of the door between the southern vestibule and the ambulatory in the eighth century.[24] The *mihrab* appears to be an addition to the church with the aim of accommodating Muslim worship. It is not entirely clear whether Christians were barred from using the church at the time Muslims added the *mihrab* or the two communities shared the same building. The church remained in use up to the eleventh century, when the structure appears to have been abandoned (Fig. 9).

In other cases, Islamic worship was simply incorporated into the varied uses already accorded to multi-layered sites. Such is the case of the Patriarch's Tomb of Hebron, which was already shared between Christian and Jewish publics in the sixth century. Sometime before the tenth century the sanctuary was transformed into a mosque, including the tombs of Isaac and Rebecca in the prayer hall, the tombs of Abraham, Sarah, Jacob, and Leah in the courtyard. Although transformed into a mosque,

8 The Dome of the Rock in Jerusalem with the dome of Holy Sepulcher on the background.
Photo: © Jerry M. Landay, *Dome of the Rock. Three Faiths of Jerusalem*, Arnoldo Mondadori Editore, 1972, p. 77

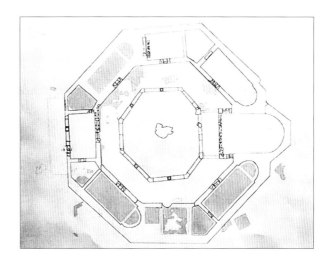

9 The Kathisma church in the eighth century.
Plan: © Israel Antiquities Authority

it is possible that non-Muslims continued to have access to it, perhaps paying a tax to the new owners of the site, as textual evidence indicates occurred after the Crusader period (after 1187) and before Baybars' order to make it temporarily an exclusively Islamic sanctuary (1266).[25]

The role the late antique churches had in shaping early Islamic aesthetic attitude and visual culture can be inferred by their presence in the list of the marvels of *Dar al-Islam* enumerated in medieval Arabic literature.[26] One of the *topoi* in such literature is the ability of Muslim builders to impose their presence onto, and thus to appropriate or alter, the inherited Christian sacred landscape. A well-known passage from al-Muqaddasi presents the construction of both the Dome of the Rock and the Great Mosque of Damascus as a reaction to the "enchantingly fair" churches, with the aim of "dazzling the minds of the Muslims" as the Christian buildings did.[27] The assonances between the artistic and architectural languages of late antique/Byzantine churches and early Islamic Friday mosques are furthermore attested by the Medinese accusations directed against al-Walid I because he renovated the great mosque of Medina (according to the descriptions, in a fashion similar to that of Damascus, with marble slabs for the dado and mosaics on the upper section of the walls) "in the style of churches".[28] Although the polemic can be attributed to Abbasid anti-Umayyad rhetoric, it is nonetheless significant that art and architecture were given a prominent place in those arguments. Similarly, al-Tabari notes that the ceilings of the Friday mosque at Kufa resemble those of the Byzantine churches (*al-kana'is al-rumiyya*), and later al-Harawi remarked that such mosaics as those in the main dome of the Great Mosque of Damascus might be admired only in the sanctuaries of the "lands of the Rum" (that is, the Byzantine empire).[29]

The coexistence and rivalry between competing sacred places, often located in proximity, implied the establishment of a sort of dialogue between the two communities. One should also mention the cases of iconophobic damages to several church mosaics in the Jordanian area during the first half of the eighth century. It seems likely that the damages were caused by the Christians as the result of the debates on the legitimacy of representing living beings among both Christians and Muslims.[30] Another case in point is the eighth-century lintel of the al-Mu'allaqa church in Cairo. Here the early Islamic Melkite Christian community adopted inscriptions as an artistic medium in order to enter and compete in the debate that had arisen around the nature and the quality of Christ, a debate that pitted the Melkite community against fellow Christians as well as against Muslims.[31]

Indeed, the continuity of several late antique sacred sites and Christian churches attests to the continued vibrancy of Christian communities during the early Islamic period. This Christian vitality, moreover, might also help to explain the choices made in the establishment of a Muslim sacred landscape in conquered cities, and in the creation of early Islamic visual culture in general.

MATTIA GUIDETTI is an assistant professor in the history of Islamic art at the University of Bologna. He held research and teaching positions at Harvard University, the Kunsthistorisches Institut of Florence, the University of Edinburgh, and Vienna University. He published the volume *In the shadow of the church: the building of mosques in early medieval Syria* (Brill, 2017). Current research projects include the reception of Ottoman artefacts in early modern Italy and Islamic objects in Bologna collections.

SUGGESTIONS FOR FURTHER READING

Avni, Gideon. *The Byzantine-Islamic Transition in Palestine: An Archaeological Approach* (Oxford: Oxford University Press, 2014).

Bashear, Sulayman. "Qibla Musharriqa and Early Muslim Prayer in Churches," *The Muslim World* 81 (1991), 267–282.

Evans, Helen C. and Brandie Ratliff, eds., *Byzantium and Islam. Age of Transition, 7th-9th Century* (New York: The Metropolitan Museum of Art, 2012).

Guidetti, Mattia. *In the Shadow of the Church. The Building of Mosques in Early Medieval Period* (Leiden: Brill, 2016).

Tannous, Jack. *The Making of the Medieval Middle East: Religion, Society, and Simple Believers* (Princeton, NJ: Princeton University Press, 2018).

NOTES

[1] For a concise introduction on Christian communities during the early Islamic period, see Brandie Ratliff, "Christian Communities during the Early Islamic Centuries," in *Byzantium and Islam. Age of Transition, 7th-9th Century*, ed. Helen C. Evans and Brandie Ratliff, (New York: The Metropolitan Museum of Art, 2012), 32–39.

[2] Hugh Kennedy, *The Great Arab Conquests. How the Spread of Islam Changed the World We Live In* (London: Weidenfeld & Nicolson, 2007), 1–33.

[3] Michele Piccirillo, "The Umayyad Churches of Jordan," *Annual of the Department of the Antiquities of Jordan* 28 (1984), 333–41; Leah Di Segni, "Christian Epigraphy in the Holy Land: New Discoveries," ARAM 15 (2003), 247–67. For a less optimistic view of Christian building activity under early Islam; see Denys Pringle, "Church-building in Palestine Before the Crusades," in *Crusader Art in the Twelfth Century*, ed. Jaroslav Folda (Oxford: B.A.R, 1982), 5–46.

[4] Arthur S. Tritton, *The Caliphs and Their Non-Muslim Subjects: A Critical Study of the Covenant of 'Umar* (London: Oxford University Press, 1930), 5–17; Mark R. Cohen, "What was the Pact of 'Umar? A Literary-Historical Study," *Jerusalem Studies in Arabic and Islam* 23 (1999), 100–57; Albrecht Noth, "Problems of Differentiation between Muslims and non-Muslims: Re-reading the 'Ordinances of 'Umar' (al-Shurut al-'Umariyya)," in *Muslims and Others in Early Islamic Society*, edited by Robert Hoyland (Aldershot: Ashgate, 2004), 103–24; Milka Levy-Rubin, *Non-Muslims in the Early Islamic Empire: From Surrender to Coexistence* (Cambridge: Cambridge University Press, 2011).

[5] Antoine Fattal, *Le statut légal des non-musulmans en pays d'islam* (Beirut: Dar al-Mashriq, 1995), 174–8.

[6] For Syria see Kennedy, *The Great Arab Conquests*, 66–97; see also the case of Cesarea where the conquest meant the destruction of the city, for which consult Amikam Elad, "The Coastal Cities of Palestine during the Early Middle Ages," *The Jerusalem Cathedra* 2 (1982), 146–67. On the reliability of the medieval narrations of the 7th-Islamic conquest, see Chase F. Robinson, *Empire and Elites after the Muslim Conquest. The Transformation of Northern Mesopotamia* (Cambridge: Cambridge University Press, 2000), 1–32. Non-Muslim sources are particularly important: Robert G. Hoyland, *Seeing Islam as Others Saw It. A Survey and Evaluation of Christian, Jewish and Zoroastrian Writings on Early Islam* (Princeton, NJ: The Darwin Press, 1997), 117–215; Andrew Palmer, *The Seventh Century in the West-Syrian Chronicles* (Liverpool: Liverpool University Press, 1993).

7   Alan Walmsley, *Early Islamic Syria: An Archaeological Assessment* (London: Duckworth, 2007), 120–6; Di Segni, "Christian Epigraphy in the Holy Land."

8   Hillary Kilpatrick, "Monasteries through Muslim Eyes: the Diyarat Books," in *Christians at the Hearth of Islamic Rule: Church Life and Scholarship in 'Abbasid Iraq*, ed. David Thomas (Brill: Leiden, 2003), 19–38; Gérard Troupeau, "Les couvents chrétiens dans la littérature arabe," *La nouvelle revue du Caire* 1 (1975), 265–79.

9   Lara Tohme, "Spaces of Convergence: Christian Monasteries and Umayyad Architecture in Greater Syria," in *Negotiating Secular and Sacred in Medieval Art: Christian, Islamic, and Buddhist*, ed. Alicia Walker and Amanda Luyster (Burlington, VT: Ashgate, 2009), 129–45; Elizabeth Key Fowden, "Christian Monasteries and Umayyad Residences in Late Antique Syria," *Antigüedad y cristianismo: monografías históricas sobre la Antigüedad tardía* 21 (2004), 565–81.

10 Hoyland, *Seeing Islam as Others Saw It*, 117–215.

11 Mattia Guidetti, *In the Shadow of the Church. The Building of Mosques in Early Medieval Syria* (Leiden: Brill, 2016), 41–45.

12 On the transition of this site in Aleppo from Late Antiquity to Middle Ages, see Jean Sauvaget, *Alèp. Essai sur le développement d'une grande ville syrienne, des origines au milieu du xix*ᵉ *siècle*, 2 vols. (Paris: Librairie Orient. Paul Geuthner, 1941), 1:58–75.

13 On this issue, see Mattia Guidetti, "The Contiguity of Churches and Mosques in Early Islamic Bilad al-Sham," *Bulletin of the School of Oriental and African Studies* 76.2 (2013), 229–258; Guidetti, *In the Shadow of the Church*, 36–70.

14 Thilo Ulbert, *Die Basilika des Heiligen Kreuzes in Resafa-Sergiupolis* (Mainz am Rhein: Zabern, 1986); Irfan Shahid, *Byzantium and the Arabs in the Sixth Century*, 2 vols. (Washington: Dumbarton Oaks Research Library and Collection, 1995–2002), vol. 1 part 2:949–962; Dorothée Sack, *Die Grosse Moschee von Resafa - Rusafat Hisham* (Mainz am Rhein: Zabern, 1996); Elizabeth Key Fowden, *The Barbarian Plain. Saint Sergius between Rome and Iran* (Berkeley, CA: University of California Press, 1999), 101–129; idem, "Sharing Holy Places," *Common Knowledge* 8 (2002), 124–146.

15 Keppel A.C. Creswell, *Early Muslim Architecture*, 2 vols. (Oxford, UK: Clarendon Press, 1932), 1:100–46.

16 Al-Baladhuri, *Kitab futuh al-buldan*, edited by Michael Jan De Goeje (Leiden: Brill, 1968), 125–6.

17 Keppel A.C. Creswell, "The Great Mosque of Hama," in *Aus der Welt der Islamischen Kunst: Festschriften für Ernst Kühnel zum 75. Geburtstagen 26.10.1957*, edited by Richard Ettinghausen (Berlin: Gebr. Mann, 1959), 48–53; Poul J. Riis, *Temple, Church and Mosque* (Copenaghen: Ejnar Munksgaard, 1965).

18 Abu al-Fida, *Mukhtasar ta'rikh al-bashar*, 4 parts in 2 vols., s.e. (Istanbul: s.e., 1869/70), 1:168.

19 Rafi Grafman and Myriam Rosen-Ayalon, "The Two Great Syrian Umayyad Mosques: Jerusalem and Damascus," *Muqarnas* 16 (1999), 1–15; Andreas Kaplony, *The Haram of Jerusalem, 324–1099: Temple, Friday Mosque, Area of Spiritual Power* (Stuttgart: Franz Steiner Verlag, 2002).

20 Charles Clermont-Ganneau, *Recueil d'Archéologie Orientale. Tome II* (Paris: Éditeur Ernest Leroux, 1896), 302–62; Heribert Busse, "Die 'Umar-Moschee im östlichen Atrium der Grabeskirche," *Zeitschrift des Deutschen Palästina-Vereins* 109 (1993), 73–82.

21 For Palmyra, see Denis Genequand, "An Early Islamic Mosque at Palmyra," *Levant* 40.1 (2008), 3–15; for Bosra, see Michael Meinecke, Flemming Aalund, Lorenz Korn and Stefan Heidemann, *Bosra: islamische Architektur und Archäologie* (Rahden: Verlag Marie Leidorf, 2005); for Jerash, see Alan Walmsley, "The Friday Mosque of Early Islamic Jarash in Jordan," *Journal of the David Collection* 1 (2003), 110–31.

22 Sulayman Bashear, "Qibla Musharriqa and Early Muslim Prayer in Churches," *The Muslim World* 81 (1991), 267–82.

23 Hoyland, *Seeing Islam as Others Saw It*, 181, 162; see also Fred M. Donner, "From Believers to Muslims: Confessional Self-Identity in the Early Islamic Community," *Al-Abhath* 50–51 (2002–3), 49.

24 See Rina Avner, "The Kathisma: a Christian and Muslim Pilgrimage Site," ARAM 18–19 (2006–2007), 550–51.

25 See Denys Pringle, *The Churches of the Crusader Kingdom of Jerusalem. A Corpus*, 4 vols. (Cambridge, UK: Cambridge University Press, 1993–2007), 1:223–39.

26 Ibn al-Fakih al-Hamadhani, *Kitab al-Buldan*, ed. M.J. De Goeje (Leiden: Brill, 1967), 50; Ibn Khurradadhbih, *Kitab al-masalik wa-l-mamalik*, ed. M.J. De Goeje (Leiden: Brill, 1967), 161–2; Ibn Shaddad, *Description de la Syrie du Nord*, translated by Anne-Marie Eddé-Terrasse (Damascus: Institut français de Damas, 1984), 231–2.

27 al-Muqaddasi, *Ahsan al-taqasim fi ma'rifat al-aqalim*, ed. Michael Jan De Goeje (Leiden: Brill, 1967), 147, 159.

28 *Encyclopaedia of Islam*, Second Edition, entry for *masjid*.

29 Al-Tabari, *Tarikh al-rusul wa-l-muluk*, 3 parts, edited by Michael Jan De Goeje (Leiden: Brill, 1964), part I, 2489; al-Harawi, *Guide de Lieux de Pèlerinage*, trans. Janine Sourdel-Thomine (Damascus: Institut français de Damas, 1957), 39.

30 Sidney H. Griffith, *A Treatise on the Veneration of Holy Icons Written in Arabic by Theodore Abu Qurrah* (Louvain: Peeters, 1997), 7; Glenn W. Bowersock, *Mosaics as History. The Near East From Late Antiquity to Islam* (Cambridge, Mass: Harvard University Press, 2006), 109–11; Mattia Guidetti, "L'Editto di Yazid II': immagini ed identità religiosa nel Bilad al-Sham dell'VIII secolo," in *L'VIII secolo: un secolo inquieto*, ed. Valentino Pace (Cividale del Friuli, 2010), 69–80; Henry Maguire, *Nectar & Illusion. Nature in Byzantine Art and Literature* (New York: Oxford University Press, 2012), 35–47; Barry Flood, "Christian Mosaics in Early Islamic Jordan and Palestine: A Case of Regional Iconoclasm", in *Byzantium and Islam*, 117–119; Robert Schick, "Die Bilderzerstörung des 8. Jahrhunderts in Palästina," in *Sakralität und Devianz. Konstruktionen – Normen – Praxis*, ed. K. Herbers and L. Düchting (Stuttgart: Franz Steiner Verlag, 2015), 139–153; Guidetti, *In the Shadow of the Church*, 86–96; Christian C. Sahner, "The First Iconoclasm in Islam: A New History of the Edict of Yazīd II (AH 104/AD 723)," *Der Islam* 94.1 (2017), 5–56.

31 Glenn Peers, "Vision and Community among Christians and Muslims: the al-Muallaqa Lintel in Its Eighth-Century Context," *Arte Medievale* 6/1 (2007), 25–46.

Early Mosques in Iran and Central Asia   MELANIE MICHAILIDIS

1 Friday Mosque, Barsian, Iran, eleventh century.
Photo: Melanie Michailidis, courtesy of the Aga Khan Documentation Center at MIT

Islam entered Iran with the defeat of the last Sasanian emperor, Yazdgerd III, in 651, and yet the earliest extant mosques in Iran, such as the Tarik Khaneh in Damghan, are dated to the late eighth or ninth century on stylistic grounds. The factors responsible for this lacuna include a slow rate of conversion to Islam in the centuries immediately following the conquest; the use of unbaked brick, a readily perishable material, for most structures until the eleventh century; and the rather peripheral nature of Iran in the Umayyad period, when high-level patronage was concentrated in Greater Syria.[1] Hence one can safely say that there were not any monumental mosques along the lines of the Great Mosque of Damascus constructed in Iran before the Abbasid period. The more modest constructions that were erected have largely perished or were later modified and incorporated into ever-evolving structures such as the Great Mosque of Isfahan.[2] Textual information on these early mosques is also exceedingly sparse, unlike the relatively detailed descriptions available for important sites like the Mosque of the Prophet in Medina or mosques in the early garrison towns such as Basra and Kufa. It is therefore difficult to generalize about early Iranian mosques, and conclusions must necessarily be tentative.

The same caveats must also be employed to some extent regarding Central Asia, although there the record of archaeological excavations is more extensive than in Iran. Islam arrived later in Central Asia, which was not part of the Sasanian realm. Samarqand, for example, did not fall until 712. Unlike the centralized Sasanian empire, which collapsed completely once Yazdgerd was killed, each Sogdian city-state in Central Asia had to be conquered separately, and rebellions were a frequent occurrence even after the conquest. The

situation required a continual influx of Muslim soldiers, so that Merv, on the former Sasanian border, was transformed into a garrison town, and large garrisons were also stationed in the main Sogdian cities. Although the Sogdians fought long and hard against the invaders, they converted in large numbers in the urban areas after it became clear around the mid-eighth century that resistance was futile. Larger Muslim populations would have logically necessitated larger mosques, although it is difficult to be conclusive with so few excavations in Iran. However, it is instructive to compare the size of the Great Mosque at Siraf, which was begun in the ninth century with a dimension of approximately fifty-five by forty-four meters, with the Friday mosque of Samarqand, which measured approximately seventy-five by eighty-five meters in its first phase of construction in the late eighth century.

In the immediate aftermath of the Arab conquest, the Zoroastrian temple in Samarqand, which was the primary religious building in the pre-Islamic city, was transformed into a mosque; later, the building was razed and a purpose-built hypostyle mosque constructed in its place.[3] This is one concrete example of a post-conquest Muslim appropriation of a structure belonging to another religion and its transformation into a mosque, first used in its original form and subsequently rebuilt or extended; another excavated example in Transoxiana is found at Rabinjan.[4] Although this phenomenon was well documented in the western Islamic world, with the Great Mosque of Damascus being the most noted example, the extent to which this occurred in Iran has been disputed, and Oleg Grabar in particular has dismissed the idea that the transformation of fire temples into mosques occurred with any frequency.[5] Yazd-i Khvast

149

is generally accepted as a fire temple from the Sasanian era converted into a mosque, but contrary to Grabar's claims, it is not unique in this regard. The Masjid-i Birun at Abarquh, the Friday Mosque at Aqda, and mosques in Qurva, Burujird, Kuhpaya, Harand, and Qihi are most likely converted fire temples.[6] Possible remains of fire temples can also be seen inside the mosques of Saveh and Bam.

Literary sources provide further evidence for such transformations in both Iran and Central Asia: local histories such as the *Tarikh-i Bukhara* and the *Tarikh-i Qumm* describe the conversion of fire temples into mosques,[7] and Zoroastrians of the ninth and tenth centuries complained about the increasing level of Muslim encroachment on their places of worship.[8] This shows that, although fire temples such as that of Samarqand were converted in the immediate aftermath of conquest, no doubt for symbolic as much as practical reasons, such conversion also occurred gradually over the centuries as Muslims gained in numbers and was still occurring in some regions during the tenth century. Moreover, it was not only fire temples which were converted: although Zoroastrianism was a state religion in Sasanian Iran, the Sogdian city-states of Central Asia were more tolerant of other religions, and Nestorian Christianity, Judaism, Manichaeism, and Buddhism, as well as Zoroastrianism, were practiced to varying degrees in different parts of Central Asia. The *Tarikh-i Bukhara* relates the transformation of Nestorian churches into mosques, during the initial Arab incursions by Qutaiba b. Muslim,[9] and in 893 when the Samanid ruler Ismail expanded to the north and captured the Turkish city of Taraz.[10] Likewise, excavations at the shrine of Hakim al-Termezi in Termez have shown that the mausoleum was appended to a Buddhist structure, which was then transformed into a mosque.[11]

Structures designed for the practices of other religions varied in their suitability for use as a mosque. The Buddhist shrine at Termez, for example, was small for a Friday mosque but was more readily adaptable as a non-congregational nine-domed mosque. Churches which were designed to hold sizable congregations lent themselves to use as mosques, as did the Zoroastrian temples of Central Asia, which were also intended to hold worshippers. The fire temples of Sasanian Iran, however, were much more diminutive, as they were designed to hold only the priests who carried out the daily rituals. Their typical form consisted of a domed square with four arched openings, called the *chahar taq*. Although lacking in directionality, the *qibla* wall of a *chahar taq* could be blocked up to transform the structure into a mosque, but its size would still be unsuitable. Most *chahar taq*s were surrounded by ambulatories or otherwise embedded within larger structures, further impeding their use as mosques, and yet textual sources and surviving examples indicate that such transformations did occur. Moreover, the frequent use of domed chambers in Iranian mosques indicates that the *chahar taq* also served as an inspiration to their architects, but until the chronology of more mosques is deciphered through archaeological excavations, the balance between conversion and inspiration will remain an open question.[12]

The earliest purpose-built mosques in Iran remained faithful to the hypostyle plan, which dates back to the Mosque of the Prophet in Medina and was used for monumental Friday mosques in Arabic-speaking regions for centuries thereafter. However, whereas in the western Islamic world, classical columns of stone were readily available as spolia, the main building material in Iran and Central Asia was brick. The use of brick in general, and unbaked brick in particular, necessarily entailed thick piers instead of the arcades composed of slender columns seen in Syrian mosques and farther west, lending the early Iranian mosques a rather squat and heavy appearance. Hence the initial Iranian adaptation of the hypostyle plan to local building materials and techniques was already aesthetically distinct from the western model. The Tarik Khaneh mosque at Damghan, probably the earliest extant mosque in Iran, is an excellent example (Fig. 2). Constructed of unbaked brick in the late eighth or early ninth century, the plan of the mosque consists of an arcade around three sides of the

2 Tarik Khaneh, Damghan, Iran, late eighth or early ninth century.
Photo: Melanie Michailidis, courtesy of the Aga Khan Documentation Center at MIT

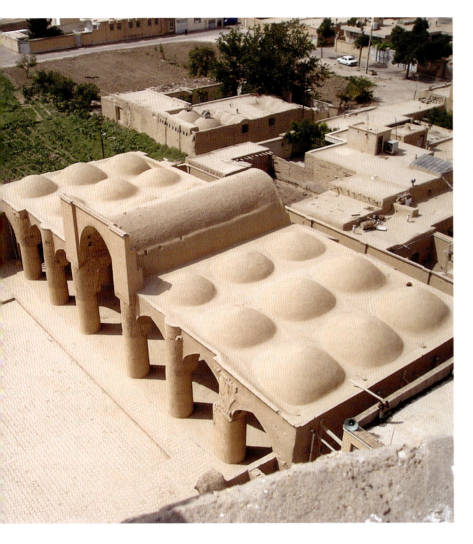

courtyard with a covered sanctuary composed of three aisles in front of the *qibla* wall: a typical hypostyle plan. However, the elliptical arches, thick piers, and small domes covering the interstices between the piers also demonstrate continuity from Sasanian materials, styles, and techniques. The raised central aisle indicating the approach to the *mihrab* is paralleled in North African mosques, and yet the barrel vault of this aisle resembles an *iwan* (Persian *ayvan*), the barrel vault closed on three-sides which is one of the distinguishing features of Iranian architecture from the Parthian period into the modern era. The height of the central aisle also resembles and foreshadows the *pishtaq*, the raised arched entrance that became a standard feature of monumental Iranian and Central Asian architecture after its first appearance in 987 at the Arab Ata mausoleum at Tim, in modern Uzbekistan.

Other early hypostyle mosques are known through excavations. The Great Mosque at Siraf was also originally constructed in the ninth century, but was considerably larger than the mosques at Damghan or Fahraj, reflecting the wealth and greater population density of this important trading center on the Persian Gulf coast. Raised on a platform two meters high, this mosque had five aisles in front of the *qibla* wall, while the arcade surrounding the other three sides of the courtyard was two aisles deep.[13] Both the platform and the rubble and mortar construction of the mosque are typical features of the pre-Islamic architecture of Fars, the large region in southwestern Iran which had been a stronghold of both the Sasanian dynasty and the ancient Achaemenids. The contemporary Friday mosque in Samarqand, in Central Asia, was even larger but had a very similar plan, with six aisles in front of the *qibla* wall and three aisles around the courtyard.

The hypostyle plan can be viewed as an import entering Iran along with the mosque as a typological form and Islam itself, but it did not remain the only mosque plan for long, and features such as the domed chamber in front of the *mihrab* and the growing prevalence of the *iwan* indicate the development of uniquely Iranian plans. As mentioned above, some of the earliest examples of domed chambers, such as the one at Yazd-i Khvast, are most likely incorporations of even earlier *chahar taq*s. This led André Godard to postulate the existence of the *mosquée kiosque*, or kiosk mosque, which he defined as a free-standing domed chamber derived from the *chahar taq*; in his view, this was the early Iranian mosque type *par excellence* and mosques such as those at Zavareh, Ardestan, and Isfahan only later acquired their arcaded courtyards as part of the ensemble.[14] Although Godard's conclusions regarding those particular buildings have been shown to be incorrect, and the known corpus of early mosques in Iran and Central Asia has expanded to show a greater variety of forms, the prominence of the domed chamber in so many Iranian mosques is still an interesting feature that requires explanation. Sauvaget proposed that these chambers served as *maqsura*s, analogous to the domed area in front of the *mihrab* at the Great Mosque of Cordoba.[15] While arguments have been put forward to counter this idea,[16] some scholars do see it as plausible.[17] Although it does seem a logical possibility that the Iranian domes could have been used as *maqsura*s, the domed chamber is much more prominent in mosques such as Zavareh or Barsian (Fig. 1) than at Cordoba, lending these mosques an overall profile which differs significantly from contemporary mosques in the western Islamic world. Moreover, apart from the Great Mosque of Isfahan, these mosques are not located in major capital cities; indeed, the surviving remnants of early mosques are spread throughout Iran and are often found in small cities and even villages, locations that would be less likely to need a *maqsura*. Early mosques with prominent domed chambers are not found in Central Asia, even though Sergei Khmel'nitskii has proposed rather unconvincingly that the central mausoleum at Uzgend was a *mosquée kiosque*.[18] The geographical concentration of the domed chambers in former Sasanian lands makes the link with either Sasanian religious or palatial architecture even more likely.

Robert Hillenbrand has drawn a link between the *iwan*, which makes an early appearance in Iranian mosque architecture, and Sasanian palace architecture.[19] The *iwan* was also used in religious architecture in Central Asia, as is evidenced by the eighth-century Buddhist *vihara* (monastery) at Adzhina-Tepe. However, since the *iwan* appears in early mosques only in places such as Nayin and Nayriz in the former Sasanian realm, and is so far not known at all in the early mosques of Central Asia, its association with palatial architecture is a reasonable one. The tenth-century mosque at Nayin is an excellent example, with triple *iwan*s on three sides of the courtyard. The mosque has been subject to later alterations, so that the plan is rather confused, with a profusion of small domes and vaults in various unexpected places, such as the southern corner and southeastern side, in addition to their customary position in front of the *mihrab*. Nevertheless, the original triple *iwan* structure is present, and it is interesting to note that the *qibla* side is not clearly marked architecturally on the courtyard façade, which lacks an obvious axiality. The overall effect gives

the sense of a tentative attempt to favor Sasanian traditions while still not entirely abandoning the Arabic hypostyle mosque plan.[20]

There is another type of plan that suddenly appeared in the ninth century throughout the Islamic world, with some examples still being constructed as late as the fifteenth century. Consisting of nine bays capped by small domes, arranged in rows of threes, these are diminutive mosques which were not designed to hold large congregations like the Friday mosques of the hypostyle and *iwan* plans. Geoffrey King has compiled a catalog of such mosques stretching from Spain to Tanzania to Central Asia, but always interpreted in local building materials and techniques. He has posited that they were an honorary type of building consistently associated with prominent local persons, and probably deriving from a lost prototype in Baghdad.[21] His list included three mosques in Central Asia: the Masjid-i Nuh Gunbad in Balkh, the Digaran Mosque at Hazara, and the mosque attached to the shrine of Hakim al-Termezi. Other Central Asian examples include the Chahar Sutun mosque at Termez, the mosque at the shrine of Khusam Ata near Qarshi, the mosque attached to the shrine of Astana Baba in southeastern Turkmenistan,[22] and the original mosque at the shrine of Qusam b. 'Abbas (Shah-i Zindeh) at Samarqand.[23] The Maghok-i Attari Mosque in Bukhara originally had a related nine-bay plan, although with only three domes.[24] The small Sar-i Kucheh mosque at Muhamadiyya, with three domes in front of the *qibla* wall, should perhaps also be seen as a variant on the nine-domed plan. Another variant can be seen in the upper story of a contemporary building at Takhmaladzh in Turkmenistan, which had nine domes and nine bays, but with separating walls between the bays; this would obviously make it unsuitable for a mosque, and the function of this building is uncertain.[25]

Of all the Central Asian nine-domed mosques, the best known is the so-called Masjid-i Nuh Gunbad at Balkh, in the eastern section of Khorasan, which is now part of Afghanistan.[26] Here the nine-domed plan was interpreted in unbaked brick, a material

3 Masjid-i Digaran, Hazara, Uzbekistan, eighth to eleventh centuries.
Photo: Melanie Michailidis, courtesy of the Aga Khan Documentation Center at MIT

that necessitated thick, heavy piers. The *qibla* side is closed, but the other three sides of the mosque are open, which would have given it a canopy-like effect in its original state. This combined with its diminutive size and lavish stucco revetment would have lent the mosque a jewel-like appearance despite the heaviness of its construction. It is positively sumptuous in comparison to the Masjid-i Digaran at Hazara, which is closed on all four sides and lacks a decorative revetment, giving the interior a dark and claustrophobic effect. This mosque exhibits a variant on the nine-domed plan, with a mixture of domes and vaults comprised of a larger central dome and domes over the four corner bays, with vaults topping the intervening bays (Fig. 3). Due to its isolated location, it is surprisingly well preserved. The Masjid-i Nuh Gunbad, on the other hand, is now in ruins, with the advantage that its essential characteristics have also been preserved. The nine-domed mosques that are an integral part of shrines have all been substantially altered; the mosque attached to the mausoleum of Hakim al-Termezi, for example, now has only three domes, and little remains of the original mosque at the Shah-i Zindeh.

One reason for the poor survival rate of early mosques in Iran and Central Asia is the use of unbaked brick in their construction. If not consistently maintained, a structure composed of this material will eventually melt away from exposure to rain. Hence many unbaked brick mosques have been rebuilt or substantially refurbished, while the remnants of others are buried awaiting excavation, and others have entirely disappeared. The few survivals, such as the Tarik Khaneh at Damghan and the Masjid-i Nuh Gunbad at Balkh, therefore give us only the barest inkling of the character of the entire corpus of early mosques. By the tenth century, builders were beginning to use baked brick more often, as is evidenced by the mosques of Nayin and Nayriz. It was considered a lavish and expensive material at this time, and

EARLY MOSQUES IN IRAN AND CENTRAL ASIA 153

unbaked brick was still the standard material for ordinary buildings. Friday mosques were obviously buildings of great religious and political significance, and hence it is hardly surprising that they were constructed of the best material available. However, the better survival prospects of baked brick undoubtedly skew our impression. In the *Tarikh-i Bukhara*, Narshakhi mentions the use of baked brick as something exceptional, even in mosques, and often it was only used for part of a building rather than the whole.[27] Interestingly, a higher proportion of extant mausolea than mosques were composed of baked brick. This could be due to their smaller size, to attitudes regarding the encasing of dead remains, or possibly to greater political importance being attached to dynastic mausolea than Friday mosques: in Bukhara in the tenth century, for example, the Samanids constructed their dynastic mausoleum of baked brick but their Friday mosque of unbaked brick.

Archaeological excavations in Central Asia support the textual sources with evidence of both baked and unbaked brick mosque remains from the tenth century. In the Merv oasis, a Friday mosque with a hypostyle plan measuring 42 meters square was excavated at Bashan, and a smaller hypostyle mosque was uncovered at Chilburj;[28] the remains of the Chahar Sutun mosque at Termez are also of unbaked brick. Baked brick remains are found in mosques at Samarqand, Dandankan in the Merv oasis, and Keder, near Otrar in modern Kazakhstan.[29] Of the intact extant mosques, the Masjid-i Nuh Gunbad is composed of unbaked brick, while the Masjid-i Digaran is constructed of a mixture, with unbaked brick used for the walls and baked brick used for the domes and vaults. Wood was also used occasionally in Central Asia for columns in structures of both baked and unbaked brick: excavations have shown this to be the case in the Samanid mosque at Samarqand,[30] and a few of the columns in the Friday mosque at Khiva date back to this period. Even a wooden *mihrab* was found in a small mosque at Iskodar, in Tajikistan. Another regionally specific material is the rubble and mortar construction of Fars province in Iran, seen in the Great Mosque of Siraf.

4 *Mihrab*, Friday Mosque, Nayin, Iran, tenth century.
Photo: Melanie Michailidis, courtesy of the Aga Khan Documentation Center at MIT

Like most early mosques, the earliest extant minarets were also made of unbaked brick, although some were later given a baked brick revetment. A number of such minarets have survived in southern Turkmenistan: Kushmelkhan, just to the north of Merv, is one example.[31] These early minarets already took the slender, rounded shape typical of the eastern Islamic world. Several unbaked brick minarets without a later baked brick cladding have survived in Tajikistan, at Zahmatabad, Rarz, and Fatmev, all dated to the ninth or tenth centuries by Khmel'nitskii on the basis of their brick sizes.[32] Baked brick seems to have become the norm for minarets by the eleventh

5 Portal, Jurjir Mosque, Isfahan, Iran, tenth century. Photo: Melanie Michailidis, courtesy of the Aga Khan Documentation Center at MIT

century, and several dated baked brick minarets survive from this era: at Mestorian, dated 1004–5; at the Tarik Khaneh in Damghan, dated 1026; and at Termez, dated 1032 (now unfortunately destroyed).

The primary decorative material in both Iran and Central Asia was stucco, which had been used to cover, brighten, and decorate brick walls since the Parthian period. This could be a simple, thin revetment, as seen on the piers of the Tarik Khaneh, or it could be thickly applied and elaborately carved, as in the Friday mosque at Nayin and the Masjid-i Nuh Gunbad at Balkh. The motifs in the stucco of the Masjid-i Nuh Gunbad are very reminiscent of the motifs seen at Samarra: at the tops of the piers are capitals formed of stucco, deeply carved in a style closely linked to Samarra style B,[33] while the soffits of the arches have realistic vine leaves symmetrically arranged and encased in linked roundels. While this is clearly similar to Samarra style A, it is also linked to the vine motifs seen in pre-Islamic Sogdian architecture, such as the palace of the Bukhar Khodahs at Varakhsha, in the Bukharan oasis. On some of the soffits, the vine leaves are interspersed with interlocked X's formed of so-called pearl borders; while interlocking geometric shapes were just beginning to grow in popularity in the ninth century, so that the mosque was at the cutting edge of the latest decorative styles, the pearl border was a motif which had been popular in Iran and Central Asia for centuries in the pre-Islamic period and was firmly absorbed into the repertoire of eastern Islamic art by this time. The stucco rosettes in the spandrels of the arches are another feature that already had a long history in this region. The overall effect of the mosque then was a very metropolitan plan executed in local materials, with rich decoration linked both to metropolitan styles and local traditions.

The stucco decoration at Nayin was less closely linked to the Samarran styles, so that it is difficult to state whether it was derived from local traditions or was a reflection of the continuing popularity of the Samarran styles (particularly since the Samarran styles themselves were derived from Iranian and Central Asian traditions). On the piers closest to the *qibla*, small vine leaves carved in high relief are densely packed into the interstices between interlocking pearl borders. The *tympanum* of the outer arch of the *mihrab* carries row upon row of these tightly packed and deeply carved vine leaves, while the *tympanum* of the inner arch bears large pear shapes in very high relief embedded within the vine leaves, resembling ripe fruits ready to be plucked (Fig. 4). The area around the *mihrab* and the soffits of the arches have small vine leaves and rosettes encased in polylobed roundels, interspersed with elongated hexagons on the soffits. Due to the depth of the carving and the sheltered location, blue paint remains on the background in many areas, a vivid reminder that the stucco revetments which now appear a dull white were brightly colored in their original state. All the stucco decoration at Nayin is concentrated on the *qibla* wall and the arcades directly in front of the *qibla*, accenting the most important area of the mosque through this medium rather than through the architecture itself. Lavishly carved *mihrab*s from this period are also found in Central Asia, in locales such as Paikend in the Bukharan oasis.

In the mosques constructed of baked brick, this material was also used for decorative revetments, as can be seen in the courtyard of the Nayin mosque, where the brickwork foreshadows the diaper patterns which would become exceedingly popular in the Seljuk period. Such diaper patterns can also be seen on the portal of the Jurjir mosque in Isfahan, with variations used in conjunction with niches and indentations to give texture and interest to this elaborate entrance. In the prototypical *muqarnas* in the tympanum of the portal, there are rows of stylized flowers, a true tour-de-force in the medium of baked brick (Fig. 5). The remainder of the mosque has been substantially reconstructed and dates to the seventeenth century, but the richness of the portal has led to the attribution of the tenth century mosque to the Buyid vizier and intellectual, Sahib Ismail b. Abbad. This linking of a patron to a specific mosque is a rare instance in the eastern Islamic world in this period, as foundation inscriptions have not survived.

The extant inscriptions of this period are almost all Quranic, and the earliest example is at Nayin. In the area in front of the *mihrab*, Quran 9.18, which refers to the construction of mosques and is consequently the verse most commonly seen in mosque epigraphy, Quran 2:131/137, 27:40, and 9:130/129 can all be seen in a floriated Kufic script. Additionally, part of the Shi'ite confession of faith appears over the *mihrab*, which is very fitting for a mosque built under Buyid rule.[34] The portal of the Jurjir mosque, also constructed under Buyid auspices, bears Quran 3.16/18, which Sheila Blair has linked to Mutazilite theologians.[35] Both are excellent examples of the type of information which can be gleaned from Quranic inscriptions, in addition to the occasional appearance of the names of patrons and even artists, as seen in the inscriptions of the oldest columns from the Friday mosque at Khiva.[36]

The inscriptions have been lost in almost every case of archaeologically excavated mosques, but there are also major problems with analyzing extant early Islamic mosques, as most of them have been substantially altered or even rebuilt in later eras. The larger and more important the mosque, the greater the likelihood of this occurring: the Great Mosque of Isfahan is an excellent case in point, and a rare example of a mosque which continues to be used but has also been excavated. By combining the excavation discoveries with information gleaned from textual sources, a picture emerges of a mosque

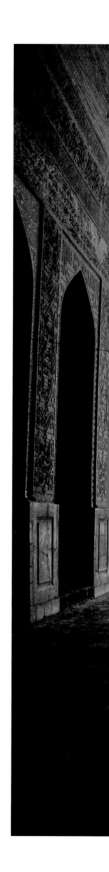

6 *Qibla iwan*, Great Mosque of Isfahan, Iran, early twelfth to fourteenth centuriy.
Photo: Melanie Michailidis, courtesy of the Aga Khan Documentation Center at MIT

originally constructed in the late eighth century of unbaked brick with a hypostyle plan, and gaining a *minbar* and *maqsura* soon after.[37] Several alterations occurred in the mid-ninth century, and again around 920. At some point before the late tenth century, a minaret was constructed on the *qibla* side. In the late tenth or early eleventh century, when Isfahan was the primary capital of the Buyid dynasty, the courtyard façade was reconstructed in baked brick, and additional buildings were appended to the corners of the mosque for specialized functions such as teaching and a library. One of the entrances from the adjoining bazaar gained a portal framed by two minarets. In the Seljuk period, Isfahan was one of the main capitals of the empire, and the mosque again attracted high-level patronage. In 1086–7, a freestanding domed chamber was constructed in front of the *qibla* by the powerful vizier Nizam al-Mulk, shortly before his downfall. In 1088, his rival and replacement Taj al-Mulk built a very similar domed chamber on the north side of the mosque; although the motive for its construction seems clear enough, the actual function of this dome is unknown and its contemporary architectural context is now lost. In the early twelfth century, partially in response to a fire which destroyed parts of the mosque, further modifications were made which gradually transformed the mosque from a hypostyle plan to a four-*iwan* plan: first the *qibla iwan*, then the eastern and western *iwan*s, and finally the north *iwan* were constructed, probably free-standing at first, and then later connected to the fabric of the mosque. The next major addition was made in 1310 under the patronage of the Ilkhanid ruler Uljaytu, who had a prayer hall constructed on the western side of the mosque, to the north of the west *iwan*, adorned with a virtuoso stucco *mihrab*. Later in the fourteenth century, when Isfahan was under the control of the Muzaffarid dynasty, the *iwan*s gained the *muqarnas* and the turquoise tiled decoration, which are still extant; by this stage, the mosque had largely taken the form it retains today, despite ongoing minor alterations in later centuries (Fig. 6). Without the availability of textual sources which mention the mosque (a rare occurrence given the reticence of medieval Islamic historians and geographers concerning architecture), as well as the Italian excavations, little would be known of this sequence, as is the case with so many mosques in Iran.

The four-*iwan* plan which evolved in the Great Mosque of Isfahan in the twelfth century became the standard mosque plan throughout Iran in the Seljuk period, and remained so up until the modern era. In addition to its use in mosques all over western Iran, such as the Friday mosques of Ardestan, Zavareh, and Gulpaygan, the four-*iwan* plan was used for *madrasa*s, *khangah*s, hospitals, and palaces, so that it is a form associated with Iran rather than with any particular building type. Since baked brick had become standard for major mosques by this time, the survival rate of Seljuk mosques is also much better. From the sparse record and somewhat clumsy interpretations of the imported hypostyle plan characteristic of the earliest Iranian and Central Asian mosques, a corpus of mosque architecture grew with a strong regional identity, which often influenced Islamic architecture far to the west for centuries thereafter.

MELANIE MICHAILIDIS (d. 2013) was a specialist in the early Islamic art and architecture of Iran and Central Asia. She earned a PhD in Islamic art and architecture from The Massachusetts Institute of Technology in 2007. From 2011, she was the Korff Postdoctoral Fellow in Islamic Art at Washington University and curated the Islamic collection of the St. Louis Art Museum.

SUGGESTIONS FOR FURTHER READING

Godard, André. "Les Anciennes mosquées de l'Iran," *Athar-é Iran* I (1936), 187–210.

Grabar, Oleg. *The Great Mosque of Isfahan* (London: Tauris, 1990).

Hillenbrand, Robert. *Islamic Architecture: Form, Function & Meaning* (Edinburgh: Edinburgh University Press, 1994).

King, G.R.D. "The Nine Bay Domed Mosque in Islam," *Madrider Mitteilungen* 30 (1989), 332–90.

O'Kane, Bernard. "Iran and Central Asia," in *The Mosque: History, Architectural Development & Regional Diversity,* ed. Martin Frishman and Hasan-Uddin Khan (London: Thames & Hudson, 1994), 118–139.

Whitehouse, David. *Siraf III: The Congregational Mosque* (Leiden: Brill, 1980).

NOTES

1. See Richard Bulliet, *Conversion to Islam in the Medieval Period: A Study in Quantitative History* (Cambridge MA: Harvard University Press 1980); Jamsheed Choksy, *Conflict and Cooperation: Muslim Elites and Zoroastrian Subalterns in Medieval Iranian Society* (New York: Columbia University Press 1997), 70–108.

2. On the evolution of this mosque, see Oleg Grabar, *The Great Mosque of Isfahan* (New York: New York University Press 1990), 45–60; Eugenio Galdieri, *Isfahan: Masgid-i Guma* (Rome: Istituto italiano per il Medio ed Estremo Oriente 1972–3).

3. Frantz Grenet and Claude Rapin, "De la Samarkand antique à la Samarkand islamique: continuités et ruptures," *Colloque international d'archéologie islamique,* ed. Roland-Pierre Gayraud (Cairo: Institut Français d'Archéologie Orientale 1998), 392–394.

4. Yu. F. Buryakov and O.M. Rostovtsev, "Arkheologicheskie issledovaniya Rabinzhana," *Istoriya material'noi kulturi Uzbekistana* 19 (1984), 158.

5. Oleg Grabar, "The Visual Arts," *Cambridge History of Iran, Vol. 4: From the Arab Invasion to the Saljuqs,* ed. Richard Frye (Cambridge: Cambridge University Press, 1975), 334.

6. See Bernard O'Kane, "Iran and Central Asia," in *The Mosque: History, Architectural Development & Regional Diversity,* ed. Martin Frishman and Hasan-Uddin Khan (London: Thames and Hudson 1994), 119; Robert Hillenbrand, *Islamic Architecture: Form, Function and Meaning* (Edinburgh: Edinburgh University Press 1994), 101–102; Mehrdad Shokoohy, "Two Fire Temples Converted to Mosques in Central Iran," in *Papers in Honour of Professor Mary Boyce,* Acta Iranica 25 (Leiden: Brill 1985), 545–72.

7. Abu Bakr Muhammad b. Jafar al-Narshakhi, *History of Bukhara,* trans. Richard Frye (Cambridge MA: Mediaeval Academy of America 1954), 21, 48.

8. Choksy, *Conflict and Cooperation*, 97–8.

9. Narshakhi, *History of Bukhara,* 53.

10. Ibid, 87.

11. V.M. Filimonov, "Obobshchayushchii Otchet po issledovaniyu, analizy arkhitekturi i dekora, datirovke otdel'niikh sooruzhenii i periodov razvitiya arkhitekturnogo kompleksa Khakim al' Termezi v gorode Termez," (Arkhiv Glavnogo Upravleniya po Okhrane Pamyatnikov Material'noi Kul'turii i Muzeev Ministerstva Kul'turii Uzbekskoi SSR, Inv. No. SD1599/F53, 1957), 167–70.

12. O'Kane, "Iran and Central Asia," 120; see also Bernard O'Kane, "Čahārtāq II. In the Islamic Period," *Encyclopedia Iranica* IV, (New York: Encyclopaedia Iranica Foundation 1982-), 639–642; Robert Hillenbrand, "Abbasid Mosques in Iran," *Rivista degli studi orientali* 61 (1987), 211.

13. See David Whitehouse, "Siraf: A Medieval Port on the Persian Gulf," *World Archaeology* 2/ 2 (Oct. 1970), 146–147.

14. André Godard, "Les anciennes mosquées de l'Iran," *Athār-e Irān* I/2 (1936), 187–210; see also André Godard, "Les anciennes mosquées de l'Iran," *Arts asiatiques* III (1956), 48–63.

15. Jean Sauvaget, "Observations sur quelques mosquées seldjoukides," *Annales de l'Institut d'Études Orientales* V (1938), 116–117.

16. Janine Sourdel-Thomine, "Inscriptions seldjoukides et salles de coupoles de Qazwin en Iran," *Revue des Études Islamiques* 42 (1974), 42–43.

17. O'Kane, EI, 640.

18. Sergei Khmel'nitskii, *Mezhdu Arabami i Tiorkami* (Berlin & Riga: Continent 1992), 91–96.

19. Hillenbrand, "Abbasid Mosques in Iran," 188.

20. Robert Hillenbrand's description of the plan is both thorough and excellent: see Hillenbrand, "Abbasid Mosques in Iran," 186–193.

21. Geoffrey King "The Nine Bay Domed Mosque in Islam," *Madrider Mitteilungen* 30 (1989), 332–90.

22. See Khmel'nitskii, *Mezhdu Arabami i Tiorkami*, 98.

23. See V.M. Filimonov "Drevnee rezone derevo iz komplekca Kusama ibn Abbasa v ansamblye Shakhi-Zinda," *Iskusstvo zodchikh Uzbekistana* I (Tashkent: Akademii nauk Uzbekskoi SSR 1962), 276.

24. Khmel'nitskii summarizes the arguments in favor of this interpretation: see Khmel'nitskii, *Mezhdu Arabami i Tiorkami*, 78–81.

25. M.E. Masson, *Srednevekovye Torgovye Puti iz Merva v Khorezm i v Maverannakhr: Trudi* YUTAKE XIII (Ashkhabad: Turkmenistan 1966), 118.

26. Lisa Golombek, "Abbasid Mosque at Balkh," *Oriental Art* XV/3 (1969), 173–189. See also Assadouleh Melikian-Chirvani, "La plus ancienne mosquée de Balkh," *Arts Asiatiques* XX (1969), 3–9.

27. See Narshakhi, *History of Bukhara*, 25, 51, 53.

28. Khmel'nitskii, *Mezhdu Arabami i Tiorkami,* 66–67.

29. Ibid, 64–71.

30. Ibid, 64.

31. Masson, *Srednevekovye Torgovye Puti*, 106.

32. Khmel'nitskii, *Mezhdu Arabami i Tiorkami*, 103–4.

33. Samarra was the Abbasid capital from 836 to 883, and its excavated remains provide much of what is known about metropolitan Abbasid art and architecture in the ninth century. The architectural decoration found at Samarra exerted a wide-ranging and long-lasting influence throughout the Islamic world: see Richard Ettinghausen, Oleg Grabar, and Marilyn Jenkins-Madina, *Islamic Art and Architecture 650–1250* (New Haven: Yale University Press 2001), 54–59.

34. Sheila Blair, *The Monumental Inscriptions of Early Islamic Iran and Transoxiana* (Leiden: Brill 1992), 38–39.

35. Sheila Blair, "The Octagonal Pavilion at Natanz: A Reexamination of Early Islamic Architecture in Iran," *Muqarnas* 1 (1983), 87–88 (69–94); see also Blair, *Monumental Inscriptions*, 52–53.

36. Blair, *Monumental Inscriptions*, 76–77.

37. See Oleg Grabar, *The Great Mosque of Isfahan,* 45–60.

Funerary Architecture in Iraq under the Abbasids and their Successors, 750–1250

MATTHEW SABA

1 Imam Dur Tomb, Samarra, c. 1085. Exterior view before destruction in 2014, taken in 1979.
Photo: Yasser Tabbaa Archive, courtesy of Aga Khan Documentation Center, MIT Libraries

Geographers in the Islamic tradition would have defined Iraq as the region encompassing lower Mesopotamia from approximately the southern edge of the Jazira at Hit and Takrit down to the Persian Gulf, and from the Zagros in the east to the Arabian and Syrian deserts in the west. The political power of the Abbasid dynasty (r. 749–1258) began to wane in Iraq in the last decades of the ninth century, greatly diminishing in 945 when administration of Abbasid territories had fallen to several vassal dynasties;[1] yet, Abbasid Baghdad continued to be a cultural center of great importance. It was the Abbasids who founded Baghdad in 762 and, in doing so, reactivated the surrounding region, once a heartland of Sasanian culture, to become the "navel of the earth" in Islamic society.[2] While the non-Abbasid western regions of Islamdom rose in prominence during the tenth century, Iraq remained an important cultural center until the ultimate demise of the Abbasids in the Mongol invasions of 1258.

Our knowledge of the history of funerary architecture in Iraq is complicated by the problem of accessibility. In Baghdad, where one might search for earlier examples, the fact that the city center has shifted over time and the early Islamic areas are largely overlaid by later developments makes archaeological research on its formative years extremely difficult.[3] Similarly, the Shi'i shrines at Baghdad, Karbala, Najaf, and Samarra represent centuries of rebuilding and renovation, meaning that their original forms are obscure. Even in rural areas, the Mesopotamian landscape has never been kind to the preservation of architecture. Recent interruptions to research in Iraq due to conflict and political instability only exacerbate these issues. One result of these difficulties has been the formation of a rather uneven scholarly landscape: a

terrain characterized by deep but narrow trenches of scholarly research on certain times and places.[4] Despite these difficulties, surveying the extant scholarship is useful, for while the narrowness of these trenches limits one's vista from within, viewing them at a distance reveals broader regional patterns.

The synthetic studies we do have collectively suggest that both the private tomb and public shrine had become part of Iraq's architectural landscape by the end of the eleventh century, and that the beginnings of this development occur in the tenth century.[5] This time period roughly corresponds to the beginnings of evidence for monumental tombs in areas outside Iraq.[6] More interesting is that the examples of funerary architecture that survive from the end of this timespan share certain elements of iconography with that of other regions but also diverge in significant ways, suggesting a well-defined, regional tradition of funerary architecture.

LITERARY EVIDENCE FOR FUNERARY ARCHITECTURE IN IRAQ

Until further research can take place at early sites like Abbasid Samarra, evidence for funerary architecture in Iraq before the eleventh century must be sought in textual sources. Fortunately, the sources for Abbasid Iraq are many – Baghdad is particularly well described – and these have allowed architectural historians to see significant developments in Muslim funerary architecture during the period in question.

One significant finding involves the burial practices of the Abbasid caliphs, who were significant patrons of monumental mosques and palaces throughout their reign. The texts indicate that the monumental tomb was not originally part of the dynasty's architectural vocabulary, but eventually become one. Studies of the written sources by Terry Allen and Thomas Leisten specifically show that contrary to the practices of later Islamic dynasties, many early Abbasid caliphs and their kin were buried in private within palaces, a form of burial related to the more widespread Near-Eastern practice of interment within the house.[7] It is only in the middle of the tenth century that an innovation in this practice occurred. From this point forward, sources specify that a number of caliphs were buried outside the palace complex in the cemetery of Khayzuran, which stood in Baghdad's Rusafa quarter on the eastern bank of the Tigris.[8] Al-Radi (d. 940) was the first caliph to be buried there, in what we hear was a "large tomb (*turba aẓīma*) upon which great wealth was spent."[9] Over the next two centuries five additional caliphs were buried at the cemetery in tombs they or their family members had constructed.[10] Seven others who were initially buried in the traditional manner on palace grounds were exhumed and transported to the cemetery, resulting in a total of thirteen caliphal burials in this manner.[11]

Textual sources indicate that some of these later Abbasid tombs were rather substantial. In the case of the burials at the dynastic cemetery, several are said to be within a *turba* (tomb) or a *qubba* (dome), both vague terms that nonetheless suggest more than a simple grave.[12] By the first quarter of the thirteenth century, it appears that we are dealing with a monumental structure, as the Baghdadi geographer Yaqat al-Hamawi (d. 1229) describes the Abbasid burials at Khayzuran as including a large *turba* housing the graves of nine caliphs, and states that charitable endowments (*awqāf*) funded its upkeep by a staff of attendants.[13]

Regarding the reason behind the shift from palace to cemetery, Allen suggests that the Sunni Abbasids began to construct more monumental tombs as a response to newly erected Shi'i shrines in Iraq, which were beginning to attract large numbers of pilgrims.[14] The shift in burial practice would thus have a political significance. Leisten, however, points to one complication in this interpretation, suggesting that the relative lack of information in earlier sources about its form and the absence of

any mention of ceremonies attached to the complex suggest an inaccessible monument.[15] In this case, the *turba* at Khayzuran may have been large, but would have served a different function from the more public-facing Shi'i shrines.

The extent to which these later caliphal tombs were visible and accessible is difficult to determine from the available evidence. To the arguments above I would add that a burial site with somewhat limited access does resonate with other tendencies in official Abbasid architecture and the system of court ceremonial with which it had evolved. The observations of the courtier Hilal al-Sabi (d. 1055/6) show that by the tenth century, the Abbasid court had become a highly ritualized space in which interaction between caliph and subjects was strictly controlled.[16] At Samarra, the palace itself evolved to become a massive complex designed to regulate such interactions between caliph and subject, being accessible but physically severed from other public institutions like the congregational mosque and markets.[17] Given the caliph's elevated and exclusive status, a tomb that was accessible, but only in certain circumstances and under strict supervision, would be fitting for his final resting place.

While the texts do not resolve the question of whether the Abbasids' extra-palatial tombs were large, public monuments, they strongly support Allen's observation that the change in Abbasid burials corresponds to the development of public funerary monuments outside the court. Already in the ninth century, there is ample textual evidence of shrines commemorating the burials of figures important to the various religious communities in Iraq, whose landscape was dotted with sites that held the memory of early Islamic conquest and, indeed, sectarian skirmishes. The Shi'a in particular had a significant history in this region and began to commemorate their martyrs and imams (spiritual leaders) from an early date. A number of old and important Shi'a shrines are located in Iraq. First and foremost are the shrine at Najaf, which marks the grave of the Prophet's son-in-law and first Shi'a imam, Ali ibn Abi Talib (d. 661),[18] and the shrine at Karbala commemorating the site where Ali's son Husayn, the third imam, was martyred in 680.[19]

In Baghdad, the shrine known as al-Kazimiyya or al-Kazimayn houses the tombs of the seventh and ninth imams, Musa al-Kazim (d. *c.* 799) and Muhammad al-Jawad (d. 835).[20] Finally, at Samarra, a shrine developed around the tombs of the tenth and eleventh imams, Ali al-Hadi (d. 868) and Hasan al-Askari (873/4).[21]

Since many of these shrines are still in use today and have been rebuilt and expanded throughout their history, little architecture is preserved that dates before 1300, but some evidence of their early histories can be gleaned from the sources.[22] In terms of form, domes were likely a common feature of the earliest structures.[23] We hear, for example, that Abu al-Hayja ibn Hamdan (d. 929), a prince from a family of governors in northern Mesopotamia with Shi'i leanings, built a domed monument with open sides over the grave of Ali at Najaf and hung it with curtains and fine tapestries.[24] In the second half of the tenth century, the Buyids, the Shi'i dynasty who ruled Iraq and western Iran in the name of the Abbasids, also added domes to the Kazimiyya shrine, one over each imam's tomb.[25] Another important architectural feature that appears in early descriptions of several shrines is a large open space surrounding the tomb chamber and an outer enclosure wall, which offered security to pilgrims congregating inside.[26] Cemeteries, mosques and schools eventually developed on the grounds, and James Allan has suggested that by the end of the eleventh century, it may be more accurate to speak of the shrines as sets of adjoined institutions rather than isolated domed tombs.[27]

While the Shi'a contributed significantly to the development of shrines in Abbasid Iraq, the sources show that this form of funerary architecture was by no means limited to Shi'i contexts. The pious of Baghdad also erected tombs over the graves of a number of important Sunni figures, serving both to distinguish their gravesites and to accommodate visitors. In the tenth century, for example, Muqaddasi reports that the Baghdad tomb of Abu Hanifa al-Nu'man (d. 767), the founder of one of the four Sunni schools of law, had acquired a *ṣuffa*, probably meaning a platform or bench.[28] In 1066, Sharaf al-Mulk al-Khwarizmi, the finance minister

of the Seljuq court in Baghdad, rebuilt the tomb, adding a school for the study of law.[29] This addition would have transformed the gravesite into a center for pilgrims, scholars and students.

Topographical descriptions of Baghdad in the eleventh century attest to how important the shrines of respected religious figures, both Sunni and Shi'i, had become for the city's identity. In the introduction to his *Ta'rikh Baghdad* (*History of Baghdad*) al-Khatib al-Baghdadi (d. 1071) tells the following story, emphasizing the sacredness endowed to the city by virtue of its housing the tombs of four saints of God (*awliyā' Allāh*), including two early Sufis, a preacher and Ahmad ibn Hanbal:[30]

> Upon leaving Baghdad, I was approached by a person who bore the mark of a devout man. He inquired, "Where are you coming from?" "From Baghdad," I said. "I fled the city, for seeing the corruption there, I feared it might be swallowed up with its populace." He said, "Return and do not fear. For in Baghdad stand the graves of four saints. They are a fortress for the people of Baghdad against every misfortune." "Who are they?" I inquired. "Buried there are the imam Ahmad ibn Hanbal, Ma'ruf al-Karkhi, Bishr al-Hafi, and Mansur b. Ammar." I did not leave the city that year, but returned and visited the graves.[31]

The same anecdote is repeated a century later by Ibn al-Jawzi (d. 1200) in his *Manaqib Baghdad* (*The Virtues of Baghdad*). As in the version cited above, the disillusioned Baghdadi is convinced to return to his city by the pious man, but Ibn al-Jawzi mentions that he is leaving specifically for the Hajj.[32] Thus, a trip to the local tombs stands in lieu of even the ultimate pilgrimage. This striking example points to a culture in which the visitation of tombs had become a widespread practice across sectarian lines.

In addition to the various roles they played in the lives of pious Muslims, these public-facing shrines were important within the sectarian political arena of ninth- and tenth-century Iraq.[33] The political aspect is perhaps most evident in the turbulent construction, destruction, and

reconstruction histories of these monuments recorded in the sources. The Sunni Abbasid caliphs sponsored construction at the great Shi'i shrines but were also known to destroy the same structures as warnings. At Karbala, for example, the caliph Harun al-Rashid (d. 809) allotted funds for the upkeep of Husayn's tomb and later destroyed it. His successor, al-Ma'mun, is credited with rebuilding the tomb, and Mutawakkil, in turn, with leveling it, apparently out of frustration with the large amount of attention it was attracting from pilgrims.[34] When the Buyids and Hamdanids, both Shi'i dynasties, rose to power during the collapse of the Abbasid Empire in the tenth century, each sponsored extensive building campaigns at several of the shrines.[35] It is possible that conspicuous patronage at these popular sites allowed emergent dynasties to visibly display their newfound wealth and to ingratiate themselves to local Shi'a.

The extent to which shrines had become sites for the demonstration of sectarian loyalties is highlighted by events like the 1051 destruction of the Kazimiyya Shrine. Heightened tensions

2 Qubbat al-Sulaybiyya, Samarra, c. 850–900. Exterior view before its reconstruction in 1969.
Photo: Marilyn Jenkins-Madina Archive, courtesy of Aga Khan Documentation Center, MIT Libraries

3 Qubbat al-Sulaybiyya, Samarra, c. 850–900. Plan of the octagonal pavilion, not including platform and ramps by Said Arida after Creswell.
Photo: Aga Khan Documentation Center, MIT Libraries. © Nasser Rabbat / Aga Khan Program for Islamic Architecture, MIT

between the Sunnis and Shi'a in Baghdad resulted in a mob of Sunnis breaking into the tomb and looting the valuables stored there as well as its fixtures made of precious metal.[36] The reports specify that the graves of Shi'i notables that had accumulated around the shrine were opened and the shrine's two domes made of teak burned to the ground. It is noteworthy that the treasures looted by the mob were then deposited at another burial site important to the Sunni community: the tomb of Ahmad ibn Hanbal (d. 855).[37]

Research on textual evidence for tombs in early Islamic Iraq has been fruitful in resurrecting a number of monuments that left no archaeological trace. These texts suggest that by the eleventh century, the cityscapes of Baghdad and other centers would have included numerous private tombs with monumental features as well as public shrines whose plans evolved to accommodate a stream of visitors seeking spiritual rewards. Iraq, like its neighbors, thus participated in the growth of the mausoleum as a form of Islamic architecture from the tenth century on, and perhaps even before. In the specific case of Iraq, the architectural form may have developed in part as a result of vying sectarian groups, including political dynasties, who sought to make themselves visible through patronage at key sites.

ARCHAEOLOGICAL EVIDENCE FOR EARLY ISLAMIC TOMBS IN IRAQ

While few, a number of standing monuments securely dated before 1250 give us an idea of the shape that the tombs described in the sources may have taken. These few monuments point to the development of a spectacular and unique regional interpretation of a more widespread tomb type. The earliest standing structure in Iraq used as a Muslim burial place is in some ways as frustrating as the textual sources, as its original purpose is still unclear. It is the Qubbat al-Sulaybiyya, an enigmatic domed octagonal building located amid the ruins of Abbasid palaces and gardens on the west bank of the Tigris (Fig. 2). The building had eight doors, one on each side of its octagonal exterior, which

led to an ambulatory covered by a roof (Fig. 3). The ambulatory surrounded a square domed chamber measuring 6.3 meters across, accessible through four doors, one per side. Each wall of the central room was decorated with two pointed niches flanking the doors. In this central, domed room, three Muslim burials of an undetermined date came to light.[38] Later excavations further revealed that the entire building sat on an elevated platform accessed by four ramps.[39] The platform measured 5.5 meters from the octagon's exterior to the outer edge and rose approximately 2.5 meters above ground level. Already situated on an escarpment overlooking the Tigris floodplain, the building was thus elevated substantially from its surroundings. The structure has been dated to the last half of the ninth century based on the similarity of its building materials to those used in the monuments of Abbasid Samarra, especially the nearby Qasr al-Ashiq built for the caliph al-Mu'tamid after 870.[40]

The Qubba's first excavator, Ernst Herzfeld, believed that it was a tomb, and this interpretation became popular among scholars.[41] More recently, Thomas Leisten and Alastair Northedge have challenged this idea based on the form of the monument and the likely later date of the burials.[42] While the original function of the Qubba remains obscure, Leisten points out that the structure still must have fulfilled local expectations of what a tomb should be: after all, it did eventually serve as a burial place for three people, and the style of a Kufic graffito found in situ suggests that the burials were likely before the twelfth century.[43] This building, then, remains important to consider in a history of early Muslim funerary architecture as an indicator of qualities that people at this time considered appropriate or desirable for tombs.

Features of the Qubba such as its situation on a height overlooking a river and its use of a dome relate to other examples of early commemorative architecture in the Islamic world. The earliest standing funerary monuments in the far eastern provinces of the Abbasid empire demonstrate the primacy of domed buildings as a tomb form.[44] The building's placement on a platform and its domed octagonal shape also have obvious resonances with the features of one monument in particular, the equally ambiguous yet paradigmatic Dome of the Rock, among whose cluster of associations by the tenth century included commemoration.[45] Another quality worth mentioning is its relative isolation. Samarra shrank quickly in size after the court abandoned it in 892 and thus the Qubba, already on the outskirts of the Abbasid city in a zone of riverside gardens, secluded palaces, and orchards, may have seemed remote to locals by the beginning of the tenth century. Isolation and a vista including major topographical features may have been one concept that united the earliest funerary monuments known in greater Iran: there, one theme is a choice of sites with vistas of mountains and rivers.[46] The Qubbat al-Sulaybiyya, situated outside a largely abandoned city and affording a view of the Tigris, may provide another example on the southwestern fringe of the Iranian cultural zone.

The next datable standing monument used for a funerary purpose in Iraq is the tomb known as Imam Dur, built in the last two decades of the eleventh century in a village just north of Samarra, where it stood intact until 2014 (Fig. 1).[47] Unlike the Qubbat al-Sulaybiyya, it is clear that the original function of this monument was as a tomb. Inscriptions in situ tell us that it was the *turba* of Abu 'Abd-Allah Muhammad, son of Musa al-Kazim, the seventh Shi'i imam, and identify an *amir* of the Banu Uqayl named Sharaf al-Dawla Muslim ibn Quraysh as the person who commissioned it. While it is uncertain who is in fact buried in the tomb, the inscriptions make its function clear and allow us to date the monument to circa 1085, the death year of the patron, or to the years immediately following.[48]

The tomb consisted of a square chamber, twelve meters high, topped by a large *muqarnas* vault. The exterior of the building was decorated in a technique known as *hazār bāf*, "thousand threads," referring to the carpet-like effect formed by the arrangement of bricks in repetitive relief patterns. In this case, a band of rhombi ran across the top of the square base. On the interior, the transition from square base to rounded vault was made through four squinches. The vault consisted of four courses, each with eight *muqarnas* cells. Adding to the visual interest of the ceiling was

4 Umm al-Awlad, Babil Governorate, southwest of Tell al-Ukhaymir, c. eleventh century? General view showing building as it stood in the 1970s.
Photo: Yasser Tabbaa Archive, courtesy of Aga Khan Documentation Center, MIT Libraries

5 Abu Hatab, Babil Governorate, 7 km west of Niliyya, c. eleventh–twelfth century? General view showing building as it stood in the 1970s.
Photo: Yasser Tabbaa Archive, courtesy of Aga Khan Documentation Center, MIT Libraries

the use of carving on each of the cells, which served to further articulate its fragmented surface.

Two architectural features separated the *muqarnas* dome of Imam Dur from *muqarnas* domes that would develop in other parts of the Islamic world. First, the dome of Imam Dur was architecturally separate from the base on which it rested, meaning that it sat on top of the cube rather than being integrated into it. Second, the shell covering the vault is not covered by a roof of any sort, meaning that the form of the *muqarnas* cells is visible on the exterior. Imam Dur's exposed *muqarnas* dome anticipated similar vaults on a number of tombs that would appear in and around Iraq a century later. Like Imam Dur, these are composed of either a polygonal or square chamber topped with a high *muqarnas* vault whose sculptural form is visible on the exterior due to the exposure of the shell without a covering.

A number of poorly understood monuments of an undetermined but very likely pre-Mongol date may help fill in the century of architectural history between Imam Dur and the next securely dated funerary monuments in Iraq, which come in the 1190s. The monuments in question are four domed cubes that stand along the banks of the ancient canal known as Shatt al-Nil, which linked the Euphrates above Hilla to the Tigris near Nu'maniyya.[49] From west to east, these are the ruined structures known as al-'Aziba, Umm al-Awlad, Abu Hatab, and Imam al-Najmi. These monuments have attracted little scholarly attention outside of two surveys of the canal conducted by Ernst Herzfeld in 1907 and Paolo M. Costa in 1966.[50] A photographic survey of the region by Yasser Tabbaa in the 1970s supplements these.[51] The form of the Shatt al-Nil monuments suggests that they functioned as tombs: in addition to being domed cubes, two have *mihrab*s, a feature that when combined with the simple domed form strongly suggests use as a tomb.[52] Their local names and the legends surrounding them also support this interpretation, as three of the names refer to people and further evoke an element of hagiography.[53]

Among them, Umm al-Awlad is perhaps the oldest.[54] Situated some few kilometers to the

6 Al-'Aziba, Babil Governorate, c. late twelfth–thirteenth century? General view of the ruin in the first decade of the twentieth century.
Photo: Arnold Nöldeke, reproduced in Sarre and Herzfeld, *Archäologische Reise im Euphrat- und Tigris-Gebiet*, vol. 3 pl. XXXVI

southeast of Tell al-Ukhaymir (ancient Kish) on the southern bank of the canal, this structure is a square chamber made of fine brick masonry measuring 8.2 meters per side, crowned with an elliptical dome. The transition from base to dome is made by an octagon formed of eight pointed arches (Fig. 4). Costa points out that the style of the brick masonry featured on the dome, characterized by a lack of plastering and the use of chamfered profiles as a sort of sparse yet elegant ornament, relates it to the domes of several dated monuments in Iran. Those constructed behind the northeast and southwest *iwan*s of Isfahan's Friday Mosque, dated to the last two decades of the eleventh century, are particularly similar.[55] If this is an indication of date, Umm al-Awlad may well be contemporary to Imam Dur or earlier. Abu Hatab, located some seven kilometers east of Umm al-Awlad, is architecturally related to Umm al-Awlad (Fig. 5).[56] The simple square chamber most likely also featured an elliptical dome. As for its date, the only clue is the plastered interior that featured a form of vine scroll which led Herzfeld to propose a vague twelfth or thirteenth century date for the monument.[57]

Al-'Aziba and Imam al-Najmi belong to a separate class, as both featured the remnants of elaborate *muqarnas* domes. Al-'Aziba is only known through a brief mention in Sarre and Herzfeld's survey of the area and a photograph (Fig. 6).[58] One wishes Herzfeld would have more fully documented the site with drawings and measurements, as it had disappeared when Costa surveyed the area in 1967.[59] The photo reproduced, then, is worth describing in detail. It shows the corner of a quadrangular

FUNERARY ARCHITECTURE IN IRAQ 167

building made of brick. On its interior, the remains of a zone of transition to an elaborate *muqarnas* dome are visible. One can see the tops of two courses of large *muqarnas* cells and what appears to be the bottom of a third in the photo. I count seven cells in the highest fully preserved course, which would mean that the full course encircling the chamber would have had around four times this many, suggesting a dome springing from a base ring of over two dozen *muqarnas* cells. The integration of the *muqarnas* cells into the walls below the springing of the dome further demonstrates that the architect used *muqarnas* to mask the transition from base to dome: here, then, is a system far more complex than at Imam Dur, whose dome remained architecturally separate from its base and featured courses of only eight cells.

7 Imam al-Najmi, c. late twelfth–thirteenth century? General view of the building as it stood in the 1970s.
Photo: Yasser Tabbaa Archive, courtesy of Aga Khan Documentation Center, MIT Libraries

This brings us to the last of the four Shatt al-Nil Monuments and the most exquisite: the so-called Imam al-Najmi (Fig. 7). The original structure must have sat in a compound, because there is evidence of a perimeter wall surrounding it along with the ruins of other structures, and ceramic sherds litter the area.[60] It consists of a chamber made of baked brick measuring 12.3 meters square at its base and tapering toward its top, which rises 11 meters high.[61] An octagonal drum made of eight pointed arches rising from the walls supports the remnants of a *muqarnas* dome, of which the circular setting only remains. The octagon formed by the arches is fully visible from the outside, and one presumes the *muqarnas* shell was also bare. The transition from square to circular setting via octagonal drum is fully integrated on the interior by *muqarnas* cells that extend from the dome down into the supporting arches, masking these architectonic elements.

When were these rather grand *muqarnas*-vaulted structures built? Herzfeld and Costa both concluded that the complexity of the domes in comparison to Imam Dur suggest a date later than 1100. I would argue further that a date before the middle of the twelfth century is unlikely, based on the extent of the leap in complexity from Imam Dur to the two Shatt al-Nil monuments. Without further research, little more is certain. Aside from excavation, one possible avenue to obtaining a *terminus ante quem* for these monuments would be better understanding settlement patterns in the Mesopotamian countryside during the Abbasid period, which depended as in other eras in this region on the maintenance of canals.[62] When exactly did the Shatt al-Nil cease to function? Answering this question is beyond the current survey, but is well worth pursuing.

Moving back to Baghdad brings us two final examples of pre-Mongol tomb architecture, related in form to the *muqarnas*-vaulted tombs of the Shatt al-Nil. These tombs, whose *muqarnas* domes are perhaps the grandest examples of the unmasked Iraqi form left standing, are products of the patronage of the Abbasid caliph al-Nasir (r. 1180–1225), who briefly reinstated caliphal authority in Iraq before its ultimate demise at the hands of the Mongols in 1258.[63] The first of these is a tomb that al-Nasir built in the last quarter of the twelfth century for his mother Zumurrud Khatun (d. 1203), although it is identified in early European scholarship as the tomb of Sitt Zubayda, the wife of Harun al-Rashid.[64]

The tomb, situated in a large cemetery in western Baghdad, is an octagonal structure covered by a cone-shaped *muqarnas* vault (Fig. 8). Like the Shatt al-Nil domes, the vault is fully integrated with the octagonal structure supporting it through nine courses of *muqarna*s cells. An innovation is that each cell is pierced by a small hole, allowing rays of light into the vault (Fig. 9). The exterior of the tomb is also more lavish, being embellished with ornamental brickwork. Each of the octagon's faces is divided into four fields, the two on top containing a pattern based on grids radiating from six- and eight-pointed stars. The bottom fields each contain a niche, also surrounded by decorative brickwork.

Around the beginning of the thirteenth century, al-Nasir commissioned a second *muqarnas*-vaulted tomb for the Sufi sheikh Shihab al-Din Umar al-Suhrawardi (d. 1234), who was recruited as an advisor and diplomatic messenger for the caliph (Fig. 10).[65] The tomb chamber consists of a square base topped by a conical *muqarnas* vault with twelve courses of cells, similar to those on the dome of the Zumurrud Khatun tomb. The dome rises to a height of 11.2 meters, making it a good three meters taller than its square base. The antechamber to the tomb and the surrounding mosque were renovated throughout history, but the tomb chamber and its vault are original.

The funerary architecture in Iraq initially resembled that of adjacent regions where the

8 Zumurrud Khatun Tomb, Baghdad, 1190s.
Photo: Kamil and Rifat Chadirji Photographic Archive, courtesy of Aga Khan Documentation Center, MIT Libraries

9 Zumurrud Khatun Tomb, Baghdad, 1190s. View of *Muqarnas* Vault.
Photo: Yasser Tabbaa Archive, courtesy of Aga Khan Documentation Center, MIT Libraries

10 Umar Suhrawardi Tomb, Baghdad, c. 1200.
Photo: A. Kerim, courtesy of Special Collections, Fine Arts Library, Harvard University

earliest examples of monumental tombs are found, but it eventually took on local flavor. The Qubbat al-Sulaybiyya, whatever its original purpose, was a domed octagon situated on the outskirts of a largely abandoned city with a view over the landscape: all qualities that relate it to early mausolea in eastern Iran and Central Asia and explain its secondary use as a tomb. The enigmatic Umm al-Awlad and Abu Hatab show that the simple domed cube remained a relevant form in Mesopotamia. An innovation comes with the exposed *muqarnas* domes, first appearing in around 1090 and being widespread in the region by around 1200, as the two tombs in Baghdad and along the Shatt al-Nil demonstrate, as do many other examples that date to the following two centuries.[66] The limited geographic distribution of this form, which only appears in Iraq and the neighboring regions of Khuzistan and Luristan, indicates that the group represents a local mutation of a global form, where the exterior of the dome itself became a sculptural surface of substantial aesthetic complexity. Yasser Tabbaa has made a convincing argument for early eleventh-century Baghdad as the possible point of origin for this local mutation of the domed cube.[67]

The development of the domed cube for tombs in Iraq raises questions regarding its potential local significance. In terms of effect, the exposed *muqarnas* vault certainly serves to increase the visibility of the structure from the outside. Both the extended height of these vaults, often as tall as the structures that support them, and their articulated surface, create a dramatic profile visible from great distances. From within, the effect is rather different: instead of a solid, well-defined mass, a person standing under the vault gazing upwards has difficulty determining where the wall ends and the ceiling begins, and the play of light and shadow on the *muqarnas* cells creates a sense of weightlessness (Fig. 9). In his discussion of these vaults, Tabbaa points to a striking resonance between the illusion of impermanence created by the *muqarnas*, in which the surface appears to change with the changing daylight and the structural forces supporting the dome are obscured, and the image of a perishable and transient universe central to theological

concepts espoused during the eleventh and twelfth centuries in Baghdad by the Abbasids and their Sunni allies.[68] Read in this way, the evolution of an architectural form made manifest an increasingly pervasive way of understanding the world.

Whatever the significance of the regionally-specific exposed *muqarnas* dome may have been, the proliferation of tombs in a locally-articulated, innovative style at some point in the eleventh century speaks to the continuing importance of publicly-performed spiritual affiliation in the checkered political landscape of Iraq under the Abbasid successor states. Imam Dur was constructed by a provincial governor whose military successes allowed him the chance to build. In making his mark, he chose to commemorate a relatively obscure member of the Prophet's family, thus emphasizing his affiliation to Shi'i Islam. Similarly, al-Nasir's patronage of monumental tombs in the late twelfth-century might be seen as part of the caliph's attempt to gain spiritual clout among the religious sects. In addition to constructing the tomb of Sufi shaykh al-Suhrawardi in Baghdad, al-Nasir sponsored renovations to the Shi'i shrines at Samarra, Najaf and Karbala, and restored the Sunni Nizamiyya *madrasa* in Baghdad.[69] While these monuments do not survive, Sheikh Suhrawardi's tomb, whose *muqarnas* vault still towers over the surrounding cemetery, stands as a testament to this caliph's strategic use of architecture to cement alliances, and to the significant role that funerary monuments played in his building program.

MATTHEW SABA is Visual Resources Librarian for Islamic Architecture at the Aga Khan Documentation Center, MIT Libraries. Before joining MIT, Matthew was as a postdoctoral curatorial fellow at the Metropolitan Museum of Art, where he worked on a project to digitize the papers of Ernst Herzfeld. His research interests include the history of early Islamic architecture, and questions related to the digitization and description of Islamic art and architecture in libraries and databases.

SUGGESTIONS FOR FURTHER READING

Allan, James W. *The Art and Architecture of Twelver Shi'ism: Iraq, Iran and the Indian Sub-Continent* (London: Azimuth Editions, 2012).

Allen, Terry. "The Tombs of the 'Abbāsid Caliphs in Baghdād," *Bulletin of the School of Oriental and African Studies, University of London* 46: 3 (1983), 421–31.

Grabar, Oleg. "The Earliest Islamic Commemorative Structures, Notes and Documents," *Ars Orientalis* 6 (1966), 7–46.

Leisten, Thomas. *Architektur für Tote: Bestattung in architektonischem Kontext in den Kernländern der islamischen Welt zwischen 3./9. und 6./12. Jahrhundert* (Berlin: Dietrich Reimer, 1998).

Rāǵib, Yūsuf. "Les premiers monuments funéraires de l'Islam," *Annales Islamologiques* 9 (1970), 21–36.

Strika, Vincenzo and Jābir Khalīl. *The Islamic Architecture of Baghdād: The Results of a Joint Italian-Iraqi Survey* (Naples: Istituto Universitario Orientale, 1987).

NOTES

[1] Marshall G. S. Hodgson, *The Venture of Islam: Conscience and History in a World Civilization. Volume 1, The Classical Age of Islam* (Chicago. University of Chicago Press, 1974), 473–95.

[2] Aḥmad ibn Abī Ya'qūb al-Ya'qūbī, *Kitāb al-Buldān*, ed. M. J. de Goeje (Leiden: Brill, 1891), 233.

[3] Studies on the topography of Baghdad during the early Islamic period include Guy Le Strange, *Baghdad during the Abbasid Caliphate* (1900; Oxford: Clarendon Press, 1924 2nd ed.); Friedrich Sarre and Ernst Herzfeld, *Archäologische Reise im Euphrat- und Tigris-Gebiet*, 3 vols. (Berlin: Dietrich Reimer, 1911–1920), 2: 106–202; K. A. C. Creswell, *Early Muslim Architecture: Umayyads, Early 'Abbāsids and Ṭūlūnids*, 2 vols. (Oxford: Clarendon Press, 1932–1940), 2: 1–38; Jacob Lassner, *The Topography of Baghdad in the Early Middle Ages: Text and Studies* (Detroit: Wayne State University Press, 1970); Vincenzo Strika and Jābir Khalīl, *The Islamic Architecture of Baghdād: The Results of a Joint Italian-Iraqi Survey* (Naples: Istituto Universitario Orientale, 1987).

[4] Compare the relatively well documented monumental architecture of ninth-century Iraq to our understanding of architecture from the tenth and eleventh.

[5] Oleg Grabar, "The Earliest Islamic Commemorative Structures, Notes and Documents," *Ars Orientalis* 6 (1966), 7–46 (entries 2, 5, 8, 14, 15 and 16); Yūsuf Rāǵib, "Les premiers monuments funéraires de l'Islam," *Annales Islamologiques* 9 (1970), 21–36; Thomas Leisten, *Architektur für Tote: Bestattung in architektonischem Kontext in den Kernländern der islamischen Welt zwischen 3./9. und 6./12. Jahrhundert* (Berlin: Dietrich Reimer, 1998), 30–31.

[6] Robert Hillenbrand, *Islamic Architecture: Form, Function, and Meaning* (Edinburgh: Edinburgh University Press, 1994), 270–75.

[7] Terry Allen, "The Tombs of the 'Abbāsid Caliphs in Baghdād," *Bulletin of the School of Oriental and African Studies, University of London* 46: 3 (1983), 421–31; Leisten, *Artchitektur für Tote*, 39–41. For House burials see Leisten, *Architektur für Tote*, 35–9.

[8] Allen, "Tombs of the 'Abbāsid Caliphs," 421–423, Leisten, *Architektur für Tote*, 45–51.

[9] Leisten, *Architektur für Tote*, 118. This quotation is taken from an obituary for the caliph included in Ibn al-Jawzī, *al-Muntaẓam fī tā'rīkh al-mulūk wa'l-umam*, 6 vols. (Hyderabad: Dā'irat al-Ma'ārif al-'Uthmāniyya, 1357–9 [1938–40]), 6: 324–5.

[10] Al-Mustakfi (d. 949), al-Muti' (d. 974), al-Ta'i' (d. 1003), al-Qadir (d. 1031) and al-Muqtafi (d. 1160). References to their obituaries given in Leisten, *Architektur für Tote*, 46–8.

[11] Al-Qa'im (d. 1075), al-Muqtadi (d. 1094), al-Mustazhir (d. 1118) al-Mustanjid (d. 1170), Al-Nasir (d. 1225), al-Zahir (d. 1226) and al-Mustansir (d. 1242). See Leisten, *Architektur für Tote*, 50, and p. 48, n. 288.

[12] Thomas Leisten, "Turba," in *Encyclopedia of Islam, Second Edition*, 12 vols. (Leiden: Brill, 1960–2005), 10: 673–5. On tomb terminology see also Grabar, "Commemorative Structures," 11–12, Allen, "Tombs of the 'Abbāsid Caliphs," 425, and Leisten, *Architektur für Tote*, 67–77.

[13] Allen, "Tombs of the 'Abbāsid Caliphs," 421. For the Arabic text, see Yāqūt ibn 'Abd-Allāh al-Ḥamawī, *Mu'jam al-buldān*, 5 vols. (Beirut: Dār Ṣādir, 1955–57) 3: 46–7.

[14] Allen, "Tombs of 'Abbāsid Caliphs," 431.

[15] Thomas Leisten, "Dynastic Tomb or Private Mausolea: Observations on the Concept of Funerary Structures of the Fāṭimid and 'Abbāsid Caliphs," in *L'Egypte Fatimide: son art et son histoire*, ed. Marianne Barrucand (Paris: Presses de l'Université de Paris-Sorbonne, 1999), 470–1 (465–79).

[16] Hilāl al-Ṣābi', *Rusūm Dār al-Khilāfa*, trans. and ed. Elie A. Salem (Beirut: American University of Beirut, 1977), especially 16–68, 29–57.

[17] Alastair Northedge, *The Historical Topography of Samarra* (London: British School of Archaeology in Iraq, 2005), 258.

[18] Su'ād Māhir Muḥammad, *Mashhad al-Imām 'Alī fī al-Najaf wa-mā bihi min al-hadāyā wa'l-tuḥaf* (Cairo: Dār al-Ma'ārif, 1969), 127–40.

19 Arnold Nöldecke, *Das Heiligtum al-Husains zu Kerbelâ* (Berlin: Mayer and Müller, 1909), 51–66.

20 Muḥammad Ḥasan Āl Yāsīn, "al-Mashhad al-Kāẓimī fī al-'aṣr al-'Abbāsī," *Sumer* 16 (1962), 119–28; Strika and Khalīl, *Architecture of Baghdād*, 3–13; Leisten, *Architektur für Tote*, 111–12.

21 Yūnus Ibrāhīm al-Sāmarrā'ī, *Marāqid al-ā'imma wa'l-awliyā' fī Sāmarrā'* (Baghdad: Majallat Ṣawt al-Islām, n.d.); Alastair Northedge, "The Shrine in its Historical Context," in *The Shi'a of Samarra: The Heritage and Politics of a Community in Iraq*, ed. Imranali Panjwani (London: I.B. Tauris, 2012), 49–66.

22 James W. Allan, *The Art and Architecture of Twelver Shi'ism: Iraq, Iran and the Indian Sub-Continent* (London: Azimuth Editions, 2012), 5–39.

23 Ibid., 16–17.

24 Grabar, "Commemorative Structures," 10.

25 Āl Yāsīn, "al-Mashhad al-Kāẓimī," 122.

26 Allan, *Art and Architecture of Twelver Shi'ism*, 27.

27 Ibid., 35–8.

28 Leisten, *Architecktur für Tote*, 125.

29 Grabar, "Commemorative Structures," 25, Leisten, *Architektur für Tote*, 126.

30 Lassner, *Topography of Baghdad*, 112. For the Arabic text, see al-Khaṭīb al-Baghdādī, *Tārīkh Baghdād*, 1: 121.

31 Ma'ruf al-Karkhi died in 815/16, Bishr ibn al-Harith al-Hafi in 841/2, and Mansur ibn 'Ammar in 839/40.

32 Ibn al-Jawzī, *Manāqib Baghdād*, ed. Muḥammad Bahja al-Atharī (Baghdad: Dār al-Salām, 1342 [1923/4]), 28–9.

33 Allan discusses the political importance of Shi'i shrines throughout history in *Art and Architecture of Twelver Shiism,* 40–79.

34 Rāġib, "Les premiers monuments," 26–7, 31, 33–4, and Leisten, *Architektur für Tote*, 189–91.

35 Allan, *Art and Architecture of Twelver Shi'ism*, 40–1.

36 For a detailed discussion of this event see Leisten, *Architektur für Tote*, 111–12. The two main Arabic sources that report the event are 'Izz al-Dīn 'Alī ibn Muḥammad ibn al-Athīr, *al-Kāmil fī al-ta'rīkh*, 13 vols. (Beirut: Dār Ṣādir, 1965–7), 9: 575–8 and Ibn al-Jawzī, *Muntaẓam*, 8: 150. For an English translation of the narrative of the event according to Ibn al-Athīr, see Allan, *Art and Architecture of Twelver Shi'ism*, 12–14.

37 Leisten, *Architektur für Tote*, 111.

38 Ernst Herzfeld, *Erster Vorläufiger Bericht über die Ausgrabungen von Samarra* (Berlin: Dietrich Reimer, 1912), 28–31. For the final report, see Leisten, *Excavation of Samarra*, 72–8.

39 Northedge, *Topography*, 230–31 and idem, "The Qubbat al-Ṣulaybiyya and its Interpretation," in *Sifting Sands, Reading Signs: Studies in honour of Professor Géza Fehérvári*, ed. Patricia L. Baker and Barbara Brend (London: Furnace Publishing, 2006), 71–82.

40 Leisten, *Architektur für Tote*, 254 and idem, *Excavation of Samarra. Volume 1. Architecture: Final Report of the First Campaign, 1910–1912* (Berlin: Philipp von Zabern, 2003), 78.

41 This argument first appears in full in Ernst Herzfeld, *Geschichte der Stadt Samarra* (Hamburg: Eckhardt and Messtorff, 1948), 277. Herzfeld's argument is paraphrased in Creswell, *Early Muslim Architecture* 2: 285.

42 For a history of interpretations of the monument as a tomb, see Leisten, *Excavation of Samarra*, 76–7, Northedge, "Qubbat al-Ṣulaybiyya," 77–9, and Northedge *Historical Topography*, 230–1.

43 Leisten, *Excavation of Samarra*, 77–8. For the graffito, see ibid., 74–6.

44 Robert Hillenbrand, "The Development of Saljuq Mausolea in Iran," in *The Art of Iran and Anatolia from the 11th to the 13th century AD* (London: University of London School of Oriental and African Studies, Percival David Foundation of Chinese Art 1975), 43 (40–59).

45 Oleg Grabar, "The Umayyad Dome of the Rock in Jerusalem," *Ars Orientalis* 3 (1959), 36–7 (33–62).

46 Richard Piran McClary, "On a Holy Mountain? Remote and Elevated Funerary Monuments in Medieval Islam," in *Tomb – Memory – Space: Concepts of Representation in Premodern Christian and Islamic Art*, ed. Francine Giese, Anna Pawlak and Markus Thome (Berlin: de Gruyter, 2018), 13–24.

47 Sarre and Herzfeld, *Archäologische Reise*, 1: 230–4, Ernst Herzfeld, "Damascus: Studies in Architecture I," *Ars Islamica* 9 (1942), 18–24 (1–53). Leisten, *Architektur für Tote*, 159–61, Northedge and Kennet, *Archaeological Atlas of Samarra*, 3 vols. (London: British Institute for the Study of Iraq, 2015), 1:151–2. The tomb was reported destroyed in October 2014. See Sam Hardy, "Islamic State destroyed the Shia Shrine of Imam al-Daur (Samarra, Iraq, 23rd October 2014)," https://conflictantiquities.wordpress.com/2014/10/30/iraq-samarra-islamic-state-destruction-shia-shrine-imam-al-daur/, accessed April 19, 2016.

48 Herzfeld "Damascus," 19–20. Leisten, *Architektur für Tote*, 160–1.

49 For the history and alternate names of the Shatt al-Nil, see Guy Le Strange, *The Lands of the Eastern Caliphate* (Cambridge: Cambridge University Press, 1905), 72–3.

50 Sarre and Herzfeld, *Archäologische Reise*, 1: 234–47 and Paolo M. Costa, "Islamic Shrines on the Šaṭ al-Nīl," *Annali dell'Istituto Orientale di Napoli* 31 (1971), reprinted in *Studies in Arabian Architecture* (Ashgate: Brookfield, VT, 1994), Part I, 1–16. Imam al-Najmi also appears in Yasser Tabbaa, "The Muqarnas Dome: Its Origin and Meaning," *Muqarnas* 3 (1985), 66–7 (61–74).

51 The photos are part of the Yasser Tabbaa Archive, Aga Khan Documentation Center, MIT Libraries, and are available on Archnet at http://archnet.org/collections/1313/details

52 Surveys have identified *mihrab*s at Abu Hatab and Imam al-Najmi. For Abu Hatab, see Costa, "Islamic Shrines," 6 and pl. VIIa. For al-Najmi, see Costa, "Islamic Shrines," 9 and pls. IXb, XIb, and XII.

53 The names Umm al-Awlad ("Mother of the Boys") and al-Aziba ("The Spinster") both refer to women, and local legends apparently attributed the tombs to two sisters (Sarre and Herzfeld, *Archäologische Reise*, 1: 246). The idea of a mother and celibate, unmarried woman both suggest pious qualities. The title of *imam* in Imam al-Najmi, of course, implies a spiritual association.

54 Sarre and Herzfeld, *Archäologische Reise*, 1: 245–6. Costa, "Islamic Shrines," 3–4.

55 Costa, "Islamic Shrines," 5 and 16.

56 Sarre and Herzfeld, *Archäologische Reise*, 1: 244 and Costa, "Islamic Shrines," 5–6.

57 Ibid., 1: 244.

58 Ibid., 1: 256 and 3, pl. XXXVI.

59 Costa, "Islamic Shrines," 3.

60 Sarre and Herzfeld, *Archäologische Reise*, 1: 238.

61 Ibid., 1: 238–9, Costa, "Islamic Shrines," 7–10, Tabbaa, "Muqarnas Dome," 66–7.

62 The relationship of settlement history to the history of irrigation agriculture in Mesopotamia is demonstrated in a number of studies, including Robert McC. Adams, *Land Behind Baghdad: A History of Settlement on the Diyala Plains* (Chicago and London: University of Chicago Press, 1964). For a discussion of method, see pp. 119-125.

63 Angelika Hartmann, *an-Nāṣir li-Dīn Allāh (1180–1225): Politik, Religion, Kultur in der späten ʿAbbāsidenzeit* (Berlin: Walter de Gruyter, 1975), 109–22.

64 Sarre and Herzfeld, *Archäologische Reise*, 2: 173–9; Vincenzo Strika, "The Turbah of Zumurrud Khātūn in Baghdad: Some Aspects of the Funerary Ideology in Islamic Art," *Annali dell' Istituto Universitario Orientale di Napoli*, 38 (new series XXVIII): 3 (1978), 283–96.

65 Sarre and Herzfeld, *Archäologische Reise*, 2: 179; Herzfeld, "Damascus," 26–7; Strika and Khalīl, *Architecture of Baghdād*, 51–3.

66 More complete lists are given in Herzfeld, "Damascus," 11–40, and Tabbaa, "Muqarnas Dome."

67 Yasser Tabbaa, "Muqarnas Dome," 62–3; see also Terry Allen, *Five Essays in Islamic Art* (Sebastapol, Ca.: Solipsist Press, 1988), 85, and Doris Behrens-Abouseif, "Muḳarnas," in The *Encyclopedia of Islam, Second Edition,* 7: 501–6.

68 Tabbaa, "Muqarnas Dome," 72, and idem, *The Transformation of Islamic Art during the Sunni Revival* (London and New York: I. B. Tauris, 2001), 124–36.

69 On his policies, see Angelika Hartmann, "al-Nāṣir li-Dīn Allāh," in *The Encyclopedia of Islam, Second Edition*, 7: 996–1003. On his architectural patronage in relation to these policies, see Hartmann, *an-Nāṣir li-Dīn Allāh*, 162–8, 198–201, and Allan, *Art and Architecture of Twelver Shi'ism*, 42.

Muslims, Byzantines, and Western Christians on the Haram al-Sharif

MEGAN BOOMER & ROBERT OUSTERHOUT

1 Dome of the Ascension, Haram al-Sharif, Jerusalem, 1200–01.
Photo: Megan Boomer

The Haram al-Sharif ("Noble Sanctuary") in Jerusalem is marked by centuries of sacred architecture and traditions that render it one of the holiest places in Islam, Judaism, and Christianity (Fig. 2).[1] Art historians celebrate the design and decoration of monuments like the Dome of the Rock and Aqsa Mosque, while worshippers laud the site's associations with Quranic and biblical history. Although some of its extant stones and sacred stories are tied to the prophetic past, the Haram has changed significantly over the course of the last two millennia. These changes led Gülru Necipoğlu to describe the site as a palimpsest, a term referring to a document that has been erased and rewritten but retains traces of its earlier forms.[2] Rather than being read, however, Jerusalem's sacred monuments are understood through the experience of the religious communities who venerate and view them. This essay traces the architectural history of the Haram al-Sharif from the destruction of the Second Temple in 70 CE to the medieval changes effected in the aftermath of the First Crusade and Salah al-Din's recapture of the city. Over the course of this period (and into the present), the monuments participated in urban, political, and religious dialogues through both their illusory permanence and their continued transformation.

The sacred area of the Haram is demarcated by the megalithic walls of the Herodian Temple precinct constructed in the first century BCE. The Temple, a focal point for Jewish devotion and identity, was destroyed by Roman armies in 70. After the quelling of the Bar Kokhba revolt in 135, Jerusalem was renamed *Aelia Capitolina* after the Emperor Hadrian and the Roman God Jupiter. As part of the city's reconstruction, a Capitolium Temple was likely built atop the Jewish Temple's ruins and statues of emperors and gods were installed on the platform.[3] The Roman outpost was not particularly important, however, and its sites are rarely mentioned before the advent of Christian topographic writing in the early fourth century. One such account, written by a pilgrim from the French city of Bordeaux in 333, records well-developed traditions associated with the platform – including events and figures from the Old Testament, New Testament, Roman history, and legend.[4] He notes a vault where Solomon tortured demons, the pinnacle

2 Aerial view of the Haram al-Sharif, Jerusalem, seen from the northwest. The Dome of the Ascension lies immediately in front of the Dome of the Rock, and the Dome of the Chain in its shadow. To the south is the Aqsa Mosque.
Photo: Albatross Aerial Photograph

where Christ was tempted, the stone the builders rejected, some rooms of Solomon's palace, and a chamber roofed by a single stone where Solomon wrote the Book of Wisdom. When speaking of the Temple, he refers to its construction by Solomon:

> There is marble in front of the altar which has on it the blood of Zacharias – you would think it had only been shed today. All around you can see the marks of the hobnails of the soldiers who killed him, as plainly as if they had been pressed into wax. Two statues of Hadrian stand there, and, not far from them, a pierced stone which the Jews come and anoint each year. They mourn and rend their garments, and then depart.[5]

The narrative maps a layered history onto the site, discussing markers of biblical martyrdom on stones, Roman rule through statues, and Jewish ritual commemorating the destroyed Solomonic structure. Reading the account, one is left with the impression that the archaeological "facts" of the ruins, whether Herodian or Hadrianic, are less important than their interpretation.

For early Byzantine Christians, the very fact that the site was in ruins allowed it to become a polemical counterpoint to the Church of the Holy Sepulcher built over the purported location of Christ's crucifixion and tomb. In his c. 337 biography of the Emperor Constantine, Eusebius of Caesarea contrasts the old Temple with the emperor's new church:

> New Jerusalem was built at the very Testimony to the Saviour, facing the famous Jerusalem of old, which after the bloody murder of the Lord had been overthrown in utter devastation, and paid the penalty of its wicked inhabitants. Opposite this then the Emperor erected the victory of the Saviour over death with rich and abundant munificence, this being perhaps that fresh New Jerusalem proclaimed in prophetic oracles.[6]

In addition to referring to the church complex as New Jerusalem, Eusebius calls the Tomb of Christ the "Holy of Holies," a term referring to the most sacred part of the Temple.[7] In early Christian scriptural interpretation, the presence of Christ in the tomb and the presence of the Church of the Holy Sepulcher in the city renewed and superseded God's Old Testament covenant commemorated on the Haram. The conspicuous absence of architecture atop the esplanade testified to this transfer, even as the ruins provided markers of earlier sacred events.

With the notable exception of Emperor Julian the Apostate's attempt to rebuild the Temple in 362/3, whose failure was widely commented upon by Christian writers, there are few references to or signs of construction on the site during the early Byzantine period. Instead, pilgrims begin mentioning the Temple's sacred objects and traditions in the Church of the Holy Sepulcher, including the Horn of the Anointing used by the Jewish kings and the altar where Zacharias was killed.[8] Many early accounts ignore the esplanade, but those that mention it most frequently refer to the Pinnacle associated with the Temptation of Christ and martyrdom of Jerusalem's first patriarch, Saint James.[9] However, the silence of the sources is hardly evidence of the site's omission from the city's devotional landscape. In addition to the Holy Sepulcher, one of Jerusalem's other major early Byzantine monuments was the Church of the Ascension on the summit of the Mount of Olives. Throughout the Easter season, Jerusalem's Christian community regularly processed to or from the church, singing as they walked from the monument to the city gates outside the Herodian precinct walls.[10] When Jerusalem's seventh-century Patriarch Sophronius exclaimed "How sweet it is to see thy fair beauty, City of God, from the Mount of Olives!," the contemplated vista would have foregrounded the Temple's ruins on the other side of the Kidron Valley (Fig. 3).[11] Seen from this angle, the esplanade's lack of construction served important commemorative functions in its own right.

An early tenth-century Christian Arabic chronicle claims that Sophronius was responsible for handing over the Haram to Caliph 'Umar following Jerusalem's capture in 638, although reports of the site's initial transfer are shrouded in

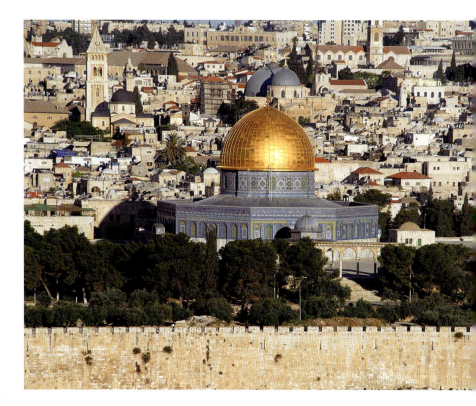

3 The Dome of the Rock, Jerusalem, seen from the Mount of Olives, with the domes of the Holy Sepulcher in the middle distance.
Photo: Gerald Carr

legend.[12] Islamic understandings of the Haram's sanctity were similarly written down centuries after the events they record, leading to significant scholarly debate regarding the original traditions associated with the site. Stories about Jerusalem's holiness circulated in Hadith collections and *fada'il* (praises) compilations dedicated to the region's sanctity and merits.[13] The latter texts have been particularly important for studies of the Haram's early Islamic associations, as the tenth- and eleventh-century compilations record chains of transmission, or *isnad*, dating back to the seventh century in order to authenticate their claims. Such records are not necessarily a secure means of dating belief or buildings, however, and the traditions are presumably only those considered accurate by the later medieval authors. Nevertheless, the early sources for the Haram's biblical associations and Islamic reinterpretation and use, like 'Umar's advisor Ka'b al-Ahbar and Palestinian families who had been orally circulating the stories for centuries are interesting in and of themselves.[14] The traditions traced to this early period also reveal much about the site's developing Islamic sanctity. Groups of early Muslims associated the Haram with the site of the Jewish Temple and the first *qibla* prior to the shift in prayer direction towards Mecca, considered Jerusalem the third holiest city after Mecca and Medina, and framed its sanctity in terms of its role at the time of resurrection.[15] Many therefore understood pilgrimage to the Haram as a beneficial activity that could absolve terrestrial sins and aid in future salvation. At some point prior to the twelfth century, the monuments on the Haram also became associated with Muhammad's night journey to "the furthest mosque" (the Quranic *Masjid al-Aqsa*) and ascension into heaven. However, using these strata of stories to date the archaeological remains is a complicated endeavor.

Recent scholarship has raised important questions about the architecture of the Haram between 638 and 692.[16] Jerusalem's Muslim community constructed the city's congregational mosque somewhere on the esplanade, but its location and architectural form are not clear. Excavations in and around the Marwani Musalla (sometimes referred to as Solomon's Stables) led Beatrice St. Laurent and Isam Awwad to identify the vaulted subterranean structure as a large seventh-century mosque.[17] According to their understanding, the Syrian governor Mu'awiya developed the Haram as a religious and political center prior to his 660 acclamation as Caliph in Jerusalem. The reconstruction and dating of this first mosque have heretofore been based on a passage attributed to a c. 680 Christian pilgrim:

> In the celebrated place where once stood the temple (situated towards the east near the wall) arose in its magnificence, the [Muslims] now have a quadrangular prayer house. They built it roughly by erecting upright boards and great beams on some ruined remains. The building, it is said, can accommodate three thousand people at once.[18]

However, Lawrence Nees recently noted that the "eyewitness" account is polemical exaggeration and contrasts the "rude" structure on the site of

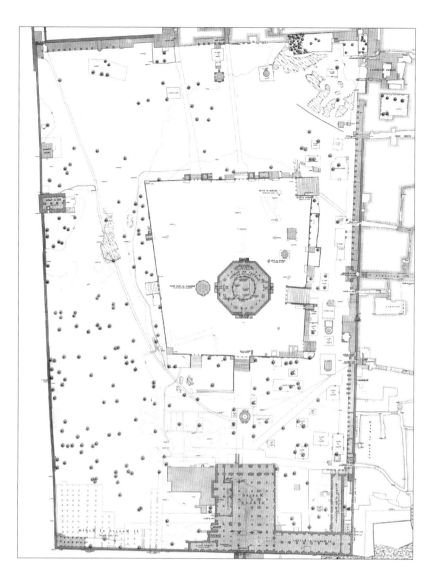

4 Plan of Haram al-Sharif.
Photo: C. W. Wilson, *Ordnance Survey of Jerusalem*, 1865

the former Temple with laudatory descriptions of Jerusalem's major churches.[19] As a result, the nature of the seventh-century mosque atop the Haram cannot yet be conclusively determined.

The Dome of the Rock is the earliest securely dated monument in Islamic art history, and its completion reconfigured both the physical site and memorial associations of the Haram.[20] A mosaic inscription running along the inner and outer faces of the octagonal arcade originally declared that the dome was constructed by the fifth Umayyad Caliph 'Abd al-Malik in the year 72 AH, or 691–2, although a later Caliph altered the name but not the date.[21] Based on the content of the inscription, the architectural characteristics of the building, the motifs of the non-figurative mosaics, and textual records, scholars have posited several interpretations of the structure's original commemorative function. The Quranic quotations lining the walls, the monument's rich ornamentation, and its prominent location make it clear that the Dome of the Rock was designed to mark Islam's presence and power in the city's saturated sacred landscape. As Oleg Grabar and others noted, however, the late-seventh-century political valences and the religious understanding of the rock at its center are difficult to decode.[22] Paradoxically, the Quranic passages quoted in the 240-meter long inscription do not refer to the reasons for the Haram's sanctity listed above. Instead, the outer face repeatedly proclaims the oneness of Allah and Muhammad's role as a prophet and concludes with the details of the monument's foundation. The interior arcade, which may have been modified shortly after 692, emphasizes the differences in Christian and Islamic interpretations of Jesus' prophetic status.[23] Much like the contrast between the Church of the Holy Sepulcher and the empty esplanade, the text suggests the Dome of the Rock appropriated and acknowledged older sacred covenants while celebrating new revelations.[24] 'Abd al-Malik may have intended the project to proclaim his Caliphal power in a manner akin to Constantine's "New Jerusalem" at the Holy Sepulcher and Justinian's "New Temple" of Hagia Sophia in Constantinople.[25] In each case, references to the relationship between the ruler and the rebuilt Temple reinforced claims to divinely-ordained sovereignty by echoing the actions of the biblical kings David and Solomon.[26] The extant Umayyad inscriptions inside the monument and on two of its exterior doors, however, do not mention David, Solomon, the Temple, or the Rock – nor do they specifically refer to the site's Islamic sanctity.[27] It is possible that some of this information may have been conveyed by now-lost texts, and also that the glass mosaics and imported marbles lining the walls served an important communicative function. For instance, scholars have observed that the images of lush vegetation and shining jewelry placed the Rock within a terrestrial and celestial paradise.[28] Rituals discussed in secondary textual sources also redefined Temple practice for and within the early Islamic monument, commemorating the site's specific history of sanctity while connecting it to Meccan pilgrimage practice.[29] Rather than searching

5 Dome of the Chain to the east of the Dome of the Rock, Jerusalem.
Photo: Megan Boomer

6 Golden Gate, Jerusalem.
Photo: Kathryn Blair Moore

for a monolithic definition of the Dome of the Rock as a site of divine or prophetic presence, the past Temple, a present proclamation of Islamic identity, or a future space of salvation, it may be more productive to view it as a structure that reshaped the terms by which all of those temporal moments were experienced and understood.

The Dome of the Rock retains more of its Umayyad architecture and decoration than any other structure on the Haram, but that does not mean it should be studied in isolation. To the contrary, the monument was designed as part of what some have referred to as a "master plan" that included the Aqsa Mosque, smaller sacred markers on and around the Dome of the Rock's elevated platform, and monumental gates leading onto the esplanade (Fig. 4).[30] Before the site was designated the Haram al-Sharif in the thirteenth century, authors and inscriptions referred to the congregational mosque and the esplanade as *al-bayt al-maqdis*, or "the house of the holy," in reference to the Temple and apply the term "mosque" to both the covered area for prayer and the totality of the precinct.[31] Myriam Rosen-Ayalon considered the Aqsa Mosque and the Dome of the Rock the axial anchors for other emplaced traditions and functional spaces, and noted the similarity with the Holy Sepulcher's division of congregational and commemorative space.[32] Andreas Kaplony and others have positioned the Dome of the Rock at the figurative and near-literal center of a "system of concentric frames".[33] The gates onto the esplanade, stairs to the elevated platform with the Dome of the Rock, and smaller sacred markers further constituted the monumental ensemble, and their names helped to concretize the association with the Temple, Muhammad, and the Resurrection.

The Dome of the Chain and Golden Gate provide two key examples of the intertwining of archaeology and associations on the Umayyad Haram. The Dome of the Chain, a small eleven-sided open structure on the eastern end of the Dome of the Rock's platform, is located near the geographic center of the Haram (Fig. 5).[34] Like the monument in whose shadow it stands, it was part of the Umayyad design of the Haram but has probably lost its original associations. Although some have considered it an architectural model for the larger Dome of the Rock or the treasury housing the money sent for the more lavish Dome's construction, it is more likely that it served a commemorative function.[35] The eponymous chain is referred to in medieval sources, and probably references a miraculous chain of judgment used by David and Solomon to adjudicate disputes. In addition to traditions regarding royal authority, the Dome of the Chain's associations with justice led pilgrims to consider it an efficacious location to appeal for the remission of their sins.[36] Divine mercy and personal repentance were also marked by the Golden Gate, a double-arched portal in the Haram's east wall (Fig. 5). As the sole gate leading to the esplanade from the Mount of Olives and the Valley of Gehenna, the site of the future Resurrection, the monumental façade both marked and extended the sacred city's limits. Although sometimes dated to the end of Byzantine rule, it is more likely part of the Umayyad monumental program.[37] Behind the long-blocked portal, three bays of double domes lead to a second monumental façade facing the Dome of the Rock's platform. By the eleventh century, and possibly from the time of its construction, its role as a gate was more symbolic than functional – a pilgrim refers the two apertures as the "Gate of Mercy" and "Gate of Repentance," and states that it was locked by 'Umar

and would only be opened on Judgment Day.[38] The gate remained open on the Haram side, however, as he describes the domed interior as a mosque on the site where God accepted David's repentance, where visitors prayed for the cleansing of their own sins.[39]

Like the Dome of the Rock, the congregational mosque shifted associations during the pre-twelfth-century period as markers of Muhammad's life became an increasingly important feature of the Haram. Rather than the "Bayt al-Maqdis," it became more commonly called the Aqsa, or "furthest," Mosque referenced within the Quran. The current Aqsa Mosque has been constructed and reconstructed so frequently that it is difficult to distinguish and date its architectural layers.[40] Like many Umayyad mosque complexes, the covered prayer hall was divided into several aisles by rows of columns and oriented towards the *qibla* wall. At the Aqsa, the location of the mosque on the esplanade was later associated with 'Umar's efforts to distinguish between Islamic Mecca-oriented prayer and earlier Jewish practice by siting the structure to the south of the Dome of the Rock.[41] This situation also facilitated connections between Umayyad buildings to the south of the Haram and the mosque.[42] Like the poorly-understood administrative structures, the Aqsa credited to either 'Abd al-Malik or his successor al-Walid I (r. 705–715) was severely damaged in multiple eighth-century earthquakes. According to the c. 985 Jerusalem-born geographer al-Muqaddasi, a reconstruction coordinated by the 'Abbasid caliphs who succeeded the Umayyads "built it [the mosque] firmer though less elegant in structure than it had been before. That older portion remained, even like a beauty spot amid the new".[43] Some of the "beauty spots" remained into the modern era, including 54 pieces of Umayyad carved woodwork, repurposed Byzantine column capitals, and parts of a marble and mosaic floor.[44]

Although the Haram al-Sharif remained an important site of visitation and patronage throughout the medieval period, Jerusalem's political significance waned when the center of Islamic power shifted from Damascus to Baghdad in the mid-eighth century. In the decades between the composition of al-Muqaddasi's account and the c. 1047 travel narrative of the Persian pilgrim Nasir-i Khusrau, however, the Cairo-based Fatimid Caliphs, the 'Abbasids' political and religious rivals, reshaped the Haram's major monuments. Their

7 *Maqsura* Dome, Aqsa Mosque, Jerusalem, c. 1035.
Photo: Megan Boomer

decision to do so was both pragmatic and political. On the one hand, earthquakes in 1016–17 and 1033–34 had again damaged the Aqsa Mosque, the precinct walls, and other structures.[45] On the other, patronage provided the rulers with an opportunity to codify centuries of circulating traditions, proclaim their control of the sacred site, and solidify their power at a time of internal upheaval. The most salient example of their efforts is the arch leading into the Aqsa Mosque's *maqsura* dome in front of the central *mihrab* (Fig. 7). A two-line mosaic inscription on the uppermost section of the wall situates the monument in Quranic, chronological, and political context, beginning:

> In the name of God, the Compassionate, the Merciful, Glory to the One who took his Servant for a Journey by Night from the Masjid al-Haram to the Masjid al-Aqsa whose precincts we have blessed (17:1). Has renovated its construction our Lord 'Ali Abu al-Hasan, the Imam al-Zahir li-A'zaz din Allah, Commander of the Faithful, Son of al-Hakim bi-'Amr Allah, Commander of the Faithful, may the blessing of God be on him, on his pure ancestors, and on his noble descendants...[46]

Unlike the ambiguities of the Dome of the Rock's seventh-century sacred citations, the eleventh-century additions to the Aqsa Mosque quote the primary passage associated with Muhammad's Night Journey in order to solidify the structure's name and sacred charge. In addition to the political claims articulated through the inscription, Jennifer Pruitt has suggested that the Fatimid use of mosaics and unusual design of the dome were intended to recall the Umayyad structures on the rest of the Haram and distill them into a single and particularly sacred

MUSLIMS, BYZANTINES, AND WESTERN CHRISTIANS ON THE HARAM AL-SHARIF 181 area.[47] As Kaplony noted, the mosaic dome of the mosque and the Dome of the Rock defined a sacred axis within a precinct that was increasingly filled with smaller domes, prayer niches, traditions, and rituals.[48] In addition to the Quranic and pre-Islamic sacred associations, the monuments were layered with the names of centuries of rulers and other patrons who left testimonies of their piety on the walls they built, the mosaics they refurbished, and the lamps and candles they donated to make the sanctuaries shine.

According to Nasir-i Khusrau, tens of thousands of Muslim pilgrims and a significant number of Christian and Jewish travelers visited Jerusalem annually in the mid-eleventh century.[49] His account enumerates a wealth of Islamic sacred traditions concentrated atop the Haram and outside the Golden Gate, extending from the prophetic past of Abraham through Muhammad into the apocalyptic future. Rather than tracing the textual precedent for these associations, he narrates the site's sanctity by specifying its physical forms. This begins with the sacred precinct's limits, which he states he recorded based on an inscription that provided the sanctuary's total length and width.[50] He further defines the boundaries by listing their thresholds, including the main Gate of David from the city's bazaar that was decorated on the exterior with a gilded brass door and glass mosaics. He notes that the tiles produced a powerful visual effect on those about to enter the sacred precinct, describing them as "dazzling to the eye" and stating that they left "the mind of the beholder...absolutely stunned".[51] On entry, he follows colonnades leading to Sufi cloisters, domes, *mihrab*s, and small mosques marking places where Jacob and Zachariah prayed, David repented, Jesus was placed in the cradle, and Mary labored. He arrives at and describes the splendors of the Aqsa Mosque before ascending to the Dome of the Rock, noting that the monument's location in the center of the platform at the center of the sacred precinct focused attention on "the third most holy place of God".[52] In addition to the Dome of the Chain on the platform, he visits domes dedicated to Gabriel and the Prophet, where Muhammad mounted the Buraq.[53]

The descriptions of the Haram's structures by Nasir-i Khusrau and al-Muqaddasi, as well as the hundreds of traditions recorded within pre-twelfth-century *fada'il* compilations, allow scholars to situate the extant material from the site's first five Islamic centuries within an architectural and devotional ensemble. Such records are particularly important because the capture of Jerusalem by the armies of the First Crusade radically reshaped the Haram's status and changed the site's major monuments. Thousands of the city's Muslim residents sought refuge on the Haram during the July 15, 1099 invasion, and were massacred there by Tancred of Antioch's forces.[54] Following the bloody events, the major monuments were rapidly "rechristened," with the Dome of the Rock considered the *Templum Domini,* or biblical Temple, and the Aqsa Mosque the *Templum* (or *Palatium*) *Salomonis.* Augustinian canons were installed in the *Templum Domini,* and the Kings of Jerusalem, who associated themselves with the biblical Solomon and David, used the *Templum Salomonis* as their royal palace before loaning the monument to the newly founded Templar Order in 1120. By the third quarter of the twelfth century, the Templar complex had expanded to fill much of the southern quadrant of the Haram, including the conversion of the Marwani Musalla into stables.[55] This institutional occupation brought both physical changes to the site and devotional shifts in how the monuments were understood and used by Christian worshippers.

In contrast to the conspicuous absence of the site in earlier Christian itineraries, twelfth-century pilgrims considered the Haram the second most sacred site in Jerusalem after the Holy Sepulcher.[56] Based on the c. 1102 narrative of the Latin pilgrim Saewulf and the c. 1106 report of the Byzantine Abbot Daniel, this shift appears to have been rapid and comprehensive, redefining the Haram's monumental topography for the gamut of Christian communities who were now seeing it with new eyes.[57] Like Nasir-i Khusrau, Saewulf and Daniel remark on the beauty of the main entrance gate, which pilgrims began to associate with a site of Apostolic healing.[58] Centuries of medieval European associations between the Golden Gate, the location of Christ's Entry into Jerusalem, and Emperor Heraclius' 630 procession to return Jerusalem's relic of the True Cross were emplaced at the eastern threshold and reinforced via liturgical ritual.[59] As for the monuments, Saewulf associates the Dome of the Rock with the biblical site of Bethel, the place where Jacob saw a ladder ascending to heaven and erected an altar, and the Solomonic Temple.[60] He refers to the cave under the rock as the Holy of Holies and the repository for the Ark of the Covenant, Manna, Rod of Aaron, and Tables of the Covenant. However, he and other twelfth-century Christian pilgrims focus on the site's New Testament associations.[61] Later in the century, the traditions surrounding the Pinnacle of the Temple were transferred to the Dome of the Chain, which was renamed in honor of Saint James' martyrdom.[62] In some cases, the Latins adopted both Islamic monuments and meanings, as with the mosque marking Mary's presence in the Temple and Christ's presence in the cradle.[63]

The c. 1170 guidebook of John of Würzburg provides one of the clearest testimonies of the physical and memorial changes to the Haram during Latin Kingdom tenure. The author attempted to organize his tour of Jerusalem in chronological order, and accordingly began with a description of Mount Moriah and the construction of Solomon's Temple.[64] Partially quoting another twelfth-century Latin author, he expressed uncertainty regarding the construction of the current Temple:

> It is not known exactly in what king's reign it was restored. Some say that it was rebuilt in the reign of the Emperor Constantine, by Helena his mother, in honour of the holy cross which was found by her; others that it was built by the Emperor Heraclius in honour of the cross of our Lord, which he had brought back in triumph from Persia; others by the Emperor Justinian; others that it was built by some Emperor of Memphis in Egypt in honour of *Allah Kebir,* that is, "God most high," because to Him all languages join in rendering their devout service.[65]

In any event, he is more interested in and quickly passes to the Christological and Marian narratives, which by his time were reinforced by inscriptions and images that asserted that pilgrims were seeing the places and events of biblical history. In one section of the Dome of the Rock, he saw the footprint Jesus left when casting the moneychangers out of the Temple inscribed in a stone.[66] This was joined to another stone with images of the infant Christ's presentation "as if on an altar" and the sleeping Patriarch Jacob, accompanied by the Latin inscription:

> Here was presented the King of Kings,
>   born of the Virgin,
> Wherefore this has rightfully been called
>   a holy place,
> Whence this place is adorned and by right
>   is called holy,
> Here Jacob saw the ladder and built an altar.[67]

The reiteration of the site's Christian holiness continued on the outside of the building, which quoted and literalized biblical passages and chants used for church dedications such as "The House of the Lord is well founded on a firm rock".[68] The Latin inscriptions and Christian images layered atop the Umayyad mosaics and marbles were presumably designed by the canons, whose cloister John saw abutting the north side of the platform.[69] Defining the Dome of the Rock in particular and the Haram in general as the biblical Temple, and reinforcing such associations through inscriptions and ritual practice, was hardly novel – the Umayyads had undertaken a similar project which was remembered and reported in the *fada'il*. However, Crusader and counter-Crusader preaching transformed the Temple from a significant absence into a recaptured presence in the Christian imagination, and a site of traumatic rupture in Islamic history.

As the continued survival of Umayyad and Fatimid mosaics and marbles in the Dome of the Rock and Aqsa Mosque attest, the Latin changes to the monuments were largely additive. Indeed, the Muslim pilgrim 'Ali ibn al-Harawi recorded the inscription on the Aqsa's Fatimid arch and stated that "the Franks did not alter any of the verses of the Mighty Quran, or the names of the caliphs".[70] On October 2, 1187, the armies led by Salah al-Din entered the city and removed the large cross atop the Dome of the Rock.[71] The sites were purified with rosewater, and the Sultan and his retinue entered the Dome to hear a Friday *khutba* praising Allah "for his cleansing of his Holy House" a week later.[72] Salah al-Din ordered the rock in the Dome of the Rock, which had been covered in marble by the canons to be unsheathed, and "commanded the repair of the Aqsa Mosque and the use of all means to beautify and adorn it and to restore its inscriptions accurately".[73] The process of clearing away the Latin layer and revealing the obscured Islamic *strata* involved repurposing a considerable quantity of Crusader sculpture under Salah al-Din and his Ayyubid successors.[74]

This process of restoring by reconfiguring earlier material seen in one of the more enigmatic medieval monuments on the Haram, the so-called Dome of the Ascension (Fig. 1). The octagonal structure stands in the Dome of the Rock's shadow and is believed to mark the spot from which Muhammad ascended to heaven. Although a dome marking the site of the Prophet's ascension and an adjacent "Dome of the Prophet" are situated in the vicinity in pre-twelfth-century *fada'il*, the standing monument has been classified by scholarship as either Crusader or Ayyubid.[75] Originally, the dome was balanced atop open pointed arches supported by slender clusters of columns. The columns' capitals are stylistically similar to other twelfth-century monuments, and Crusader architectural historians have argued that the building was originally designed and used as the Haram's Latin baptistery.[76] Islamic archaeologists, in contrast, have observed that the masonry of the southern *mihrab* niche is consistent with the base of the columnar arcade, and argued that the structure was assembled in the Ayyubid period using largely spoliated stones.[77] A marble slab inserted over the entrance provides information regarding the building's construction (or restoration) and dedication (or rededication). After an opening line with the *bismallah* and Quranic quotations, it continues:

> This is the Dome of the Prophet (*qubbat al-nabiyy*) – may God pray upon him and his family – which the historians mentioned in their books. There took in charge its exposure after its loss and its rebuilding after its destruction by himself and his money, the poor for his Lord's mercy, the great *amir*, the great general, the unique, the glorious, the more special, the confident, the hero of (of holy war), the conqueror, the fighter (at the boundaries), 'Izz al-Din, the beauty of Islam, the happy of the happiest, the sword of the prince of believers Abu 'Umar 'Uthman b. Ali b. 'Abdullah al-Zanjili, governor of Jerusalem. And that is in the months of 597 [1200–1201].[78]

In addition to providing a name and date for the monument and identifying the patron, the inscription provides us with an alternate frame for understanding the architecture of the Haram. The Dome declares itself to be authenticated by deep-rooted textual tradition, but architecturally lost and recovered. Regardless of whether the monument's structural skeleton was "Christian" or "Islamic," the inscription and the prominent reuse of Crusader

sculpture elsewhere on the Ayyubid Haram suggest such juxtapositions of styles were part of a recovery project for a deeper past.

As the inscription makes clear, the Haram's monuments are invested with the power to both witness and recover histories. These forms of commemoration through creation continue into the present, and occasionally involve returning to the pasts discussed within this paper. In 1969, an arsonist destroyed the *minbar* of the Aqsa Mosque made between 1168 and 1176 for the Syrian ruler Nur al-Din, who hoped to install it on the recaptured Haram. His nephew Salah al-Din fulfilled this desire, and the masterpiece of Islamic woodwork stood for centuries within the mosque.[79] The man who burned it believed doing so would enable the reconstruction of the original Temple and that destroying millennia of history would result in a millenarian Apocalyptic return. Instead, it was the *minbar* that was recreated after this act of violence. The medieval methods and materials were reproduced insofar as possible, and years were spent working to replicate the geometric harmony and complexity of the original design.[80] In 2007, the new *minbar*, which replicated the inscriptions, dimensions, and appearance of the medieval object insofar as possible, was installed in the Aqsa. Much like the one made for Nur al-Din, it testifies to the site's enduring sanctity and to its continued project of remembering by both recording and remaking.

ROBERT G. OUSTERHOUT is Professor Emeritus in the History of Art at the University of Pennsylvania. He is the author most recently of *Visualizing Community: Art, Material Culture, and Settlement in Byzantine Cappadocia*, Dumbarton Oaks Studies 46 (Washington, D.C., 2017); and *Eastern Medieval Architecture: The Building Traditions of Byzantium and Neighboring Lands* (Oxford University Press, 2019). His fieldwork has concentrated on Byzantine architecture, monumental art, and urbanism in Constantinople, Thrace, Cappadocia, and Jerusalem.

MEGAN BOOMER, Andrew W. Mellon Postdoctoral Fellow in the Department of Art History & Archaeology at Columbia University, specializes in the architectural history of the medieval Mediterranean. Her current book project focuses on the construction and transformation of sacred monuments in the Latin Kingdom of Jerusalem.

SUGGESTIONS FOR FURTHER READING

Grabar, Oleg. *The Shape of the Holy: Early Islamic Jerusalem* (Princeton: Princeton University Press, 1996).

Grabar, Oleg, and Benjamin Z. Kedar, eds. *Where Heaven and Earth Meet: Jerusalem's Sacred Esplanade* (Jerusalem: Yad Ben-Zvi, 2009).

Kaplony, Andreas. *The Haram of Jerusalem 324–1099: Temple, Friday Mosque, Area of Spiritual Power* (Stuttgart: Franz Steiner Verlag, 2002).

Kühnel, Bianca, ed. *The Real and Ideal Jerusalem in Jewish, Christian and Islamic Art.* Jerusalem, 1998. Issued as *Jewish Art* 23/23 (1997–98).

Necipoğlu, Gülru. "The Dome of the Rock as Palimpsest: 'Abd al-Malik's Grand Narrative and Sultan Süleyman's Glosses," *Muqarnas* 25 (2008): 17–105.

Raby, Julian, and Jeremy Johns, eds. *Bayt al-Maqdis: 'Abd al-Malik's Jerusalem* (Oxford: Oxford University Press, 1992).

Rosen-Ayalon, Myriam. *The Early Islamic Monuments of al-Haram al-Sharif: An Iconographic Study* (Jerusalem: Qedem Monographs of the Institute of Archaeology, Hebrew University, 1989).

NOTES

[1] Due to the site's long history it has been known by several names, many of which carry a political or ideological charge. We have chosen to refer to the area as the "Haram al-Sharif" or "Haram" in keeping with modern Arabic and English convention, although the formal usage of the term to refer to the precinct postdates the period covered within the essay. Because of the site's association with the Jewish Temple, readers may also know it as the Temple Mount.

[2] Gülru Necipoğlu, "The Dome of the Rock as Palimpsest: 'Abd al-Malik's Grand Narrative and Sultan Süleyman's Glosses," *Muqarnas* 25 (2008), 17–105. This view also accords with Oleg Grabar, *The Shape of the Holy: Early Islamic Jerusalem* (Princeton: Princeton University Press, 1996) and Andreas Kaplony, *The Haram of Jerusalem 324–1099: Temple, Friday Mosque, Area of Spiritual Power* (Stuttgart: Franz Steiner Verlag, 2002).

[3] The location of Jerusalem's Capitolium is debated, as discussed in Yoram Tsafrir, "70–638: The Temple-less Mountain," *Where Heaven and Earth Meet: Jerusalem's Sacred Esplanade,* eds. Oleg Grabar and Benjamin Z. Kedar (Jerusalem: Yad Ben-Zvi Press, 2009), 80–82.

[4] Jaś Elsner, "The Itinerarium Burdigalense: Politics and Salvation in the Geography of Constantine's Empire," *The Journal of Roman Studies* 90 (2000), 181–195.

[5] Itinerarium Burdigalense, trans. John Wilkinson, *Egeria's Travels to the Holy Land* (Warminster: Aris & Phillips, 1981), 155–56.

[6] Eusebius, *V. Const.* 3.33.1–2, trans. Averil Cameron and Stuart G. Hall, *Eusebius Life of Constantine* (Oxford: Oxford University Press, 1999), 135; with extensive commentary, 273–91.

[7] Robert Ousterhout, "New Temples and New Solomons: The Rhetoric of Byzantine Architecture," in *The Old Testament in Byzantium*, eds. Paul Magdalino and Robert Nelson (Washington, D.C.: Dumbarton Oaks, 2010): 223–253.

[8] One of the most complete lists of the Holy Sepulcher's Temple-related objects and associations is the so-called Brevarius A, dated to the late fourth century. For a translation, see "Brevarius A and B," trans. John Wilkinson, *Jerusalem Pilgrims Before the Crusades* (Warminster: Aris & Phillips, 2002), 118–119.

[9] Cecily Hennessy, "Saint James the Just: Sacral Topography in Jerusalem and Constantinople," *Tomb and Temple: Reimagining the Sacred Buildings of Jerusalem,* eds. Eric Fernie and Robin Griffith-Jones (Woodbridge: Boydell, 2018), 194–210; Kaplony, *The Haram of Jerusalem,* 191–193.

[10] See the account of the pilgrim Egeria in *Egeria's Travels,* 133–142.

[11] Sophronius of Jerusalem, "Anacreonticon 19," in *Jerusalem Pilgrims before the Crusades,* 161.

[12] Michael Breydy, *Das Annalwerk des Eutychios von Alexandrien: ausgewählte Geschichten und Legenden kompiliert von Sa'id ibn Batriq um 935 AD* (Leuven: Peeters, 1985), vol. 1, 139–140; vol. 2, 118–120.

[13] Amikam Elad, *Medieval Jerusalem and Islamic Worship: Holy Places, Ceremonies, Pilgrimage* (Leiden: Brill, 1995); Suleiman Ali Mourad, "The Symbolism of Jerusalem in Early Islam," in *Jerusalem: Idea and Reality,* eds. Tamar Mayer and Suleiman A. Mourad (London: Routledge, 2008), 86–102. Marcus Milwright, *The Dome of the Rock and its Umayyad Mosaic Inscriptions* (Edinburgh: Edinburgh University Press, 2016), 5–8 cautions against an overreliance on such sources.

[14] On Ka'b al-Ahbar, *see* Paul M. Cobb, "Virtual Sacrality: Making Muslim Syria Sacred before the Crusades." *Medieval Encounters* 8.1 (2002), 44–45. On the familial sources for the *isnad* chains and an argument for their early dating, Elad, 15–21.

[15] On the literary sources and debate regarding these early traditions, Izhak Hasson, "The Muslim View of Jerusalem: The Qur'an and Hadith," *The History of Jerusalem: The Early Muslim Period, 638–1099,* eds. Joshua Prawer and Haggai Ben-Shammai (New York: New York University Press, 1996), 352–359. On early associations with the Temple, see Kaplony, *Haram,* 38–48.

[16] For a summary of relevant primary sources and secondary scholarship prior to 2002, Kaplony, *Haram,* 200–212.

[17] Beatrice St. Laurent and Isam Awwad, "The Marwani Musalla in Jerusalem: New Findings," *Jerusalem Quarterly* 54 (2013), 7–30; Beatrice St. Laurent and Isam Awwad, "Archaeology & Preservation of Early Islamic Jerusalem: Revealing the 7th Century Mosque on the Haram al-Sharif," *Proceedings of the 9th International Congress on the Archaeology of the Ancient Near East,* vol. 2, ed. Susanne Bickel, Bruno Jacobs, Jean-Marie Le Tensorer, and Denis Genequand (Wiesbaden : Harrassowitz Verlag, 2016), 441–454.

[18] Denis Meehan translation quoted and analyzed in Lawrence Nees, *Perspectives on Early Islamic Art in Jerusalem* (Leiden: Brill, 2016), 34–5. The parentheses are original to the translation, although the authors of the present article have elected to translate the Latin "Saracini" as Muslims rather than Nees and Meehan's "Saracens."

[19] Nees, *Perspectives on Early Islamic Art,* 35–55. Nees also proposes a radical reinterpretation of the Dome of the Chain as the original *mihrab,*

minbar, and *maqsura* for Mu'awiya's open-air mosque. This understanding of architectural typology conflicts with the analysis of Arabic sources in Heba Mostafa, "The Early Mosque Revisited: Introduction of the *Minbar* and *Maqsura*," *Muqarnas* 33 (2016), 1–16. On the author's purpose and the text's use, see Kathryn Blair Moore, *The Architecture of the Christian Holy Land: Reception from Late Antiquity through the Renaissance* (Cambridge: Cambridge University Press, 2017), 7.

[20] It is possible that the decoration of the structure continued into the mid-690s and that the notion of monumentalizing the rock preceded 'Abd al-Malik's 685–705 reign, but the inscription nonetheless situates the Dome of the Rock within a precise religious and political context.

[21] For the full text, see Grabar, *Shape of the Holy*, 59–60. The mosaic inscription, along with two plaques originally affixed to the Dome of the Rock's east and north doors, were later modified to efface 'Abd al-Malik's name in favor of his 'Abbasid successor al-Ma'mun (r. 813–833). However, the mosaic's date, the paleography of all three texts, and later medieval texts all testify to 'Abd al-Malik's patronage.

[22] Grabar, *Shape of the Holy*, 53–115; Oleg Grabar, *The Dome of the Rock* (Cambridge, MA: Harvard University Press, 2006), 96–119.

[23] Milwright, *Dome of the Rock*, 160–170.

[24] Scholarship has typically framed this discourse in language of either "triumphalism" or "ecumenicism" – see in particular the evolving attitudes of Oleg Grabar summarized in *The Shape of the Holy*, 133.

[25] This comparison is also noted by Andreas Kaplony, "635/8–1099: The Mosque of Jerusalem," *Where Heaven and Earth Meet*, 113. For a summary of the arguments for and against the counter-Ka'ba claim, Necipoğlu, "The Dome of the Rock as Palimpsest," 36–7.

[26] On 'Abd al-Malik's expressions of biblical sovereignty, Nasser Rabbat, "The Meaning of the Umayyad Dome of the Rock," *Muqarnas* 6 (1989), 12–21; Nasser Rabbat, "The Dome of the Rock Revisited: Some Remarks on al-Wasiti's Accounts," *Muqarnas* 10 (1993), 66–75.

[27] The association with the Temple in particular produced a constellation of additional emplaced biblical, Quranic, and eschatological narratives summarized in Kaplony, *The Haram of Jerusalem*, 38–41. Later medieval references to and the possibility of lost mosaic inscriptions are discussed in Necipoğlu, "The Dome of the Rock as Palimpsest," 46.

[28] Myriam Rosen-Ayalon, *The Early Islamic Monuments of al-Haram al-Sharif: An Iconographic Study* (Jerusalem: Hebrew University of Jerusalem, 1989), 68. Priscilla Soucek, "The Temple of Solomon in Islamic Legend and Art," *The Temple of Solomon,* ed. J. Gutmann (Missoula, MT: Scholars Press for American Academy of Religion, 1976), 73–123 argues the vegetation and gems are intended to reference Islamic descriptions of Solomon's Temple.

[29] On Umayyad rituals in the Dome of the Rock, Elad, *Medieval Jerusalem and Islamic Worship,* 51–61. Other associations within early *fada'il* are summarized in Robert Hillenbrand, "Medieval Muslim Veneration of the Dome of the Rock," *Tomb and Temple,* 125–45. A constellation of connections to Mecca are summarized in Grabar, *The Dome of the Rock,* 112–14.

[30] Necipoğlu, "The Dome of the Rock as Palimpsest," 80; Kaplony, *Haram of Jerusalem,* 33–48; Rosen-Ayalon, *Early Islamic Monuments,* 1.

[31] Kaplony, *Haram,* 560–569.

[32] Rosen-Ayalon, *Early Islamic Monuments,* 7. "Functional spaces" is here intended to refer to the ablution fountains, minarets, and treasury referenced on the site as well as the likely administrative complex adjacent to the Haram's south wall.

[33] Kaplony, "635/8–1099," 106; Necipoğlu, "The Dome of the Rock as Palimpsest," 39.

[34] Although modified in subsequent centuries, the columns, capitals, bases, and original floor level of the Dome of the Chain all indicate that the monument was constructed at around the same time as the Dome of the Rock and retains its original plan. Rosen-Ayalon, *Early Islamic Monuments,* 27.

[35] Rosen-Ayalon, *Early Islamic Monuments,* 25–29; Kaplony, *Haram,* 298–306.

[36] Kaplony, *Haram,* 303.

[37] Rosen-Ayalon, *Early Islamic Monuments,* 33–45; Michael Hamilton Burgoyne, "The Gates of the Haram al-Sharif," in *Bayt al-Maqdis,* 105–124.

[38] Kaplony, *Haram,* 276–280.

[39] Naser-e Khosraw, *Naser-e Khosraw's Book of Travels,* Trans. W.M. Thackston (Albany: Bibliotheca Persica, 1986), 25–6.

[40] Scholars have done so by relying or commenting on R.W. Hamilton's excavations published in *The Structural History of the Aqsa Mosque: A Record of Archaeological Gleanings from the Repairs of 1938–1942* (London: Oxford University Press, 1949). A variety of possibilities for Hamilton's "Aqsa I, II, and III" are proposed in Grabar, *Shape of the Holy,* 120.

[41] Elad, *Medieval Jerusalem,* 30–31.

[42] As most scholars working on the site note, deficits in recording and publishing information during the excavations of the site now referred to as the "Jerusalem Archaeological Park" present a major obstacle to analysis of the so-called administrative quarter.

[43] Al-Muqaddasi, Muhammad ibn Ahmad, *The Best Divisions for Knowledge of the Regions: Ahsan al-Taqasim fi Ma'rifat al-Aqalim,* trans. Basil Collins (Reading: Garnet, 2001), 153.

[44] Robert Hillenbrand, "Umayyad Woodwork in the Aqsa Mosque," *Bayt al-Maqdis: 'Abd al-Malik's Jerusalem, Part II,* ed. Jeremy Johns (Oxford: Oxford University Press, 1999), 271–310; John Wilkinson, "Column Capitals in the Haram al-Sharif," in *Bayt al-Maqdis: Abd al-Malik's Jerusalem,* eds. Julian Raby and Jeremy Johns (Oxford: Oxford Universiy Press, 1992), vol. I, 125–140; Hamilton, *Structural History,* 60–61.

[45] Grabar *Shape of the Holy,* 135.

[46] Grabar *Shape of the Holy,* 149–51. According to a c. 1173 pilgrim, another inscription dated the dome's completion to 1035.

[47] Jennifer Pruitt, "The Fatimid Holy City," *The Medieval Globe* 3.2 (2017), 50–51 and eadem, *Building the Caliphate: Construction, Destruction, and Sectarian Identity in Early Fatimid Architecture* (New Haven: Yale University Press, 2020), 127–152.

[48] Kaplony, *Haram,* 98–107.

[49] *Safarnameh,* 21.

[50] *Safarnameh,* 23; Max van Berchem, *Matériaux pour un Corpus Inscriptionum Arabicarum,* pt. 2, vol. 2 (Cairo : Institut français d'archéologie orientale, 1927), 84–97.

[51] *Safarnameh,* 24.

[52] *Safarnameh,* 31–32.

[53] *Safarnameh,* 33.

[54] Translated twelfth-century Latin accounts of the massacre can be consulted in F.E. Peters, *The First Crusade: "The Chronicle of Fulcher of Chartres" and Other Source Materials,* 2nd ed. (Philadelphia: University of Pennsylvania Press, 1998), 245–260. For a summary of the Arabic sources and political context, Paul M. Cobb, *The Race for Paradise: an Islamic History of the Crusades* (New York: Oxford University Press, 2014), 99–103.

[55] Denys Pringle, *Churches of the Crusader Kingdom of Jerusalem,* vol. 3 (Cambridge: Cambridge University Press, 2007), 420–32.

[56] Sylvia Schein, "Between Mount Moriah and the Holy Sepulchre: The Changing Traditions of the Temple Mount in the Central Middle Ages," *Traditio* 40 (1984), 175–195.

57 Saewulf, "A Reliable Account of the Situation of Jerusalem," 104-105 and Daniel the Abbot, "The Life and Journey of Daniel," 132-133 in *Jerusalem Pilgrimage 1099-1185,* eds. John Wilkinson, Joyce Hill, and W.F. Ryan (London: Hakluyt Society, 1988).

58 Saewulf, 104, Daniel, 133.

59 Iris Shagrir, "*Adventus* in Jerusalem: The Palm Sunday Celebration in Latin Jerusalem," *Journal of Medieval History* 41.1 (2015): 1-20.

60 Saewulf, 104-5.

61 On the stone, see Yamit Rachman-Schrire, "The Stones of the Christian Holy Places of Jerusalem and Western Imagination: Image, Place, Text (1099-1517)," PhD Dissertation, Hebrew University of Jerusalem, 2015, 39-44. On the shift to Crusader and Marian associations, Moore, *Architecture,* 86-91.

62 Pringle, 182-185.

63 Priscilla Soucek, "The Temple after Solomon: The Role of Maryam Bint 'Imran and her *Mihrab*," *The Real and Ideal Jerusalem in Jewish, Christian and Islamic Art*, ed. Bianca Kühnel (Jerusalem, 1998), issued as *Jewish Art* 23/23 (1997-98), 32-41; Kaplony, *Haram,* 600-603; Moore, *Architecture,* 91.

64 Robert Ousterhout, "'Sweetly Refreshed in Imagination': Remembering Jerusalem in Words and Images," *Gesta* 48 (2009), 153-68.

65 *Description of the Holy Land by John of Würzburg,* trans. Aubrey Stewart (London: Palestine Pilgrim's Text Society, 1890), 11. A handful of twelfth-century authors ascribe the building to "Amor" or the Caliph 'Umar, including the aforementioned Daniel.

66 John of Würzburg, 246.

67 Translation Pringle, 404. Despite the visual and textual efforts to juxtapose these two moments in biblical history, John unequivocally declared that Jacob's Dream "did not happen here."

68 Jaroslav Folda, *The Art of the Crusaders in the Holy Land, 1098-1187* (Cambridge: Cambridge University Press, 1995), 252; Daniel Weiss, "Hec est Domus Domini Firmiter Edificata: The Image of the Temple in Crusader Art," *The Real and Ideal Jerusalem,* 210-17.

69 For another example of the canons' refashioning of biblical material for present purpose, Julian Yolles, "The Maccabees in the Lord's Temple: Biblical Imagery and Latin Poetry in Frankish Jerusalem," *The Uses of the Bible in Crusader Sources,* eds. Elizabeth Lapina and Nicholas Morton (Leiden: Brill, 2017), 421-439.

70 *A Lonely Wayfarer's Guide to Pilgrimage: 'Ali ibn Abi Bakr al-Harawi's Kitab al-isharat ila ma'rifat al-ziyarat,* trans. Josef W. Meri (Princeton: Darwin Press, 2004), 72. Other accounts of Jewish and Muslim visitors to the Latin Haram are mentioned in Benjamin Z. Kedar and Denys Pringle, "1099-1187: The Lord's Temple (*Templum Domini*) and Solomon's Palace (*Palatium Salomonis*)," *Where Heaven and Earth Meet,* 132-49.

71 *The Chronicle of Ibn al-Athir for the Crusading Period from Al-Kamil fi'l Ta'rikh,* vol. 2, Trans. D.S. Richards (New York: Routledge, 2016), 334 and *The Rare and Excellent History of Saladin or al-Nawadir al-Sultaniyya wa'l-Mahasin al-Yusufiyya by Baha al-Din Ibn Shaddad,* trans. D.S. Richards (Aldershot: Ashgate, 2001), 78.

72 *Ibn Khallikan's Biographical Dictionary,* vol. 2, trans. W. M. Mac Guckin de Slane (Paris: Oriental Translation Fund of Great Britain and Ireland, 1843), 635-7

73 Ibn al-Athir, 334.

74 Finbarr Barry Flood, "An Ambiguous Aesthetic: Crusader Spolia in Ayyubid Jerusalem," *Ayyubid Jerusalem: The Holy City in Context 1187-1250,* eds. Robert Hillenbrand and Sylvia Auld (London: Altajir Trust, 2009), 202-215.

75 Kaplony, 486-492.

76 Pringle, 413-414; Folda, 253-54.

77 Mahmoud K. Hawari, *Ayyubid Jerusalem (1187-1250): An Architectural and Archaeological Study* (Oxford: Archaeopress, 2007), 90 and Michael Hamilton Burgoyne, "1187-1260: The Furthest Mosque (*al-Masjid al-Aqsa*) under Ayyubid Rule," *Where Heaven and Earth Meet,* 150-75.

78 Hawari, 84 and van Berchem, 37-54.

79 Sylvia Auld, "The *Minbar* of Nur al-Din in Context," *Ayyubid Jerusalem,* 72-93; Yasser Tabbaa, "Originality and Innovation in Syrian Woodwork of the Twelfth and Thirteenth Centuries," *Material Evidence and Narrative Sources: Interdisciplinary Studies of the History of the Muslim Middle East,* eds. Daniella J. Talmon-Heller and Katia Cytryn-Silverman (Leiden: Brill, 2015), 188-215.

80 Lynette Singer, ed., *The Minbar of Saladin: Reconstructing a Jewel of Islamic Art* (New York: Thames and Hudson, 2008).

Mosques under the Ayyubids   STEPHENNIE MULDER

1 Al-Jarrah Mosque, Damascus, 1250, minaret. Photo: Stephennie Mulder

The Ayyubid Sultanate (1171–1250) was a Sunni dynasty founded by the Kurdish general Salah al-Din (Saladin). The Ayyubids controlled Syria, Egypt, upper Iraq, and Yemen in the twelfth and thirteenth centuries. Although the Ayyubid era was a period of intensive architectural patronage which saw the construction of castles like Crac des Chevaliers, citadels in cities like Cairo and Damascus, as well as hundreds of new *madrasa*s (legal schools), shrines, tombs, and *khanqah*s (Sufi convents), it was not a period of large-scale mosque construction. Indeed, few examples of Ayyubid purpose-built mosques survive, and the reasons typically given are twofold: First, by the twelfth and thirteenth centuries, most major cities within Ayyubid domains already had major congregational mosques. Second, the Ayyubid sovereigns were not leaders of a vast empire, but princes ruling a loosely-allied group of local principalities, subject to shifting and competing political alliances. Perhaps because they did not have imperial tax revenues at their disposal, and perhaps because they needed to secure and strengthen these local relationships, Ayyubid patrons appear to have found it desirable to invest not in congregational mosques but in smaller institutions of a more populist character, such as neighborhood mosques, *madrasa*s, *khanqah*s, and shrines.

Yet in contrast to the remaining material evidence, the Arabic textual sources appear to report a more significant investment in mosque architecture than has typically been understood for this period. In Damascus, for example, according to the medieval historian and topographer Ibn 'Asakir (d. 1175), at the time of Saladin's rise to power there were nearly 430 mosques in the city and its suburbs.[1] A hundred years later, Ibn Shaddad (d. 1284) lists 660 mosques, meaning that in the brief tenure of the Ayyubids the number of mosques swelled by nearly a third, with the city adding some 230 structures.[2] While at first glance this seems impressive, the difficulty is to identify precisely what the medieval sources mean when they refer to the construction of mosques (*masjid,* pl. *masajid*) in Ayyubid times.

Two problems arise when discussing the nature of the mosque in this era. The first is the tendency of some authors to conflate architectural terminology when describing buildings. Ibn 'Asakir, for example, is notorious for doing so. Writing about a shrine (*mashhad*) for al-Husayn located within the Umayyad mosque in Damascus, he describes it as

> a mosque (*masjid*) at the door of the Congregational Mosque, known as the Mashhad al-Ra's (the Shrine of the Head). It has a water source, and they say the head of al-Husayn ibn 'Ali (upon him be peace) was placed in it when it was brought to Damascus. It has an imam (prayer leader) and a *waqf* (perpetual endowment for its maintenance and upkeep).[3]

Although it would seem difficult to make a case that a shrine located within the congregational mosque is itself a separate mosque, still, some medieval authors frequently call such sites mosques. However, at around the same time, some of Ibn 'Asakir's contemporaries – for example the pilgrimage guide author al-Harawi (d. 611/1215) and the Spanish pilgrim Ibn Jubayr (d. 613/1217), as well as Ibn Shaddad (d. 685/1284), who wrote a century later – call the site a *mashhad*, or shrine. Thus, in the Ayyubid period the term *masjid* itself was a flexible one, and it encompassed many types of buildings in which prayer could occur, such as *madrasa*s, shrines, oratories, and tombs.[4]

2 Madrasa al-Firdaws, Aleppo, 1235–36.
Photo: Yasser Tabbaa Archive, courtesy
of Aga Khan Documentation Center,
MIT Libraries (AKDC@MIT)

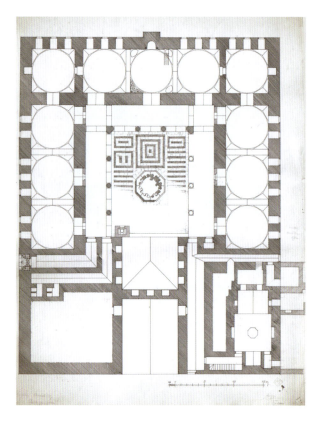

3 Madrasa al-Firdaws, Aleppo, 1235–36, plan.
Drawing: The Ernst Herzfeld Papers,
Department of Islamic Art, The Metropolitan
Museum of Art, eeh1622_001

Furthermore, some of the difficulty in categorizing these buildings arises from the trend – still nascent in the Ayyubid era – toward incorporating previously separate building types into unified, single architectural units: a trend that would reach its full expression a century later in the enormous pious complexes of Mamluk Cairo. Probably the earliest example of this type is the Madrasa al-Firdaws (built 1235–36) in Aleppo (Fig. 2).[5] Its plan, in the north, west, and east, consists of three large chambers and numerous residential units, organized around a rectangular courtyard (Fig. 3). The south chamber, however, functioned as a prayer hall. As in many an Ayyubid multifunctional complex, the most elaborate decoration is reserved for the prayer hall. It included a large central dome with a *muqarnas* transitional zone, flanked by two smaller domes, and, under the central dome, what is arguably the most spectacular stone inlaid *mihrab* (prayer niche) in Ayyubid architecture (Fig. 4).[6] Such embellishments, and the fact that the most elaborate decoration is reserved for the prayer hall, indicate that although the primary use of the building was as a *madrasa* (legal school), its function as a place for prayer (*masjid*) was no less significant. Indeed, at least from an aesthetic perspective, the prayer hall with its elaborate *mihrab* received even greater emphasis. Furthermore, that many neighborhood residents used such buildings for daily prayer is suggested both by the textual accounts and by common practice observable today. Daily prayers were held in *madrasa*s, and the *waqfiyya* (endowment deed) of the Madrasa al-Salahiyya in Jerusalem specifically stipulated that the students and professors pray in the prayer hall.[7] Indeed, based on aesthetic prioritization of space and patterns of use, such buildings could even, for the sake of argument, be considered to be mosques foremost with other, secondary functions appended to them. In truth, any definition calls for a complex understanding of these buildings not as mosques or *madrasa*s alone, but as inherently multifunctional and multivalent works of architecture.

The second difficulty, noted previously, is what is typically perceived to be the numerical paucity of remaining mosques dating to the Ayyubid era.

4 Madrasa al-Firdaws, Aleppo, 1235–6, *mihrab*.
Photo: Yasser Tabbaa Archive, courtesy of Aga Khan Documentation Center, MIT Libraries (AKDC@MIT)

But like the semantic issue of the *masjid* explored above, this problem is less one of quantity than of interpretation. Although it is indeed true that most major cities already had large congregational mosques, and thus the need for new construction was minimal, a major aspect of Ayyubid patronage consisted in the restoration and renovation of these already-extant mosques, particularly those of venerable and ancient pedigree – such as the Umayyad mosques in Damascus (705–715) and Aleppo (710), or the Mosque of 'Amr in Fustat (641, rebuilt in 827)– all of which were restored under Zangid and Ayyubid patronage. Such works of restoration were no mere "touch-up" projects. On the contrary, they were frequently interventions that contributed significantly to the upkeep and continuation of these structures: in the case of the Umayyad Mosque in Damascus, for example, which was renovated multiple times under Ayyubid patronage, walls were repeatedly plastered, several rounds of costly new marble facings were ordered for the decoration of the interior, and new doors were commissioned, manufactured, and installed.[8] Under Saladin, the Mosque of 'Amr in Fustat received new marble facings for the *mihrab* and was graced with new inscriptions.[9] Such works of renovation and restoration were a major focus of the architectural patronage of the Ayyubid family; in fact, they constituted nearly half of all known acts of construction by them.[10] That the wealthiest members of Ayyubid society so actively concerned themselves with restoration is an indication such measures were seen not as secondary to new foundations, but rather, as equally prestigious (and in the case of these prominent mosques, perhaps even more prestigious) than acts of foundation *ex nihilo*.

Nevertheless, new mosques were built in the Ayyubid era, in both Egypt and the region of Greater Syria (*Bilad al-Sham*).[11] In general, they tended to be small in scale, of a type sometimes called the "neighborhood mosque," and were often part of other types of buildings, such as citadels, tombs, and palaces. Among the better known is the Jami' al-Tawba (Mosque of Repentance) in Damascus (Fig. 5), built in 1231–35 by the Ayyubid Sultan al-Malik al-Ashraf Musa, located just

MOSQUES UNDER THE AYYUBIDS 191

5 Al-Tawba Mosque, Damascus, 1231–35.
Photo: Stephennie Mulder

6 Al-Tawba Mosque, Damascus, 1231–35, plan. Drawing: The Ernst Herzfeld Papers, Department of Islamic Art, The Metropolitan Museum of Art, eeh1504_001

7 Al-Tawba Mosque, Damascus, 1231–35, prayer hall. Photo: Stephennie Mulder

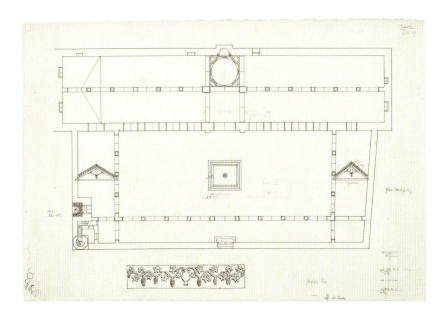

200 meters northwest of the northern gate of Bab al-Faradis. Its name derives from the fact that it is said to have been built on the site of a caravanserai that had become a place of ill repute and prostitution; and perhaps to emphasize the site's re-dedication to holiness, al-Ashraf chose a plan which mimicked that of the Umayyad mosque, with its long, rectangular courtyard oriented parallel to the *qibla* and surrounded by three arcades. Similar to the Umayyad mosque, too, is its prayer hall, which extends slightly beyond the courtyard on the east and west to form a kind of T-plan (Fig. 6). The prayer area consists of two long halls oriented parallel to the *qibla*, with a low transept marking the direction of the *mihrab* (Fig. 7). At the end of the transept, the *mihrab* is covered by a small dome.[12]

Another, even simpler, example of an Ayyubid neighborhood mosque is the Jami' al-Jarrah (al-Jarrah mosque), also in Damascus, located just south of the city, slightly west of the gate of Bab al-Saghir (Fig. 8). It borders the eponymously-named cemetery of Bab al-Saghir, in which many famous Damascenes are buried.[13] The cemetery is the focus of much pilgrimage activity, meaning the building functioned as a kind of cemetery mosque. It is likely that in medieval times, as today, this mosque was a haven for pilgrims from diverse lands. This small structure was newly-built on the site of an older mosque by the Amir Mujahid al-Din Muhammad Qilij in 648.[14] It is far more modest in plan and in decoration than the Mosque of al-Tawba. In plan, it is nearly square, with a small arcaded courtyard on three sides facing a simple prayer hall entered via three arched doorways (Fig. 9). The façade consists of a central portal crowned by a pointed arch and surmounted by a largely unadorned, square minaret with an octagonal upper storey and a wooden balcony (Fig. 1). On either side of the portal, two windows give a view over the northern portico across a square pool and toward the entrance to the prayer hall. The prayer hall itself is a single, large room parallel to the *qibla*, largely unadorned, and with a simple, wood-trussed roof.

8 Al-Jarrah Mosque, Damascus, 1250.
Photo: Stephennie Mulder

Nevertheless, not all Ayyubid mosques were so small or so restrained in architectural embellishment. The minaret of the Ayyubid-era congregational mosque in the city of Balis, on the Euphrates in northern Syria, was built by the Ayyubid Sultan al-Malik al-'Adil in 1210–11 in the form of an octagon and using ornamental brick. Both features are unusual for Ayyubid mosques and more commonly associated with eastern Islamic influence. The minaret also bore a Shi'izing inscription, a feature that perhaps – in association with Balis' geographical proximity to the eastern Islamic world – explains its unusual form and decoration (Fig. 10).[15]

Despite their differences, the Madrasa al-Firdaws, the al-Tawba Mosque, the al-Jarrah mosque, and the minaret at Balis are, each in their own way, examples of the diversity of mosque architecture in the Ayyubic period. Such buildings – their varied patterns of use, patronage, and multiple functions within the city fabric – invite the expansion of simplistic categorizations and challenge our assumptions about the nature of the mosque in the middle Islamic period.

STEPHENNIE MULDER is Associate Professor of Islamic Art and Architecture at the University of Texas at Austin. She has conducted archaeological and art historical fieldwork in Syria, Egypt, Turkey, and elsewhere in the region, and is the author of an award-winning monograph, *The Shrines of the 'Alids in Medieval Syria: Sunnis, Shi'is and the Architecture of Coexistence*. She has published articles on Islamic art, architectural history, archaeology, heritage preservation, and the trade in looted antiquities.

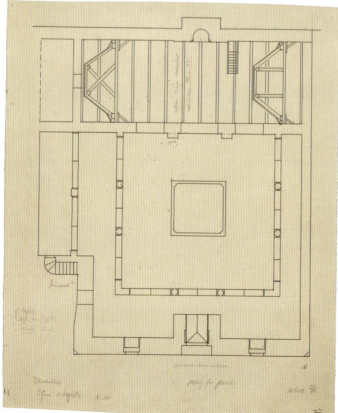

9 Plan, al-Jarrah Mosque, Damascus, 1250.
Drawing: The Ernst Herzfeld Papers, Department of Islamic Art, The Metropolitan Museum of Art, eeh1507_001

10 Minaret at Balis (Meskene), Syria, 1210–11.

Photo: Stephennie Mulder

SUGGESTIONS FOR FURTHER READING

Allen, Terry. *Ayyubid Architecture*, Sixth Edition (Occidental, Cal.: Solipsist Press, 1999). Electronic Publication, accessed July 9, 2021. http://www.sonic.net/~tallen/palmtree/ayyarch/

Humphreys, R. Stephen. "Politics and Architectural Patronage in Ayyubid Damascus," in C. E. Bosworth et al., *The Islamic World from Classical to Modern Times*, (Princeton: Darwin Press, 1989).

Korn, Lorenz. *Ayyubidische Architektur in Ägypten und Syrien*, 2 vols. (Heidelberg: Heidelberger Orientverlag, 2004).

Tabbaa, Yasser. *Constructions of Power and Piety in Medieval Aleppo* (University Park: Pennsylvania State University Press, 1997).

Talmon-Heller, Daniella. *Islamic Piety in Medieval Syria: Mosques Cemeteries and Sermons under the Zangids and Ayyubids* (Leiden: Brill, 2007).

NOTES

1. Ibn 'Asakir, *Ta'rikh madinat Dimashq*, ed. Salah al-Din al-Munajjid (Damascus, Matbu'at al-Majma' al-'Ilmi al-'Arabi, 1951).
2. Ibn Shaddad, *al-A'laq al-khatira fi dhikr umara' al-'Iraq wa'l-Jazira: Ta'rikh Madinat Dimashq*, ed. Sami al-Dahhan. (Damascus: al-Ma'had al-Faransi lil-Dirasat al-'Arabiyya, 1956), 92–166.
3. Ibn 'Asakir, *Ta'rikh madinat Dimashq*, 2: 72.
4. On the shifting architectural terminology in the medieval sources, see Oleg Grabar, "The Earliest Islamic Commemorative Structures, Notes and Documents," *Ars Orientalis* 6 (1996), 11–12, and Josef Meri, *The Cult of Saints among Muslims and Jews in Medieval Syria* (Oxford: Oxford University Press, 2002), 268.
5. Yasser Tabbaa, *Constructions of Power and Piety in Medieval Aleppo* (University Park: Pennsylvania State University Press, 1997), 168–82.
6. Terry Allen, "Madrasah al-Firdaus", in *Ayyubid Architecture* (Occidental, Cal.: Solipsist Press, 1999), http://www.sonic.net/~tallen/palmtree/ayyarch/ch8.htm - alep.firdaus (accessed July 9, 2021); Tabbaa, *Constructions*, 46–8, 142, 168–71.
7. Daniella Talmon-Heller, *Islamic Piety in Medieval Syria: Mosques Cemeteries and Sermons under the Zangids and Ayyubids* (Leiden: Brill, 2007), 48.
8. Lorenz Korn, *Ayyubidische Architektur in Ägypten und Syrien* (Heidelberg: Heidelberger Orientverlag, 2004), 1: 44.
9. Ibid., 2:15.
10. Allen, "Doorways in the Great Mosque of Damascus," in *Ayyubid Architecture*, http://sonic.net/~tallen/palmtree/ayyarch/ch1.htm#damas.ummosque (accessed July 9, 2021); R. Stephen Humphreys, "Politics and Architectural Patronage in Ayyubid Damascus," in *The Islamic World from Classical to Modern Times,* eds. C. E. Bosworth et al. (Princeton: Darwin Press, 1989), 154.
11. For a comprehensive catalogue and complete bibliography for each, see Korn, *Ayyubidische Architektur*, vol. 2.
12. Ibid., 143–4.
13. Stephennie Mulder, *The Shrines of the 'Alids in Medieval Syria* (Edinburgh: Edinburgh University Press, 2014), 114–185.
14. Ibid., 158–9.
15. Janine Sourdel and Dominique Sourdel, "La Date de construction du minaret de Bâlis," *Les Annales Archéologiques de Syrie* 3 (1953), 103–5; Robert Hillenbrand, "Eastern Islamic influences in Syria: Raqqa and Qal'at Ja'bar in the later 12th century," in *The Art of Syria and the Jazira 1100–1250*, ed. Julian Raby (Oxford: Oxford University Press, 1985), 21–48; Stephennie Mulder, *The Shrines of the 'Alids in Medieval Syria* (Edinburgh: Edinburgh University Press, 2014), 28–9.

Shrines in the Central Islamic Lands   STEPHENNIE MULDER

1 Shrine for al-Husayn, Cairo, Egypt, 1154 and 1873.
Photo: Author

The Islamic world is replete with devotional sites, perhaps nowhere more densely concentrated than in the area known as the central Islamic lands, a designation that includes Iraq, Egypt, and *Bilad al-Sham*, or Greater Syria (today Israel, Palestine, Syria, and Jordan). Many of the most important Muslim shrines are located here, and their veneration forms a major engine of the economic, spiritual, and devotional life of the area today as it did in the medieval period. This region has a special place within Muslim piety for two reasons. First, it contains the territory perceived by adherents of all three monotheistic faiths to be the Holy Land (*al-ard al-muqaddasa*), where the events of the Bible and New Testament took place and where many Muslim holy figures also resided. Second, for the Shiʻa, Syria and Iraq are home to many of the holiest shrines and shrine cities, sites that commemorate key events in the early Shiʻi communal narrative.

Prior to the coming of Islam, the Holy Land had been envisioned by Jews and Christians as the Biblical terrain of coastal Palestine and, above all, the city of Jerusalem. Thus, when Muslims initially settled in this region, they encountered a longstanding, vibrant landscape of devotion centered on worship at sites commemorating Biblical prophets, Talmudic sages, and Christian saints. Indeed, the growth and development of varied cults of saints dedicated to holy men, pious women, martyrs, and ascetics was one hallmark of the late Antique and early medieval period in the Eastern Mediterranean.[1] Among Christians in the fourth and fifth centuries, these cults had spurred the development of a formalized, interlinked itinerary of pilgrimage sites that had instigated major architectural patronage in the form of mausolea, churches, martyria, and vast pilgrimage complexes. Sites in and around the

city of Jerusalem were the primary objects of pilgrimage for Christians and Jews, although other locales also received generous patronage in this period, particularly under the Byzantine emperor Justinian: for example Rusafa (Sergiopolis) (fourth century CE)[2] and Qalʻat Semʻan (475 CE) in northern Syria,[3] or sites of intensive interfaith pilgrimage and worship like Saydnaya (547 CE), northeast of Damascus.[4] Similarly, in both Iraq and Egypt Muslims encountered a vibrant Jewish and Christian pilgrimage landscape. In Iraq, sites holy to Biblical prophets such as Ezekiel were beloved by both Jews and Christians, while in Egypt, a network of Coptic pilgrimage sites had flourished.[5] Subsequently, in the centuries following the Islamic conquest, and becoming pronounced in the middle Islamic period, a uniquely Islamic sacred topography was generated, one that often coexisted with these previous sites and at the same time marked the landscape as holy to Muslims. In particular, over the course of the eleventh to thirteenth centuries, the initial Jerusalem-centric boundaries of the old Jewish and Christian Holy Land expanded, generating a new Islamic sacred landscape that now encompassed much of the area of Greater Syria.[6]

SAINT VENERATION IN ISLAM

Islamic shrines have many names, and an equally varied architectural legacy. They may be called *qubba* (dome), *turba* or *darih* (burial place), *mashhad* (place of witnessing), or *mazar* (place of visitation). These terms are fluid and tend not to be consistent in their application to specific architectural types. However, in terms of form, most shrines fall into two broad categories: a simple, cubical funeral chamber surmounted by a dome (often called a *qubba* or *turba*), or a more complex plan having some variation on a courtyard, domed tomb chamber, and assembly rooms/prayer hall.[7] Assembly rooms may be domed, flat roofed, or covered by *iwan*s (barrel-vaulted halls). Thus, aside from the typical presence of the cubical, domed form over the burial chamber, there is no single architectural pattern for Muslim shrines.

Regardless of architectural form or the term employed, all Islamic shrines share the characteristic of memorializing the vestiges or traces (*athar*) of the holy person – who either passed by the place in question, performed some miracle on the spot, or was buried there – or of memorializing a relic associated with them. Such cults of relics were less frequent in the earlier periods, but became popular by the twelfth and thirteenth centuries when we find reports of pieces of fabric, weapons, footprints, and frequently, sacred stones associated with saintly Muslims.[8] The geographer Yaqut (d. 1229), for example, lists the relics held in the Umayyad mosque in Damascus, while the pilgrimage guide author 'Ali al-Harawi (d. 1215) speaks about a stone from which Moses had drawn water during the Exodus.[9] Such references are frequent in the Arabic sources. These objects were revered for their powers of healing, both spiritual and physical. As with such practices in other religious traditions, the veneration of holy figures in Islam is closely reliant on both the experiential and phenomenological aspects of devotion – on feeling, touching, and tasting traces of the saint and thus partaking of their *baraka* (blessing).[10] At the same time, holy sites validate and reify oral and textual narratives describing concrete religio-historical events. Practices related to reverence for holy figures are therefore among the primary vehicles for the performance and reaffirmation of historical or communal memory.

The veneration of holy figures in Islam is a complex of informal, loosely associated beliefs and practices with numerous local and confessional variations. Furthermore, while the Muslim veneration of saints shares certain characteristics with other religious traditions, it also differs in some ways. Similar in most traditions are the general reasons believers visit holy locales: like Christians, Jews, Buddhists, and Hindus, Muslims

also visit shrines to pay homage to the memory of a deceased holy figure, to make vows of repentance, and to receive some tangible spiritual or physical assistance by means of the saint's mediating power (*shafa'a*). Also similar are the sorts of benefits one might expect to receive: a deepening of spiritual connection, healing from disease, the observation or experience of miracles, and the communal experience of connection with other believers. Muslim saints, like those of other traditions, are envisioned as intercessionary figures, who occupy a liminal space between the believer and God and who have powers to mediate on behalf of supplicants. Muslim saints acquired their holy status through a rather eclectic process of becoming "beloved by the people." Simply put, if a figure came to be loved and venerated, and particularly if they were associated with the performance of miracles (*karamat*), then he or she was considered a saint. The term "saint" then, although used here for the lack of a better English term, should be understood as an indication of holy status based on communal consensus and religious practice.[11] Because veneration of saints in Islam is somewhat informal, Muslim scholars and writers appear to have been less focused on a tradition of official hagiography. Instead, the medieval sources on saints and saintly locales reflect an integration of saint worship into the realm of the everyday. Accordingly, accounts of saints' lives and descriptions of their shrines tend to be found within a rich corpus of texts having a broader focus: including chronicles, pilgrimage guides, biographical dictionaries, and *fada'il* (praise) literature. These sources often contain accounts of miracles, saintly manifestations, and visions associated with holy figures.[12]

In Islamic legal thought, the practice of shrine visitation, called *ziyara*, is distinguished from formal pilgrimage (Hajj) to Mecca. The Hajj is incumbent upon all Muslims at least once in their lifetime (if their economic situation allows): indeed, Hajj is one of the five basic ritual obligations of Islam. The role and status of shrine visitation, on the other hand, differs between the sects. While *ziyara* was always an integral part of both Sunni and Shi'i worship, for Sunnis the legality of the practice was cause for some debate, whereas for Shi'is, the central place of devotion to members of the Prophet's family ensured that the performance of *ziyara* always had a vital role in religious life. Consequently, some of the earliest shrines are located at sites associated with the Family of the Prophet. These figures were beloved by both Sunnis and Shi'is, but their veneration traditionally had a more prominent role in Shi'i devotional practice. Unlike within Sunnism, Shi'ism never developed a tradition of interrogating the legality of the practice of shrine visitation – on the contrary, practices associated with *ziyara* became an essential aspect of Shi'i religious experience. However, within Sunni legal circles, *ziyara* held a more contested theological place, and critiques of it arose in Iraq as early as two centuries after the founding of Islam.[13] Thus, we find that among the earliest collections of Hadith (the Islamic Tradition, or corpus of legal exemplars deriving from the behavior and words of the Prophet Muhammad), there were admonitions derived from the Prophet's preference for the *taswiyat al-qubur*, or "leveling of tombs" to the ground, in other words, a preference for a simple burial in the bare earth, without elaborate grave goods and particularly without building any structure over the grave. This was a practice envisioned as the appropriate expression of the Islamic doctrine of the equality of all human beings in death.[14]

However, Sunni opposition to shrine visitation was by no means uniform, and criticisms that did exist probably reflected an anxiety among Sunnis about the popularity of the practice of *ziyara* and its association with certain Christian and Jewish devotional rituals.[15] Indeed, it is difficult to find Hadith advocating the wholesale rejection of the practice of *ziyara*. More common are critiques of specific activities at burial places: for example, praying at gravesites, making sacrifices, marking the grave or making an inscription for it, and erecting buildings over it. However, the detail and specificity of the legal sanctions marshaled against shrine visitation probably only confirm the widespread persistence and ubiquity of these activities in practice.[16] Thus, it should be emphasized that despite the early criticism noted above and some

later condemnations that arose after the fourteenth century in the discussions of Ibn Taymiyya and others,[17] there is little evidence of broad resistance to the practice of shrine visitation *per se* by more than a restricted group of legal scholars. In general, in all eras and among most Muslims of both elite and popular backgrounds, it was seen as at best, a highly meritorious – and at worst, a sometimes suspect but nevertheless, largely beneficial – adjunct to canonical religious practice.[18] Ayyubid and Mamluk-era scholars such as al-Ghazali (d. 1111), Ibn Qudama (d. 1223), and al-Nawawi (d. 1277), were deeply concerned with the proper etiquette of pilgrimage, but never forbade visitation itself, indeed they advocated for its performance, often enthusiastically.[19]

Furthermore, as just noted, protestations against saint veneration should probably be read not as reflective of normative practice and attitudes, but rather as evidence for the very popularity of such devotion. Support for this proposition abounds: for example, elaborate grave markers and structures appear to have existed from the earliest periods, and they attracted the believers in large enough numbers for some legal scholars to exhort against them.[20] Shrines and other commemorative structures, including vast cemeteries filled with lavishly ornamented mausolea, were built from the earliest years after the establishment of the Islamic community and are among the most frequently patronized architectural constructions in Islamic lands from medieval times until the present. The medieval sources are replete with descriptions of people from all walks of life visiting shrines, performing acts of devotion, and of the miracles associated with saintly locales. Thus, from the outset, there was a tension between legal disapproval of saint veneration among some Sunni religious scholars and actual practice: for in all periods, ordinary Muslims and members of the religious and ruling elite alike embraced these activities, apparently without regard for scholarly sanction. Thus, while Sunni and Shi'i shrine visitation is often discussed in the academic literature as two separate and non-overlapping phenomena – in which Sunnism abjured the practice while Shi'ism embraced it and even perhaps caused the growth of the phenomenon – this division is artificial and has probably been exaggerated.[21] Saint veneration was widespread at all times and regardless of sectarian affiliation, and differences between the two sects with respect to such practices are probably differences of emphasis, not of kind.

In the central Islamic lands, among both Sunnis and Shi'is, the practice of *ziyara* seems to have been a natural outgrowth of three things: the continuation and elaboration of pre-Islamic devotional practices for the Biblical prophets and holy figures of the Jewish and Christian traditions; reverence for the Prophet's family – a sentiment shared by all Muslim communities, though particularly pronounced within Shi'ism; and, lastly, veneration of learned rulers, preachers, scholars and Sufis, a phenomenon that becomes widespread in the twelfth and thirteenth centuries.[22]

VENERATION OF BIBLICAL PROPHETS AND JEWISH AND CHRISTIAN HOLY FIGURES

Muslims revered the Biblical prophets and other Jewish and Christian holy figures.[23] Research for this aspect of devotional practice is still in its early stages, however, some preliminary observations can be made. Shrines for Biblical prophets such as Abraham and Ezekiel are mentioned in the earliest Arabic praise literature and pilgrimage guides, as are some shrines for Christian holy figures. For example, the medieval geographer al-Muqaddasi, writing in 986, begins his narrative by saying that "Syria is the abode of the prophets, the habitation of the righteous, the home of the successors to the Prophet," indicating that a kind of hierarchy of holy figures was in place from an early date.[24] By the early thirteenth century, such references are commonplace, and authors such as al-Harawi and Yaqut recount legions of traditions regarding the locations of shrines for the prophets and also for Christian figures such as 'Isa (Jesus), Maryam (Mary), and John the Baptist, although like many Muslim sites, their accounts are frequently marked by some skepticism as to whether the sites were genuine and accompanied by opinions and arguments for the authenticity of one location over another. Some sites, such as the competing shrines for Moses in Jericho and Damascus, remained contested, leading to active competition for pilgrims well into modern times.[25] Meanwhile, others transformed over time, as the site of a shrine for Joshua near Tiberias did, later becoming a shrine for Jesus.[26]

Jerusalem was Islam's third-holiest city, after Mecca and Medina. Thus, as was the case for Christians and Jews, the city was also the focus of Muslim veneration of the Biblical prophets. Jerusalem was the original *qibla*, or direction Muslims faced for prayer, until Muhammad received a revelation to change the *qibla* to Mecca (Quran 2.144). Still, despite the change, the city remained an important site. Its holiest location, the raised platform and *temenos* area of the ruined Temple of Solomon, was soon graced with one of Islam's most notable and enigmatic buildings, the Dome of the Rock (691) (Fig. 2), located alongside the expansive and elegant al-Aqsa Mosque (709–15). Muslims call the site the Haram al-Sharif (Noble Sanctuary). In addition to the prophets Solomon and Muhammad, the Dome of the Rock

2 Dome of the Rock, Jerusalem, 691.
Photo: Kathryn Blair Moore

200 MULDER

is also associated with the Biblical Abraham, for the rock is thought to have been the location where Abraham prepared to sacrifice his son. The area continued to be revered for its Biblical associations, but later, came to be associated with the *mi'raj* (the Ascension or Night Journey) of the Prophet Muhammad. In the narrative of the *mi'raj*, Muhammad is guided by the angel Gabriel through the various levels of heaven, until he is eventually ushered into the presence of the throne of God. The Dome of the Rock, built by the Umayyad caliph 'Abd al-Malik (r. 685–705), was likely originally intended to convey a message of religio-political sovereignty by linking Islam to the region's biblical past, but was later identified as the site from whence Muhammad began this heavenly journey.[27] Thus, although the Dome of the Rock does not memorialize the burial place of a holy person, it fulfils many of the same functions as a shrine – Muslims make *ziyara* to the site and perform a sequence of shrine visitation-related activities such as prayer, observation of and entreaty for miracles, and ritual activities such as circumambulation and recitation of narratives associated with the holy place.[28] In addition to Abraham, Jerusalem is linked with many other Biblical prophets and Christian figures, including David and Solomon, who are buried there; Jonah, whose family came from Jerusalem; and Saint Joseph, who fled to Egypt from the city with Mary and Jesus.[29]

Judging from the frequency of their appearance in the Arabic sources, shrines for the Biblical prophets were visited by Muslims as often as exclusively "Islamic" ones. Indeed, countless shrines for the prophets are described by medieval writers. The prophet Abraham, father of all three monotheistic faiths, had many holy sites associated with him, from multiple locales commemorating his birthplace – for example outside of Damascus, in Sawad in the Hawran, or Iraq[30] – to several sites at which he prepared to sacrifice his son[31] and the location of his house.[32] In some towns, including Aleppo and Mosul, there was a sacred itinerary associated with Abraham, with multiple stations.[33]

The place of Abraham's burial in the Cave of the Patriarchs, known in Arabic as the Haram al-Ibrahimi Mosque in Hebron/al-Khalil, is one of the most venerable pilgrimage places in Greater Syria (Fig. 3).[34] It is the second-holiest Jewish site after the Temple Mount, and for the Muslims of Greater Syria it was likewise considered the second-holiest site for *ziyara*.[35] Indeed, Sanjar al-Jawali, a powerful *amir* under the Mamluk sultan al-Nasir Muhammad (r. 1293–4, 1299–1309, and 1309–41), was given the title *Amir al-Haramayn* (Amir of the two Sacred Enclosures) to indicate that he oversaw the administration of both the Dome of the Rock in Jerusalem and the mosque in Hebron.[36] The Haram al-Ibrahimi Mosque is one of the oldest continuously venerated sites in the central Islamic lands, and has intact Roman-era (Herodian) foundations and a medieval superstructure. In the Islamic era, it was first remodeled in the late eleventh century by the Fatimid general Badr al-Jamali. It was then transformed into a Romanesque basilica in Crusader times, and subsequently completely renovated by Saladin in 1187, who changed the basilica into a mosque after his reconquest of Hebron. Later, no less than three phases of restoration occurred in the Mamluk period, under the Amir Tankiz al-Nasiri, Mamluk governor in Bilad al-Sham from 1312–40; and later

3 Haram al-Ibrahimi Mosque (Cave of the Patriarchs), Hebron, Palestine, C. 20 BCE–1455 CE
Photo: Museum With No Frontiers [MWNF] / Discover Islamic Art

4 Pulpit of Haram al-Ibrahimi Mosque (Cave of the Patriarchs), Hebron, West Bank, 1091–92.
Photo: Creswell Archive, Ashmolean Museum, ©Victoria and Albert Museum, London

under the Amir 'Alam al-Din Sanjar al-Jawali (early fourteenth century) and Sultan al-Zahir Barquq (1382–9 and 1390–9). Today, the shrine – built over a grotto containing the graves of the patriarchs Abraham, Isaac, Jacob, and their wives – consists of a large, rectangular outer enclosure (approximately 60 m by 34 m), a courtyard, and a mosque with two Mamluk-era minarets. The spectacular *minbar* (pulpit) dated to 1091–2, is one of the masterworks of Islamic wooden marquetry and possibly the earliest wooden *minbar* still in use (Fig. 4). It is an important early example of geometric strapwork integrated with vegetal arabesque designs.[37] The pulpit was originally commissioned by Badr al-Jamali for the shrine of the head of Husayn – the revered grandson of the Prophet Muhammad and one of the earliest martyrs in Islam – in Ascalon and was subsequently moved to Hebron by Saladin. The *mihrab* (niche indicating the direction of prayer) and the walls of the prayer area are decorated with elegant interlaced polychrome decoration added by Tankiz al-Nasiri in 1332.

Other shared Biblical sites were also revered. In the village of Ramah (Nabi Simwayl) outside Jerusalem, a shrine for the Prophet Samuel was an important Jewish pilgrimage site and appears to have had a mosque or prayer room to accommodate the site's many Muslim visitors,[38] while in Petra an ostensibly Jewish shrine for Aaron was maintained by Muslims.[39] Shrines for some prophets, like Elijah/al-Khidr, were actively patronized by all groups.[40] Many of these sites were "rediscovered" during the Zangid and Ayyubid periods, probably in response to a heightened awareness of the holiness of the land of Palestine and Syria in the aftermath of the Crusades.[41] Although most Biblical and Christian holy sites were located in Palestine and Syria, other locales in the central Islamic lands were also dedicated to such figures. In Egypt there were shrines for Joseph, Jacob, and Moses, among others, marking key events in the Biblical narratives associated with them,[42] and Iraq had numerous sites linked to prophets. Near the village of Thamanin on the upper Tigris, for example, is the site where Noah's ark alighted.[43] In the citadel of Mosul was a shrine for Abraham and the tomb of St. George, over which a Chaldean church, now ruined, was built.[44] Al-Harawi mentions a shrine for Ezekiel, known in Arabic as Dhu al-Kifl, south of al-Hilla, and a shrine for Daniel exists inside the 4,600-year-old citadel in Kirkuk.[45]

It was also not uncommon for shrines to commingle Jewish and Christian saints and relics, as at the Station of Abraham in the Aleppo citadel, where according to the medieval pilgrimage guide author 'Ali al-Harawi, there was a piece of John the Baptist's head (the remainder of which was enshrined in a special enclosure inside the Umayyad Mosque in Damascus, where it remains until today).[46] Other ostensibly Christian sites were, and continue to be, venerated by Muslims, including Jesus's birthplace in Bethlehem, the tomb of Mary in Jerusalem, and the minaret of Jesus at the Great Mosque of Damascus, which has a key place in Muslim eschatology as the location at which Jesus will descend to herald the arrival of the last days.[47] Major sites of pilgrimage like the church of Saint Sergius at Sergiopolis/Rusafa in Syria had long histories of shared Christian-Muslim interaction, indeed the cathedral and mosque directly abut each other, sharing a wall and facilitating direct passage between the two buildings.[48] The pilgrimage church at Saydnaya, commemorating

Mary, continues to be among the most important shared sites of pilgrimage in Syria and is visited each Friday by numerous Muslim pilgrims who make entreaties before its icon,[49] while the long-abandoned medieval Christian site of Mar Musa al-Habashi (Saint Moses the Ethiopian), 80 km north of Damascus, has been reinvented in the past few decades by local Syrians as a site of active interfaith exchange.[50] There is every reason to believe that in the past, as they frequently do today, Jews, Christians, and Muslims shared such sites.

VENERATION OF THE FAMILY OF THE PROPHET

The earliest shrines of a distinctly Islamic character appeared at the burial places of the Prophet's family, and the sources indicate reverence for their tombs from the nascent years of the Islamic community.[51] The shrines no doubt flourished as part of a culture of mourning that developed in the aftermath of the martyrdom of numerous holy figures central to Shi'i communal identity, but they were also frequently visited by Sunnis. While the Prophet's daughter Fatima and the second Shi'i Imam, al-Hasan, were buried in the cemetery of al-Baqi in Medina, most of the other descendants of the Prophet were buried in the central Islamic lands or in Iran. Tombs and *mashhad*s (places of memorial) for the family of the Prophet and for the 'Alids (the Prophet's descendents through the lineage of his cousin and son-in-law, 'Ali ibn Abi Talib) were present in this region already in the second half of the ninth century.

The largest concentrations of individual shrines are found in Cairo, in the great Qarafa al-Kubra cemetery to the south of the city,[52] and in Damascus, where members of the Prophet's family and martyrs from the battle of Karbala are buried in the Bab al-Saghir cemetery.[53] Most of these are quite modest in plan, however, in Iraq, where the Shi'i population was larger, they became great shrine cities, centered around *ziyara* as a central economic engine, supporting illustrious scholarly communities, large libraries, and immense shrine complexes. In addition to the shrine for the Prophet's grandson al-Husayn's body at Karbala, the Iraqi sites include Najaf, burial place of the Prophet's cousin and son-in-law (and first Imam of the Shi'a), 'Ali ibn Abi Talib (Fig. 5); Kazimayn, where the Seventh and Ninth Imams Musa al-Kazim and Muhammad al-Taqi are resting; and sites such as Samarra, where shrines for the Tenth and Eleventh Imams 'Ali al-Hadi and Hasan al-'Askari are located, and where there is also a shrine to the Twelfth Imam al-Mahdi, who went into occultation on the spot. Today, many of

5 Shrine of Imam 'Ali, Najaf, Iraq, founded in the late eighth century and continuously renovated (most recently in 2008).
Photo: Hussain Aldurazi

these shrines are vast complexes situated around a large open courtyard preceding a domed shrine area, with numerous rooms and buildings attached that are used for teaching and religious assembly. A number of the shrines, for example at Kazimayn, date to the Buyid period (934–1055) or earlier, and at other locations the present shrines date to periods of reconstruction under the Safavid Shahs in the sixteenth and seventeenth centuries.[54] But some evidence indicates earlier histories for many sites. 'Ali ibn Abi Talib's shrine at Najaf, for example, is believed to have been founded by the 'Abbasid caliph Harun al-Rashid (786–809),[55] and the Hamdanid ruler of Syria and Northern Iraq 'Abdallah ibn Hamdan (905–929) is said by the tenth century geographer Ibn Hawqal to have built a stately dome over the site.[56] Al-Muqaddasi (d. 1000) also records shrines at the graves of 'Ali and al-Husayn in Iraq.[57]

Among the first, and certainly the most beloved, of the Shi'ite martyrs was al-Husayn ibn 'Ali ibn Abi Talib, the grandson of the Prophet Muhammad and the third Imam of the Shi'a. He was killed on the battlefield of Karbala in Iraq on the orders of the Sunni Umayyad caliph Yazid on the tenth of Muharram, year 61 of the Islamic calendar (CE 680). Following his death, his body was buried at Karbala, while his head was carried as a trophy back to the Umayyad caliph in Damascus. Its journey from Iraq to Syria was soon traced by the appearance of a trail of shrines to mark each place along the route where the head rested, paused, or a drop of blood fell on a stone in its passing.[58] These *mashhad*s (shrines) for al-Husayn were some of the earliest outside of the Hijaz (the region of the holy cities of Mecca and Medina in Arabia), and the constellation of shrines that stretched from Karbala to Damascus and eventually to Cairo are among the most important sacred routes within Islam. Al-Harawi mentions at least seven shrines for him, at Mosul, Balis and Nisibin in northern Syria, Damascus, Ascalon, Cairo, and al-Mahalla in lower Egypt.[59] Nor were the sites static, for shrines to al-Husayn continued to be discovered and "rediscovered" throughout Islamic history: in fact, the rediscovery of shrines is one of the main mechanisms by which devotional culture was perpetuated and sustained in the medieval period.[60]

The anniversary of al-Husayn's death, called the 'Ashura ("Tenth" after the tenth day of the month of Muharram on which he was killed), marks the climactic date of the Shi'i liturgical calendar, and its commemoration is the central moment of the reaffirmation of the memory of this archetypal tragedy for the Shi'a. Today, among the Twelver (*ithna 'ashariyya*) Shi'a, ceremonies include processions of devotees who chant and beat their chests in symbolic empathy with the suffering of al-Husayn, and in some regions of the Shi'i world a select group will intensify this experience of identification with the suffering of the holy figure by practicing rituals of mortification of the flesh, such as whipping the back with chains or cutting the forehead. These intensificatory practices, along with the more widely embraced procession itself, are always carried out in proximity to the shrine of the person in question or with the shrine as the end goal of the processional activity (Fig. 6).[61] However,

6 Twelver Shi'i devotees in procession to the shrine of al-Husayn in the Umayyad Mosque, Damascus, Syria, during the observance of the 'Ashura, 2005.
Photo: Stephennie Mulder

7 Shrine for al-Husayn, Aleppo, Syria, 1183–1260.
Photo: Stephennie Mulder

many Shi'is, particularly those from the Isma'ili communities and others, reject these practices.

In addition to the burial place for al-Husayn's body at Karbala, two of the shrines for his head came to particular prominence, one at Ascalon on the coast of Palestine (now destroyed), where the head itself was miraculously rediscovered by the Fatimid *vizir* Badr al-Jamali in 1091. Later, toward 1153–4, to protect the relic from the advancing Crusaders it was removed and placed in a shrine in the Eastern Palace in Cairo, where it rested in the tomb of the Fatimid caliphs, the Turbat al-Za'faran.[62] The Cairene site remains an important holy place and is visited by multitudes of pilgrims daily (Fig. 1). But other sites also played an important role. In Syria, there was a *mashhad* for al-Husayn in Damascus at the site where the head had been displayed as a trophy by the Umayyad caliph inside Bab al-Faradis, and until today, a shrine exists inside the Umayyad mosque. It is the focal point of visitation by pilgrims from around the Islamic world.

The most architecturally prominent of the Syrian shrines for the Prophet's family was the Mashhad al-Husayn in Aleppo, located to the west of the city on a hill known as the Jebel Jawshan (Fig. 7). It was rediscovered in 1177–8 by a local shepherd.[63] This building has been called the most important medieval Shi'i structure in Syria.[64] Indeed, it is among the more remarkable of the Ayyubid buildings and an aesthetic rival to the more famous *madrasa*s from the period. However its pedigree as a "Shi'i" building is open to scrutiny, for its main patron was the Sunni Ayyubid Sultan of Aleppo, the son of Saladin, al-Malik al-Zahir (r. 1193–1216).[65] He contributed to the building campaign in the form of a monumental entrance portal, but was only one of several Sunni patrons to embellish the site.

In plan, the building resembles many Ayyubid *madrasa*s (Fig. 8). Oriented around a central

SHRINES IN THE CENTRAL ISLAMIC LANDS 205

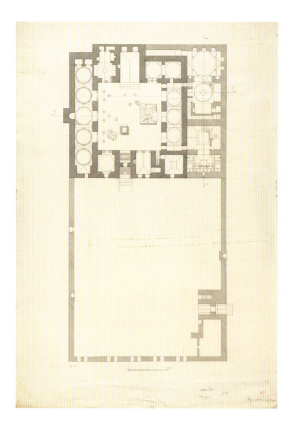

8 Plan, Shrine for al-Husayn, Aleppo, Syria, 1183–1260. Drawing: The Ernst Herzfeld Papers, Department of Islamic Art, The Metropolitan Museum of Art, eeh1514_001

9 Portal, Shrine for al-Husayn, Aleppo, Syria, 1196. Photo: Author

courtyard, its main features are a five-bay domed prayer hall in the south, a large *iwan* to the west, and numerous smaller rooms. Al-Zahir's large, elaborately decorated portal, located at the entrance to the shrine on its eastern face and today preceded by a large exterior courtyard, is among the finest examples of the virtuosic tradition of Ayyubid stereotomy (stone cutting and fitting) (Fig. 9). The portal contains inscriptions praising both the Twelve Imams of the Shi'a and the four Rightly Guided Caliphs of the Sunnis, apparently a deliberately conciliatory choice by the patron al-Zahir. By his patronage of the shrine, the lavishness and visibility of its decoration, and the skillful juxtaposition of seemingly opposing messages, the Ayyubid Sultan al-Zahir, ruling over the largely Shi'i population of Aleppo, seems to have used the shrine as a rallying point for a policy of pragmatic sectarian coexistence. It would not be the first time 'Alid shrines were used for such a purpose: shrines for the Prophet's family in Iraq were also heavily patronized by al-Zahir's contemporary the Abbasid Caliph al-Nasir li-Din Allah (r. 1180–1225), most famously the site of the occultation of the Twelfth Imam al-Mahdi at Samarra, for which he provided a lavish mosque and *mashhad* in the year 1209.[66]

Not all 'Alid shrines in the central Islamic lands received such obvious exhortations for sectarian coexistence, and indeed shrines were just as frequently the focal points of sectarian conflict, particularly in Iraq, where sectarian tensions reached a high point in the mid-eleventh century.[67] But it is important to note that 'Alid shrines were also particularly open to sectarian-neutral interpretive stances, and that they seem to have been used by patrons to engender awareness of a shared devotional culture. This is often overlooked in the academic literature, which tends to emphasize conflict over cooperation, and to still refer to such sites as "Shi'i" shrines, despite sparse evidence they were used exclusively, or even primarily, by Shi'is. On the whole, shrines are interpretively fluid sites and tend toward pluralism, a fact particularly relevant for 'Alid shrines, beloved as they are by both Sunnis and Shi'is. This is not to deny the undoubtedly more central role of the 'Alid shrines in Shi'i piety, but rather to emphasize the rather underappreciated function reverence for the 'Alids serves also among Sunnis.[68]

Perhaps the most obvious example of this fluidity is in Cairo, though in there, the sectarian dynamic was opposite to that in northern Syria. In Cairo, the Shi'i Fatimid Caliphate (969–1171) patronized the largest concentration of individual 'Alid shrines in the central Islamic lands.[69] The Fatimids were Isma'ili Shi'is, but their Egyptian subjects were largely Sunni. Over the course of the early twelfth century, they built and renovated numerous shrines. But the Fatimids did not invent the practice of reverence for the 'Alids in Cairo – rather they capitalized on a long-established tradition of Sunni reverence for members of the Prophet's family, many of whom are buried in the Qarafa al-Kubra' cemetery to the south of Cairo. There, Sunni reverence for the 'Alid saints dates to at least the early ninth century, with the foundation of a shrine for Sayyida Nafisa, a pious 'Alid descendant, in 824.[70] Later, between 1122 and 1154, the Fatimid caliphs officially sponsored this long-flourishing cult of 'Alid saints, hoping to capitalize on the popularity of the practice to bolster support for their political and religious claims to the caliphate.

VENERATION OF RULERS, SCHOLARS, AND SUFIS

Muslims also make *ziyara* to the graves of saintly figures like Sufis, scholars, theologians, and rulers, people who had important religious, military, and political roles in the centuries subsequent to the establishment of Islam. Particularly in the twelfth-

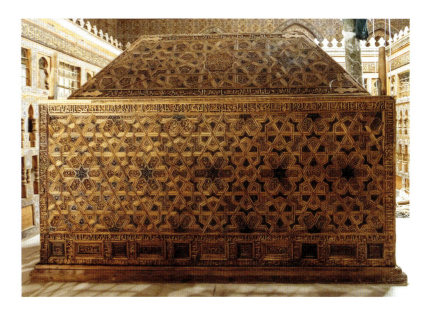

10 Cenotaph of Imam al-Shafi'i, Cairo, Egypt, 1178. Photo: Bernard O'Kane

fifteenth centuries, such shrines proliferated.[71] The company and mentorship of learned and charismatic men (and occasionally also women) was ardently sought during these figures' lifetimes, and their graves became objects of veneration after death. Rulers like Nur al-Din and his successor Saladin became saints because of their piety and heroic deeds, and supplicants began to visit their graves shortly after their burials. Two famous female saints were especially beloved, Rabi'a al-Shamiyya in Damascus, and Rabi'a al-'Adawiyya in Basra, and there were many more.[72]

The graves of the founders of the Sunni law schools like Abu Hanifa (d. 767), in Baghdad, and Imam al-Shafi'i (d. 820), in Cairo, came to be important sites of pilgrimage, with *madrasa*s built adjacent to their tombs and frequent intraconfessional struggles over their meanings and identities. In Cairo, one of Saladin's first actions after becoming Sultan was to support the construction of a lavish mausoleum and *madrasa* at al-Shafi'i's grave, completed in 1176–7.[73] The site had been visited since the jurist's death, and Saladin's *madrasa* quickly became a popular site for legal study and veneration of the beloved scholar. The centerpiece of his shrine was a magnificent carved wooden cenotaph, a tour de force of medieval woodcarving (Fig. 10). The foundation inscription

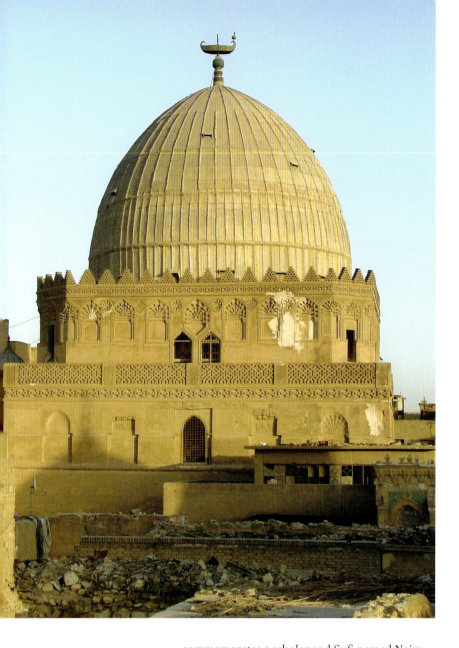

11 Tomb of Imam al-Shafi'i, Cairo, Egypt, 1211.
Photo: Author

commemorates a scholar and Sufi named Najm al-Din al-Khabushani as the instigator of the project, and contains a clear statement in support of the Ash'ari theology embraced by the Shafi'i school. In 1211, Saladin's successor al-Malik al-Kamil ordered the expansion of the site, constructing a vast complex including a *madrasa*, kitchens, and an enlarged mausoleum (Fig. 11). With its towering dome over twenty-nine meters high, the shrine was the largest freestanding mausoleum in Egypt and one of the largest in the Islamic world, competing in visual prominence with such illustrious buildings as the Dome of the Rock in Jerusalem. Medieval visitors described the throngs of pilgrims, students, and scholars that visited the site, and who gave the complex the air of a city unto itself.[74] The shrine complex played a significant role in the growth of the city of Cairo when its construction spurred the further development of the Qarafa al-Kubra cemetery below the Citadel.[75]

Sufi saints were known as *wali*s "Friends (of God)" or as shaykhs (leaders) of the Sufi brotherhoods, and their burial places also attracted many visitors, particularly after the expansion of institutionalized, *tariqa*-based Sufism in the twelfth–fifteenth centuries.[76] The spread of Sufism contributed to the development of new architectural types such as the *ribat* (lodge/hospice), *khanqah* (hostel) and *zawiya* (oratory) in cities like Cairo and Damascus. These were often built at the graves of beloved Sufi shaykhs, with a tomb chamber attached. In contrast to the somewhat more advanced state of knowledge on such shrines in Turkey and Iran, the subject of Sufi shrines in the central Islamic lands is yet in the early stages of investigation, and many important sites of *ziyara* have yet to be researched or published. But it is nonetheless apparent that such sites played a critical and growing role in the lives of pious Muslims from the medieval period onward.[77] Pilgrimage guides like those written by Ibn al-Zayyat and al-Sakhawi in the fourteenth and fifteenth centuries mention numerous *zawiya*s and *ribat*s that attracted pilgrims.[78] Indeed, by the early fourteenth century, a traveler like Ibn Battuta could journey for a quarter of a century and never pay for a night's lodging, relying instead on the network of *madrasa*s and shrine centers that grew up around the graves of Sufis and other holy figures.

In Egypt, such sites have a long history. Although initially Sufi shaykhs lodged humbly in the "corners" (*zawiya*s) of mosques, it was not long before purpose-built *khanqah*s and formally-planned *zawiya*s began to appear. In Cairo in the Mamluk period, the construction of *khanqah*s and *zawiya*s at the graves of Sufi saints proliferated, such that intense competition developed for land and resources. The desire of pious Muslims to be buried near saints in order to benefit from their *baraka* (blessing) led to abuses in some cases – as when a corrupt shrine overseer accepted payments for allowing the burial of impious people.[79] Many shrines evolved over time into complexes with

12 Dome, Shrine of Zayn al-Din Yusuf, Cairo, Egypt, 1298–1336.
Photo: Creswell Archive, Ashmolean Museum, © Victoria and Albert Museum, London

13 Shrine of Suhrawardi, Baghdad, Iraq, thirteenth-nineteenth centuries.
Photo: Creswell Archive, Ashmolean Museum

multiple functions. The shrine of Zayn al-Din Yusuf, a popular Sufi saint who died in 1297, is located in the Qarafa al-Kubra cemetery (Fig. 12). Although it initially consisted only of a small space adjacent to the tomb, in 1325 it was enlarged to a four-*iwan* plan, creating areas that could serve various needs, from Friday prayer to Sufi gatherings for recitation and dancing. Eventually the building was graced with a tall, gadrooned dome, an elegant *muqarnas* entrance portal, and living quarters for Sufi followers.[80] In addition to Cairo, many towns and villages continue to benefit from the presence of such tombs, as at the shrine of the important Shaykh Ahmad al-Badawi in the delta town of Tanta. Each year, on the saint's *mawlid* (birthday celebration), Tanta is filled with pious revelers who spend the week in an atmosphere of carnival. Similarly, the shrine for Shaykh Yusuf Abu'l Hajjaj at Luxor, located at the center of the ruined Pharaonic Temple of Karnak, is a beloved site of pilgrimage.[81]

In the Syrian region and in Iraq, too, such sites proliferated in the medieval period, and many continue to be visited today. In the twelfth-fifteenth centuries, the Sufi order of the Qadariyya spread into the Syrian region from Iraq, becoming prominent in Jerusalem and many other Palestinian cities.[82] Sufi saints played an important role in the Islamization of the landscape by virtue of their numerous *ribat*s and tombs, which became sites of pilgrimage and devotion.[83] In Syria, a similar expansion of Sufi orders and affiliations occurred in the same period.[84] Until today, Damascenes visit shrines built for medieval Sufis like Ibn 'Arabi and Shaykh Arslan,[85] and Sufism retains a prominent place in contemporary worship.

Shrines initially built in the medieval period were continuously added to and enlarged. In Iraq, birthplace of many of the Sufi orders, the founder of the Qadariyya order 'Abd al-Qadir al-Jilani (1077–1166) is venerated at his shrine in Baghdad, and is one of the most important sanctuaries in Iraq.

SHRINES IN THE CENTRAL ISLAMIC LANDS   209

Originally, the site was his *madrasa*, but after his death, it was transformed into a site for pilgrimage. It has undergone no less than five documented reconstructions since its founding in the twelfth century.[86] Another Sufi site, the Suhrawardi shrine, located in Baghdad's eastern quarter of al-Rusafa, is also an example of this pattern (Fig. 13). It was built at the grave of the Sufi shaykh and Shafi'i scholar 'Umar al-Suhrawardi (d. 1234). One of the great medieval mystics, 'Umar al-Suhrawardi was a nephew of the founder of the Suhrawardiyya order and a close confidante of the 'Abbasid caliph al-Nasir. Sometime after his death in the thirteenth century, a cubical tomb was built over his grave, with a towering conical stalactite dome. It was renewed a century later in 1334, then again in 1511, when a spacious mosque was added to the tomb. Finally, this mosque was replaced by the present one in the Ottoman period, with episodes of construction in 1833 and 1855.[87]

Such continuous processes of restoration and renovation speak to one of the primary characteristics of shrines in Islamic lands: their representation of a true, living form of architecture. For unlike many more conservative structures, such as mosques or *madrasa*s, shrines were, and are, subjected to a continual process of intervention and renewal. It is not unusual for such transformations to have entirely obscured the original building.[88] While these tangled architectural legacies often make shrines a difficult object of study, they also speak more powerfully than words of their histories as flexible sites of communal cohesion and identity, and of their place in the hearts of the people.

STEPHENNIE MULDER is Associate Professor of Islamic Art and Architecture at the University of Texas at Austin. She has conducted archaeological and art historical fieldwork in Syria, Egypt, Turkey, and elsewhere in the region, and is the author of an award-winning monograph, *The Shrines of the 'Alids in Medieval Syria: Sunnis, Shi'is and the Architecture of Coexistence*. She has published articles on Islamic art, architectural history, archaeology, heritage preservation, and the trade in looted antiquities.

SUGGESTIONS FOR FURTHER READING

McGregor, Richard J.A., *Islam and the Devotional Object* (Cambridge: Cambridge University Press, 2020).

Meri, Josef, *The Cult of Saints among Muslims and Jews in Medieval Syria* (Oxford, Oxford University Press: 2002).

Mulder, Stephennie, *The Shrines of the 'Alids in Medieval Syria: Sunnis, Shi'is, and the Architecture of Coexistence* (Edinburgh: Edinburgh University Press, 2014).

Talmon-Heller, Daniella, *Islamic Piety in Medieval Syria: Mosques, Cemeteries, and Sermons under the Zangids and Ayyubids (1146–1260)* (Leiden: Brill, 2007)

Williams, Caroline "The Cult of 'Alid Saints in the Fatimid Monuments of Cairo, Part II: The Mausolea," *Muqarnas* 3 (1985), 37–52.

NOTES

1. Recent research on Jewish and Christian saint veneration includes James Howard-Johnston and Paul A. Hayward, *The Cult of Saints in Late Antiquity and the Early Middle Ages* (Oxford: Oxford University Press, 1999), and Josef Meri, *The Cult of Saints among Muslims and Jews in Medieval Syria*, (Oxford: Oxford University Press: 2002).

2. Michael Mackinson et. al., *Resafa* I–VI, Deutsches Archäologisches Institut, 6 vols. (Mainz am Rhein: P. von Zabern, 1984–2002).

3. J.-L. Biscop and Jean-Pierre Sodini, "Travaux récents au sanctuaire syrien de saint Syméon le Stylite (Qal'at Sem'an)," *Comptes rendus des séances de l'Académie des inscriptions et des belles lettres* (April–June 1983), 335–372; A. Hadjar, *The Church of St. Simeon the Stylite and other Archaeological Sites in the Mountains of Halaqat* (Damascus: Sidawi, 1995), 24–46.

4. Earl Baldwin-Smith, *Early Churches in Syria* (Princeton: Princeton University Press, 1929); Dianne Van de Zande, "The Cult of Saint Sergius in its Socio-Political Context," *Eastern Christian Art* 1 (2004), 141–52.

5. On the shrine of Ezekiel, see Meri, *Cult*, 229–40; on Coptic sites in Egypt, see David Frankfurter, *Pilgrimage and Holy Space in Late Antique Egypt* (Leiden: Brill, 1998).

6. Zayde Antrim, *Routes and Realms: The Power of Place in the Early Islamic World* (New York: Oxford University Press, 2012). Stephennie Mulder, *The Shrines of the 'Alids in Medieval Syria: Sunnis, Shi'is and the Architecture of Coexistence* (Edinburgh: Edinburgh University Press, 2014).

7. For detailed descriptions of Muslim shrine types, see Oleg Grabar, "The Earliest Islamic Commemorative Structures, Notes and Documents," *Ars Orientalis* 6 (1966), 9–12; Robert Hillenbrand, *Islamic Architecture: Form, Function, and Meaning* (New York: Columbia University Press, 1994), 253–330; Christopher S. Taylor, *In the Vicinity of the Righteous: Ziyara and the Veneration of Muslim Saints in Late Medieval Egypt* (Leiden: Brill, 1999), 26–38; and Meri, *Cult*, 262–72.

8. Richard J.A. McGregor, *Islam and the Devotional Object* (Cambridge: Cambridge University Press, 2020).

9. Yaqut al-Hamawi, *Kitab Mu'jam al-Buldan* (Dictionary of Countries), ed. F. Wüstenfeld (Leipzig, 1866), 2: 589; 'Ali al-Harawi, *Kitab al-isharat ila ma'rifat al-ziyarat* (A Lonely Wayfarer's Guide to Pilgrimage), trans. Josef Meri (Oxford: Oxford University Press, 2004), 34–5. Other sources on relics include D.S. Margoliouth, "The Relics of the Prophet Mohammed," *The Moslem World* 27 (1937), 20–7; J.-M. Mouton, "De quelques reliques conservés à Damas au Moyen-Âge: Stratégie politique et religiosité populaire sous les Bourides," *Annales Islamologiques* 27 (1993), 245–54; Meri, *Cult*, 17 and 108–17; Daniella Talmon-Heller, *Islamic Piety in Medieval Syria: Mosques, Cemeteries, and Sermons under the Zangids and Ayyubids (1146–1260)* (Leiden: Brill, 2007), 55–7.

10. On *baraka*, see Taylor, *Vicinity*, 51–5, 127–67; Meri, *Cult*, 101–8.

11. On the differences between Muslim and Christian terminology and practices regarding saint veneration, see Meri, *Cult*, 5, 118–19.

12. However, some biographical dictionaries did approach a form that resembles Christian hagiography, for example Diya' al-Din al-Maqdisi al-Hanbali (d. 1245), *al-Hikayat al-uqtabbasa fi Karamat Mashayikh al-Ard al-Muqaddasa* (The Cited Tales of the Wondrous Doings of the Shaykhs of the Holy Land), pt. 3, MS. Al-Asad Library, Damascus, no. 1039 (formerly MS. al-Zahiriyya, Damascus, fols. 91–99), ed. and trans. Daniella Talmon-Heller, *Crusades* 1 (2002), 111–54. See also Talmon-Heller, *Islamic Piety*, 16.

13. Werner Diem and Marco Schöller, *The Living and the Dead in Islam: Epitaphs in Context*, 3 vols. (Wiesbaden: Otto Harrassowitz, 2004), 2: 67; Meri, *Cult*, 127.

14. Mulder, *Shrines*, p. 3; Diem and Schöller, *Living and the Dead*, 2: 171, for a comprehensive discussion of tomb building in Sunni legal theory and practice, see 2:169–293.

15. Oleg Grabar, "The Earliest Islamic Commemorative Structures, Notes and Documents," *Ars Orientalis* 6 (1966) 8 (7–46).

16. Ibid., 12. On the scholarly debate over the permissibility of shrine visitation, see Diem and Schöller, *Living and the Dead*, 2: 67–82. For prior discussions, see Yusuf Raghib, "Les premiers monuments funéraires de l'Islam," *Annales Islamologiques* 9 (1970), 21–36; Christopher Taylor, "Reevaluating the Shi'i Role in the Development of Monumental Islamic Funerary Architecture: The Case of Egypt," *Muqarnas* 9 (1992), 1–10; Thomas Leisten, *Architektur für Tote* (Berlin: D. Reimer, 1998); and then more recently Leor Halevi, *Muhammad's Grave. Death Rites and the Making of Islamic Society* (New York: 2007).

17. Niels H. Olesen, *Culte des saints et pèlerinages chez Ibn Taymiyya (661/1263–728/1328)* (Paris: Geuthner, 1991).

18. Leor Halevi, *Muhammad's Grave. Death Rites and the Making of Islamic Society* (New York: Columbia University Press, 2007); Taylor, *Vicinity*, 195–218; Meri, *Cult*, 126–40.

19. Talmon-Heller, *Islamic Piety*, 183.

20. Diem and Schöller, *Living and the Dead*, 251–23; Thomas Leisten, "Between Orthodoxy and Exegesis: Some Aspects of Attitudes in the Shari'a toward Funerary Architecture," *Muqarnas* 7 (1990), 14 (12–22).

21. For a critique of the notion that Shi'ism caused the growth of saint veneration, see Taylor, "Reevaluating the Shi'i Role."

22. Janine Sourdel-Thomine, "Les Anciens lieux de pèlerinage damascains d'après les sources arabes," *Bulletin d'Études Orientales* 14 (1952–4), 65–85.

23. Meri, *Cult*, 48 (table); and Talmon-Heller, *Islamic Piety*, 184–87, 199–202.

24. Al-Muqaddasi, *Ahsan al-taqasim fī ma'rifat al-aqalim* (The Best Divisions for the Knowledge of the Regions), ed. M. J. De Goeje (Leiden: Brill, 1906), 151, 184; English transl. by B. Collins, *The Best Divisions for the Knowledge of the Regions* (Reading: Center for Muslim Contribution to Civilisation, 2001), 128, 155.

25. McGregor, *Islam and the Devotional Object*, 145; J. Sadan, "Le Tombeau de Moïse à Jéricho et à Damas. Une Compétition entre deux lieux saints principalement à l'époque ottomane," *Revue des Études islamiques* 49 (1981), 59–100; John Renard, *Friends of God* (Berkeley: University of California Press, 2008), 199–200.

[26] E. Reiner, "From Joshua to Jesus: The Transformation of a Biblical Story to a Local Myth: A Chapter in the Religious Life of the Galilean Jew," in *Sharing the Sacred. Religious Contacts and Conflicts in the Holy Land*, eds. A. Kofsky and G. Stroumsa (Jerusalem: Yad Izhak Ben-Zvi Publications, 1998), 223–72.

[27] Nasser Rabbat, "The Meaning of the Umayyad Dome of the Rock," *Muqarnas* 6 (1989), 12–21.

[28] Saïd Nuseibeh and Oleg Grabar, *The Dome of the Rock* (New York: Rizzoli, 1996), 43–51; Julian Raby and Jeremy Johns, *Bayt al-Maqdis*, 2 vols. (Oxford: Oxford University Press, 1999).

[29] Renard, *Friends*, 197–98.

[30] Al-Harawi, *Kitab al-isharat*, 24, 36, and 160.

[31] Ibid., 66.

[32] Ibid., 178.

[33] Ibid., 12, Anne-Marie Eddé, *La Principauté Ayyoubide d'Alep (579/1183–658/1260)* (Stuttgart: Franz Steiner, 1999), 429–31.

[34] Michael Meinecke, *Die Mamlukische Architektur in Ägypten und Syrien (648/1250 bis 923/1517)*, 2 vols. (Glückstadt: J. J. Augustin, 1992), 1: 72, 2: 30.

[35] Meri, *Cult*, 195–199.

[36] Palestinian Authority, *Pilgrimage, Sciences and Sufism: Islamic Art in the West Bank and Gaza* (Vienna: Museum with No Frontiers, 2004), 204.

[37] L.H. Vincent and E. J. H. Mackay, *Hébron: Le Haram El-Khalil, Sépulture des Patriarches* (Paris: Éditions Leroux, 1923), 218–25; Max van Berchem, "La Chaire de la mosquée d'Hébron et la martyrion de la tête de Husain à Ascalon," in *Festschrift Eduard Sachau* (Berlin, 1915), 298–31; Yasser Tabbaa, *The Transformation of Islamic Art during the Sunni Revival* (Seattle: University of Washington Press, 2001), 80–81 (For the later date of many sections of the minbar, see Tabbaa's n. 29); Daniella Talmon-Heller, Benjamin Z. Kedar and Yitzhak Reiter "Vicissitudes of a Holy Place: Construction, Destruction and Commemoration of Mashhad Husayn in Ascalon," *Der Islam* 93 (2016), 182–215.

[38] Meri, *Cult*, 240–1.

[39] Ibid., 244.

[40] Meri, "Re-Appropriating Sacred Space: Medieval Muslims Seeking Elijah and al-Khadir," *Medieval Encounters: Jewish, Christian and Muslim Culture in Confluence and Dialogue* 5 (1999), 1–28.

[41] Talmon-Heller, *Islamic Piety*, 190; Mulder, *Shrines*, 247–66.

[42] Al-Harawi, 104.

[43] Ibid., 176–7.

[44] Ibid., 178, on the vestiges of the Chaldean Church, see Friedrich Sarre and Ernst Herzfeld, *Archäologische Reise im Euphrat- und Tigris Gebiet*, 4 vols (Berlin: D. Reimer, 1922–12), 2: 236–38.

[45] For Ezekiel, see al-Harawi, 198. Al-Harawi places the Daniel shrine in Mosul, not Kirkuk where it is located today, see 178.

[46] Al- Harawi, 32.

[47] Ibid., 76, 74, 32, respectively. Sourdel-Thomine, "Les Anciens Lieux," 73–74.

[48] Elizabeth Key Fowden, *The Barbarian Plain: Saint Sergius between Rome and Iran* (Berkeley: University of California Press, 1999), 174–193. Dorothée Sack, *Die Grosse Moschee von Resafa – Rusafat Hišam* (The Great Mosque at Rusafa – Rusafat Hisham) (Mainz: P. von Zabern, 1996).

[49] Immerzeel, "The Monastery of Saydnaya." See notes 2–4 (above) for other sources on Christian sites of pilgrimage in Syria.

[50] Erica Dodd, *The Frescoes of Mar Musa al-Habashi: a Study in Medieval Painting in Syria* (Toronto: Pontifical Institute of Mediaeval Studies, 2001), xvi. For more on contemporary shared sites, see Dionigi Albera and Maria Couroucli, eds., *Sharing Sacred Spaces in the Mediterranean Christians, Muslims, and Jews at Shrines and Sanctuaries* (Indiana: Indiana University Press, 2012).

[51] Grabar, "Earliest Islamic Commemorative Structures," 39.

[52] Caroline Williams, "The Cult of 'Alid Saints in the Fatimid Monuments of Cairo, Part II: The Mausolea," *Muqarnas* 3 (1985), 55; Galila El Kadi and Alain Bonnamy, *Architecture for the Dead: Cairo's Medieval Metropolis* (Cairo: The American University in Cairo Press, 2007), 21–127.

[53] Mulder, *Shrines*, 114–85.

[54] James Allan, *The Art and Architecture of Twelver Shi'ism: Iraq, Iran and the Indian Sub-continent* (London: Azimuth Editions, 2011); Moojen Momen, *An Introduction to Shi'i Islam* (New Haven: Yale University Press, 1985), 40.

[55] Su'ad Mahir, *Mashhad al-Imam 'Ali fi al-Najaf wama bihi min al-hadaya wa-al-tuhaf* (The Mashhad of Imam 'Ali at Najaf and its Pious Gifts and Art) (Cairo: Dar al-Ma'arif, 1969), 123.

[56] Muhammad Ibn Hawqal, *Kitab surat al-ard* (The Book of the Image of the Earth), (Beirut: Dar Maktabat al-Hayah, 1964), 240.

[57] Al-Muqaddasi, *Ahsan al-taqasim*, 130.

[58] Mulder, *Shrines*, 247–66.

[59] al-Harawi, 30, 80, 96, 112, 156, 164, 178. Meri, *Cult*, 191–5.

60 Meri, *Cult*, 190–8, Mulder, *Shrines*, Introduction; Talmon-Heller *et al.*, "Vicissitudes of a Holy Place."

61 Momen, 240.

62 Al-Harawi, 80, 83, Williams, 52, Mulder, *Shrines*, 247–66.

63 See, for example, [limit list to 3] Jean Sauvaget, "Deux sanctuaires chiites d'Alep," *Syria* 9 (1928), 224–37; Ernst Herzfeld, *Matériaux pour un Corpus Inscriptionum Arabicarum, pt. 2, Syrie du Nord. Inscriptions et monuments d'Alep* (Materials for a Corpus of Arabic Inscriptions, pt. 2, Northern Syria. Inscriptions and Monuments of Aleppo) (Cairo: Institut français d'archéologie orientale, 1954–56), 236–48, pl. 237; Tabbaa, *Constructions*, 110–121; and Mulder, *Shrines*, 63–113.

64 Tabbaa, *Constructions of Power and Piety in Medieval Aleppo*, (University Park, Pennsylvania: Pennsylvania State University Press, 1997), 110.

65 Mulder, *Shrines*, pp. 82–99.

66 Ibid.

67 Allan, *Art and Architecture.*

68 Mulder, *Shrines.*

69 Williams, "Cult, Part II," 55.

70 Ibid., 39–40.

71 For the Zengid-Ayyubid period (1146–1260), see Talmon-Heller, *Islamic Piety*, 184–98; for the Mamluk period (1250–1517) see Y. Frenkel, "Baybars and the Sacred Geography of *Bilad al-Sham*: A Chapter in the Islamisation of Syria's Landscape," *Jerusalem Studies in Arabic and Islam* 25 (2001), 153–170.

72 Margaret Smith, *Rabi'a The Mystic and Her Fellow-Saints in Islam* (Cambridge: Cambridge University Press, 1928 [reprinted 2010]); John Renard, *Friends of God: Islamic Images of Piety, Commitment, and Servanthood* (Berkeley: University of California Press, 2008), 155–163. On their tombs, see Meri, *Cult*, 81 and Sourdel-Thomine, "Les Anciens Lieux," 83.

73 Mulder, "The Mausoleum of Imam al-Shafi'i," *Muqarnas* 23 (2006), 15–46.

74 Ibn al-Jubayr, *Rihlat ibn Jubayr* (The Travels of Ibn Jubayr) (Beirut: Dar wa-Maktabat al-Hilal, 1981), 21. Broadhurst, *The Travels of Ibn Jubayr* (London, J. Cape: 1952), 40.

75 al-Maqrizi, *Mawa'iz wa-l-i'tibar fi dhikr al-khitat wa-al-athar* (Advice and Counsel in Describing the Quarters and Antiquities), (Bulaq, Dar al-Tiba'a al-Misriyya, 1853), 2: 444.

76 J. Spencer Trimingham, *The Sufi Orders in Islam* (Oxford: Oxford University Press, 1971); Marshall G. S. Hodgson, *The Venture of Islam: Conscience and History in a World Civilization* (Chicago: University of Chicago Press, 1974), 2: 201–54; Erik S. Ohlander, *Sufism in an Age of Transition: 'Umar al-Suhrawardi and the Rise of the Islamic Mystical Brotherhoods* (Leiden: E. J. Brill, 2008).

77 Korn, *Ayyubidische Architektur*, 60–67.

78 Meri, *Cult*, 261, n. 54.

79 Taylor, *Vicinity*, 51.

80 Sheila S. Blair, "Sufi Saints and Shrine Architecture in the Early Fourteenth Century," *Muqarnas* 7 (1990), 35–49.

81 Renard, *Friends of God*, 203–4.

82 Daphna Ephrat, *Spiritual Wayfarers, Leaders in Piety* (Cambridge: Harvard Center for Middle Eastern Studies, 2008).

83 Nimrod Luz, "Aspects of Islamization of Space and Society in Mamluk Jerusalem and its Hinterland," *Mamluk Studies Review* 6 (2002), 133–153.

84 For Damascus, see Louis Pouzet, *Damas au VIIe/ XIIIe siècle: Vie et structures religieuses d'une métropole islamique* (Beirut: Dar el-Machreq, 1991), 208–13; for Aleppo, see Eddé, *Principaute*, 416–435.

85 Meri, *Cult*, 174–177, 209–210.

86 Vincenzo Strika and Jabir Khalil, *The Islamic Architecture of Baghdad* (Naples: Istituto Universitario Orientale, 1987), 39–42.

87 Ibid., 51.

88 Mulder, *Shrines*, 186–243.

Shrines and Mausolea in Iran and Central Asia   MELANIE MICHAILIDIS

1 Samanid mausoleum, Bukhara, Uzbekistan, c. 914–43.

Photo: Melanie Michailidis, courtesy of the Aga Khan Documentation Center at MIT

Despite ostensible disapproval in Islamic law, funerary architecture has been one of the most enduring and impressive manifestations of visual culture in lands governed by Islamic rulers. This genre has been particularly popular in the eastern Islamic world, where extensive shrines and hubristic memorials to rulers have been constructed from at least the tenth century to the present day. Some of the earliest extant Islamic mausolea are to be found in Iran and Central Asia, indicating that this architectural form first became a focus of patronage in the region in the ninth century, soon after the initial stages of Islamization. The tenth-century Samanid mausoleum and the eleventh-century Gunbad-i Qabus, two undisputed masterpieces of Islamic architecture, are also among the early constructions. They are superb examples of the two forms which emerged during this early stage of development: the domed square, widespread through Central Asia and also found in Iran, and the tomb tower, a form specifically associated with the mountainous region south of the Caspian Sea in northern Iran. These two structures served as memorials to secular rulers, but mausolea were also constructed to house the remains of religiously significant individuals from the early Islamic period onwards.

EARLY FUNERARY ARCHITECTURE

The Quran does not specifically address the construction of funerary architecture, but there are Hadiths, which are the canonical records of the sayings and actions of the Prophet and constitute the second most authoritative text in Islam, that prohibit many pre-Islamic funerary customs including wailing and lamentation and the erection of tents or other structures over graves.

Many scholars have taken this to mean a blanket prohibition on funerary architecture in Islam and have viewed the construction of mausolea as a breaking of the rules. Scholars of architectural history, therefore, have generally followed K.A.C. Creswell, who posited that the originally strict prohibition on any sort of burial apart from being wrapped in a simple shroud was eventually abandoned after the initial transgression, the construction of open canopy mausolea beginning in the mid-ninth century.[1] Surveys of Islamic art and architecture have explained Islamic funerary architecture in these terms, and have used selections of the extant buildings to trace a linear trajectory: the earliest extant mausoleum, the ninth-century Qubbat al-Sulaibiyya at Samarra, is taken to be the first Islamic mausoleum, with the form then proliferating in the tenth and eleventh centuries, the date of the next extant examples, in areas of the Islamic world deemed peripheral by Western scholars. According to this scenario, the mausoleum only gradually came to be accepted over most of the Islamic world.

Many scholars have also viewed the emergence of funerary architecture, after a supposed lacuna during the earliest two centuries of Islam, as a widespread yet unorthodox phenomenon. Diez, for example, stressed that the Shi'ites were the first to transgress, since many early examples are from Iran and Central Asia as well as from Fatimid Egypt (despite the fact that Iran and Central Asia were mostly Sunni at this time).[2] Oleg Grabar also noted the existence of early mausolea in Central Asia and in upper Egypt, and he posited that the location along the frontiers of the Islamic world was responsible for this transgression; he attributed this to a *jihad* mentality amongst *ghazi* warriors fighting for the faith, and suggested that their martyrdom allotted them a special place deserving of an otherwise forbidden mausoleum.[3]

Yusuf Raghib challenged this approach of looking only at extant buildings, and he reviewed the literary sources and concluded that mausolea were built from the very earliest Islamic period, particularly for the Prophet (whose house burial was later enclosed in the mosque of Walid I), Companions of the Prophet, descendants of the Prophet ('Alids in particular), Quranic/Biblical figures, martyrs, and caliphs, so that these religiously significant people were considered exceptional enough to warrant a mausoleum.[4] These buildings stretch from Cairo to Khorasan and constitute prototypes from the Islamic heartland for a type of building that was new to Central Asia. Yet some of the earliest extant mausolea are found in Central Asia: several of these structures can plausibly be dated to the ninth century, and hence could conceivably pre-date the Qubbat al-Sulaibiyya. Even if they were constructed at about the same time or slightly later, some are located in such remote areas that their presence can only be explained by a tradition of monumental funerary construction in the Islamic world that had already existed for some considerable time. The early remains of Central Asian mausolea therefore correlate with Raghib's argument based upon textual sources.

Although none of these early mausolea have extant inscriptions, two have been dated to the ninth century on stylistic grounds: Kiz Bibi, in the Merv oasis, and Khaja Mashhad, in southwestern Tajikistan. Three others have been dated to the ninth or tenth centuries, also on stylistic grounds: Shir Kabir, at Dehistan in western Turkmenistan; Tilla Halaji, in southwestern Tajikistan on the Afghan border; and Khaja Bulkhak, near Isfara, in the Ferghana Valley in northern Tajikistan. Kiz Bibi could potentially even be dated earlier: as Sergei Khmel'nitskii points out, its architecture, and particularly its squinches and the proportions of the dome, were already archaic in the ninth century, and the closest analogy to the building is the nearby Lesser Qiz Qala, dated to the sixth or seventh century by Galina Pugachenkova.[5] The

Tajik mausolea also have archaic features more commonly found in the pre-Islamic architecture of their regions, while the Samarra-style stucco decoration of the Shir Kabir has parallels dating to the ninth to tenth centuries in Iran.

The corpus of mausolea dating from the ninth century, or even slightly earlier, was undoubtedly substantial, given that there are many remains of unbaked brick mausolea in Central Asia.[6] Though difficult or sometimes impossible to date accurately in their current state, brick sizes and, in some regions, archaic local building techniques date many to the Samanid period (874–1000) and earlier. The function can be ascertained by the size of the buildings, their plans, their presence in cemeteries, and in some cases by their status as places of pilgrimage. Given that unbaked brick is not a very durable material, extant buildings and fragments of buildings are undoubtedly a small fraction of what once existed. Hence it seems likely that the mausoleum as a building type became popular throughout Central Asia shortly after the Muslim conquest of the region, and much earlier than the generally accepted narrative would allow. In Iran as well, Huff has pointed out the possibility that many of the *chahar taq*s (domed structures with four arched openings) in the southern provinces may well be Islamic mausolea rather than Zoroastrian fire temples.[7]

In pre-Islamic Iran and Central Asia, the majority religion was Zoroastrianism, which dictates that corpses should be exposed rather than buried. Nevertheless, funerary architecture per se was not entirely new to Central Asia: a diminutive structure called the *naus*, usually not more than five or six feet tall, was sometimes built to hold ossuaries. But the scale of the Islamic mausoleum was something entirely new, as was the level of individual glorification that it often entailed (seen, for example, in royal mausolea such as the Gunbad-i Qabus, which lauds its intended occupant through its dramatic form as well as its inscriptions). The *naus* not only held multiple ossuaries, but the names of the incumbents were not recorded on the ossuaries themselves or on the building, even though local inhabitants must have been aware that particular buildings housed particular families. In contrast, Soviet excavations of mausolea have shown that, while some did contain multiple burials, many housed single individuals. This was a significant break from the pre-Islamic funerary tradition, as of course was the act of burial itself.

Contrary to Grabar's assertions, *ghazi* activity seems an unlikely explanation for this new phenomenon of building mausolea. Looking at the five earliest extant mausolea in Central Asia, only two, Shir Kabir and Khaja Bulkhak, were on the edges of the Islamic world, in areas where Grabar argues that such activity would have taken place. Shir Kabir is located in Dehistan, which the geographical text the *Hodud al-'Alam* states was a frontier post subject to constant attacks by the Ghuzz, and the location of a *ribat* with a *minbar* and the tomb of 'Ali b. Sukhari.[8] It is possible that this 'Ali b. Sukhari was the incumbent of the Shir Kabir, which later became part of a larger complex with facilities for pilgrims. Khaja Bulkhak is located in the Ferghana Valley, which had long been a border region between the Sogdians and the Turks and was still at this time on the outer boundary of the Islamic world, with Qarluq tribes surrounding the valley on three sides. The *Hodud al-'Alam* describes the region as a major emporium for Turkish slaves,[9] but does not allude to the incessant fighting which characterized regions bordering the Ghuzz. Kiz Bibi was located in the Merv oasis, an area that was not anywhere remotely near the frontier by the mid-eighth century. Tilla Halaji and Khaja Mashhad are both located in a mountainous region in southwestern Tajikistan near the Afghan border. This remote area was ruled even throughout the Samanid period by local dynasties who had converted to Islam but who were periodically accused of apostasy. Muslims were still a minority amongst the population, which would have been composed of Zoroastrians and Buddhists (the eighth century Buddhist monastery at Azhina-Tepe is in this region). This area was firmly within the sphere of Iranian-speaking peoples, as it has remained down to the present. One forbidding mountain range is located next to the other; this is decidedly not the type of landscape where Turkish nomads

could graze their flocks, and it was never a region of *ribat*s and *jihad*. The remnants of ruined unbaked brick mausolea are also spread widely in a variety of locations, and many are not in areas where fighting with Turkish tribes occurred. The early mausolea listed by Raghib are also not on the frontiers, but in central locations such as Medina, Cairo, Najaf, Karbala, and Samarra, where religiously significant individuals were interred.

The presence of early mausolea in both central, important locations and remote areas which were not fully Islamicized and had not previously known burial or the memorialization of the individual dead indicates that there is something inherently Islamic about the mausoleum, despite the often-noted disapproval of it in the Hadith. As Thomas Leisten has pointed out, objections to funerary architecture in the Hadith and commentaries were by no means absolute. The Hadith prohibiting funerary architecture are not found in the compilation of al-Bukhari, or in the early Shi'ite collections. Abu Hanifa did not condemn the construction of mausolea, and the three other main schools only considered this as *makruh* (discouraged), not as *haram* (forbidden). A debate took place in the commentaries, with some theologians arguing that mausolea were allowed because the Prophet himself was buried inside a built structure. Even those who disagreed with the building of mausolea in principle did not challenge the right of others to do so on their own private land.[10] So the legal position of mausolea in the early centuries can best be described as ambivalent and contested, rather than universally condemned.

It is unfortunate that we do not know more about the form of the earliest mausolea, but it is safe to assume that they were domed. Domed structures had long been associated with the mausoleum, and plenty of examples of classical and Byzantine martyria were still extant in the Umayyad heartland. The Qubbat al-Sulaibiyya took the form of a domed octagon, echoing the Dome of the Rock, which was itself based upon classical prototypes. All of the earliest Central Asian mausolea were domed squares; no octagons are known from this region. But beyond having a square shape topped by a dome supported by squinches, there is a great deal of diversity in these buildings.

One of the early mausolea, Tilla Halaji, took the form of a *chahar taq*, the domed square with an arched opening on each side, which had been used in Zoroastrian fire temples in pre-Islamic Iran. The Kiz Bibi mausoleum had only one entrance, but a deep niche on each side, forming a plan similar to that of a *chahar taq* with three of its sides closed. This plan had previously been seen in Central Asia in the *naus* group at Bit-tepe; it would also continue to be used for mausolea in the tenth and eleventh centuries. The Shir Kabir has a single, off-center entrance and three shallow niches on each side, one of which is a *mihrab*. Khaja Bulkhak has two entrances, centered on the eastern and western sides of the building. Khaja Mashhad has the same plan, but the eastern entrance opens into an *iwan* (Persian *ayvan*), which connects the mausoleum to another domed square; the only other extant example of such an arrangement is the eleventh-century core of the Sultan Saodat complex, at nearby Termez. Khaja Mashhad was the only one of this early group to be constructed of baked brick; the others are all made of the unbaked brick, which was the usual building material at that time. The baked brick of Khaja Mashhad was used decoratively in ways simpler than, but definitely foreshadowing, the later Samanid mausoleum. Shir Kabir is also notable for its decoration, in this case the elaborate stucco *mihrab*; no stucco decoration remains on any of the others.

Kiz Bibi, Tilla Halaji, and Khaja Bulkhak all contained single burials; it is not known whether this was the case at Shir Kabir and Khaja Mashhad, as they have not been excavated. Both Shir Kabir and Khaja Mashhad functioned as part of larger complexes appended to them several centuries later. At Khaja Mashhad these appendages were constructed of unbaked brick in the eleventh to twelfth centuries and probably served as a *madrasa*. Across from the mausoleum and its *ziyaratkhana* (structure for pilgrims), two other domed rooms connected by an *iwan* were built; small rooms around the courtyard and two additional *iwan*s on the eastern and western sides gave the complex a typical four-*iwan* plan. At Shir Kabir, the complex has been destroyed and its form cannot be ascertained, but a later baked brick revetment on the northern side of the building appears to be of the twelfth century.

Both Khaja Mashhad and Shir Kabir, given their status as pilgrimage sites, their more elaborate decoration and, in the case of Khaja Mashhad, its construction of baked brick, must have contained the graves of holy figures. It is impossible to say who the incumbents of Kiz Bibi, Tilla Halaji, Khaja Bulkhak, and the many ruined unbaked brick mausolea would have been, particularly in the absence of foundation inscriptions. In their building materials and techniques, as well as in the plan with four deep niches, they drew on local traditions. Other plans, as well as the idea of the mausoleum itself, were imported as funerary practices gradually changed and conversions grew. These early mausolea show that these changes had occurred, and that precedents had been set, by the time the Samanid mausoleum was constructed.

MAUSOLEA OF THE SAMANID PERIOD

It is exceedingly difficult, if not impossible, to delineate a definitive corpus of funerary architecture from the Samanid era (874–1000). There is no abrupt change in building techniques and materials or in architectural and decorative styles from the pre-Samanid to the Samanid era and from the Samanid to the Qarakhanid eras; instead, the architecture of Central Asia evolved gradually, and the changes that occurred did not coincide with any change of dynasty. Only the Samanid mausoleum itself, located in the Samanid capital, Bukhara, and the mausoleum of Arab Ata at Tim, which is dated to 977, can be attributed to the Samanid period with absolute certainty. Other mausolea which probably date to the tenth century include Hakim al-Termezi, in Termez; Khalifa Rajab, at Mizdakhan, a necropolis near Nukus; Iskhak Ata, in the complex of Khusam Ata near Qarshi; Ataulla Said Vakkos, Aq Astana Baba, and Khoja Roshan, all in Surkhandariya Province; Aisha Bibi and Babaji

2 Mausoleum of Arab Ata, Tim, Uzbekistan, 977.
Photo: Melanie Michailidis, courtesy of the Aga Khan Documentation Center at MIT

Khatun, near Taraz; and Baba Hatem and Baba Roshan, near Balkh.

Although these mausolea are all domed squares, their plans are varied. The Samanid mausoleum has a *chahar taq* plan, with slightly battered walls, engaged columns on the four exterior corners, and an arcaded gallery that encircles the building and allows additional light to penetrate the interior (Fig. 1). Iskhak Ata also has a *chahar taq* plan, although one side is emphasized with a hint of a *pishtaq*, or raised entrance. The *pishtaq* is pronounced in the neighboring mausoleum attributed by locals to the daughter of Iskhak Ata, and at Arab Ata, which has the earliest dated example of this feature, which was to later become so prevalent in the eastern Islamic world (Fig. 2). Both of these mausolea have a single entrance, as do the mausolea of Khalifa Rajab, Ataulla Said Vakkos, and Khoja Roshan. However, before it was reconstructed in the early twenty-first century, the entrance at Khoja Roshan was unique, with a long passageway and ramp leading down into the tomb chamber. This arrangement is reminiscent of the tombs of Central Asian nomads, indicating a possible Turkish connection for the incumbent, the patron or the builder.[11] The plan of Hakim al-Termezi is also highly unusual, with a second opening towards the mosque but a drastic difference of approximately five feet in floor level (Fig. 3). Aq Astana Baba, with deep niches on all four sides, is analogous to Kiz Bibi, and can be seen as a variation on the *chahar taq* plan.

Most of the extant tenth-century mausolea in Central Asia are composed of baked brick, a sure indication of importance and extra expense at this period, when most buildings were made of unbaked brick, and even major mosques, such as the Friday mosque of Bukhara, were made of a mixture of the two. The Samanid mausoleum in particular is celebrated for its brickwork, which lends a

3 Mausoleum of Hakim al-Termezi, Termez, Uzbekistan, tenth century.
Photo: Melanie Michailidis, courtesy of the Aga Khan Documentation Center at MIT

4 Gunbad-i Qabus, Gurgan, Iran, 1006–7.
Photo: Melanie Michailidis, courtesy of the Aga Khan Documentation Center at MIT

magnificent woven effect to the exterior. Hakim al-Termezi, Iskhak Ata, and the adjoining mausoleum attributed to the daughter of Iskhak Ata, Arab Ata and Aq Astana Baba are also all constructed of baked brick. Khoja Roshan was made of unbaked brick with a dome of baked brick, a combination typical of the period. Khalifa Rajab was constructed of unbaked brick interspersed with reeds, a technique unique to Khorezm; this was covered by a baked brick revetment. Before its reconstruction in the early twenty-first century, Ataulla Said Vakkos was made wholly of unbaked brick, as were many other mausolea that have not survived intact.

At the Samanid mausoleum, brick is not only the medium of construction, but also the medium of decoration; the very surface texture is a tour-de-force virtually unrivalled in later brick architecture. Motifs which would normally be composed of cheaper materials such as wood or stucco are replaced by expensive baked brick, conveying an image of conspicuous consumption befitting a dynastic monument. The sophistication of the Samanid mausoleum, in the division of the squinches in the zone of transition, the brickwork, and many details of the decoration, is unparalleled in any contemporary mausolea. The decoration of Arab Ata, Iskhak Ata, and Aq Astana Baba is much simpler and less ambitious but nevertheless effective, involving decorative brickwork with a few areas of carved stucco as an accent. The geometric shapes formed by areas of raised brick at Aq Astana Baba are a dramatic exaggeration of a decorative effect seen to a lesser extent elsewhere: the palmettes in the zone of transition, for example, are similar to those seen in stucco at Shir Kabir.

A sizable proportion of tenth-century mausolea in Central Asia contained the bodies of holy figures. The mausoleum of Hakim al-Termezi definitely housed the remains of a religiously esteemed individual; those of Arab Ata, Ataulla Said Vakkos, Iskhak Ata, Khalifa Rajab, Aq Astana Baba, and Khoja Roshan were probably in this group as well. All of these were buried as individuals; later burials may have clustered round them, but these were contained within their own separate graves or mausolea. All, moreover, became sites of at least local pilgrimage and veneration; the shrine of Hakim al-Termezi is still a major focus of local piety (which only lacks pilgrims from afar because of its location in a militarily sensitive area). Patronage of these structures is likely to have been at a high level: inscriptions in the mausoleum of Hakim al-Termezi show that the building was refurbished by the Qarakhanid Ahmad b. Hizr (r. 1082–95). Textual sources also show that rulers of this period built the mausolea of the religiously significant: the tomb of 'Ali at Najaf, for example, was re-constructed by the Hamdanid governor Abu'l Hayja 'Abdallah (r. 906–29), while that of Husayn at Karbala was rebuilt by 'Adud al-Dawla in 979. Hence it is quite likely that the original construction of the mausoleum of Hakim al-Termezi and the transformation of the

5 Mil-i Radkan, Radkan, Iran, early eleventh century.
Photo: Melanie Michailidis, courtesy of the Aga Khan Documentation Center at MIT

existing pre-Islamic shrine into a significant Islamic one was carried out by one of the early Samanids.

However, the expense lavished on religiously significant mausolea pales in comparison to the level of detail and conspicuous consumption seen at the Samanid mausoleum. It was constructed by Ismail, the founder of the Samanid dynasty (d. 907), as a visible link between the new rulers and the new capital, Bukhara. The mausoleum was a clever synthesis of Islamic funerary practices, which were still relatively new to Central Asia, local traditions, and references to the Persian past. This re-interpretation of the past glory of Sasanian Iran, rather than the past glory of Bukhara, coalesced with the Samanid promotion of New Persian as a language of government and literature in the formation of new local identity.[12] Ismail attached himself strongly to the city of Bukhara, and the three bodies which Soviet excavators found underneath the mausoleum probably belong to him, his father, and his grandson, Nasr b. Ahmad, whose name appears in an inscription carved in the wooden lintel over the eastern doorway (the only inscription anywhere on the building). The structure became a focal point of local pilgrimage, and other graves and mausolea clustered around it, so that three of the four entrances were blocked when Soviet work at the site began. These agglomerations were all cleared away, and the dome, which had partially collapsed, was rebuilt.

When the Turkic Qarakhanid dynasty superseded the Samanids in 1000, the tradition of

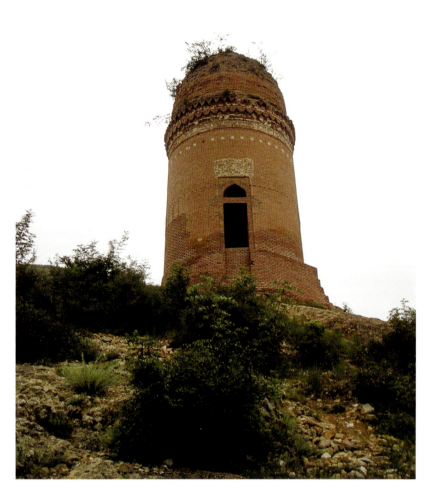

6 Tomb Tower near Resget, Iran, early twelfth century.
Photo: Melanie Michailidis, courtesy of the Aga Khan Documentation Center at MIT

constructing domed square mausolea continued, both for rulers and for religiously significant individuals. At Uzgend, one of the Qarakhanid capitals, now located in Kirghizstan, three royal mausolea are clustered together. The earliest tomb is the one in the center, and the later flanking mausolea show a clear progression in the elaboration of their decoration, executed in both stucco and brick revetments. At Termez, a local dynasty of religious notables constructed a funerary complex in the eleventh century referred to as Sultan Saodat. The original part of the complex consisted of two domed square mausolea linked by an *iwan*, an arrangement seen earlier at the nearby complex of Khaja Mashhad, but unknown elsewhere. The mausoleum known as Mir Sayyid Bahram, built for either the Qarakhanid Mansur b. 'Ali or 'Ali b. Hasan in the second quarter of the eleventh century, also fits well with corpus of earlier mausolea. With its *pishtaq* and its framing inscription, it is very similar to Arab Ata, while its shallow interior niches reflect those of the contemporary mausoleum of Sultan Saodat, and its engaged exterior corner columns recall the Samanid mausoleum. In size and in decoration, however, it is a modest building. The most lavish of the Qarakhanid mausolea is the tomb known as Shah Fazl, constructed at Safid Buland in 1055–60 for Muhammad b. Nasser by his son, Mua'izz al-Daula 'Abbas (and containing the bodies of both). From the outside it appears to be a typical mausoleum of the period, but the inside is covered with an exquisitely carved stucco revetment bearing the earliest extant foundation inscription in Persian.

TOMB TOWERS OF THE ZIYARIDS AND BAVANDIDS

In 1006–7, shortly after the Samanids were defeated by the Qarakhanids, an exceedingly monumental mausoleum of a type very different to the domed squares of Central Asia was constructed at Gurgan, the capital of the Ziyarid dynasty, in northern Iran. This tomb tower reaches the staggering height of 65 meters, including a ten-meter foundation extending down into an artificial mound. Ten flanges encircle the building, which is topped by a conical dome.

Known as the Gunbad-i Qabus, this is the earliest extant example of a group of tomb towers in northern Iran; since it is also the most dramatic and self-assured of the group, it is very unlikely to have actually been the first, and must have been preceded by monuments which are now lost (Fig. 4). The other tomb towers are located in or near the Alborz Mountains, just south of the Caspian Sea in northern Iran; the only exception is the Gunbad-i 'Ali, near Abarquh in Fars. None approach the height of the Gunbad-i Qabus: the second tallest is the Mil-i Radkan, at 35 meters (Fig. 5). With the exception of the Pir-i 'Alamdar and Chehel Dukhtaran at Damghan, which are sited on flat land and in an urban area which was located on a major trading route, most tomb towers are situated on hillsides in remote, mountainous areas. Constructed to commemorate rulers of the Bavandid dynasty, these structures would have been very visible to their constituents but were too remote to advertise Bavandid power much beyond their realm.

The tomb towers are all topped by double domes, and the association between the domed form and mausolea was such a strong one that several of the foundation inscriptions (at Lajim, Pir-i 'Alamdar and Chehel Dukhtaran) refer to the buildings they adorn as *qubba*, meaning "dome." Unlike the domed squares, which were so prevalent in Central Asia, the tomb towers all have a single entrance, and most lack any windows, so that their single chambers are very dark. Most have entrances high off the ground, seemingly designed to discourage entry. With the exception of the Gunbad-i 'Ali, which is composed of the rubble and mortar often used in Fars, all the buildings are constructed of baked brick. The interior chambers are undecorated apart from the Pir-i 'Alamdar, which has a Quranic inscription painted around the base of the dome. In the earliest towers, the Gunbad-i Qabus and Mil-i Radkan, exterior decoration is limited to the inscription bands and panels. Bands of terracotta decoration then started appearing next to the inscription bands, and at the tomb tower near Resget, painted stucco decoration was added as well (Fig. 6). The stucco motifs enable this mausoleum to be dated to the early twelfth century, but it clearly corresponds to

the other early eleventh century Bavandid mausolea in every other way, and appears to be closely modeled on the nearby tower at Lajim.

All of the tomb towers have foundation inscriptions, and Pir-i 'Alamdar and Resget have Quranic inscriptions as well (verses 39:54/53 in the Pir-i 'Alamdar; verses 21:36 and 112 on the tower at Resget). The foundation inscriptions indicate that these mausolea were all constructed for secular rulers, apart from Chehel Dukhtaran. The Gunbad-i Qabus was built by and for the Ziyarid ruler Qabus b. Vushmgir during his lifetime; Mil-i Radkan, Lajim, and Resget were all constructed for rulers of the Bavandid dynasty; Pir-i 'Alamdar was built by a Ziyarid who was serving as a Seljuk governor; and the Gunbad-i 'Ali was built for a Firuzanid amir and his wife. Although ruling as Buyid vassals in a part of Fars, the Firuzanids came from the Caspian region, where the tomb tower form prevailed. Textual sources indicate that the Buyids of Rayy also constructed tomb towers, which Muqaddasi compared to the pyramids.[13] The association of the tomb tower form with kingship in the Caspian region is clear, but the actual usage of the buildings is less obvious, since excavators and restorers have failed to find bodies under some of the monuments. According to medieval legends about the Gunbad-i Qabus, the body of Qabus b. Vushmgir was placed in a crystal coffin and suspended from the roof by chains (excavators also failed to find any evidence of this). Many features of the buildings themselves, including inscriptions in Middle Persian on the Bavandid towers, correspond to contemporary textual descriptions of royal Sasanian funerary practice, indicating that the Ziyarids and Bavandids were emulating their eponymous ancestors. This would entail placing the bodies on a platform inside the towers rather than burying them, and then sealing up the entrances.[14]

When the Seljuk Turks invaded Iran, they were inspired by the tomb tower form, although not by its Sasanian connotations, and they adapted the tomb tower to their own tastes and to conventional Islamic funerary practice. Seljuk tomb towers were wider in relation to their height, had windows and easily accessible entrances, and were located on flat ground, with burial crypts underneath to house the bodies. The two towers at Kharraqan, constructed in 1067 and 1093, are excellent examples. The easternmost tower also has painted interior decoration, consisting of peacocks flanking a tree, and a staircase to access the area between the two domes. Both towers exhibit lavishly detailed brick revetments, with a variety of geometric patterns typical of the Seljuk period. With the Seljuks, the tomb tower spread as far west as Anatolia, but the domed square form retained popularity as well. The most monumental example is the tomb of Sultan Sanjar at Merv, where the exterior gallery recalls that of the Samanid mausoleum. The dome covered in glazed blue tiles dramatically exhibits the addition of color in Seljuk architectural decoration, and foreshadows the monumental tombs to come, such as the mausoleum of Uljaytu. The funerary architecture of Iran and Central Asia, which became a focal point of high-level patronage beginning with the Samanid dynasty, would continue to attract considerable resources and exhibit the latest developments in techniques of dome construction and tiled decoration through the Ilkhanid and Timurid periods, while the elaboration and expansion of funerary shrines would continue up to the present day.

MELANIE MICHAILIDIS (d. 2013) was a specialist in the early Islamic art and architecture of Iran and Central Asia. She earned a PhD in Islamic art and architecture from The Massachusetts Institute of Technology in 2007. From 2011, she was the Korff Post-doctoral Fellow in Islamic Art at Washington University and curated the Islamic collection of the St. Louis Art Museum.

SUGGESTIONS FOR FURTHER READING

Blair, Sheila. *The Monumental Inscriptions from Early Islamic Iran & Transoxania* (Leiden: Brill, 1992).

Grabar, Oleg. "The Earliest Islamic Commemorative Structures," *Ars Orientalis* VI (1966), 7–46.

Hillenbrand, Robert. *Islamic Architecture: Form, Function & Meaning* (Edinburgh: Edinburgh University Press, 1994).

Leisten, Thomas. *Architektur für Tote* (Berlin: D. Reimer, 1998).

Michailidis, Melanie. "Landmarks of the Persian Renaissance: Monumental Funerary Architecture in Iran and Central Asia in the Tenth and Eleventh Centuries." PhD diss., Massachusetts Institute of Technology, 2007.

Raghib, Yusuf. "Les premiers monuments funéraires de l'Islam," *Annales Islamologiques* 9 (1970), 21–36.

NOTES

[1] K.A.C. Creswell, *Muslim Architecture of Egypt*, vol. I (Oxford: Clarendon Press, 1952), 110–3; see also Creswell, *Early Muslim Architecture*, vol. II (Oxford: Clarendon Press, 1969), 371.

[2] Ernst Diez, *Churasanische Baudenkmäler* (Berlin: D. Reimer, 1918), 89.

[3] Oleg Grabar, "The Earliest Islamic Commemorative Structures," *Ars Orientalis* VI (1966), 41–2. See also Robert Hillenbrand, "The Development of Saljuq Mausolea in Iran," in *The Art of Iran & Anatolia from the 11th to the 13th Centuries,* ed. W. Watson (London: University of London, 1973), 41; Hillenbrand *Islamic Architecture: Form, Function & Meaning* (Edinburgh: Edinburgh University Press, 1994), 264.

[4] Yusuf Raghib, "Les premiers monuments funéraires de l'Islam," *Annales Islamologiques* 9 (1970), 3–36.

[5] Sergei Khmel'nitskii, *Mezhdu Arabami i Tiorkami* (Berlin & Riga: Continent, 1992), 123.

[6] N.M. Bachinski, "Sirtsoviye zdaniya Drevnego Termeza," *Termezskaya Arkheologicheskaya Ekspeditsiya: Trudi* AN UzSSR (Tashkent: Akademii Nauk, 1945), 196–225; see also Sergei Khmel'nitskii, *Mezhdu Samanidami i Mongolami: Arkhitektura Srednei Azii* XI-*nachala* XIII *vv., Chast' I* (Berlin & Riga: Continent, 1996), 204–5.

[7] D. Huff, "'Sasanian' Chahar-Taqs in Fars," in *Proceedings of the Third Annual Symposium on Archaeological Research in Iran*, ed. Firouz Bagherzadeh (Tehran: Iranian Centre for Archaeological Research, 1975), 243–54.

[8] V. Minorsky, trans., *Hudud al-'Alam* (London: Luzac & Co., 1970), 133.

[9] *Hudud al-'Alam*, 115–6.

[10] Thomas Leisten, "Between Orthodoxy & Exegesis: Some Aspects of Attitudes in the Shari'a Toward Funerary Architecture," *Muqarnas* VII, 1990, 12–22.

[11] On nomadic Central Asian tombs, see Sergei Rudenko, *Frozen Tombs of Siberia: the Pazyryk Burials of Iron Age Horsemen,* trans. M. Thompson (Berkeley: University of California Press, 1970); Jeannine Davis-Kimball, Vladimir Bashilov & Leonid Yablonsky, *Nomads of the Eurasian Steppes in the Early Iron Age* (Berkeley: University of California Press, 1995).

[12] Melanie Michailidis, "Landmarks of the Persian Renaissance: Monumental Funerary Architecture in Iran and Central Asia in the Tenth and Eleventh Centuries" (PhD diss., Massachusetts Institute of Technology, 2007), 242–258.

[13] Muqaddasi, *The Best Divisions for Knowledge of the Regions*, trans. B.A. Collins (Reading: Garnet, 1994), 210.

[14] Michailidis, "Landmarks of the Persian Renaissance," 103–114.

The Ilkhanids and their Successors SHEILA BLAIR

1 Courtyard of the Madrasa Imami in Isfahan; view toward towards the *qibla iwan*.
Photo: Sheila Blair and Jonathan Bloom

In the middle of the thirteenth century, Mongol troops under Qubilay's brother Hulagu moved west across much of what is now Iran and adjacent territories in Iraq, Azerbaijan, and Turkey. Their campaigns culminated in 1258 in the conquest of Baghdad and the termination of the 'Abbasid caliphate there. For the next century and a half Hulagu, his descendants, and his successors ruled the region, first as the Ilkhanid dynasty (1256–1353) in the northwest, along with various local families such as the Muzaffarids (1314–93) in central Iran and the Injuids (1325–53) in Fars, and then as the Jalayirids (1340–1432) in Iraq, Kurdistan, and Azerbaijan. The Mongols themselves were originally Shamanists and had been exposed to most of the major religions practiced in Eurasia: Buddhism, Zoroastrianism, Manichaeism, at least four types of Christianity (Nestorian, Jacobite, Armenian, and Catholic/Latin), Judaism, and several approaches to Islam (notably Sunnism, Shi'ism, and Sufism). But after the Ilkhanid ruler Ghazan officially converted to Islam in 1295, practice of other religions was curtailed, and most of the religious architecture that survives from the Ilkhanid domains in Iran and adjoining areas is therefore Muslim.[1] Many of the building types traditional in the area – mosques, *madrasa*s, *khanqah*s (hospices for Sufis), and tombs – were continued, but the most notable feature of the period is the combination of these individual units into multipart complexes, many of them very large and decorated with sumptuous revetments and furnishings.[2]

Most communities already had congregational mosques, so only a few new ones were needed, and they generally followed the traditional Iranian plan with a domed chamber behind one or more *iwan*s (barrel-vaulted spaces open at one end). At Veramin, just south of Rayy, for example, the local family of governors under the Ilkhanid ruler Abu Sa'id had a new mosque erected between 1322 and 1326.[3] A large, freestanding rectangle (66 by 43 meters), the mosque centers on a court, with four *iwan*s connected by two-story arcades at the center of each of its sides. The four *iwan*s are not equal in size; rather, the monumental portal, the wider *qibla iwan*, and the majestic dome behind it create a strong longitudinal axis leading in the direction of prayer.

The four-*iwan* plan was not the only one used in the period. Other mosques, such as those at Ashtarjan and Faryumad, have two *iwan*s,[4] while one of the largest congregational mosques of the period, that ordered at Tabriz by the vizier 'Ali Shah sometime between 1311, the year he became co-vizier, and 1324, the year he died, now consists of a single monumental *iwan* measuring some sixty-five meters in depth and thirty meters across (Fig. 2).[5] Enormous walls ten meters thick were needed to support the vault, whose springing lines are set some twenty-five meters above ground level.

2 Mosque of 'Ali Shah, Tabriz, 1311–24.
Photo: Sheila Blair and Jonathan Bloom

A semicircular bay projecting from the rear of the *qibla* wall houses a tall *mihrab* with superposed keel-shaped arches set inside a rectangular frame. Flanking the *mihrab* are two enormous windows whose sills sit several meters above ground level; they served to light the vast interior.

Contemporary sources tell us that this tremendous construction was intended to surpass the celebrated *iwan* in the palace at Ctesiphon (mid-6th century?), the Sasanian site near the Ilkhanid's winter capital at Baghdad. The huge size and massive walls of 'Ali Shah's mosque also set the standard for buildings in Cairo such as the tomb complex of Sultan Hasan (1356–62), the largest and most impressive of all Mamluk buildings in the city. In the nineteenth century the enormous *iwan* in Tabriz served the Qajars as fort, prison, and arsenal, whence its nickname the Arg (citadel) of 'Ali Shah. The site was an apt choice for a stronghold, since cannon shots produced only pockmarks on the excessively thick walls, which remain a testament to the Mongols' passion for monumentality.[6]

The severe winters in northwest Iran made open-air worship unfeasible at certain times of the year, and various types of hypostyle mosque had no courtyard. The congregational mosque rebuilt at Ardabil in the early fourteenth century consists of a square dome chamber preceded by a rectangular hall with a flat roof supported on two rows of tree trunks and interior walls covered with hard white plaster with stenciled decoration in vivid blue, green, red, and other colors.[7] The mosque at Asnaq is square with four monolithic stone columns supporting the flat wooden roof.[8] Smaller mosques in central Iran often consisted of a single dome chamber, as in the group built along the Zayanda River downstream from Isfahan at Kaj, Dashti, and Aziran.[9]

Since so many large congregational mosques already existed by this period, individual elements were often added to extant ones. The most famous example is the stupendous carved plaster *mihrab* inserted in the winter prayer hall of the congregational mosque at Isfahan in July 1310 during the reign of Sultan Uljaytu (r. 1304–16) (Fig. 3).[10] Measuring over six by three meters, the *mihrab* displays a series of concentric niches within rectangular frames and is remarkable for its extraordinary carving on several levels. Densely covered in writing, it has inscriptions with Quranic verses, sayings of the Prophet's family, and pious

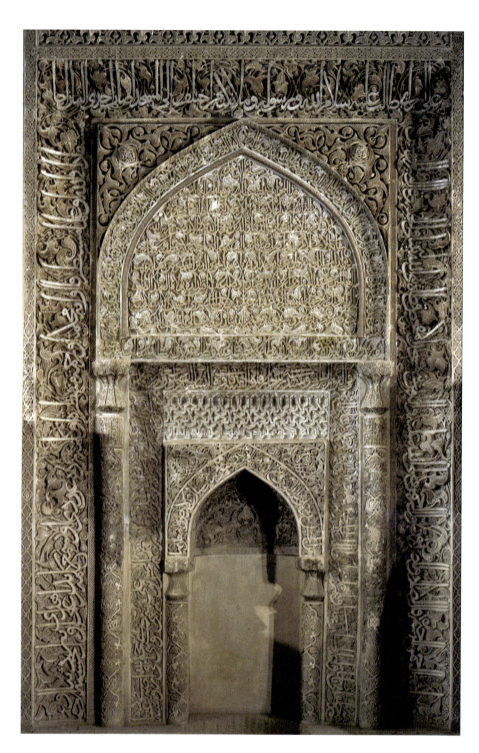

3 *Mihrab* added to the congregational mosque at Isfahan in 1310.
Photo: Sheila Blair and Jonathan Bloom

228 BLAIR

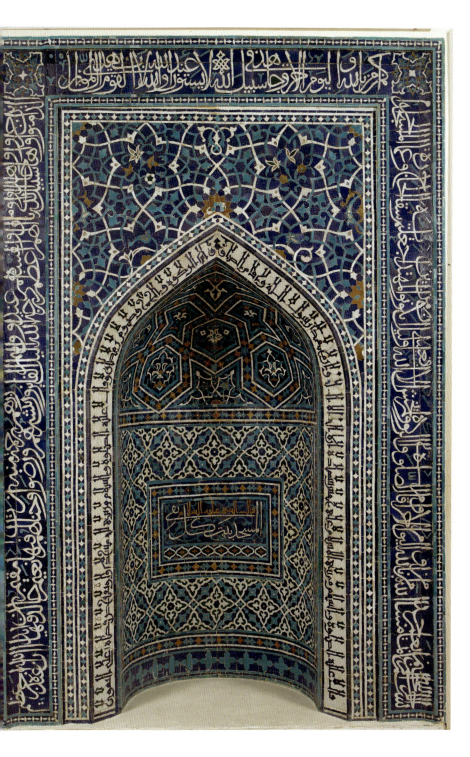

4 *Mihrab* from the Madrasa Imami, Isfahan, 1354.
New York: Metropolitan Museum of Art, 39.20 (Public domain)

invocations in addition to a long foundation text. The large framing band, for example, opens with a Prophetic Hadith saying that God will build a house (*bayt*) in Paradise for anyone who builds a mosque as a nesting place for a partridge. The inscription continues with a saying by the Prophet's cousin and son-in-law 'Ali on a similar theme, relating that whoever frequents a mosque will acquire one of eight blessings. The juxtaposition of Prophetic and 'Alid Hadiths implies that 'Ali is the worthy successor to Muhammad, and the texts were likely chosen in light of the sultan's conversion from Sunnism to Shi'ism at the end of the previous year, a decision that reportedly caused much upheaval and rioting in the city of Isfahan, whose inhabitants were staunch Sunnis.

Other types of religious buildings designed for communal use, such as *madrasa*s and *khanqah*s, also followed the *iwan* plan. The Madrasa Imami built at Isfahan in 1354 is a near-perfect example, with four *iwan*s grouped around a central court and connected by two-story arcades with living chambers (Fig. 1).[11] The *iwan*s on the north and south along the *qibla* axis are larger, and a portal leads from the southern one into a square chamber crowned by a dome. The south wall once contained a fine *mihrab* in tile mosaic, perhaps moved from another building and now in the Metropolitan Museum of Art (Fig. 4).[12] Measuring 3.43 by 2.8 meters, it is composed of pieces of tile glazed in white and light and dark blue, with secondary elements in manganese brown shading towards yellow and green. The outer framing inscription band has a bold Quranic text about visiting mosques (Quran 9:18–22), and a smaller rectangular text across the back of the niche contains a Prophetic hadith saying that the mosque is the dwelling place of the pious.

Both the Madrasa Imami and the tile mosaic *mihrab* testify to the florescence of Isfahan under the provincial family of Muzaffarid governors, who also had a *madrasa* added to the east side of the congregational mosque in their capital city between 1366–67 and 1376–77.[13] The *madrasa* comprises a court with a wide *iwan* on the south originally facing a corresponding one on the north and connected to it by two-story arcades on the lateral sides. Behind the south *iwan* is a transverse rectangular hall with a *mihrab* inserted in the back (south) wall. Like its counterpart from the Madrasa Imami, this *mihrab* is composed of tile mosaic in the typical Muzaffarid palette of five colors worked in

5 Tomb of Shaykh Buraq at Sultaniyya, c. 1310.
Photo: Sheila Blair and Jonathan Bloom

exuberant floral patterns, not only arabesques but also Chinese-inspired motifs such as lotus flowers.

Tombs too followed forms established in earlier periods, notably the tomb tower and the domed square. Mausolea built for minor figures such as descendants of the imams or princelings were relatively small, freestanding buildings. For example, the Imamzada Ja'far at Isfahan, built for a descendant of the fifth imam and 'Alid sheikh who died in 1325, is an octagonal tomb tower measuring seven meters in diameter but eleven meters high.[14] The elegant proportions of its blind arcading are thus more refined than earlier examples. Although its exterior decoration in terracotta and three colors of tile is much restored, its general appearance and architectural details are extremely close to another tomb tower further north at Sultaniyya (Fig. 5). Sometimes known as the tomb of Chelebi Oghlu, and dated c. 1330 on the basis of the adjacent *khanqah* dated 1333, the tomb in fact marks the grave of the sufi sheikh Buraq, who died in 1306–7 or 1307–8 during Sultan Uljaytu's campaign in Gilan, and should therefore be dated c. 1310.[15] The close connection between the two tomb towers suggests that a team of artisans might have moved from Sultaniyya to Isfahan, thereby exemplifying one of the characteristic features of this period – the movement of teams of architectural specialists from site to site.

The Imamzada Baba Qasim, built in 1340–41 for a local Sunni theologian in Isfahan, is slightly more complicated.[16] A small *muqarnas*-vaulted portal on the north leads to the square tomb chamber (five meters on a side) crowned by a hemispheric inner dome and exterior polyhedral tent dome. Beside it is an octagonal chamber that was converted into a square tomb in 1880, but may originally have served for gatherings of the sheikh's disciples. The small but charming monument has tasteful tile decoration in four colors (light and dark blue, white, and a sparing use of manganese brownish yellow) arranged in formal floral patterns.

Wealthier patrons, mainly rulers and their courtiers, built much larger tombs and incorporated them into elaborate funerary complexes. The best surviving example – and the undisputed gem of extant Ilkhanid architecture and a masterpiece

THE ILKHANIDS AND THEIR SUCCESSORS 231

6 Tomb of Uljaytu, Sultaniyya, 1306–20.
Photo: Sheila Blair and Jonathan Bloom

of world architecture – is the mausoleum of Uljaytu at Sultaniyya (Fig. 6).[17] Like the name of the newly founded city, Sultaniyya ("imperial"), everything about the construction is grand. It is a huge octagon measuring thirty-eight meters in diameter. The north wall of the structure projects laterally to meet the side walls, and the triangular spaces in the corners are filled with stairs to the upper stories. Another turret stair fills the southwest corner. The exterior walls with blind reveals likely abutted various subsidiary structures on several sides as they are undecorated at the bottom. Above the octagon floats the ethereal blue-tiled dome, which measures fifty meters in height and is ringed by eight minarets. It is constructed with a double shell, which served to both lighten the load and increase rigidity. Some scholars have suggested that the dome served as the model for the one that Filippo Brunelleschi constructed over the cathedral of S. Maria del Fiore in Florence (1418–36), often reckoned a structural marvel in its time.[18] However, the precise method of architectural transmission is undocumented and the connection remains speculative at best.[19] An inscription in cut tile over the east portal on the tomb at Sultaniyya with the date 1310 probably marks the completion of the outer decoration in brick and glazed tile.[20]

A ring of galleries on the exterior of Uljaytu's tomb provides stunning views of the surrounding plain and a visual transition from the plain walls below to the glazed dome above. The subtle design of interpenetrating volumes is complemented by the sophistication of the gallery vaults (Fig. 7). Each of the two dozen is decorated differently. They display a variety of carved and stamped plaster motifs, painted in red, yellow, green, and white. Many of the strapwork panels closely resemble contemporary manuscript illumination. The close similarities suggest that designers provided patterns that could be used on different scales in architecture and book painting.[21]

The central octagonal space of Uljaytu's tomb at Sultaniyya is vast, measuring twenty-five meters in diameter and divided by eight arched openings with balconies. The interior was decorated in at least two phases. In the original decorative scheme, the decoration swept upward from the floor to the base of the dome. The bays on the four corners were also distinguished from the four cardinal ones: the corner bays were decorated with a revetment of light buff fired brick laid in common bond, with patterns executed in square-ended light blue glazed bricks, whereas the bays on the cardinal axes had more elaborate decoration in all-over geometric patterns of specially cut brick, thin light blue glazed strips, dark blue glazed strips, and unglazed terracotta cut to special shapes. The cardinal bays were decorated with *muqarnas* vaulting. An inscription in unglazed terracotta set against a ground of light and dark blue tile mosaic in the soffit of the east bay ends with the date (written out in words) of 1313–14 and probably marks the end of the first stage of the interior decoration.

At some point, this brick and tile interior was redecorated in tile and painted plaster following a new scheme that emphasized horizontality and the equality of all eight interior *iwan*s. The lower walls were covered with a four-meter dado of light blue hexagonal tiles, with corner colonnettes completely covered in three colors of tile mosaic (light and dark blue and white), some of the first surviving examples of complete tile mosaic in these three colors. Above the dado the upper walls were covered with a thick coating of white plaster displaying traces of polychrome ornament and inscriptions in light blue, red, black, green, reddish brown, and yellow gold, partly executed in low relief on two levels.

Inscriptions here play not just an integral but a dominant role. They are written in a range of scripts, from a huge three-meter band in *thuluth* ringing the dome to smaller ones in Kufic, sometimes inserted in the stems of the larger inscriptions. The texts contain a variety of well-known Quranic excerpts and canonical Hadith, including the entire Surat al-Fath (Chapter of Victory, 48) ringing the dado and Traditions about prayer in a mosque, the tomb as a center of pilgrimage and circumambulation like the

7 Gallery vaults in the tomb of Uljaytu at Sultaniyya.
Photo: Sheila Blair and Jonathan Bloom

Kaaba, the superiority of the Quran over previous revelation, the rewards of paradise for believers, and the uniqueness of God. A date in numbers of 1320–21 known only from old photographs of the plaster revetment on the interior probably marks the end of this phase of redecoration, which therefore continued three years after the death of the patron Uljaytu into the reign of his son and successor Abu Sa'id (r. 1317–35). This dating is confirmed by a

THE ILKHANIDS AND THEIR SUCCESSORS   233

plaster inscription with the name of 'Ali Shah, the wily politician who became chief vizier following the execution of his rival in 1317.

To the south of the main room is a rectangular hall measuring fifteen by twenty meters that was probably added as part of the reconstruction when the interior of the main hall was revetted. The vaults now covering the hall are modern reconstructions, but the rectangular space must have had some sort of innovative transverse vaulting. Transverse vaulting on diaphragm arches had been a feature of the region since Parthian times and became particular popular through the Near East in the first centuries of Islam.[22] In the constructions from early Islamic times, the crown of the vault is horizontal along its entire length. The spandrels are built up to a level just above the crown of the arch, and the wall then serves to support a series of vaults set perpendicularly to the main axis. The transverse vaults that occur in the Ilkhanid period are more developed, with the cross vaults terminating in groin vaults, cloister vaults, lanterns, and the like (Fig. 8).[23] The system was typically used to cover rectangular prayer halls, whether the so-called "*masjid* (mosque) type," in which the *mihrab* is set in an enlarged central bay of the long side, or the so-called "oratory type," in which the short side is parallel to the *qibla*, thereby eliminating the need for a wider central bay.[24] The rectangular hall in the tomb of Uljaytu at Sultaniyya belongs to the former type, with a dome set over the wider central bay. The walls below still bear traces of fine decoration with superbly cut plaster above a dado tile mosaic with interlocking palmettes in light blue and white against a dark blue ground. The tile mosaic designs, datable to the second stage of reconstruction (1313–20), are some of the earliest to contain white and mark the beginning of a transition from geometric to floral motifs.

Scholars have long speculated about the reasons for the expansion and redecoration of the interior of the tomb at Sultaniyya. Donald Wilber and others connected it to Uljaytu's conversion to Shi'ism, suggesting that the sultan decided to convert the building into a tomb for 'Ali and Husayn by moving their bodies from Najaf and Karbala, but then gave up the plan and had the tomb renovated to serve

as his own mausoleum.[25] Such an argument is not entirely convincing, for none of the inscriptions on either level of decoration makes much mention of 'Ali and Husayn and the story of a tomb for 'Ali and Husayn occurs in no historical source before 1600. Another argument suggests that the redecoration was an allusion to Uljaytu's brief tenure over Mecca and Medina and his desire to control the Hijaz.[26] Both of these explanations may contain hints of a broader purpose: the sultan's desire to change a simple tomb into a shrine complex and center of pilgrimage. Architecturally, the tomb stands as the culmination of a steady line of prototypes of increasingly large mausolea with dome chambers and side galleries, from the tenth-century tomb of the Samanids in Bukhara to that of the Seljuk Sultan Sanjar in Merv (r. 1118–53), as well as the model for a series of imperial Mongol mausolea, including the Gur-i Mir at Samarqand, which served as the tomb of the warlord Timur (r. 1370–1405), and the Taj Mahal at Agra, the tomb of the Mughal emperor Shah Jahan (r. 1628–58) and his wife Mumtazz Mahal.

While it now stands in splendid isolation, Uljaytu's tomb at Sultaniyya was once the center of a large pious foundation that included places for prayer, instruction and Quran reading, residence, and meditation.[27] The buildings were grouped loosely around a courtyard, and the same spaces may have fulfilled more than one function. The foundation was one of the largest pious endowments of its time. According to a report by a sheikh who taught there, in the sultan's lifetime the endowments exceeded one hundred *tuman*s, some one million dinars and one-twentieth of the entire tax revenue due to the state in the 1330s.[28] The building's decoration was also described as some of the most elaborate of the time, with courtyards paved in white marble, roofs covered with *muqarnas*, silvered domes, and painted and plastered walls. Although such descriptions undeniably contain some hyperbole and poetic license, they do indicate the imperial scale of the complex, and the richness and quality of the surviving fragments attest to the prodigious funding behind it.

The tomb's glory was still visible in the sixteenth century, as documented in the earliest representation of the city, a painting in a unique manuscript dated 1537–38 by Nasuh Matrakçi.[29] The Ottoman court artist had accompanied Sultan Süleyman on his campaigns through the region a few years before and presumably painted the illustration from sketches made en route. The tomb with its eight minarets and ring of gallery vaults is unmistakable. Matrakçi's depiction also shows a gallery in front on the north. Flanked by tall minarets, it has two stories supporting five domes. Such a domed gallery has not survived, although it is found in later buildings in the region, notably the Blue Mosque built by the Qaraqoyunlu ruler Jahanshah in 1465 as well as covered mosques in Bursa.[30] Uljaytu's tomb shows no evidence of such a gallery, which is probably part of Matrakçi's conventions. We are on surer grounds when looking at Matrakçi's depiction of the nearby building, which must represent Sultaniyya's now-destroyed congregational mosque. The image depicts a domed portal with flanking minarets, covered side hall, and large dome over the *qibla*. Illustrations by travelers in the eighteenth and nineteenth centuries show the same features.[31]

Uljaytu's tomb complex at Sultaniyya was one of several constructed in the Ilkhanid period. After converting to Islam, his brother and predecessor Ghazan had built one in a suburb to the west of Tabriz known as Sham (Syria) or Shemb.[32] According to contemporary chronicles, the complex known as the Ghazaniyya included a congregational mosque, two *madrasa*s for followers of the Shafi'ite and Hanafite schools, a *khanqah*, a hospital, a palace, a library, an observatory, a courtyard, and a hot-water bath-fountain in addition to the dodecagonal tomb. Fragments collected at the site in the 1930s show that it was extensively decorated in three colors of glazed tile (light and dark blue and black). A somewhat stylized depiction of the complex in a copy of Rashid al-Din's *History of the Mongols* completed at Herat a century later shows an open courtyard enclosed by arcades, with various large buildings on the sides.[33]

The counterpart of the Ghazaniyya was the Rab'-i Rashidi, the quarter founded by the vizier Rashid al-Din on a hilltop east of Tabriz. The surviving text of its endowment dated 9

8 Transverse vaults in the tomb at Garlandan, c. 1315.
Photo: Sheila Blair and Jonathan Bloom

August 1309 with later emendations, allows a fuller reconstruction of its parts and personnel.[34] A gateway complex gave access to the founder's tomb, a hospice, a *khanqah*, and a hospital. Over three hundred people were permanently attached to the foundation: more than one hundred salaried employees and day laborers, along with 220 slaves. The endowment amounted to almost five hundred thousand dinars, about half that of Sultan Uljaytu for his funerary complex at Sultaniyya.

The focus of the Rab'-i Rashidi was the tomb where the Quran was recited around the clock and feasts and special readings were held on holidays. The depiction of the "Bier of Alexander" from a magisterial copy of the *Shahnama* or *Book of Kings* made in the 1330s, probably under the auspices of Rashid al-Din's son Ghiyath al-Din, gives a reasonable depiction of the setting and the activities carried out in these Mongol tombs.[35] The frame of the room represents the typical construction of reddish bricks inset with light blue glazed ones. The lower walls are covered with a dado of hexagonal glazed tiles. Above, the white walls with a row of blue palmettes represent plaster with stenciled decoration. All of these elements are found at Uljaytu's tomb at Sultaniyya. The cenotaph fills the center of the space, surrounded by crowds of wailing mourners. Several figures, both male and female,

THE ILKHANIDS AND THEIR SUCCESSORS   235

weep over the coffin. Large tapers and hanging lamps illuminate the room.

The endowment for the Rab'-i Rashidi also provided for an atelier to produce books. Every year, scribes were to copy a thirty-volume manuscript of the Quran and a collection of Prophetic Traditions; the addenda to the endowment directed the overseer to include copies of Rashid al-Din's own works to be transcribed yearly in both Arabic and Persian. The form of all these manuscripts was carefully specified (good Baghdadi paper, neat script, careful collation with the original, and leather binding), and the few examples that have survived, such as an illustrated Arabic copy of his *Jami' al-tawarikh* or *Compendium of Chronicles* dated 1314–15 or several copies of his compendium of four theological books entitled *Majmū'a Rashīdiyya*, one dated 1307–11, show that the patron's instructions were faithfully executed.[36]

The tomb complexes of Ilkhanid rulers and their courtiers seem to have been somewhat randomly planned to fit the exigencies of the sites. Despite their haphazard quality, they provided the model for Ottoman sultans in Bursa, whose tomb complexes or *külliye*s in Bursa and elsewhere were combined in more regular conglomerations. From northwest Iran at the opening of the fourteenth century, the idea of a personal funerary complex also spread quickly to central Iran. The best evidence is from Yazd, a prosperous town in central Iran where at least twelve mosques, one hundred *madrasa*s, and two hundred tombs were erected during the fourteenth century in addition to the congregational mosque.[37] The most notable patrons came from a family of local notables, the Al-i Nizami, including the *qadi*s Rukn al-Din (d. 1331–32) and his son Shams al-Din (d. 1332–33), who both built their own tomb complexes, the Rukniyya and the Shamsiyya.[38] The one for Rukn al-Din erected near the main congregational mosque once comprised a mosque, a *madrasa*, a library, a hospice for descendants of the Prophet, and an observatory known as the Mu'asasa-yi Vaqt-u Sa'at (Institute of Time and the Hour) because of its ingenious mechanical devices. All that survives is the square dome chamber surmounted by a tiled dome. The entire interior is revetted with a coat of hard white plaster lavishly decorated with painted and stenciled designs in blue, green, and brown with traces of gilding.[39] Rukn al-Din's son Shams al-Din built a similar funerary ensemble combining a mosque and adjoining *madrasa*, library, hospital, hospice for descendants of the Prophet, bazaar, and bath. Surviving parts include a narrow, arcaded forecourt with a monumental *iwan* flanked by rectangular halls and leading to the rectangular tomb chamber. Interior surfaces here too are revetted with plaster and painted with an array of polychrome designs in low relief in addition to tile mosaic. The multiple rectangular halls of the Shamsiyya show that elaborate systems of transverse vaulting was readily used in Yazd by the 1330s, and textual sources allow us to trace the exact source of architectural transmission. Shams al-Din, who was the son-in-law of the chief vizier Rashid al-Din, spent much of his life in Tabriz. When he died, his body was shipped to Yazd in an ebony and sandalwood casket along with his marble tombstone. According to the local history, the *Tarikh-i Yazd*, plans for his tomb complex drawn in Tabriz were sent to Yazd.[40] This is some of our first solid evidence for the use of architectural plans on paper, facilitated perhaps by the introduction of gridded paper.[41]

The innovative types of transverse vaulting, begun in northwest Iran and transferred to Yazd, were further developed there, as shown by the new congregational mosque begun under the auspices of the notable Rukn al-Din.[42] In 1325 he purchased land to the south of the old mosque and ordered the construction of an *iwan* or *ṣuffa*, a dome chamber (*gunbad*), a place of prayer (*maqṣūra*), and upper rooms (*ghurfahā*). Maxime Siroux's thorough survey

9 Transverse vaults in the west hall of the congregational mosque, Yazd, 1364–76.
Photo: Sheila Blair and Jonathan Bloom

of the mosque shows that these correspond to the two-story *iwan*, with flanking galleries and the dome chamber behind.[43] Early work also included a soaring monumental portal on the west, much rebuilt, that opens to a rectangular court connecting the new mosque with the bazaar. Later in the century under the Muzaffarids, new decoration was installed, including a dazzling tile *mihrab* dated 1375–76, and prayer halls were added on both sides of the *iwan* and dome chamber. These long rectangular spaces are broken by transverse arches joined by vaults running in the direction of the cross arches. Windows in the small lantern domes flood the interiors with light (Fig. 9). The innovative vaulting produces some of the most serene interiors in Iranian architecture.

From central Iran techniques of transverse vaulting spread to the northeast. At Turbat-i Shaykh Jam, for example, the rectangular room known as the Masjid-i Kirmani added c.1360 is divided by transverse arches into five bays with a central lantern dome and *muqarnas* semidomes over the end bays.[44] These rectangular halls provided models for architects working under the Timurids at the end of the fourteenth and beginning of the fifteenth centuries who developed the decorative possibilities of transverse vaulting by reducing the load-bearing elements and opening the room to increased light and applied decoration.

In addition to personal tomb complexes, other funerary complexes built or enlarged in the Ilkhanid period were shrines for Sufi saints, both contemporary figures, and those long dead. Lisa Golombek labeled these shrines "the little cities of God" and singled out five as the most brilliant and best preserved: the shrine of 'Abd al-Samad at Natanz; that of Shaykh Safi, eponym of the Safavid dynasty, at Ardabil; the shrine for Pir-i Bakran near Isfahan; the shrine of Bayazid at Bistam; and the complex of Shaykh Ahmad at Turbat-i Shaykh Jam.[45] The shrine at Natanz, a small town 130 kilometers north of Isfahan on the old road connecting Qum and Kashan with Ardistan and Yazd, provides a good example of the growth and development of such complexes in the Ilkhanid period.[46] It contains the tomb of 'Abd al-Samad, a spiritual master of the Suhrawardi order who taught at Natanz. After his death in 1299–1300, one of his wealthy disciples, Zayn al-Din Mastari, a vizier in the Ilkhanid administration, turned the site into a major shrine complex. An earlier building on

the site became the sheikh's square tomb.[47] On the interior, rectangular side niches transform the square space into an octagon. The upper walls are covered with a hard plaster coat. At the top is a superb carved plaster inscription with the date 1307, crowned in turn by a stunning *muqarnas* vault, the most spectacular to survive from the Ilkhanid period (Fig. 10). A blue-glazed tent dome protects the vault on the exterior.

Traces in the walls show that the lower walls of the tomb chamber at Natanz were once extensively revetted with luster tiles, in which an already glazed and fired tile is painted with metallic oxide and fired a second time in a reducing kiln. Many of these expensive and shiny tiles were removed from the site in the nineteenth century and are now in museum collections around the world.[48] Traces in the plaster show that the tomb originally had a dado of six tiers of star and cross tiles was surmounted by a frieze of rectangular tiles, including one in the Metropolitan Museum (12.44) with the date Shawwal 707/March–April 1307. Many of these tiles depict birds whose heads have been later chipped away by a zealous iconoclast. The *mihrab* niche has a convex hood, probably to be identified with the luster one dated 1307–8 in the Victoria and Albert Museum in London (71–1885). The rectangular cenotaph now bears underglaze-painted tiles with the name of Khadija Sultan and the date 1635–36, but the cenotaph was likely once covered with another set of three molded luster tiles (Metropolitan Museum of Art 09.87) inscribed with the name Hasan ibn 'Ali ibn Babawayh, the builder – the same artisan whose name appears on the colonnettes below the frieze in the tomb.

To the west of the tomb at Natanz rises a tall entrance portal, all that remains of a *khanqah* destroyed sometime before the 1930s when a mosque was built on the site. Between it and the tomb rises a soaring multi-tier minaret employing the most innovative materials and techniques of the period. Further to the east on the other side of a corridor from the street is a rebuilt four-*iwan* mosque that incorporates a domed pavilion dated 998–99, the earliest dated dome to survive in central Iran.[49] During the expansion of the shrine in the early fourteenth century, other luster tiles were also added to the interior of the octagonal pavilion that now served as the dome chamber of the congregational mosque.[50]

10 *Muqarnas* vault over the tomb of 'Abd al-Samad, Natanz, 1307–8.
Photo: Sheila Blair and Jonathan Bloom

Major work on the complex at Natanz seems to have halted abruptly when the patron was put to death in 1312. Minor work resumed in 1324–25 under a local shrine official, Shams al-Dawla Muhammad ibn 'Ali, who had rooms inserted over the entrance corridor and an inscription added at the base of the minaret. Doors, fireplaces, and other furnishings were supplied over the centuries, but most of the shrine represents architectural work from the first decade of the fourteenth century.

The complex around the grave of 'Abd al-Samad at Natanz is typical of the many shrines that developed in Iran and adjacent areas in the first two-thirds of the fourteenth century. Despite formal variety, most of these complexes share similar functions of commemoration, piety, and worship. Most display an increasing reverence for the family of the Prophet and the 'Alid line. Most exemplify the dual patronage of government officials and clerics, many of them members of Sufi orders, who were instrumental in converting the Mongols to Islam. These patrons were able to invest substantial sums in the construction and decoration of these complexes, which represent some of the finest architectural decoration of their time, especially in their extensive use of glazed and luster tile revetment. They were also furnished with luxury textiles, lamps, books, and other portable objects.[51]

Architecturally, the buildings in all these funerary complexes for both secular figures and sufi saints exemplify the increasing refinement of forms typical of Ilkhanid architecture, as shown by taller rooms, arches with a more pointed profile, and more attenuated minarets. This new verticality can be seen as well in the monumental portals with soaring double minarets preserved in Isfahan, Yazd, Abarquh, and elsewhere. Architects also paid increasing attention to innovative methods of covering spaces, particularly rectangular ones, as the solid walls of earlier buildings were pierced with openings and bays, new types of transverse vaulting with ramping vaults were developed to admit light and air, and *muqarnas* became standard to cover entire vaults and semi-domes. Color was used more extensively, as exteriors were revetted in tile mosaic in a broadening palette with more fluid floral designs. Color was also extended to interior surfaces, which were plastered, carved, and painted in a bewildering variety of epigraphic and floral designs. Collectively these large and elaborate buildings show the wealth that patrons invested in religious architecture under the Ilkhanids and their successors and set the stage for developments under the Timurids and their contemporaries in the later fourteenth and fifteenth centuries.

SHEILA BLAIR retired recently as Norma Jean Calderwood University Professor of Islamic and Asian Art at Boston College and Hamad bin Khalifa Endowed Chair of Islamic Art at Virginia Commonwealth University, positions she shared with her husband and colleague Jonathan Bloom. Author, co-author or editor of nearly two dozen books and hundreds of articles on all aspects of Islamic art, she specializes in the uses of writing and the art of the Mongol period.

SUGGESTIONS FOR FURTHER READING

Sheila S. Blair, *The Ilkhanid Shrine Complex at Natanz, Iran* (Cambridge, M A: Harvard University Press, 1986).

Sheila S. Blair and Jonathan M. Bloom, *The Art and Architecture of Islam 1250–1800*, Pelican History of Art (London and New Haven: Yale University Press, 1994).

Linda Komaroff, ed. *Beyond the Legacy of Genghis Khan* (Leiden: E J Brill, 2006).

L. Komaroff and S. Carboni, eds. *The Legacy of Genghis Khan: Courtly Art and Culture in Western Asia, 1256–1353* (New York: Metropolitan Museum of Art, 2002).

Donald Wilber, *The Architecture of Islamic Iran: The Il Khānid Period* (Princeton: Princeton University Press, 1955).

NOTES

[1] Sheila Blair, "Religious Art of the Ilkhanids," *The Legacy of Genghis Khan: Courtly Art and Culture in Western Asia, 1256–1353*, ed. L. Komaroff and S. Carboni (New York: Metropolitan Museum of Art, 2002), 104–33. Many other types of religious architecture have not survived; see, for example, the Buddhist sites mentioned in texts as collected by Roxann Prazniak, "Ilkhanid Buddhism: Traces of a Passage in Eurasian History," *Comparative Studies in Society and History* 56/3 (2014), 650–80. The one surviving example is likely the ruined site at Viar near Sultaniyya, for which see Sheila Blair, *Text and Image in Medieval Persian Art* (Edinburgh: Edinburgh University Press, 2014),139–46.

[2] The basic survey of architecture in this period is Donald Wilber, *The Architecture of Islamic Iran: The Il Khānid Period* (Princeton: Princeton University Press, 1955). The major buildings are covered in Sheila Blair and Jonathan Bloom, *The Art and Architecture of Islam 1250–1800*, Pelican History of Art (London and New Haven: Yale University Press, 1994), chapter 2, 5–20, and in Sheila Blair, "Iran and Central Asia, 1250–1500," chapter 43 of *Sir Banister Fletcher's A History of Architecture*, 21st ed. (London: Bloomsbury Publishing, 2019), 559–83.

[3] Wilber, *Architecture of Islamic Iran*, no. 64; Blair and Bloom, *Art and Architecture of Islam*, 13–14 and Figs. 14–15; H. Nakha'ī, *Masjid-i Jāmi'-i Varāmīn* (Tehran: Ruzana1, 1397/2018).

[4] Wilber, *Architecture of Islamic Iran*, nos. 49 and 61.

[5] Wilber, *Architecture of Islamic Iran*, no. 51; Blair and Bloom, *Art and Architecture of Islam*, 11–12 and Fig. 13; Sheila Blair "'Arg-i 'Alī Shāh," *Encyclopaedia Islamica* (London: Institute of Isma'ili Studies, 2010), vol. 3, 610–14.

[6] Bernard O'Kane, "Monumentality in Mamluk and Mongol art and Architecture," *Art History* 19 (December 1996), 499–522.

[7] Wilber, *Architecture of Islamic Iran*, no. 40.

[8] Bernard O'Kane, "The Friday Mosques of Asnak and Saravar," *Archaeologische Mitteilungen aus Iran* 12 (1979), 341–51.

[9] Wilber, *Architecture of Islamic Iran*, nos. 69, 70, and 71.

[10] Blair and Bloom, *Art and Architecture of Islam*, 10–11 and Fig. 12. Sheila Blair, "Writing about Faith: Epigraphic Evidence for the development of Shi'ism in Iran," *People of the Prophet's House: Artistic and Ritual Expressions of Shi'i Islam*, ed. F. Suleman (London: Ismaili Institute in association with the British Museum Press in Association with the British Museum and Azimuth Editions, 2015), 102–10.

[11] Wilber, *Architecture of Islamic Iran*, no. 100; Bernard O'Kane, "Architecture in the Interregnum: The Mozaffarid, Jalayerid and Kartid Contributions," *Iran after the Mongols*, ed. S. Babaie (London: I. B. Tauris, 2019), 211–14.

[12] Mary Crane, "A Fourteenth-century Mihrab from Isfahan," *Ars Islamica* 7/1 (1940), 96–100. Details also available on the museum website: https://www.metmuseum.org/art/collection/earch/449537?searchField=All&sortBy= Relevance&ft=39.20&offset= 0&rpp= 20&pos=1. On the development of tilework in the period, see Douglas Pickett, *Early Persian Tilework: The Medieval Flowering of Kāshī* (Cranberry, NJ: Associated University Presses, 1997).

[13] Wilber, *Architecture of Islamic Iran*, no. 109; O'Kane, "Architecture in the Interregnum," 216–17.

[14] Wilber, *Architecture of Islamic Iran*, no. 68; Blair and Bloom, *Art and Architecture of Islam*, 14 and Fig. 18.

[15] Wilber, *Architecture of Islamic Iran*, no. 80; Sheila Blair, "The Mongol Capital of Sultaniyya, 'The Imperial'," *Iran* 24 (1986), 139–51; Blair and Bloom, *Art and Architecture of Islam*, 14.

[16] Wilber, *Architecture of Islamic Iran*, no. 27.

[17] Wilber, *Architecture of Islamic Iran*, no. 47; Blair, "The Mongol Capital of Sultaniyya"; Blair and Bloom, *Art and Architecture of Islam*, 6–8 and Figs. 4, 5, and 7; Farnaz Akhavan Tavakoli, *A Bibliography of Sultanyeh* (Tehran: Iranian Cultural Heritage Organization, 202); Blair, *Text and Image*, chapter 4; and Marco Brambilla, "The Mausoleum of Oljeitu and the Citadel of Sultaniyya," *Iran after the Mongols*, ed. S. Babaei (London: I. B. Tauris, 2019), 129–41.

[18] Piero Sanpaolesi, "La Cupola di Santa Maria del Fiore ed il Mausoleo de Soltanieh," *Mitteilungen des kunsthistorischen Institutes in Florenz* 16/3 (1972), 221–60; Rowland J. Mainstone, *Developments in Structural Form* (Cambridge, Ma: MIT Press, 1975), 123–25.

[19] Howard Saalman's definitive study of the building, *Filippo Brunelleschi: The Cupola of Santa Maria del Fiore* (London: Zwemmer, 1980), 29, for example, mentions Sanpaolesi's reference merely in passing, but does not take up the issue.

[20] The inscriptions are discussed in Sheila Blair, "The Epigraphic program of Uljaytu's tomb at Sultaniyya: Meaning in Mongol architecture," *Islamic Art* 2 (1987), 43–96; 'Abdallah Qūchānī, *Gunbad-i Sulṭāniyya bih istinād-i katībah-hā* (Tehran: Intisharat-i Ganjinah-i Hunar,1381/2002), 8–9; and Blair, *Text and Image*, 112–27.

[21] Eleanor Sims, "The 'Iconography' of the internal decoration in the mausoleum of Uljaytu at Sultaniya," *Content and Context of Visual Arts in the Islamic World*, ed. P. Soucek (University Park, PA: College Art Association, 1988), 139–76.

[22] For its development in early Islamic times, see Ignacio Arce, "From the diaphragm arches to the ribbed vaults: An hypothesis for the birth and development of a building technique," *Proceedings of the First International Congress on Construction History, Madrid, 20th–24th January 2003*, ed. S. Heurta (Madrid: Instituto Juan de Herrera, Escuela Técnica Superior de Arquitectura, 2003), 225–41.

[23] Lionel Bier, *Sarvistan: A Study in Early Iranian Architecture* (University Park, PA, and London: College Art Association, 1986), 34–39.

[24] Lisa Golombek, *The Timurid Shrine at Gazur Gah*, Royal Ontario Museum Art and Archeology Occasional Paper 15 (Toronto: Royal Ontario Museum, 1969), 55–56, coined the terms "*masjid*" and "oratory" types and gave a preliminary list of examples from the Timurid and pre-Timurid periods, beginning with the *iwan* at Garlandan, near Isfahan, built 1315 (see Fig. 8). Some of the most spectacular from the period are in the Khan Mirjan in Baghdad, built by the eponymous governor in 1358–59, for which see Tariq Jawad al-Janabi, *Studies in Medieval Iraqi Architecture* (Baghdad: Ministry of Culture and Information, 1982), 140–46 and O'Kane, "Architecture in the Interregnum," 221. For later developments, see Lisa Golombek and Donald Wilber, *The Timurid Architecture of Iran and Turan* (Princeton: Princeton University Press, 1988), 110–11.

[25] Wilber, *Architecture of Islamic Iran*, no. 47.

[26] Blair, "Epigraphic program."

[27] Blair, "The Mongol Capital of Sultaniyya" and *Text and Image*, 128–35.

[28] For comparable prices in the Ilkhanid economy, see I. P. Petrushevsky, "The Socio-Economic Condition of Iran under the Īl-Khāns," *The Cambridge History of Iran*, vol. 5, *The Saljuq and Mongol Periods*, ed. J. A. Boyle (Cambridge: Cambridge University Press, 1968), 483–537, especially 498.

[29] Istanbul, University Library, Yildiz Y5964, fols. 31b and 32a; fascimile edition with introduction by H. G. Yurdaydin, *Beyān-i Menāzil-i Sefer-i 'Iraḳeyn-i Sulṭān Süleyman Hān* (Ankara: Türk Tarih Kurumu Basimevi, 1976); Blair, 'The Mongol Capital of Sultaniyya," pl. 1B; Blair and Bloom, *Art and Architecture of Islam*, Fig. 3; Blair, *Text and Image*, Fig. 4.32.

30 Golombek and Wilber, *Timurid Architecture of Iran and Turan*, no. 214.

31 Blair, "The Mongol Capital of Sultaniyya," especially pls. VA and VB.

32 Wilber, *Architecture of Islamic Iran*, no. 27.

33 Paris, Bibliothèque nationale de France, mss. Or. Suppl. pers. 1113; Wilber, *Architecture of Islamic Iran*, Fig. 31; Blair, *Text and Image*, Fig. 4.13. The manuscript has been redated c. 1430–34 by Francis Richard, *Splendeurs persane: Manuscrits du XIIe au XVIIe siècle* (Paris: Bibliothèque nationale de France, 1997), no. 40.

34 Sheila Blair, "Ilkhanid architecture and society: an analysis of the endowment deed of the Rab'-i Rashidi," *Iran* 22 (1984), 67–90. For the dating of the amendations, see Nourane Ben Azzouna, "Rashīd al-Dīn Faḍl Allāh Hamadhānī's Manuscript Production Project in Tabriz Reconsidered," *Politics, Patronage and the Transmission of Knowledge in 13th–15th Century Tabriz*, ed. J. Pfeiffer (Leiden: Brill, 2014), 187–200.

35 Freer Gallery of Art 1938.3; Oleg Grabar and Sheila Blair, *Epic Images and Contemporary History: The Illustrations of the Great Mongol Shahnama* (Chicago and London: University of Chicago Press, 1980), no. 39.

36 Sheila Blair, *A Compendium of Chronicles: Rashid al-Din's Illustrated History of the World*, The Nasser D. Khalili Collection of Islamic Art, vol. XXVII, ed. J. Raby (London: The Nour Foundation in association with Azimuth Editions and Oxford University Press, 1995); eadem, "Patterns of Patronage and Production in Ilkhanid Iran: The Case of Rashid al-Din," *The Court of the Il-khans 1290–1340*, ed. J. Raby and T. Fitzherbert, Oxford Studies in Islamic Art 12 (Oxford: Oxford University Press, 1997), 39–62; eadem, "Writing and Illustrating History: Rashid al-Din's *Jami' al-tavarikh*," *Theoretical Approaches to the Transmission and Edition of Oriental Manuscripts*, papers from an international conference held in Istanbul in 2001, ed. J. Pfeiffer and M. Kropp, *Beiruter Texte und Studien* 111 (Beirut: Orient-Institut der Deutschen-Morganländischen Gesellschaft, 2007), 57–66; Nourane Ben Azzouna and Patricia Roger-Puyo, "The Question of Manuscript Production Workshops in Iran according to Rashīd al-Dīn Faḍl Allah al-Hamadhānī's *Majmū'a Rashīdiyya* in the Bibliothèque nationale de France," *Journal of Islamic Manuscripts* 7/2 (2016), 152–94.

37 Iraj Afshar, *Yadgarha-yi Yazd*, 3 vols. (Tehran: Ziba, 1965–1975).

38 Wilber, *Architecture of Islamic Iran*, nos. 67 and 107, the latter mistakenly dated there c. 1365, although the patron had died several decades earlier; Jean Aubin, "'Le Patronage culturel en Iran sous les Ilkhans: Une grande Famille de Yazd," *Le Monde Iranien & Islam* 3 (1975), 107–18.

39 Yuka Kadoi, "Aspects of frescoes in fourteenth-century Iranian architecture: the case of Yazd," *Iran* 43 (2005), 217–40.

40 Jonathan Bloom, "Paper: The Transformative Medium in Ilkhanid Art," *Beyond the Legacy of Genghis Khan*, ed. L. Komaroff (Leiden: Brill, 2006), 289–302, esp. 296.

41 Jonathan Bloom, "Lost in Translation: Gridded Plans and Maps along the Silk Road," *The Journey of Maps and Images on the Silk Road*, ed. P. Forêt and A. Kaplony (Leiden: Brill, 2008), 83–96. For the example of a stucco plan used to construct the *muqarnas* vault at the palace of Takht-i Sulayman, see Yvonne Dold-Samplonius and Silvia L. Harmsen, "The Muqarnas Plate Found at Takht-i Sulayman: A New Interpretation," *Muqarnas* 22 (2005), 85–94.

42 Wilber, *Architecture of Islamic Iran*, no. 66; Afshar, *Yadgarha-yi Yazd*, II: 109–60; Blair and Bloom, *Art and Architecture of Islam*, 14 and Fig. 17; O'Kane, "Architecture in the Interregnum," 217–18.

43 Maxime Siroux, "La Masdjid-é Djum'a de Yezd," *Bulletin de l'Institut français d'archéologie orientale* 44 (1947), 119–76.

44 Wilber, *Architecture of Islamic Iran*, no. 81; Lisa Golombek, "The Chronology of Turbat-i Shaykh Jām," *Iran* 9 (1971), 27–44.

45 Lisa Golombek, "The Cult of Saints and Shrine Architecture in the Fourteenth Century," *Near Eastern Numismatics, Iconography, Epigraphy, and History: Studies in Honor of George C. Miles*, ed. D. K. Kouymjian (Beirut: American University of Beirut, 1974), 419–30. For Pir-i Bakran, see also Ana Marija Grbanovic, "The Ilkhanid Revetment Aesthetic in the *Buq'a* Pir-i Bakran: Chaotic Exuberance or a Cunningly Planned Architectural Revetment Repertoire?," *Muqarnas* 34 (October 2017), 43–83.

46 Wilber, *Architecture of Islamic Iran*, no. 39; Sheila Blair, *The Ilkhanid Shrine Complex at Natanz, Iran*, Harvard Middle East Studies Papers, Classical Series 1 (Cambridge, MA: Center for Middle Eastern Studies, Harvard University, 1986); Ḥusayn Aẓam Wāqifī, *Mīrāth-i Farhangī-yi Naṭanz* (Tehran: Intishārāt-i 'Ilmī wa Farhangī, 1374s/1995).

47 For the evidence dating the building to the Saljuq period, see Richard McClary and Ana Marija Grbanovic, "On the Origins of the Shrine of 'Abd al-Samad in Natanz: The Case for a Revised Chronology," *Journal of the Royal Asiatic Society* (forthcoming).

48 Oliver Watson, *Persian Lustre Tiles* (London: Faber and Faber, 1985); Tomoko Masuya, "Persian Tiles on European Walls: Collecting Ilkhanid Tiles in Nineteenth-Century Europe," *Ars Orientalis* 30 (2000), 39–54; Richard McClary, "Re-contextualising the Object: Using New Technologies to Reconstruct Lost Interiors of Medieval Islamic Buildings," *International Journal of Islamic Architecture* 7/2 (2018), 263–68.

49 Sheila Blair, "The Octagonal pavilion at Natanz: a reconsideration of early Islamic architecture in Iran," *Muqarnas* 1 (1983), 69–94.

50 For the reassignment of the tiles from the covering of the cenotaph to the installation in the *mihrab*, see Sheila Blair, "Luted letters: The relief inscriptions on Kashan luster *mihrab*s" (forthcoming).

51 Many discussed and illustrated in Sheila Blair, "On giving to shrines: 'Generosity is a quality of the people of Paradise'," *Gifts to the Sultan: The Art of Giving at the Islamic Courts*, ed. L. Komaroff (New Haven: Yale University Press, 2011), 51–74.

Religious Architecture of Central Asia under the Timurids and Their Successors

BERNARD O'KANE

1 Gur-i Mir, Samarqand, 1403.
Photo: Bernard O'Kane

The Timurids, who ruled over most of Iran and Central Asia in the late fourteenth and early fifteenth centuries, left an imposing body of religious architecture. Their legacy extended far beyond these monuments, however, for their architecture was adapted in varying ways not only by the dynasties that supplanted them, such as the Uzbeks and Safavids, but also in empires further afield, those of the Ottomans and Mughals.[1]

Timur (r. 1370–1405), the founding figure of the dynasty, looms overlarge in any assessment of its initial architectural trends. A monumentality to match his ego was characteristic of his major projects, be they secular (the Aq Saray palace at Shahr-i Sabz) or religious (Shrine of Shaikh Ahmad Yasavi, Samarqand Friday Mosque). Members of his family were the only other significant patrons of the time, but they played a limited role.

Samarqand, which became his capital early in his reign, also played a dominant role in the siting of new projects. The Shah-i Zinda necropolis on the outskirts of Samarqand saw the beginnings of Timurid architecture in the numerous mausoleums built on the pathway that led from the city to the shrine of the "Living King" (i.e. the *shah-i zinda*) himself, Qutham b. 'Abbas, a companion of the prophet. A respect for holy men and their shrines was a characteristic of Timur throughout his lifetime, and in fact what is probably the single most impressive tiled cenotaph in Islamic art, that of the Shah-i Zinda, may well be a Timurid construction of the 1360s, rather than, as is usually thought, an earlier Chaghatayid monument (Fig. 2).[2] One rather surprising common characteristic of Timurid mausolea, including those at the Shah-i Zinda, is their lack of *mihrab*s, perhaps indicating that prayer within them was neither expected nor encouraged.[3] Other indications of this are the *masjid* (c. 1404)

2 Shah-i Zinda, Uzbekistan, Samarqand, tiled cenotaph of Qusam ibn 'Abbas, 1360s.
Photo: Bernard O'Kane

that Timur's wife Tuman Agha built beside her mausoleum, and an early fifteenth one (replacing an earlier one) adjacent to the shrine of Qutham ibn 'Abbas himself.[4]

Timur's defeat of the Golden Horde ruler Tughtamish in 1395 enabled funds to be channeled to more ambitious projects. The first was another shrine, that of Khvaja Ahmad Yasavi (1397–9) (Fig. 3). Although the site had an earlier Seljuk mausoleum, this was incorporated within a new multifunctional complex.[5] Exactly how the different spaces within it functioned is not clear, but the Timurid historian Sharaf al-Din 'Ali Yazdi gave a description of the complex mentioning its lofty portal with two minarets, a large dome chamber; another smaller one that served at the mausoleum; two further cruciform rooms that served as meeting halls, and smaller rooms together with their appurtenances and dependencies.[6] There is no doubt, however, that it housed Sufis of the long-established Yasaviyya sect, and can therefore be viewed as a funerary *khanqah*, albeit on an unprecedented scale.[7] What also makes

this different from earlier *khanqah*s, and indeed from earlier Iranian architecture in general, is the treatment of the outer walls, with a complete revetment of tile decoration of various kinds (apart from the unfinished entrance portal).

This use of complete exterior decoration is also found in Timur's other major religious building, the Friday mosque of Samarqand (1398–1405, also known as the Bibi Khanum mosque) (Fig. 4).[8] This is more surprising, since, unlike the Ahmad Yasavi complex, it was erected in the middle of a dense urban setting. However, a key to understanding Timur's ability to cut a swathe through the old town is given in Ruy Gonzalez de Clavijo's account of the building of a new bazaar in the old town, which makes it clear that, despite the opposition of those whose property stood in the way, many houses were demolished in the process.[9] Only a ruler as autocratic and ruthless as Timur could have ridden roughshod over the *shari'a* to achieve his desired results. This is also shown in his reaction to the building on the return from his Indian campaign in 1404: it was too small for his taste and its two supervisors were executed. He ordered it built higher, but it was never fully completed before his death in the following year.

Although the mosque was built on the familiar four-*iwan* courtyard plan, a major innovation was the placing of dome chambers behind the side *iwan*s (in addition to that of the *qibla iwan*). These would have been the inspiration for their other prominent appearance, in Shah 'Abbas's new congregational mosque at Isfahan in the early seventeenth century. The tall minarets that flanked both the *qibla* and entrance *iwan*s (in addition to the four at the corners) would also have been striking; their form may have been derived from the now destroyed Ilkhanid Friday mosque at Sultaniyya.[10]

Timur's grandson Muhammad Sultan built a *madrasa* and *khanqah* opposite one another at Samarqand around 1400. These have not survived (their site has been eclipsed by the adjacent tomb built for him by Timur, the Gur-i Mir (Fig. 1), which eventually became Timur's own mausoleum), but the combination proved to be of lasting popularity in the following century.

3 Shrine of Shaykh Ahmad Yassavi, Kazakhstan, Turkistan City, view of exterior, 1397–99.
Photo: Bernard O'Kane

4 Mosque of Bibi Khanum, Samarqand, 1399–1405.
Photo: Bernard O'Kane

Shah Rukh, Timur's eventual successor (r. 1409–47), transferred the capital to the city where he had formerly been governor, Herat. He himself built a *madrasa* and *khanqah* (no longer extant) in the shade of its citadel (1410–11). Although this was praised by contemporary chroniclers, its fame was eclipsed by the monuments erected by his wife Gawhar Shad, in particular the *madrasa* and congregational mosque at Herat (1417–38), and the Friday mosque and other additions to the shrine at Mashhad (1418).

We may divide the major religious monuments of the Timurids in the fifteenth century into three groups, mosques, *madrasa*s and funerary structures. Of the numerous *khanqah*s which are also mentioned in the sources unfortunately none, or at least none of the major examples, has survived intact.

Most towns in Iran already had a congregational mosque by the fifteenth century. Mashhad was an exception; known as the town of Sanabad until the fourteenth century, it seems to have been the foundations of Gawhar Shad at the shrine that propelled its status into a major pilgrimage center, to the tomb of the Shi'a Imam Riza. Chief among these buildings was her mosque (completed in 1418) (Fig. 5).[11] It was unusual in its lack of a major portal facing the exterior; the *iwan* opposite the *qibla* led instead to another of her buildings, the Dar al-Siyada, adjacent to the dome chamber of the imam. Its four-*iwan* plan displays one feature that

CENTRAL ASIA UNDER THE TIMURIDS AND THEIR SUCCESSORS   245

5 Mosque of Gawhar Shad, Mashhad, 1418.
Photo: Bernard O'Kane

was first used (to lesser effect) at the Yazd Friday mosque: the removal of the rear wall of the *qibla iwan*, enabling the spectator in the courtyard to see the interior of the *qibla* dome chamber. The *qibla iwan* at Mashhad, however, is both much shallower and taller than that of Yazd, enabling not only much more penetration of light into the sanctuary, but also of the spectator's gaze. The position of the spectator in the courtyard is also privileged by the treatment of the facades between the *iwans*. These appear to be in two stories, but the upper storey is merely a façade, echoing the bays of the lower one below which lead to the prayer halls.

Gawhar Shad's Friday mosque in Herat (1417–37) was built (as part of a complex including a funerary *madrasa*) outside the city walls,[12] which may have counted as a separate urban entity, although the Hanafi rite, to which the Timurids adhered, permitted Friday prayer in more than one congregational mosque. Although only a fragment of a minaret now remains standing, some detailed descriptions and a nineteenth-century sketch give us a good idea of its main features. Several descriptions mention upper storey living units flanking the side *iwan*s, but it is probable that they misinterpreted the type of upper gallery that appeared as façade architecture at the Mashhad mosque.

The unusually long twenty-year building period of Gawhar Shad's complex[13] can probably be explained by employment of the court architect, Qavam al-Din Shirazi, first at her complex in Mashhad, and secondly on Shah Rukh's shrine for 'Abd Allah Ansari at Gazur Gah (1428–9). The latter is described in a variety of terms in the sources (*mazar*, *khanqah*, *buq'a*, and *hazira*); it probably functioned as a funerary *khanqah*, and raises the question of Timurid attitudes to funerary structures. There seem to have been divergent attitudes depending on whether the deceased was Sunni or Shi'a, religious or secular, and whether the grave had previously been uncovered or already had a domed mausoleum erected over it. As far as Sunni religious figures were concerned (e.g., at Gazur Gah, Taybad, and Turbat-i Jam), if the grave was previously uncovered, then a commemorative structure was likely to be erected adjacent to it. With Shi'a religious figures (e.g., the Mazar-i Sharif shrine, tombs of Qasim-i Anvar at Langar, and Farid al-Din 'Attar at Nishapur) however, the Timurids built dome chambers over their graves long after their death. There is likely to have been still have been some opposition by the *ulama* to erecting mausoleums, otherwise it is hard to explain the almost invariable location, at least in Khurasan, of mausolea for secular patrons within *madrasa*s, rather than the free-standing buildings that were erected for Timur and his family in Transoxiana. Unlike mausoleums in contemporary Egypt, they rarely have *mihrab*s, a lack that is again more likely to be explained by the objections of the *ulama* than the scruples of the patrons. The blurring of functions between *khanqah*, tomb, and *madrasa* should also be noted, a consequence of the blurring of distinctions between the *ulama* and Sufis in Timurid society.[14] Classes were given in at least one domed mausoleum at Herat, at the Shrine of Abu'l-Walid at Azadan (Fig. 6) and at the *hazira* of Sultan Ahmad.[15]

The single most common religious building type was the *madrasa*. As mentioned above, they frequently incorporated the patron's mausoleum, a factor that may explain much of the wealth that was poured into these buildings. Their plans are more consistent that other buildings types, rarely departing from a four-*iwan* courtyard with two-storey living quarters in between. One notable innovation was the entrance complex that many of them display, a set of rooms leading off the vestibule that did not communicate with the cells around the courtyard. A prototype is seen at the shrine at Gazur Gah mentioned above, but the most developed is at the *madrasa* of Khargird (1442–3) (Fig. 7).[16] In each case one of the rooms is a mosque. The other room at Khargird is a domed lecture hall which displays the most advanced vaulting of it time. Its use of intersecting ribs was preceded by the Gawhar Shad's Dar al-Siyada at Mashhad and the dynastic mausoleum in her *madrasa*, but here there is an uninterrupted flow of the ribs from the base of the lantern at the top of the dome down to the recesses of the cruciform plan. The earlier tripartite zone of

6 Shrine of Abu'l-Walid, Azadan, c. 1475–1500.
Photo: Bernard O'Kane

CENTRAL ASIA UNDER THE TIMURIDS AND THEIR SUCCESSORS 247

7 Madrasa al-Ghiyathiyya, Khargird, 1436–43.
Photo: Bernard O'Kane

transition is now divided into a lower square and an upper zone which blends into the dome.

Whether on secular or religious buildings, the advances of the Timurids in decoration should also be noted. Tilework was used much more extensively than previously, sheathing exteriors and courtyards. Interiors displayed a tiled dado but above that painted plaster was the norm. The remains within the domed rooms of the *madrasa*s of Gawhar Shad, Tuman Agha and Pir Ahmad Khvafi[17] show that in their original state painting of the quality of contemporary illuminated manuscripts could be found.

8 Masjid-i Kalan, Bukhara, 1514.
Photo: Bernard O'Kane

POST TIMURID CENTRAL ASIA

The ruling dynasty that succeeded the Timurids is commonly known as Uzbek, which was the most common tribal affiliation of its amirs, although its rulers, the khans, were normally of Chingizid affiliation, and comprised several groups, principally the Shibanids (1500–99) and the Toqay Timurids (also known as the Janids or Ashtarkhanids) (1599–1747). More importantly, they ruled over a more decentralized state, with the four major appanages, Bukhara, Samarqand, Balkh, and Tashkent, some times divided between two or more khans.[18] This had obvious repercussions for architectural patronage,[19] as it became harder to accumulate wealth, and although we shall see impressive buildings, none is of the scale of either Timur's grandest foundations or of Shah Abbas's in Isfahan. Although as nomadic descendants of Chingis Khan they looked down upon Timur's unrelated genealogy, they soon realized that the cultural patronage of urban centers instituted by the Timurids was essential to their prestige.[20]

As with the Timurids, Friday mosques had already been built in the major towns. However, sometimes these needed refurbishment or, in the case of the Kalan (Great) Mosque at Bukhara (Fig. 8), probably considerably more. The entrance portal of this is dated to 1514, and the large tiled mosaic *mihrab* is definitely also datable to the sixteenth century. It has been suggested that the tilework of the courtyard facades matches the period of Ulugh Beg,[21] but its patterns are much simpler than typical Timurid work, so it would be safer to assume that the whole mosque was completely rebuilt in the early sixteenth century. Whether its four-*iwan* form follows an earlier prototype is therefore uncertain, but not unlikely; the shallow *iwan*s and massive supports for the relatively small *qibla* dome chamber would otherwise suggest an

9 Mir-i 'Arab Madrasa, Bukhara, 1535.
Photo: Bernard O'Kane

10 Registan Square, Samarqand, from left to right: Ulugh Beg Madrasa, 1421; the Tila-Kari Madrasa, 1646–60; and the Shir Dar Madrasa, 1619–36.
Photo: Bernard O'Kane

unwillingness to compete with the grandeur of Timur's Samarqand Friday mosque.

Opposite it is the Mir-i 'Arab Madrasa (1535) (Fig. 9), a building that in many ways epitomizes Uzbek style and its continuity with Timurid prototypes. It was built by the Shibanid 'Ubaydallah Khan for Sayyid Mir 'Abd Allah Yamani, his spiritual advisor. At first glance it owes much to the previously mentioned *madrasa* at Khargird, with twin dome chambers above a façade consisting of an entrance *pishtaq*, corner towers with a group of three arches between them, an entrance complex and a beveled four-*iwan* courtyard. However, differences are soon also apparent. The entrance is in the form of a semi-octagon (for the first time in a *madrasa*); the entrance complex now communicates with both the exterior and the interior rooms, and the group of three arches on the façade is in two storeys, not one. The horizontality of Khargird is replaced by a much taller entrance *pishtaq* and by drums which markedly increase the height of its two flanking domes. The two side courtyard *iwan*s project also vertically much more than their Khargird counterparts. One of the dome chambers is a mausoleum (containing the tombs of both Shaykh Yamani and the patron 'Ubaydallah Khan).

The single most common form of building type erected by the Uzbeks was indeed the *madrasa*. This was, as we have seen already a trend established by the Timurids, but greater urgency was now given to their proliferation as they formed a bulwark of Sunni orthodoxy against their Shi'a rivals to the

south, the Safavids. The *madrasa* form continued for the most part to be similar to the Timurid tradition, with two dome chambers incorporated within an entrance complex preceding a four-*iwan* courtyard. Two of the most notable examples were erected at the Registan, one of the main squares in Samarqand, by Yalangtush Bahadur, the semi-independent ruler of the eponymous appanage (Fig. 10). The first was the Shir Dar Madrasa (1619–36); it took the place of the *khanqah* of Ulugh Beg formerly on the site, and was built to rival Ulugh Beg's *madrasa* opposite it. The name derives from the ornamentation of the spandrels of the entrance portal, which show a hybrid creature with tiger-like (or even leopard-like) stripes but with a mane; the term *shir* is also ambiguous, referring to a lion or a tiger. The sun emblem behind the lion (or tiger) is a royal symbol that was used in Buyid coinage. Given that the form of the building is so similar to its predecessor, its ability to compete rests on the fineness of its decoration. Here, unfortunately, the quality of the tilework has declined from the Timurid period; although the patterns are as impressive as ever, the colors do not have the same vibrance as before, there is an over-insistence of yellow, and the use of larger tile pieces results in coarser designs.

Yalangtush's second building, the Tila-Kari (gold-bearing) *madrasa* (1646–60) (Fig. 11), framed a third side of Registan. This was in fact a multi-functional complex, its west side being occupied by a Friday mosque, necessary since the Bibi Khanum mosque, mentioned above, had become dilapidated

CENTRAL ASIA UNDER THE TIMURIDS AND THEIR SUCCESSORS 251

11 Tila-Kari Madrasa, Samarqand, 1646–60. Photo: Bernard O'Kane

12 *Khanqah, madrasa,* and mosque complex at the Char Bakr necropolis, Bukhara, 1559–69. Photo: Bernard O'Kane

13 Afaq Khvaja mausoleum, Kashgar, late eighteenth century. Photo: Bernard O'Kane

by this time. The portal is as grand as the other two monuments on the square, but apart from the lavishly decorated *qibla* dome chamber (Fig. 11) the interior is an anticlimax, with just one storey of cells around three sides of the courtyard. Its massive dome (recently rebuilt) on a high drum, flanked by low domed prayer halls, dominated the *qibla* side.

Built at the same time as this (1651–52) was the *madrasa* of the most powerful political figure of the time, 'Abd al-'Aziz Khan, at Bukhara, in this case also opposite a previous one of Ulugh Beg. This was also larger than its predecessor, and ambitious in its decorative program of tile mosaic on the entrance and courtyard facades, and painting in its two dome chambers. The latter included some realistic landscapes in a sinicising style reminiscent of contemporary blue and white ceramics; it has been suggested that the cultural links with Mughal India may have influenced this unusual choice.[22]

One building type that is rarely found in most of the Islamic world, but is common in the Indian subcontinent and in Khurasan and Central Asia, is the *namazgah*. Referred to as a *musalla* in the Arab world, and sometimes as an *'idgah*, it refers to a structure marking the *qibla* at an open prayer ground outside a town, that was large enough to accommodate all of the population at the times of the two major feasts. The form can be as simple as a wall with a *mihrab*, such as that of Bukhara in its original form (12th century). The slightly more elaborate form of a dome chamber flanked by two rooms is found at Nysa (10th–14th centuries), Turbat-i Jam (late fifteenth century), and Mashhad (16th century). Later examples increase the number of flanking bays (four: Kasan, 19th century; six: Samarqand, 17th century; eight: Tashkent, 19th century).

The buildings erected at the Char Bakr necropolis west of Bukhara provide an opportunity to examine a multifunctional complex built in a funerary setting (Fig. 12). Although the principal buildings, a *khanqah*, *madrasa*, and mosque, were apparently built between 1559–69 by the ruler of Bukhara, 'Abd Allah ibn Iskandar Sultan, the actual endowment deeds that survived were in the name of Khvaja Sa'd al-Din, a local shaikh whose ancestors' graves at the site were the focus of pilgrimage, and a person who was both a notable member of the *ulama*, a wealthy landowner, and one of the most prominent architectural patrons in Bukhara.[23] The *khanqah* is typical of those of the period, constructed as a large domed hall fronted by an *iwan*. The mosque at the site is a slightly smaller version of this, but the *madrasa* in the middle is quite atypical, consisting of one *iwan* flanked by two small chambers, the whole forming a U-shaped ensemble. It overlooked a number of platforms and small enclosures filled with graves.

Domed mausolea, either for secular or religious figures, were now almost completely abjured, although there are a few exceptions. One is the

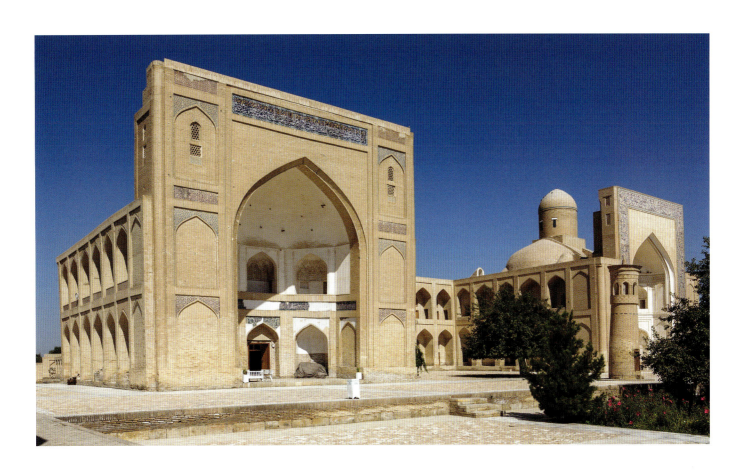

CENTRAL ASIA UNDER THE TIMURIDS AND THEIR SUCCESSORS 253

funerary mausoleum at Balkh erected by its ruler 'Abd al-Mu'min ibn 'Abd Allah Khan in 1596–7.[24] It was situated opposite the platform on which is located the grave of Khvaja Parsa, a fifteenth-century religious figure. It replaced an earlier fifteenth-century building at the site which was both a shrine (*mazar*) and a mausoleum. It is likely that 'Abd al-Mu'min intended the replacement for himself; beneath its spacious domed prayer hall is a crypt, and by honoring the saint at the same time he may have assuaged any lingering religious objections to building a mausoleum for himself. Another important exception is the Afaq Khvaja mausoleum at Kashgar (late 18th century), which in time became the nucleus of a shrine complex, accumulating many prayer halls and some rooms for students (Fig. 13). Existing mausolea, however, could be extensively renovated, for example that at Khiva of the fourteenth-century poet Pahlavan Mahmud, which also acquired shrine status and was provided with new tilework in the nineteenth century, perhaps because it had become a dynastic mausoleum in the meantime.[25]

A distinctive element of many Central Asian buildings is a wooden columned porch; this was used in both *khanqah*s (Zayn al-Din, Bukhara, 16th century)[26] and mosques (Buland, Bukhara, 16th century), and could also be found on the outside of a wooden columned hypostyle hall (Kokand, 1815). If the interior also had a wooden ceiling (e.g., the early twentieth-century Bala Hauz mosque at Bukhara), then painted wood rather than tilework became dominant in the decorative repertory. Another example of the wooden columned hypostyle hall is found at the 'Atiqa (or 'Idgah) mosque at Kashgar. Exact information regarding the chronology of its many different elements is unfortunately lacking; the main prayer hall is hardly earlier that the nineteenth century. It also includes a quadripartite garden court, two sides of which have cells that could have been used by students. Its monumental entrance consists of an *iwan* flanked by two minarets, and its northwest exterior wall is lined with booths, forming a bazar, all forming an elegant demonstration of the flexibility of the Central Asia mosque plan.

14 Amin Mosque, Turfan, 1777.
Photo: Bernard O'Kane

This is also demonstrated by one of its most famous examples, that of the Amin mosque at Turfan (Fig. 14). Although built in 1777, supposedly to commemorate the ruler Amin Khvaja by his son Hakim Sulayman,[27] this has elements that are most unlike other mosques. It is surprising to build a congregational mosque 2 kms outside of the city. It contains no epigraphy. From the outside it looks more like a fortified caravanserai, a role hardly mitigated by the enormous tower at one corner, which also seems more suited to a military role than the call to prayer. Subtract the hypostyle covered central courtyard, and the division of the surrounding spaces on three sides into small chambers is that of a caravanserai.[28] In fact viewed from above one can see that there was originally a parapet above the walls of the courtyard, and that the central space supported by wooden columns is a later addition. Its later conversion into a prayer hall is more evidence of the flexibility of mosques, but it clearly was not designed to be one from the beginning.

BERNARD O'KANE is Professor of Islamic Art and Architecture at the American University in Cairo, where he has been teaching since 1980. He has also been a visiting professor at Harvard University and the University of California at Berkeley. He is the author of eleven books, among the most recent being *Mosques: the 100 Most Iconic Islamic Houses of Worship* (2019).

SUGGESTIONS FOR FURTHER READING

Badr, Jasmin and Mustafa Tupev, "The Khoja Zeinuddin Mosque in Bukhara," *Muqarnas* 29 (2012), 213–44.

Golombek, Lisa and Donald Wilber, *The Timurid Architecture of Iran and Turan* (Princeton: Princeton University Press, 1988).

McChesney, Robert, "Economic and Social Aspects of the Public Architecture of Bukhara in the 1560's and 1570s," *Islamic Art* 2 (1987), 217–42.

O'Kane, Bernard, *Timurid Architecture in Khurasan* (Costa Mesa: Mazda Publishers, 1987).

O'Kane, Bernard, "The Uzbek Architecture of Afghanistan," *Cahiers d'Asie Centrale* 8 (2000), 122–60

NOTES

[1] The Mughals in their own writings still referred to themselves as the Timurids.

[2] Bernard O'Kane, "The Development of Iranian *Cuerda Seca* Tiles and the Transfer of Tilework Technology," in *And Diverse Are Their Hues*, ed. Sheila Blair and Jonathan Bloom (Yale: Yale University Press, 2011), 174–203. The earliest Timurid work at the necropolis may be the mausoleum of 1361, sometimes attributed to Qutlugh Agha, one of Timur's wives.

[3] Unlike the situation with their contemporaries, the Mamluks, who incorporated *mihrab*s within almost all their mausoleums, and even specified in *waqf* documents that the mausoleum was a *masjid*, to encourage prayer there.

[4] Lisa Golombek and Donald Wilber, *The Timurid Architeture of Iran and Turan* (Princeton: Princeton University Press, 1988), cat. nos. 11, 21.

[5] Golombek and Wilber, *Timurid Architeture*, cat. no. 53.

[6] Sharaf al-Din 'Ali Yazdi, *Zafar Nama*, 2 vols, ed. Muhammad 'Abbasi (Tehran, 1336/1957), 2:16. He was presumably quoting from a *waqf* document (he includes the phrase for appurtenances and dependencies, *tavabi' va lavahiq*, that is characteristic of them), and he was also able to give the diameters of the principal rooms in cubits, indicating an even more intimate acquaintance with the building – perhaps from other personal documents. The fact that he was also a noted mathematician may have encouraged his interest in measurement: Mahdi Farhani Monfared, "Sharaf al-Din 'Ali Yazdi: Historian and Mathematician," *Iranian Studies* 41 (2008), 537–47.

[7] Thierry Zarcone, "Yasawiyya," *Encyclopaedia of Islam,* 2nd ed. 11:294. For a description of a visit to the shrine in the early 16th century by the historian Fazl Allah Khunji, see Michele Bernadini, "À propos de Fazlallah b. Ruzbehan Khonji Esfahani et du mausolée d'Ahmad Yasavi," *Cahiers d'Asie Centrale* 3–4 (1997), 281–96.

[8] Bernard O'Kane, "Bibi Khanom Mosque," *Encyclopaedia Iranica*, 4:197–8.

[9] Ruy Gonzalez de Clavijo, *Via y hazañas del gan Talorlan con la descripcion de las tierras de su imperio y señorio*, tr. Guy le Strange as *Clavijo, Embassy to Tamerlane 1403–1406* (London, 1928), 278–80.

[10] Michael Rogers, *The Making of the Past: The Spread of Islam* (Oxford: Oxford University Press, 1976), 21.

[11] Bernard O'Kane, *Timurid Architecture in Khurasan* (Costa Mesa: Mazda Publishers, 1987), cat. no. 2.

[12] Ibid., cat. no. 14.

[13] Ibid., cat. no. 9.

[14] A similar blurring of the roles of *madrasa*, mosque and *khanqah* is visible in 15th-century Mamluk Cairo.

[15] Ibid., 24–5. The domed mausoleum was the no longer extant Gunbad-i Chihil Gazi.

[16] Ibid., cat. no. 22.

[17] Ibid., figs. 14.6–7, 19.5–7.

[18] For a convenient historical summary see Robert D. McChesney, "Central Asia vi. In the 10th-12th/16th-18th Centuries," *Encyclopaedia Iranica*, 5:176–93.

[19] A monograph on Uzbek architecture is still awaited; the earlier sources in Russian are now partially out of date. Some convenient sources in English are Robert D. McChesney, "Economic and Social Aspects of the Public Architecture of Bukhara in the 1560s and 1570s," *Islamic Art* 2 (1987), 217–42; Bernard O'Kane, "The Uzbek Architecture of Afghanistan," *Cahiers d'Asie Centrale* 8 (2000), 122–60; Sergej Chmelnizkij, "The Shaybanids and the Khan Princedoms. Architecture," in *Islam: Art and Architecture*, ed. Markus Hattstein and Peter Delius (Cairo: American University in Cairo Press, 2007), 436–46.

[20] Maria Eva Subtelny, "Art and Politics in Early 16th century Central Asia," *Central Asiatic Journal* 27 (1983), 121–48.

[21] Golombek and Wilber, *Timurid Architecture*, 1:229.

[22] Yves Porter, "Le kitab-khana de 'Abd al-'Aziz Khan (1645–1680) et le mécénat de la peinture à Boukhara," *Cahiers d'Asie Centrale* 7 (1999), 130.

[23] Detailed in McChesney, "Economic and Social Aspects."

[24] O'Kane, "Uzbek Architecture," 130–47.

[25] Michael Rogers, "Nineteenth Century Tilework at Khiva," in *Islamic Art in the 19th Century: Tradition, Innovation and Eclecticism*, ed. Doris Behrens-Abouseif and Stephen Vernoit (Leiden: Brill, 2006), 363–85.

[26] Jasmin Badr and Mustafa Tupev, "The Khoja Zeinuddin Mosque in Bukhara," *Muqarnas* 29 (2012), 213–44.

[27] Liu Zhengyin, "Architecture. Part Three: The Eastern Region of Central Asia," in *History of Civilizations of Central Asia*. Volume v, *Development in Contrast: from the Sixteenth to the Mid-Nineteenth Century*, ed. Chahryar Adle and Irfan Habib (Paris, UNESCO Publications, 2003), 532.

[28] Or possibly a *madrasa*, although the defensive character argues more for a caravanserai that a *madrasa*. There is an earlier example of a caravanserai being converted to a *madrasa*, that of Nadir Divan Beg at Bukhara (1622).

Religious Architecture of Safavid Iran   FARSHID EMAMI

1 Shaykh Lutfullah Mosque, Isfahan, view of the dome and forecourt.
Photo: Courtesy of Daniel C. Waugh

The dome chamber of the Shaykh Lutfullah Mosque, built in Isfahan between around 1595 and 1619, is one of the most mesmerizing religious spaces that exists today in Iran. Upon entering the prayer hall – a domed cube covered with calligraphic, geometric, and vegetal decoration – the visitor's eyes are drawn upward to the intricate scheme on the surface of the cupola (Fig. 2). Eight tiers of pointed-oval figures, fashioned in glazed mosaic tiles on a plain brick ground, gradually dwindle in size as they ascend toward a sunburst, forging a sense of spatial illusion that renders the dome loftier than it actually is. The dome rests upon a cylindrical drum rimmed by two inscription bands and pierced by sixteen windows alternating with tile-covered blind arches. The apertures are screened by scrolling branches whose interstices are open to allow daylight in. During the day, shafts of light filtered through these perforated screens traverse the hall, creating shimmering light patches that gently move on glazed tiles.

The Shaykh Lutfullah Mosque is the epitome of a series of stunning religious edifices that were sponsored by the rulers of the Safavid dynasty (1501–1722) in early modern Iran. With regard to architectural form and decorative idiom, Safavid religious buildings drew inspiration from the legacy of their predecessors, Timurids and Turkmens, polities that dominated Central Asia and Iran in the fifteenth century. The visual hallmarks of Safavid architecture – harmonious geometric schemes and glazed ceramic revetment – had reached a remarkable level of intricacy in Timurid-Turkmen monuments. But the architects and art practitioners of the Safavid era did not merely replicate these inherited aesthetic trends. Rather, they considerably refined and expanded established prototypes to create dazzling sanctuaries that were unprecedented in terms of spatial coherence

and visual effect. Furthermore, a dual religious identity – the proclamation of Twelver Shi'ism as the official imperial creed and the dynasty's origin in a Sufi order – imbued Safavid religious architecture with distinctive devotional feelings and symbols. The novelty of Safavid religious edifices, then, does not arise from their stylistic or structural traits. Instead, it issues from the manner in which deep-seated spatial forms and decorative patterns were harmonized with Shi'i and Sufi elements to engender spiritual experiences that resonated with the devout sensibilities of a new age. An overview of the landmarks of Safavid religious architecture reveals how these monuments enacted unique pious sentiments and affective encounters through a careful arrangement of visual and material emblems – icons, texts, and relics – in architectural space.

SAINTS AND SHRINES

Sufism was inextricably intertwined with Safavid religious identity. The first monarch of the dynasty, Shah Isma'il (r. 1501–24), was the hereditary spiritual leader (*pir*, *shaykh*) of the Safaviyya order, a Sufi brotherhood (*tariqa*) based in the city of Ardabil in northwest Iran. Founded by the eponymous Sufi Shaykh Safi al-Din Ishaq (d. 1335), the order gradually morphed into a militant, messianic movement in the second half of the fifteenth century. Under the leadership of Isma'il's father and grandfather, Haydar and Junayd, the Safaviyya order attracted a large following among the Turkmen pastoralist tribes of northwestern Iran and eastern Anatolia. The fervent support of these Turkic tribesmen, who became known as the Qizilbash (literally, "red-head" after the color of their headgears which they wore as a sign of their allegiance to the Safavid cause), was fundamental to the rise of the Safavid household to imperial power. During their rise to political and spiritual prominence, the Safavids also became staunch adherents of Twelver Shi'ism, which was upheld and propagated as the official sectarian creed of the state throughout the rule of the dynasty.

One of the earliest manifestations of the merger of Safavid ideological tenets and Shi'i piety with Timurid-Turkmen architectural heritage can be seen in the shrine of Harun-i Vilayat in Isfahan (Fig. 3), a rare surviving work of architecture from the reign of Shah Isma'il.[1] In the early sixteenth century, the shrine was reconstructed and augmented by the city's Qizilbash governor, Durmish Khan, and his deputy Mirza Shah Husayn, a local architect who later became a high-ranking statesman. The focus of the shrine is the burial chamber of a holy figure, who appears to have been revered as the "patron saint" of Isfahan but whose precise identity remains uncertain.[2] The sectarian appropriation of the shrine by the Safavids is reflected in its foundation inscription, which refers to the building as a *mashhad* (place of martyrdom) as well as a *dar al-vilayat* (abode of guardianship). The latter phrase appears to have had deliberate punning connotations; it likely referred to the *madrasa*, or religious seminary, which was dedicated to the study of the "guardianship" of Imam Ali (*vilayat* in this sense is a key tenet of Shi'ism), while also alluding to the literal meaning of the term (*vilayat* can also denote "district" or "dominion"). The co-option of the shrine as a specifically Shi'i pilgrimage site was likely facilitated by Isfahan's local Shi'i community, from whose lineage the architect-builder of the complex, Mirza Shah Husayn, descended.

The most impressive component of the Harun-i Vilayat shrine complex is its ornate portal, dated by inscription to 1513, which opens onto the courtyard of the *madrasa* (Fig. 3). Sheathed in glazed mosaic tiles, the portal consists of an *iwan* (open-air hall enclosed on three sides) framed by a rectangular

2 Shaykh Lutfullah Mosque, Isfahan, view of the prayer hall.
Photo: Daniel C. Waugh

3 Harun-i Vilayat shrine, Isfahan, view of the portal.
Photo: Daniel C. Waugh

4 Detail view of the portal of the Harun-i Vilayat shrine, showing the tile mosaic panel with a pair of peacocks.
Photo: Bernard O'Kane

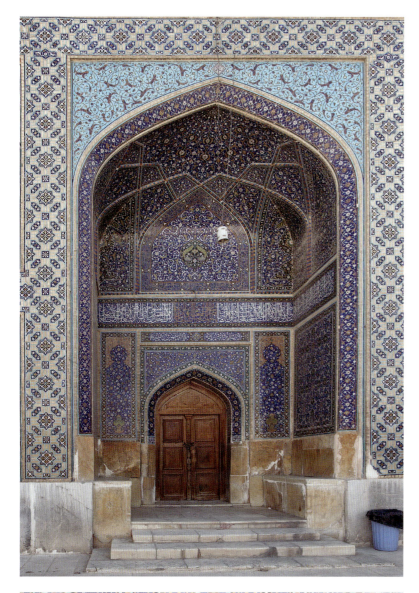

screen (*pishtaq*). Although not large scale, the portal originally overlooked an urban square known as the Maydan-i Harun-i Vilayat, which accentuated its visibility in the cityscape. The *iwan* is crowned by a semi-dome decorated with intersecting arches that spring from atop the band containing the foundation inscription. Executed in white *thuluth* script on an azure blue ground, the foundation text extolls Shah Isma'il as a descendant of Imam Ali (the first Shi'i imam) and a warrior on the frontiers of Islam (*ghazi*). In keeping with an established custom, the name and honorifics of Shah Isma'il are rendered in a golden color above the doorway. The visual affinity between the decorative patterns employed in the portal of the Harun-i Vilayat Shrine and those that can be found in contemporary illuminated manuscripts, vessels, and carpets suggests that the royal atelier (*kitabkhana*) was involved in the design process.[3]

The immediate prototype for the portal's form and decorative scheme can be found in a series of shrines built in the Isfahan region in the second half of the fifteenth century. A noteworthy precursor is an ornate portal at the Darb-i Imam shrine, completed in 1453 under the Turkmen ruler Jahanshah (r. c. 1438–67) of the Qaraquyunlu ("black sheep") confederation.[4] Yet several novel features distinguish the portal of the Harun-i Vilayat shrine from its predecessors, imbuing it with distinctive metaphoric and ideological associations. These new elements are particularly manifest in the tile panel installed in the *tympanum* (Fig. 4). Here, looming above the doorway, a pair of peacocks are depicted in a lobed medallion set amid a field of interlacing scrolls of split palmettes (*islimi*), lotuses (*nilufar*), and cloud bands (*abr*).[5] This scene is in turn framed by an Arabic inscription that contains invocations to the twelve Shi'i imams.

Bounded by holy names, this intricate tile mosaic scene was certainly conceived as a symbolic representation of heaven. The swirling white clouds (a motif of Chinese origin common in Persianate book arts), in particular, evoke a celestial image. Epigraphy complements this visual metaphor: the name and titles of Shah Isma'il, prominently displayed below the paired peacocks, is rendered in the same golden hue deployed for the names of the imams, visualizing the sanctity of the Safavid ruler and his alleged descent from the holy saints of Shi'ism. The shah's name and titles are indeed inscribed directly below the cartouche that contains

RELIGIOUS ARCHITECTURE OF SAFAVID IRAN 259

the epithet of the twelfth Imam (*sahib al-zaman*, "lord of the age"). Known as the Mahdi ("the rightly guided one"), the twelfth Imam is believed to have been in occultation since the ninth century and is expected to return as an eschatological savior at the end of time. This juxtaposition represents Isma'il as the harbinger of the awaited imam of Shi'ism, highlighting the Safavid monarch-saint as an intermediary between terrestrial and spiritual spheres. Integrated into the material fabric of the portal, these verbal and visual signs of the divine create a holy axis linking earth to paradise, with Shah Isma'il appearing at the junction of two realms. Rather than a mere functional entrance, the ornate portal of the Harun-i Vilayat shrine was conceived as a symbolic gate, a sacred locus invested with ideological messages.

The most intriguing feature of the portal's decoration is perhaps the use of figurative imagery – the peacocks – for which there are few precedents in the religious monuments of the pre-Safavid period. A bird native to South Asia, the peacock had long been a symbol of paradise and eternal life across cultures in west and south Asia, with precedents in Sasanian and Byzantine art.[6] In medieval Islamic texts, the peacock is described as a heavenly creature

5 Shrine of Shaykh Safi, Ardabil, view of the courtyard with the entrance *iwan* and dome of the Jannatsara seen in the background.
Photo: Daniel C. Waugh

6 Aerial view of the Tawhidkhana and Ali Qapu, Isfahan, with the Shaykh Lutfullah Mosque and the arcades of the Maydan-i Naqsh-i Jahan seen in the background.
Photo: Reza Noor Bakhtiar/Source: *Isfahan, muzeh-ye hamisheh zendeh* (Shahrdari-yi Isfahan, 1993).

who was complicit in seducing Adam and Eve, and hence was expelled from the garden of paradise along with the serpent. Yet the visual prominence of the peacock image on the portal of the Harun-i Vilayat shrine – and in many other works of Safavid art and architecture – suggests that it was likely seen as more than a generic paradisal emblem. Several sects that sprang from the Kurdish-speaking regions (most notably, Yazidis and Ahl-i haq) venerate the peacock as a sublime holy entity and since the Safavids arose from the same geography it is likely that the same belief was common among members of the Safaviyya order.[7] In the world of the early Safavids, the Imams, Shah Isma'il, and the peacock were all heavenly beings who mediated divine grace.

A similar blend of dynastic legitimacy and Shi'i religiosity informs the sixteenth-century additions to the most sacred sites for the Safavids: the ancestral shrine of Shaykh Safi al-Din in Ardabil. Formed around the convent (*khanqah*, *zawiya*) of Shaykh Safi, the core buildings of the ensemble – the cylindrical tomb of the shaykh and the adjacent Dar al-Huffaz – date from the fourteenth century. But it was in the first half of the sixteenth century, during the reign of Shah Isma'il's son and successor, Shah Tahmasp (r. 1524–76), that the shrine was expanded to create a uniform religious complex befitting the imperial status of the Safavid household.[8] These additions consisted of a monumental domed hall known as Jannatsara (abode of paradise) which faced the so-called Dar al-Hadith (hall for the study of Hadith) across a rectangular courtyard (Fig. 5). There are indications in the sources that the Jannatsara may originally have been intended as the mausoleum of Shah Isma'il, though the term may also refer to the Sufi sessions, which were similarly described as paradisal in contemporary sources.[9] In any event, the Jannatsara at the Ardabil shrine appears to have primarily been used for the performance of Sufi rituals while the Dar al-Hadith was dedicated to the scriptural study of Shi'ism.

THE MOSQUE AND THE SUFI SANCTUARY

The harmonious juxtaposition of Sufi and Shi'i modes of piety in an imperial complex can also be discerned in an axis of religious edifices built on the Maydan-i Naqsh-i Jahan (Image-of-the-World Square) in Isfahan. Surrounded by a two-storied arcade containing a bazaar, this massive square was laid out as the new civic center of Isfahan, which became the seat of Safavid throne under the fifth and mightiest ruler of the dynasty, Shah Abbas I (r. 1588–1629). Laid out in the 1590s as part of the plan for the development of Isfahan as the imperial capital, the *maydan*'s sacred axis consisted of three monuments: the Tawhidkhana (Hall of Unity), the Ali Qapu (Lofty Gate), and the Shaykh Lutfullah Mosque (Fig. 6).

The Tawhidkhana was the Sufi institution of this religious ensemble (Fig. 7). It sat in a rectangular

7 The Tawhidkhana, view from the Ali Qapu.
Photo: Daniel C. Waugh

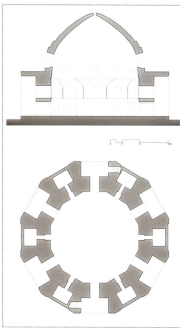

8 Plan and section of the Tawhidkhana.
Drawing: Jessie Li and Farshid Emami, after a survey by Cultural Heritage Organization, Isfahan

 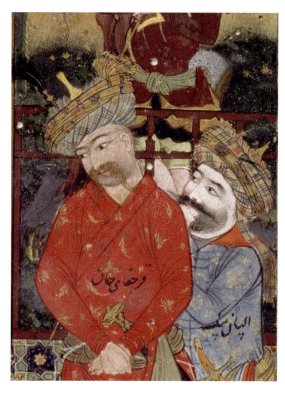

9 Portrait of a "royal gatekeeper" (Sufi resident of the Tawhidkhana), with the twelve-faceted Safavid *taj* (crown) sticking from the turban.
Source: Cornelis de Bruyn, *Reizen over Moskovie, door Persie en Indie: Verrykt met driehondert konstplaten* (Amsterdam: Gedrukt voor den auteur door Willem en David Goeree, 1711), 88

10 Detail from an early-seventeenth-century painting, depicting Safavid courtiers Alpan Beg (right) and Qarachaqay Khan (left) wearing the *taj*.
Photo: Walters Art Museum/Walters Art Museum, Baltimore, Acquired by Henry Walters (W691)

courtyard within the palace complex (*dawlatkhana*) and was accessed via an alleyway running behind the Ali Qapu – a five-storied tower with reception halls on its upper floors – that marked the principal entrance into the royal precincts. Passing through the arcaded alleyway that stretched beyond the vestibule of the Ali Qapu, one reached a recess that opened onto the entrance to the Tawhidkhana. In terms of architectural form, the Tawhidkhana consists of a twelve-sided domed hall nestled in a peripheral ring consisting of six arched *iwans* alternating with six rooms (Fig. 8). These rooms were probably used for spiritual seclusion and meditation (*chilla-nishini*). The courtyard was surrounded by residential cells for the dervishes, who also served as the shah's bodyguards and wardens of the palace complex (*qapuchi*).[10] The dodecagonal blueprint of the Tawhidkhana was likely a deliberate reference to the twelve imams. The shape of the building thus would have matched the *taj-i haydari* (crown of Haydar), the headgear worn by the Sufi disciples as well as the Qizilbash tribesmen and courtiers who had been initiated into the Safaviyya order.

Allegedly devised by Shah Isma'il's father, Shaykh Haydar, the *taj* consisted of a twelve-faceted red baton with a cone-shaped finial, around which the turban was wrapped (Fig. 9).[11]

In seventeenth-century Isfahan, the Tawhidkhana served as a communal prayer hall, where the ritual of *dhikr* (literally "remembrance," a form of Sufi prayer that involves repetition of a pious formulaic phrase) was conducted according to the custom of the Safaviyya order known as *halqa-yi tawhid* (circle of unity).[12] The ritual occurred weekly, on Thursday evenings, when the dervishes performed the *dhikr-i jali* (vocal invocation) by chanting the *tahlil* ("there is no god but God"). The participants of these prayer sessions were not, however, confined to the resident Sufis; the assemblies were also attended by state officials, amirs, and courtiers who had been "honored to wear the *taj*" and would send "a cash payment as votive offering (*nazr*)".[13] In the age of Shah Abbas, the courtiers and officials wearing the *taj* included both the Turkmen tribesmen and the *ghulam* (military slaves) as is evident in an early-seventeenth-century painting of a royal banquet, where a *ghulam* (Qarachaqay Khan) as well as a Turkmen courtier (Alpan Beg) are both depicted wearing the *taj* (Fig. 10). The weekly ritual performed at the Tawhidkhana reaffirmed the role of the Safavid shahs as spiritual guides of a Sufi order, enabling the ruling elite to showcase their allegiance to the dynasty.

The performance of the *dhikr-i jali* implies that the prayer sessions held at the Tawhidkhana likely took the form of an audition (*sama'*) accompanied by music and ritual dance. On Thursday evenings, the sound of hundreds of Sufis chanting a litany would have reverberated in the dome, spilling out into the *maydan*. The Safavid ritual of initiation was probably performed in the Tawhidkhana as well. It is no coincidence, then, that the building resembles the Jannatsara at the shrine of Shaykh Safi in Ardabil; similar rites and ceremonies were probably staged in both edifices.[14] Although located on the palace grounds, the Tawhidkhana was not an exclusively royal building; together with the Ali Qapu, it functioned as a sanctuary (*bast*) for those seeking asylum in the blessed abode of the shah.

Towering over the Tawhidkhana, the Ali Qapu was a multi-functional building that mediated between the palace complex and the *maydan*. The palace-gateway also marked a hallowed locus, for it contained a sacred threshold (likely a relic from a Shi'i shrine) on which nobody would step and "on certain occasions they kiss it as if it is sacred".[15] The dynastic legitimacy of Safavid rulers did not solely rest upon their status as hereditary spiritual guides of a Sufi order but also issued from their alleged descent from the seventh Shi'i imam (and ultimately Imam Ali and the Prophet Muhammad via his daughter Fatima). Through the rituals and holy materials that they contained and accommodated, the Tawhidkhana and the Ali Qapu represented the Safavid shahs as divinely sanctioned monarchs who emanated spiritual blessing (*baraka*) and provided protection from injustice.

Erected across from the Ali Qapu on the Maydan-i Naqsh-i Jahan, the Shaykh Lutfullah Mosque (Fig. 1) mirrored and complemented the sanctified realm formed by the Ali Qapu and Tawhidkhana. The foundation inscription refers to the building as a "blessed mosque" (*masjid al-mubarak*) and extolls its founder, Shah Abbas, as the reviver (*muhiy'*) and propagator (*muravvij*) of the creed (*madhab*) of his saintly ancestors.[16] The mosque was built in honor of the eponymous cleric Shaykh Lutfullah al-Maysi al-'Amili (d. c. 1622), a native of the region of 'Amil (in present-day Lebanon) who taught and led the congregational and Friday prayers there. Since the reign of Shah Isma'il, scores of Shi'i clerics had relocated from the Arabic-speaking provinces of the Ottoman empire to the Safavid lands, where they received lavish royal patronage and participated in the imperial project of indoctrinating the masses in the tenets of Shi'ism.[17] According to the chronicler Fazli Beg Khuzani, upon the foundation of the mosque the shah requested that Shaykh Lutfullah supervise the construction of the prayer halls (*shabistanat*), chambers (*ghurafat*), and other dependencies (*havali*) – which would be the residence of worshippers (*'ubbad*) and ascetics (*zuhhad*) – and perform Friday prayer and other obligatory duties (*fara'iz*) in the mosque after the its completion. The shah further decreed that an amount from the revenues of the royal estates be paid to Shaykh Lutfullah every year to cover the expenses of "his mosque."[18] Building work commenced in the mid-1590s and continued for more than two decades, through around 1619. The latter date appears in an inscription at the prayer niche (*mihrab*) of the mosque which contains the signature of the architect: "Work of the lowly poor, in need of God's mercy, Muhammad Riza son of Master Husayn architect from Isfahan, 1028 H (1618–19)".[19]

The Shaykh Lutfullah Mosque is commonly described as a royal "chapel-mosque" or a "private mosque for the royal household".[20] However, these designations hark back to the speculations of twentieth-century authors and are not borne out by any textual or epigraphic evidence. Instead, documentary sources – Fazli's above-mentioned chronicle and an Arabic epistle written by Shaykh Lutfullah – reveal that the mosque was intended to serve as a locus of congregational prayer and other normative pious practices.[21] The mosque was

11 Shaykh Lutfullah Mosque, Isfahan, plans of the first floor (bottom) and the basement (top).

Drawing: Enrico Milletti and Farshid Emami, after Mario Ferrante, "La Mosquee de Saih Lutfallah a Ispahan: relevés planimétrique," in Giuseppe Zander, ed., *Travaux de restauration de monuments historiques en Iran* (Rome: IsMEO, 1968), 441–64

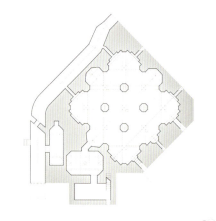

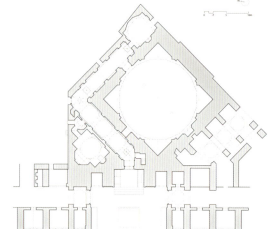

12 Old photograph of the Shaykh Lutfullah Mosque, Isfahan, showing the forecourt with fallen tiles.

Photo: Joseph Papazian, c. 1880–85/Source: Tehran, Gulistan Palace Photo Archive, Album 199, no. 14

in fact built adjacent to a now-vanished *madrasa*, and there are references to the "*madrasa* of Shaykh Lutfullah" in seventeenth-century sources.[22] Hence, the domed chamber of the Shaykh Lutfullah Mosque can be more accurately described as the worship hall of a religious-educational complex, signifying the imperial patronage of the clerical establishment. In his epistle, Shaykh Lutfullah quotes Shah Abbas as saying: "I want to build you a congregational mosque facing my abode, which can fit from a thousand to two thousand people, that Turkmens (*al-atrak*), slaves (*al-'abid*), and every other willing person including myself, may come to you".[23] This passage implies that the mosque's original congregation included the Safavid nobility and the *ghulam*; the state officials who attended the *dhikr* on Thursday evenings at the Tawhidkhana were to participate in the Friday service and its preceding sermon (*khutba*) delivered by Shaykh Lutfullah at noon on the following day.[24] Architectural space and rituals operated in tandem to create a variegated arena of devotion hosting both normative and Sufi forms of piety.

Lacking the key components of a traditional Friday mosque – a minaret or courtyard – the architectural form of the Shaykh Lutfullah Mosque might seem unusual for an Islamic house of worship intended to host daily congregational or Friday prayers. An overview of precedents indicates, however, that the mosque's architectural form derived from an established typology of multifunctional mosques common in the fourteenth and fifteenth centuries in Anatolia and Iran, such as the Green Mosque (*yesil camii*) in Ottoman Bursa (1419–24) and the Blue Mosque (*masjid-i kabud* or *muzaffariyya*) in Turkmen Tabriz (1465). The presence of several chambers and halls (arranged in three levels around a central domed sanctuary) render the Shaykh Lutfullah Mosque particularly akin to these precedents. An immediate prototype appears to have existed in the former Safavid capital of Qazvin. A recent study has shown that the Haydariyya Mosque, a single-dome sanctuary built in the early twelfth century, originally lay on the south side of the now-vanished Maydan-i Asb (Hippodrome), the

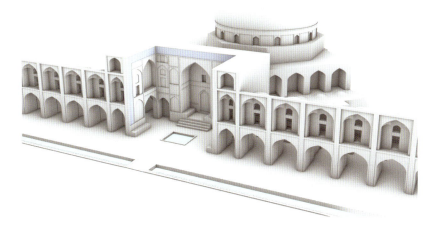

13 Reconstructed view of the Shaykh Lutfullah Mosque showing the original configuration of the forecourt with its now-vanished basin and inscription band (highlighted in dark blue).
Model: Jessie Li

royal square adjacent to the palace complex in Qazvin. Like the Shaykh Lutfullah Mosque, the Qazvin mosque too was provided with a U-shaped entrance block in Safavid times, defining a forecourt for the sanctuary that faced the entrance to the palace complex.[25]

While certainly informed by these prototypes, the Shaykh Lutfullah Mosque presents distinctive features in its architectural configuration. In terms of formal structure, the mosque consists of three major components: the entrance block that forms a setback in the arcaded façade of the Maydan-i Naqsh-i Jahan; the prayer hall, which is oriented toward the *qibla*; and a bent corridor with attendant rooms that leads from the portal to the domed chamber.[26] Two staircases alongside the corridor give access to an underground prayer hall beneath the domed chamber and an upper floor gallery (above the corridor) that culminates in a loggia overlooking the main prayer hall. Facing the *mihrab*, this elevated loggia – which is reminiscent of the one that exists in the Green Mosque – was probably intended for the presence of distinguished figures such as the shah or royal ladies.

Carved out of the building mass around the Maydan-i Naqsh-i Jahan, the U-shaped entrance block defines an elegant forecourt for the mosque. This setback was part of the coordinated urban design of the *maydan*; in its initial state (that is, before the construction of the pillared hall in the 1640s), the Ali Qapu too featured a recess that mirrored the one that exists in front of the Shaykh Lutfullah Mosque.[27] The mosque's plan in fact echoes the overall configuration of the Ali Qapu/Tawhidkhana ensemble: a rectangular recess leads via a corridor to a domed prayer hall in both ensembles. At the Shaykh Lutfullah Mosque, however, the domed sanctuary was dedicated to the performance of the canonical prayer and other normative forms of worship rather than Sufi rituals.

The Shaykh Lutfullah Mosque is also grander and far more lavishly ornamented than the Sufi chantry. Covered with interlaced vegetal scrolls – executed in light blue, white, and black tiles on a buff brick ground – the dome rises above the drum, which is decorated with the "beautiful names of God" (*asma' al-husna*) penned in a large checkerboard script legible from afar (Fig. 1). The use of such graceful arabesques on the dome is unprecedented and speaks to the distinct urban sensibility that characterized the religious architecture of Safavid Isfahan; the dazzling cupola of the Shaykh Lutfullah Mosque was designed as an urban landmark to adorn the *maydan*, while creating a visual counterpart for the Ali Qapu. It must be noted, though, that the exterior decoration of the mosque was heavily restored in the twentieth century, and in the process the forecourt has lost its original appearance (Fig. 12). Late nineteenth-century photographs indicate that most of the tiles had fallen by the 1880s, when the remaining pieces were removed, and the facade was whitewashed.[28] The tile revetments that now cover the surfaces of the forecourt were only installed between around 1930s and the late 1950s. Old photographs indicate that the forecourt originally featured a basin as well as a monumental inscription running on its three side walls. This now-lost three-dimensional inscription, which may have contained the endowed properties of the mosque, was clearly conceived as part and parcel of the physical fabric of the *maydan* (Fig. 13). With its dazzling vegetal and epigraphic ornamentation, the forecourt embellished the royal square while creating a prelude to the encounter with the inner sanctuary.

The most salient idiosyncrasy of the mosque is its bent corridor (Fig. 14). Running along two sides of the prayer hall, the hallway resolves the 45-degree shift in axis between the *maydan* and the *qibla*, enabling worshippers to enter the sanctuary

RELIGIOUS ARCHITECTURE OF SAFAVID IRAN 265

14 Shaykh Lutfullah Mosque, Isfahan, view of the corridor leading to the prayer hall.
Photo: Daniel C. Waugh

on the sacred axis of prayer facing the *mihrab*. This transitional space also creates physical and temporal distance between the square and the mosque, accentuating the passage from the profane urban arena to the sacred domain of prayer. Passing through the fairly dark, low-vaulted hallway, the domed chamber would appear as a holy locus detached from the mundane world that surrounds it.

The splendid prayer hall of the Shaykh Lutfullah Mosque is commonly described as the culmination of the centuries-long tradition of erecting domed cubes. The chamber is built atop an underground hall – borne out by four piers that divide the space into nine bays – which functioned as a *shabistan*, or "night-time hall," where "dervishes and others would pray and sleep at night".[29] Such enclosed halls intended for wintertime or nocturnal sojourns (also known as *bayt al-shata'* or *tabkhana*) had been a common element of mosque design in Iran and Anatolia since the fourteenth century. The main chamber features four corner squinches upon which the cylindrical drum of the single-shell dome rests. Mediating the gap between a square base and a circular dome through polygonal registers has a long pedigree in Iranian architecture. Here, though, the squinches of the zone of transition have been unified with the cubic base; rimmed by turquoise blue moldings, the eight arches rise from atop the dadoes to the base of the drum. The 135-degree angle between the eight arches (which form an octagon) are in turn bridged by smaller arches, creating a sixteen-sided polygon upon which the circular base of the drum rests. An immediate precursor of this manner of treating the zone of transition can be found in the Ali Mosque, completed in 1522 in the vicinity of the Harun Vilayat shrine in Isfahan. This early sixteenth-century mosque (which also features an underground prayer area beneath the domed hall) likely served as the model for Muhammad Riza b. Husayn, the Isfahani architect of the Shaykh Lutfullah Mosque.

The structural harmony of the domed sanctuary of the Shaykh Lutfullah Mosque is accentuated by its ornamental and epigraphic programs. Above a dado of overglaze-painted tile panels fashioned in the black-line (or *cuerda seca*, "dry cord") technique, the walls are sheathed with glazed mosaic tiles on a plain ground (Fig. 15). Monumental inscription bands, executed in white and azure blue mosaic tiles, are equally crucial in defining the mosque's visual character. The inscriptions are penned by calligraphers Ali Riza Abbasi and Baqir Banna in *thuluth*, a proportional cursive script. Following a long-established tradition in the writing of monumental *thuluth*, the vertical strokes of the letters *alif* and *lam* are rhythmically clustered together to strike an exuberant aesthetic effect. The calligraphers have also regularly elongated the tail of the letter *ya* in the reverse direction to create an overlapping rhythm of horizontal strokes and

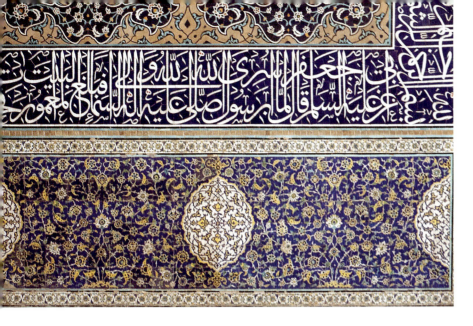

15 Detail view of the wall decoration of Shaykh Lutfullah Mosque, Isfahan, showing the polychrome glazed tiles on the dadoes topped by an inscription band in *thuluth* penned by Ali Riza Abbasi. Photo: Daniel C. Waugh.

balance the flow of vertical letters (Fig. 16). Although epigraphy is a ubiquitous element of Islamic religious spaces, in the Shaykh Lutfullah Mosque the inscriptions play a particularly central role. Exuding an unprecedented sense of order and harmony, the texts gracefully highlight structural forms.

The content and placement of the epigraphic bands are as carefully devised as their calligraphic appearance. The texts comprise quotations from the Quran and Hadith (recorded sayings of the Prophet Muhammad and the Shi'i imams), including the Sura al-Jumu'ah (Friday, Quran 62), which contains a mandate on the performance of Friday prayer, as well as Hadith by the Prophet Muhammad and Imam Sadiq (the sixth Shi'i imam, Ja'far al-Sadiq, d. 765) on the spiritual merits of praying at mosques. The core theme of the inscriptional program is the abundant blessing that the faithful could receive from visiting mosques for prayer. The inscribed texts also include two devotional poems composed by Shaykh Lutfullah and his contemporary cleric Shaykh Baha'i (Baha' al-Din al-'Amili, d. 1621), who served as Isfahan's chief religious authority (*shaykh al-Islam*). Inscribed on the facing bays that flank the *qibla* axis, these Arabic poems are the only texts signed by Baqir Banna (Fig. 16). Though composed in different meters and rhymes, these devout poems echo each other in overall thematic structure: in an impassioned tone, they invoke the "fourteen immaculate ones" (the Prophet Muhammad, his daughter Fatima, and the twelve imams), seeking God's mercy – through the intersession of these saints – for Baha'i and Lutfullah on the day of resurrection (both clerics are personally named in their respective poems).[30] The prayer composed by Shaykh Lutfullah mentions the name of Baqir Banna in the last verse, suggesting that the cleric and calligrapher (who was likely a building professional as his epithet *banna* suggests) closely collaborated in devising the epigraphic program.

16 Interior view of the Shaykh Lutfullah Mosque, showing the bay inscribed with an Arabic versified prayer composed by Shaykh Baha'i. Photo: Daniel C. Waugh.

RELIGIOUS ARCHITECTURE OF SAFAVID IRAN 267

By naming the holy saints and sites of Twelver Shi'ism, this pair of versified prayers grant a Shi'i character on the Shaykh Lutfullah Mosque, a feat that would have been impossible by solely drawing on the Quran, which does not contain any direct reference to the twelve imams. Like the Quranic passages, these versified supplications were not just visual ornamentation; they also had a sonic resonance and would have been recited in the mosque during vigils and prayers. Yet through their aural and visual presence, the poems do not merely spell out the mosque's sectarian orientation; they articulate the core devotional tenor of the sanctuary, revealing the spiritual associations of its architectural form and ornamental program. In particular, the emphasis on the themes of repentance and salvation confers an eschatological character to the mosque, for the ultimate intercession of the Prophet and his saintly family on behalf of the faithful will occur on the Judgment Day.

It is in light of the themes conveyed by epigraphy that the meaning of the ceiling's decorative pattern may be interpreted. Centered on a sunburst at the dome's apex, the scheme can be read as radiating rays of light, signifying the effusion of divine grace (*fayz*). But this unusual design appears to represent more than a mere conventional image of the cosmos; the ascending flame-shaped medallions can also be interpreted in mystical terms as human souls rising through celestial spheres toward the divine. The pointed-oval shape is a multivalent ancient symbol that was commonly deployed as an aureole in Christian art and was associated with light in Islamic art as well.[31] In pre-Safavid Islamic architecture, the pattern was frequently used in perforated screens installed atop doorways. Shaykh Baha'i, whose devotional poem is inscribed on the wall of the mosque, composed Persian and Arabic verse with mystical undertones and penned an epistle on the Sufi concept of the "unity of existence" (*vahdat-i vujud*), which posits that all essences are

17 View of the Shah Mosque on the south side of the Maydan-i Naqsh-i Jahan, Isfahan.
Photo: Daniel C. Waugh

divine.³² Yet the message of the dome's design was not merely metaphoric, since the scheme also resembles the pattern on the feathers of the peacock, the angelic bird of paradise, an effect accentuated by the reflection of light on the tiles. Contemporary viewers were likely able to read these multivalent symbolic and mimetic forms that were ubiquitous in the religious architecture of Safavid Iran.

THE IMPERIAL FRIDAY MOSQUE

The Shaykh Lutfullah Mosque is a singular masterpiece of Safavid architecture, unparalleled in the intricacy of its design and ornamentation. The most spectacular monument of Safavid religious architecture is, however, the Shah Mosque (*masjid-i shah*, known as *masjid-i imam* since the 1979 Revolution in Iran). Laid out in 1611 on the south side of the Maydan-i Naqsh-i Jahan (Fig. 17), this enormous congregational mosque was founded at the time when the Safavid empire had reached a greater level

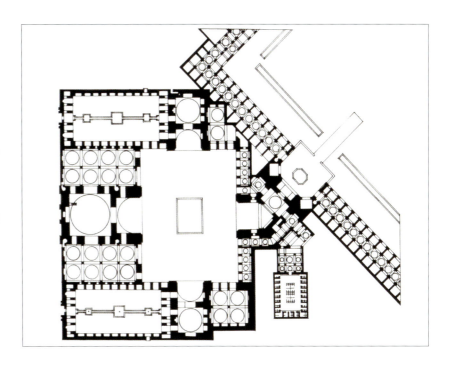

18 Plan of the Shah Mosque, Isfahan.
Drawing: Keith Turner after Henri Stierlin, courtesy of MIT Libraries, Aga Khan Documentation Center

19 View of the courtyard of the Shah Mosque.
Photo: Daniel C. Waugh

RELIGIOUS ARCHITECTURE OF SAFAVID IRAN 269

20 Mosaic tile panel on the portal of the Shah Mosque, showing confronted peacocks flanking a vase.
Photo: Farshid Emami

of material prosperity and territorial expansion. With regard to formal typology, the Shah Mosque belongs to a genealogy of four-*iwan* mosques that first emerged in the eleventh century and flourished as the principal model for imperial congregational mosques in Iran and Central Asia during the Ilkhanid and Timurid periods. At the heart of the monument lies a courtyard, which is dominated by four *iwan*s at the center of each side (Fig. 18). Flanked by minarets, the *iwan* on the *qibla* side is grander than the other three and precedes a massive double-shell dome in

front of the *mihrab*. Sheathed in glazed blue tiles, the courtyard is surrounded by arched recesses on the upper floor (Fig. 19). But only on the northwestern side do these recesses front chambers; on the other sides the arched recesses simply form a gallery. But this does not mean that the upper floor gallery was merely ornamental. Likely, these loggias were occupied by women during religious ceremonies and sermons. Several sixteenth-century Safavid manuscript paintings depict women in the upper-floor galleries of mosques.

As with the Shaykh Lutfullah Mosque, the Shah Mosque resolves the shift in axis between the Maydan-i Naqsh-i Jahan and the *qibla* axis through an elaborate transitional zone. From the square, one would first enter a recessed forecourt dominated by a lofty entrance portal crowned by a semi-dome filled with *muqarnas* tiers and flanked by two minarets. Like the Harun-i Vilayat shrine, the portal of the Shah Mosque is decorated with the image of confronted peacocks (Fig. 20), which are joined by a host of other heavenly birds in the adjacent tile panels. Beyond the doorway lies a vestibule on the axis of the *maydan*, whence one could view the *qibla* dome and *iwan* (Fig. 21). To reach the courtyard, however, one should pass through either of the two corridors that branch off from the sides of the vestibule. It is at the end of these two passages that the luminous courtyard reappears to the visitor.[33]

Built on a grand scale, the Shah Mosque was explicitly designated as a congregational mosque (*jami'*) for the performance of Friday prayer in its inscriptions and in Safavid official sources. The full-fledged espousal of Friday prayer (which had been deemed impermissible during the occultation of the twelfth imam in the traditional clerical discourse) does not mean, however, that the new congregational mosque was conceived as an ecumenical sanctuary. Popularly known as the mosque of the "Imam of the Age" (*sahib al-zaman*), the mosque was consecrated to the twelfth Imam and was inscribed with texts, drawn from the Hadith collections, which proclaimed particularly Shi'i tenets of faith.[34] Further, the relics of the Imams, including a blood-stained shirt attributed to Imam Husayn (the grandson of the Prophet Muhammad and the third Imam) were reportedly kept in a closet above the *mihrab* of the mosque.[35] The incorporation of these relics in the most sacred area of the mosque granted a sectarian identity to the sanctuary. Although housed in a fairly small closet, the relics must have had an affective presence for the worshippers by recalling the most tragic event for Shi'i Muslims: the martyrdom of Imam Husayn at the battle of Karbala in 680.

At first glance, the Shah Mosque might appear as a mere reiteration of Timurid architectural trends. Yet it held a very different meaning for contemporary worshippers: the mosque's consecration to the twelfth imam – along with the heavenly birds, holy relics, and sectarian texts –

21 View of the southwest (*qibla*) *iwan* of the Shah Mosque, Isfahan.
Photo: Daniel C. Waugh

exerted a tremendous impact on the contemporary perception and experience of the monument. Equally crucial in imparting a distinctive character on the Shah Mosque was its visual appearance as a civic landmark and its urban configuration: as in the Shaykh Lutfullah Mosque, the elaborate liminal zone of the Shah Mosque dramatized the encounter with the mosques' inner sanctuary and augmented its sense of sanctity.

To gain a nuanced understanding of the character of Safavid religious monuments, then, requires a shift of focus from stylistic and technical aspects to the perception and experience of the monuments. Religious edifices are not static statements about faith. Rather, they acquire sociocultural meanings and spiritual associations by those who worship in them and interact with them. Seen in this light, the harmonious integration of a multitude of pious rituals and material sacred emblems were crucial to bestowing a distinct character on Safavid religious architecture.

FARSHID EMAMI (PhD Harvard University, 2017) is Assistant Professor in the Department of Art History at Rice University. He specializes in the art and architecture of early modern Islamic empires, with a focus on Safavid Iran. His book manuscript offers a new narrative of architecture and urbanism in seventeenth-century Isfahan, the Safavid capital, through the analytical lens of urban experience. Besides articles on Safavid art and architecture, he has written on topics such as lithography in nineteenth-century Iran and modernist architecture and urbanism in the Middle East.

SUGGESTIONS FOR FURTHER READING

Canby, Sheila R., ed. *Shah 'Abbas: The Remaking of Iran* (London: British Museum Press, 1999).

Emami, Farshid. "Inviolable Thresholds, Blessed Palaces, and Holy Friday Mosques: The Sacred Topography of Safavid Isfahan," in *The Friday Mosque in the City: Liminality, Ritual, and Politics*, eds. A. Hilâl Ugurlu and Suzan Yalman (Bristol: Intellect, 2020), 159–95.

Hillenbrand, Robert. "Safavid Architecture," in *Cambridge History of Iran*, vol. 6, eds. Peter Jackson and Lawrence Lockhart (Cambridge: Cambridge University Press, 1986), 759–842.

Rizvi, Kishwar. *The Safavid Dynastic Shrine: Architecture, Religion and Power in Early Modern Iran* (London: I. B. Tauris, 2011).

Stierlin, Henri. *Ispahan, image du paradis* (Genève: Sigma, 1976).

NOTES

[1] See Robert Hillenbrand, "Safavid Architecture," in *Cambridge History of Iran*, vol. 6, eds. Peter Jackson and Lawrence Lockhart (Cambridge: Cambridge University Press, 1986), 762–63; and Sussan Babaie, "Building on the Past: The Shaping of Safavid Architecture, 1501–76," in *Hunt for Paradise: Court Arts of Safavid Iran, 1501–76*, eds. Jon Thompson and Sheila Canby (London: Rizzoli, 2003), 27–47 (esp. 32–35).

[2] The phrase Harun-i Vilayat literally means "guardian of the realm," though later sources describe Harun, the biblical "Aaron," as the name of the descendent of the Shi'i imams interred in the tomb.

[3] Walter Denny, "The Anhalt Medallion Carpet," in *Masterpieces from the Department of Islamic Art in the Metropolitan Museum of Art*, ed. Maryam D. Ekhtiar et al. (New York: Metropolitan Museum of Art, 2011), 257–58; Sheila R. Canby, *The Golden Age of Persian Art, 1501–1722* (New York: Abrams, 2000), 26–28.

[4] The portal was built during the governorship of Jahanshah's son, Muhammadi, in Isfahan (c. 1451–67). See Lutfullah Hunarfar, *Ganjina-yi asar-i tarikhi-yi Isfahan* (Isfahan: Saqafi, 1965), 343. Other precedents include the portal of the Khanqah and Madrasa of Shaykh Abu'l Qasim Nasrabadi (1450–52).

[5] For the ornamental nomenclature in Safavid art, see Yves Porter, "From the 'Theory of the Two Qalams' to the 'Seven Principles of Painting': Theory, Terminology, and Practice in Persian Classical Painting," *Muqarnas* 17 (2000), 109–18. For early Safavid art, Jon Thompson and Sheila R. Canby eds., *Hunt for Paradise*.

[6] On the peacock as a symbol of paradise, see Abbas Daneshvari, "A Preliminary Study of the Iconography of the Peacock in Medieval Islam," in *The Art of the Saljuqs in Iran and Anatolia: Proceedings of a Symposium Held in Edinburgh in 1982*, ed. Robert Hillenbrand (Costa Mesa: Mazda, 1994), 192–200.

[7] Martin van Bruinessen, "The Peacock in Sufi Cosmology and Popular Religion: Connections between Indonesia, South India, and the Middle East," *Epistemé* 15.2 (2020), 177–219.

[8] On the shrine of Shaykh Safi, see Kishwar Rizvi, *The Safavid Dynastic Shrine: Architecture, Religion and Power in Early Modern Iran* (London: I. B. Tauris, 2011).

[9] Sheila Blair, *Text and Image in Medieval Persian Art* (Edinburgh: Edinburgh University Press, 2014), 250–53.

[10] Willem Floor, "The Khalifeh al-kholafa of the Safavid Sufi Order," *Zeitschrift der Deutschen Morgenländischen Gesellschaft* 153.1 (2003), 75–77 (51–86).

[11] Barbara Schmitz, "On a Special Hat Introduced During the Reign of Shah 'Abbās the Great." *Iran: Journal of Persian Studies* 22 (1984), 103–12.

[12] For the reference to *halqa-yi tawhid*, see Eskandar Beg Monshi, *History of Shah 'Abbas the Great = Tārīk̲-e 'Ālamārā-ye 'Abbāsī*, trans. Roger M. Savory, 3 vols. (Boulder: Westview Press, 1978–86), 1:463.

[13] Vladimir Minorsky, trans., *Tadhkirat al-Muluk: A Manual of Safavid Administration (circa 1137/1725)* (London: 'E. J. W. Gibb memorial', Luzac & co., 1943), 33, 55.

[14] Rizvi, *Safavid Dynastic Shrine*, 130.

[15] Pietro della Valle, *Viaggi di Pietro della Valle, il Pellegrino*, ed. G. Gancia, 2 vols. (Brighton, England, 1843), 1:458–59.

[16] Hunarfar, *Ganjina*, 402.

[17] See Rula Jurdi Abisaab, *Converting Persia: Religion and Power in the Safavid Empire* (London: I.B. Tauris, 2004).

[18] Fazli b. Zayn al-Abidin Khuzani Isfahani, *A Chronicle of the Reign of Shah 'Abbas,* ed. Kioumars Ghereghlou (Cambridge, UK: Gibb Memorial Trust, 2015), 146 and 617–18; Charles Melville, "New Light on Shah 'Abbas and the Construction of Isfahan," *Muqarnas* 33 (2016), 155–76, esp. 162–63.

[19] Hunarfar, *Ganjina*, 402.

[20] Sussan Babaie, "Sacred Sites of Kingship: the Maydan and Mapping the Spatial-spiritual Vision of the Empire in Safavid Iran," in *Persian Kingship and Architecture: Strategies of Power in Iran from the Achaemenids to the Pahlavis*, ed. Sussan Babaie and Talinn Grigor (London: I.B. Tauris, 2015), 187 (175–218).

21. Shaykh Luftallah al-Maysi, "Risalat al-I'tikafiya," in *Miras-i Islami-yi Iran*, ed. Rasool Ja'fariyan (Qum: Kitabkhana-yi Ayat Allah Mar'ashi Najafi, 1994), 316–37.

22. Muhammad Tahir Nasrabadi, *Tazkira-yi Nasrabadi: Tazkirat al-shu'ara*, ed. Mohsen Naji Nasrabadi, 2 vols. (Tehran: Asatir, 1378/1999), 1:223.

23. Shaykh Luftallah al-Maysi, "Risalat al-I'tikafiya," 336. Translated in Abisaab, *Converting Persia*, 84.

24. The mosque reportedly contained a portable wooden *minbar* (pulpit) and could accommodate a large congregation in its compound.

25. Hamidreza Jeyhani and Fatemeh Rajabi, "Maydan-i Asb-i Shahi: Jilaukhan-i daulatkhana-yi Safavi-yi Qazvin," *Pazhuhishha-yi Mi'mari-yi Islami* 22 (1398/2019), 43–66.

26. For an architectural survey of the mosque, see Mario Ferrante, "La Mosquée de Saih Lutfallah a Ispahan: relevés planimétrique," in Giuseppe Zander, ed., *Travaux de restauration de monuments historiques en Iran* (Rome: IsMEO, 1968), 441–64.

27. Eugenio Galdieri, *Esfahan, 'Ali Qapu: An Architectural Survey* (Rome: IsMEO, 1979).

28. Muhammad Mahdi b. Muhammad Riza al-Isfahani, *Niṣf-i jahan fi ta'rīf al-Isfahan*, ed. Manuchehr Sotudeh (Tehran: Amir Kabir, 1340/1961), 65–66.

29. Muhammad Husayn b. Khalaf-i Tabrizi, *Burhan-i qati'*, ed. Muhammad Mu'in (Tehran: n.p., 1951), s.v. "shabistan".

30. For the poems, see Hunarfar, *Ganjina*, 412–15.

31. Rostislava Todorova, "The Aureole and the Mandorla: Aspects of the Symbol of the Sacral from Ancient Cultures to Christianity," in *Transition from Late Paganism to Early Christianity in the Architecture and Art in the Balkans*, Studia academica šumenensia; vol. 3, ed. Ivo Topalilov and Biser Georgiev (Shumen: Shumen University Press, 2016), 199–223.

32. Shaykh Baha'i, *Kulliyat-i asar va ash'ar-i Shaykh Baha'i*, ed. Sa'id Nafisi (Tehran: Nashr-e Chakame, 1361/1982).

33. For more on the liminal zones of the Isfahan mosques, see Farshid Emami, "Inviolable Thresholds, Blessed Palaces, and Holy Friday Mosques: The Sacred Topography of Safavid Isfahan," in *The Friday Mosque in the City: Liminality, Ritual, and Politics*, eds. A. Hilâl Ugurlu and Suzan Yalman (Bristol: Intellect, 2020), 159–95.

34. For the inscriptions, see Hunarfar, *Ganjina*, 427–64. On the mosque's consecration to the twelfth Imam, see Engelbert Kaempfer, *Exotic Attractions in Persia, 1684–1688: Travels* & *Observations*, trans. Willem Floor & Colette Ouahes (Washington, D.C.: Mage, 2018), 141, 148; Adam Olearius, *The Voyages and Travels of the Ambassadors Sent by Frederick, Duke of Holstein*, trans. John Davies (London: printed for John Starkey, and Thomas Basset, 1699), 221.

35. Jean Chardin, *Voyages de Chevalier Chardin, en Perse et en autres lieux de l'Orient*, ed. L. Langlès, 10 vols. (Paris: Le Normant, Imprimeur-libraire, 1810–11), 7:349–50.

Islamic Architecture in Medieval Anatolia, 1150–1450

OYA PANCAROĞLU

1 Burmalı Minare Mosque, Amasya, Turkey, 1242–43. Photo: Cobija / Wikimedia Commons / CC BY-SA 4.0

The recession of Byzantine political and military power in Anatolia from the end of the eleventh century opened the way for a protracted process of emigration, displacement, and settlement with both local and regional demographic ramifications.[1] From among the various groups of newcomers to Anatolia – consisting mostly of Turkic Muslim populations who arrived especially in the wake of the Battle of Manzikert (1071) – there emerged and declined through the twelfth century new dynasties that vied for territory, power and prestige among themselves. Further tensions and conflicts arose from frictions with the Great Seljuk and Byzantine empires and from the tumultuous passage of the First and Third Crusades. The uncertainty of much of the twelfth century helps to explain the time lag of several decades between the formation of the first Turkic dynasties (including the Seljuks, Danishmendids, Mengujekids, and Saltukids) and the earliest identifiable examples of Islamic architecture in Anatolia. By the early thirteenth century, the local Seljuk state became the dominant power in Anatolia and attained a notable degree of economic ascendancy. New construction projects gained momentum in this context and continued remarkably unabated through the Mongol invasion of 1243, the dissolution of the Seljuk dynasty in the beginning of the fourteenth century, and the political divisions of the so-called Beylik ("principality") period which lasted until the final extension of Ottoman authority over Anatolia in the late fifteenth century. The period of 1150–1450 is thus defined by a continuously changing state of political divisions in Anatolia, bracketed between the periods of Byzantine and Ottoman imperial hegemony.[2] This medieval *longue durée* of political division was accompanied by ongoing social mobility and socio-religious diversity, which affected the nascence of Islamic architecture in the country.

Throughout the medieval period, a large proportion of Anatolia's urban and rural inhabitants consisted of native Christian populations – mostly Greek and Armenian – who had well established ritual practices and sites. The religious life of the new Muslim settlers have been often described in modern historiography with such terms as "eclectic," "syncretistic," or "heterodox." Though these labels are problematic in implying deviation from a presumed religious norm, they nonetheless communicate the absence of a homogeneous practice/manifestation of the Muslim faith in Anatolia, much like the lack of unity in the realm of politics. Adherence to Islam in medieval Anatolia came in various forms and layers – notably, though not exclusively, through the agency of numerous Sufi orders – and often incorporated concepts, traditions, and imagery which can be identified either as survivals of the ancient belief system of Turks or as the product of intimate contact with active Christian cults in the country.[3] By the late eleventh century, the wider Islamic world had also attained a significant degree of pluralism borne of difference – whether social, cultural or political – across a vast geography. The notion of religious difference in this period disclosed itself in multiple dimensions and channels including theological sectarianism, legalistic factionalism, and increasingly more organized and numerous forms of Sufi mysticism. When seen against this complex and often politicized wider panorama of faith and practice, it becomes apparent that the diverse courses of the Muslim faith in medieval Anatolia cannot be explained simply by a reductive interpretation of the nature or degree of

Islamization among the settlers who, furthermore, were far from constituting a single monolithic group. The new settlers comprised not only nomadic and sedentary Muslim Turkic peoples coming from such diverse directions as Iran, Syria, and the Caucasus but also immigrants of Iranian (especially eastern Iranian and Central Asian) and Arab ethnic identity. The religious, cultural, and intellectual background of these immigrants was therefore, by definition, considerably mixed.

The combination of social, political, and religious multiplicity in medieval Anatolia was a key factor in the development of Islamic religious architecture, which rested upon networks of community, patron, and craftsman. In a highly mutable and mobile society engaged with the challenges of settlement, these social networks provided a sense of cohesion and encouraged the development of socio-religious affiliations identified with one or more building types. Among such affiliations were numerous Sufi orders that comprised followers and supporters of mystical forms of devotion; scholars and students of curricular Islamic sciences who were associated with the institution of the *madrasa*; and a form of grassroots social organization whose members (known as *ahis*) pledged themselves to upholding the *futuwwa* – a code of ethical conduct combining mystical spirituality with the ideals of a productive professional life. Religious architecture in Anatolia developed largely in connection with these networks of affiliation and in relation to the changing sources of political authority.[4] Examination of architectural forms, inscriptions, decoration, patronage and, when available, endowment (*waqf*) deeds allows the reconstruction of the workings of such networks and the means by which the diversity of medieval Anatolia created its own brand of cohesive social, political, and religious structures.

MOSQUES

The idea that the mosque is the quintessential religious building in any Muslim community is seldom questioned. The obligation of Muslim men to congregate for Friday noon prayer and sermon is so central in most – though, it must be said, not all – traditional communities that the large congregational mosque (or "Friday mosque") is perceived as, or expected to be, the principal religious building of a Muslim community. Moreover, Islamization of a region is often assessed in material terms by reference to mosque architecture believed to represent the epitome of religious building activity in that community. Inasmuch as the basic importance of the mosque for most medieval Anatolian Muslim communities need not be disputed, it should also be noted that the mosque did not hold institutional monopoly for the communal exercise of piety. The testimony of Ibn Battuta who travelled extensively through the country in the 1330s – by which time the process of Islamization had been underway for over two centuries – is telling in this regard.[5] Ibn Battuta had much to say about Muslim religious life in Anatolia, which he experienced first-hand, but relatively little to say about mosques because most of the devotional activities to which he was invited were evidently localized elsewhere, in particular in the lodges of *ahis*. This does not mean that Muslim men of medieval Anatolia did not congregate in mosques on Fridays or in small neighborhood mosques; rather, it implies that the locus of religious activity was not solely centered on the mosque or the Friday congregation.

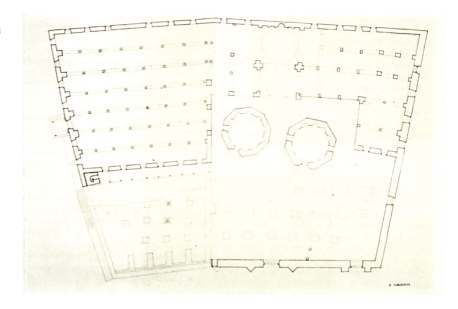

2 Alaeddin Mosque, Konya, Turkey, twelfth–thirteenth century, plan.
Source: XIII. *Vakıf Haftası Kitabı*, Ankara, 1996, 170

Some of the issues surrounding the mosque in medieval Anatolia can be illustrated by the case of Konya, the city that served as a capital of the Seljuk dynasty from the beginning of the twelfth century. The ancient mound in the center of the roughly circular walled city served as the Seljuk citadel. Within this once-walled citadel and in conspicuous proximity to the only surviving portion of the palace stands the Seljuk royal mosque known as the Alaeddin Mosque after its last major patron, sultan 'Ala al-Din Kayqubad I (r. 1220–37).[6] The irregular plan of the building is the result of multiple building phases, quite likely starting with the conversion of a Byzantine church in the early twelfth century and attaining the present irregular form of its large prayer hall in the early thirteenth century (Fig. 2). The prayer hall consists of two discrete parts: a domed *mihrab* area to the west in which early thirteenth-century Persianate tilework is showcased and a large hypostyle hall to the east comprising spoliated Byzantine columns (Fig. 3). The carved wooden *minbar* of the mosque is dated to the year of the accession of sultan Qılıch Arslan II (r. 1156–92) and proclaims, through its inscriptions, the grand self-image of the new ruler.[7] The two tomb towers in the courtyard – one from the reign of sultan Qılıch Arslan II and serving as the Seljuk dynastic mausoleum (discussed further below), the other left unfinished and possibly initiated by sultan 'Izz al-Din Kaykawus I (r. 1211–20) – constitute the earliest known case of a funerary structure within an Anatolian congregational mosque precinct which would become characteristic with the development of a continuous ritual and spatial association between tombs and mosques in Anatolia.[8]

The complex history and disparate appearance of the Alaeddin Mosque, the conspicuous use of Byzantine spolia (especially the columns of the hypostyle hall in the east as well as on both tombs and the exterior main façade of the courtyard), and the evidence of multiple building phases all point to at least the partial dependence of this mosque on earlier Byzantine structures. One Middle Byzantine church, dedicated to the local saint Amphilochios, was located just to the south of the mosque at the highest point of the mound. Destroyed in the early twentieth century, this church appears to have been used as a palace church for Christian members of the Seljuk ruling family (especially the wives and mothers of the sultans), a possibility that has also been suggested for the Byzantine chapel in the citadel of Alanya.[9] St. Amphilochios was mentioned by al-Harawi, the Syrian author of a Muslim pilgrimage guide who visited Konya around 1179–80, as a church (*kanisa*) believed to contain the tomb of Plato (its conversion to a mosque occurred only in the fourteenth century).[10] The structural and functional preservation of this highly visible church constituted a notable counterpoint to the metamorphosis of the royal mosque and its remarkably monumental dynastic tomb tower.

The interventions of the early thirteenth century resulted in the creation of a highly composite monument reflected both in the absence of regularity in the covered spaces and in the articulation of the exterior of the northern wall of the courtyard which became the mosque's main façade (Fig. 4). Furnished with new entrances and several inscriptions with consecutive claims of construction, this façade oriented towards the city reflects the rivalry between the sibling sultans, 'Izz al-Din Kaykawus I (r. 1211–20) and his successor, 'Ala al-Din Kayqubad I (r. 1220–37), each of whom exploited this façade for the projection of their political power and identity in the early decades of the thirteenth century.[11] The resulting disjointed nature of the architecture is indicative of the tentative and cumulative conceptualization of the royal mosque in Konya which evidently developed less as a discrete and integral building and more as an ongoing project shaped, on the one hand, by a perceived need for enlargement and, on the other hand, by the impulsive assertion of rival identities in the ruling house. This was a space that was tested and contested especially in view of its political signification as the royal mosque of the capital city. The transformations carried out in the early thirteenth century amounted to an unprecedented re-centering of the mosque's dynastic imprint within a religious framework designed to bolster and project an aura of sanctity.[12]

3 Alaeddin Mosque, Konya, Turkey, twelfth–thirteenth century, hypostyle hall.
Photo: Alexostrov / Wikimedia Commons / CC BY-SA 3.0

4 Alaeddin Mosque, Konya, north exterior façade.
Photo: Christian Mathis / Wikimedia Commons / CC BY-SA 3.0

Located within the citadel which was also home to the Seljuk palace, the Alaeddin Mosque in Konya can be considered as belonging to the family of citadel mosques among which are some of the earliest mosques constructed in Anatolia.[13] As a citadel mosque, however, the Alaeddin Mosque stands apart on account of its sizable courtyard, which is generally absent from most medieval Anatolian mosques. In Konya, this courtyard seems to have been related more to the presence of the Seljuk dynastic tomb rather than to the prayer hall, which clearly evolved in a piecemeal fashion. More typical of Anatolian citadel mosques of the late twelfth century is the Kale ("Citadel") Mosque of Divriği, perched at the zenith of a high citadel in the upper Euphrates valley region ruled in the twelfth and thirteenth centuries by a local branch of the Mengujekid dynasty (Fig. 5).[14] A rectangular stone building with a prominent portal opposite the *mihrab*, its interior consists of three aisles carried on two arcades. The patrons of such mosques probably did not impose any particular mosque morphology on the builders who were free to adapt the basic rectangular aisled building type – generally described as "basilical" – to the one fundamental exigency of a mosque, a prayer hall with *qibla* orientation. So-called basilical mosques of medieval Anatolia are primarily distinguished by the longitudinal morphology of the prayer hall and the absence of a courtyard.[15] The portal of the Kale Mosque, constructed in a decorative combination of stone and brick with a limited use of colored tiles, diverges from the regional character of the interior's stone architecture, and can be related most closely with designs prevalent at the same time in the greater Iranian world; this has been explained by the tentative reading of a signature on the portal announcing the name of a master builder from Maragha in Azerbaijan.[16]

The main building material for monumental architecture in Anatolia from the ancient periods has been stone. With the introduction of Islamic

5 Kale ("Citadel") Mosque, Divriği, Turkey, 1180–81.
Photo: Oya Pancaroğlu

6 Eşrefoğlu Mosque, Beyşehir, Turkey, 1296–99.
Photo: Oya Pancaroğlu

brick building styles and traditions from the east (especially Iraq, Iran, and Central Asia), instances of brick architecture (and colored tile decoration) also entered the medieval Anatolian Islamic repertoire as could be seen in a limited manner in the Kale Mosque of Divriği or, more extensively, in the İplikçi Mosque. A notable, though certainly not the earliest, example of brick architecture is the Great Mosque (Turkish: Ulu Cami) of Malatya within the old city walls that reflects the inspiration of mosque architecture developed under the Great Seljuks in Iran in the late eleventh and early twelfth centuries.[17] This is evident especially in the brick architecture of the dome in front of the *mihrab* with its tripartite squinches in the zone of transition combined with a large *iwan* opening to the compact courtyard, and the extensive use of glazed tiles and bricks. Although parts of the mosque have been significantly altered in subsequent periods, these features are certainly from its initial foundation which could be dated to 1247, if not to 1224 and the reign of sultan 'Ala al-Din Kayqubad I when the Seljuks were involved in the consolidation of their power in the east and against the Ayyubids.[18] Malatya, located at the eastern cusp of Seljuk Anatolia and with an extensive frontier history, had been incorporated into the Seljuk domains only in 1178. Whether the employment of a distinct Iranian style and technique here was intended as a deliberate statement – perhaps directed towards the Ayyubids of Syria, the main regional rivals of the Seljuks in the early thirteenth century – or carried a particular meaning in the local social context is not possible to know. It does, however, demonstrate that no single style or technique of mosque architecture dominated at this time in Anatolia. The extant examples underline the variety of styles available to patrons, either by way of local traditions and resources or through the agency of émigré builders and artisans who brought distinct architectural styles and techniques into Anatolia. Furthermore, these imported styles and techniques that, like the *muqarnas*, were equally applied to the architecture of *madrasa*s and tombs, were reincarnated in the medium of stone and were naturalized fairly swiftly and smoothly. In the case of Malatya, two artists' signatures point to the work of a father and son team from Malatya itself who were responsible for the tilework, revealing the availability of local resources in the city for the implementation of an Iranian architectural style in the first half of the thirteenth century.

The question of imported style and technique is also raised by a most distinct type of medieval Anatolian mosque that consists of an inner structure composed of wooden columns and a ceiling of wooden beams, enclosed by stone walls. Extant examples date from the end of the thirteenth century to the end of the fourteenth century and are located in and around towns such as Ankara, Beyşehir, Sivrihisar, Kastamonu, Konya, and Afyon.[19] The roots of this architecture appear to lie in Central Asia, which furnishes important examples, notably the Friday Mosque of Khiva that has carved wooden columns dating to the

eleventh, thirteenth, and fourteenth centuries, thereby demonstrating the early establishment and continuity of this tradition in the region of Khwarazm.[20] The connection between this Central Asian tradition and its manifestation in Anatolia from the thirteenth century cannot only be explained in terms of the geographic availability of high-quality timber in both regions. The sophistication of the construction technique visible especially in the complex superstructure composed of transverse beams, in the refined proportions of the parts to the whole and in the surviving carved and painted decoration points towards craftsmen possessing a particular technical know-how with an extensive accumulation of experience in this medium. Some of the most sophisticated examples of such mosques – the Eşrefoğlu Mosque in Beyşehir (1296–9) built by Suleyman Bey, the first ruler in the eponymous Eşrefoğlu *beylik* west of Konya (Fig. 6) and the Arslanhane Mosque in Ankara (1289–90) built by leading members of a local *ahi* organization – correspond to the twilight of Seljuk hegemony and the emergence of local *beylik*s when the swift fragmentation of political power provided renewed opportunities of patronage to specialized building craftsmen.[21] This is also evident from the fact that both of these mosques were the second mosque to be built in their respective cities, each foundation representing a new phase in local politics. The dissemination of wooden mosques with a genetic similarity between them from the thirteenth through the fourteenth century suggests that these mosques were constructed by itinerant craftsmen and their descendants whose work could be commissioned even by smaller settlements (including villages), thanks no doubt to the availability and affordability of timber in the mountainous zones of Anatolia. Smaller mosques constructed entirely of wood are found especially in the mountains of the Black Sea region where dendrochronological dating of the wood in at least two of them has suggested possible construction dates as early as the first decade of the thirteenth century.[22]

Mosque construction in medieval Anatolia thus developed in direct relation to the changing political and social circumstances as well as the sources of both local and imported traditions of building. Islamic architecture in medieval Anatolia is characterized by its highly receptive nature, for reasons that have to do as much with necessity as with choice. Perhaps more than any other type of building, mosques reflect the susceptibility and receptivity of the medieval Anatolian polities and their search for means of reinforcing their status. The disparate picture that arises from a survey of mosques furnishes important clues to the standing of these polities both within and beyond Anatolia. In the fourteenth century, Mamluk Egypt and Syria loomed large on the Anatolian horizon as the main regional force and left important traces in the architecture of the Beylik period. Syrian architects had been employed in Seljuk building projects in the early thirteenth century, at a time when Seljuk-Ayyubid rivalry had peaked notably under sultan 'Ala al-Din Kayqubad I.[23] From the last decades of the thirteenth century, Mamluk involvement in the politics of Seljuk decline and in the destabilization of Mongol and Armenian authority in eastern and southern Anatolia were followed by the importation of current Mamluk styles into Beylik architecture.[24]

The most notable cases come from the western *beylik*s of the Aegean region whose engagement of Mamluk architectural resources was realized through the maritime channels.[25] The İsa Bey Mosque, built in 1375 by 'Isa Bey (r. 1360–90) of the *beylik* of Aydın in Ayasuluk (Byzantine Hagios Theologos, modern Selçuk, near Ephesus), was signed by a Damascene architect who clearly sought to evoke the Umayyad Mosque of his hometown in a contemporary Mamluk guise (Fig. 7). The courtyard mosque first made an appearance in western Anatolia with the Great Mosque (Ulu Cami) of Manisa (1366–7), which reflects the plans of mid-fourteenth-century Mamluk mosques in Cairo and Damascus.[26] The prayer hall of the İsa Bey Mosque is a scaled-down version of its Umayyad prototype with two aisles parallel to the *qibla* wall punctuated by a central perpendicular nave with two domes. The courtyard façade of the prayer hall also recalls the Umayyad mosque in its articulation of this nave with a triple-arch entrance. Upon this

7 Isa Bey Mosque, Selçuk, Turkey, 1374–75.
Photo: Carlos Delgado / Wikimedia Commons / CC BY-SA 3.0

Umayyad design, the Damascene architect stamped the Mamluk brand especially with the two-tier fenestration around the courtyard and the bichrome interlacing stonework over the main elevated portal accessed by a double staircase that is characteristic of fourteenth-century portals from Syria and Egypt. The two-tier arrangement of windows framed with carved and two-color stonework was applied to mosques built in western Anatolia until the early fifteenth century, demonstrating an ongoing Mamluk inspiration for buildings undertaken by the Aegean *beylik*s of Menteşe, Aydın, and Saruhan as well as a number of early Ottoman mosques.

The Mamluk connection in the architecture of the Aegean *beylik*s can be seen as a natural extension of their overseas commercial and political ties established in the face of ongoing Ottoman-Karamanid tension and expansionism along their eastern flanks through most of the fourteenth century. The choice for Mamluk architecture can also be considered in the newly-Islamizing context of this part of Anatolia with its extensive remains of classical antiquity. Ayasuluk, the capital of the *beylik* of Aydın, was a stone's throw away from the ruins of Ephesus and the cult site of the Seven Sleepers' Cave. The İsa Bey Mosque was built in the neighborhood of the renowned Temple of Artemis (albeit destroyed and rebuilt as a church in the early Christian period) and at the foot of the Byzantine citadel, home to the sixth-century Church of St. John built by the emperor Justinian. Besides providing ready sources of building material that are attested by the reused columns and capitals of the mosque, these ancient structures in varying degrees of preservation in the fourteenth century undoubtedly created a close and charismatic horizon of antiquity in terms of their visual and cultic import. The importation of a Syrian architect for the contemporary recreation of one of Islam's most venerable ancient mosques against this particular backdrop was probably more than a matter of simple expediency and constituted a meaningful corollary to the signs of local antiquity and sanctity. The intentionality of the design of this mosque is also supported by the fact that its patron, 'Isa Bey, was highly renowned for his active patronage of science and literature, creating perhaps the most intellectually dynamic court in fourteenth-century Anatolia.[27]

TOMBS

Among the surviving Islamic buildings of medieval Anatolia, tombs built primarily for the ruling elite stand out in terms of their fine architecture and decoration as well as their sheer number in the

282 PANCAROĞLU

hundreds, wide distribution, and relationship to the human-made environment.[28] In addition to these, Anatolia's rural landscape is home to an even greater number of tombs of holy persons, which are known by the Turkish term *yatır*.[29] These are significant cult sites generally preserving their sacred qualities for the local populations. Although many of the *yatır*s would have been established in the medieval period (and some appear to have had a continuous history of sanctity going back to the period before Manzikert), dating and attribution are often impossible since most are simple structures and many have been rebuilt over time. Given this variety of tomb types, it is difficult to give a comprehensive overview to account for all of the permutations of form and style and the mostly uninvestigated issues of social and religious practice informing this architecture. If the mosques speak to the multiplicity and variability of medieval Anatolia's political context, the tombs further compound the pluralism of religious architecture in terms of function and meaning. As in the case of funerary architecture in other parts of the medieval Islamic world, beliefs concerning the hereafter, the socio-political obligation to represent and preserve memory and the appeal of pious visitation all played a role in the construction of tombs across the Anatolian landscape. What makes the Anatolian case especially interesting are the ways in which tombs lent distinct meanings to the newly emerging Islamic fabric of towns and the countryside alike. As with all types of religious buildings, tombs were built both as freestanding structures and as integral part of complexes.

Freestanding monumental tombs in Anatolia were built most often as polygonal structures with conical domes although other types – including cubical structures with hemispherical dome and cylindrical structures with conical domes – are also attested. The tower-like appearance of most tombs recall the earlier brick examples of Iran and Azerbaijan, but the prevalent use of stone in the Anatolian context and its attendant decorative elements also make the case for an architectural affiliation with the conical domes raised on high drums typical of Armenian and Georgian church architecture. An important difference is, of course, the fact the conical domes of Armenian and Georgian churches belong to the superstructure of their respective buildings, whereas the tombs are independent structures standing on ground level. A common practice was to situate freestanding tombs just at the boundary of settlements either in a pre-existing cemetery or in an area that would subsequently become a cemetery and/or a new settlement. Examples of these can be seen throughout Anatolia, including Konya where the spiritually and politically important figure of Mawlana Jalal al-Din Rumi, who died in 1274, was buried just beyond the eastern gate of the city. Other medieval tombs associated with holy men or the ruling elite dot the extramural landscapes of major cities such as Konya, Kayseri, and Sivas where they became the focus of visitation, engendering further building activity or burials in the vicinity. The case was similar in towns of moderate political importance such as the Mengujekid centers of

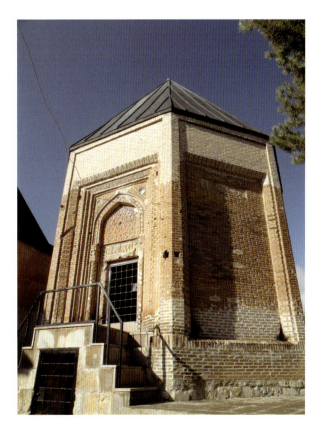

8 Sultan Melik Tomb, Kemah, Turkey, 1190s.
Photo: Oya Pancaroğlu

ISLAMIC ARCHITECTURE IN MEDIEVAL ANATOLIA 283

Divriği, and Kemah (Fig. 8), where the surviving late twelfth- and early thirteenth-century tombs punctuate the medieval urban outskirts in which they watched over the formation of extensive cemeteries in the subsequent centuries.[30]

Not all tombs, however, were built outside of the urban context. In Konya, the Alaeddin Royal Mosque in the citadel features two tombs in its courtyard.[31] Although the relationship of these two tombs to each other or to the puzzling building history of the mosque discussed above remains unresolved, it is seems clear that the construction of the earlier one was a deliberate projection of Seljuk dynastic identity at a decisive juncture. The visibility of this tomb from afar was ensured by its elevation (22.6 meters) and its conical dome once apparently clad entirely in blue tiles (Fig. 9). Its two-line foundation inscription, though undated, states that it was built during the reign of sultan Qılıch Arslan II who was responsible for the political ascendance of the Seljuks in the second half of the twelfth century, defeating the Byzantines in the Battle of Myriokephalon in 1176 and eliminating their Turkmen rivals in central Anatolia, the Danishmendid dynasty, in 1178. These victories are hinted in the inscription where Qılıch Arslan II is refered to as the "sultan of the lands of Rum and Syria" (*sultan bilad al-Rum wa al-Sham*).[32] Based on this, it is suggested that the tomb was built sometime after these two victories but before Qılıch Arslan II's death in 1192. The name of the same sultan is also inscribed on one of the eight cenotaphs in the interior. The other seven cenotaphs must belong to subsequent – though not necessarily consecutive – Seljuk sultans although there is no accurate information concerning the identity of royal interments after Qılıch Arslan II due to the damage and retiling of the cenotaphs. Two inscriptional friezes encircle the tomb around its cornice but both of them are severely damaged. The upper one was a tile frieze with the Throne Verse from the Quran written in white on a dark blue background while the lower frieze below, in stone, contained an inscription in Persian of which only a few words could be read.

Constructed of fine ashlar masonry with both original and spoliated decoration, the tomb is a decagonal structure on two levels. Its decagonal form, unique among the extant freestanding tombs of medieval Anatolia most of which are octagonal, may indicate a connection to northwestern Iran

9 Tomb of Qılıch Arslan, Konya, Turkey, before 1192.
Photo: Oya Pancaroğlu

where two decagonal tombs (Mu'mina Khatun in Nakhchevan dated 1186–7 and the Gunbad-i Qabud in Maragha dated 1196–7) were built in the last decades of the twelfth century. The upper level of the Konya tomb contains the royal tiled cenotaphs and is accessed from an arched entrance reached by a double staircase. Unlike most tombs that feature a *mihrab* in the interior for the proper *qibla* orientation of prayers by visitors, the interior of the tomb of Qılıch Arslan II is articulated by elongated niches on each of the nine sides. The lower level, serving as the crypt, is a common feature in Anatolian tombs and is furnished with its own entrance. Although there is, to date, no significant study on the procedures followed for interment in such tombs, it seems that burial of the deceased in the ground – the most common form of Muslim funerary practice – was not *de rigueur* in medieval Anatolia and that methods of embalming without burial were also practiced especially, but not exclusively, among elite members of society.[33] Accordingly, reports from Konya dating to the beginning of the twentieth century relate that just such embalmed bodies were present in the crypt of this tomb.[34] The late twelfth-century Mengujekid tomb in Kemah known by the name of Sultan Melik also contains in its crypt a preserved body that was the object of an annual rite of veneration until the early decades of the twentieth century and continued to be visited until relatively recently (Fig. 8).[35] A group of embalmed bodies said to belong to the Mongol elite of the late thirteenth century are today on view at the Amasya Museum; several of these were reported to have been brought from the tomb attached to the Burmalı Minare Mosque (Fig. 1) built during the reign of sultan Ghiyath al-Din Kaykhusraw II (r. 1237–47).[36]

A glimpse into the funerary rites and architectural processes involving embalming is provided by Ibn Battuta's eyewitness account from the western Anatolian city of Manisa, which he visited in the early 1330s when it was the capital of the *beylik* of Saruhan:

> [W]hen we arrived in this town we found [the ruler of Saruhan] at the tomb of his son, who had died some months earlier. He and the boy's mother spent the eve of the Eid and the following morning at his tomb. The boy had been embalmed and placed in a wooden coffin covered with tinned iron; it was suspended in an unroofed tower (*qubba*) so as to expel its odor after which the tower would be roofed, his coffin placed manifestly on the ground surface (*zahiran 'ala wajh al-ard*), and his clothes laid on it. I have seen this [practice] also with other princes.[37]

Although Ibn Battuta makes no mention of a crypt in this anecdote, his portrayal of visitation and the deferred completion of the dome suggest an established funerary custom to which the architecture, or at least its construction, was adapted. Moreover, his matter-of-fact reporting and mention of other cases indicate a fairly prevalent custom among the elite. Indeed, some fifty years after Ibn Battuta's report, Hacı Paşa (d. 1424), a renowned physician and judge (*qadi*) from Konya in the service of 'Isa Bey of the *beylik* of Aydın, included a section on the method of embalming in a medical compendium he completed in 1380.[38]

The practice of embalming probably carried particular significance that may be related at least

in part to the survival of pre-Islamic Turko-Mongol traditions in Anatolia.[39] A wide range of funerary customs are known to have been practiced among Altaic peoples, including the postponement of burial according to the seasons for which embalming would have been practiced for the elite, as well as the placing of the deceased in a coffin and suspending it from the top of a tree until such time as the bones could be collected and buried or, less frequently, incinerated. Embalming of some form was also practiced in Byzantine Anatolia, which is borne out both by textual evidence[40] and by the numerous discoveries of preserved bodies in Christian contexts especially in the region of Cappadocia.[41] One significant difference between the Byzantine Christian and the Turkic Muslim tradition in Anatolia is that generally the Christian bodies were laid to rest in fairly inaccessible places such as rock-hewn graves in Cappadocia whereas the Muslim bodies were placed into crypts with potentially accessible entrances.

The possible sources of inspiration for the practice among Turks in Anatolia is further complicated by the fact that, in the Caspian region of Iran, some of the earliest examples of freestanding tombs dating to the tenth and eleventh centuries built by the Persian Bavandid and Ziyarid dynasties – which lack evidence of burial in them – have been identified as part of a particular medieval conceptualization of Sasanian Iranian funerary customs probably involving the embalming of the deceased.[42] Moreover, the well-known post-Seljuk tombs in Azerbaijan, such as that of Mu'mina Khatun in Nakhchevan, were also built with crypts. In the present state of knowledge, it is not possible to relate every instance of a crypt with the practice of embalming or to know to what extent the crypts were made accessible. Yet, the frequent spatial articulation of the tomb structure on two accessible levels coupled with the sheer number of tombs built in the medieval period indicate a particular conceptualization of the funerary context that requires more study.

The visitation of tombs in Islamic societies from the medieval period onwards appears to have held a particularly special place in women's piety and worship. Equally significant in this regard are the tombs that were built in Anatolia for women of prominence. This is in keeping with the general trend of women's patronage of architecture in Anatolia, which is attributed to the status of women in the traditional framework of Turko-Mongol political customs, and to the role played by women in the particular context of Anatolia's political divisions in creating critical political alliances by means of marriage. The standing of women in the power structure can be sensed from both the impressive visibility of the architecture sponsored by them and from their deployment of great financial resources necessary to carry out major building projects.[43] Moreover, a certain degree of gender identity seems to have subsisted with buildings founded by women such that subsequent generations of women continued to invest in buildings founded by women. This is certainly the case, for example, with the hospital built in 1228–9 in Divriği by the Mengujekid princess Turan Malik for which additional endowments continued to be made especially by women well into the Ottoman period.[44]

An important example of a tomb built by an elite woman is that which is believed to belong to Mama Khatun in Tercan (a town midway between Erzincan and Erzurum). Mama Khatun, a daughter of the Saltukid ruler 'Izz al-Din Saltuk II (r.1132–68), emerged as the ruler of Erzincan and its surroundings around 1191 and was apparently unseated by a nephew around 1201 when she reportedly made an attempt to secure a marriage alliance between herself and the Ayyubids.[45] This suggests that she must have been fairly young and perhaps unmarried when she assumed power around 1191 or that her husband had died sometime before her attempt to find a suitable Ayyubid groom for herself. She appears to have been a significant figure in the fierce political playing field of the last decade of the twelfth century and probably even in the early thirteenth century after her "retirement" around 1201. Soon thereafter, the Seljuks annexed the Saltukid realms in 1202. Although not much information about Mama Khatun has come to light (besides her military engagements in eastern Anatolia in the 1190s), it is generally assumed that she retired (or was exiled) to Tercan where she apparently built a caravanserai, a bathhouse, a mosque, and a tomb sometime probably in the early decades of the thirteenth century. Of these structures, the tomb, the bathhouse, and the caravanserai have all been restored in varying degrees while the mosque has been entirely rebuilt.[46] The caravanserai, though much restored and without a surviving inscription, could be interpreted as a sign of Mama Khatun's

interest in exerting her influence on the traffic between Erzincan and Erzurum – a segment of the main east-west route connecting central Anatolia to Tabriz and beyond. This idea is also supported by a nearby bridge (now ruined), which is believed to be part of Mama Khatun's building project.[47] At the same time, the building project comprising pious, charitable, and commercial functions must have also allowed Mama Khatun to consolidate her finances in the face of Seljuk expansionism by means of a pious endowment.

Mama Khatun's tomb is composed of an octagonal chamber with unusual lobed sides built above a crypt and capped by a conical dome. Even more unusual is a circular enclosure wall surrounding the tomb with rectangular arched alcoves on its interior. The portal of the enclosure wall is highly decorated and inscribed with Quranic verses in Kufic script and with the name of the architect from the eastern town of Ahlat. Some of the alcoves contain tombstones, one of which is dated 1247; it can be assumed that the structure was completed before this date, although it is not possible to know whether the alcoves were originally intended as sites of burial. Despite the absence of an inscribed date or name, the association of these structures with Mama Khatun seems fairly secure. The combination of the tomb with an enclosure wall represents a particular approach to funerary architecture that may have functioned to reserve the space around the tomb proper as a sanctified zone. This may have been conceived to facilitate or encourage ritual visitation; such a function may also have necessitated the large courtyard of the Alaeddin Mosque in Konya containing two tombs.[48] A more mundane reason for the enclosure at Mama Khatun may have to do with a wish to shield the tomb and its visitors from the commercial traffic of the caravanserai situated just thirty meters away.

The possibility of a particular ritual function, however, cannot be entirely ruled out and it may be that other freestanding tombs of the twelfth or thirteenth centuries were also provided with some type of perimeter wall that has not survived. Another extant example of a medieval Anatolian tomb with an enclosure wall is found on the outskirts of Kayseri and is dated to 1339.[49] Known by its later name of Köşk Medrese ("Kiosk Madrasa"), the structure consists of a tomb chamber placed in the middle of a large outer enclosure of high walls, porticos on the three inner sides, and two rooms on two levels on either side of the entrance. The grand proportions and the spatial differentiation of the enclosure make the case for the provision of functions which probably had to do with the accommodation of visitors and their rituals at the site. A seventeenth-century Ottoman court record suggests the probability of the building being used as a dervish lodge, although whether this was the original intention remains unclear. The four rooms by the entrance could provide temporary shelter and provisions while the high walls of the enclosure indicate a defensive aspect that probably has to do with the rural location of the site. More intriguing when considered in the light of the tomb of Mama Khatun is the fact that, according to the inscription, this tomb was also built for a woman, in this case Suli Pasha, the wife of the Mongol emir Eretna.

Tombs thus reveal some of the ways in which women negotiated politics and piety simultaneously and the margins of maneuver that were available to them especially in times of instability. A case in point is the tomb known as Çifte Kümbet built on the outskirts of Kayseri in 1247–48 for sultan 'Ala al-Din Kayqubad I's Ayyubid wife who had been strangled to death in Ankara in the fierce struggle over dynastic succession upon the unexpected death of her husband in 1237 (Fig. 10).[50] At this time, her two sons were also killed, while her daughters moved into the security of their mother's Ayyubid background in Syria and Egypt as the Seljuk throne in Konya was claimed by their half-brother, Ghiyath al-Din Kaykhusraw II. The tomb in Kayseri was built a decade after these events, on the heels of sultan Ghiyath al-Din Kaykhusraw II's death in the winter of 1245–6, when the daughters returned to Anatolia, had their mother's remains transported from Ankara to Kayseri and, as stated in the foundation inscription, ordered the building of this tomb as her martyrium (*mashhad*). The inscription constitutes a righteous message, reinstating their mother's royal rank and personal virtues with reference to her Ayyubid lineage. The tomb, built as an octagonal tower above a crypt in fine ashlar masonry with a portal containing a *muqarnas* niche surrounded by low-relief geometric interlace, represents the best of Seljuk craftsmanship in the middle of the thirteenth century. The location of the tomb at a considerable distance from the urban limits of medieval Kayseri may have been intended as an alternative site for visitation, competing with but also distanced from the Huand Hatun complex of Mahpari Khatun, 'Ala al-Din Kayqubad I's more powerful wife and the mother of sultan Ghiyath al-Din Kaykhusraw II.

COMPLEXES WITH MULTIPLE FUNCTIONS

The social, political and religious aspects of tombs developed in tandem with a growing trend in the establishment of building complexes with multiple religious and social functions in medieval Anatolia. From the turn of the thirteenth century onwards, patrons of *madrasa*s, hospitals, or Sufi and *ahi* lodges frequently incorporated a tomb chamber into the buildings they sponsored, similar to examples from twelfth-century Syria such as the *madrasa* and tomb complex of Nur al-Din Zangi in Damascus. An even earlier example of a complex with a funerary element is the congregational

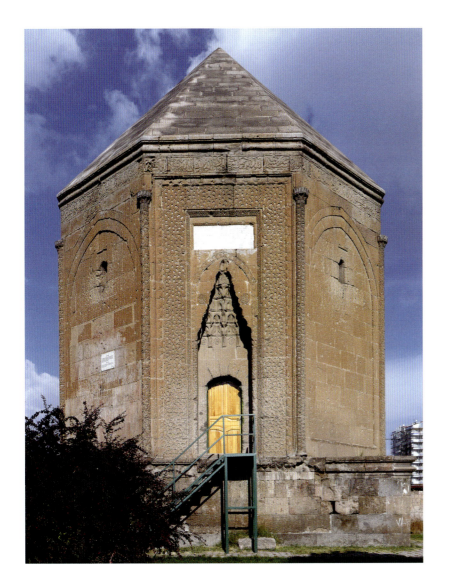

10 Çifte Kümbet Tomb, Kayseri, Turkey, 1247–48.
Photo: Peter J. Lu

mosque of Kayseri built by the Danishmendid ruler Malik Muhammad (r. 1135–42).[51] Adjacent to the *qibla* wall of the mosque was a *madrasa* – no longer extant – that contained the tomb of the founder who died in 1142.[52] This appears to be not only the earliest instance of a *madrasa* burial in Anatolia but also the first combination of a mosque and a *madrasa* into a complex.[53] Although an early thirteenth-century document mentions in passing a royal *madrasa* in the citadel of Konya,[54] no physical evidence for it has yet been found nor does the source clarify what, if any, relationship this *madrasa* had to the royal mosque.

From the middle of the thirteenth century onward, new congregational mosques in Anatolia were frequently built together with the tomb of the patron, a phenomenon that is not encountered to the same degree elsewhere in the medieval Islamic world. This may be related to the process of fragmentation and rivalry beginning with the Mongol invasion of 1243, which probably encouraged the new local rulers to cast newly built mosques as signs of political and personal power bolstered by the presence of their future tomb. A telling and early example of this phenomenon is the Burmalı Minare Mosque in Amasya built in 1242–43 by an amir named Farrukh and his brother Yusuf, titled as "treasurer" (Fig. 1).[55] This mosque, adhering to the basilical type, appears to have been the first one to be built in Amasya, evidently superseding the initial Danishmendid Fethiye Mosque that was a modest church conversion. A tomb tower with a crypt was constructed to the left of the entrance and its upper level chamber was accessed from the interior of the mosque. The date on the foundation inscription, 640 H. (July 1242–June 1243), places the Burmalı Minare Mosque on the eve of the Mongol invasions of the summer of 1243 that resulted in Seljuk defeat and reduction of the autonomy of the Seljuk state. The previous two years (when this mosque and tomb must have been under construction) were racked by the Baba'i Revolt, affecting a large portion of Anatolia and especially Amasya, which was home to the spiritual leader of the revolt.[56] Although the foundation inscription names Ghiyath al-Din

Kaykhusraw II as the reigning sultan, the Burmalı Minare Mosque with its tomb attachment was built at a highly unstable conjuncture when the prospect of a unified Seljuk state was especially dim and opened the door to local claims to power. Before the 1240s, the only example of a prominent juxtaposition of tomb tower with mosque in Anatolia was the Alaeddin Mosque in Konya and it is likely that the royal Seljuk mosque and dynastic tomb tower served as a meaningful model for the patrons of the Burmalı Minare Mosque in Amasya. Such conspicuous combination of a congregational mosque with a tomb became a trend especially in the waning years of Seljuk power in the late thirteenth century by such upstarts on the *beylik*-period political scene as Sulayman Bey who built the Eşrefoğlu Mosque with an attached tomb in his capital of Beyşehir, or the leading *ahi* family of Ankara who built the Arslanhane Mosque with an associated freestanding tomb.[57]

The addition of a funerary aspect to mosque architecture in medieval Anatolia occurred in tandem with an increasing emphasis on building projects conceived to aggregate multiple functions in a single complex. These projects either brought together two or more buildings as part of a complex or, more simply, accommodated two or more activities in single buildings – notably *madrasa*s and Sufi or *ahi* lodges.[58] The demands of the *longue durée* of migration and settlement – a period that may be extended from the end of the eleventh century to the establishment of Ottoman hegemony in the late fifteenth century – created conditions in which the idea of incorporating multiple functions in architecture acquired a particular significance for reasons that were probably fundamentally socio-economic and political. This is also evident especially in the building of hundreds of caravanserais in the Anatolian countryside from the end of the twelfth century onwards in tandem with the intensification of commercial activity brought about by Seljuk ascendancy and policy.[59] These caravanserais embodied the very idea of functional multiplicity in their accommodation of the basic needs of their visitors from food and shelter to medicine and shoe repair, as well as the provision for their animals as outlined in their endowment deeds.⁶⁰ Moreover, caravanserais were almost always designed with a small mosque so that the Muslim travelers could fulfill their religious obligations while on the road.

The surviving endowment deeds of buildings such as *madrasa*s and lodges often also make provisions for the accommodation of travelers, which suggests that social mobility figured highly on the charitable consciousness of medieval Anatolian patrons as much in the countryside as in the towns. Ibn Battuta's experience as a traveler in fourteenth-century Anatolia is a vivid testament to the dynamics of hospitality institutionalized especially in the lodges run by *ahis* who were generally merchants and craftsmen and who integrated the communal activities of eating and camaraderie with the fulfillment of religious rites in the codified framework of mystical Islam.⁶¹ Hagiographical literature produced in medieval Anatolia also indicates that spaces such as *madrasa*s could often be used for functions – including spectacles performed by itinerant dervishes or the provision of accommodation to guests – other than the educational. From the available textual evidence on the organization and occupation of buildings such as lodges and *madrasa*s, it is possible to deduce that communal and religious functions were conceived in a fluid continuum in response to the condition of mobility borne of both the process of settlement and the drive for commercial activity.

This fluid continuum on the functional level came to be explored in building projects in which, initially, two or more buildings were conjoined to create complexes that typically juxtaposed social or educational services with religious functions. The Mosque and Hospital of Divriği built in 1228–9 by the Mengujekid ruler Ahmadshah and Turan Malik, his cousin (and perhaps wife) from Erzincan, adjoined two discrete institutions in a complex (Fig. 11).⁶² Although justly celebrated and studied for

11 Mosque and Hospital Complex, Divriği, Turkey, 1228–9.
Photo: Oya Pancaroğlu

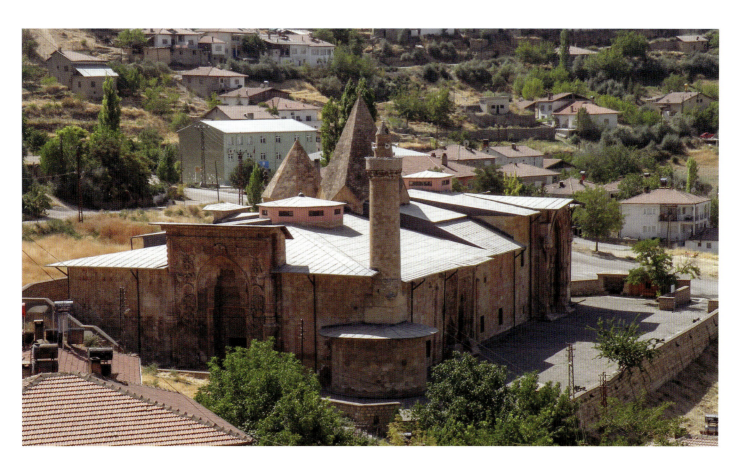

ISLAMIC ARCHITECTURE IN MEDIEVAL ANATOLIA 289

the remarkable decoration concentrated especially on the portals of the two buildings, Divriği's combination of the two institutions into a single conjoined socio-religious complex located below and beyond the citadel walls has garnered less attention. It was a major project on the part of the patrons and represented a significant investment of their respective resources. It is remarkable that this grand construction is dated to the same year (1228–9) as the annexation of the Mengujekid lands of Erzincan and Kemah by the Seljuks. With this annexation, Dawudshah, the senior Mengujekid ruler of Erzincan and the brother of Turan Malik, was sent into exile in Seljuk central Anatolia, an event that must have created some anxiety in Divriği, which, curiously enough, escaped this instance of Seljuk expansionism. Certainly, the complex could not have been simply a quick means to secure the resources of the patrons in the form of an endowment in uncertain times. All evidence points to a proactive rather than reactive undertaking and one that was meant to recast Divriği as a significant nexus in the network of Anatolia's cultural resources and shifting political landscape. The dynastic identity of the complex was augmented by the presence of the tomb chamber in the hospital marked by a high conical dome and its social functions were enhanced by an associated bath nearby, now in ruins.

Just a decade later in Kayseri, a similar institutional combination was undertaken by Mahpari Khatun, the widow of sultan 'Ala al-Din Kayqubad I and the mother of sultan Ghiyath al-Din Kaykhusraw II (Fig. 12).[63] Known as the Huand Hatun, the complex consists of a mosque attached at one corner to a *madrasa* and a detached double bathhouse (now partly rebuilt). The tomb of the founder was built within the walls of the mosque but as a freestanding tower raised above a base in the northwestern corner where the two buildings were adjoined. Of these structures, only the mosque bears a date (1237–8), which is the year of 'Ala al-Din Kayqubad I's sudden death in Kayseri, and Ghiyath al-Din Kaykhusraw II's subsequent controversial accession to power. It has been suggested that this complex was built in

12 Huand Hatun Complex, Kayseri, Turkey, 1230s, view towards the tomb enclosure.
Photo: Oya Pancaroğlu

stages, possibly starting with the *madrasa* that may have been built (or started) by sultan 'Ala al-Din Kayqubad I a few years earlier.[64] According to this suggestion, the mosque was occasioned by the accession of Mahpari Khatun's son to the Seljuk throne. The tomb is assumed to have been the last structure to be added, probably a few decades after the construction of the mosque.[65]

Like the complex at Divriği, the Huand Hatun was located outside of the city walls, but situated directly opposite its main eastern gates by the citadel, thereby creating a kind of plaza that must have been also conceived in relation to the traffic entering and leaving the city proper. Its patron, Mahpari Khatun, sponsored a number of major building projects in the Seljuk realms, especially in the short period between the accession of her son to the throne in 1237 and the Mongol invasion of 1243.[66] Known to have retained her Christian identity at least until the death of her husband, she played an important role in the power structure of the dynasty, which is also reflected by her apparent detainment in the hands of Bayju, the commander of the Mongol forces in Anatolia, after the disaster of 1243.[67] The seeming dual ambiguity of Mahpari Khatun's religious affiliation is also reflected in the inscription of her cenotaph, which compares her to both Maryam (the mother of Jesus) and Khadija (the wife of the Prophet Muhammad).[68]

By its location and incorporation of multiple functions, the Huand Hatun complex shaped the urban space around it and, in this regard, may have been seen as a model for architectural patronage by Seljuk statesmen in the aftermath of the Mongol invasion. In the latter half of the thirteenth century, building activity attained a new momentum driven especially by high-ranking Seljuk officials who, more than the sultan himself, negotiated the fragile political relations of the state with their Mongol overlords while maneuvering the unsettled power relations among themselves. Statesmen such as Jalal al-Din Qaratay (d. 1256) or Parwana Mu'in al-Din Sulayman (d. 1277) undertook major building projects in a number of locations across the country, paralleling the web of political networking in which they engaged. Among these, the architectural legacy of the vizier Fakhr al-Din 'Ali, who acquired the epithet of Sahib 'Ata (Master of Giving) thanks to his numerous endowments, stands out.[69]

Sahib 'Ata's prolific patronage of socio-religious complexes is especially notable for its geographic spread across Anatolia and reveals the significant impact of such projects on the urban centers.[70] Two of his major undertakings are located in Sivas and Konya: the former consisting of a *madrasa* (Gök Medrese, 1271) with an associated (though no longer standing) hostel, the latter (Sahib Ata Complex, 1258–83) including a mosque, a Sufi lodge, the founder's tomb, and probably a bathhouse undertaken over the course of a few decades. The surviving redaction of the endowment document of the Sivas complex illustrates the workings of a major charitable foundation that was dedicated not only to the teaching of law but also to the provision of room and board to travelers in the hostel and the regular distribution of food to the poor from the *madrasa*.[71] The façade of the *madrasa*, with its monumental marble portal, was also fitted with a fountain, further enhancing the charitable function of the building oriented towards the public at large (Fig. 13). The inclusion of a separate hostel

13 Gök Medrese, Sivas, Turkey, 1271.
Photo: Dosseman / Wikimedia Commons / CC BY-SA 4.0

ISLAMIC ARCHITECTURE IN MEDIEVAL ANATOLIA 291

underscores Sahib 'Ata's recognition of the value of engaging with visitors and outsiders which can be seen as a major consideration in the patron's choice of location as well. The Gök Medrese complex in Sivas was located within the city walls but near the southern gate and the Sahib 'Ata Complex in Konya was just outside of the Larende Gate. Similarly, Sahib 'Ata's complex in Akşehir consisting of a *madrasa*, mosque and a Sufi lodge was on the outskirts of the city on the road to Çay.

The building of multifunctional complexes continued with the Ottomans starting in the fourteenth century in Bursa where each of the sultans between Orhan and Mehmed II built their own complexes, making provisions for guests, students, and the maintenance of piety in the form of continuous Quran recitations.[72] According to their inscriptions, the central building in these complexes was called an *'imara* (*imaret* in Turkish) or a *zawiya* (lodge) but never a mosque (*jami'* or *masjid*) and incorporated a central prayer hall as well as subsidiary rooms for accommodation and socio-religious activity. Other buildings in the complex typically included a *madrasa* and the tomb of the founder and, occasionally, commercial buildings or bathhouses. Although the architecture of Bursa showcases the particular development of the socio-religious complex in the early Ottoman period, the practical and conceptual foundations of such foundations in Anatolia can be traced all the way back to the Danishmendid congregational mosque and *madrasa* of Kayseri built in the first half of the twelfth century.

In the early fifteenth century, Ibrahim Bey (r. 1423–64), one of the last rulers of the Karamanid dynasty that superseded the Seljuks in central Anatolia, built his own multifunctional socio-religious complex, which epitomizes key aspects of Islamic architecture in late medieval Anatolia, on the eve of the Ottoman conquests.[73] Situated just outside of the walls of his capital, Larende (modern Karaman), and known as the Imaret of Ibrahim Bey (dated 1432–3), the complex was conceived much in the same spirit as its counterparts in Bursa or its predecessors in the towns of central Anatolia. Its surviving original endowment

deed delineates a highly detailed and developed conceptualization of the social and devotional functions of such architectural projects in medieval Anatolia. The Imaret of Ibrahim Bey consists of a two-story building with numerous rooms and halls of various size disposed around a central domed court. A prayer hall occupied part of the ground floor; it was highlighted by a magnificent tile *mihrab* (now in the Çinili Köşk of the Archaeology Museum in Istanbul), which was probably executed by the same itinerant group of craftsmen from Tabriz who signed similar work in Bursa and Edirne around the same time. Attached to the building at the rear with entrances both from the interior and the exterior is the tomb of the founder. The complex was enclosed by a perimeter wall with a gate (no longer extant) and includes a fountain.

According to its endowment deed, the imaret was founded with a double mission comprising devotional and charitable activities.[74] For the former, Ibrahim Bey stipulated the fulltime employment of twelve men for the continuous and daily recitation of the Quran. Of these, one would also serve as the imam, another as the *muezzin*, and a third as an instructor (*mudarris*) who would be charged with teaching *tafsir* (Quranic exegesis) and Hadith (traditions of the Prophet). As for the charitable activities, these included primarily the provision of room and board to travelers of any rank and the needy. The travelers were defined in the foundation inscription as "comers and goers from among any group (*ta'ifa*) of Muslims" who could stay for free for up to three days. The provisions detailed in the endowment deed stipulated the preparation of between one hundred to two hundred bowls of food twice a day, to be served with a minimum of 150 loaves of bread. The staff employed for this output and maintenance were listed as a cook, sweepers, porters, a man in charge of the pantry, and another responsible for the lighting. The Imaret of Ibrahim Bey thus signaled itself as a religious institution by its inclusion of Quranic recitation and religious instruction as a fundamental act of piety. This act of piety was enshrined as the constant and diurnal inner axis of the institution, which was conceived to function much as a revolving door, actively geared towards the needs of a mobile society both by its location beyond the city walls and its significant mission of hospitality.

Ibrahim Bey was clearly mindful of the fact that, for the population of late medieval Anatolia, roads continued to function not only as physical arteries but also as channels through which various configurations of social cohesion could be promoted in multifunctional institutions that allowed for communal, religious, and political interaction and influence. The transplantation of Islamic forms of architecture – notably the mosque – was realized as a matter of course alongside a sense of adaptableness that moved in tandem with the changing political and social circumstances of settlement. As everywhere else, architecture served as a means for the articulation of political identity but with a notable degree of conceptual flexibility that allowed for such developments as the close association of mosques with tombs or the multifunctional socio-religious complex.

In 1475, after more than a century of bitter rivalry and violent confrontation punctuated by ineffective attempts at marriage ententes, the Ottomans brought the *beylik* of Karaman to an end. The toll of subjugation was excessively high and was said to have resulted in the destruction of six congregational mosques, four *madrasa*s, and thirty-three neighborhood mosques.[75] Among the mosques that were destroyed was the fourteenth-century Mosque of Alaeddin Bey. The Ottomans used the stone blocks of this Karamanid mosque in the re-fortification of the citadel of Larende but left the tomb of its founder – once attached to the mosque – standing. This was a deliberate act of the obliteration of a polity, the identity of which was clearly seen to inhere architecturally in the congregational mosque. The preservation of the tomb was perhaps ensured by a reticence to desecrate the funerary structure. Apparently, the notion of sanctity could be withheld from the mosque when deep-seated enmity and suspicion on the part of the victors gained the upper hand in a brutal process of subjugation. In this connection, the fact that the Ottomans also spared the Imaret of Ibrahim Bey in 1475 acquires a particular

meaning. Just as the idea of sanctity of mosques could be ignored when destruction was deemed politically necessary, so could political identity be disregarded when the building in question – in this case, an *imaret* – offered an apposite and valued combination of social and religious functions. In ensuring the integrity of the Imaret of Ibrahim Bey both as a building and as an endowment, the Ottomans were also recognizing the particular social dynamics of medieval Anatolia. By the turn of the next century, however, a newly attained imperial identity with its attendant imposition of centralized religious orthodoxy would cast the long shadow of Ottoman hegemony over Anatolia, eventually obscuring its medieval social order with its distinct architectural formulations.

OYA PANCAROĞLU is Professor in the Department of History at Boğaziçi University. She obtained her PhD from the Department of History of Art and Architecture at Harvard University in 2000 and has since taught at the University of Oxford and Bilkent University. Her research interests include Islamic architecture in medieval Anatolia (12th–15th centuries), figural representation in early and medieval Islamic art, and ceramic production in the medieval eastern Islamic lands.

SUGGESTIONS FOR FURTHER READING

Blessing, Patricia. *Rebuilding Anatolia after the Mongol Conquest: Islamic Architecture in the Lands of Rum, 1240–1330* (Burlington: Ashgate Variorum, 2014).

McClary, Richard P. *Rum Seljuq Architecture, 1170–1220: The Patronage of Sultans* (Edinburgh: Edinburgh University Press, 2017).

Pancaroğlu, Oya. "Devotion, Hospitality and Architecture in Medieval Anatolia," *Studia Islamica* 108 (2013), 48–81.

Peacock, A.C.S. "Islamisation in Medieval Anatolia," in *Islamisation: Comparative Perspectives from History*, ed. A.C.S. Peacock (Edinburgh: Edinburgh University Press, 2017), 134–55.

Redford, Scott. "City Building in Seljuq Rum," in *The Seljuqs: Politics, Society and Culture*, eds. Christian Lange and Songül Mecit (Edinburgh: Edinburgh University Press, 2014), 256–76.

Wolper, Ethel Sara. *Cities and Saints: Sufism and the Transformation of Urban Space in Medieval Anatolia* (University Park: Pennsylvania State University Press, 2003).

NOTES

[1] Anatolia is defined in this essay approximately as the region west of the Euphrates valley. It thus excludes much of the eastern highlands and southeastern lowlands of the modern Republic of Turkey for the simple purpose of examining the development of Islamic architecture in regions where no such tradition existed prior to the twelfth century.

[2] Osman Turan, *Selçuklular Zamanında Türkiye* (Istanbul: Turan Neşriyat Yurdu, 1971); Speros Vryonis, *The Decline of Medieval Hellenism in Asia Minor and the Process of Islamization from the Eleventh through the Fifteenth Centuries* (Berkeley: University of California Press, 1971); Claude Cahen, *La Turquie pré-ottomane* (Istanbul: Institut français d'études anatoliennes, 1988); Rudi Paul Lindner, "Anatolia, 1300–1451," in *The Cambridge History of Turkey*, vol. 1, *Byzantium to Turkey, 1071–1453*, ed. Kate Fleet (Cambridge: Cambridge University Press, 2009), 102–37.

[3] F.W. Hasluck, *Christianity and Islam under the Sultans*, 2 vols, (Oxford: Clarendon Press, 1929); Mehmet Fuat Köprülü, *Islam in Anatolia after the Turkish Invasion: Prolegomena*, trans. and ed. Gary Leiser (Salt Lake City: University of Utah Press, 1993); Ahmet Yaşar Ocak, "Social, Cultural and Intellectual Life, 1071–1453," in *The Cambridge History of Turkey*, vol. 1, *Byzantium to Turkey, 1071–1453*, ed. Kate Fleet, (Cambridge: Cambridge University Press, 2009), 353–422; A.C.S. Peacock, "Islamisation in Medieval Anatolia," in *Islamisation: Comparative Perspectives from History*, ed. A.C.S. Peacock (Edinburgh: Edinburgh University Press, 2017), 134–55; Michel Balivet, *Romanie byzantine et pays de Rûm turc: Histoire d'un espace d'imbrication gréco-turque* (Istanbul: Isis, 1994); Keith Hopwood, "Christian-Muslim Symbiosis in Anatolia," in *Archaeology, Anthropology and Heritage in the Balkans and Anatolia: The Life and Times of F.W. Hasluck, 1878–1920*, vol. 2, ed. David Shankland (Istanbul: Isis Press, 2004), 13–30; Rustam Shukurov, "The Crypto-Muslims of Anatolia," in *Archaeology, Anthropology and Heritage in the Balkans and Anatolia: The Life and Times of F. W. Hasluck, 1878–1920*, ed. David Shankland, vol. 2 (Istanbul: Isis Press, 2004), 135–57; idem, "Christian Elements in the Identity of the Anatolian Turkmens (12th-13th Centuries)," in *Cristianità d'occidente e cristianità d'oriente [secoli VI–XI]* (Spoleto: Fondazione centro italiano di studi sull'alto

Medioevo, 2004), 707–64; Ethel Sara Wolper, "Khidr, Elwan Çelebi and the Conversion of Sacred Sanctuaries in Anatolia," *Muslim World* 90 (2000), 309–22; Oya Pancaroğlu, "Caves, Borderlands and Configurations of Sacred Topography in Medieval Anatolia," *Mésogeios* 25–26 (2005), 249–82; eadem, "The Itinerant Dragon Slayer: Forging Paths of Image and Identity in Medieval Anatolia," *Gesta* 43 (2004), 151–64.

[4] Ethel Sara Wolper, *Cities and Saints: Sufism and the Transformation of Urban Space in Medieval Anatolia* (University Park, Penn.: Pennsylvania State University Press, 2003); Gary Leiser, "The Madrasah and the Islamization of Anatolia before the Ottomans," in *Law and Education in Medieval Islam: Studies in Memory of Professor George Makdisi*, ed. Joseph E. Lowry et al. (Cambridge: E.J.W. Gibb Memorial Trust, 2004), 174–191; Oya Pancaroğlu, "Devotion, Hospitality and Architecture in Medieval Anatolia," *Studia Islamica* 108 (2013), 48–81.

[5] Ibn Battuta, *The Travels of Ibn Battuta, A.D. 1325–1354*, trans. H.A.R. Gibb, vol. 2 (Cambridge: Published for the Hakluyt Society at the University Press, 1962), 413–68.

[6] Haluk Karamağaralı, "Konya Ulu Cami," *Rölöve ve Restorasyon Dergisi* 4 (1982), 121–33; Scott Redford, "The Alaeddin Mosque in Konya Reconsidered," *Artibus Asiae* 51 (1991), 54–74; Doğan Kuban, *Selçuklu Çağında Anadolu Sanatı* (Istanbul: Yapı Kredi Yayınları, 2002), 128–32; Neslihan Asutay-Effenberger, "Konya Alaeddin Camisi Yapım Evreleri Üzerine Düşünceler," *Middle East Technical University Journal of the Faculty of Architecture* 23 (2006), 113–22; Suzan Yalman, " Sanctifying Konya: The Thirteenth-Century Transformation of the Seljuk Friday Mosque in to a House of God," in *The Friday Mosque in the City: Liminality, Ritual, and Politics*, eds. A. Hilal Uğurlu and Suzan Yalman (Bristol: Intellect Books, 2020), 127–55.

[7] M. Zeki Oral, "Anadolu'da San'at Değeri Olan Ahşap Minberler, Kitabeleri ve Tarihçeleri," *Vakıflar Dergisi* 5 (1962), 29–34.

[8] It has recently been argued that the unfinished tomb tower could be associated with the later sultan Ghiyath al-Din Kaykhusraw II (r. 1237–46); Richard P. McClary, *Rum Seljuq Architecture, 1170–1220: The Patronage of Sultans* (Edinburgh: Edinburgh University Press, 2017), 164–6.

9 V. Macit Tekinalp, "Palace Churches of the Anatolian Seljuks: Tolerance or Necessity?" *Byzantine and Modern Greek Studies* 33 (2009), 148–67; Rustam Shukurov, "Harem Christianity: The Byzantine Identity of Seljuk Princes," in *The Seljuks of Anatolia: Court and Society in the Medieval Middle East*, eds. A.C.S. Peacock and Sara Nur Yıldız (London: I.B. Tauris, 2013), 115–50. Two further examples of medieval palace churches built in Muslim-held citadels in northeastern Anatolia have recently been discussed in idem, "Churches in the Citadels of Ispir and Bayburt: An Evidence of 'Harem Christianity'?" in *Polidoro: Studi offerti ad Antonio Carile*, ed. Giorgio Vespignani (Spoleto: Centro italiano di studi sull'alto Medioevo, 2013), 713–23.

10 Josef W. Meri, *A Lonely Wayfarer's Guide to Pilgrimage: ʿAli ibn Abi Bakr al-Harawi's Kitab al-Isharat ila Maʿrifat al-Ziyarat* (Princeton: Darwin Press, 2004), 152–3. See also, Suzan Yalman, "From Plato to the Shahnama: Reflections on Saintly Veneration in Seljuk Konya," in *Sacred Spaces and Urban Networks*, eds. Suzan Yalman and A. Hilal Uğurlu (Istanbul: Koç University Research Center for Anatolian Civilizations, 2019), 119–40.

11 Redford, "The Alaeddin Mosque in Konya Reconsidered" and Yalman, "Sanctifying Konya."

12 Yalman, "Sanctifying Konya."

13 Ali Boran, *Anadoludaki İç Kale Cami ve Mescitleri* (Ankara: Türk Tarih Kurumu, 2001).

14 Max van Berchem and Halil Edhem, *Matériaux pour un Corpus Inscriptionum Arabicorum Troisième partie, Asie mineure. Tome premier, Siwas, Diwrigi*, (Cairo: Institut français d'archéologie orientale du Caire, 1917), 56–62; Boran, *Anadoludaki İç Kale Cami ve Mescitleri*, 60–5; Necdet Sakaoğlu, *Türk Anadolu'da Mengücekoğulları*, (Istanbul: Yapı Kredi Yayınları, 2004), 217–26; Oya Pancaroğlu, "The House of Mengüjek in Divriği: Constructions of Dynastic Identity in the Late Twelfth Century," in *The Seljuks of Anatolia: Court and Society in the Medieval Middle East*, eds. A.C.S. Peacock and Sara Nur Yıldız (London: I.B. Tauris, 2013), 25–67.

15 Ali Uzay Peker, " Anadolu Bazilika Geleneği ve Selçuklu Anıtsal Mimarisine Etkisi," in *Anadolu Selçukluları ve Beylikler Dönemi Uygarlığı 2: Mimarlık ve Sanat*, eds. Ali Uzay Peker and Kenan Bilici (Ankara: Kültür ve Turizm Bakanlığı Yayınları, 2006), 55–65.

16 Michael Meinecke, *Fayencedekorationen seldschukischer Sakralbauten in Kleinasien*, vol. 1, (Tübingen: Wasmuth, 1976), 15, n. 40. Colored glazed tiles highlighting the spandrels of the portal arch were visible until recently.

17 M. Oluş Arık, "Malatya Ulu Camiinin Asli Planı ve Tarihi Hakkında," *Vakıflar Dergisi* 8 (1969), 141–8; Meinecke, *Fayencedekorationen seldschukischer Sakralbauten in Kleinasien*, vol. 1, 47–8; vol. 2, 390–400; Walter Denny, "Points of Stylistic Contact in the Architecture of Islamic Iran and Anatolia," *Islamic Art* 2 (1987), 27–41.

18 For the epigraphic evidence concering the questions over dating, see Meinecke, *Fayencedekorationen*, vol. 2, 390–3 and Arık, "Malatya Ulu Camiinin Asli Planı."

19 Katharina Otto-Dorn, "Seldschukische Holzäulenmoscheen in Kleinasien," in *Aus der Welt der islamischen Kunst. Festschrift für Ernst Kühnel zum 75. Geburtstag am 26.10.1957*, ed. Richard Ettinghausen (Berlin: Gebr. Mann, 1959), 59–88; Aptullah Kuran, "Anadolu'da Ahşap Sütunlu Selçuklu Mimarisi," in *Malazgirt Armağanı* (Ankara: Türk Tarih Kurumu, 1972), 179–86; Yılmaz Önge, "Selçuklularda ve Beyliklerde Ahşap Tavanlar," *Atatürk Konferansları* 5 (1971–72), 179–95; Kuban, *Selçuklu Çağında Anadolu Sanatı*, 146–50, 299–303.

20 Otto-Dorn, 84–88; Sheila Blair, *The Monumental Inscriptions from Early Islamic Iran and Transoxiana* (Leiden: Brill, 1992), 76–7.

21 On the Eşrefoğlu Mosque, see Yaşar Erdemir, *Beyşehir Eşrefoğlu Süleyman Bey Camii ve Külliyesi* (Beyşehir: Beyşehir Vakfı, 1999); Ahmet Çaycı, *Eşrefoğlu Beyliği Dönemi Mimari Eserleri* (Ankara: Türk Tarih Kurumu, 2008), 24–56. On the Arslanhane Mosque (also known as the Ahi Şerafettin Mosque), see Gönül Öney, *Ankara Arslanhane Camii* (Ankara Kültür Bakanlığı Yayınları, 1990).

22 Peter Ian Kuniholm, "Dendrochronologically Dated Ottoman Buildings," in Uzi Baram and Lynda Carroll (eds.), *A Historical Archaeology of the Ottoman Empire* (New York: Kluwer Academic, 2000), 128, 130–2; E. Emine Naza-Dönmez, *Wooden Mosques of the Samsun Region, Turkey* (Oxford: Archaeopress, 2008), 8–22.

23 Redford, "The Alaeddin Mosquein Konya Reconsidered" and Erdal Eser, "Anadolu-Suriye Sanat İlişkileri," in *Anadolu Selçukluları ve Beylikler Dönemi Uygarlığı 2: Mimarlık ve Sanat*, eds. Ali Uzay Peker and Kenan Bilici (Ankara: Kültür ve Turizm Bakanlığı Yayınları, 2006), 67–73.

24 For example, see Nermin Şaman Doğan, "Kültürel Etkileşim Üzerine: Karamanoğulları – Memluklu Sanatı," *Hacettepe Üniversitesi Edebiyat Fakültesi Dergisi* 23 (2006), 131–49.

25 Michael Meinecke, *Die mamlukische Architekture in Ägypten und Syrien*, vol. 1 (Glückstadt: Verlag J.J. Augustin, 1992), 135–41; idem, *Patterns of Stylistic Changes in Islamic Architecture* (New York: New York University Press, 1996), 91–9.

26 Meinecke, *Die mamlukische Architekture*, 136–7.

27 Clive Foss, *Ephesus after Antiquity: A Late Antique, Byzantine and Turkish City* (Cambridge: Cambridge University Press, 1979); Erdoğan Merçil, "Aydınoğulları," *Türkiye Diyanet Vakfı İslam Ansiklopedisi* (hereafter TDVIA), vol. 4 (Istanbul: Türkiye Diyanet Vakfı, 1991), 239–41; Sara Nur Yıldız, "From Cairo to Ayasuluk: Hacı Paşa and the Transmission of Islamic Learning to Western Anatolia in the Late Fourteenth Century," *Journal of Islamic Studies* 25 (2014), 263–97.

28 The most recent comprehensive typological survey of tombs up to the fourteenth century is Hakkı Önkal, *Anadolu Selçuklu Türbeleri*, 2nd ed. (Ankara: Atatürk Kültür Merkezi Yayınları, 2015) where 118 extant tombs are listed. For an earlier surveys, see Ülkü Ü. Bates, "The Anatolian Mausoleum of the Twelfth, Thirteenth, and Fourteenth Centuries," PhD thesis, University of Michigan, 1970; Orhan Cezmi Tuncer, *Anadolu Kümbetleri 1: Selçuklu Dönemi* (Ankara: n.p., 1986).

29 Altan Gökalp, "Les *Yatır, Idukut*, ou la part de la Providence," in *Cimètieres et traditions funéraires dans le monde islamique. İslam Dünyasında Mezarlıklar ve Defin Gelenekleri*, vol. 2, eds. Jean-Louis Bacqué-Grammont and Aksel Tibet (Ankara: Türk Tarih Kurumu, 1996), 121–4.

30 Rahmi Hüseyin Ünal, "Monuments salguqides de Kemah (Anatolie orientale)," *Revue des études islamiques* 35 (1967), 151–61; Önkal, *Anadolu Selçuklu Türbeleri*, 37–53; Sakaoğlu, *Türk Anadolu'da Mengücekoğulları*, 51–4, 94–5, 389–402; Pancaroğlu, "The House of Mengüjek in Divriği."

31 Redford, "The Alaeddin Mosque in Konya Reconsidered"; Önkal, *Anadolu Selçuklu Türbeleri*, 64–9, 185–90; Yalman, "Sanctifying Konya."

32 On the inscriptions of the tomb, see Zeki Oral, "Konyada Alâûd-din Camii ve Türbeleri," *Yıllık Araştırmalar Dergisi* 1 (1956), 55–56; Kerim Türkmen, "Konya Sultanlar Türbesi İçerisindeki Sandukalar Üzerinde Yer Alan Kitabeler," in *Konya Kitabı X: Rüçhan Arık – M. Oluş Arık'a Armağan*, eds. Haşim Karpuz and Osman Eravşar (Konya: Konya Ticaret Odası, 2007), 665–72.

33 Osman Turan, Şemseddin Altun-Aba, Vakfiyyesi ve Hayatı," Belleten 11 (1947), 208–11; Faruk Sümer, "The Seljuk Turbehs and the Tradition of Embalming," in *Atti del Secondo Congresso Internazionale di Arte Turca, Venezia, 26–29 settembre 1963* (Naples: Istituto universitario orientale, 1965), 245–8; Zehra Efe, "Türkiye Müze ve Türbelerindeki Mumyaların Tarihi ve Bugünkü Durumları," *Süleyman Demirel Üniversitesi Fen-Edebiyat Fakültesi Sosyal Bilimler Dergisi* 34 (2015), 279–92.

34 İbrahim Hakkı Konyalı, *Abideleri ve Kitabeleri ile Konya Tarihi* (Konya: Yeni Kitap Basımevi, 1964), 576–85.

35 31. Sakaoğlu, *Türk Anadolu'da Mengücekoğulları*, 51–3.

36 Albert Gabriel, *Monuments turcs d'Anatolie*, vol. 2, (Paris: E. de Boccard, 1931), 17–20; Abdizade Hüseyin Hüsameddin, *Amasya Tarihi*, vol. 1 [rendered into modern Turkish by Ali Yılmaz and Mehmet Akkuş], (Ankara: Amasya Belediyesi Kültür Yayınları, 1986), 155–6. For other human remains visible in the various crypts of turn-of-the-century Amasya, see Hüsameddin, 147–8, 158, and 164.

37 Translation based on the Arabic text in Ibn Battuta, *Voyages d'Ibn Batoutah*, vol. 2, ed. and trans. (into French) C. Defrémery and B. R. Sanguinetti (Paris: Imprimerie Nationale, 1854), 313.

38 Cemil Akpınar, "Hacı Paşa," TDVIA, vol. 14, (Istanbul: Türkiye Diyanet Vakfı, 1996), 495 and A. Süheyl Ünver, *Hekim Konyalı Hacı Paşa: Hayatı ve Eserleri* (Istanbul: Tıp Tarihi Enstitüsü Yayınları, 1953), 74–8.

39 Jean-Paul Roux, *La mort chez les peuples altaïques anciens et médiévaux* (Paris: Maisonneuve, 1963), 136–40, 157–9, 179–84; John Andre Boyle, "The Thirteenth-Century Mongols' Conception of the After Life: The Evidence of Their Funerary Practices," *Mongolian Studies* 1 (1974), 5–14.

40 Pancaroğlu, "Caves, Borderlands and Configurations of Sacred Topography." See also Anthony Bryer and David Winfield, *The Byzantine Monuments and Topography of the Pontos*, vol. 1 (Washington, D.C.: Dumbarton Oaks, 1985), 171, for a site called Mumya Kalesi ("Mummy Citadel") in Şiran (Cheriana) in the Pontic hinterlands of Anatolia's eastern Black Sea region which Bryer suggests may have been a source for the substance "mummy" used in embalming.

41 As an example, see Muhsin Endoğru and Demet Kaya, "Aksaray Akhisar Köyü Çanlı Kilise Kurtarma Kazısı," in VIII. *Müze Kurtarma Kazıları Seminesi* (Ankara: Kültür Bakanlığı Yayınları, 1997), 585–606.

42 Melanie Michailidis, "In the Footsteps of the Sasanians: Funerary Architecture and Bavandid Legitimacy," in *Persian Kingship and Architecture: Strategies of Power in Iran from the Achaemenids to the Pahlavis*, eds. Sussan Babaie and Talinn Grigor (London: I.B. Tauris, 2015), 135–73.

43 Durukan, "Anadolu Selçuklu Sanatında Kadın Baniler"; Ethel Sara Wolper, "Princess Safwat al-Dunya wa al-Din and the Production of Sufi Buildings and Hagiographies in Pre-Ottoman Anatolia," in *Women, Patronage, and Self-Representation in Islamic Societies*, ed. D. Fairchild Ruggles (Albany: State University of New Press, 2000), 35–52; Patricia Blessing, "Women Patrons In Medieval Anatolia and a Discussion of Māhbarī Khātūn's Mosque Complex in Kayseri, *Belleten* 78 (2014), 475–526; Suzan Yalman, " The 'Dual Identity' of Mahperi Khatun: Piety, Patronage and Marriage across Frontiers in Seljuk Anatolia, in *Architecture and Landscape in Medieval Anatolia, 1100–1500*, eds. Patricia Blessing and Rachel Goshgarian (Edinburgh: Edinburgh University Press, 2017), 224–52.

44 Oya Pancaroğlu, "The Mosque-Hospital Complex in Divriği: A History of Relations and Transitions," *Anadolu ve Çevresinde Ortaçağ* 3 (2009), 171, n. 9.

45 Gary Leiser, "Saltuk Oghullari," *Encyclopaedia of Islam*, 2nd ed. vol. 8, 1001; Dursun Ali Şeker, "Mama Hatun," in TDVIA, vol. 27 (Istanbul: Türkiye Diyanet Vakfı, 2003), 548; Faruk Sümer, *Selçuklular Devrinde Doğu Anadolu'da Türk Beylikleri* (Ankara: Türk Tarih Kurumu, 1990), 35–6.

46 Rahmi Hüseyin Ünal, *Les monuments islamiques anciens de la ville d'Erzurum et de sa région* (Paris: Maisonneuve, 1968), 129–142, 146–52; Ayşe Denknalbant, "Mama Hatun Külliyesi," TDVIA, vol. 27 (Istanbul: Türkiye Diyanet Vakfı, 2003), 549–50; Önkal, *Anadolu Selçuklu Türbeleri*, 437–43; S. Kemal Yetkin, "Mama Hatun Türbesi," *Yıllık Araştırmalar Dergisi* 1 (1956), 75–91 (includes English translation); Hüseyin Yurttaş, "Tercan Mama Hatun Külliyesi Hakkında Bazı Düşünceler ve Yapılan Son Onarımlar," in *Prof. Dr. Zafer Bayburtluoğlu Armağanı: Sanat Yazıları* (Kayseri: Kayseri Büyükşehir Belediyesi Kültür Yayınları, 2001), 637–51.

47 Denknalbant, "Mama Hatun Külliyesi," 550.

48 Indeed, a particular ceremonial ritual to be carried on Fridays was introduced into the Alaeddin Mosque precinct in connection with the interment of sultan Ghiyath al-Din Kaykhusraw I in the dynastic tomb tower following his martyrdom in a battle against the Byzantines in 1211; Yalman, "Sanctifying Konya," 139.

49 Gabriel, *Monuments turcs d'Anatolie*, vol. 1, 67–70; Nermin Şaman and Turgay Yazar, "Kayseri Köşk Hânikâhı," *Vakıflar Dergisi* 22 (1991), 301–14.

50 The tomb is known as the Çifte Kümbet ("Double Mausolea") which probably indicates a one-time pairing with another tomb which is not extant; see Gabriel, *Monuments turcs d'Anatolie*, vol. 1, 76–7; Halil Edhem, *Kayseriye Şehri* (Istanbul: Tarih-i Osmani Encümeni, 1334/1915), 85–88; Önkal, *Anadolu Selçuklu Türbeleri*, 103–7; Ahmet Akşit, "Melike-i Adiliye Kümbetinde Selçuklu Devri Saltanat Mücadelesine Dair İzler," *Türkiyat Araştırmaları Dergisi* 11 (2002), 239–45.

51 Gabriel, *Monuments turcs d'Anatolie*, vol. 1, 32–5; Osman Eravşar, "Cami-i Kebir (Ulu Camii, Sultan Camii," in *Kayseri Ansiklopedisi* vol. 1 (Kayseri: Kayseri Büyükşehir Belediyesi Kültür Yayınları, 2015), 295–300.

52 Osman Eravşar, "Melik Mehmed Gazi Medresesi ve Türbesi," *Kayseri Ansiklopedisi*, vol. 4 (Kayseri: Kayseri Büyükşehir Belediyesi Kültür Yayınları, 2015), 371–2; Mehmet Çayırdağ, "Kayseri'de Zamanımıza Kadar Gelememiş Bazı Mühim Tarihi Binalar," in IX. *Türk Tarih Kongresi*, vol. 2 (Ankara: Türk Tarih Kurumu, 1981), 718–9; Ahmed Nazif, *Mir'at-i Kayseriyye veya Kayseri Tarihi*, ed. Mehmet Palamutoğlu (Kayseri: Kayseri Özel İdare Müdürlüğü ve Kayseri Belediyesi Birliği Yayınları, 1987), 14, 18.

53 When Malik Muhammad was buried in his *madrasa* next to the congregational mosque in Kayseri in 1142, the Alaeddin Mosque in Konya was without a funerary component as the dynastic tomb tower was only built in the latter decades of the twelfth century.

54 Turan, "Şemseddin Altun-Aba," 201, 221.

55 Gabriel, *Monuments turcs d'Anatolie*, vol. 2, 17–20; Semavi Eyice, "Burmalı Minare Camii ve Türbesi," TDVIA, vol. 6 (Istanbul: Türkiye Diyanet Vakfı, 1992), 444–5; İsmail Hakkı Uzunçarşılı, *Kitabeler* (Istanbul: Maarif Vekaleti, 1927), 99–100; Ali Yardım, *Amasya Burmalı Minare Camii Kitabeleri* (Ankara: Amasya Valiliği Kültr Yayınları, 2004); Önkal, *Anadolu Selçuklu Türbeleri*, 94–8.

56 Ocak, Ahmet Yaşar, "Babai," in *Encyclopaedia of Islam*, THREE. Consulted online on 15 February 2021 <http://dx.doi.org/10.1163/1573-3912_ei3_com_23862>

57 On these two mosques, see note 22 above.

58 Pancaroğlu, "Devotion, Hospitality and Architecture in Medieval Anatolia."

59 Kurt Erdmann, *Das anatolische Karavansaray des 13. Jahrhunderts*, 3. vols. (Berlin: Gebr. Mann, 1961–76); Ayşıl Tükel Yavuz, "The Concepts That Shape Anatolian Seljuq Caravanserais," *Muqarnas* 14 (1997), 80–95.

60 For an example of a Seljuk caravanserai endowment, see Osman Turan, "Selçuklu Devri Vakfiyeleri III: Celaleddin Karatay Vakıfları ve Vakfiyeleri," *Belleten* 12 (1948), 17–173.

61 Ibn Battuta, *Travels*; Pancaroğlu, "Devotion, Hospitality and Architecture in Medieval Anatolia."

62 Doğan Kuban, *Divriği Mucizesi: Selçuklular Çağında İslam Bezeme Sanatına Üzerine Bir Deneme* (Istanbul: Yapı Kredi Yayınları, 1999); Sakaoğlu, *Türk Anadolu'da Mengücekoğulları*, 239–385; Pancaroğlu, "The Mosque-Hospital Complex in Divriği."

63 Gabriel, *Monuments turcs d'Anatolie*, vol. 1, 39–51; Haluk Karamağaralı, "Kayseri'deki Hunad Camiinin Restitüsyonu ve Hunad Manzumesinin Kronolojisi Hakkında Ba'zı Mülahazalar," *Ankara Üniversitesi İlahiyat Fakültesi Dergisi* 21 (1976), 199–245; Durukan, "Anadolu Selçuklu Sanatında Kadın Baniler," 16–7; Blessing, "Women Patrons in Medieval Anatolia"; Yalman, "The 'Dual Identity' of Mahperi Khatun."

64 This sequence was proposed by Karamağaralı, "Kayseri'deki Hunad Camiinin Restitüsyonu." For a sequence which posits the mosque as the first structure, see Kuban, *Anadolu Çağında Selçuklu Sanatı*, 134–7.

65 Karamağaralı, "Kayseri'deki Hunad Camiinin Restitüsyonu," 208–10.

66 Durukan, "Anadolu Selçuklu Sanatında Kadın Baniler," 16–8; Blessing, "Women Patrons in Medieval Anatolia"; Yalman, "The 'Dual Identity' of Mahperi Khatun."

67 Shukurov, "Harem Christianity."

68 Halil Edhem, *Kayseriye Şehri*, 63–85; Yalman, "The 'Dual Identity' of Mahperi Khatun."

69 Ethel Sara Wolper, "Understanding the Public Face of Piety: Philanthropy and Architecture in Late Seljuk Anatolia," *Mésogeios* 25–26 (2005), 311–36; Patricia Blessing, "Buildings of Commemoration in Medieval Anatolia: The Funerary Complexes of Şāḥib 'Aṭā Fakhr al-Dīn 'Alī and Māhperī Khātūn," *Al-Masaq* 27 (2015), 225–52.

70 Pancaroğlu, "Devotion, Hospitality and Architecture in Medieval Anatolia."

71 Sadi Bayram and Ahmet Hamdi Karabacak, "Sahib Ata Fahr'üd-din Ali'nin Konya İmaret ve Sivas Gök Medrese Vakfiyeleri," *Vakıflar Dergisi* 13 (1981), 31–70; Pancaroğlu, "Devotion, Hospitality and Architecture in Medieval Anatolia."

72 Pancaroğlu, "Devotion, Hospitality and Architecture in Medieval Anatolia" and eadem, "Architecture, Landscape, and Patronage in Bursa: The Making of an Ottoman Capital City," *Turkish Studies Association Bulletin* 20 (1995), 40–55. On the architecture of these complexes in Bursa, see Albert Gabriel, *Une capitale turque: Brousse, Bursa*, 2 vols., (Paris: E. de Boccard, 1958).

73 Ernst Diez, Oktay Aslanapa and Mahmut Mesut Koman, *Karaman Devri Sanatı* (Istanbul: Istanbul Üniversitesi Edebiyat Fakültesi Yayınları, 1950), 67–84; Aynur Durukan, "İbrahim Bey İmareti ve Kümbeti," TDVIA 21 (Istanbul: Türkiye Diyanet Vakfı, 2000), 287–90; Osman Nuri Dülgerler, *Karamanoğulları Dönemi Mimarisi* (Ankara: Türk Tarih Kurumu, 2006), 116–9; İbrahim Hakkı Konyalı, *Abideleri ve Kitabeleri ile Karaman Tarihi* (Istanbul: Faha Matbaası, 1967), 405–52.

74 İsmail Hakkı Uzunçarşılıoğlu, "Karamanoğulları Devri Vesikalarından İbrahim Beyin Karaman İmareti Vakfiyesi," *Belleten* 1 (1937), 56–144 (German summary translation, 145–64).

75 Şikari, *Karamannâme*, ed. Metin Sözen and Necdet Sakaoğlu (Istanbul: Karaman Valiliği - Karaman Belediyesi, 2005), 181.

Three Sufi Shrines under the Ottomans ZEYNEP YÜREKLI

1 Shrine of Ibn 'Arabi, Damascus, 1518, view from the southeast.
Reproduced from: Gérard Degeorge, *Damascus* (Paris: Flammarion, 2004), 154

More than two centuries posthumously, three medieval Sufis found themselves in the twists and turns of early modern religio-politics. Each of these Sufis had Ottoman opponents who thought his teachings were un-Islamic, and proponents who considered him a saint. We will never know what Muhy al-din Ibn al-'Arabi (d. 1240), Jalal al-din al-Rumi (d. 1273), and Haji Bektash al-Khurasani (d. late thirteenth century) would think of the Ottomans, a dynasty that was not even born when they died, but this did not stop early modern devotees from imagining that they had prophesied – even facilitated with their blessing – the coming of the Ottomans.[1] There is a particularly complex relationship between the incorporation of these figures into Ottoman religio-political and historical consciousness and the architectural remodeling of their shrines.[2]

Chroniclers from the late fifteenth century onwards claimed that when 'Osman Ghazi (d. 1324), the founder of the Ottoman dynasty, emerged as ruler of one of the small Turkish principalities that mushroomed in late medieval Anatolia, he had one foot firmly planted in the mystical realm. Poorly documented as the circumstances of this allegedly illiterate frontier warrior were, there was room for a great degree of imagination. Legend had it that 'Osman used to frequent the convent of the Sufi shaykh Ede Bali, and eventually married his daughter. The Sufi author 'Ashiq-Pasha-zade (d. after 1484) relates in his *Chronicles of the Ottoman Dynasty* that 'Osman had a dream immediately before his first conquest: A moon, which we soon learn symbolizes Ede Bali's daughter and 'Osman's future bride, rises from the shaykh's lap and enters the warrior's bosom. Then an enormous tree grows out of 'Osman's belly. Its shade covers the world, underneath it waters flow, and people drink from

them and water their gardens.[3] When 'Ashiq-Pasha-zade was writing this in the last decades of the fifteenth century, generations after the events, the Ottomans had indeed cast an enormous shadow on central Eurasia. With the conquest of Constantinople in 1453 and the subjugation of Byzantine successor states in Morea and Anatolia by 1461, Mehmed II (r. 1444–6, 1451–81) had achieved a complete takeover of the Byzantine Empire, and had quickly moved on to subdue the remaining Muslim polities in Anatolia. Born from the union of martial and devotional realms that is encapsulated in the dream narrative, the Ottomans' recent expansions into the lands of Christian and Muslim neighbors appeared natural, predestined, and legitimate.

However conscious of this extraordinary transformation from principality to empire, the chroniclers of the late fifteenth century – writing in a period of somewhat stalled territorial expansion under Bayezid II (r. 1481–1512) – could not have guessed the scale of things to come. Selim I (r. 1512–1520) would conquer eastern Anatolia, Syria, Egypt, and a part of the Hijaz including Mecca and Medina. By the end of Süleyman I's reign (1520–1566) the empire would be a superpower competing with the Habsburgs in the west and the Safavids in the east, having incorporated a large part of Eastern Europe (up to and almost including Vienna) as well as the Arab world (including much of coastal North Africa).

For military success of such magnitude, the blessing of Sufi saints was considered essential in the Turco-Mongol Muslim realm. Numerous accounts of saintly interventions facilitating major Ottoman conquests, which we find in Sufi hagiographies as well as dynastic chronicles, reveal that the Ottomans were no exception in this regard. However, compared to their eastern contemporaries, their relationship with the cult of the saints was markedly constrained. While the Safavids (1501–1722 in Azerbaijan, Iran, and surrounding regions), Shibanids (1500–98 in Central Asia), and Mughals (1526–1739 in the Indian subcontinent) broadly continued the Turco-Mongol patterns of the public veneration of shrines expected of Asian rulers, the Ottoman sultans' interest in Sufism was largely contained within the private realm. Their endorsement of Sufi establishments rarely extended beyond the enhancement of endowments or cash sums given to Sufis as alms. All public acts of royal Sufi devotion, including architectural patronage, were limited to shrines of long deceased shaykhs whose orthodoxy was established by prominent religio-legal scholars. The sultans prayed and distributed alms at the tombs of such esteemed shaykhs on their way to and from military campaigns. However, they still avoided acts of extreme humility, such as walking barefoot to a shrine or sweeping its floors, which Safavid and Mughal rulers performed publicly.[4]

These differences may be explained by various factors. One of them is the Ottoman imperial aspiration that gained momentum after Mehmed II's conquest of Byzantium. This entailed not only fiscal and military but also religio-legal centralization, which brought the Sufi networks affiliated with the ascetic movements of Central Asia under the scrutiny of a newly centralized hierarchy of Sunni religio-legal scholars (in Ottoman, 'ilmiyye). Mehmed's empire thus drifted away from the devotional practices that continued to flourish under its eastern contemporaries. This divergence was then exacerbated by the sectarian conflict with the Shi'ite Safavids that arose during the reign of Bayezid II and persisted throughout the sixteenth century. As the emergence of the Safavids from a shrine in Ardabil made the Ottoman state increasingly suspicious of Sufi networks, the sultans restricted their architectural patronage of Sufi shrines to a select few. Even the convent-shrine of Ede Bali, who figured prominently in the dream narrative that was supposed to have presaged the dynasty's political success, remained otherwise absent from dynastic chronicles or ceremonies.

Architecturally, it seems to have hardly changed between the time of Orhan (r. 1324–62), who built the tombs over the shaykh and his daughter, and the time of 'Abdülhamid II (r. 1876–62), who rebuilt the convent.[5]

The select few that attracted royal patronage in the early modern period included, most notably, the shrine of Muhy al-din Ibn al-'Arabi (henceforth Ibn 'Arabi) in Damascus, which was constructed on the order of Selim I (r. 1512–20) in 1518, and the shrine of Jalal al-din al-Rumi (henceforth Rumi) in Konya, which benefited from imperial patronage throughout the sixteenth century. In both cases, the orthodoxy of the buried saint was confirmed by responsa (*fatwa*s) issued from the top of the Ottoman 'ilmiyye. These included one which declared Ibn 'Arabi orthodox, by the chief jurisconsult (*muftī*) Ibn Kamal (a.k.a. Kemal-Pasha-zade, d. 1534) who had been supreme judge of Anatolian provinces at the time of the construction of Ibn 'Arabi's shrine.[6] Although the later chief *muftī* Chivi-zade (d. 1547) challenged his opinion around 1540 and declared the followers of both Ibn 'Arabi and Rumi heretics, he was soon removed from the post, and the orthodoxy of both shaykhs

2 Shrine of Ibn 'Arabi, Damascus, 1518, view of entrance.
Photo: Ross Burns/Manar al-Athar

was reestablished by Abu al-Su'ud, chief *muftī* from 1545 until his death in 1574.[7] We will now consider the architectural transformation of the shrines of Ibn 'Arabi and Rumi against this background, before turning to another Sufi shrine which unlike them remained outside the pale of Ottoman orthodoxy. The shrine of Haji Bektash al-Khurasani, as we will see, underwent extensive architectural transformation in the same period, but in very different circumstances of patronage and religio-legal standing vis-à-vis the Ottoman establishment.

IBN 'ARABI

Ibn 'Arabi's shrine in Damascus (Fig. 1) was commissioned by Selim I following the Battle of Ridaniyya (Egypt), where he vanquished the Mamluk army in 1517. This was the second one of Selim's two crowning military achievements, the first being the Battle of Chaldiran (near the modern Iranian-Turkish border), where he had defeated Isma'il I (r. 1501–24) three years earlier, crushing the credibility of the Safavid shah's claim to God-given invincibility. Selim's decisive victory in Egypt in the winter of 1517 brought an end to Mamluk sovereignty, resulting in the annexation of Egypt, Syria, Palestine, and the Hijaz, and thus the three holiest cities of Islam (Mecca, Medina and Jerusalem), to the Ottoman empire. Perhaps in order to justify his bold assault on such sacred territory, Selim's first two architectural commissions following the victory were shrines: that of Prophet David near Aleppo, where in 1516 Selim had defeated the Mamluk army for the first time, and that of Ibn 'Arabi in Damascus.[8]

The construction of Ibn 'Arabi's shrine was completed during the winter of 1517–18, which Selim, returning victoriously from Egypt, spent in Damascus.[9] It is located away from the commercial hub of the city, but on the main thoroughfare of Salihiyya, an extramural quarter that teemed with theological scholars and students who were attracted there by a number of *madrasa*s. Crucially, it was home to a longstanding community of Hanbali jurists and students. Hostile to the cult of the saints as well as Ibn 'Arabi's teachings, the

Hanbalis in Salihiyya had quite possibly hindered the construction of his shrine under the Mamluks.[10] The Ottoman complex has a daringly prominent presence in that setting, flanking the thoroughfare with Ibn 'Arabi's domed mausoleum and an adjacent Friday mosque on one side, and a soup kitchen for the distribution of food to the poor (an Ottoman institution known in the region as *takiyya*) on the other side, which according to its inscription was renovated on the order of sultan Süleyman I in 1554. The mosque and tomb share a small courtyard surrounded by porticos, accessible from the street through a gateway topped by a single minaret (Figs. 2 and 3). The Arabic foundation inscription over the entrance, dated February 1518, announces Selim's caliphal status as *al-imām al-aʿẓam* (greatest

3 Shrine of Ibn 'Arabi, Damascus, 1518, minaret above the entrance.
Photo: Ross Burns/Manar al-Athar

SUFI SHRINES UNDER THE OTTOMANS 301

Imam), immediately followed by two significant items of Islamic regnal titulature previously used by the Mamluks: *malik al-ʿarab wa al-ʿajam* (king of Arabs and Persians), perhaps alluding to his victories against the Mamluks in 1517 and the Safavids in 1514, and *khādim al-ḥaramayn al-sharīfayn* (custodian of the two noble sanctuaries in Mecca and Medina).

Ibn Tulun (d. 1546), a local scholar who witnessed the initial construction process and then found employment as prayer leader and Quran reciter in the mosque, wrote that Selim first ordered the demolition of an unfinished Mamluk mosque at the site.[11] Although this might seem to indicate Selim's desire to stamp the site with an Ottoman identity, stylistically and in terms of construction methods and materials, the buildings are in keeping with the architecture of the region. The mosque is a hypostyle structure; although it was renovated and enlarged in the twentieth century, there is no indication that the original structure followed the domical mosque type prevalent in the central Ottoman lands. Furthermore, the polychrome masonry of the courtyard facades and the entrance, the minaret sitting on an octagonal base above the gate, and the pointed dome of the mausoleum are elements shared with the Mamluk architecture of Syria. This conformity with regional practice did not escape the attention of a late sixteenth-century author, who noted that the mosque reflects the building traditions of the "Arab lands".[12] Indeed, the manifestly Ottoman elements of decoration are limited to a few finishing touches. A conical cap, characteristic of the slender Ottoman minaret type, sits awkwardly atop the Mamluk-style octagonal minaret of polychrome masonry (Fig. 3). The roofs of the mosque, the entrance into its courtyard, and the dome of the mausoleum were covered with lead as was standard practice in Ottoman imperial complexes. Finally, the interior walls of the mausoleum were decorated, perhaps under Süleyman or later, with tiles that were probably produced locally but in the same underglaze painted technique as Iznik tiles, and similar to them in style (Fig. 4).[13] The tile decoration includes a monumental Quranic inscription (55: 1–6) above the *mihrab* in the tomb chamber.

Selim's choice of Ibn ʿArabi's shrine as one of his first commissions in the conquered lands could not have been accidental. Ibn ʿArabi had been a controversial figure in Islamic jurisprudence since the early fourteenth century, and perhaps more than anywhere else, in the Salihiyya quarter

4 Shrine of Ibn ʿArabi, Damascus, tiles inside the tomb chamber, probably sixteenth century.
Photo: Michael Greenhalgh/Manar al-Athar

of Damascus. Here, proponents of his monistic doctrine had been attacked by the Hanbali jurist Ibn Taymiyya (d. 1328), initiating a polemic between generations of Hanbali scholars and Sufis. From the inception of the dynasty, the Ottomans appeared on the pro-Sufi side and offered patronage to scholars who were followers of Ibn ʿArabi. In 1330 Orhan appointed one of them, Daʾud al-Qaysari (d. 1350), to the professorship of the first Ottoman *madrasa* in Iznik. Ibn ʿArabi's teachings were no doubt part of the curriculum there, and endured in Ottoman religious scholarship through subsequent generations,[14] especially from the reign of Murad II (r. 1421–44 and 1446–51) onwards.[15] By contrast, he seems to have remained a highly controversial figure in Mamluk Egypt.[16] The renowned Ottoman scholar Shams al-din al-Fanari (d. 1431) taught Ibn

'Arabi's *Fuṣūṣ al-Ḥikam* (The Bezels of Wisdom) as a canonical text in the *madrasa*, but following the advice of concerned colleagues, he was careful not to mention this to anyone during his sojourn in Cairo.[17]

Whatever the actual motives behind Selim's patronage were, it seems to have raised his profile among certain Sufi circles in the Arab lands. In a treatise that purports to contain prophesies by Ibn 'Arabi, we find a couplet that alludes to the construction of his tomb in the aftermath of Selim's conquest: "When the *sīn* [initial of *Selīm*] enters the *shīn* [initial of *Shām*, i.e. Syria] / There will appear the tomb of Muhy al-din".[18] Although the actual date of composition cannot be ascertained, this indicates that the shrine came to be seen as owing its existence to this crucial Ottoman victory. On a local level, Selim's patronage of the shrine was no doubt greatly appreciated by Sufis in Damascus.[19] However, his motives probably transcended the local milieu, given that shortly afterwards he commissioned a Sufi scholar who had studied with 'Abd al-Rahman al-Jami (d. 1492) in late Timurid Herat to compose a treatise defending the orthodoxy of *Fuṣūṣ al-Ḥikam* (The Bezels of Wisdom).[20] This treatise was composed in Persian and thus would have had limited readership in the newly conquered Arab lands, or in the Ottoman heartlands. However, it would still have resonated with the defensive mode of the proponents of Ibn 'Arabi in Ottoman Anatolia and Balkans, who included Sufi (in particular Khalwati) shaykhs as well as religio-legal scholars who were associated with them. They were doubly likely to face accusations of heresy in the wake of Selim's conquests, with sensitivity concerning the Sufi cult of saints heightened by the Ottoman-Safavid conflict, and with the prospect of Hanbali scholars from the conquered Mamluk lands having an influence on the Ottoman *'ilmiyye*. Indeed, it was such an accusation that led to Ibn Kamal's *fatwa* concerning Ibn 'Arabi. The chief *muftī* was asked: "What should be done with those who accuse Ibn 'Arabi of heresy?" In an official endorsement rarely afforded as clearly to a Sufi's legacy, he responded that the sultan had a duty to punish those accusers.

The shrine complex of Rumi (d. 1273) in Konya, the center of the Mawlawi order of dervishes, was fairly established by the time Ottoman forces captured the city from the Qaramanids (central Anatolia, circa 1250–1474) in 1467. It underwent considerable remodeling and expansion under the Ottomans, but the construction phases remain unclear.[21]

A Persian hagiography of Rumi, by Aflaki (d.1360), recounts that the mausoleum was sponsored immediately upon Rumi's death in 1273 by a group of late Seljuk grandees, including the commander (*amīr*) 'Alam al-din Qaysar, the chancellor (*parvāna*) Mu'in al-din Sulayman, and his wife Gurji Khatun, to be built by a polymath named Badr al-din from Tabriz, who excelled not only in architecture but also in alchemy and philosophy.[22] Later, according to Shikari's (d. 1584) Turkish chronicle based on a lost Persian verse account of the Qaramanid dynasty, the ruler 'Ala al-din 'Ali (r. circa 1357–97) had the tomb reconstructed and covered with green tiles in fulfilment of a vow, following a victorious assault against the Armenian Kingdom of Cilicia (1198–1375).[23] The tomb chamber that contains the sarcophagi of Rumi and his father Baha al-din Walad is topped by a tower with a double-shelled roof. Layers of rebuilding and redecoration make the construction phases of the mausoleum impossible to determine with certainty; nonetheless, the formal and structural similarities of the tomb tower to that of Sayyid Mahmud Khayrani in nearby Akşehir (1409–10) have been noted.[24]

The painted decoration on the interior south wall of the tomb chamber, and on the piers carrying the tomb tower rising above it (Fig. 5), was signed by a Mawlawi craftsman named 'Abd al-Rahman b. Muhammad during the reign of Bayezid II (r. 1481–1512).[25] Though the decoration was heavily overpainted in later periods, a recent restoration has recovered its initial state during Bayezid's reign. Besides the rich calligraphic program including mirrored script (*muthannā*) compositions, also found in the interior painted decoration of the tomb of Princes Mustafa and Cem in Bursa (circa 1480),[26] a variation on the theme of paradise garden with rivers, cypresses, and date palms decorates the area around the south window.[27] Further landscape

5 Shrine of Rumi, Konya, interior view towards the tomb chamber.
Photo: Zarifa Alikperova

6 Shrine of Rumi, Konya, aerial view from the west.
Source: "Mevlana Müzesi Havadan Görüntülendi," *Yeni Haber*, 14 December 2015

scenes with rivers, trees, and fortresses, evidently also from Bayezid's reign, have recently been discovered underneath later layers of decoration on the top tier of each of the four piers that carry the vault of the tomb tower.[28]

The core of the shrine consists of a domed hall for the Mawlawi *samāʿ* ritual, a domed mosque, and a structure that now encompasses the tomb tower in one of its eight square bays (Fig. 6). The latter structure functions as a funerary vestibule entered from the western façade. It contains an elongated area of circulation for pilgrims, surrounded by burials including the tomb of Rumi in one of its bays and sarcophagi of later saints in the other bays, and provides access to the ritual hall. A depiction of Konya

7 Shrine of Rumi, Konya, left, and Friday mosque built by Süleyman. Photo: Ömer Tanoğlu

from circa 1537 (Fig. 8) shows the tomb as adjoined by two further sections and a minaret,[29] indicating that all the components in the core of the shrine (tomb and its vestibule, ritual hall and mosque) were complete by that time. The painting also shows the fountain in the courtyard, commissioned by Selim I in 1512.[30] Ottoman chronicles mention Süleyman I as a major architectural patron of the shrine, but the nature of his patronage, mentioned in chronicles, remains uncertain.[31]

In all likelihood, Süleyman commissioned the domed Friday mosque next to the shrine in 1559–60 (Fig. 7).[32] It occupies an area immediately outside the shrine compound proper, but its staff members were paid from the shrine's endowment.[33]

Süleyman's patronage of this monument possibly followed the war of succession between two of his sons, resulting in the victory of the designated heir-apparent Selim (II) over his brother Bayezid. A contemporary chronicle adds a hagiographic flavor to the course of events: during the battle between the two princes, a cloud of dust rises from the shrine of Rumi, and descends upon Bayezid and his soldiers, who are thus thrown into chaos.[34] The author attributes Selim's triumph to the spiritual aid of Rumi and contends that this was a punishment that Bayezid deserved for disobeying his father. The story seems to have been generated and circulated by the Mawlawi community in Konya and was incorporated by the Mawlawi dervish Mahmud

SUFI SHRINES UNDER THE OTTOMANS 305

8 View of Konya with the shrine of Rumi in the lower right corner, from Matrakçı Nasuh's *Beyān-i Menāzil*, 1537–38. Istanbul University Rare Books Library, T 5964, fol. 17a.
Photo: Istanbul University Rare Books Library

9 Battle between Ottoman princes at the shrine of Rumi, from a manuscript of *Terceme-i Şevākıb-ı Menākıb*, 1590s. The Morgan Library & Museum, New York, Ms M.466, fol. 131a.
Photo: The Morgan Library & Museum, New York

into the hagiography of Rumi in 1590 (Fig. 9).[35] The shrine may indeed have played a significant role in a network of loyalty to Prince Selim, who had been governor in Konya. Following his enthronement in 1566, he had a soup kitchen, now demolished, constructed next to the shrine complex.[36] Although the administration of this soup kitchen was independent from the shrine, its endowment deed allocates a specific amount for daily food to be provided to the Mawlawi dervishes there, honoring a special request from the judge of Konya.[37] The involvement of this local representative of the Ottoman religio-legal cadre in soliciting royal patronage on behalf of the Mawlawis confirms their acknowledged orthodoxy, as established by the *fatwa* of the current chief *muftī* Abu al-Su'ud.

The inscription on the gateway into the shrine compound, dated 1584–85, mentions the patronage of Murad III (r. 1574–95).[38] This possibly refers to the entire west wing, which was renovated in the nineteenth century and includes residential rooms for dervishes behind an L-shaped arcade defining the northwestern corner of the courtyard, a communal room, and the kitchen at the southwest corner.

Ottoman sultans and grandees visited the shrine on military campaigns and government missions. Conveniently located as it was on the main route from Istanbul to the southeastern parts of the empire, it was also home to Sufi leaders whose influence extended widely through Mawlawi convents throughout the empire. The Mawlawi network was immensely influential among the learned circles, in accordance with its high regard for refined skills in Persian poetry, music, and calligraphy. The Ottoman commander Lala Mustafa Pasha (d. 1580) visited the shrine on his way to the Safavid front in 1578, listened to music, and had the outcome of the campaign predicted based on a page he randomly opened from

HAJI BEKTASH

a manuscript of Rumi's *Mathnawī-i Maʿnawī* (Spiritual Couplets), a Persian poetic work that was kept in the shrine in several richly illuminated copies and recited in rituals.[39] One of the illustrations for the account of this campaign written by Mustafa ʿĀli (d.1600), who had been the chief clerk for the campaign and personally arranged for the illustration of his account, depicts the commander with the *Mathnawī-i Maʿnawī* in hand, accompanied by the author and the Mawlawi shaykh, sitting between the tomb chamber and the ritual hall packed with whirling dervishes.[40] The image encapsulates not only the Mawlawis' deep-seated interest in the culture of books and the communal appreciation of Persian poetry, but also their pro-establishment stance, which accounts for the unbroken chain of Ottoman royal patronage throughout the sixteenth century.

The close relationship of the shrine with the Ottoman military elite is reflected in the burial of three individuals who served as *beylerbeyi* (governor-general) of the province of Qaraman in mausolea next to Rumi's: Khurram Pasha (d. 1526), who died in battle against Turcoman insurgents in the region; Hasan Pasha (d. 1573–74), husband of a daughter of Selim II, and vizier after serving as *beylerbeyi* of Qaraman; and Sinan Pasha (d. 1573–74), a Georgian prince who converted to Islam and entered Ottoman service during the Safavid campaign of Lala Mustafa Pasha.[41] Also buried there was a daughter of Kuyuji Murad Pasha (d. 1611), who died in 1585–86 while he was *beylerbeyi* of Qaraman.[42] Other grandees embellished the tomb and its vestibule with precious objects and decoration, which included silver furnishings: the silver grill and gate separating the tomb chamber from the vestibule (Fig. 5) were donated in 1597–98 by Mahmud Pasha, *beylerbeyi* of the province of Marʿash in southeast Anatolia, while the silver-plated door panels at the main entrance of the vestibule were donated in 1599–1600 by vizier Hasan Pasha, a son of the former grand vizier Soqollu Mehmed Pasha (d. 1579).[43] Several grandees also donated books to the shrine's library. These included three lavishly illuminated Quran manuscripts given to the shrine by the grand-vizier Rustam Pasha, who also gave one to the tomb of Rumi's companion Shams al-Tabrizi in the same city.[44]

At the same time as the Ottomans endorsed certain Sufi communities whose beliefs and practices were considered uncontentious by Hanafi scholars (Mawlawis and the various branches of the Khalwatis in particular) and molded them further into Sunni orthodoxy, antinomian Sufis gradually united under the legacy of Haji Bektash, a thirteenth-century Khurasanian Sufi who had settled near Kırşehir in the late thirteenth century. The social network around Bektashi shrines and convents was comprised of not just dervishes but also laypeople and villagers who embraced latitudinarian versions of Islam and faced persecution under Ottoman orthodoxy, as well as raider commanders (in Turkish, *akıncı beyleri*) in the Balkans whose autonomy was curbed by centralizing imperial policies.[45] This social convergence among dervishes, villagers, and frontier warriors is reflected in a new genre of hagiography (*velāyetnāme*) that emerged in the late fifteenth century and associated Bektashi saints with the culture of the Ottoman frontiers. Frontier warriors' cherished idols, including the early Ottoman rulers and their commanders as well as the Umayyad warrior Sayyid Battal Ghazi, made anachronistic appearances in these texts. Written in plain Turkish, captured from imaginative oral accounts and geared towards a mixed community of shrine-goers, the *velāyetnāme*s provided an interpretive framework in which the Bektashi shrines could be perceived from the peripheries of the now centralized social order. They told an alternative version of the history of the Ottomans that simultaneously highlighted the importance of the culture of holy war in the Ottoman success and claimed a crucial role in it on behalf of Haji Bektash, his associates, and their followers.[46]

The hagiographic undertaking of the late fifteenth century was followed by the architectural remodeling of key Bektashi shrines. In particular, two rural Anatolian shrines, namely Haji Bektash (near Kırşehir) and Sayyid Battal Ghazi (near Eskişehir), were extensively rebuilt from the 1490s onwards, and transformed into monumental building complexes.[47] Their new ritual and cooking facilities catered not only to pilgrims around the year, but also to huge crowds during

SUFI SHRINES UNDER THE OTTOMANS 307

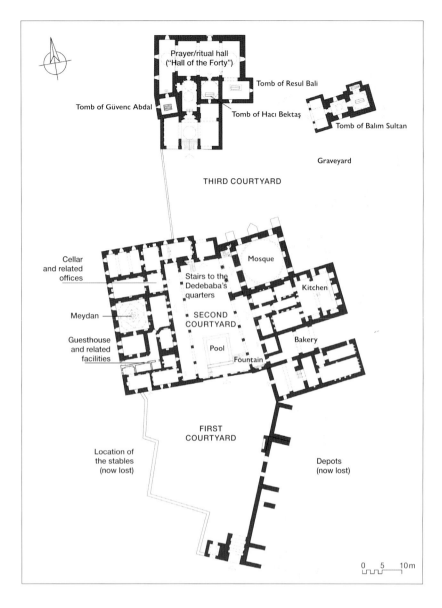

10 Shrine of Haji Bektash, Hacıbektaş near Kırşehir, plan.
Drawing: Zeynep Yürekli

annual festivals in each shrine. Unsurprisingly, the principal architectural patrons appear to have been members of families of raider commanders based in the Balkans. As the exemplary representatives of the culture of frontier warfare, these families (descendants of early Ottoman warriors Evrenos, Mikhal, and Malqoch) had been among the most influential power brokers of early Ottoman history. At the end of the fifteenth century, as their autonomy in the Balkans began to wane under the pressure of imperial centralization, they became the primary cultural patrons of the emerging Bektashi network – offering their patronage to unorthodox dervishes, poets and writers.[48]

The shrine of Haji Bektash is arranged around a succession of three courtyards (Fig. 10).[49] The only part of the complex that predates the late fifteenth century is the core of the shrine in the innermost (third) courtyard, and includes the tomb of Haji Bektash, though its vestibule was enlarged and renovated as a mosque by a local Ottoman governor in 1560–61. A freestanding tomb for Khidr Bali (a.k.a. Balım Sultan), a descendant of Haji Bektash who assumed the leadership of the shrine during the reign of Bayezid II, was built in 1519 by 'Ali b. Shahsuwar, a Dulqadirid vassal of the Ottomans. The middle (second) courtyard is a palimpsest of constructions that may have been initiated in the 1490s and continued in the 1550s under the patronage of the raider commander Bali, a descendent of the early Ottoman warrior Malqoch based in the Balkans, with subsequent renovations in the eighteenth and nineteenth centuries documented by inscriptions and archival documents. It is the administrative core of the shrine, with a mosque, a kitchen, and a bakery on one side, and the ritual hall (*meydan*) and the quarters of the leader of the Bektashi order on the other side (Fig. 11). Contrary to what has been generally assumed in scholarship, the inscription dated 1368, which is now above the gate into the ritual hall to the west of the second courtyard but is quite likely not in its original location, does not refer to Ottoman patronage.[50] The buildings around the outermost (first) courtyard have not survived but included a guesthouse, stables and storage facilities.[51]

Thus the Ottoman-period remodeling of the shrine, with the addition of a series of new buildings to the south of the core of the shrine, created a building complex arranged around a linear succession of courtyards on the north–south axis leading to the tomb. The particular arrangement of courtyards flanked by individual buildings which provided for food preparation facilities on a massive scale, assembly rooms, offices, accommodation, stables, and storage facilities, bears a striking resemblance to the arrangement of Ottoman palaces, particularly the Topkapı Palace in Istanbul, although much smaller in scale.[52] On the other hand, it is also similar to the Safavid shrine in Ardabil, with which the shrine of Haji Bektash shared a group of devotees known as Qizilbash.

11 Shrine of Haji Bektash, Hacıbektaş near Kırşehir, second courtyard looking towards the south, with (from left to right) the mosque, kitchen and museum offices (constructed in the twentieth century) in the eastern wing, the entrance from the first courtyard in the middle, and the western wing with the entrance to the ritual hall (*meydan*).
Photo: Gücügür Görkay

12 Kitchen of the shrine of Haji Bektash, 1560–61.
Photo: Gücügür Görkay

In particular, the predominance of the kitchen in the second courtyard (Figs. 11 and 12) finds parallels in Ottoman palaces as well as the Safavid shrine in Ardabil, and draws on the Turco-Mongol tradition of providing food to the masses in shrines, a practice documented also for the Timurid and Mughal milieus.[53]

CONCLUSION

The influence of a Sufi shrine tended to go deep into society and far beyond its immediate surroundings, through the mediation of discipleship, pilgrimage, legend, and scholarly debate. Whilst attracting pilgrims from far-away lands, Sufi shrines were maintained by close-knit communities. Their patronage could therefore serve as a dual-purpose political tool, one that enabled patrons to address not only a wide and varied audience, but also a more limited local audience with specific messages. However, the use of this tool by the Ottomans was complicated by clashing opinions concerning the cult of the saints amongst Ottoman religio-legal bureaucrats, especially after the rise of the Safavids from a Sufi shrine as the Ottomans' fervent ideological enemy and hostile neighbor. Thus no Sufi shrine in the Ottoman empire acquired a level of ceremonial import comparable to the shrine of Shaykh Safi al-din in Ardabil under the Safavids or that of Muin al-din Chishti in Ajmer under

SUFI SHRINES UNDER THE OTTOMANS 309

the Mughals.[54] The shrine that was most closely connected to the Ottoman dynasty belonged to a martyr rather than a Sufi saint, namely Abu Ayyub al-Ansari, one of prophet Muhammad's "helpers" (*anṣār*) who had died during Yazid ibn Muawiya's (d. 683) siege of Constantinople outside the city walls (in the area known today as Eyüp).[55] The shrine constructed there by Mehmed II after the conquest later came to play a significant role in royal ceremonies that no Ottoman Sufi shrine played.[56]

Given how circumspect the Ottoman religio-legal establishment was vis-à-vis the cult of Sufi saints, none of our three thirteenth-century Sufis would have acquired the shrine he has, had he not found his niche in sixteenth-century religio-politics, from where proponents came to his defense. Both in Damascus and Konya, royal architectural patronage accompanied the pro-Ottoman stances taken by local Sufi communities. In both cases, sultanic patronage was legitimized by responsa that established the orthodoxy of the enshrined saints. These two factors – sympathy for Ottomans, and confirmed orthodoxy – seem to have attracted a certain level of royal patronage. Meanwhile, in the case of Haji Bektash, raider commanders from the Balkans were drawn to the shrine by legends that established a connection between the saint and the early Ottoman warriors, attesting to the power of hagiography in building a sociopolitical network around the cult of a saint.

ZEYNEP YÜREKLI is Associate Professor of Islamic Art and Architecture at the University of Oxford. She researches late medieval and early modern Islamic architecture and illustrated manuscripts. Her book, *Architecture and Hagiography in the Ottoman Empire: The Politics of Bektashi Shrines in the Classical Age* (Ashgate), was published in 2012.

SUGGESTIONS FOR FURTHER READING

Doğan, Ahmet Işık. *Osmanlı Mimarisinde Tarikat Yapıları, Tekkeler, Zaviyeler ve Benzer Nitelikteki Fütuvvet Yapıları* (Istanbul: İstanbul Teknik Üniversitesi, 1977).

Lifchez, Raymond, ed. *The Dervish Lodge: Architecture, Art, and Sufism in Ottoman Turkey* (Berkeley: University of California Press, 1992).

Tanman, Baha. "Tariqah Buildings / Tekkes in Ottoman Architecture," in Halil Inalcık and Günsel Renda, eds., *Ottoman Civilization*, 2 vols. (Ankara: Ministry of Culture, 2003), 1: 288–307.

Yürekli, Zeynep. *Architecture and Hagiography in the Ottoman Empire: The Politics of Bektashi Shrines in the Classical Age* (Farnham: Ashgate, 2012).

Yürekli, Zeynep. "Writing Down the Feats and Setting Up the Scene: Hagiographers and Architectural Patrons in the Age of Empires," in John J. Curry and Erik S. Ohlander, eds., *Sufism and Society: Arrangements of the Mystical in the Muslim World, 1200–1800* (London and New York: Routledge), 94–119.

NOTES

1. See, for example: Pseudo-Ibn al-'Arabi and Pseudo-Sadr al-din al-Qunawi, *Al-shajara al-nu'māniyya*, ed. Mamduh al-Zubi (Beirut and Damascus: Al-Manāra, 2001) [Ibn al-'Arabi's prophesies concerning the Ottomans]. Lokmanî Dede, *Menâkıb-ı Mevlâna*, ed. Halil Ersoylu (Ankara: Türk Dil Kurumu, 2001), 35–6 [on Rumi's views concerning the Ottomans]. Anon., *Velâyetnâme*, ed. Hamiye Duran (Ankara: Türkiye Diyanet Vakfı, 2007), 528–41 (fols. 119b-122b); Anon., *Manzûm Hacı Bektâş Veli Velâyetnâmesi*, ed. Bedri Noyan (Aydın: B. Noyan, 1986), 347–53; Zeynep Yürekli, *Architecture and Hagiography in the Ottoman Empire: The Politics of Bektashi Shrines in the Classical Age* (Farnham: Ashgate, 2012), 65–6 [on the investiture of 'Osman or his father Ertughrul as a frontier warrior by Haji Bektash].

2. Parts of this essay focusing on the shrines of Ibn 'Arabi and Rumi were published previously in a conference publication by the Research Centre for Anatolian Civilizations (ANAMED) of Koç University in Istanbul: Zeynep Yürekli, "Ibn al-'Arabi and Rumi in the Twists and Turns of Ottoman Religio-Politics," in *Sacred Spaces and Urban Networks*, ed. Suzan Yalman and A. Hilal Uğurlu (Istanbul: Koç University Research Centre for Anatolian Civilizations, 2019), 159–75. For an extensive treatment of the shrine of Haji Bektash, see Yürekli, *Architecture and Hagiography*.

3. Friedrich Giese, *Die altosmanische Chronik des 'Āšiķpašazāde* (Osnabrück: Otto Zeller, 1972), 9–10; Colin Imber, "The Ottoman Dynastic Myth," *Turcica* 19 (1987), 20–22 (7–27); Cemal Kafadar, *Between Two Worlds: The Construction of the Ottoman State* (Berkeley: University of California Press, 1995), 8

4. Charles Melville, "Shah Abbas and the Pilgrimage to Mashhad," *Pembroke Papers* 4 (1996): 191–229; S.A.I. Tirmizi, "Mughal Documents Relating to the Dargah of Khwaja Mu'inuddin Chishti," in *Muslim Shrines in India: Their Character, History and Significance*, ed. Christian W. Troll (Delhi: Oxford University Press, 1989), 48–59; Abu al-Fazl b. Mubarak, *The Akbarnāma of Abu'l Fazl*, trans. Henry Beveridge, 3 vols. (Calcutta: Royal Asiatic Society, 1897), 2: 476–7.

5. M. Baha Tanman, "Edebâli Zâviyesi," *Türkiye Diyanet Vakfı İslâm Ansiklopedisi*, 44 vols. (Istanbul: Türkiye Diyanet Vakfı, 1983–2013), vol. 10, 394–5; Ekrem Hakkı Ayverdi, *İlk 250 Senenin Osmanlı Mimârîsi* (Istanbul: İstanbul Fetih Cemiyeti, 1976), 35–6.

6. Éric Geoffroy, *Le Soufisme en Égypte et en Syrie sous les derniers Mamelouks et les premiers Ottomans: Orientations spirituelles et enjeux culturels* (Damascus: Institut Français de Damas, 1995), 133–4, 511; Richard C. Repp, *The Müfti of Istanbul: A Study in the Development of the Ottoman Learned Hierarchy* (London: Ithaca Press, 1986), 231–2.

7. Ibid., 250, 252; Gülru Necipoğlu, *The Age of Sinan: Architectural Culture in the Ottoman Empire* (London: Reaktion, 2005), 60–1.

8. Ibid., 60.

9. Celâl-zâde Mustafa, *Selim-nâme,* ed. Ahmet Uğur and Mustafa Çuhadar (Ankara: Kültür Bakanlığı, 1990), 209; *Tārīḫ-i Nişāncı Meḥmed Paşa* (Istanbul: Maṭbaʿa-i ʿĀmire, 1290H/1873), 215–16; Saʿd al-din, *Tācü't-ṭevārīḫ*, 2 vols. (Istanbul, 1279–1280H/1862–1864), 2: 379–80; Muhammad Adnan Bakhit, *The Ottoman Province of Damascus in the Sixteenth Century* (Beirut: Librairie du Liban, 1982), 15–16, 115–16; Richard van Leeuwen, *Waqfs and Urban Structures: The Case of Ottoman Damascus* (Leiden: Brill, 1999), 95–101; Abd al-Qadir al-Rihawi and Émilie E. Ouéchek, "Les deux takiyya de Damas: la takiyya et la madrasa Sulaymaniyya de Marg et la takiyya as-Salimiyya de Salihiyya," *Bulletin d'Etudes Orientales* 28 (1975): 217–25.

10. Ryad Atlagh, "Paradoxes of a Mausoleum," *Journal of the Muhyiddin ibn 'Arabi Society* 22 (1997), 5–7 (1–24).

11. Ibn Tulun, *Al-Qalā'id al-jawhariyya fī tarikh al-Ṣāliḥiyya* (Damascus: Maktab al-Dirāsāt al-Islāmiyya, 1949), 64–6, 69–70; idem, *Mufākahat al-khillān fī ḥawādith al-zamān: Tārīkh Miṣr wa al-Shām*, 2 vols. (Cairo: Wizārat al-Thaqāfa wa al-Irshād al-Qawmī, 1962–1964), 2: 68–80.

12. Necipoğlu, *Age of Sinan*, 224; Çiğdem Kafescioğlu, "'In the Image of Rūm': Ottoman Architectural Patronage in Sixteenth-Century Aleppo and Damascus," *Muqarnas* 16 (1999), 80 (70–96); Âşık Mehmed, *Menâzırü'l-Avâlim*, ed. Mahmut Ak, 3 vols. (Ankara: Türk Tarih Kurumu, 2007), 2: 633–4; MS. Süleymaniye Library, Halet Efendi 616, fol. 229b.

13. Gérard Degeorge, *Damascus* (Paris: Flammarion, 2004), 161–2.

14. Mehmet Bayraktar, "Dâvûd-i Kayserî," *Türkiye Diyanet Vakfı İslam Ansiklopedisi*, vol. 9, 32–5; M. Erol Kılıç, "İbnü'l-Arabî, Muhyiddin," *Türkiye Diyanet Vakfı İslam Ansiklopedisi*, vol. 20, 513–15 (493–516).

15 Hüseyin Yılmaz, *Caliphate Redefined: The Mystical Turn in Ottoman Political Thought* (Princeton: Princeton University Press, 2018), 131–2.

16 Alexander D. Knysh, *Ibn 'Arabi in the Later Islamic Tradition: The Making of a Polemical Image in Medieval Islam* (Albany: State University of New York Press, 1999), 201–23.

17 Şevkiye İnalcık, "İbn Hâcer'de Osmanlılar'a Dair Haberler III," *Ankara Üniversitesi Dil ve Tarih-Coğrafya Fakültesi Dergisi* 6 (1948), 520, 527 (517–29), quoting from Ibn Hajar al-Asqalani, *Ibnā' al-ghumr fī abnā' al-'umr*; Repp, *Müfti of Istanbul*, 86–7.

18 *Al-shajara al-nu'māniyya*, ed. al-Zūbī, 61–2; Atlagh, "Paradoxes," 16–21; Denis Gril, "L'énigme de la Šağara al-nu'māniyya fîl-dawla al-'utmāniyya, attribuée à Ibn 'Arabi," in *Les traditions apocalyptiques au tournant de la chute de Constantinople*, ed. Benjamin Lellouch and Stéphane Yérasimos [Varia Turcica 33] (Paris and Montreal: L'Harmattan, 1999), 133–51; Michel Chodkiewicz, *An Ocean Without Shore: Ibn Arabi, the Book, and the Law* (Albany: State University of New York Press, 1993), 17, 137 n.55; Geoffroy, *Le Soufisme en Égypte et en Syrie*, 134–5.

19 Ibid., 452–65.

20 Shaykh Makki Muhammad b. Muhammad, *Al-Jānib al-gharbī fī ḥall mushkīlāt al-shaykh Muḥyī l-Dīn ibn al-'Arabī* (Tehran: Mawlā, 1364 [1985–1986]).

21 For a summary of the architectural development of the complex, see Haşim Karpuz, "Mevlânâ Külliyesi," in *Türkiye Diyanet Vakfı İslam Ansiklopedisi*, vol. 29, 448–52. Zarifa Alikperova's forthcoming work revisits the chronology of buildings and uncovers previously unknown aspects of patronage, not addressed here.

22 Suzan Yalman, "Badr al-dīn Tabrīzī," *Encyclopaedia of Islam*, Third Edition, vol. 4, 9–10; Shams al-din Ahmad al-Aflaki al-'Arifi, *Manāqib al-'Ārifīn*, ed. Tahsin Yazıcı, 2 vols. (Ankara: Türk Tarih Kurumu, 1976), 1: 141, 193, 387–9; 2: 792.

23 Yalman, 10; Şikârî, *Karamannâme: Zamanın Kahramanı Karamanîler'in Tarihi*, ed. Metin Sözen and Necdet Sakaoğlu (Karaman: Karaman Valiliği, 2005), 177–8, 89b–90a.

24 Karpuz, "Mevlânâ Külliyesi," 449.

25 *Nuqisha al-qubba al-khaḍrā fī ayyām dawlah al-sulṭān al-mu'ayyad bi-ta'yīd allah al-musta'ān Sulṭān Bāyazīd bn Muḥammad Khān 'alā yad al-'abd al-ḍa'īf al-Mawlawī 'Abd al-Raḥman bn Muḥammad al-Ḥalabī* [possibly *al-Chalabī*] *wa anshada fī tārīkhihi hādhayn al-baytayn* […]. I have previously suggested a reading of the last words as *hadīr al-tanbīr*, which as a chronogram would give the date 912H (1506/7) but after a close look at photographs taken during restoration, I revert to Konyalı's reading as *hādhayn al-baytayn*, which must have been followed by two couplets that contained a chronogram, now unfortunately lost; see İbrahim Hakkı Konyalı, *Abideleri ve Kitabeleri ile Konya Tarihi* (Konya: Yeni Kitap Basımevi, 1964), 644–5.

26 Serpil Bağcı, "Osmanlı Mimarisinde Boyalı Nakışlar," in *Osmanlı Uygarlığı*, ed. Halil İnalcık and Günsel Renda, 2 vols. (Ankara: Kültür ve Turizm Bakanlığı, 2004), 2: 737–59. For other examples of *muthannā* compositions, see Esra Akın-Kıvanç, *Muthanna / Mirror Writing in Islamic Calligraphy* (Bloomington, Indiana: Indiana University Press, 2020).

27 Though there has been some confusion about the dating of this landscape scene, Serpil Bağcı argued that despite being heavily overpainted, in terms of mode of representation it is to be dated to Bayezid II's reign. The recent restorations have proven her correct. See Bağcı, "Osmanlı Mimarisinde Boyalı Nakışlar," 741.

28 Ali Fuat Baysal and Ayşe Zeyra Sayın, "Restorasyon Sonrası Kubbe-i Hadrâ Kalem İşleri Üzerine Bir Değerlendirme," *İSTEM İslam Sanat, Tarih, Edebiyat ve Musiki Dergisi* 33 (2019): 39–64; Ali Fuat Baysal, *Kubbe-i Hadrâ Kalemişi Tezyînâtı ve Onarımı* (Konya: Palet Yayınları, 2020).

29 Ms. Istanbul, Istanbul University Library, T 5964, 17a; Naṣūḥü's-Silāḥī (Maṭrākçī), *Beyān-ı Menāzil-i Sefer-i 'Irāḳeyn-i Sulṭān Süleymān Ḫān*, ed. Hüseyin G. Yurdaydın (Ankara: Türk Tarih Kurumu, 1976).

30 Konyalı, *Konya Tarihi*, 646.

31 Ibid., 649.

32 Necipoğlu, *Age of Sinan*, 63.

33 Konyalı, *Konya Tarihi*, 534–5.

34 Matrakçı Nasuh, *Rüstem Paşa Tarihi Olarak Bilinen Târîh-i Âl-i Osmân (Osmanlı Tarihi 699–968/1299–1561)*, ed. Göker İnan (Istanbul: Türkiye Yazma Eserler Kurumu Baskanlığı, 2019), 479.

35 Dervish Mahmud, *Terceme-i Şevāḳıb-ı Menāḳıb*, ms. New York, Morgan Library, MS M.466, fols. 130b–131b.

36 Konyalı, *Konya Tarihi*, 969–80.

37 Ibid., 977; İbrahim Ateş, "Hz. Mevlânâ Dergâhı ile ilgili Vakıf ve Vakfiyeler," IX. *Vakıf Haftası Kitabı: Türk Vakıf Medeniyetinde Hz. Mevlânâ ve Mevlevihânelerin Yeri ve Vakıf Eserlerde Yer Alan Türk-İslâm Sanatları Seminerleri* (Ankara: Vakıflar Genel Müdürlüğü, 1992), 34 (29–66).

38 Konyalı, *Konya Tarihi*, 649–50.

39 Necipoğlu, *Age of Sinan*, 64, 66; Mustafa Eravcı, *Mustafa 'Âli's Nusret-nâme and Ottoman-Safavi Conflict* (Istanbul: MVT, 2011), 21; Mustafa Âli, *Nuṣretnâme*, ms. London, British Library, Add. 22011, fols. 34a-36a; ms. Istanbul, Topkapı Palace Library, H.1365, fol. 36a.

40 Necipoğlu, *Age of Sinan*, 64, 66; Serpil Bağcı et al., *Osmanlı Resim Sanatı* (Ankara: T.C. Kültür ve Turizm Bakanlığı Yayınları, 2006), 166, 168.

41 Konyalı, *Konya Tarihi*, 612–13, 616–19, 736–8.

42 Ibid., 692–6.

43 Ibid., 687–90.

44 Mss. Konya, Mevlana Museum 2, 3, 5, 6; Abdülbaki Gölpınarlı, *Mevlânâ Müzesi Müzelik Yazma Kitaplar Kataloğu* (Ankara: Türk Tarih Kurumu, 2003), 3–7.

45 Yürekli, *Architecture and Hagiography*, 25–50.

46 Kafadar, *Between Two Worlds*, 97–8; Yürekli, *Architecture and Hagiography*, 4–8, 58–78.

47 Yürekli, *Architecture and Hagiography*, 79–133.

48 Machiel Kiel, "Yenice Vardar (Vardar Yenicesi-Giannitsa): A Forgotten Turkish Cultural Center in Macedonia of the 15th and 16th century," in *Studia Byzantina et Neohellenica Neerlandica* III, ed. Willem F. Bakker, Arnold F. van Gemert, and Willem J. Aerts (Leiden: Brill, 1972), 300–29; Kafadar, *Between Two Worlds*, 147, 190; Hiclâl Demir, *Çağlarını Eleştiren Divan Şairleri: Hayretî – Usûlî – Hayâlî*, MA thesis (Bilkent University, Ankara, 2001); Mariya Kiprovska, "The Mihaloğlu Family: Gazi Warriors and Patrons of Dervish Hospices," *Osmanlı Araştırmaları* 32 (2008): 193–222; Yürekli, *Architecture and Hagiography*, 126–33; Mariya Kiprovska, "Shaping the Ottoman Borderland: The Architectural Patronage of the Frontier Lords from the Mihaloğlu Family," in *Bordering Early Modern Europe*, ed. Maria Baramova, Grigor Boykov and Ivan Parvev (Wiesbaden: Harrassowitz, 2015), 185–220.

49 See Mahmut Akok, "Hacıbektaşi Veli Mimari Manzumesi," *Türk Etnografya Dergisi* 10 (1967): 27–57; Baha Tanman, "Hacı Bektâş-ı Velî Külliyesi," in *Türkiye Diyanet Vakfı İslam Ansiklopedisi* (Istanbul, 1988–), vol.14, 459–71; idem., "Hacıbektaş-ı Veli Külliyesi," in *Nevşehir* (Ankara: Kültür Bakanlığı, 1996), 144–61; Yürekli, *Architecture and Hagiography*.

50 Zeynep Yürekli, "Bir Kitabenin Söylemeye Çalıştıkları," *Journal of Turkish Studies – Türklük Bilgisi Araştırmaları Dergisi* 31 (2007), 339–48; idem, *Architecture and Hagiography*, 107–9.

51 Sirri Pasha, *Mektūbāt-ı Sırrı Paşa*, ed. Arakel [Tozliyan] (Istanbul: Şirket-i Mürettibiye Maṭbaʻası, 1303/1886), 175; Akok, "Hacıbektaşi Veli," 28; Tanman, "Hacı Bektâş-ı Veli," 461; Yürekli, *Architecture and Hagiography*, 149–52.

52 Tanman, "Hacı Bektâş-ı Velî Külliyesi," 462; Yürekli, *Architecture and Hagiography*, 143–9.

53 Tirmizi, "Mughal Documents," 50–51; Syed Liyaqat Hussain Moini, "Rituals and Customary Practices at the Dargah of Ajmer," in *Muslim Shrines in India*, ed. Troll, 62–3 (60–75); Gülru Necipoğlu, *Architecture, Ceremonial, and Power: The Topkapı Palace in the Fifteenth and Sixteenth Centuries* (Cambridge, Mass.: MIT Press, 1991), 55, 69–72; Rhoads Murphey, *Exploring Ottoman Sovereignty: Tradition, Image and Practice in the Ottoman Imperial Household, 1400–1800* (London and New York: Continuum, 2008), 28–35, 200–3; Kishwar Rizvi, *The Safavid Dynastic Shrine: Architecture, Religion and Power in Early Modern Iran* (London: I.B. Tauris, 2010), 129, 155–6; Yürekli, *Architectue and Hagiography*, 149–52.

54 See P.M. Currie, *The Shrine and Cult of Muʻin al-Din Chishti of Ajmer* (New Delhi: Oxford University Press, 1989); S. Liyaqat H. Moini, *The Chishti Shrine of Ajmer: Pirs, Pilgrims, Practices* (Jaipur: Publication Scheme, 2004); Rizvi, *Safavid Dynastic Shrine*; Zeynep Yürekli, "Writing Down the Feats and Setting Up the Scene: Hagiographers and Architectural Patrons in the Age of Empires," in *Sufism and Society: Arrangements of the Mystical in the Muslim World, 1200–1800*, ed. John J. Curry and Erik S. Ohlander (London and New York: Routledge, 2012), 96–7, 100–4 (94–119).

55 See Feray Coşkun, *Sanctifying Ottoman Istanbul: The Shrine of Abū Ayyūb al-Anṣārī*, doctoral thesis (Freie Universität, Berlin, 2016); Çiğdem Kafescioğlu, *Constantinopolis/Istanbul: Cultural Encounter, Imperial Vision and the Construction of the Ottoman Capital* (University Park: Pennsylvania State University Press, 2009), 45–51.

56 Nicolas Vatin, "Aux origines de pèlerinage à Eyüp des sultans ottomans," *Turcica* 27 (1995), 91–9; Cemal Kafadar, "Eyüp'te Kılıç Kuşanma Törenleri," in *Eyüp: Dün-Bugün Sempozyum 11–12 Aralık 1993* (Istanbul: Tarih Vakfı Yurt Yayınları, 1994), 50–61; Gülru Necipoğlu, "Dynastic Imprints on the Cityscape: The Collective Message of Imperial Funerary Mosque Complexes in Istanbul," in *Cimetières et traditions funéraires dans le monde Islamique*, ed. Jean-Louis Bacqué-Grammont and Aksel Tibet, 2 vols. (Ankara: Türk Tarih Kurumu, 1996), 2: 23–36; idem, *Age of Sinan*, 66–7.

Seljuk and Ottoman Mosques

ALI UZAY PEKER

1 Mihrimah Mosque, Edirnekapı, 1560, domed central space with western main arch and arcade.
Photo: Ali Uzay Peker

Before the Seljuks, the Muslim presence in Anatolia consisted of periodic Arabic incursions into its southeastern lands. Seljuks brought to Anatolia the architectural traditions and high culture of the early Islamic cities that had flourished in Central Asia, Iran, and upper Mesopotamia. Seljuk and later Ottoman architects also learned a great deal from existing Anatolian traditions.

MOSQUES IN PRE-OTTOMAN ANATOLIA

The traditional hypostyle mosque of Arabia and the kiosk mosque of Iran were brought to Anatolia immediately after the arrival of the Muslims. Early great mosques from the eleventh and twelfth centuries like Diyarbakır (1092) (Fig. 2), Siirt, Bitlis, Mardin, Harput, Kızıltepe, Urfa, and Silvan in southeastern Anatolia incorporated Arab-style columned halls wider than they are long, while the neighborhood mosque continued the Iranian prototype of the domed cube.[1] At the end of the twelfth century, a new type, longer than it was wide, started to appear.[2] Examples include the Sivas, Kayseri (Fig. 3), and Erzurum great mosques; Kayseri's Külük Mosque; and the Citadel Mosques of Erzurum and Divriği. In the thirteenth century, almost all mosques of Anatolia included a nave with *maqsura* dome and *oculus* (e.g. Divriği's Niğde Alaeddin, Kayseri's Hacı Kılıç, Amasya's Burmalı Minare, Amasya's Gök Madrasa, and Kayseri's Develi Mosques). While Amasya's Burmalı Minare (Fig. 4), Niğde's Alaeddin (1223) (Fig. 5), and Amasya's

2 Great Mosque, Diyarbakır, 1092, *mihrab* and eastern wing.
Photo: Ali Uzay Peker

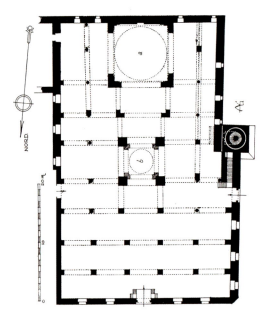

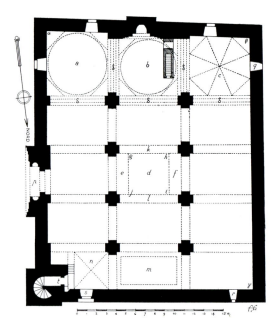

5 Alaeddin Mosque, Niğde, 1223, plan.
Albert Gabriel, *Monuments Turcs d'Anatolie*. Paris: E. De Boccart, 1934

3 Great Mosque of Kayseri, 1205, plan.
Albert Gabriel, *Monuments Turcs d'Anatolie*, Paris: E. De Boccart, 1934

4 Burmalı Minare Mosque, Amasya, 1247, *qibla* wall and eastern façade.
Photo: Ali Uzay Peker

Gök Madrasa (1267) (Fig. 6) mosques look like complete basilicas with nave and flanking aisles, some others like Kayseri's Hunat (1238) (Fig. 7) comprise a basilica core surrounded by several vaulted aisles. Evidently the basilical impulse outstripped the hypostyle in shaping thirteenth-century mosques.[3]

Seljuk architects were exposed to the example of a dominant dome in the Great Mosque of Silvan (1157), which contains an octagonal *maqsura* dome fourteen meters in diameter. The mosque is an attempt to obtain a large clear space at the center while retaining side spaces in the form of vaulted aisles, which crest much lower than the *maqsura* dome. The aisles are parallel to the *mihrab* wall and form dark and narrow corridors cut off from the center. This box-like, quadrangular building is crowned by a pyramidal cap over the dome. Silvan was a bold attempt to insert a large *maqsura* dome into a plan with multiple aisles, but it fell short of creating a well-balanced interior and its experiments were not revived until the Early Ottoman period.

The "multiplication of domes" is another Seljuk trend that can be regarded as significant to the later Ottoman predilection for centralized mosques. The nave and side aisles of the Alaeddin Mosque in Niğde (1223), for example, each have a dome above their final, square bays. This gesture differentiates the prayer row closest to the *mihrab* wall, extending the impact of the prominence given in Early Islamic architecture to the space in front of the *mihrab*. In Amasya's Burmalı Minare Mosque, a similar order of three domes cover three bays over the nave leading to the *mihrab*, hence emphasize the *qibla* direction.

It is less clear why this triple dome arrangement is carried over to the aisles in Amasya's Gök Madrasa Mosque. In that case, it emphasizes the *mihrab* wall prayer line, the *qibla* axis, and spaces around the enclosed inner court scheme in front of the entrance gate. The latter section includes a lantern dome. Rectangular vaulted rooms flank the entrance vestibule. These rooms must have constituted a multi-functional prayer space, one in which, for example, educating children or gathering

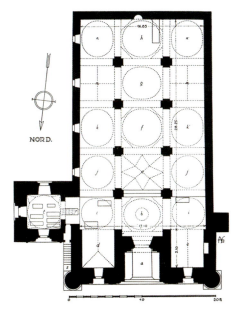

6 Gök Madrasa Mosque, Amasya, 1267, plan.
Albert Gabriel, *Monuments Turcs d'Anatolie*. Paris: E. De Boccart, 1934

7 Hunat Mosque, Kayseri, 1238, central aisle.
Photo: Ali Uzay Peker

of visiting scholars of Islamic lore was possible. Seljuk *madrasa*s often contain a central *iwan* facing an open or enclosed court with aligned student cells. The Gök Madrasa Mosque with cells and inner court appeared as a precursor of the so-called "Inverted T" type Ottoman mosque in Bursa.

The trend towards mosques with more than one dome diverted Anatolian mosque architecture from the early Islamic path. Previously, in Iran, a comparable local transformation took place where extensive *iwan*s reshaped the central space of mosques, creating semi-open voids overlooking an open circulation area. Inside, bulbous domical vaults in brick reinforced square units. As a matter of fact mosques with more than one dome over a nine-bay plan appeared earlier in Central Asia. Examples are the Haji Piyada (Noh Gumbad) Mosque in Balkh (ninth century), the Chor Sutun at Termez (tenth century) and the Masjid-i Diggaran at Hazara (eleventh century, north of Bukhara). Bernard O'Kane explains that this type as "simply a domed variation of one of many pre-Islamic versions (e.g. the Parthian temple at Nysa) featuring a flat roof supported by four piers".[4] Indigenous design traditions and extraneous impacts are molded in novel products all over the world. In the case of the nine-fold plan and organization of the domes on it, the "nine-fold categorizing system" that we find in Chinese / Central Asiatic cosmography seems to have exerted a profound influence.[5] Transference of the multi-domed mosque from Central Asia to Anatolia by the way of Iran is another instance of migration of architectural ideas together with culture.

The cultural context of Anatolia prompted the appearance of this new type, the multiple-domed mosque. This mosque type developed through the assimilation of the Anatolian basilica of vaulted nave and two aisles to the hypostyle plan of early mosques. The Samanid and Kharakhanid domed and Iranian Seljuk domical-vaulted prayer halls in Central Asia and Iran provided models for this later development in Anatolia. Breaking the rigidity of the basilica aisles provided designers with the possibility of creating cubic independent units to be covered either with vigorous vaults, as in Divriği's Great Mosque (1228), or multiple domes, as in Niğde's Alaeddin and Amasya's Gök Madrasa Mosques. Introduction of a lantern dome resembling domed transept basilica over the inner court in a number of Seljuk mosques is another factor that instigated this trend.

EARLY OTTOMAN MOSQUES

The multiplication of domes in basilica-type mosques led to new formations in the Early Ottoman period. The tradition of embracing local features gave birth to a new type, which appeared around Bursa, hence the name Bursa-type, also known as the "Inverted T" type.[6] This type is comprised of a central unit consisting of two successive domed spaces on the *qibla* axis. The first dome after the entrance gate houses a pool; the second generally has a raised floor reached by a few steps. This second domed unit houses the *mihrab* and *minbar*; in effect, a cubical domed *masjid* is made a part of this sort of building. As a cubical room it opens to the inner court in the north. Among the scholars of Ottoman architecture, there is a consensus that these spaces in Bursa type mosques were not initially intended to be permanently used as *masjid*; often the existing *mihrab*s are later additions. Some uncertainty still exists as to its real function (or functions) and the term *zawiya* (hospice) alluding to multifunctional use is used to name this type.[7]

In the Hüdavendigar Mosque in Bursa, the *masjid* part is roofed with a barrel vault (Fig. 8). It has *iwan*s, covered by vaults opening to the inner court. Corner rooms flank them. In effect it produces a multi-functional building integrating the Seljuk domed *madrasa* concept and the Byzantine quincunx pattern. In Anatolia, pre-Ottoman *zawiya*s, *khan*s, *madrasa*s, and *darussifa*s (hospitals) housed such multi-functional spaces. This mosque exemplifies the accumulation of different functions like education, prayer, communion, recitation, and sermon that accorded with the Islamic practice of sheltering communal activities in the body of a single building.[8] In the Early Ottoman period, a familiar, welcoming atmosphere was created with the aim to unite religious and state authority and strengthen the bond between the sultan and his subjects.

The Gök Madrasa Mosque in Amasya can be regarded as the transitional building between the enclosed type of *madrasa* with *iwan*s around an inner court and the early Ottoman mosques in Bursa and Edirne. The mosque has an oblong prayer space with rooms on both sides of the entrance vestibule and an inner court. The vestibule resembles the typical entrance *iwan* of a *madrasa*. The size of the meeting rooms and the prayer space make it clear, however, that the intent was to

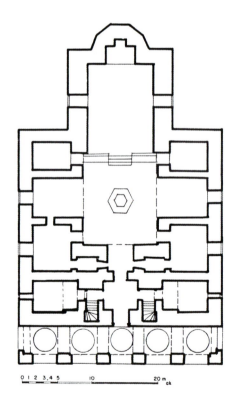

8 Hüdavendigar Mosque, Bursa, 1385, plan. Kuran (after Gabriel), Aptullah Kuran, *Osmanlı İlk Devir Mimarisinde Cami*, Ankara: ODTU Mimarlık Fakültesi, 1964

9 Hüdavendigâr Mosque, Bursa, 1385, inner domed court with pool, western *iwan* and southern *iwan* with *mihrab*, and western *iwan*. Photo: Ali Uzay Peker

combine a Friday mosque with a *madrasa*; hence the compound name, "Gök Madrasa Mosque."

In Bursa, with examples like Hüdavendigar (Fig. 9), Yıldırım (1395) and Yeşil (1419), there is the contrary trend, where a mosque is added to a multi-functional meeting space. In these mosques, the inner court around the pool underneath the lantern dome seems to have had no clear religious use. In the Yeşil Mosque, however, the Sultan's loge above the entrance directly opposite the *mihrab* has the *qibla* orientation and hints its use as a private prayer alcove. Their multi-functionality does not preclude the primacy of the *qibla* axis; rather the *qibla* axis is emphasized by the alignment of the entrance and the two successive domed units. Two semi-open rooms flank the entrance vestibule of the Yeşil as in the Gök Madrasa Mosque. This type gained a monumental expression in Amasya's Bayezid II Mosque, where separation between the *masjid* and the inner court almost disappeared and the central two-domed core became an independent entity (Fig. 10). The side domed spaces are low and distinct, but still connected with arches. On the other hand, in the Gedik Ahmet Pasha Mosque in Afyon (1472), domed side spaces flank *iwan*s, which face outside in eastern and western façades. These *iwan*s contain entrances to the side rooms, which open with doors to the inner core. This late development realizes the independence of the side rooms from the central prayer space.

The Great Mosque of Bursa appeared at the end of the fourteenth century as an ideal Friday mosque with domes (Fig. 11). The central nave is flanked by two

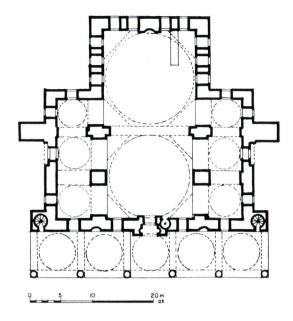

10 Bayezid II Mosque, Amasya, 1486, plan.
Kuran (after Gabriel), Aptullah Kuran, *Osmanlı İlk Devir Mimarisinde Cami*, Ankara: ODTU Mimarlik Fakültesi, 1964

11 Great Mosque, Bursa, 1400, central aisle with pool and *mihrab*.
Photo: Ali Uzay Peker

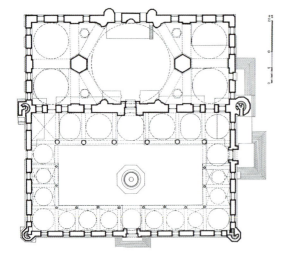

12 Üç Şerefeli Mosque, Edirne, 1447, plan.
Kuran (after Ayverdi), Aptullah Kuran, *Osmanlı İlk Devir Mimarisinde Cami*, Ankara: ODTU Mimarlık Fakültesi, 1964

aisles on the east and west, and it is higher than the others. It attained the synthesis of the basilical plan with domed transept and the Arab hypostyle plan. There is a grand pool with a lantern in the second bay from the entrance on the *qibla* axis. The pool emphasizes the *mihrab* direction, but also obstructs it.

The presence of a pool inside the mosque recalls, in a much reduced form, the Iranian tradition of inner open courtyards as in the Isfahan Great Mosque. A number of other mosques from the thirteenth century, like the Kayseri's Great Mosque, Niğde's Alaeddin, Amasya's Gök Madrasa, and Divriği's Great Mosque have an essentially enclosed plan with a lantern dome; the wooden pillared Eşrefoğlu Mosque in Beyşehir has a deep pit at the center of the nave. Seljuk *madrasa*s of the thirteenth century, like the İnce Minareli and Karatay Madrasas in Konya, also contain enclosed courts with opposed *iwan*s, and a central pool below a lantern dome.

The Üç Şerefeli Mosque in the former Ottoman capital city of Edirne plays a prominent role in the evolution of a distinct Ottoman mosque plan (Fig. 12). This mosque has a dome twenty-four meters in diameter in the center of a plan consisting of just two aisles. Here, for the first time, a large *maqsura* dome breaks through the aisles to span from the *mihrab* to the courtyard wall. The hexagonal dome sits on two colossal pillars and northern and southern walls. This central core is further elaborated with pairs of domes in the east and west. Since the Üç Şerefeli mosque was built rather near to the so-called Eski Cami (1414), which is a large hypostyle Friday mosque with multiple domes like Bursa's Great Mosque, it seems that the architect's intention was to introduce a novel variant on the "large-scale *maqsura* type" instead of a rival Friday mosque of the same kind. This type already had appeared in Anatolia in the Great Mosque of Silvan (1157) and was then elaborated in the Great Mosque of Manisa (1367). Both of these mosques include vaults on four parallel aisles surrounding a broad, central, octagonal dome, and separate side spaces.

OTTOMAN MOSQUES AFTER THE CONQUEST OF CONSTANTINOPLE

It is somewhat surprising, in light of subsequent developments, that the first mosques built in İstanbul after the conquest followed the Bursa pattern. Mahmud Pasha Mosque (1462), for example, has two central domes and enveloping side spaces. As late as the Sultan Selim I Mosque (1522), architects still followed the scheme of the domed cube of the Bayezid II Mosque in Edirne. Ottoman architects were quickly lured into the challenge presented by the Church of Hagia Sophia.

The Church of Hagia Sophia comprises a central dome flanked by two half domes topping an oblong structure with double exedrae at both ends (Fig. 13). It has a two-part narthex and aisles with upper galleries, but the nave dominates, being almost double the width of the flanking aisles. The designers Anthemius and Isidorus sought to connect large halls with the domed core. They used arcades of *porphry* and *verde antiqua* columns to screen these spaces from the *cella*. The arching system in the aisles and galleries on the north and south remains low to counterweight the thrust of the piers. The resultant structural instability was caused in part by the demand of Eastern Orthodox Divine liturgy for individual space units.

Structural troubles have in fact plagued the dome of Hagia Sophia ever since its collapse shortly after the inauguration. Since the nave's north and south faces lack semi-domes to balance the thrust of the huge dome, a number of bulky buttresses were added in the reconstruction, compromising structural clarity and integrity. These additions aimed at filling the structural gap

13 Church of Hagia Sophia, İstanbul, 537, domed central hall with eastern semidome and apse.
Photo: Ali Uzay Peker

created in the aisles and galleries, which became darker spaces. Given that the great Church is on the highly active North Anatolian fault line, it is remarkable that a building of such size created with technological means of the sixth century still stands. Hagia Sophia's builders sought to place a dome over the essentially open structure of a basilica. The oversize transept dome joins with the walls by means of semi-domes, apse, and exedra recesses in the east and west that form two grand ovals underneath the dome, ultimately combining the incompatible forms of the rectangle and circle.

The Mosque of Bayezid II in İstanbul has the appearance of a miniature Hagia Sophia (Fig. 14). Its oblong prayer hall includes a dome over the nave, two semi-domes with pendentives, and two aisles flank it on all sides. Since there was no need for galleries in an Islamic house of prayer, its architect, Hayreddin (or Yakubşah bin Sultanşah), was free to eliminate the obstructive screening arcades. Hayreddin also roofed the side aisles with four smaller domes. This use recalls the Seljuk basilica mosques with domes, like the Gök Madrasa. The unaccompanied semi-domes, the uniformly

SELJUK AND OTTOMAN MOSQUES 321

domed aisles, the high drum, and projecting mass of the dome are all independent units, composed together. Multi-functional rooms are attached at northeastern and northwestern corners; they were probably used as hospices (*tabhana*), as in Bayezid II's mosque (1488) in Edirne. They have separate entrances and were once totally detached from the prayer hall. Later, partition walls were removed in order to integrate these side spaces to the central hall. The full segregation of the side spaces heralds the end of the "Inverted T" type mosque. The Mosque of Sultan Selim I in İstanbul was the last building with central prayer hall and detached side rooms.

MOSQUES OF MIMAR SINAN

The Ottoman mosque reached the zenith of its formal development with grand architect Sinan's idiosyncratic structures in the sixteenth century. At the Şehzade Mosque (1548), Sinan created a new

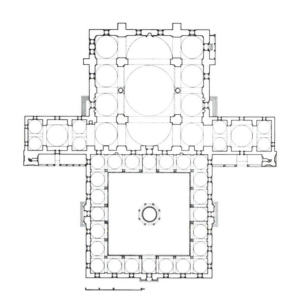

14 Bayezid II Mosque, İstanbul, 1506, plan.
Aptullah Kuran, *The Mosque in Early Ottoman Architecture*, Chicago/London: The University of Chicago Press, 1968

15 Şehzade Mosque, İstanbul, eastern façade, 1548.
Photo: Ali Uzay Peker

spatial arrangement that yields a new approach to the façade (Fig. 15). The idea of removing the elements of aisle and gallery arcades had already been established by Hayreddin. Sinan, working within the tradition of the master-apprentice system of the Ottoman architectural profession, borrowed Hayreddin's innovation and furthered it by shifting the arcades to the exterior side façades of the Şehzade Mosque.[9] This articulated the outer walls with columns and arches, created lines of well-balanced solids and voids, and revealed the supporting and supported systems in relation to the great unity of the dome and its substructure.

Earlier, at the Mihrimah Mosque in Üsküdar (1547) Sinan maintained the conventional rectangular form of the classical Friday mosque, but added semi-domes on the east, west, and south sides. Not long after the start of Mihrimah's construction, Sinan designed Şehzade with a revolutionary idea of expanding a cubic mosque type by adding four semi-domes around the central one.[10] Şehzade's four semi-domes expanded space in all directions and unified the three entrances and the *mihrab* on two cross axes, giving the upper structure total symmetry. This plan provided Sinan with a fully centralized structure.

Sinan began construction of the Süleymaniye Mosque in 1550 shortly after completing Şehzade (Fig. 16). This monument has been regarded as a successor of Hagia Sophia's domed basilica.[11] The north-south extension of the mosque incorporated a central dome with two semi-domes that are further elaborated with double semi-domes, which is to say, it reiterates the configuration of Hagia Sophia. Exedrae are not present in the Süleymaniye since there are no galleries, nor do arcades separate the aisles from the nave. At the level underneath the cornice between the curvilinear upper structure and the rectilinear lower part, Süleymaniye turns out to be an entirely different structure. Süleymaniye has a rectangular plan with the *mihrab* on its longer side (Fig. 17). This longer east-west alignment is a return to the traditional design of the "Friday mosque type." Its domed aisles recall the domed side units of the İstanbul Bayezid Mosque, in which the center is expanded on the two sides. The central domes of these side aisles in the Süleymaniye are higher and wider, and thus open to the baldachin with higher and wider pointed arches on the east and west sides.

At the Süleymaniye, the introduction of an east-west axis and the enhancement of the interior space in these directions introduce a crosswise development embedded in the oblong nave. The triumphal arch-like arcade of the triple arches in the center leans on the back corners of the four colossal pillars hence create deep recesses like *iwan*s. Their interrelatedness to the colored voussoirs of the background arches in the aisles creates a concentric rhythm around the nave. This last characteristic makes an ambulatory space behind the pillars like in a centralized rotunda. Hence, what we have is an archetypal building that melded Roman rotunda and Hagia Sophia's domed basilica with earlier traditions of Islamic architecture. Mosques in Seljuk and Ottoman architectural traditions incorporated rhomboid, basilical and Kufa type plans. Süleymaniye incomparably synthesized these (Table 1).

In designs for later mosques, Sinan adapted the polygonal baldachin to the Islamic Friday mosque pattern. His Rüstem Pasha Mosque in İstanbul (1563), Selimiye in Edirne, Sokollu in Kadırga (1571), Sokollu in Azapkapı (1578), and Mehmed Pasha in Nişancı (1589) mosques comprise a rectangular shell with hexagonal or octagonal domed baldachin cores. The last in this chain, Nişancı Mosque, embodies Sinan's work on this type, which contains contours adapted to the inner octagon, but only on the southern side. In Zal's Mahmud Pasha Mosque (1579), side spaces envelop the central square domed-baldachin inside a rectangular shell of walls.

Sinan's great masterpiece, the Mihrimah Sultan Mosque near Istanbul's Edirne city gate, also has a rectangular prayer space (1560s) (Fig. 1). The central dome rises elegantly on a square base like a tower, overshadowing the rectilinear lower structure. The rectangular shell of the walls creates a backdrop for the domed units. Sinan pierced the wall façades with windows to the point of rendering them mere screens. Sinan always puts an emphasis on the tension between covering and supporting units, which had to be separately resolved in order to be integrated; the way the surrounding rectangular walling system is interrelated with the square or polygonal dome core is a second major feature of his designs. In the Mihrimah Mosque, the central core of the dome with four corner towers erupts out of the rectangular shell. Sinan ingeniously links the two in the south façade through corbelled arches on two sides. Interrelated proportions in fenestration in the tympanum and the *mihrab* wall beneath it help to create a tuned correlation. In the Mihrimah Mosque,

Sinan achieved an extensively fenestrated elegant building with a vast dome (20m.) as high as possible (37m.) saved from the mass of a complex structural system of supports.

LATE OTTOMAN MOSQUES

Seventeenth-century Ottoman mosque architecture largely continued along the path set out by Sinan. Both the Yeni Valide (1603, 1663) in the Eminönü district and the famous Sultanahmad Mosque (1617) replicate the quatrefoil plan of the Şehzade Mosque in having a central dome, four semi-domes, and four corner domes. While Sultanahmad reproduces the principles of Sinan's façade system with great sophistication, Yeni Valide developed mannerist tendencies like the elongated drum and turrets, hence fragmenting covering and supporting elements. With these two exceptions, the seventeenth century did not produce monumental mosques. The following century proved more

16 Süleymaniye Mosque, İstanbul, main dome, southern semi dome and western arch, 1557
Photo: Ali Uzay Peker

17 Süleymaniye Mosque, İstanbul, 1557, plan
Ali Saim Ülgen, *Mimar Sinan Yapıları: Külliyeler*. Ankara: Türk Tarih Kurumu, 1989

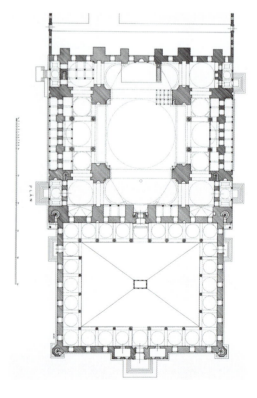

TABLE I: SELJUK AND OTTOMAN MOSQUE TYPOLOGY AFTER THE LENGTH OF THE QIBLA WALL

RHOMBOID **(KIOSK)**	Konya Hacı Hasan (13th c.) (from A. Atun)	Bursa Alaeddin Bey (1335) (from A. Kuran)	Edirne II. Bayezid (1505) (from A. Kuran)	Istanbul Yavuz Selim (1522) (from G. Goodwin)	İstanbul Şehzade (1548) (from A. Kuran)
SHORTER QIBLA WALL **(BASILICAL)**	Istanbul Aya Sofya (536) (from R. Mainstone)	Niğde Alaeddin (1223) (from A. Gabriel)	Amasya Burmalı Minare (1247) (from A. Gabriel)	Amasya Gök Medrese (1267) (from A. Gabriel)	Bursa Murad Hüdavendigar(1385) (from A. Kuran)
	Iznik Yeşil (1392) (from A. Kuran)	Edirne Eski (1413) (from A. Kuran)	Amasya Bayezid Paşa (1419) (from A. Kuran)	Bursa Muradiye (1426) (from A. Kuran)	Istanbul Mahmut Paşa (1462) (from A. Kuran)
	Istanbul Mahmut Paşa (1462) (from A. Kuran)	Afyon Gedik Ahmet Paşa (1472) (from A. Kuran)	Istanbul II. Bayezid (1505) (from A. Kuran)		
LONGER QIBLA WALL **(KUFA)**	Silvan Ulu (1157) (from A. Altun)	Manisa Ulu (1376) (from A. Kuran)	Bursa Ulu (1399) (from A. Kuran)	Edirne Üç Şerefeli (1447) (from A. Kuran)	Eski Fatih (1471) (from A. Kuran)
	Üsküdar Mihrimah (1547) (from A. Kuran)	Istanbul Süleymaniye (1557) (from A. Kuran)	Edirnekapı Mihrimah (1565) (from A. S. Ülgen)	Edirne Selimiye (1574) (from A. Kuran)	

productive of sultanic mosques. Gülnüş Emetullah Mosque in Üsküdar (Yeni Valide) (1709) and Damat İbrahim Pasha Mosque in Nevşehir (1726) carry on the seventeenth-century mannerist style.

In the middle of the eighteenth-century, Nuruosmânîye Mosque, initiated by Mahmud I and completed by Osman III, embodied new social and cultural circumstances that had been developing for a half century. The mosque reflects an encounter with West European culture through intensified diplomatic interaction and trade relations. One sign of this is that the building superintendent was a Greek named Simyon (Simeon) Kalfa. The Nuruosmânîye has features that have been characterized as Baroque. Stately stairs lead to the entrance portals and the cornices of the prayer hall are undulating. The domed baldachin, portals, porch, and façade of the mosque nonetheless recall features of Sinan's mosques.[12] The successor of the Nuruosmânîye Mosque, such as Ayazma (1760), Laleli (1763), Beylerbeyi (1778), and Selimiye (1792) Mosques reproduced the hybrid body of the Nuruosmânîye, though in a more constrained manner. They represent a return to the lucidity of Sinan's structure, but with minor Baroque designs and Rococo ornamentation.

In the eighteenth century, state dignitaries founded a number of rather modest building complexes. The mosques of Çorlulu Ali Pasha (1708), Damat Ibrahim Pasha (1720), Ismail Efendi (1724), Hekimoğlu Ali Pasha (1735), Hacı Beşir Ağa (1745), Zeynep Sultan (1769), and Şebsefa (1787) are prominent examples. Except for the Hekimoğlu Mosque, which is hexagonal and larger, all others are unassuming traditional cubic *masjids* with Rococo ornamentation. Eyüp's Sultan Mosque (1800) represents the end of the great age of Ottoman mosque architecture. It was the last attempt to create a monumental polygonal mosque with structural precision, which proved to be unattainable in an age of disintegration of institutional conventions.

The neighborhood mosque type with four walls and dome in monumental size dominated the following century and signals the end of an age of inquiry. Prominent examples are Nusretiye (1826),

Mecidiye (1855), Hirka-ı Şerif (1851), Ortaköy (1854), Kağıthana (1864), Pertevniyal Valide Sultan (1871), Yıldız (1886), Hidayet (1887), and Cihangir (1889) Mosques. Architects began to employ fashionable European ornamental styles like Empire, Baroque, Rococo, Neoclassical, Orientalist, and Neo-Gothic in order to provide repetitive and structurally dull mosques with a modicum of "style." Raimando D'Aranco's Karaköy Mosque (1903) in the florid Art Nouveau manner represents a full capitulation to trends in European design. Yet, it was also a bold attempt to stick to a current global mode. Its demolition in the 1950s during an urban development project, a rare incident of deliberate destruction of a mosque, is maybe a proof of public disapproval of a truly modernist style mosque across the historical peninsula housing a number of traditionalist mosques in its silhouette on the other side of the Golden Horn.

Revivalism followed this period of Western influence. Ottoman Turkish architects strived to revive an assumed classicism in the first decades of the twentieth century. The architect Kemalettin Bey's mosques, such as the Kamer Hatun (1911) in Beyoğlu, Bebek (1913), and Bostanci (1913) were attempts to revisit the "Ottomanness" of the classical style, but did not go beyond sheathing the domed-*masjid* type of the nineteenth century with classical ornamentations instead of Western motifs. The nineteenth-century Friday mosque with four walls and a dome, in a few words, a former neighborhood mosque realized at a grand scale, replaced Sinan's glorious buildings.

ALI UZAY PEKER, PhD, is currently a Professor at Middle East Technical University, Graduate Program in Architectural History, teaching courses on Seljuk and Ottoman Architecture. He is an art and architectural historian with published articles in a number of national and international journals and edited books. His research on symbolism in medieval architecture in Turkey revealed theoretical backgrounds of architectural symbols in medieval Anatolia in the Islamic period. He also studied eighteenth-century Ottoman architecture.

SUGGESTIONS FOR FURTHER READING

Goodwin, Godfrey. *A History of Ottoman Architecture* (Baltimore: Johns Hopkins Press, 1971).

Kuban, Doğan. *The Miracle of Divriği* (İstanbul: Yapı Kredi, 2001).

Kuban, Doğan. *Sinan's Art and Selimiye* (İstanbul: İş Bankası, 2011).

Kuran, Aptullah. *Sinan: The Grand Old Master of Ottoman Architecture* (İstanbul: Ada Press, 1987).

McClary, R. P., *Rum Seljuq Architecture. 1170–1220: The Patronage of Sultans* (Edinburgh: Edinburgh University Press, 2017).

NOTES

[1] For introductory surveys on Seljuk (a general name used for the architecture of the period spanning between eleventh-fourteenth centuries) mosques in Anatolia, see Oktay Aslanapa, *Anadolu'da İlk Türk Mimarisi* [Earlier Architecture of the Turks in Anatolia] (Ankara: AKM, 1991) and Ara Altun, *An Outline of Turkish Architecture in the Middle Ages* (Istanbul: Arkeoloji ve Sanat Yayınları, 1990). For a detailed account of the twelfth-century Artukid (a local dynasty in southeastern Anatolia) mosques see Ara Altun, *Anadolu'da Artuklu Devri Türk Mimarisinin Gelişmesi,* [Evolution of Turkish Architecture in Anatolia under the Artuks] (Istanbul: Kültür Bakanlığı, 1978).

[2] Kuban calls this "the new Anatolian type" in *Muslim Religious Architecture* II: *Development of Religious Architecture in Later Periods* (Leiden: E. J. Brill, 1985), 19.

[3] For the influence of basilica on Seljuk architecture see A. U. Peker, "Anadolu Bazilika Geleneği ve Selçuklu Anıtsal Mimarisine Etkisi" [Basilica Tradition in Anatolia and its Influence on Seljuk Monumental Architecture] in *Selçuklu Uygarlığı,* eds. A. U. Peker and Kenan Bilici (Ankara: Kültür Bakanlığı, 2006), 55–65.

[4] Bernard O'Kane, "Iran and Central Asia," in *The Mosque: History, Architectural Development and Regional Diversity*, eds. Martin Frishman and Hasan-Uddin Khan, (London: Thames and Hudson, 2002), 121 (119–40).

[5] For the history of the nine-fold division in Chinese cosmography see J. C. Didier, "In and Outside the Square," *Sino-Platonic Papers* 192/3 (September, 2009) 170–192; for the Chinese nine-fold diagram named Ming-t'ang see A. C. Soper, "The "Dome of Heaven" in Asia," *The Art Bulletin*, 29/4 (Dec., 1947), 240 (225–48).

[6] Aptullah Kuran calls this type "the eyvan mosque" in *The Mosque in Early Ottoman Architecture* (Chicago and London: The University of Chicago Press, 1968), 76.

[7] For example recently by Doğan Kuban in *Osmanlı Mimarisi* [Ottoman Architecture] (Istanbul: YEM Yayın, 2007), 83; Gülru Necipoğlu employs "convent masjid" in *The Age of Sinan: Architectural Culture in the Ottoman Empire* (Princeton and Oxford: Princeton University Press, 2005), 50. This latter term was proposed by Semavi Eyice, "İlk Osmanlı Devrinin Dinî-İçtimai bir Müessesesi: Zaviyeler ve Zaviyeli Camiler" [Convents and Mosques with Convents], *Istanbul Üniversitesi İktisat Fakültesi Mecmuası* 23/1–4 (1963), 1–80.

[8] For *masjid* as a multifunctional space see Ahmet Önkal and Nebi Bozkurt, "Cami," in *İslâm Ansiklopedisi* (İstanbul: TDV, 1993) 46–56; also Martin Frishman, "Islam and the Form of the Mosque," in *The Mosque: History, Architectural Development and Regional Diversity*, eds. Martin Frishman and Hasan-Uddin Khan (London: Thames and Hudson, 2002), 32.

[9] Sinan explains how indebted is he to his masters in his biography: Sâî Çelebi, *Tezkiret ül-Bünyan* [The Book of Buildings], ed. H. Develi, trans. H. Develi - S. Rifat (Istanbul: Koçbank, 2002) 135.

[10] Doğan Kuban regards the domed baldachin in Sinan's structures as the core of the design in "The Style of Sinan's Domed Structures," *Muqarnas* 4 (1997), 76 (72–97).

[11] Rowland J. Mainston, "The Suleymaniye Mosque and Hagia Sophia," in *Uluslararası Mimar Sinan Sempozyumu Bildirileri*, ed. Azize A. Yasa (Ankara: TTK Basımevi, 1996), 221–29; On how Sinan filtered lessons of Hagia Sophia through Early Ottoman architecture see Gülru Necipoğlu-Kafadar, "The Emulation of the Past in Sinan's Imperial Mosques," in *Uluslararası Mimar Sinan Sempozyumu Bildirileri*, ed. Azize A. Yasa (Ankara: TTK Basımevi, 1996), 177–89.

[12] For an account on this mosque's idiosyncratic features see A. U. Peker, "Return of the Sultan: Nuruosmânîye Mosque and the İstanbul Bedestan," in *Constructing Cultural Identity, Representing Social Power*, eds. N. Kısakürek, O. Rastrick, K. Esmark and C. Bilsel (Pisa: Plus - Pisa Univertsity Press, 2010), 139–57.

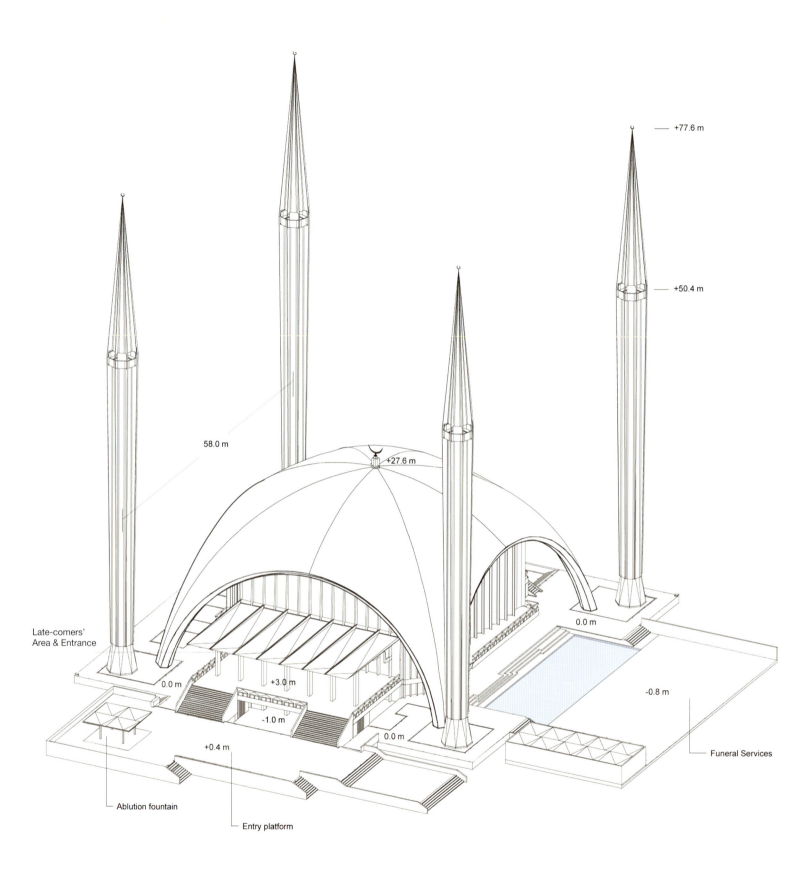

Kocatepe: The Unbuilt State Mosque of Turkey

IMDAT AS

1 Vedat Dalokay, unbuilt Kocatepe Mosque, Ankara, 1957, bird's eye view.
Drawing: Imdat As

Vedat Dalokay (1927–91) won a competition for the Kocatepe State Mosque in the newly established capital city of modern Turkey, Ankara, held in 1957 and organized by the Foundation of Religious Affairs. As a student of Paul Bonatz at Istanbul Technical University, Dalokay used his rationalist-modernist architectural training to reinterpret the classical Ottoman mosque typology with contemporary materials and building technologies. However, his design was abandoned and some parts of his project that were already constructed were torn down. In 1967, a new competition was held, and the current neo-classical Ottoman mosque was built instead. Dalokay was able to implement his design vision outside of Turkey, specifically in the Gulf States, Saudi Arabia, and most famously in Islamabad, Pakistan, with the King Faisal Mosque. A long time after his death, Dalokay's impact can be seen in some of the new mosque projects in Turkey, for example, the Sakirin Mosque in Istanbul (2009), the Ahmet Hamdi Akseki Mosque in Ankara (2013) – the main mosque of the Religious Affairs – and many more projects around the country. Ironically, Dalokay's mosque design was simply a modern interpretation of the sixteenth-century Ottoman imperial mosque type. However, the disposition of liturgical elements, the surface treatments, and the design of a particular path of movement raise the interesting possibility that Dalokay might have been also partially inspired by fourteenth-century heterodox Seljuk convent-mosques surrounding him in central Anatolia.

The drawings of Dalokay reveal a deceptively simple building (Fig. 1). There is a large entry platform with an ablution fountain; a higher positioned covered space for late-comers; a main prayer hall; and a separate open-to-the-air platform for funeral services, which incorporates a large reflecting pool. This mosque was to be the central piece of a larger religious affairs complex that he designed. Some of the ancillary buildings of this complex have been constructed and are still in use today.

THE PATH

Disposition of liturgical elements, treatment of surfaces, and a particular path of movement, are all elements which raise the interesting possibility that Dalokay might have been partially inspired by fourteenth-century heterodox Seljuk convent-mosques surrounding him in central Anatolia. At Dalokay's Kocatepe Mosque one enters the open platform with the ablution fountain, cleanses, steps up the monumental staircases to the late-comers area, and from there continues into the main prayer hall. The sequence ends at the *qibla* wall, which culminates with a panoramic view of a flower garden. Dalokay has perhaps proposed a concept of a ritual path, which is peculiar in Ottoman mosque architecture, since there is usually no hierarchy of access structures in sacred Islamic space.

Such neutral space conditions metaphorically symbolize limitless space, in part due to the absence of a dominating path construct. The space of such buildings acts like an empty field or container with no sense of a governing moment, space, or central point. One can enter the mosques from any of its eight gates, that is, the three courtyard gates or the five gates of the enclosed prayer hall. There is no hierarchy of gates, and no particular path to follow. Indeed, as much as the dome geometrically dictates a center of gravity, these mosques offer a surprisingly neutral space. David Gebhard, in *The Problem of Space in the Ottoman Mosque*, elaborates on this peculiar condition of space and argues that

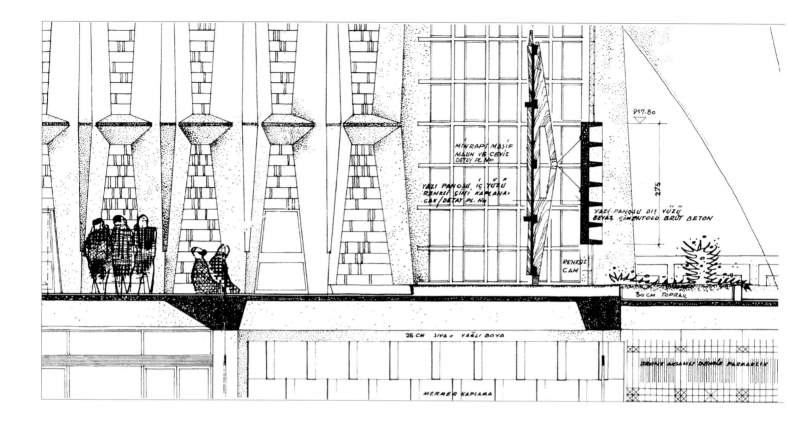

2 Vedat Dalokay, unbuilt Kocatepe Mosque, Ankara, 1957, detail of section drawing, showing the lower band of window openings on the *qibla* wall.
Drawing: Vedat Dalokay Foundation

"even the *mihrab* on the *qibla* wall does not create any directional force".[1]

The Kocatepe Mosque contradicts the field condition of earlier Ottoman imperial mosques. The prayer hall has two gates on the northern façade. Perhaps influenced by the ideas of the "architectural promenade," Dalokay obliges mosque-goers to experience the building in a particular way. For example, once in the mosque and sitting on the prayer carpet, only then is one allowed to view the flower garden through the lower band of windows on the *qibla* wall (Fig. 2). The path gives a highly controlled and sequenced awareness of architectural elements, landscape, and their symbolic meaning.

THE FORM

The Ottoman imperial mosque synthesized the expansive architectural vocabulary of its domain into a complete and unified style. It came to a syncretic stage in the sixteenth century. From thereon variations of this style emerged, for example, the Ottoman Baroque of the late eighteenth-century. The main characteristics of Ottoman classical architecture are the establishment of a nondirectional neutral space, the juxtaposition and individuality of its architectural components, and the concomitant structural clarity.[4]

The modern understanding of structural "honesty" is one of the hallmarks of Ottoman mosque architecture. The architectural components that form the interior space, such as domes, semidomes, and vaults, are always exposed on the exterior of the building. Therefore, one can easily read the structure of the interior space by looking at its exterior forms. This clarity was more important for Ottoman architects than to impress a smoother integration of architectonic elements upon the viewer. Splendid decoration and smooth surface treatments among architectural components "were deliberately rejected in favor of an appearance of strength and durability".[2]

The effect of Ottoman architecture, therefore, is what we could call a continuous differentiation: the architectural components are treated as several distinct and separate elements that are delicately held together to form a unified whole. The dome, its satellites, its square base, and the numerous porches and minarets, all stress an independent existence. The building systems have complex correlations between elements and subsystems. The aesthetics of the whole is derived from the elegance of the ordered complexity of these elements and give the impression of discrete fluidity. The common concept of structural clarity and the rich formal repertoire and its tectonic logic crystallized a unique style for Ottoman classical architecture. Dalokay's mosque in essence can be regarded as a continuation within this conceptual framework. The building components, such as the minarets, the dome, the liturgical elements, and pools remain distinctively individual building components. Yet, they are interwoven.

On the other hand, Dalokay reinterpreted the central dome component of the mosque. When looking at the layouts (Fig. 3), one can recognize Dalokay's reconfiguration of the dome and its pillars. At the Selimiye Mosque, Sinan creates an uninterrupted and absolute domical space by pushing the eight supporting pillars all the way to the outer limits of the drum of the dome. Consequently, the dome dominates the entire space. Dalokay stretched Sinan's dome expansion even further by putting the supporting piers outside the enclosed prayer hall. He proposed a thin concrete shell structure that would have established a dome sixty-seven meters in diameter. As a result, the visitor would have been praying in the ultimate dome, as opposed to a mediating square structure that holds the dome underneath. This expansion of the central dome, thereby eliminating the square base, was heavily criticized by famous Turkish architect Turgut Cansever. In his book *Not to Put the Dome on the Ground,* Cansever questions Dalokay's expansion of the dome:

3 Mimar Sinan, Selimiye Mosque, Edirne, 1574 (left); Vedat Dalokay, the unbuilt Kocatepe Mosque, Ankara, 1957 (right); plan comparison. Drawings: Imdat As

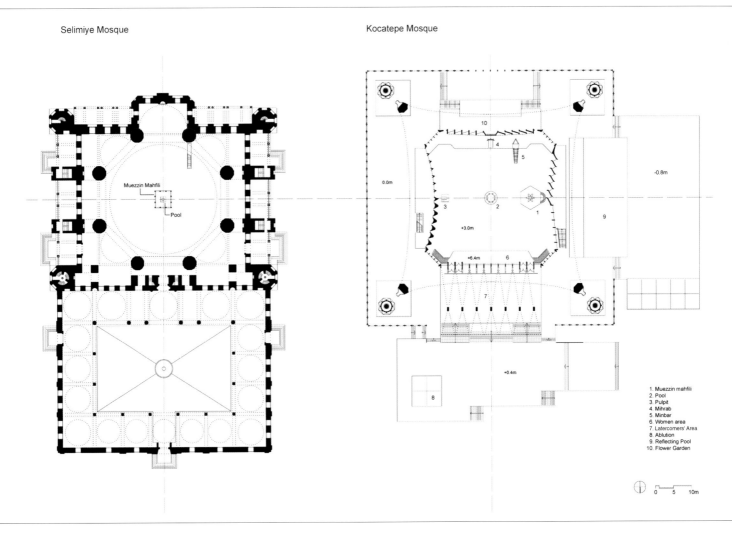

These shell-structured "modernist" mosques are a dilemma of keeping the visual memories of the Ottoman domes, and deny all historical references related to it. The dominant dome and minarets to accentuate corners would be preserved, but they would be designed in a "modernist" vocabulary. (...) Do architects have the right to select some useful components from this meaningful treasury and ignore others? Can a unity of architectural realities, which gives reference to religious or non-religious formation for over 500 years be "renewed" arbitrarily as such? Should the dome, which is more than a plain structural element and carries rich allusions, be taken disrespectfully and "put on the ground"?[3]

Cansever was known for his historicist approach to architectural design and was generally critical of modernism. In this case, he particularly criticized the purging of symbolic references by "putting the dome on the ground." In the next section, I will discuss the symbolic significance of these building components, which will shed some light on Cansever's criticism.

THE NARRATIVE

In order to understand the symbolic references in Dalokay's mosque, I will first describe Seljuk convent-mosques in fourteenth-century Anatolia; second, the transition from there to the Suleymaniye (1557) and Selimiye (1574) mosques; and third, conclude with how Dalokay absorbed the rich and diverse repertoire of religious symbolism of sacred architecture in Turkey.

Convent-mosques are religious congregational buildings that were widely used by Sufi orders in Anatolia. They typically follow T-shape layouts and consist of a central space with three *iwan*s (Fig. 4). According to written documents, there were over a hundred of these types of mosques in Anatolia.[4] The interior was usually double centered, with a main dome over the main central space and a prayer hall located in one of the *iwan*s. The ground of the prayer space was slightly raised above the central floor level. Moreover, the central space had an oculus or lantern hovering over a pool located directly underneath. Followers of these mosques sang, danced, and used liturgical tools and terminology as part of their rituals. It has been argued that in these mosques many old belief systems from Asia were wedded with principles of Islam. They produced syncretic rituals that were often received as heretical according to mainstream Sunni doctrine. However, they laid the basis for influential Sufi orders, such as the Bektashis and the Mevlevis.[5]

One of the best-known convent-mosques is the Yesil Mosque (1421) in Bursa (Fig. 4). Here, the

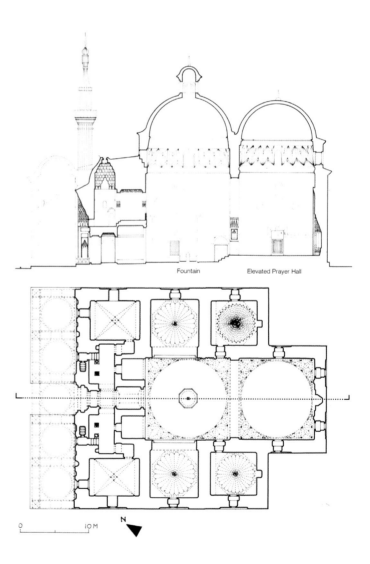

4 Haci Ivaz Pasa, Yesil Mosque, Bursa, 1420, plan and section drawing of a double-centered T-plan convent-mosque with fountain and elevated prayer hall.
Source: Harvard Fine Arts Library, Visual Collections

pool and the *oculus* were eliminated when convent-mosques were ripped from their sectarian functions and turned into solely prayer halls in the sixteenth century. In the case of the Yesil Mosque, the central space was filled up to the prayer-floor level and the pool was removed entirely.[6]

According to architectural historian Gunkut Akin, domical spaces with *oculi* and pool have a long history in Asia. In Anatolia, they were common in sacred spaces of various sects. The *oculus* was often open to the sky and the four cardinal directions were represented by invisible gateways, symbolized by *iwan*s surrounding the central space.[7] According to these sects, this arrangement of physical and idealized space represented the cosmos, the celestial roof, and an invisible axis mundi. In the Sunni doctrine, such an axis mundi happened at the Dome of the Rock in Jerusalem, when Prophet Muhammed ascended to heaven (*miraj*) to unite with God. However, some of the Sufi orders like the Bektashis believed that Ali – the prophet's cousin and son-in-law – accompanied him in this journey. For them, the *miraj* is an allegory for meeting the divine. In their rituals, they perform mystical experiences by staging the *miraj* and singing hymns to the event. These ceremonies end by participants telling each other that they witnessed the *miraj*.[8]

The pool in these sacred spaces fulfilled vital practical and symbolic functions. Practically, these functions were cleansing and drinking. However, it is difficult to conceive the pool for ablution purposes only, since one cannot enter a mosque before cleansing oneself. This is the reason why, in mosque layouts, the ablution fountains are usually placed outside the prayer hall. Therefore, it is not credible to view the pool solely for these two purposes.

The pool is a source of countless metaphors and allegories in Islam and, in order to understand its function, let us look at how Islamic orders used to employ the pool in their rituals. For example, when some of these sects use a space without a pool, they place a basin at the center of their ritual space and perform specific rituals around it. These are related to the symbolism of the physical architectural

elements like the *oculus*, four cardinal directions, and axis mundi.[9] In combination with these elements, the basin represents the pool of *kawthar*, the fountain in heaven, into which the four heavenly rivers flow. The real function of the pool is perhaps more related to these heterodox rituals than to practical needs of cleansing and drinking.

This may explain why the pool component has been purged from its central location in later orthodox Ottoman mosques. Mostly, it was relocated to the mosque courtyards, as in the Suleymaniye Mosque. However, the symbolic references to the *kawthar* remained. In fact, there are plenty of historic sources equating the pool at the Suleymaniye Mosque to the *kawthar*. Moreover, the two side entrances to the courtyard bear inscriptions referring to paradise: "Peace be unto thee! Enter the Garden of Eden because of what ye used to do."[10] Obviously, through this process of fragmentation and recombination the pool has lost its sectarian connotations. The dissociation from convent mosques was also made through the choice of inscriptions. At the Suleymaniye Mosque, inscriptions were solely chosen from the Quran. In earlier mosques, the repertoire of inscriptions included quotes from the Hadith or, occasionally, even Persian poetry.[11] As a result, we see that orthodox rituals were clearly separated from the more mystical sectarian traditions in the height of Ottoman power.

In the later Selimiye Mosque, however, mystical underpinnings and themes resurfaced, at least in terms of liturgical components and inscriptions. One of the peculiar novelties of the Selimiye Mosque is both the return of the pool into the main prayer hall and its position in a central location under the *muezzin mahfili* – the place where the *muezzin* performs his call for prayers. The *muezzin mahfili* is usually located in an inconspicuous place within the prayer hall. Therefore, the central placement at the Selimiye Mosque has been much debated by scholars of Islamic architecture. For example, Akin argues that the *muezzin mahfili,* in addition to accentuating the central space, conceals and dominates the

5 Mimar Sinan, Selimiye Mosque, Edirne, 1574, the fountain under the *muezzin mahfili*.
Photo: Bulent Oniz

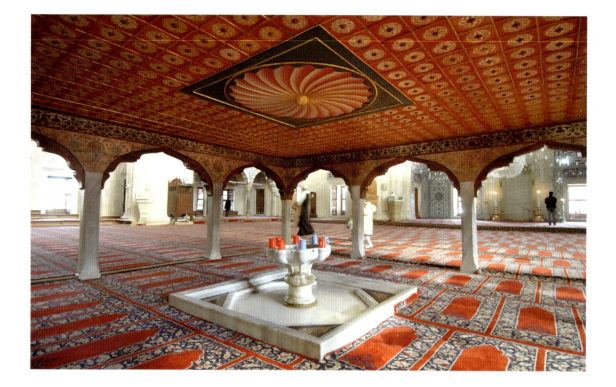

symbolism of the pool, that is, orthodox Sunnism suppresses heterodox sects.[12] Indeed, the *muezzin mahfili* is indeed three meters elevated above the prayer floor and an octagonal pool is put underneath (Fig. 5). The pool has a goblet-shaped drinking bowl in the middle, which is surrounded by eight protruding semicircles. The ceiling on top of the pool is divided into small spiraling patterns with a larger one on top of the pool.

The Selimiye Mosque also uses secondary sources for its inscriptions in addition to the Quran. Gülru Necipoğlu-Kafadar describes in detail the differences of inscriptions of Ottoman imperial mosques and highlights the peculiar Sufi references made at the Selimiye Mosque. For example, the central dome is decorated with eight medallions inscribed with divine names. Under these medallions, the ninety-nine beautiful names of God are placed, which Sufi dervishes chant in their rituals. Thus, Necipoğlu argues that they are the "visual counterparts of Sufi's oral recitations".[13]

In addition to this tacit link, the inscriptions also include quotations from the Hadith. The pool, in combination with the inscriptions at the Selimiye Mosque, builds a strong referential link to earlier convent-mosques.

Dalokay's drawings also show clear references to convent-mosques: the symbolism of paradise, the *kawthar*, the four cardinal directions, and the raised floor in the prayer hall. Dalokay shows in detail what he envisioned for the interior spaces and facades. For example, sometimes they are detailed so as to guide construction workers in how to build the framework for concrete castings, in order to ensure that the patterns on the exposed concrete follow the design intentions of interior surface decoration. As in the Selimiye Mosque, Dalokay's inclusion of an octagonal pool inside the prayer hall created a marker to accentuate the center of the mosque interior space. But, more importantly, it created an axis mundi in combination with the stylized *oculus* on the dome. Moreover, the pool's design – an octagonal geometry with eight goblet-shaped drinking bowls – strikingly mimics the ones found at convent-mosques. The theme of paradise was also articulated in his design. In his drawings, Dalokay shows a flower garden on the *qibla*-wall side (Fig. 2). Regarding the large openings on four sides, one could argue that Dalokay made references to the *iwan*s in convent mosques, which represent the four cardinal directions. Furthermore, the slightly elevated floor along the *qibla* wall also augments the reference to the differences in level in double-centered convent mosques. Dalokay's design, with his central octagonal pool and oculus, the flower garden, and the four *iwan*-shaped elevations, creates a strong referential link to convent-mosques. Like the Bektashis, he perhaps regarded the prayer space as a metaphor for paradise on earth, where the divine and the people can spiritually unify into a single body.

THE VISUAL CONSTRUCT

Walls, roofs, ceilings, and floors were conceived as continuous flat and unbroken two-dimensional planes by Ottoman architects. Decoration and inscriptions were applied over these uninterrupted surfaces. Dalokay surely builds on the continuity of surfaces in his design. However, at the Kocatepe Mosque, the three-dimensional nature of space is constantly brought into awareness. This is certainly true for the view of the mosque from a distance, as part of Ankara's skyline, but also for experiences in close proximity. His design has been clearly shaped by the modern perspectival construct. The way he located the monumental shell structure, the way he positioned the liturgical elements in space, and the way he designed visual moments along a loosely prescribed path, all command a three-dimensional perception of space.

It can be inferred from his drawings that Dalokay was thinking about the prayer space as a panoramic device. By entering the space, one is immersed within a 360-degree panoramic view of the immediate environment. The location of Kocatepe on a hill in Ankara further strengthens this condition. He introduced varying thick and deep vertical sun-shading devices on all four sides that made the view unfold with bodily movement in space. The movement in the prayer hall is built through a loosely knit system of architectural constants: the sun-shading devices, the liturgical elements in space, the texture and material qualities

of the prayer hall, the dome decorations, as well as the continuous planes extending outside the enclosed prayer space.

Dalokay's detailed deliberations on texture and material applications on the exterior surfaces of the continuous ground plane are important cues for depth perception. Dalokay thereby controls the way people walk or stroll through space. His construction drawings are crowded with many notes clarifying his design intentions; in one of them he characterizes the marble stones on the eastern and western sides beyond the enclosed space as mainly crimson superseded with green marble pieces. Dalokay clearly intended a strong continuity between the inside and outside of the prayer hall, thereby creating a visual continuity on the floor level, from the inside crimson and green carpets to the exterior crimson and green marble surface. These features would have immersed the mosque-goers within an expanded perception of space, stretching well beyond the enclosed prayer hall.

Therefore, the Kocatepe Mosque suggests that continuities, not boundaries, are Dalokay's major concern for his design. These are physical and visual continuities: the relation of the city to his mosque, and the relation of architectural components to each other and to the entirety of the mosque. The deep relationship between city and building, building and individual components, the development of a peculiar visual construct, and the firm control of dispersed phenomena suggest a unifying intellectual rigor to which Dalokay aspired in his form-giving exercise.

It is relatively easier to deal with a referential theory of meaning and to analyze how the Kocatepe Mosque incorporated particular precedents of paths, forms, and narratives, and translated them into modern architecture. The religious references are so pervasive that it is easy to understand the temptation to take them as a program of design; however, they do not tell us how Dalokay specifically produced architecture with them. How does Dalokay's work indeed contribute to our understanding of translating textual or visual heritage into "brick and mortar?" To some extent this question is related to what consists in

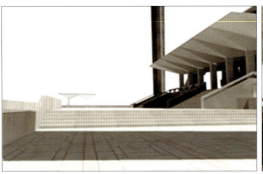
Main Approach

Late-comers' Area & Entrance

Prayer Hall

6 Vedat Dalokay, unbuilt Kocatepe Mosque, Ankara, 1957, sequence of views and goblet-shaped fountain.
Computer renderings: Imdat As

the act of design formulation that produces the Kocatepe Mosque.

Once Dalokay established his repertoire of references, the design is not developed through reiterations of references but rather through its own inherent logic. At some point in design formulation, Dalokay perhaps associated the design of the Kocatepe Mosque with a spontaneous questioning of architecture's fundamental premises: durability, utility, and beauty. Therefore, the translation is not a mere reproduction but a reformulation of the original artifact and, as such, it has a life on its own. With the help of computer graphics, we can partially simulate that life and go beyond the referential meaning of the mosque. We can simply look into Dalokay's work for what it is and analyze the more evident qualities of his design concept, the form, the spatial quality, the bodily experience, and make a non-referential judgment of his architecture (Fig. 6).

Indeed, the pool in the center of the mosque could refer to the *kawthar* as described earlier. However, the water in the pool can offer by itself spiritual tranquility that is comparable to the phenomena communicated in religious scripts, that is, the pool can affect, and not only symbolize, the idea of paradise and, through that, can practically emanate purity and pleasure. If we investigate Dalokay's work in this way, the relationships of references to building lose their importance. Although the pool symbolizes *kawthar,* potentially it affects purity and pleasure regardless of its connection to the symbolism. The references to Ottoman classical architecture or Seljuk convent-mosques are thus with hindsight secondary.

Therefore, referential meaning alone cannot account for the power of Dalokay's design, even though reference is so central to the program of the mosque. The power of Dalokay's mosque lies in the experience of formal properties upon personal feelings, perceptions, insights, and conditions. His Kocatepe Mosque proposal demonstrates how architecture can speak on its own – through its own coherent formal, structural, and aesthetic qualities – even in the absence of any references.

IMDAT AS is an international research fellow at Istanbul Technical University (ITU). He received the prestigious TUBITAK 2232 grant to head the City Development through Design Intelligence lab at ITU to research the impact of emerging technologies on the future of the city. Imdat co-authored *Dynamic Digital Representations in Architecture: Visions in Motion* (Taylor & Francis, 2008), and is currently working on two upcoming books on Artificial Intelligence in Architecture and Urban Planning for Routledge and Elsevier.

Goblet-Shaped Fountain

SUGGESTIONS FOR FURTHER READING

Akin, Gunkut. "The muezzin mahfili and pool of the Selimiye Mosque," *Muqarnas* 12 (1995), 63–83.

As, Imdat, and Schodek, Daniel. *Digital Representations in Architecture: Visions in Motion* (New York: Taylor & Francis, 2008).

Faroqhi, Suraiya. *Der Bektaschi–Orden in Anatolien* (Vienna: Verlag des Institutes fur Orientalistik der Universitat Wien, 1981).

Gebhard, David. "The problem of space in the Ottoman mosque," *Art Bulletin* 45 (1963), 271–5.

Necipoğlu-Kafadar, Gülru, "Religious Inscriptions on the Great Mosques of the Ottoman, Safavid and Mughal Empires," *Hadeeth Ad-Dar* 25 (2008), 34–40.

Necipoğlu-Kafadar, Gülru. "The Süleymaniye complex in Istanbul: an interpretation" *Muqarnas* 3 (1985), 92–117.

NOTES

[1] Thomas F. Mathews, *The early churches of Constantinople: architecture and liturgy* (University Park: Pennsylvania State University Press, 1971), 126.

[2] Gülru Necipoğlu-Kafadar, "The Süleymaniye complex in Istanbul: an interpretation," *Muqarnas* 3 (1985), 107 (92–117).

[3] Turgut Cansever, as quoted in Ugur Tanyeli, "Cagdas Mimarlikta Islami icerik sorunu ve Cansever," *Arredamento Dekorasyon* (1991), 83 (83–89).

[4] Suraiya Faroghi, *Der Bektaschi–Orden in Anatolien* (Vienna: Verlag des Institutes fur Orientalistik der Universitat Wien, 1981), 191–2.

[5] John Kingsley Birge, *The Bektashi order of dervishes* (London: Luzac Oriental, 1994), 15.

[6] Eyice Semavi, "Ilk Osmanli devirinin dini – ictimai bir muessesi: Zaviyeler ve zaviyeli camiiler," *Istanbul Universitesi Iktisat Fakultesi Mecmuasi* 23 (1963), 7 (3–80).

[7] Cavit Sunar, *Melamilik ve Bektasilik* (Ankara: Ankara Universitesi Ilahiyat Fakultesi Yayinlari, 1975), 71.

[8] Enver Behnan Sapolyo, *Mezhepler ve tarikatlar tarihi* (Istanbul: Turkiye Yayinevi, 1964), 317.

[9] Gunkut Akin, "The muezzin mahfili and pool of the Selimiye Mosque," *Muqarnas* 12 (1995), 67 (63–83).

[10] Necipoğlu-Kafadar, "The Süleymaniye complex in Istanbul: an interpretation," 109.

[11] Gülru Necipoğlu-Kafadar, "Religious Inscriptions on the Great Mosques of the Ottoman, Safavid and Mughal Empires," *Hadeeth Ad-Dar* 25 (2008), 36 (34–40).

[12] Akin, "The muezzin mahfili and pool of the Selimiye Mosque," 79.

[13] Necipoğlu-Kafadar, "Religious Inscriptions on the Great Mosques of the Ottoman, Safavid and Mughal Empires," 36.

Regionalist Expressions of the Mosque in the Arabian Peninsula and the Middle East

JAMES STEELE

1 Abdel Wahid El-Wakil,
Corniche Mosque, Jeddah.
Photo: Mohammad Akram

The Kingdom of Saudi Arabia developed rapidly during the 1970s and early 1980s, especially due to the escalating price of oil, and subsequently lost much of its architectural heritage. The most extensive changes occurred in the capital city of Riyadh, the holy cities of Mecca and Medina, and in the historic core of the Red Sea port of Jeddah. This loss is especially regrettable because of the nomadic Bedouin roots of this culture and the subsequent scarcity of traditional architecture in the Kingdom.

At the end of the 1980s enlightened political, religious, and academic leaders started to voice concern about this loss of heritage and sought ways to protect it, noting that history is especially important in the nation where Islam originated and its holiest sites are located. After most major infrastructure was in place, official attention turned to mosque construction, in response to the perceived dangers of moving too far, too fast.

At the time of the twin "oil shocks" that drove up prices in 1973 and 1976, Egyptian architect Hassan Fathy (1900–89) achieved international fame with his book *Architecture for the Poor*, in which he described his frustration in trying to complete his village of New Gourna, near Luxor. He based his design on traditional typologies that he had discovered in the central, medieval district of Cairo, combined with Nubian methods of mud-brick construction. Fathy believed that this synthesis represented the essence of Egyptian tectonic identity, which he put forward as an alternative to European architectural styles. Several disciples who have since designed many of the most important mosques throughout the region adopted his system.

HASSAN FATHY'S ARCHITECTURAL LANGUAGE

When Hassan Fathy graduated in 1926, Egypt was still under colonial rule. After a brief flirtation with Bauhaus Modernism, he joined a group of ultra-nationalistic intellectuals who were expressing their idealism through their art. Fathy's contribution involved the search for an authentic Egyptian alternative to Western influence. He started by documenting medieval Cairene houses such as the Beits Kathoda, Souheimi, and Gamal adin Dahabi. He substantiated his field surveys with historical sources, such as Napoleonic-era *Description de l'Égypte*, or Description of Egypt, at the Institut français d'archéologie orientale (French Institute for Oriental Archaeology), in Cairo.[1]

Fathy discovered consistent typologies in each of the houses he studied, derived from a common set of socio-religious and environmental constraints. These start with the *magaz*, or indirect entrance from the street, which prevents a direct view into the house and provides security. The *magaz* typically leads into a primary forecourt, usually paired with a second, smaller one located on the windward side of the house. These two courts are joined by an open breezeway, or *taktaboosh*, with a long narrow room bridging over it. The forecourt is paved and the windward court is planted, which allows cool evening air trapped in the vegetation to rush forward in a convective current to the front of the house as the sun rises and heats the paving. A *maqaad*, or raised covered porch, was located on the first floor of the street side of the forecourt to take advantage of the cooler prevailing breeze at sunset. A *qa'a*, or reception room for male guests, completed Fathy's spatial ensemble. It was covered with a tower, or *shuksheika*, paired with a *malkaf*, or second tower oriented toward the prevailing breeze.

2 Hassan Fathy, New Gourna Mosque, New Gourna near Luxor, entrance façade.
Photo: Christopher Little/ Aga Khan Award for Architecture

3 Plan of the New Gourna Mosque.
Photo: Aga Khan Award for Architecture Archives, Geneva

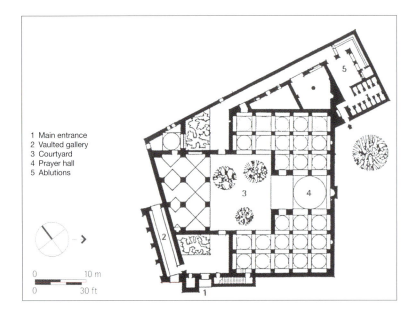

1. Main entrance
2. Vaulted gallery
3. Courtyard
4. Prayer hall
5. Ablutions

As air heated inside the house, it rose by convection up through the *shuksheika*, and was expelled.

Fathy felt that this set of Cairene typologies, of *magaz*, paired paved and planted courtyards, *taktaboosh*, *maqaad*, *qa'a*, *shuksheika*, and *malkaf*, still did not adequately represent the profoundly diverse heritage of his nation, so he traveled to Nubia, in Upper Egypt, to study the vernacular architecture there. The Nubians had devised an ingenious system of building in mud brick without any centering, or scaffolding, due to a shortage of wood in this barren region, which spans the border with Sudan. The Nubian system is based on a parabolic arch inscribed on a mud brick wall with successive courses leaning in compression against it; this system could also be employed to create domes.

Fathy first used this integrated system of Cairene typologies and Nubian construction techniques at New Gourna, intended to relocate 5000 villagers from Old Gourna, on the slopes of the Valley of the Kings and Queens, to the west bank of the Nile. Due to resistance from the Gournii themselves, who were reluctant to be separated from direct access to the tombs that provided them a lucrative income, only a small portion of the village was completed.

The portion of New Gourna that was built includes a mosque completed in 1948, which still survives (Fig.2). It is the only mosque designed by Fathy in the Arab world to have been realized and is clearly a synthesis of Cairene typologies and Nubian building traditions. The mosque has a *magaz*, leading past an ablution or washing area into a large forecourt, which precedes a domed, hypostyle prayer hall (Fig. 3). Its sturdy minaret and massive dome were modeled on those of a mosque he had seen in a Nubian village; Fathy described these and additional elements in an unpublished manuscript entitled *Mosque Architecture*, which also influenced his disciples.[2] One of the most important of these elements is a series of repetitive, chevron-like crenellations inspired by those on the top of the wall surrounding the Ibn Tulun Mosque in Cairo, which Fathy described as visually interlocking the mosque and the horizon.

ABDEL WAHID EL-WAKIL'S EXPANSION OF FATHY'S PRINCIPLES

Fathy's ideas have been perpetuated to a remarkable degree by several of his disciples, who were active in the Gulf region since the early 1980s with the region's evaluation of the historical cost of "progress." The Egyptian architect, Abdel Wahid El-Wakil (b. 1943) is unquestionably first among these, working with Fathy after graduating from Ain Shams University in 1965. He first received international recognition by winning an Aga Khan Award in 1980 for the Halawa house, in Agamy Egypt, which was cited for its use of traditional typologies, such as the *magaz, maqaad*, and courtyard, and Nubian domes, vaults, and arches.

With the Halawa house, as with all subsequent projects, El-Wakil was clearly proclaiming an important philosophical departure from his mentor's approach. Rather than adopting the confrontational go-it-alone, truth-against-the-world posture that Fathy had assumed, he has

deliberately sought out the patronage of the rich and powerful, in the belief that Fathy's principles must be accepted by people at the top in order to be more effectively disseminated.

El-Wakil decided to relocate to the Kingdom of Saudi Arabia in 1975, soon after the Halawa house was finished and found his first two important patrons in Jeddah. These were Sheikh Abdel-Aziz al-Sulaiman and Mayor Muhammed Said al-Farsi. Sheikh Sulaiman commissioned El-Wakil to design a residence for him in the Andalus district of Jeddah. El-Wakil responded with a new scheme that not only eloquently elaborates on the Fathyesque lexicon used at Agamy, with the addition of a soaring *qa'a*, not present in the Halawa house, but also provides a commentary on the traditional tower house, once found throughout old Jeddah. By literally turning the tower house on its side and aligning it with the Corniche, El-Wakil makes a critical observation about how a vernacular, vertical typology can be meaningfully transformed into its contemporary, horizontal equivalent, driven by the prevalence of free-standing villa construction throughout the Kingdom today (Fig. 4).

As a result of this project, El-Wakil was then commissioned to design a mosque in memory of the late Sheikh Abdullah Al-Sulaiman, across the Corniche from the house, near the coast (Fig. 5). El-Wakil used this opportunity to engage in an unexplored aspect of Islamic architectural heritage; by doing so he re-invigorated and perpetuated a precious body of knowledge that was then threatened with extinction. Using the groundbreaking research of his mentor Hassan Fathy as his starting point, El-Wakil investigated scarcely recorded building techniques involving complex, sacred Islamic geometries. Alpay Ozdural has demonstrated that such methods were partially transcribed, dispelling the popular notion that they were only transferred verbally.[3] In his own extensive field surveys, El-Wakil recorded the most prominent surviving examples of historic Islamic architecture available to him, focusing on specific aspects, such as the geometric complexities of *muqarnas*. Many times, he was just steps ahead of the wrecker's ball, sometimes even purchasing

4 Abdel Wahid El-Wakil,
Al-Sulaiman Palace, Jeddah.
Photo: Abdel Wahid el Wakil

5 Abdel Wahid El-Wakil,
Al-Sulaiman Mosque, Jeddah.
Photo: Abdel Wahid el Wakil

assemblies that had already been demolished and storing them for further study. This led him to write his own computer program on *muqarnas* geometry, long before digital access was ubiquitous. He has succeeded in finally codifying an entire field of knowledge that had been difficult to access.

El-Wakil's testing ground came with a dome, which at twelve meters in diameter in 1976 was the largest masonry hemisphere of its kind at the time. He insisted on using the same unsupported, ancient Nubian method used by Fathy at New Gourna, in spite of the risk and vastly larger scale, in order to prove its effectiveness. Like Hagia Sophia in Istanbul, this mosque also has side domes that buttress the main dome, but they are fully round and located on the sides of the big circumference, rather than on its longitudinal axis. But, consistent with his mission of always moving traditional knowledge forward, he decided against adopting the octagonal model used by his mentor at Luxor, in favor of the hexagonal base of the dome of the Sokullu Mehmet Pasha Mosque built by Sinan in Turkey in 1572, generally considered as that master's finest work. The Sulaiman Mosque demonstrates Abdel Wahid El-Wakil's determination to master the technical limits of the structural language that he inherited from Fathy and to advance the contemporary knowledge of Islamic architecture.

The Sulaiman Palace and Mosque brought El-Wakil to the attention of people at the highest positions of power within the Kingdom, including then Prince Fahd ibn Abdul-Aziz, who was soon to become King, as well as Prince Sultan bin Salman. They were among those in the royal family who recognized the threat that unchecked modernization posed to Saudi values and identity. They had voiced their concerns about the need to join past and present to then Mayor of Jeddah, Muhammed Said al-Farsi, whose city was one of those at the forefront of development. They agreed that the bridge would best be achieved with an architectural language that would both reflect the proud Islamic heritage of the nation and its core importance in the Muslim world, while still being progressive and modern. Local historian Haroon Sugich has described the appearance of El-Wakil, who clearly embodies this difficult juncture, as a fateful coincidence, since: "the mayor finally found someone who could articulate the vision of the King in his designs, blending the traditional and modern with integrity and depth".[4]

El-Wakil has been able to creatively extrapolate the synthesis first formulated by Hassan Fathy. It was the impact of the Sulaiman Palace, Sugich explains, that propelled El-Wakil into Said Farsi's inner circle and placed him "under the direct patronage of King Fahad".[5] Farsi, under the auspices of the Ministry of Pilgrimage and Endowments and its Deputy Director Husam Hussein Khasoggi, which had been solely entrusted with the restoration, construction, administration, and maintenance of all mosques within the Kingdom, then commissioned El-Wakil to design four small mosques. These acted as what the architect has

described as "religious sculpture" intended to encourage a return to traditional values. Khashoggi recalls that, "the Ministry became deeply involved in the preservation of Islamic cultural heritage, establishing a link between the past and the present day" and that it had the task of "preserving the integrity of Islamic architecture in the country through a program of building, re-building and renovating mosques." As part of this plan, the idea was "to set up a number of main mosques as "model" mosques, comprising the main mosque in each principal town and each provincial capital in the Kingdom".[6] The four mosques that El-Wakil had been commissioned to design on prominently visible sites on the seaside of the Corniche were an important part of this strategy.

The Island Mosque (1985), which was the first of these, sets the tone for the Ruwais, Abraj, and Corniche mosques. A tight budget made it necessary for the architect to appeal to the Jeddah Municipality for variances on critical requirements such as ablution and air conditioning. He argued that worshippers would be coming directly from home and would have already washed. Trusting in Fathy's teaching, he also contended that natural ventilation alone, assisted by prevailing sea breezes, could provide the same level of comfort as mechanical cooling, if traditional techniques were implemented. Each of these mosques, then, are case studies in the effectiveness of traditional methods of natural cooling and the use of thermal mass to prevent overheating through convective radiation. In the Island Mosque, the prayer area is strategically placed behind an arcade and an open courtyard, so that it captures and contains the cool sea breezes that filter into it (Fig. 6). The thick clay brick walls and a tile floor of the prayer hall assure that solar gain and people using the space only gradually heat the air. When the temperature finally does increase, the air rises up and out of an opening in the dome

6 Abdel Wahid El-Wakil, Island Mosque, Jeddah Corniche.
Photo: Christopher Little/ Aga Khan Award for Architecture

REGIONALIST EXPRESSIONS OF THE MOSQUE 343

above, which acts like the *shuksheika* in the *qa'a* of a Cairene house. So, the dome has an environmental purpose as well as symbolically representing the heavenly vault of the sky covering the earthlike solidity of the cube below.

The Corniche Mosque, which followed soon after in 1986, is also prominently sited, at the tip of a large coral based dune (Fig. 1). It has a dramatically vaulted entrance, reminiscent of several Egyptian precedents, which introduces worshippers to a carefully choreographed series of spatial and visual experiences before they reach the central prayer hall. The entrance also funnels ocean breezes into the interior.

The al-Ruwais Mosque, the third of these four distinctive structures to be built along the Corniche, is larger than the first two (Fig. 7). Its double bank of catenary vaults, which are stacked to guide the maximum amount of cool air into the rectilinear prayer hall at the back, seems to have been inspired by the New Baris Market designed by Hassan Fathy, in Kharga, Egypt. The main dome above the *mihrab* bay, along with smaller domes on each side, contribute to this extremely effective system of air circulation and create a memorable massing of forms. The mosque occupies a high knoll that makes it a dominant landmark when crossing the bridge that leads to the downtown area of Jeddah, when approaching the city from the north.

The Abraj Mosque, which is the last of the four small Jeddah to be built, is located on a main avenue in a residential neighborhood. It was originally named after the Binladen Construction Company, which helped sponsor it. Unlike the other small mosques, Turkish rather than Egyptian precedents inspired this, specifically the centralized dome typology introduced by Mimar Sinan at the Selimiye, in Edirne. El-Wakil once again displays his creative translation of important prototypes here by skillfully reducing Sinan's stately formal vocabulary to a much smaller scale. The curving dome rests on a hexagonal base that allows for four half domes to be used as squinches. The result is a compact, well-balanced jewel–like structure with a visual power that far exceeds its diminutive size.

While these small structures were being designed and built, El-Wakil received commissions for four additional mosques in the same city. The first of these, from the Ministry of Hajj and Awqaf, was eventually sponsored by the firm of E.A. Juffali and Brothers and bears their name. The second commission came from Muwaffak Mohammed al-Harithy in honor of his father, Al-Sharif Mashour al-Harithy. The third was from Ragab Abdel Aziz and Silsila Abdullah, for a site in the Baghdadiyah district. The fourth was for the King Saud Mosque located on the Medina Road in the Al-Sharafiyyah district of Jeddah (Fig. 8). Each of these, like the Sulaiman Mosque completed in 1980, was designed to accommodate between 1000 and 2000 worshippers, and so have been classified as "community" mosques.

The Juffali Mosque is situated in the midst of a lush garden beside the lagoon of the old city, near the Ministry of Foreign Affairs. El-Wakil echoed elements of the buildings nearby, such as the *roshan*, or wood latticed windows and massive walls that are part of the vernacular language of the historic core. The Harithy Mosque is located on Sari Street, near the Medina road in Jeddah, on a site that is at a thirty degree angle from the *qibla* direction toward Mecca. This presented a challenge for the architect,

7 Abdel Wahid El-Wakil, al-Ruwais Mosque, Jeddah.
Photo: Abdel Wahid el Wakil

8 Abdel Wahid El-Wakil, King Saud Mosque, Jeddah.
Photo: Abdel Wahid El-Wakel

which he solved with extensive landscaping, used to reconcile the angle created between the mosque and the street line. This strategy extends into a large central courtyard, which contains many palm trees and a large fountain, covered by a retractable tent, for shade during the hottest times of the day. A pair of Ottoman-style pencil minarets flank the main street-front entrance; these, along with a large dome over the square prayer space at the opposite end of the central courtyard, provide visual balance when the rectilinear structure is seen from the side. Matching arcades, capped with small domes over each bay along the extended elevations, modulate the long walls and connect the prominent, bracketing features of the minarets at one end and with the large dome at the other. Exquisite tiles in the prayer hall, made in Kutahye, Turkey in the Iznik tradition, and a carved marble *mihrab* reinforce the Turkish reference established by the minarets.

After the Azezeyia Mosque, which is the third in this series and for which little information exists, El-Wakil designed the King Saud Mosque (1980), which is the last of his larger community *masjid*s in Jeddah. It is also located ear the Medina road in the Al-Sharafiyyah district of the city. The stature of the mosque's patron, King Fahad bin Abdul Aziz al-Saud, and its scale clearly convey the level of influence the architect had attracted by this point, when construction started in 1986. This building replaced an existing reinforced-concrete structure of the same name built on the same site in 1956. This had been the first modern mosque in Jeddah, but had been closed due to engineering safety concerns. The historical reference that El-Wakil chose, in this instance, was the Sultan Hasan Mosque in Cairo, built in 1356. This Mamluk-era mosque has a square central courtyard surrounded on each side by *iwan*s.

While the King Saud Mosque follows the Sultan Hasan typology, it differs in several important ways. Rather than being aligned with the street, it was shifted within the orthogonal grid to align with the *qibla* direction. The mosque has a roughly square, compact plan that allows it to fit inside its

REGIONALIST EXPRESSIONS OF THE MOSQUE 345

9 Abdel Wahid El-Wakil, Quba Mosque, near Medina.
Photo: Abdel Wahid el Wakil

10 Abdel Wahid El-Wakil, Qiblatain Mosque, Medina.
Photo: Abdel Wahid el Wakil

site boundary. This shift creates many interesting formal conditions on the periphery, most obvious at the main entrance, which dominates the northwest corner of the site, along Asad Allah Street. This impressive portal, which is capped with a sixty-meter high minaret, is an exact, photogrammetric reproduction of the Sultan Hasan doorway. It extends at right angles from the main wall of the mosque enclosure, to both intercept and turn the 5000 worshippers who pass through it into a long corridor leading to the central courtyard inside. The main dome of the King Saud Mosque is twenty meters in diameter, just one meter less than that of the Sultan Hasan Mosque, in deliberate deference to its precedent. Yet, it is sizable nonetheless, considering that the dome of the Hagia Sophia in Istanbul, which was the largest covered space in antiquity prior to the Renaissance, has a diameter of twenty-three meters.

After the construction of the King Saud Mosque, El-Wakil moved beyond the confines of Jeddah and achieved the highest level of national recognition by being asked to renovate the Masjid al-Quba, or Quba Mosque, just south of Medina (Fig. 9). Khalifa Uthman ibn Affan, a *sahabi*, or companion, of the Prophet, first extended the Quba Mosque. Khalifa Al-Walid ibn Abd al-Malik, the builder of the Great Mosque of Damascus, then altered it. Subsequent alterations further weakened the integrity of the structure, and all concerned felt that there was no alternative but to tear it down. El-Wakil replaced it with a large courtyard configuration, paved in black, red, and white marble and a prayer hall covered by three ribbed, white domes. A minaret marks each corner. The re-building was completed in 1986.

The Masjid al-Qiblatain, or Two Qiblas Mosque, followed this important project, in 1987 (Fig. 10). It is where the Prophet received a revelation that Muslims should turn their direction of prayer from Jerusalem to Mecca. Two domes of different height, connected by a vault, with their brickwork exposed, reflect this crucial change, with the northern one representing the original *qibla*, while the higher, main dome on the south, commemorates the historic shift toward Mecca. Two minarets, inspired by Yemeni precedents, frame the domes, which

seem to rise between them. The plan of the mosque is raised on a plinth above street level and centers around a hypostyle prayer hall for 2,000 people where intricate plasterwork articulates repetitive arches and the *mihrab*. It includes a women's gallery at an upper level at the rear of the hall.

Al-Miqat Mosque, at Dhul Hulayfa, which Abdel Wahid El-Wakil also designed at this time, is 9 kilometers from al-Masjid al-Nabawi, or the Prophet's Mosque, and was conceived as a gateway to Mecca for pilgrims coming from Medina. Al-Miqat was inspired by the Ibn Tulun mosque in Cairo and so is also rotated within a *ziyadah*, or surrounding precinct wall to conform to the *qibla* direction. Access requirements caused by the main highway nearby, however, dictated that the *ziyadah* in this case be parallel to the road. It contains public facilities on its northwestern edge and ablution on its southeastern and southwestern sides.

An additional aspect of al-Miqat design is the transformation of the original prototype presented by the Mosque of the Prophet and its commemoration at a smaller scale as a rotated square. By doing so, El-Wakil has intentionally revitalized the sacred geometry of the past. The square has historically been used as a platform to indicate the cardinal points, from which, as Hassan Fathy has said in his *Mosque Architecture*, "the movement of the sun and moon and stars in their unequal course is re-enacted, with their meeting and reconciliation giving fresh promise of one more coincidence." Rather than implying temporality, the sequentially diminished, rotated squares of al-Miqat symbolize infinity with the final deflection toward the *qibla* direction, which closes the series, placing this gesture in its earthy context.

Millions of pilgrims come to the Kingdom each year to visit the Quba and Qiblateen mosques, *en route* to the Mosque of the Prophet. The original, nearly square, 98 × 115 foot, or 11,270 square foot compound, with a large courtyard and hypostyle covered area in front of the *mihrab*, has served as a prototype for many subsequent mosques. Renovations took place under the Umayyads (661–750), Abbasids (750–1258), Mamluks (1250–1517), and Ottomans (1299–1923), as well as under

King Abdul Aziz Al-Saud, from 1949 to 1951 and King Fahad bin Abdul Aziz al-Saud in 1991–1992.[7] The final renovation, which essentially surrounds the old mosque and is materially distinguished from it, also includes notable engineering innovations. These include twenty-seven movable domes on rails which can be opened and closed to control internal heat gain and twelve hydraulically powered fabric umbrellas, with six used in each of two smaller courtyards for the same purpose. Mahmoud Rasch and his team at Sonderkonsruktionen und Leichtbau engineered these and Dr. Kamal Ismail was the architect (Fig. 11).

A communiqué released by El-Wakil Associates in 1990 lists thirteen mosques as having been completed and five designed between 1980 and 1990 with one of those, the Yateem mosque in Bahrain, under construction. Of those completed, only the Maydani mosque in Riyadh has not been described here. Subsequent accounts have added the Friday mosque in Medina, as well as the Hafeyer mosque in Mecca, completed in 2008, bringing the final total in the Kingdom to fifteen. By any measure, the realization of these projects in such a short period of time at such a high level of artistic and technical skill, not to mention their investigation into and contribution to the knowledge of Islamic architecture is a remarkable achievement. From his beginnings in Jeddah in 1980, with four small symbolic and highly visible structures along the Corniche, to the community mosques of Sheikh Suliaman, al-Harithy, Azezeyiah, Juffali, and King Saud in that city, followed by the historically significant pilgrimage and congregational Quba and Qiblateen Mosques, joined by the new Miqat Mosque near Medina, Abdel Wahid El-Wakil has demonstrated an aesthetic trajectory that has had a profound impact on subsequent designers working within the same typological framework, in either a reflexive or reactive way. Rasem Badran is one of the most important of these.

RASEM BADRAN – AN ALTERNATIVE READING OF FATHY

Jordanian architect Rasem Badran (b. 1945) is also a disciple of Hassan Fathy, although in contrast to El-Wakil, he never worked with him. Badran first came to prominence with his entry into the Baghdad State Mosque competition in 1982 (Fig. 12). Although it was never realized, the design firmly established him as a rising talent. Since then, he has carried out extensive research into the history and context of the region, resulting in a hauntingly beautiful design that evoked the essence of Abbasid-era Mesopotamia. He was prompted by what he calls "narratives" to produce a concept based on the platforms historically used for religious structures in the region, breaking down the monumentality resulting from the large program with both this raised dais, which reduced visual awareness of scale and the use of a repeated fifteen meter square grid of cubes, that recall the Kaaba in Mecca. Three years after the Baghdad State Mosque competition, Badran was selected by the Riyadh Development Authority as the architect for the Qasr al-Hokm project in Riyadh (Fig. 13). As in Baghdad, this complex included a mixture of sacred and secular elements, but here the mosque accommodates 20,000 worshippers divided between an enclosed prayer hall for 14,000 and a courtyard for 6,000, replacing an ancient mud-brick mosque on the site. It was connected to

11 Umbrellas at the Mosque of the Prophet, Medina.
Photo: Abdel Wahid el Wakil

12 Rasem Badran, Baghdad State Mosque competition 1982 entry.
Photo: *Mimar: Architecture in Development*

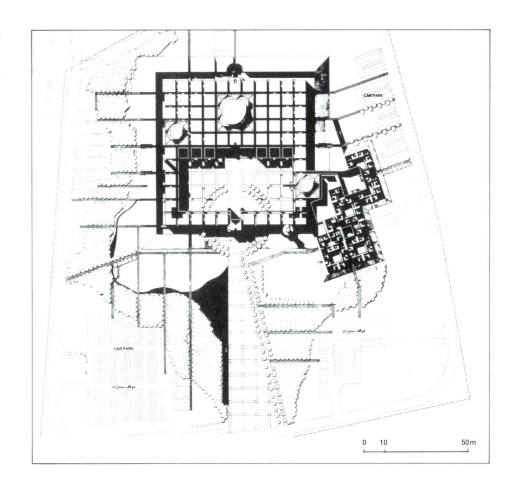

13 Rasem Badran, Qasr al Hokm Mosque and Justice Palace complex, Riyadh, 1985.
Photo: Aga Khan Award for Architecture

REGIONALIST EXPRESSIONS OF THE MOSQUE 349

14 Beeah Architects, al-Kindi Plaza, Riyadh.
Photo: Reha Gunay / Aga Khan Award for Architecture

a palace that also served as a hall of justice, which Badran also replaced.

Qasr al-Hokm is laden with layers of memories since it is located at the core of the old district of the capital city of Riyadh, where the nation of Saudi Arabia originated. It has also suffered from the wholesale destruction of its historical fabric beginning with the oil boom in the late 1970s. Rasem Badran was determined to both uncover and express the many layers of symbolic meaning attached to this site, searching beyond it to discover sources such as the historic mosque at Ad-Darriyah, above the Wadi Hanifah, the ancestral home of the ruling Saud family, which served as prototypes for him.

Badran's final design revolves around a series of courtyards, starting with the 11,200 square meter Mohammad Ibn-Saud Plaza in front of his new Palace of Justice, followed by the smaller Al-Safa Plaza, which then leads to the mosque. One of the most important aspects of Badran's design is a triangular commercial zone that mediates between this linear sequence and the street. This zone is significant because it re-introduces the historical connection between secular economic and sacred uses, which had been severed during the rush toward modernization, often leaving the mosque as an isolated object, surrounded by parking, within the urban landscape. Badran has not only managed to retain the spiritual and temporary authority of the Qasr al-Hokm Justice palace and mosque in this connection to commercial use, but has also managed to revive and preserve the precious cultural memories of this singular place and to balance tradition and modernity within it.

The Al-Kindi Mosque and Plaza in Riyadh, designed by Ali Shuaibi and Abdul-Rahman Hussaini of Al-Beeah Group Consultants, is also inspired by traditional elements of the Islamic Arab city, with a similar connection between secular, commercial activity and sacred use, it spans two curving parallel streets (Fig. 14). The Al-Kindi

15 Mohammed Ali al-Ameri, Sheikh Zayed Grand Mosque, Abu Dhabi.
Photo: Awani Arrar

16 Mohammad Makiya, Kuwait State Mosque.
Photo: Mohammad Makiya

Mosque and Plaza presents a wall to each of these streets, in order to clearly define the border between public, semi-public, and private spaces. This edge is perforated by metaphorical gates that lead to a tranquil courtyard within, terminated by a large, rectilinear prayer hall, diagonally cutting across one end.

The Al-Kindi Mosque shares the natural mud beige Najdi palette, as well as the double minarets, mixed use, and contextual integration that distinguish the Qasr al-Hokm project. But, both of these stand in stark contrast to the uniform whiteness, eclectic regional borrowing, and statuesque individuality of El-Wakil's mosques, regardless of scale.

THE INFLUENCE OF EL-WAKIL IN ABU DHABI

The pervasiveness of the imageability of El-Wakil's approach is evident throughout the region, but perhaps most obviously in the Sheikh Zayed Grand Mosque in Abu Dhabi by Mohammed Ali al-Ameri, completed in 2007 (Fig. 15). Dedicated to Sheikh Zayed bin Sultan al-Nahyan, the founder and first

17 Mohammad Makiya, Sultan Qaboos Grand Mosque, Muscat.
Photo: Mohammad Makiya

president of the United Arab Emirates, who is also buried there, it was inspired by both the Hassan II Mosque in Casablanca, Morocco and the Badshahi Mosque in Lahore, Pakistan, with a prayer hall that can accommodate up to 40,000 worshippers. It has a 180,000 square foot courtyard in its midst, with a 377-foot-high minaret at each of its four corners. Its most distinctive features are the fifty seven bulbous domes of various sizes which serrate the desert skyline. The powerful message that al-Ameri perpetuates here, following El-Wakil, is unity in diversity and Dar al-Islam, or the totality of the Muslim diaspora, in ascendance, once again.

MOHAMMED SALEH MAKIYA

Mohammed Saleh Makiya (1914–2015) was born in Iraq and belongs to Fathy's generation. However, Makiya created his own distinctive aesthetic, setting up an alternative for his native region. After study abroad, he returned to Iraq in 1946 and founded the College of Engineering at Baghdad University in 1959, which he led until 1968, influencing a large cadre of loyal students. During this time he designed the Khulafa Mosque in Baghdad in 1960 as well as the Siddique mosque in Doha (1978) and the Kuwait State Mosque (1984) after his departure (Fig. 16).

His Sultan Qaboos Grand Mosque in Muscat, Oman of 1993, named after Sultan Qaboos bin Said and intended to commemorate the fiftieth year of his reign, is perhaps most typical of Makiya's monumental, yet highly refined tectonic style. This is characterized by magnificent domes, layered blind niches of layered, telescoping arches, arcades open to one side, and a revitalization of craft (Fig. 17). He has been inspired by the Bilad Bani Bu Ali Mosque in Sharqiya, Oman, but his composition is more massive and uses a centralized dome. Makiya has also placed his mosque on a podium constructed of 300,000 tons of Indian sandstone, with a square prayer hall that can hold up to 6,500 people. A pair of outer and inner courtyards can accommodate an additional 13,500, bringing the total to 20,000. One main minaret and four smaller ones symbolize the five pillars of Islam, and an exceptionally beautiful *mihrab* demonstrates his ability to incorporate the finest crafts into his work.

Unlike Fathy and his disciples, who have had such a profound impact on the religious architecture of the region, Makiya and his advocates follow a heuristic rather than typological path. Of the myriad of mosques that now exist in the Kingdom of Saudi Arabia and throughout the Middle East, those designed in an architecturally informed way address these two theoretical positions.

JAMES STEELE is an architect, teacher, and writer. He received his architecture degrees at the University of Pennsylvania, and a PhD in Urban Planning from the University of Southern California (USC). He set up and directed programs at several universities around the globe before joining the School of Architecture at USC Los Angeles. His writing and editing includes more than fifty titles on a wide variety of topics, mainly related to architecture in the Islamic world.

SUGGESTIONS FOR FURTHER READING

Eisheshtawy, Yasser, ed. *The Evolving Arab City: Tradition, Modernity and Urban Development* (London, Routledge, 2008).

Fathy, Hassan. *Architecture for the Poor* (Chicago, University of Chicago Press, 1973).

Holod, Renata and Hassan-Uddin Khan. *The Mosque and the Modern World* (London, Thames and Hudson, 1997).

Serageldin, Ismail and James Steele eds. *Architecture of the Contemporary Mosque* (London, Academy Editions, 1996).

Steele, James. *Architecture for People: The Complete Works of Hassan Fathy* (London, Thames and Hudson, 1997).

Steele, James. *The Architecture of Rasem Badran: Narratives on People and Place* (London, Thames and Hudson, 2005).

NOTES

[1] *Description de l'Égypte, ou Recueil des observations et des recherches qui ont été faites en Égypte pendant l'expédition de l'armée française* (Paris: Imprimerie Imperiale, 1809–29).

[2] Hassan Fathy, *Mosque Architecture*, undated manuscript (Geneva: Aga Khan Award for Architecture Archives)

[3] Alpay Ozdural, "Omar Khayyam, Mathematicians, and 'Conversazioni' with Artisans," *Journal of the Society of Architectural Historians* 54.1 (March 1995), 54–71.

[4] Haroon Sugich, "Traditional Architecture Finds a Royal Patron," *Arts and the Islamic World* 3.1 (Winter-Spring 1988), 46 (45–50).

[5] Ibid., 50.

[6] Husam Hussein Khashoggi, "Mosques: Houses of God," *Al Benaa* 34.6 (April–May 1987), 12.

[7] Osamah El-Gohary, "Regionalism and El-Wakil's Architecture," *Al Benaa* 34.6 (April-May 1987), 11.

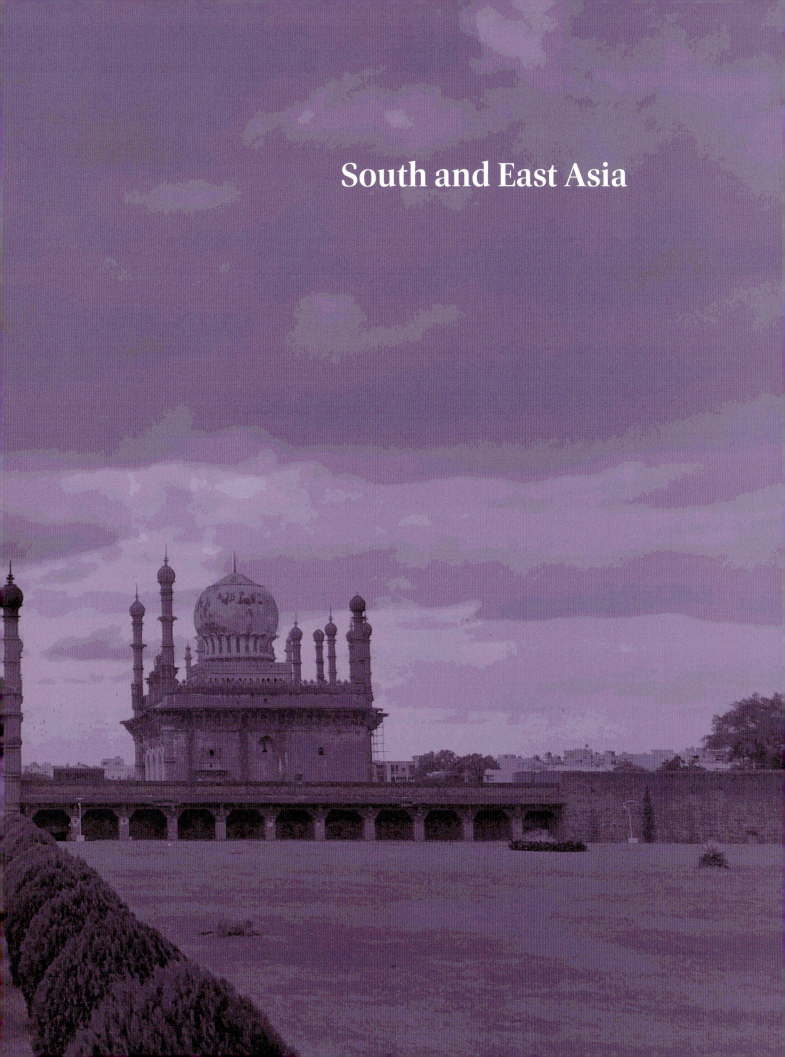

South and East Asia

The Sultanates in South Asia, 700–1690   ALKA PATEL

1 Tomb of Shaikh Rukn-i Din
Rukn-i Alam, c. 1315, Multan,
Pakistan. General View.
Photo: Aga Khan Award for
Architecture

The sultanates of South Asia (c. 1190–1690) were
independent states throughout present-day
Pakistan, India, and Bangladesh. While similar
politico-economic formations had existed
previously, such as the emirates of Sindh based
at Mansura and Multan (ninth-tenth centuries),
the later sultanates are characterized by a de-
emphasis on caliphal investiture and recognition
from Baghdad in favor of a reliance on prominent
local rulers as the primary political arbiters of
the region. Collectively, the sultanates were not
only predecessors – and in the case of the Deccani
sultanates, rivals as well – of the Mughal imperium
(1526–1857). The sultanates' rulers, nobles, and
merchants also oversaw transitions in strong,
regionally based artistic traditions as indigenous
practices were reinvented to accommodate Islamic
religious and cultural norms, frequently giving
way to significant innovations in the centuries-old
architectural conventions of South Asia.

Probably because of the great variety
and independence of the regional traditions
flourishing within each of these sultanates,
this fascinating five-hundred-year period of
South Asian history has been one of the most
challenging for scholars. Resisting accepted
scholarly constructs such as dynastic rubrics
and transcending religion-based categories
such as "Hindu" and "Muslim," sultanate-period
architecture in particular has been relatively
little studied. Fortunately, it is receiving increased
attention, and serving as a salutary exhortation
to re-examine often overly inflexible categories
prevalent in scholarship. This essay begins with a
brief examination of the early presence of Islam
in South Asia (eighth to mid-twelfth centuries).
It then lays out the major, representative
architectural developments in various sultanates,

emphasizing the combination of indigenous and
imported conventions creating new forms that were
long-lived throughout the history of South Asia.

EARLY ISLAM IN SOUTH ASIA c. 700–1150

A discussion of South Asia's sultanates would
be incomplete without some reference to earlier
developments, specifically the architecturally and
textually documentable presence of Islam in the
region by the late seventh-early eighth century that
continued uninterrupted into the sultanate period.
A comparison between this earlier Islamic presence
– a substantial one by many accounts – and the later
sultanates provides an important perspective on the
history of Islam in South Asia.

The sultanate period did not constitute the
first contact between Islamic and Indic cultural
forms. Rather, commercial and cultural links
connecting the Near East and South Asia from the
first centuries CE and earlier conveyed Islam into
the subcontinent, which in turn only strengthened
the transregional connectivity between the western
and eastern reaches of Asia.[1] But there was a
noteworthy difference between early Islam in South
Asia and the sultanate period: while eighth- through
mid-twelfth-century Muslim communities were
mostly integrated into Hindu kingdoms, during the
sultanate period we see the proliferation throughout
South Asia of principalities ruled by Muslim
politico-military elites. It is noteworthy, however,
that despite the establishment of Islamic states in
the Indus Valley and Gangetic plains by the twelfth
century, reliance on and reinventions of indigenous
architectural traditions are evident in both early
Islamic and sultanate-period buildings.

Islam was introduced into the subcontinent
through mercantile activity and related state-

2 Congregational Mosque. Banbhore, Pakistan. Probably founded early eighth century. Surviving remains from ninth-tenth centuries.
Photo: Wikimedia Commons – Anwar Ahmed

sponsored expansion within the first century of the Hijra (622). Archaeological evidence from the mid-seventh century indicates that new Muslim converts continued to engage in extensive commerce along well-established maritime and overland routes linking the eastern Mediterranean, Iran, and China. The subcontinent and the island of Sarandib (modern Sri Lanka) served as indispensable entrepôts as well as target markets in this nexus.[2]

Indeed, the Umayyad campaigns into Sindh of the late seventh through early eighth centuries can be seen as attempts at bringing within state control some of the mercantile activity that was already flourishing in the region. The commercial pragmatism of the Umayyad "conquest" of Sindh has long been known from the *Chachnama*, a thirteenth-century Persian account of the Umayyad campaigns.[3] The extension of the status of *dhimma*, or protected people, to Sindh's Buddhists and Hindus (expanded beyond Judaism and Christianity to Zoroastrianism already during the conquest of Iran) led to the continuation of many of the region's Buddhist monasteries and Hindu temples.[4] These institutions served not only religious but also commercial purposes, so that their maintenance and continuation was profitable to the new Arab forces in Sindh.

Recent re-examination of the excavated mosque at Banbhore (probably ancient Daybul) (Fig. 2) – previously considered the subcontinent's earliest mosque – attributes it to the Habbari Amirs based at Mansura in the ninth-tenth centuries, well after the initial Umayyad conquest.[5] Since a mosque was commonly among the first structures erected upon Islamic conquest, its absence in a region as strategically and commercially important as Sindh could indicate that the Umayyad forces were not immediately able to commandeer local labor and other means of production.[6] It is possible that consolidation of the territory and stable political rule in Sindh were not achieved until the ninth or tenth century by the Amirs of Mansura and Multan. Notwithstanding these tentative political beginnings, Islam as a socio-religious practice was integrated into the area's cultural landscape, so that by the tenth-eleventh centuries mosques in the Indus Delta evince a successful combination of imported and indigenous architectural traditions.[7]

In contrast to the absence of an early Umayyad mosque in Sindh, at Gwalior in north-central India an eighth-century *mihrab* (Fig. 3) – perhaps originally integrated into a mosque or open prayer area (*musalla*) – indicates the presence of a Muslim community in the vicinity.[8] The group had no evident ties with the Arabs in Sindh, rather being based at the important fort town of Gwalior within the realms of the Mauryas (seventh-eighth centuries), who had territories spanning the modern Indian states of Uttar Pradesh, northern Madhya Pradesh, and Bihar (ancient Gopaksetra) and were likely a junior clan of the Paramaras (ninth-fourteenth centuries) of north-central India.[9] Due to the strategic location of Gwalior at the intersections of east-west and north-south routes of communication and trade, the town's Muslim community likely engaged in commerce and very possibly contributed to making it a significant market center by the ninth century.[10]

The Muslim community's patronage of the local architectural traditions and labor is borne out in the form and decoration of the *mihrab*. The *mihrab* itself is a slightly pointed hemispherical niche framed by plain pilasters with two circular medallions in the spandrels. The pediment consists of varying fractions of the dormer-

3 *Mihrab*. Gwalior, Madhya Pradesh. Eighth century.
Photo: Alka Patel

window motif (*chandrashala*), not dissimilar to the base iconographic components comprising the curvilinear spires of northern Indian temples (*shikhara*). The niche's background is diaper-patterned and bordered by a continuous chain of four-petal flowers, all of which are also commonly found on the region's temple architecture. The fashioning of the *mihrab* – the focal point of Islamic ritual – within an indigenous rather than imported architectural language indicates this Muslim community's reliance on local labor and the group's medium if not long-term socio-economic integration within Maurya realms. Moreover, the innovative use of iconography traditionally associated with Hindu temple architecture in the fashioning of a *mihrab* – with the attendant omission of figural imagery – results in an object that transcends the scholarly constructs of "Hindu" or "Islamic."

Muslim communities continued to thrive in many of South Asia's coastal and inland localities during the ninth through twelfth centuries, well before the ascendancy of South Asia-based Muslim politico-military elites in the 1190s. Although no architectural remains survive, Arab travelers and geographers such as Ibn Khurdadbih (fl. 912), al-Mas'udi (fl. 915), al-Istakhri (fl. 951), Ibn Hauqal (fl. 943–68), and the unidentified author of the *Hudud al-'Alam* (*Boundaries of the World*, 982) among others all make note of Muslim settlements along the western coasts of South Asia[11] – understandable in light of the long-enduring connections with the Near East and Iran. The writers also mention that these communities were integrated into the domains of the Rashtrakutas (northern and southern branches, ninth-fifteenth centuries), with some Muslims holding important positions in imperial administrations.[12] Coasts were not the only areas with an Islamic presence: Akin to the eighth-century Muslim community at the inland fort-market town of Gwalior, bilingual Arabic-Sanskrit inscriptions from the Tochi Valley (northwestern Pakistan) signal the presence of a Muslim community within Hindu Shahi domains (c. 850–1026).[13] In the Ganga-Jamuna *doab*, a Sanskrit inscription from Kanauj (northwest of Gwalior) refers to the *Turushkadanda* – possibly a Muslim poll tax – indicating the presence of Muslims also within the realms of the later Gahadavalas (c. 1075–1200).[14]

As noted before, there were a few Islamic states in the northern and northwestern reaches of South Asia, and the Islamic architecture in some of these areas also evinces strong, regionally based rather than imported construction methods and

THE SULTANATES IN SOUTH ASIA 359

aesthetics. Following the Amirs of Sindh (ninth-tenth centuries), the Ghaznavids of Afghanistan (c. 990–1175) brought much of present-day Pakistan within their control by the mid-eleventh century. A mosque at Udegram (Fig. 4), Upper Swat, attests to an established Ghaznavid presence in the region, which effectively constituted both a way station on the seasonal capillary routes through the Karakorum Range[15] and a crucial frontier between the Ghaznavids, the recently deposed Hindu Sahis of Afghanistan and the Punjab, and the Loharas of Kashmir (c. 1000–c. 1170).[16]

The mosque combines both imported and indigenous components. It consists of the expected elements of courtyard, ablution pool, and *qibla* with prayer area, within a hypostyle plan of stone-based wood columns originally supporting the roof – all part of a mosque building tradition imported from the central Islamic lands. However, the construction method of layered schist and the angular keyhole shape of the single *mihrab* both place it firmly within Gandharan practices,[17] recalling the image niches found in Gandhara's Buddhist monasteries. Furthermore, the mosque's construction within local Gandharan traditions distinguishes it from the brick and stucco buildings of Ghazna, the dynastic capital in central Afghanistan, thereby establishing a discernible pattern of area-specific architectural practice even within a politically unified region under dynastically centralized control.

By the mid-twelfth century at the height of the Chaulukya dynasty (c. 940–1303) in the modern Indian states of Gujarat and Rajasthan, architectural evidence attests to a sizeable and prosperous Muslim community at Bhadreshvar on the southern coast of Kachh, the western extension of Gujarat. Two mosques, one tomb and another commemorative *chhatri*, and a stepwell – the stepwell a recognizably South Asian structure – from the 1150s, as well as inscribed epitaphs dating through the mid-thirteenth century, all indicate the long settlement of a Muslim community at this coastal town strategically situated near the Gulfs of Kachh and Khambhat (Cambay), the latter a central node in the Indian Ocean network.[18] Analysis of the epitaph inscriptions indicates that many of the inhabitants were of southern Iranian origin, particularly from Siraf, a Persian Gulf port that had been commercially prominent during the Sassanian and early Islamic periods.[19]

Similar to the architectural patronage of Gwalior's Muslim community, the Bhadreshvar group also relied on local architectural labor for the construction of the site's tombs and mosques, as exemplified by the Chhoti Mosque (c. 1150).[20] The building clearly demonstrates the innovative use of

4 Mosque at Udegram Castle, Swat, Pakistan. Eleventh century.
Photo Wikimedia Commons – Tan Afridi

360 PATEL

5 Chhoti Masjid, Bhadreshvar, with its rows of multi-sectioned (*misraka*) columns.
Photo: Alka Patel

the regional conventions of temple architecture. In keeping with its temple counterparts, the mosque is built of stone with an interior revealing its trabeate construction of rows of multi-sectioned (*misraka*) columns upholding a flat stone roof (Fig. 5). Rather than a temple's pillared hall leading into a small, dark sanctum, however, the mosque is configured as a rectangular hypostyle hall in front of the *qibla* wall with a single *mihrab*. Moreover, while the mosque's columns are replete with auspicious floral iconography, they are devoid of the extensive figural programs that were a hallmark of the region's temples. The plain concave *mihrab* was likely hung with a more decorative but perishable textile or wooden element to emphasize its centrality. The regional architectural vocabulary, developed from the ninth century onward principally through the construction of temples, was by the mid-twelfth century innovatively applied to Islamic buildings and thereby underwent an important rejuvenation.

THE SULTANATES c. 1190–1690

The Ghurid conquests of Delhi and Ajmer (eastern Rajasthan) in 1192–3 signaled the beginnings of Islam as a dominant political force in South Asia. While Muslim communities had long flourished throughout the region principally within non-Muslim kingdoms, the Ghurid annexation of the Indus Valley and modern north India led to the emergence of a Muslim politico-military elite in the region. Moreover, the Ghurids set a historical momentum in motion: over the next 350 years, various groups originating in the northwestern reaches of South Asia made their way into the Gangetic plains and established at Delhi the successive dynasties of the Khaljis (c. 1290–1320), Tughluqs (c. 1320–1415), Sayyids (c. 1415–1450), and Lodis (1450–1526). Although the Khaljis and Tughluqs were centered in the north, they conducted campaigns of conquest into the Deccan

THE SULTANATES IN SOUTH ASIA 361

6 Qutb Minar. Part of Qutbi Complex, Delhi. General View. Founded 1199.
Photo: Wikimedia Commons – Jorge Laskar

7 Congregational Mosque, Qutbi Complex. Delhi. General View. Founded 1192–93.
Photo: Wikimedia Commons

as well. The Tughluqs in particular created a far-flung empire that disintegrated into various principalities ("sultanates") that were ultimately independent of Delhi and its many changing dynasties. Existing as political formations with regional rather than pan-Indic power bases, most sultanates with the possible exception of Mandu (see below) are characterized by architectural patronage that is, to varying degrees, reflective of their localized ambits.

The Ghurid presence in northern India also led to the introduction of new architectural forms. The Qutb Minar (Fig. 6), founded in 1199 and completed in 1236 with repairs and additions through the fourteenth century, is the only freestanding minaret east of the Indus that survives.[21] It stands outside the southeastern corner of the Qutb Mosque (Fig. 7), founded in 1192, the region's earliest monumental mosque. Together, the minaret and the mosque are the architectural manifestations of the establishment of Islam as a political force in northern India. The site's significance continued unabated through the fourteenth century for Delhi's successive dynasties, many of which extended and maintained the complex. But despite the political change instituted by the Ghurids on an elite level, the conquering military commanders still patronized locally trained labor for the construction of the mosque and minaret.[22]

While mosques had been constructed in northern South Asia since the ninth century and probably earlier (albeit on considerably smaller scale), the minaret constituted a new architectural form in northern India. The Qutb Minar combines formal precedents from Iranian and Afghani towers with indigenous building materials and techniques. The minaret of the probable Ghurid summer capital of Jam-Firuzkuh (c. 1175), in central Afghanistan, and the commemorative towers of sultan Mas'ud III (r. 1098–1115) and Bahram Shah (r. 1117–49) at Ghazna (southeastern Afghanistan) clearly provided some formal elements, namely the stellate plans, elevations divided with *muqarnas* bands and balconies, tapering profile, and calligraphic decoration.[23] However, the Qutb Minar is not constructed of brick but of stone, the

8 Firuz Shah Tomb and Madrasa bordering Hauz Khas, northwest of Delhi.
Photo: Wikimedia Commons

preferred building material in India, and the plan consists of alternating angular and hemispherical projections. Also, stone allowed for the use of cursive scripts rather than Kufic for the calligraphic program. These formal and technical elements of the Qutb Minar, together with the expert reuse of building materials in the mosque and the corbeled arches of its *iwan* façade, all indicate that the Ghurid forces relied on local rather than imported building traditions as they set out to create an enduring presence of political Islam east of the Indus.

After the decline of the Ghurids in the 1210s, the Delhi-based Islamic dynasties were effectively independent states; indeed, the Khalji ruler Qutb al-Din Mubarak Shah I (r. 1316–20) even briefly adopted the caliphal title of Amir al-Muminin.[24] With the Tughluqs and their successor states, buildings generally took on a distinctly and recognizably South Asian character, with few direct architectural references in the central Islamic lands.

The tomb and *madrasa* complex of Firuz Shah Tughluq (r. 1351–88) northwest of Jahanpanah (the third of eight urban enclaves collectively constituting Delhi), demonstrates the combination of imported and adapted architectural referents with simplified indigenous building vocabularies (Fig. 8). The tomb and *madrasa* are seamlessly joined as a series of domed and trabeated cells bordering the Hauz Khass, or Royal Reservoir. The tomb chamber itself is square and low in its proportions, with a small entry and low hemispherical dome. Its battered walls and general austerity – features in all Tughluq-patronized structures[25] – recall the tomb complexes of the northwestern reaches of South Asia. The well-known tomb of the Suhrawardiya shaikh Rukn-i Din Rukn-i Alam (c. 1315) (Fig. 1) in Multan, where Ghiyath al-Din Tughluq (r. 1320) was posted as a Khalji-deputed governor, provides a comparative example. Both structures have a militaristic appearance with their heavy, battered walls and minimal decoration. The Multan tomb had its formal antecedents in earlier Islamic funerary buildings such as the tomb of Uljaytu in Tabriz, northern Iran, but the form was well integrated into the Multan region's architecture by the early fourteenth century.[26] Firuz Shah's *madrasa* and some parts of his tomb also evince identifiably Indic iconography, such as the stylized lotus petals on the column capitals in the *madrasa*'s cells, and the tomb's exterior railing, which recalls Buddhist stupa railings (*vedika*).

Thus, Firuz Shah's allowance of Indic elements in royally patronized architecture in some ways contradicts the Tughluq court chronicles' descriptions of the sultan's overtly Sunni stance and desecration of temples. Although this discrepancy is explicable in part by the literary conventions of the genre of royal biography, it also serves as a timely reminder of the importance of architectural evidence in creating a balanced view of any historical period.

Soon after the ascendancy of the Tughluqs and their expansions southward into the Deccan (1320s) and eastward into Bengal (1330s), these farther provinces became de facto independent sultanates. As noted above, the regional power bases of the sultanates were to varying degrees reflected in their architectural patronage. At the Adina Mosque (Fig. 9) of Pandua (1374–5), for example, though the large-scale plan with integrated courtyard was exceptional in Bengal, the use of intricately carved terracotta

THE SULTANATES IN SOUTH ASIA 363

9 Main entrance façade of the Adina Mosque, 1374–5, at Pandua, West Bengal, India.
Photo: Wikimedia Commons – Amitabha Gupta

10 Adina Mosque, *tympanum*.
Photo: Wikimedia Commons – Amitabha Gupta

panels (Fig. 10) for parts of exterior and interior decoration was directly linked to regional practices of temple decoration.[27] Similarly, the mosques of Karim al-Din (c. 1320) and Khwaja Jahan (fourteenth century) in Bijapur both served to transplant north Indian mosque-building conventions to the Deccan, including the block-like monumental gateway leading into a spacious courtyard and the strategic reuse of building materials. But they also encapsulated the continuation of local architectural styles in their squat, multi-sectioned (*citrakhanda*) columns and *mihrab* frames recalling Hindu temple entrances (Fig. 11).[28]

Unlike the Deccan and Bengal, the sheer proximity of the Tughluq provinces in northern India to the capital region of Delhi helped to maintain them longer within Tughluq control, until the demise of the dynasty in the 1390s. The regional capitals of Jaunpur to the immediate east of Delhi, Malwa directly to the south, and Gujarat to the west continued to receive centrally deputed provincial governors through the end of the fourteenth century. The Tughluqs were dealt a final blow with the sack of Delhi in 1398 by the legendary Timur (r. 1370–1405) and his forces. Thereafter the Delhi-deputed provincial governors in northern India declared themselves independent of the last important Tughluq sultan Firuz Shah III (r. 1389–91?), adopting royal prerogatives such as the striking of coins in their own names, and effectively establishing the sultanates of Jaunpur (1394–1531), Mandu (1402–1562), and Gujarat (c. 1400–1573).

Despite the long-standing political association between the Tughluqs and their eastern, western, and southern provinces, each of these successor states developed a distinct architectural vocabulary that had little to do with Tughluq-patronized architecture in Delhi. The buildings of Jaunpur and Mandu evince eclectic but identifiable architectural styles that incorporate some general elements of Indic iconography and, in the case of Mandu, also refer to the Timurid heritage of Khorasan (eastern Iran and Central Asia). Overall, however, they are all unique to their territories. The buildings of the Gujarat sultanate – extending through modern Rajasthan and parts of eastern Sindh – are further distinguished by a close formal relationship to the region's temples and other architectural typologies.

Shortly after the official declaration of Jaunpur's independence, the Atala Mosque (1408) (Fig. 12) was erected supposedly atop a pre-existing temple to the local deity Atala Devi, an assertion that is circumstantially supported by the inscriptions on the reused material found within the mosque. The interior displays trabeate construction, with square columns upholding a flat roof. Decorative motifs, such as stylized lotus petals grace column capitals and heavy rounded brackets create transitions between the column capitals and the ceiling. These elements certainly recall the interiors of some of Delhi's Tughluq-patronized buildings (for example, Firuz Shah's *madrasa*, and can be more

11 Tomb and Mosque Complex of Ibrahim II
Adil Shah ("Ibrahim Rauza"). General View.
Bijapur, Karnataka. Founded 1627.
Photo: Katherine Kasdorf

12 Atala Mosque at Jaunpur, Uttar
Pradesh. Colored etching by
William Hodges, 1786.
Photo: Wikimedia Commons –
Welcome Library public domain

THE SULTANATES IN SOUTH ASIA 365

13 Tomb of Hoshang Shah, also called Husang Shah Ghuri. Mandu, Madhya Pradesh (India). General View, 1435–36.
Photo: Wikimedia Commons – Bernard Gagnon

broadly placed within later Indic traditions of ornamentation.

It is the mosque's exterior areas, however, that provide the distinguishing features of Jaunpur's architectural idiom. The gateways leading into the mosque precinct, as well as the monumental arches (*pishtaq*) marking the central axis of the *iwan*, are both extremely tall and solid blocks punctured by various blind niches with pendant stylized lotus petals. The *iwan* archway conceals the principal dome of the prayer area. These monumental arches far exceed the *pishtaq*s in Tughluq architecture, being much more attenuated in their proportions and having more decorative detail that the remarkably spartan surfaces of the latter. Moreover, these tall and comparatively slender *pishtaq*s are unique to Jaunpur, recognizable as the distinct feature of this sultanate's architecture.[29]

Like the buildings of Jaunpur, the Mandu sultanate's architecture also had some elements recalling Tughluq Delhi, while simultaneously distinguishing itself as part of a recognizable regional style that referred, more than any other sultanate, to the Timurid legacies of eastern Iran and Central Asia. The city of Mandu is focused on the royally sponsored complex comprised of the tomb of Sultan Hushang Shah Ghuri (r. 1406–35) the congregational mosque and the Madrasa of the Heavenly Vault (*madrasa-i bam-i bihisht*, 1436-c. 1470). Although little survives of the *madrasa*, Shihab Hakim's *Ma'athir-i Mahmudshahi* (completed 1468), the primary textual source for the Mandu sultanate, provides an archaeologically verifiable description of the structure, including the presence of a tomb and minaret, and its function as both a *khanqah* (Sufi lodge) and *madrasa*. While Shihab Hakim gives no explanation regarding the name of the *madrasa* or its jurisprudential affiliation (*madhhab*), the minaret's approximate height of 45 meters, calculated from the author's description, seems to add substance to the *madrasa*'s lofty pretensions. Shihab Hakim's mention of artisans from Khorasan being employed in the *madrasa*'s construction helps explain the use of Quranic calligraphy in the building's arches, a characteristic also of Timurid architecture in Central Asia and eastern Iran.[30]

The tomb of Hoshang Shah (Fig. 13) is representative of Mandu architecture because of its balance between integration within and distinctiveness from this important complex. The building, set to the west of the congregational mosque just beyond the latter's *qibla* wall, is compact and square in plan, clad in white marble.

14 Stepwell. Adalaj, near Ahmadabad, Gujarat. Interior, c. 1500.
Photo: Hasan-Uddin Khan

The white marble contrasts with the surrounding beige stone of the *riwaq*s, which directly refer to the *riwaq*s and *iwan* of the neighboring mosque. Moreover, while the *riwaq*s are clearly of trabeated construction, the tomb possesses a lofty domical interior. Thus, the beige *riwaq*s with their Indic-order columns and ornately carved brackets serve as a foil for the sparkling white tomb in the center.

The block-like form of the tomb, its lack of polychromy, and proportionally small entrance and windows all hearken to the austere aesthetic of Tughluq tombs. However, the use of intricately carved white marble, as well as the much more prominent hemispherical dome on its tall drum, both set it apart. The tomb's decorative elements are derived from a pan-Indic iconography: the undulating brackets that support projecting eaves, the deeply carved lotus medallions in the arch spandrels, the bands of tightly wound vine and floral motifs framing the entry, and the written (rather than figural) rendition of Allah in the entry frame's center. Although all of these elements ultimately derived from temple architecture, by the fourteenth century, if not earlier, they were common to Islamic buildings throughout the subcontinent. It is the abundant use of Indic iconography in sparkling white marble, however, that makes this tomb not only different from its Tughluq predecessors but also unique in the Islamic funerary architecture of South Asia through the sixteenth century, even presaging imperial Mughal tomb complexes such as the Taj Mahal (1632–40).

Similar to Jaunpur and Mandu, the architectural patronage of the Gujarat sultanate also evinces a regional preference, constituting a building style that is unique to this political formation. In contrast to Jaunpur and Mandu, however, the Gujarat sultanate's architecture maintained a direct and palpable connection with preceding and contemporaneous temples and other types of architecture in the region in both typology as well as iconography. While the Jaunpur and Mandu buildings are replete with elements belonging to a pan-Indic iconography, the Gujarati buildings adopt the medium, types, and decorative programs specifically of western Indian temples and stepwells.

With its water-purveying and social functions, its multi-level subterraneous construction, and wealth of floral and other auspicious iconographies, the stepwell (*vav, baoli*) was a distinctly South Asian building type. Moreover, due to its monumental character and importance in social as well as practical realms, the structural type was patronized by both Muslim and non-Muslim elites throughout the region since at least the twelfth century, as seen at Bhadresvar and other sites.[31] A nobleman of the Gujarat sultanate commissioned the stepwell at Adalaj (c. 1500) (Fig. 14), outside the capital city of Ahmadabad.[32] Its elite patronage demonstrates that western Indian architectural types as well as iconographies were thoroughly integrated into Islamic building practices within the Gujarat sultanate during the fifteenth-sixteenth centuries.

Along with a ground-level entrance marked by two rectangular towers, the stone stepwell consists of five trabeate tiers progressively deepening to the circular well shaft. Each of the tiers consists of multi-sectioned, square-order (*bhadraka*) columns and is ornamented with floral and zoomorphic motifs – the former, particularly, seen also in sultanate-period mosques and tombs. Overall, the structure strikes a pleasing balance between plain and ornamented surfaces, and the stone

maintains a cooler subterranean temperature than above ground.

The regionally based building tradition of western India had been adapted to suit varying contexts throughout the Gujarat sultanate by the fifteenth century. Along with stepwells and temples, mosques and tombs were also constructed in stone trabeation with a restrained application of carved ornament. The Congregational Mosque of Ahmadabad (1424) and the Jain Chandraprabha Temple of Jaiselmer (mid-fifteenth century) serve to demonstrate the wide use of the regional building tradition, not only encompassing all religious affiliations but also cutting across the categories of religious (mosques, tombs, temples) and secular (stepwells) structures. All three of these buildings are multi-storied and trabeated; they also display a selective use of ornamentation. In fact, the neighboring region of Sindh under the later Sammas (c. 1290–c. 1520) and Arghuns (c. 1520–91) also benefited from Gujarati building techniques and shows a similar application of the regional tradition in many of its mosques and tombs.[33] The strongly entrenched, regionally based architectural conventions of western India continued to be patronized, then, by all of the elite groups – sultans, nobles, and Jain merchants and bankers – who were integral to the functioning of the Gujarat sultanate and nearby territories.

After the fourteenth century Tughluq campaigns into the Deccan, the region's sultanates maintained a trajectory independent of the northern political formations. The Vijayanagara empire (1336–1565), one of the pre-eminent states of South Asia, was temporally contemporaneous and geographically contiguous with the Bahmani sultanate (1347–1538) to the north. The Bahmani sultanate eventually disintegrated into five separate rulerships – the Barid-shahis (1487–1619), the Adil-shahis (1490–1686), the Nizam-shahis (1490–1636), Imad-shahis

15 The Congregational or Jama Masjid of Ahmedabad, Gujarat, 1424. Photo: Wikimedia Commons – Shyamengineer

(1491–1574), and the Qutb-shahis (1496–1687) – three of which embraced Shi'ism. Vijayanagara was eventually absorbed by these five sultanates, which in turn were annexed by the Mughal Empire only in the late seventeenth century. Although Vijayanagara was an exception to the otherwise Muslim-ruled sultanates, it was nonetheless a participant – at least in court ceremonial – of the Perso-Islamic courtly culture that pervaded the Deccan.[34]

The city of Bijapur in the west-central Deccan underwent an intensive construction program with the rise of the Adil-shahis, exemplified by the tomb and mosque complex commissioned by Ibrahim II Adil Shah's (r. 1579–1626) principal wife Taj Sultana – a complex also known as the Ibrahim Rauza (Fig. 11). Although the tomb is built on a more intimate scale than the Gol Gumbad (1656) or tomb of Muhammad Adil Shah (r. 1626–56), it is representative of the Adil-shahi sultanate's visual identity, particularly in its ornamentation.[35] Moreover, the tomb complex's horizontal emphasis, bulbous domes, extremely intricate carved-stone motifs, and pencil-thin minarets are also characteristic of Deccani sultanate architecture in general.

Similar to north Indian sultanate architecture, Deccani Islamic buildings also integrate a discernible pan-Indic decorative iconography into their fabrics. The tomb and mosque both have lofty, domed interiors, tall exterior arcades, and the tomb has an extensive calligraphic program, all recalling architectural conventions from the central Islamic lands. Upon close examination, however, the specifically South Asian character of the structures becomes clear: the arcades' flat ceiling soffits are fitted with stone floral panels, not unlike the ceilings of the region's Hindu temples; the undulating brackets upholding projecting eaves are replete with floral ornamentation; and the addorsed minaret bases are essentially large multi-sectioned columns of the Indic orders. The combination of indigenous and imported building conventions continued throughout the Deccan as well, indicating that the elite-patronized architectural style relied on local labor and ideas for its formation and execution.

CONCLUSIONS

With this review of Islamic architecture in South Asia from its beginnings in the eighth century through the establishment of Mughal rule in the early sixteenth, it becomes evident that Islam and Muslim communities, both elite and non-elite, had a long and entrenched presence in South Asia. Thus, the period of the sultanates (1190–1690) was by no means the first contact between Indic and Islamic cultural forms; while Muslim mercantile communities had long resided throughout the subcontinent, the later centuries are marked by the espousal of Islam among most of the politico-military elites of the region.

The social, ritual, and iconographic features of Islam led to the introduction of new forms into the South Asian architectural repertory. By the eighth century, Muslim groups settled at commercially important localities in India were patronizing local artisans for the construction of mosques and tombs. Moreover, with the emergence of Islam on a political level by the 1190s, the monumental minaret and mosque also came to be important features of the South Asian landscape. The Muslim communities of South Asia were full participants in local culture, also taking part in the regional conventions they encountered. Thus, Muslim elites and others were patrons of Indic structures such as stepwells. Overall, the Muslim-patronized structures of South Asia were catalysts for the rejuvenation of indigenous architectural practices, which local craftspeople adapted to the needs of their Muslim patrons.

ALKA PATEL's (UC-Irvine) interests encompass South Asia within the Indian Ocean and Persianate worlds during the thirteenth–eighteenth centuries. Her works include *Building Communities in Gujarat: Architecture and Society during the Twelfth-Fourteenth Centuries* (Brill, 2004), and *Iran to India: the Shansabānīs of Afghanistan, ca. 1150-1215*, the first in a two-book project with Edinburgh University Press (2021). Patel has also guest-edited *Ars Orientalis* XXXIV (2004) and *Archives of Asian Art* LIX (2007), along with several collaborative volumes.

SUGGESTIONS FOR FURTHER READING

Flood, Finbarr B. "Before the Mughals: Material Culture of Sultanate North India," *Muqarnas* 36 (2019), 1–39.

Haidar, Navina Najat, and Marika Sardar, eds. *Sultans of the South: Arts of India's Deccan Courts, 1323–1687* (New York & New Haven: Metropolitan Museum of Art & Yale University Press, 2011).

Hasan, Perween. *Sultans and Mosques: The Early Muslim Architecture of Bangladesh* (London: I.B. Tauris, 2007).

Hillenbrand, Robert. "The Architecture of the Ghaznavids and Ghurids," in *The Sultan's Turret: Studies in Persian and Turkish Culture. Studies in Honor of Clifford Edmund Bosworth*, ed. Carole Hillenbrand, vol. 2 (Leiden: Brill, 2000), 124–206.

Mumtaz, Kamil Khan ed. *Architectural Heritage of Pakistan* 11: *Sultanate Period Architecture* (Lahore: Anjuman-i Mimaran, 1991).

NOTES

[1] While the literature on the topic is vast, overviews are provided by Vimala Begley et al., eds., *Rome and India* (Madison: University of Wisconsin Press, 1991); Ranabir Chakravarti, ed., *Trade in Early India* (New Delhi: Oxford University Press, 2001); Alka Patel, ed., *Communities and Commodities: Western India and the Indian Ocean, 11th-15th Centuries.* Ars Orientalis 34 (Washington, D.C.: Smithsonian Institution, 2007).

[2] See especially John Carswell, "The Excavation of Mantai," *Ancient Ceylon* 1 (1990), 17–28; Osmund Bopearachchi, "Seafaring in the Indian Ocean: Archaeological Evidence from Sri Lanka," in *Tradition and Archaeology: Early Maritime Contacts in the Indian Ocean*, eds. H.P. Ray and Jean-François Salles (New Delhi: Manohar, 1996), 59–71.

[3] Ali ibn Hamid Kufi, *The Chachnama: an Ancient History of Sind*, trans. Mirza Kalichbeg Fredunbeg (Lahore: Vanguard Books, Ltd., 1985); Derryl N. Maclean, *Religion and Society in Arab Sind* (Leiden: E.J. Brill, 1989).

[4] The two regional conquests were explicitly compared by the jurist al-Baladhuri (d. 892), cited in Maclean, *Religion and Society,* 41; see also Francesco Gabrieli, "Muhammad ibn Qasim ath-Thaqafi and the Arab Conquest of Sind," *East and West* NS 15, 3–4 (September–December 1965), 281–95.

[5] For a seventh-century dating of the Banbhore mosque, see S. M. Ashfaque, "The Grand Mosque of Banbhore," *Pakistan Archaeology* 6 (1969), 182–209; for the ninth-tenth-century re-dating, see Muhammad Ishtiaq Khan, "The Grand Mosque of Banbhore: A Reappraisal," *Ancient Pakistan* 15 (2002), 1–6.

[6] J. Pedersen et al., "Masdjid," in *Encyclopaedia of Islam (2nd edition)*, eds. P. Bearman et al. (Leiden: Brill, 2010) Brill Online.

[7] See especially Monique Kevran, "Le port multiple des bouches de l'Indus: Barbarike, Deb, Daybul, Lahori Bandar, Diul Sinde," *Res Orientales* 8 (1996), 45–92; also Finbarr Barry Flood, *Objects of Translation: Material Culture and Medieval "Hindu-Muslim" Encounter* (Princeton: Princeton University Press, 2009), 46.

[8] The Gwalior *mihrab* was found at the Man Mandir palace (c. 1500) and first published by Michael D. Willis, "An Eighth Century Mihrab in Gwalior," *Artibus Asiae* 46, 3 (1985), 227–46.

9   H. C. Ray, *The Dynastic History of Northern India, Early Medieval Period* 2 vols. (New Delhi: Munshiram Manoharlal Publishers, 1973 2nd ed.), 1: 5–6; 2: 1156ff.

10   For a review of Gwalior within the economic networks of northern India, see Brajadulal Chattopadhyaya, "Trade and Urban Centres in Early Medieval India," in *The Making of Early Medieval India* (Delhi: Oxford University Press, 1997), 130–54.

11   For translations see H. M. Elliot, *The History of India as Told by Its Own Historians: The Muhammadan Period*, ed. John Dowson (Calcutta: Susil Gupta, 1956 2nd ed.).

12   See especially Ranabir Chakrabarti, "Monarchs, Merchants and a Matha in Northern Konkan (c. AD 900–1053)," *Indian Economic and Social History Review* 27.2 (1990), 189–208.

13   Ahmad Hasan Dani et al., "Tochi Valley Inscriptions in the Peshawar Museum," *Ancient Pakistan* 1 (1964), 125–35. For the Hindu Shahis, see Ray, *Dynastic History*, 1: 55–106; and Abdur Rehman, *The Last Two Dynasties of the Sahis* (Delhi: Renaissance Publishing House, 1988).

14   Sten Konow, "Sarnath Inscription of Kumaradevi," *Epigraphia Indica* 9 (1907–8), 319–28.

15   See the recent reconsideration of the connections between Swat, the Kashmir river valleys, and Central Asia by Jason Neelis, "*La Vieille Route* Reconsidered: Alternative Paths for Early Transmission of Buddhism Beyond the Borderlands of South Asia," *Bulletin of the Asia Institute* 16 (2002), 143–64.

16   Ray, *Dynastic History*, 1: 107–84.

17   For Udegram, see Muhammad Nazir Khan, "A Ghaznavid Historical Inscription from Udegram, Swat," and Umberto Scerrato, "Research on the Archaeology and History of Islamic Art in Pakistan: Excavation of the Ghaznavid Mosque on Mt. Raja Gira, Swat," *East and West* NS 35 (September 1985), 153–166 and 439–450 respectively; and Alessandra Bagnera, "Preliminary Note on the Islamic Settlement of Udegram, Swat: The Islamic Graveyard (11th–13th century A.D.)," *East and West* 56, No. 1.3 (September 2006), 205–228.

18   A thorough catalogue of the site of Bhadresvar is available in Mehrdad Shokoohy and Natalie Shokoohy, *Bhadresvar: the Oldest Islamic Monuments in India* (Leiden: E.J. Brill, 1988).

19   See ibid., 50–59. For Siraf, see especially David Whitehouse, "Excavations at Siraf: First Interim Report," *Iran* 6 (1968), 1–22.

20   Alka Patel, *Building Communities in Gujarat: Architecture and Society during the Twelfth through Fourteenth Centuries* (Leiden: E.J. Brill, 2004), 105–24.

21   For a possible precedent to the Qutb Minar in Lahore, see Finbarr B. Flood, "Between Ghazna and Delhi: Lahore and Its Lost Manara," in *Cairo to Kabul*, eds. Warwick Ball and Leonard Harrow (London: Melisende, 2002), 102–12.

22   Alka Patel, "Toward Alternative Interpretations of Ghurid Architecture in Northern India (Late Twelfth–Early Thirteenth Century CE)," *Archives of Asian Art* 54 (2004), 35–61; and *idem*, "Ghurid Art," *Encyclopaedia of Islam* (3rd ed.), Leiden: E.J. Brill (online 2014).

23   Jonathan Bloom, *Minaret: Symbol of Islam* (Oxford: Oxford University Press, 1989), 170–4.

24   Clifford Edmund Bosworth, *The New Islamic Dynasties* (New York: Columbia University Press, 1996), 303.

25   For an overview of Tughluq architectural patronage, see Anthony Welch and Howard Crane, "The Tughluqs: Master Builders of the Delhi Sultanate," *Muqarnas* 1 (1983), 123–66.

26   For an analysis of Rukn-i Din mausoleum, see Robert Hillenbrand, "Turco-Iranian Elements in the Medieval Architecture of Pakistan: The Case of the Tomb of Rukn-i Alam at Multan," *Muqarnas* 9 (1992), 148–74; on the tombs of Multan, see Ahmad Nabi Khan, *Multan: History and Architecture* (Islamabad: Institute of Islamic History, Culture and Civilisation, 1983), especially 169–298.

27   See especially Pika Ghosh, "Problems of Reconstructing Bengal Architecture of the 14th-16th Centuries," in *The Architecture of the Indian Sultanates*, eds. Abha Narain Lambah and Alka Patel (Mumbai: Marg Publications, 2006), 92–103.

28   See Katherine Kasdorf, "Translating Sacred Space in Bijapur: the Mosques of Karim al-Din and Khwaja Jahan," *Archives of Asian Art* 59 (ed. Alka Patel, 2009), 57–80.

29   See Abha Narain Lambah, "The Sharqis of Jaunpur: Inheritors of the Tughluq Legacy," in *Architecture of the Indian Sultanates*, eds. Lambah and Patel, 42–55.

30   See Michael Brand, "The Sultanate of Malwa," in *The Architecture of the Indian Sultanates*, eds. Lambah and Patel, especially 87–91.

31   For an overview of the Gujarat sultanate's architecture, see Alka Patel, "From Province to Sultanate: The Architecture of Gujarat during the 12th through 16th Centuries," in ibid., 68–79. For stepwells, see Jutta Jain-Neubauer, *The Stepwells of Gujarat in Art-Historical Perspective* (New Delhi: Abhinav Publications, 1981).

32   See Patel, "From Province to Sultanate," in *Architecture of the Indian Sultanates*, eds. Lambah and Patel, 75.

33   Alka Patel, "Of Merchants, Courtiers, and Saints: the Islamic Architecture of Sindh," in *Sindh: Past Glory Present Nostalgia*, ed. Pratapaditya Pal (Mumbai: Marg Publications, 2008), 80–95.

34   See Phillip B. Wagoner, "'Sultan among Hindu Kings': Dress, Titles, and the Islamicization of Hindu Culture at Vijayanagara," *The Journal of Asian Studies* 55 (November 1996), 851–80.

35   See Deborah Hutton, *Art of the Court of Bijapur* (Bloomington: Indian University Press, 2006), especially 121–30.

Mughal Religious Architecture

LAURA E. PARODI

1 Jami Masjid, Fatehpur Sikri, view of prayer hall from Salim Chishti's tomb.
Photo: Laura E. Parodi

The Indian Timurids, conventionally known as Mughals or Moguls, ruled over parts of present-day Uzbekistan, Afghanistan, Pakistan, India, and Bangladesh between 1494 and 1858. They were descended from Timur – known in the West as Tamerlane the Great (r. 1370–1405). The Timurids had earlier ruled over parts of present-day Iran, Afghanistan and Central Asia. In the early sixteenth century they were displaced by the Shibanids, but the elite reassembled around Babur (r. 1494–1530), today regarded as the first Mughal. In 1504 he made Kabul his capital and in 1526 shifted his court to Hindustan (the upper Gangetic plains), which would become the heartland of the Mughal empire. Between 1540 and 1555 Mughal authority was temporarily limited to the Kabul region under Babur's sons Humayun (r. 1530–40 and 1545–56) and Kamran (r. 1540–45). A real phase of expansion began under Akbar (r. 1556–1605) and continued through the reigns of Jahangir (r. 1605–27), Shah Jahan (1627–58), and 'Alamgir, a.k.a. Aurangzeb, (1658–1707). Vast tracts of the Indian subcontinent were subjugated through military conquest, treaty or marriage alliance – most notably Gujarat (1573), Bengal (1576), Kashmir (1586), and the Deccan (culminating in 1687). After 'Alamgir's demise Mughal authority was eroded by emerging regional powers – such as the Marathas and the Nizam in the Deccan and the Nawab of Oudh (Awadh) in the north – and by the British. Between the sack of Delhi in 1739 at the hands of the then ruler of Iran, Nadir Shah, and the deposition of the last emperor in 1858, Mughal rulers ceased to be the preeminent patrons of architecture.

Mughal religious architecture is well-preserved yet little-studied compared to Mughal palaces, gardens, and mausolea. The Timurids were as a rule Hanafi Sunnis, but many of them were disciples of Sufi mystics and devoted to the family of the Prophet. The Mughals complemented this with an interest in Indic religions. Whereas the Timurids had patronized Sunni institutions such as *madrasa*s as well as Shi'ite shrines (*mashhad*s) and Sufi convents (*khanaqa*s), the Mughals and their elite followed Indian practice in their preference for mosques and Sufi establishments: *madrasa*s are scarcely mentioned until the rise of reformist movements such as the Deobandi in the nineteenth century. Religious or charitable functions were also associated with Mughal funerary complexes, which often hosted reciters of the Quran, mosques, or soup kitchens. Temples, churches and non-Islamic charitable foundations were also built and patronised in the Mughal realm.

Even as construction and ornament testify to ample reliance on locally available expertise and materials, the imperial Mughal style deliberately harked back to Timurid architecture, reproducing many of its features: scale, massive walls, tall portals, pointed arches, and double domes raised on tall drums.[1] Minarets, another hallmark of the Timurid style, were only introduced in the second Mughal century, and stone – except where scarce, as in the Indus Valley and Bengal – commonly replaced ceramic revetments. Imperial religious architecture had a stronger Timurid flavor than secular buildings – although trabeate construction and Indic architectural components such as tall podiums, columns, flat roofs, eaves (*chajja*), and domed rooftop pavilions (*chatri*) were widely employed. The Mughals exercised strict control over their elite: accordingly, the buildings commissioned by Mughal officers were not only smaller but seldom displayed features associated with the imperial style; the vast majority followed local architectural traditions of the subcontinent.

CONGREGATIONAL MOSQUES

Few congregational mosques were built at the direct behest of members of the Mughal royal family. From a strictly formal point of view, a Mughal imperial mosque "type" may be postulated, characterized by imposing dimensions (from about 70 × 70 up to 170 × 170 meters), red sandstone exteriors inlaid with contrasting stones such as white marble, a high stepped podium, a vast porticoed or columned courtyard, a three-domed prayer hall to the west in accordance with Indian practice, and a skyline marked by *chatri*s or minarets. All these features have precedents in the subcontinent, but the Mughals combined them together consistently for the first time, along with the tall arched portals (*pishtaq*) characteristic of Timurid architecture.

The earliest mosque built in the imperial style (Fig. 1) was commissioned by Akbar in 1571 in thanksgiving for the birth of three sons, foretold by the mystic Salim Chishti, a resident of Sikri, southwest of Agra. The village was renamed Fatehpur Sikri (Victory City) and developed into the largest Mughal metropolis of its time, with an estimated 200,000 inhabitants; the court resided there until 1585. The mosque is on a ridge to the southwest of the palatial complex. It measures about 110 × 140 metres and is accessed through grand portals with monumental staircases on the east and south sides.[2] The southern access, known as

2 Jami Masjid, Fatehpur Sikri, prayer hall dome.
Photo: Laura E. Parodi

3 Tomb of Salim Chishti (on the left) and tomb of his descendants, Fatehpur Sikri.
Photo: Laura E. Parodi

Buland Darwaza (Victory Gate), is Fatehpur Sikri's main landmark, visible from afar. Its stately *pishtaq* and superimposed niches create a play of light and shade reminiscent of Timurid architecture, while the multicolored stone inlays and *chatri*s of varying sizes and heights impart a distinctive Indo-Islamic flavor. At the rear, *chatri*s cascade down in tiers to the courtyard roof. A continuous row of *chatri*s lines the roof above the false arches behind which are pillared porticoes. The prayer hall is accessed through a *pishtaq* inlaid with white marble; its three domes are built in the pre-Mughal style of Delhi, with single shells, straight sides and inverted lotus finials. Their blackened surface points to the loss of decoration – probably tiles, as in the recently restored tomb of Humayun in Delhi. Remains of polychrome painted decoration, including medallions with floral scrolls inside the main dome (Fig. 2), suggest that the color scheme may have been originally richer. The mosque has multiple bays, three *mihrab*s, a stepped stone *minbar* and small "service rooms" at either end.

The courtyard hosts the tomb of Salim Chishti and that of his descendants (Fig. 3). Both are airy domed structures raised on podiums, with latticed screens for walls.[3] Salim Chisti's tomb is the earliest Mughal building whose visible surfaces are entirely of white marble. The screens (*jali*) allow visitors to catch glimpses of the cenotaph while circumambulating the tomb before entering the chamber. Like the serpentine brackets they are inspired by Gujarati architecture, but they are carved with Timurid-inspired geometric interlaces. White marble has been interpreted as a means to visualize light, an attribute of sanctity, but only indirect support for this may be gleaned from Mughal sources; however it is certain that marble was the most valuable building material the Mughals had at hand.

Marble continued to be used only sparingly in congregational mosques, even in the case of imperial commissions and even though by the seventeenth century it had become the preferred material for palaces. Other reasons may be adduced besides continuing adherence to the Fatehpur Sikri model. The Mughals had ample access to

4 Jami Masjid, Agra, view of prayer hall from courtyard.
Photo: Laura E. Parodi

sandstone – extracted in the Sikri environs – but not to marble, which had to be sourced from Makrana in present-day Rajasthan, with the involvement of the Kachwaha Raja.[4] The sheer size of imperial congregational mosques may have made a full marble revetment impractical. Additionally, the exclusive use of marble may have been viewed as inappropriate in buildings endowed for the use of the cities' populace: in Mughal halls of public audience, marble is similarly reserved for the area occupied by the ruler.[5]

During the seventeenth century, the three main Mughal metropoles – Agra, Delhi and Lahore – were endowed with imperial congregational mosques. At Agra, the mosque (Fig. 4) was built at the behest of Shah Jahan's eldest daughter Jahanara in 1643–48.[6] Smaller than the mosque at Fatehpur Sikri yet similarly set on a tall podium, it has a simpler and more symmetrical plan with three gateways on the north, east (now lost) and south, with a neat separation between the block of the prayer-hall and the courtyard, surrounded by a single row of porticos. The skyline with corner turrets and a row of *chatri*s closely recalls the Fatehpur Sikri mosque, save for the three domes, which are bulbous in compliance with the Shah Jahani style.

Shah Jahan's own 1650–56 mosque in Delhi (Fig. 5) is similar in conception but built on a more ambitious scale (c. 100 x 100 meters).[7] Located across the river from Shah Jahan's brand new palace complex (1639–48)[8] and raised on a truly imposing podium, with open loggias for walls, it is at once a landmark and a place from which views of the palace, city, and river could be enjoyed – it was known in its day as Jahannuma Masjid (Belvedere Mosque). There are no *chatri*s around the courtyard; two tall minarets flank the façade of the prayer hall. They had been introduced only a few years earlier in Mughal funerary and religious architecture: in Lahore, at the tomb of Jahangir (1628–38)[9] and the 1634–35 congregational mosque built by the governor Wazir Khan;[10] and in Agra, at the Taj Mahal (1632–48, discussed below). The prayer hall is more lavishly decorated with marble inside and out than at Jahanara's mosque, but the side aisles exemplify the preference for a palette dominated by red and white that will characterize all later Mughal architecture (Fig. 6) and come to be identified with the "classic" Mughal style.[11] Marble slabs atop the arches of the façade bear an inlaid black stone inscription praising the building and its patron.

Lahore's congregational mosque, commissioned by 'Alamgir in 1673-4 and known today as Badshahi Masjid (Imperial Mosque) (Fig. 7),[12] is again stylistically similar yet much larger (170 x 170 meters) in order to serve at once as a mosque and occasionally as an *'idgah* (large, open-air prayer-space) capable of hosting 60,000 worshippers during festivals. The red and white stone revetments, imported from afar, proclaim its imperial status. Massive octagonal minarets rise from the four corners of the courtyard and turrets reinforce the corners of the prayer hall. Marble is used sparingly on the walls but lavishly expended on the

5 Jami Masjid, Delhi, view of prayer hall from courtyard.
Photo: Laura E. Parodi

6 Jami Masjid, Delhi, interior of prayer hall, side aisle.
Photo: Laura E. Parodi

7 Badshahi Masjid, Lahore.
Photo: Laura E. Parodi

8 Maryam al-Zamani Mosque, Lahore.
Photo: Laura E. Parodi

superstructure; calligraphy is not prominently used, at variance with the Jahannuma.[13] The exterior exudes a novel sense of weight and the arches and interior are decorated with opulent floral stucco reliefs reminiscent of palatial architecture.

The Fatehpur Sikri model also inspired a congregational mosque built by Shah Jahan in the Agra fort (1653), known as Moti Masjid (Pearl Mosque) today.[14] It reproduces the same combination of courtyard, three-domed prayer-hall and courtyard surrounded by arcades and a continuous row of *chatri*s, but differs in the absence of a *pishtaq* and in the exclusive use of marble as fitting a royal residential site.

A purely formal approach facilitates stylistic comparison but fails to account for some key aspects. A gap of nearly seventy years separates Akbar's 1571 mosque from the remaining three, built over just three decades between 1643 and 1674. The gap is far from coincidental and reflects shifts in Mughal religious policy: by 1580 Akbar proclaimed a policy of universal tolerance, or "peace-for-all" (*sulh-i kull*) and promoted his image as a charismatic sovereign transcending religious differences by discontinuing Islamic prayers and adopting syncretic practices such as meditation and reverence for the sun. His son Jahangir also adhered to *sulh-i kull*, which may explain why no mosques are attributed to his patronage. Indeed, the only mosque securely associated with imperial patronage during his reign was endowed in Lahore (1611–12) by his mother, Maryam Zamani, a Rajput princess who was not herself a Muslim. It is the oldest surviving mosque in Lahore, built in close proximity to a gate to the palace complex.[15] A relatively modest-scale building with five bays and a tall *pishtaq* facing onto a courtyard once accessed through three entrances, of which two remain, it is built on a brick core revetted in painted stuccowork (Figs. 8–9). Its vaults are lavishly decorated with intersecting arches bearing minute tracery and the Holy Names of God.

By contrast, in the course of Shah Jahan's reign the Mughals returned to emphasize normative, Sunni Islam – a shift that may well have been prompted by political considerations. In the late 1630s Mughal expansion directly targeted the last remaining polities of the Deccan: Bijapur and Golconda. Like the Mughal state, they were multiethnic and multireligious, but the ruling houses were Muslim, and a war against Muslims needed some rhetorical justification: typically, some

9 Maryam al-Zamani mosque, Lahore, interior.
Photo: Laura E. Parodi

claim of apostasy or deviance from rightful Islam. Bijapur and Golconda both had Shi'ite leanings, and the renewed emphasis on Sunni Islam in the Mughal realm was possibly not coincidental. It began shortly after Ahmadnagar was annexed and the remaining Deccani states accepted Mughal suzerainty in 1636 (Jahanara requested permission to build the Agra mosque the following year) and continued throughout the period leading to their final capitulation (1686 and 1687 respectively). In the same years Mughal cities were further "islamicized" with a network of smaller mosques and charitable

10 Govind Deva Temple, Brindavan.
Photo: Laura E. Parodi

endowments,[16] along with *'idgah*s for the celebration of religious festivals.[17]

Not only the resurgence of mosques (and minarets) under Shah Jahan, but their relative lack of importance for nearly a century calls for an explanation; a reference to wider Islamic trends may prove useful. The militant Shi'ism propounded by the first two Safavid shahs (Isma'il, r. 1501–24, and Tahmasp, r. 1524–76) had been accompanied by a disregard for congregational mosques: as the spiritual as well as political leaders of their community and as the Imams of their time, the sole interpreters of Divine will, early Safavid rulers claimed to have superseded other religious authorities. Pilgrimage to the ancestral shrine in Ardabil (northern Iran) and the graves of the Imams was then regarded as more meritorious than Friday or daily prayers. Besides direct military confrontation, their Sunni neighbors – the Ottomans and Shibanids – challenged the Safavids through rhetoric in diplomatic exchanges, and in architectural patronage. Both the Ottomans and Shibanids patronized Sufi orders, but the Ottomans are best known for a series of impressive congregational mosques and the Shibanids for their *madrasa*s – both were buildings closely associated with Sunnism. Conversely, the Safavids' allies in the Deccan followed their example: no congregational mosques were built at Ahmadnagar, annexed by the Mughals in 1636;[18] in Bijapur one was only begun in 1576 – the year Tahmasp died – and never finished.[19] In Golconda a modest one was built in 1518 and a

11 Govind Deva Temple, Brindavan, interior.
Photo: Laura E. Parodi

larger one only finished in 1597;[20] it may have been endowed in 1591, the same year the Safavids began building a congregational mosque for the first time (today the Masjid-i Imam, previously known as the Masjid-i Shah in Isfahan). The Mughals chose to remain neutral in the Shi'ite-Sunni conflict due to their close ties to the Safavids, who had supported Babur and Humayun in their attempts to secure a throne. Thus the emperors' choice not to patronize congregational mosques for nearly a century may have been influenced by considerations of domestic as well as foreign policy.

Among non-imperial patrons, perhaps the best known is Raja Man Singh Kachwaha, Jahangir's brother-in-law and one of the leading officers of the Mughal realm under three rulers (Akbar, Jahangir, and Shah Jahan).[21] Man Singh patronized both mosques and Brahmanical temples, most notably congregational mosques at Lahore (now lost) and at Rajmahal in Bengal, and temples at Brindavan in present-day Madhya Pradesh and at his ancestral home of Amber in present-day Rajasthan. In size and style, the buildings proclaim Man Singh's connection with the Mughal lineage. The c. 1595 mosque at Rajmahal, now partly ruined, measures a remarkable 77 × 65 m. and its prayer hall includes features of the imperial Mughal style such as "service rooms" and a now-lost *pishtaq*. It may be contrasted with a coeval mosque built at Malda by an anonymous patron in the local Bengali style, with brick construction, curved cornices, elongated engaged turrets, and plain wall surfaces relieved by relatively inconspicuous doorways.[22]

The temples endowed by Man Singh, all of which date to Akbar's *sulh-i kull* period, even though Man Singh's career extended into Shah Jahan's reign, were either politically instrumental for the Mughals or motivated as memorials to Man Singh's deceased relatives – or in other words, as the Rajput equivalents of mausolea. Their architectural vocabulary further articulates this asymmetrical relationship: the exteriors and, to a large extent, the interiors are devoid of figural sculpture, as had long been customary in Hindustan under Islamic rule. Yet these buildings were among the most innovative of their time. An example is the 1590 Govind Deva temple at Brindavan (Figs. 10–11), built as a memorial to Man Singh's father, which combines arches, vaults, and domes with pillars and brackets in a distinctly Mughal manner, while achieving "a sense of open longitudinal and vertical space unprecedented in Akbari architecture ... anticipat[ing] trends yet to develop in imperial Mughal architecture".[23]

The later Mughals inherited fully-provisioned cities and districts and controlled limited resources compared to their predecessors. Mosques endowed during the eighteenth and nineteenth centuries are with few exceptions single-aisled, three-domed structures, as the more modest among non-imperial commissions in the previous centuries. Imperial patronage dwindled and was mostly limited to

12 Taj Mahal, Agra.
Photo: Wikimedia Commons
CC BY-SA 3.0 © Dhirad

Delhi's Chishti shrines: 'Alamgir's son Bahadur Shah I (r. 1707–12) endowed a mosque and tomb at the *dargah* (shrine) of Bakhtiar Kaki,[24] while his successors often patronized and were ultimately buried at the *dargah* of Nizamuddin.[25] Meanwhile, by the 1720s, a redistribution of power and resources meant a wider group of patrons endowed mosques, funerary monuments, residences, and gardens in Delhi – mostly built outside the walled city and often in connection with burgeoning new districts. Holy sites were powerful catalysts of patronage: these ranged from Sufi establishments appealing to all denominations and faiths to Shi'ite shrines reflecting the rising importance of Iranian émigrés in north India following the decline and dissolution of the Safavid empire in Iran.[26] Under British rule, an increasing number of religious buildings was provided by commoners, identified only by their name.[27]

FUNERARY COMPLEXES

The Mughals are best known not for their mosques but for their palaces and gardens, including funerary gardens such as the world-famous Taj Mahal. Mughal funerary gardens were widely perceived as images of Paradise, and it has been suggested that the Taj Mahal played a particular role as a source of inspiration for contemporary religious architecture. Imperial Mughal funerary complexes comprise large walled gardens laid out on a regular grid, with gates or pavilions oriented towards the cardinal points and a mausoleum set on a tall plinth (*takht, kursi*) at the center or – in the case of the Taj Mahal – at one end. The three largest complexes, in Delhi, Agra and Lahore respectively, host the tombs of emperors Humayun (1562–71),[28] Akbar (1605–13),[29] and Jahangir (1628–38). Three more were built for imperial consorts: Nur Jahan, Jahangir's chief queen in the latter part of his reign (d. 1645), in Lahore;[30] Mumtaz Mahal, Shah Jahan's favorite wife, in Agra (this is the famous Taj Mahal) (Fig. 12);[31] and 'Alamgir's queen Rabi'a Daurani. Known as Bibi-ka Maqbara, the latter is the only imperial mausoleum the Mughals built in the Deccan, at Aurangabad in present-day Maharashtra.[32] Other

imperial relations and high officers were buried in smaller compounds built along similar principles: examples are the Khusrau Bagh in Allahabad (present-day Bihar), hosting the tombs of Jahangir's wife Shah Begum, her son Khusrau, and the patron, her daughter Sultan-Nisar Begum;[33] the tomb of Nur Jahan's parents in Agra (known as the tomb of I'tmad ud-Dawla after her father's title, though originally built for her mother);[34] the tomb of Nur Jahan's brother Asaf Khan in Lahore;[35] and the tomb of 'Alamgir's sister Roshanara in Delhi.[36] Still other members of the Mughal family were buried in the imperial compounds – most notably at the tombs of Humayun and Akbar; some, as mentioned, chose to be buried in simple graves at the feet of their spiritual mentors: among them emperor 'Alamgir, buried at the *dargah* of Shaykh Burhanuddin (Khuldabad, present-day Maharashtra)[37] and his sister Jahanara, buried at the shrine of Nizamuddin in Delhi.[38] Shah Jahan was buried alongside his wife in the Taj Mahal.

Imperial mausolea follow the principle of Timurid burials in crypts surmounted by domed chambers containing cenotaphs, although crypts are replaced by a burial chamber inside the plinth, above which there may or may not be a commemorative structure. Mughal mausolea display a variety of forms: Humayun's tomb, the Taj Mahal, the Bibi-ka Maqbara, and the tomb of Asaf Khan are domed buildings; Akbar's tomb (Fig. 13) and the tomb of Shah Begum are stepped structures with a much more markedly Indian flavor; the tombs of Jahangir (Fig. 14) and Nur Jahan are but large platforms containing a burial chamber (the former complemented by four tall minarets at the corners; the tomb of I'tmad ud-Dawla (Fig. 15) is a low building with engaged turrets at the corners and a pavilion in the center; while Roshanara's is an open-air quadrangular pavilion. Humayun's tomb (Fig. 16), built by a Timurid architect, most likely provided inspiration for the Taj Mahal, which in turn inspired the Bibi-ka Maqbara (Fig. 17): all three have complex radial plans, *pishtaq*s on all four sides flanked by superimposed niches, and culminate in a bulbous dome; each combines this with a different kind of Indic decorative treatment:

13 Akbar's tomb, Sikandra.
Photo: Laura E. Parodi

14 Jahangir's tomb, Lahore.
Photo: Laura E. Parodi

15 Tomb of I'tmad ud-Dawla, Agra.
Photo: Laura E. Parodi

16 Tomb of Humayun, Delhi.
Photo: Laura E. Parodi

17 Bibi-ka Maqbara, Aurangabad.
Photo: Laura E. Parodi

red sandstone with perforated screens and colored stone inlays in Humayun's tomb; white marble with floral reliefs and colored inlays in the Taj Mahal; and Deccani-inspired stucco reliefs in the Bibi-ka Maqbara. In the latter two, minarets rise from the four corners of the podium.

Imperial Mughal mausolea are typically located outside the city walls and along a prominent road: this is the case with Humayun's and Akbar's tombs and the funerary compound at Shahdara outside Lahore which hosts the tombs of Jahangir, Nur Jahan, and Asaf Khan. A riverside location is seen at Humayun's tomb, Akbar's tomb, the Taj Mahal and the tomb of I'tmad ud-Dawla. Proximity to the river provided a scenic setting, water to feed the garden's numerous canals and fountains, and access by boat.[39]

The gardens also display a variety of layouts: Humayun's tomb is divided into nine parts (a number regarded as auspicious by the Timurids), with the mausoleum occupying the central unit; the tombs of Akbar, Shah Begum and I'tmad ud-Dawla have a cruciform plan with causeways connecting the central platform to entrances or pavilions. The garden at the Taj Mahal is similarly cruciform, but a pool lies at the intersection while the mausoleum sits on a riverside terrace at the northern end. Jahangir's tomb is divided into sixteen identical plots, while the Bibi-ka Maqbara is oblong, with four main causeways and further subdivisions. A reduction of such variety to a single "type" purportedly imbued with symbolic significance is questionable. A philological approach may be more profitable and help to explain the seemingly sudden appearance of Mughal funerary gardens in a fully-developed form in the sixteenth century.

Gardens held special importance for the Timurids, who did not reside in palaces but in large suburban estates known from the late fifteenth century onwards as *chaharbaghs*.[40] Textual sources suggest the Timurids occasionally buried their dead in gardens, and mausolea within walled compounds existed in late-fifteenth century Herat (then the Timurid capital);[41] but there seems to be no Timurid precedent for the distinctive Mughal combination of geometrically laid-out gardens and mausolea. A possible exception is the early sixteenth-century tomb of Ulugh Beg "Kabuli" (today named after his son 'Abdurrazzaq) in Ghazni (present-day Afghanistan), a radially symmetrical building bearing strong resemblance to the tomb of Humayun.[42] Entrances with staircases on all four sides suggest it may conjecturally have been located at the center of a garden.

Tombs were without doubt the most common Islamic buildings in the Indian subcontinent. This may have prompted a response from the Mughals, especially since their direct antagonists – the Surs – who had displaced them from Hindustan for fifteen years between 1540–55, had built large-scale mausolea. Sher Shah Sur's tomb in Sasaram (in present-day Bihar, not far from Varanasi) is a stepped stone building measuring c. 75 × 75 meters, sitting on a platform in the middle of an artificial lake and centered on an octagonal funerary building almost covered by tiers of *chatri*s.[43] Akbar's mausoleum, whose plinth measures over 100 × 100 meters, is similarly articulated as a stepped composition of *chatri*s.

At the same time, Mughal burials follow Timurid precedents in several respects. Various types of burial had been practised by the Timurids, depending on period, region, and individual preference. As mentioned, burials in crypts surmounted by domed buildings or chapels were common, whether in cemeteries or in *madrasa*s. In the later period in Khurasan, burials marked by simple gravestones were preferred, sometimes grouped within enclosures. Babur's tomb in Kabul, possibly commissioned by his son Kamran (c. 1540–44) in a terraced garden known today as the Bagh-i Babur, exemplifies the latter type: his grave was once surrounded by a latticed stone enclosure, now replaced by a modern structure.[44] The garden was previously and subsequently used as a family cemetery by the Mughals, and attracted Mughal patronage as late as Shah Jahan's reign, when a still extant small, domeless three-bayed marble mosque was added along with a now lost monumental gateway.[45]

Babur's tomb (a secondary burial dating from the time when the dynasty was temporarily ousted from Hindustan)[46] failed to influence subsequent imperial Mughal burials, which seem more closely inspired by four extant Timurid mausolea, all of which may, interestingly, be connected with the patronage of Babur's paternal grandfather Abu Sa'id (r. 1451–69) or his relations: the "Ishrat Khana" and "Aq Saray" in Samarkand, the tomb of Yunus Khan in Tashkent and the cited tomb of Ulugh Beg "Kabuli" (Babur's uncle) in Ghazni.[47] All four are large multichambered structures strikingly reminiscent of Timurid shrines in plan and elevation. They are accessed through a vestibule on the south side and comprise a crypt, a funerary chamber and a number of ancillary rooms whose function is unclear but presumably associated with burial rituals and ceremonies associated with death anniversaries. Mughal mausolea are invariably accessed through a vestibule on the south side and many of them, including Humayun's tomb, Akbar's tomb, the Taj Mahal, and the Bibi-ka Maqbara, feature ancillary rooms.

Limited information is available on the rituals associated with burial and mourning, but they lasted forty days and must have been quite elaborate. Death anniversaries were observed by the Timurids and Mughals: the family sojourned in proximity to the tomb, prayers were recited, offerings made, and food distributed to the poor. References in Babur's memoirs testify that circumambulation – probably aimed at absorbing the deceased's blessing (*baraka*) – was practised in his time at secular tombs as well as shrines.[48] Thus a convergence between secular mausolea and shrines may be postulated both at the formal and functional level, at least among the Mughals' direct ancestors. Why this occurred in the first place is unclear. Humayun and Akbar were descended on the maternal side from a prominent Sufi saint (Ahmad Jami, d. 1141),[49] but further research is needed in order to clarify whether their ancestors had previously intermarried with saintly lineages.

Besides this intriguing connection, the alleged symbolic meaning of imperial Mughal mausolea needs to be considered. Wayne E. Begley famously suggested that the plan of the Taj Mahal may replicate a diagram developed by the medieval Iberian mystic Ibn al-'Arabi (d. 1240), representing the Plain of Assembly and the Throne of God on Judgment Day.[50] According to this interpretation, the mausoleum – whose portals are decorated with excerpts from the Quran dealing with the end of time – would occupy the place of God's Throne, flanked by the seats of the Elect (a mosque and symmetrical *mehmankhana* or guest house on either side of the mausoleum). The pool at the center of the garden would reproduce the paradisiacal well of Kawthar at the feet of God's Throne. Other scholars rejected this theory, most notably Ebba Koch, who showed that the Taj Mahal is but a large-scale version of the standard Agra riverside garden in Shah Jahan's reign.[51]

In fact, the widespread assumption that Mughal tombs were part of a centuries-old tradition conceiving gardens as images of Paradise in quadripartite form receives no support from either archaeological data or textual sources. The interpretation of the term *charbagh* or *chaharbagh* (literally "four-garden") as a quadripartite or cross-axial plan imbued with Paradisiacal symbolism was first proposed by Pope and Ackerman in the *Survey of Persian Art*, who based their claims merely on the Persian origin of the word "paradise" and a suggested parallel between the purported "four gardens" and the four rivers of Eden, without even basic support from textual or archaeological evidence.[52] Their hypothesis was later embraced and popularized by textbooks for garden designers in the 1970s and 1980s, none of which was written by specialists of Persian or Islamic art. The fact that Islamic art was then coming into its own and garden studies were still at an early stage may possibly explain why the idea rapidly gained momentum and voices of dissent[53] were consistently ignored. To this day, a survey of available evidence turns out no quadripartite gardens in the Islamic world except for a few Andalusian courtyards dating no earlier than the eleventh century and some gardens built in South Asia from about the late sixteenth, none of which are called *chaharbagh* in textual sources. Additionally, despite the scholarly assumption of an Iranian origin of the alleged Paradise-garden form, there is no trace of quadripartite gardens in Iran at any time – whether before or during the Islamic era.[54] The oft-quoted Persian panegyrics that extol the beauty of gardens by comparing them to heavenly or earthly Paradise never suggest a quadripartition – at most, they mention eight Paradises (*hasht bihisht*). Finally, textual sources indicate that the term *chaharbagh*, whatever its etymology, was applied exclusively to gardens where the ruler or his deputies resided, which hosted administrative and public functions.[55] Far from being an Islamic universal, the *chaharbagh* would seem to be closely associated with the Timurids and their immediate successors – the Shibanids, Safavids, and Mughals – between the fifteenth and seventeenth centuries.[56] Textual as well as archaeological evidence suggests *chaharbagh*s were not quadripartite but typically laid out on a natural or artificial slope, with a building facing onto a pool on the top terrace, and a larger pool at the opposite end.[57] From the seventeenth century onwards, the term *chaharbagh* only occurs sporadically as the Safavids and Mughals by then resided in palaces which took over the functions of suburban estates. Accordingly, when Mughal quadripartite gardens do appear, they are never called *chaharbagh* – either because they host tombs, in which case sources refer to them as *rawza* (also a word for a garden, but specific to the funerary context), or because they are pleasure gardens, known as *bagh* (a generic word for garden or orchard) or *baghche* (usually, though not exclusively, smaller gardens or palace courtyards).[58]

Interestingly, Ibn al-'Arabi's diagram presents numerous parallels with the plan of the Taj Mahal but not a quadripartition, even as it includes the Kawthar – the alleged source of the Rivers of Paradise. While tombs are sometimes compared to Paradise, whether in panegyrics or inscriptions, there is no proof of a connection with a quadripartition or a cosmic diagram. It is premature to say whether the cruciform plan of some Mughal gardens resulted from pure formal experimentation or whether it implied references to Indic cosmology, in which the four cardinal points and the centrality of Mount Meru held some importance; but interestingly enough the only emperor buried in a quadripartite garden is Akbar. His tomb is the most Indic-looking of all Mughal mausolea and his funerary complex the only one where neither a mosque nor a *mihrab* are featured, in accordance with the emperor's attempt to transcend sectarian differences, including his own Muslim beliefs.

Ironically, in spite of the great variety of garden designs in the Islamic world, quadripartite gardens have become a perceived hallmark of the Mughals, the Timurids, and more generally Islam, inspiring architects, landscape designers, and artists in recent decades – a phenomenon which deserves to be studied in its own right, yet falls beyond the scope of this survey.

To sum up, religious architecture under the Mughals seems to have followed prior Indo-Muslim practice in several respects, from the relative importance assigned to funerary buildings to the form and distribution of neighborhood mosques. At the same time, references to the Timurid architectural style were almost invariably present in imperial commissions. Mughal religious architecture has not yet received the attention it deserves: the variety of burial types and the alternate fortune of congregational mosques are among the topics that would deserve further attention, ideally in a comparative perspective extending beyond the chronological and geographical limits of the Mughal realm.

LAURA E. PARODI (PhD) teaches at the University of Genoa. She is the author of numerous essays on Mughal art and architecture. Her interests range from gardens to manuscript culture and court ceremonial. She has taught courses and seminars at the University of Oxford, University College Dublin, the Massachusetts Institute of Technology, and various Italian universities. She edited *The Visual World of Muslim India: The Art, Culture and Society of the Deccan in the Early Modern Era* and co-edited *Comparative Oriental Manuscript Studies: An Introduction.*

SUGGESTIONS FOR FURTHER READING

Asher, Catherine B. *Architecture of Mughal India. The Cambridge History of India* 1.4 (Cambridge: Cambridge University Press, 1992).

Asher, Catherine B. "The Architecture of Raja Man Singh: A Study of Sub-Imperial Patronage," in *The Powers of Art: Patronage in Indian Culture*, ed. Barbara Stoler Miller (Delhi: Oxford University Press, 1992), 183–201

Chagatai, M. Abdullah. *The Badshahi Masjid (Built by Aurangzeb in 1084/1674): History and Architecture* (Lahore: Kitab-Khana-i-Nauras, 1972)

Koch, Ebba. *Mughal Architecture* (Munich: Prestel-Verlag, 1991).

Koch, Ebba. *The Complete Taj Mahal and the Riverfront Gardens of Agra* (London: Thames & Hudson, 2006).

Wescoat, James L., Michael Brand, and M. Naeem Mir. "The Shahdara Gardens of Lahore: Site Documentation and Spatial Analysis," *Pakistan Archaeology* 25 (1990), 333–66.

NOTES

[1] For a survey of Timurid architecture see Lisa Golombek and Donald Wilber, *The Timurid Architecture of Iran and Turan* (Princeton: Princeton University Press, 1988).

[2] Catherine B. Asher, *Architecture of Mughal India. The Cambridge History of India* 1.4 (Cambridge: Cambridge University Press, 1992), 53–8; Ebba Koch, *Mughal Architecture* (Munich: Prestel-Verlag, 1991), 65–6. On earlier Mughal mosques see Asher, *Architecture of Mughal India*, 25–32 and 34–6; Koch, *Mughal Architecture*, 32, 35; Bianca Maria Alfieri, *Islamic Architecture of the Indian Subcontinent* (London / Ahmedabad: Laurence King Publishing and Mapin, 2000), 185–94.

[3] Koch, *Mughal Architecture*, 56–8; Asher, *Architecture of Mughal India*, 56–7.

[4] Ebba Koch, *The Complete Taj Mahal and the Riverfront Gardens of Agra* (London: Thames & Hudson, 2006), 94–5.

[5] Ebba Koch, "Diwan-i 'Amm and Chihil Sutun: The Audience Halls of Shah Jahan," *Muqarnas* 11 (1994), 143–65.

[6] Asher, *Architecture of Mughal India*, 189–91.

[7] Ibid., 202–3; Koch, *Mughal Architecture*, 119.

[8] Koch, *Mughal Architecture*, 109–14; Asher, *Architecture of Mughal India*, 191–200.

[9] Asher, *Architecture of Mughal India*, 172–4.

[10] Ibid., 225–6; Koch, *Mughal Architecture*, 118–19.

[11] Cf. Chanchal B. Dadlani, *From Stone to Paper: Architecture as History in the Late Mughal Empire* (New Haven and London: Yale University Press, 2018).

[12] M. Abdullah Chagatai, *The Badshahi Masjid (Built by Aurangzeb in 1084/1674): History and Architecture* (Lahore: Kitab-Khana-i-Nauras, 1972); Koch, *Mughal Architecture*, 129–30; Asher, *Architecture of Mughal India*, 257–9.

[13] On baluster columns see Koch, *Mughal Architecture*, 93–5.

[14] Koch, *Mughal Architecture*, 121–2; Asher, *Architecture of Mughal India*, 187–9.

[15] Asher, *Architecture of Mughal India*, 116–17.

[16] Koch, *Taj Mahal*, 212–13; Asher, *Architecture of Mughal India*, 201, 266–90.

[17] Asher, *Architecture of Mughal India*, 202, 222–3, 255, 259–60.

[18] Pushkar Sohoni, "Patterns of Faith: Mosque Typologies and Sectarian Affiliation in the Kingdom of Ahmadnagar," in *Envisioning Islamic Art and Architecture: Essays in Honor of Renata Holod*, ed. David J. Roxburgh (Leiden: E.J. Brill, 2014), 112–17 (110–27).

19 George Michell and Mark Zebrowski, *Architecture and Art of the Deccan Sultanates. The Cambridge History of India* 1.7 (Cambridge: Cambridge University Press, 1999), 88–9.

20 Michell & Zebrowski, *Art of the Deccan*, 98–101.

21 Catherine B. Asher, "The Architecture of Raja Man Singh: A Study of Sub-Imperial Patronage," in *The Powers of Art: Patronage in Indian Culture*, ed. Barbara Stoler Miller (Delhi: Oxford University Press, 1992), 183–201.

22 Asher, *Architecture of Mughal India*, 94–6.

23 Ibid., 68.

24 Ibid., 293–4.

25 Ibid., 296, 307.

26 Dadlani, *From Stone to Paper*, esp. Chapter 2.

27 Asher, *Architecture of Mughal India*, 308–9.

28 Laura E. Parodi, "The Posthumous Portrait of Hazrat Jannat Ashiyani: Dynastic, Saintly, and Literary Imagery in the Tomb of Humayun," *Islamic Art* 6 (2009), 129–58; Glenn D. Lowry, "Humayun's Tomb: Form, Function and Meaning in Early Mughal Architecture," *Muqarnas* 4 (1987), 133–48; Koch, *Mughal Architecture*, 43–4; Asher, *Architecture of Mughal India*, 43–6.

29 Asher, *Architecture of Mughal India*, 105–10; Koch, *Mughal Architecture*, 70–2.

30 Asher, *Architecture of Mughal India*, 174.

31 Koch, *Taj Mahal*.

32 Laura E. Parodi, "The Bibi-ka Maqbara in Aurangabad. A Landmark of Mughal Power in the Deccan?" *East & West* 48/3–4 (1998): 349–83.

33 Asher, *Architecture of Mughal India*, 146–8; Koch, *Mughal Architecture*, 78–9.

34 Asher, *Architecture of Mughal India*, 130–33; Koch, *Mughal Architecture*, 74–5.

35 James L. Wescoat, Michael Brand, and M. Naeem Mir, "The Shahdara Gardens of Lahore: Site Documentation and Spatial Analysis," *Pakistan Archaeology* 25 (1990), 333–66.

36 Koch, *Mughal Architecture*, 127–8.

37 Asher, *Architecture of Mughal India*, 260.

38 Ibid., 265.

39 Laura E. Parodi, "The Taj Mahal and the garden tradition of the Mughals," *Orientations* 48/3 (May/Jun 2017): 118–25.

40 Laura E. Parodi, "Kabul, a forgotten Mughal capital: gardens, city and court at the turn of the sixteenth century," *Muqarnas* 38 (2021).

41 Terry Allen, *Timurid Herat* (Wiesbaden: Reichert, 1983), 24–26.

42 John D. Hoag, "The Tomb of Ulugh Beg and Abdu Razzaq at Ghazni, A Model for the Taj Mahal," *Journal of the Society of Architectural Historians* 27/4 (Dec. 1968), 234–48.

43 Catherine B. Asher, "The Mausoleum of Sher Shāh Sūrī," *Artibus Asiae* 39/3–4 (1977), 273–98; Alfieri, *Islamic Architecture*, 196–7.

44 Laura E. Parodi, "Of Shaykhs, Bībīs and Begims: sources on early Mughal marriage connections and the patronage of Babur's tomb," in *Proceedings of the 6th European Conference of Iranian Studies* (Wiesbaden: Reichert, 2007), ed. Maria Szuppe, Anna Krasnowolska and Claus Pedersen, *Cahiers de Studia Iranica* 45 (2011), 121–38. Maria Teresa Shephard-Parpagliolo, *Kabul: The Bagh-e Baburi. A Project and Research into the Possibilities of a Complete Restoration* (Rome: IsMEO, 1972); Ratish Nanda and Jolyon Leslie, "Rehabilitating the Garden of Babur and Its Surroundings in Kabul," in *Urban Conservation and Area Development in Afghanistan* (Aga Khan Historic Cities Programme, s.l., 2007), 21–42.

45 Parodi, "Kabul, a forgotten Mughal capital."

46 Parodi, "Of Shaykhs, Bībīs and Begims."

47 Golombek & Wilber, *Timurid Architecture*, vol. 1, nos. 35, 36, 49, 65.

48 Parodi, "Posthumous Portrait," note 68.

49 Parodi, "Of Shaykhs, Bībīs and Begims."

50 Begley, Wayne E., "The Myth of the Taj Mahal and a New Theory of Its Symbolic Meaning," *The Art Bulletin* 61 (March 1979), 7–37.

51 Koch, *Mughal Architecture*, 99.

52 Arthur Upham Pope and Phyllis Ackerman, "Gardens," in *A Survey of Persian Art from Prehistoric Times to the Present*, eds. A.U. Pope and Ph. Ackerman, vol. 2, 1427–45.

53 Ralph Pinder-Wilson, "The Persian Garden: *Bagh* and *Chahar-Bagh*," in *The Islamic Garden*, eds. Elizabeth MacDougall and Richard Ettinghausen (Washington, D.C.: Dumbarton Oaks, 1976), 71–85; Mahvash Alemi, "Chahar Bagh," *Environmental Design* 1 (1986), 28–45.

54 Laura E. Parodi, review of D.F. Ruggles, *Islamic Gardens and Landscapes* (Philadelphia: University of Pennsylvania Press, 2008), *Journal of Islamic Studies* 21 (2010), 439–43.

55 Laura E. Parodi, "Mughal garden typologies reconsidered," in *The Art and Culture of Mughal India: New Studies*, ed. Roda Ahluwalia (New Delhi: Niyogi Books, 2021), 156–81.

56 Parodi, "Kabul, a forgotten Mughal capital."

57 Ibid.

58 Parodi, "Mughal garden typologies."

Badshahi Masjid, Lahore   KAMIL KHAN MUMTAZ

1 Badshahi Masjid, Lahore, 1674. Detail.
Photo: Wikimedia Commons/ Muhammad Umair Mirza

The Badshahi Masjid (Figs. 1–2) is the last and the largest of the series of *jami* (congregational) mosques built in their capital cities by the Mughal emperors: Akbar in Fatehpur Sikri (1571), Shah Jahan in Delhi (1644–58), and Aurangzeb in Lahore (1674). Surprisingly, there is no mention of this mosque or of its architect in contemporary histories. The only definite information we have is from a royal *farman* (order) about the erection of a new mosque at Lahore, and the sanctioning of a sum of Rs 30 lakhs (3,000,000 Rupees),[1] and the inscription on the entrance of the mosque itself which states that this "mosque of Abul Zafar Muhy-ud-Din Muhammad Alamgir, the victorious and valiant king, [was] constructed in 108 AH (1674 CE), under the superintendence of the humblest servant of the royal household, Fidai Khan Koka." This last named person was the foster brother of Aurangzeb, and a Governor of Lahore.[2]

The Mughal Empire declined after the reign of Aurangzeb. In 1799 Ranjit Singh became master of Lahore. During his rule the mosque was used as a magazine for military stores. Light guns mounted on the minarets bombarded the fort in 1841. After the annexation of the Punjab in 1849, the British also used it as a powder magazine but carried out some of the first repairs of urgent nature in 1850. To defray the costs, the British authorities chose to sell its red sand-stone slabs. But as this was strongly resented by the Muslim population, further sale of the stone was stopped. The mosque was restored to the Muslims in 1856 only after dismantling the eastern cells to prevent its use as a stronghold against the British.[3]

In its essence, the plan of the Badshahi Masjid conforms to the type established by Akbar's mosque at Fatehpur Sikri (Fig. 3). This includes a large courtyard enclosed by cells, often connected to form a continuous gallery; a domed prayer chamber at the western end, or more precisely, the *qibla* side in the direction of Mecca; and one, two, or three monumental gateways on the major axes, their number and placement depending on the specific locations in the urban context of the three mosques, the respective topographies of their sites and their relationships with adjoining structures.

Apart from its expansive scale and refined proportions, what distinguishes the Badshahi Masjid is the dominating presence of its eight *minar*s (minarets). Despite the precedent established by the monumental Qutub Minar in Delhi (1199), minarets did not appear as distinctive elements of mosque architecture in Hindustan before the mid-seventeenth century. Several forms of corner buttresses topped by stubby pylons or domed *chatri* (umbrella) pavilions continued to be employed, particularly in the outlying kingdoms and sultanates of Bengal and the Deccan. But none of the major mosques of the first four Mughal emperors had any *minar*s. The first Mughal *minar*s appeared in the tombs of Akbar at Sikandara, I'tmad ud-Dawla at Agra, Jahangir at Shahdara, and the Taj Mahal at Agra. The Fatehpur Sikri mosque has no minarets; the Delhi Jami introduced two *minar*s, one at each end of the prayer hall façade. At Lahore, the architect provided two sets of four *minar*s each, an inner set marking the corners of the prayer hall, and an outer set marking the corners of the courtyard. The sizes of the minarets are correspondingly scaled down for the prayer chamber and increased for the courtyard (Fig. 4).

Another divergence from the established precedents is that while most large mosques have the longer axis of the courtyard along the east west direction aligned to the *qibla*, the Badshahi Masjid courtyard has its shorter axis in line with the *qibla*

2 Badshahi Masjid, Lahore, 1674, main façade of the prayer chamber from the courtyard.
Photo: Wikimedia Commons/ Ali Imran

direction. Similarly, while the prayer chamber of the Fatehpur mosque projects beyond the rectangle of the courtyard, the Badshahi Masjid follows the Delhi example in which the prayer chamber extends into the courtyard. In most other respects too, each of the *jami* mosques had their own distinctive features of architectural form and decorative details.

Located at the north-western extreme of the old city and citadel, with the old bed of the river Ravi immediately to its north, the Masjid is separated from the city on its south by a public open space and from the fort on its east by the Huzuri Bagh garden. This garden is formally laid out, with a marble *baraderi* pavilion in its centre and four gates, one at each end of the two axes. The Roshnai Gate on its north wall that once provided access to the landing point on the river for boats and ferries is now blocked off by the Samadi buildings containing the ashes of Ranjit Singh and Guru Arjun Dev. The southern gate leads to the city. The Alamgiri Gate on the east connects the garden with the fort and imperial residences. On the west is the formal entrance to the Masjid. Thus the Huzuri Bagh acts as a forecourt to the mosque (Fig. 3).

Like its predecessor at Delhi, the Badshahi Masjid is elevated on a high platform. But unlike the Delhi Jami it has only one gateway that is from the Huzuri Bagh on the east (Fig. 4). This imposing structure, with a half-domed double-storied portal, stands on a high terrace approached by twenty-foot high flights of twenty-one steps that form three sides of a pyramid. The terrace measuring 65 × 35 ft. is paved with red-stone slabs. Indeed red sandstone, imported from quarries in the Fathpur Sikri range in the Agra district, is the main cladding material over the brick masonry structures.

With its own height of seventy-seven feet, the gateway rises to about one hundred feet above ground level (Fig. 5). This double-storied building functions both as a ceremonial entry to a royal mosque and as residential quarters for the imam, visiting scholars, and other functionaries.[4]

3 Fatehpur Sikri Mosque, Fatehpur Sikri, India, 1571, plan and elevation.
Redrawn from H. Steirlin, *Encyclopedia of World Architecture*, London: Macmillan Press, 1983, 342

4 Badshahi Masjid, Lahore, 1674, plan and sectional elevations.
Drawings: Kamil Khan Mumtaz

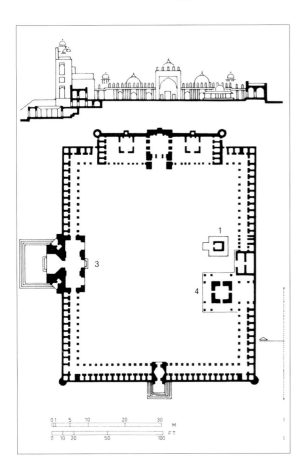

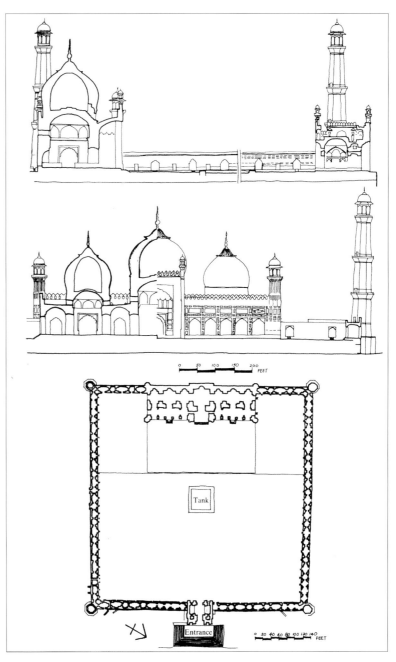

Its front and rear elevations are almost identical. The flanking bays on either side of the central arches have pairs of smaller arched recesses, placed vertically one above the other, as balconies with windows to the rooms of the upper floors. At the corners of the square structure are four minarets. The external surfaces are divided into recessed (*pas o pesh*) rectangular panels and are sparingly carved in low relief. The material throughout is red sandstone with white marble veins, embellished by an occasional rosette or sunflower. Slender shafts, attached to the sides of the slightly projecting central bay, terminate above the roof in the form of *guldasta* (bouquet) vases with white marble orbs placed in full-blown lotuses. Between these shafts and above the central arch is an elaborate array of twelve merlons, which carry above them an open arcade, topped by eleven white marble *gumbati*s (miniature solid domes). Between this balustrade and each corner minaret is an airy *chatri* kiosk with projecting eaves and square white marble domes. The four corner minarets have projecting square platforms surmounted by similar square kiosks.

The recessed surfaces below the arches on the outer and inner facades, as well as the walls and ceilings of the passage through the gateway, are decorated with fresco murals painted on lime plaster. Floral and geometric motifs are mostly placed in the rectangular wall panels while the spherical surfaces of the domes and pendentives are decorated respectively with net-like curvilinear *badroon* designs and geometric *ghalibkari* patterns of interlocking ribs.

On either side of the main passage through the gateway are double-storied verandas attached to rooms that may have served as reception parlours or class-rooms adjoining independent apartments in the north and south wings. Above the double height passage is a hemispherical dome which does not exceed the height of the parapets of the gateway.[5]

The gateway opens onto the courtyard measuring 530 feet square and enclosed within a wall of eighty cloisters or *dalan*s. The floor of the courtyard, including that of the gateway, is one step higher than that of the outer terrace. A further change in level defines the two parts of the courtyard. The lower level is called the *fina*, where funeral prayers may be offered, and this also contains the ablution tank. The upper part is further divided into three areas, with the central area a step higher than the areas on either side. The present floor of red-stone slabs is the recent work of the Renovating Committee. The original courtyard contained a number of shady trees and was paved, as was the main prayer chamber, in small bricks laid on edge, making a pattern of *musallah*s or prayer mats. The original source of water for the mosque appears to have been an ancient well with a Persian wheel in an independent enclosure, just outside the south-eastern minaret.[6] The surface water was carried by an elaborate drainage system under the courtyard floor into the River which flowed along the northern enclosure wall.[7]

The enclosing cloisters or *dalan*s, which may have served as class-rooms or lecture halls, have a plinth of about three feet above the courtyard and a parapet at a height of about 21 feet, studded with a continuous row of crockets. The inner and outer walls are about a yard thick and have a usable space of some thirteen feet between them, divided into cells which are connected to form long corridors. The present emergency exit on the southern wall is a modern intervention. Other than this the exterior walls on the south and west had

5 Badshahi Masjid, Lahore, 1674, the formal entrance portal to the mosque, with the seventeenth-century Huzuri Bagh pavilion and garden in the forecourt. Photo: Hasan-Uddin Khan

6 Badshahi Masjid, Lahore, 1674, Courtyard pool with the entrance gateway in the background. Photo: Hasan-Uddin Khan

no openings, while those on the east and north have rectangular apertures like large windows. The walls, divided into the familiar *pa so pesh* scheme of rectangular panels, are plastered with a thick layer of lime and ornamented with multi-foiled (*marghola*) pointed arches.[8]

The eastern *dalan*s, demolished by the British, have been rebuilt, with arrangements for ablutions, and some arrangements for ablution for ladies have been added within the southern *dalan*s.[9] The corners of this vast courtyard are marked by tall minarets (Fig. 7). Standing on a plinth of about 20 feet, they rise to over 160 feet in three storeys. The original octagonal *chatri* pavilions on top of the *minar*s were lost in the earthquake of 1840 and were restored as part of the works carried out by the Public Works Department between 1939 and 1960.[10]

Raised above the courtyard in the centre of the west side is the *iwan* or main prayer chamber, about 275 feet in length and 85 feet deep with 51 feet high enclosing walls. This prayer chamber, following the tradition of the Imperial mosques of the Mughals at Agra and Delhi, consists of two oblong, arcaded chambers. The central bay is in the form of a *pishtaq* or fronton, reflecting the scheme of the eastern gateway but with a wider and taller half-domed recess. The central arch rises past the general roof line and is framed in a border with a pair of slender minarets marking the corners and a crown of merlons along the top edge. "The height of the fronton up to the very edge of the parapet is about 80 feet from the floor of the courtyard and is 55 feet wide, excluding the turrets".[11] This high vault is flanked by five smaller arched openings on each side. The corners of the building are marked by four sturdy minarets with projecting platforms, surmounted by domed kiosks with projecting eaves. The parapet is formed by a horizontal row of merlons shaped like broad leaves resembling *naga* (serpent) hoods.

The red sandstone façade of the central prayer chamber is treated in a similar fashion to the entrance gateway but with a more liberal use of white marble. The isolated sunflowers in the spandrels of the outer entrance are replaced by a florid vine that fills the triangular spaces between

7 Badshahi Masjid, Lahore, 1674, courtyard with its tall corner minarets during Eid prayers.
Photo: Samina Quraeshi

8 Badshahi Masjid, Lahore, 1674, *mihrab* and surrounding *qibla* wall.
Photo: Hasan-Uddin Khan

the multi-cusped *surahi* or *vangrhian wala* arch
and its rectangular frame. The rectangular *tilli*
and square *murabba* recessed panels framing the
outer entrance are replaced in the inner *peshtaq*
by an embossed chain-like cursive version in
white marble.

Below the high central arch is a rectangular
recessed porch with a half domed vault above.
Beyond a smaller arched opening is the central
square hall with the inlaid white marble *mihrab*
recess in the centre of the *qibla* wall, while on
either side stretch out long halls or loggias (Fig. 8).
Parallel with the loggias and on either side of the
central hall are two wide wings. Three high domes,
one over the middle bay of each wing and one over
the central hall, are of white marble that tower
above the roof of the prayer chamber. All three
are double domes with the outer domes raised on
cylindrical drums, constricted at the necks and
crowned by inverted lotus-like *maujpa* (finials)
with gilded *kala*s (pinnacles). The rectangular bays
between the domes are roofed with domical vaults
with concave margins called *qalamdani*, and with
central ribs. The plinth of this prayer chamber,
raised about 5 ft. above the courtyard level, is
approached by flights of steps in the porticos.
The marble and stone floor and much of the fresco
work in the ceiling is later repair work.[12]

The parapet all around the building has a
regular range of crockets (*kungra*s), having an
elegant *mudakhal* design. The crockets of the
parapet of the prayer chamber in particular are
faced with red stone slabs, ornamented with white
marble inlaid in parallel outline and fretted designs
in relief, and the crockets of the *dalan*s are covered
with a thick layer of lime plaster.[13]

The arches used throughout the Badshahi
Masjid are a form of multi-foil pointed arch called

*marghola*s by the local masons. After their initial
appearance in the Diwan-i-Khas of the Agra Fort
(1635), they emerged as a prominent feature of Shah
Jahan's reign and have therefore come to be known
as Shah Jahani arches.

But the most remarkable aspect of the Lahore
jami are not the niceties of architectonic forms,
materials, stylistic characteristics and historical
precedents, but its powerful manifestation
of the qualities of majesty (*jalal*) and beauty
(*jamal*), which are at once the two categories into
which the qualities and names of the Divine are
traditionally divided, and the hallmark of the
masterpieces of Mughal, or for that matter all
traditional architecture.

The entire complex is composed within a perfect
square. The size and placing of every element on
plan, section and elevation is derived from a system
of proportionate sub-division of the whole. Thus
while mathematical rigor governs the rhythms and
symmetries and provides the basis for the *jalali*
aspect of majesty, it is the balance, harmony, and
proportions that govern the lyrical arabesques and
traceries of its surface decorations and reflect the
jamali aspect of beauty. Moreover, the elements
are orchestrated into a hierarchy in which the
scale is modulated to match the experience of the
monument by the observer as he approaches it from
a distance and moves in and through its spaces.

KAMIL KHAN MUMTAZ As practicing architect, educator, author,
and pioneer in the movement for conservation of architectural
heritage Kamil Khan Mumtaz, has been a leading influence in
raising standards of architectural design in general and in the
search for a contemporary, appropriate architecture for Pakistan
responsive to climate, economy and materials yet rooted in the
indigenous culture.

SUGGESTIONS FOR FURTHER READING:

Chaghatai, Abdullah. *The Badshahi Masjid: History and Architecture* (Lahore: Kitab Khana-i-Nauras, 1972).

Mumtaz, Kamil Khan. *Architecture in Pakistan* (Singapore: Concept Media Ltd., 1985).

Khan, Ahmad Nabi. *Development of Mosque Architecture in Pakistan* (Islamabad: National Hijra Council, 1990).

Khan, Muhammad Wali Ulla. *Lahore and its Important Monuments* (Karachi: Anjuman Press, 1973).

Koch, Ebba. *Mughal Architecture* (New Delhi: Oxford University Press, 2002).

Nadiem, Ihsan H. *Historic Mosques of Lahore* (Lahore: Sang-e-Meel Publications, 1998).

NOTES

[1] Abdullah Chaghatai, *The Badshahi Masjid: History and Architecture* (Lahore: Kitab Khana-i-Nauras, 1972), 10.

[2] Ibid., 12.

[3] Ihsan Nadiem, *Historic Mosques of Lahore* (Lahore: Sang-e-Meel Publications, 1998), 122.

[4] Chaghatai, *The Badshahi Masjid*, 16.

[5] Ibid., 17.

[6] Ibid., 19.

[7] Kamil Khan Mumtaz, *Architecture in Pakistan* (Singapore: Concept Media Ltd., 1985), 75.

[8] Chaghatai, 18.

[9] Ibid., 20.

[10] Ibid., 23.

[11] Ibid., 21.

[12] Mumtaz, 76.

[13] Chaghatai, 19.

The Architecture of Sufi Shrines in Pakistan   KAMIL KHAN MUMTAZ

1 Shrine of Daata Ganj Bakhsh, at Lahore, originally built in the late eleventh century and expanded several times, most recently in the twenty-first century; general view from the courtyard.

Photo: OCOO Images, Lahore

In his account of the design and construction of the tomb of a Sufi saint, Hazrat Dawood Bandagi (1530–75) at Shergarh, some 80 kilometers from Lahore (Fig. 2), the sixteenth-century Lahore architect,[1] Ustad Bazid, tells us that:

Before every brick that we put in place I would invoke God's blessings upon the holy Prophet, may Allah's blessings and peace be upon him. Virtuous men, devotees and seekers of the spiritual path would recite the chapter *Ikhlas* [Quran 112] twice over as they passed on each load of bricks or mortar. There were so many people and such a crowd that each turn to hand over the bricks would take rather a long while and with great difficulty. In this manner the construction of the radiant tomb was accomplished in four years.

The following chronogram was written on its completion, circa 1580:[2]

This pure tomb of Hazrat Dawood
May God forever spread its shadow wide
By the radiant beauty of its appearance
The eyes gain sight of the light of God
He who looks upon it with the eye of
    meditation
Cannot take his gaze away from it
To the chant of "*La ilaha illah hoo*"
    (there is no God but He)
When recited beneath this dome
From this which has no parallel comes forth
    the sound of "*wahdahoo la shareek*"
    (He is one and has no associate)
To determine the year of its completion
It has been said "*muddi zillahoo abda*"
    (extend its shadow to eternity)

We see that the tomb is conceived and built as an act of devotion by pious souls. It embodies the spiritual presence, or *hadra*, of a saint, and the intention or purpose of its construction is to "spread its shadow wide," to propagate the teachings of the saint. The "radiant beauty of its appearance" is designed to enable the seeker to "gain sight of the light of God," and for the adept on the Sufi path, "who looks upon it with the eye of meditation." The tomb is a support, a vehicle that brings him into communion with the Divine.

The intimate relation of the architecture of the Sufi shrine to Islamic spirituality illustrates the profound connection between the traditional arts and crafts and the metaphysical and idealist world-view common to all traditional societies. Traditionally the term "art" is applied to making or doing anything that meets the dual criteria of utility and beauty. But beauty is traditionally understood as a quality of the Divine. In the traditional cosmology everything in the created universe is a manifestation of the Divine. However, some objects and acts are more "transparent," that is, the ideal forms are more readily recognized in them than in others which are more "opaque." For example, qualities such as proportion, harmony, balance, symmetry etc. are more readily recognized in certain mathematical relationships and in music. Similarly, a human form, or a tree or a sunset, may strike us as "perfect" because it corresponds with our idea of a perfect man, tree, etc. Indeed every earthly object, artifice, or act, takes on a symbolic meaning to the extent that it is perceived as reflecting its heavenly archetype.

Every craftsman acquires his art from a recognized master, who in turn, traces it to a divinely inspired source - a prophet, a saint, a sage, or a great master who was both skilled in his art and spiritually enlightened. But none of these

2 Shrine at Okara, c. 1580: entrance view.
Photo: Yasmin Cheema

sources claim to be the originators or creators of the art in question, only to have been the vehicles or recipients of these gifts from the Divine Spirit. This is why the great classical forms in every traditional art are held in such veneration and esteem. They are handed down from master to apprentice, from generation to generation. These forms are copied by students as a means of perfecting their technical skills, but also as a means of purifying the spirit or acquiring a special blessing. They are used by professionals as exemplars, points of reference, guiding framework, or grounds for their own work.

The ideal forms, in themselves can be read as a language of symbols whose meanings may be implicit, as in architectonic elements, in geometric patterns, and floral motifs, or explicit as in the case of iconographic sculpture and painting but, in Islamic art and architecture, more often in calligraphy.

The basic form of the Sufi tomb is a cube or octagonal chamber, symbolizing the earthly, material body, with a hemispherical dome, representing the heavenly sphere above. In this metaphor the body of the lover rises upwards towards the Beloved, and the Spirit descends halfway to meet it. This meeting of the lover and the Beloved is the *wissal*, the union, the ultimate goal of the Sufi.

The transition from the square to the circle is at once the most challenging and intriguing aspect of the tomb's structure and geometry, as can be seen in many of the shrines and tombs, for example the thirteenth-century Shah Rukn-i-Alam in Multan, sited on a platform atop a low hill (Fig. 3). One method of achieving the transition is by interposing a third element, a zone of transition, between the cube and the spherical dome. This third element may appear as a cylindrical neck or drum, or as an octagonal base below the dome. In rare examples the octagonal form rises directly from the ground, so that on entering the tomb chamber, we are already in the zone of transition. Among other devices used to make the transition are squinches, pendentives and *muqarnas*. This last device, a series of tiny niches, is a marvelous invention that seems to have appeared, at about the same time, throughout the Islamic world (Fig. 4).

The *muqarnas* can be found at the base of domes, in the corners of arched entrances, as cornices and column capitals, in an amazing variety of forms. The basis is always a complex three dimensional geometry of half arches and segmented domes forming a honeycomb of niches corbelling one above the other. But each region has its distinct system, and each system allows for an infinite variety of permutations and combinations.

A somewhat related form of articulation is *ghalibkari* or *qalabkari*, a lattice or network of ribs in stucco plaster or brick masonry applied to the curved surface of domes and vaults. The word "*qalab*" probably refers to the formwork or centering used in the construction of domes and arches, but sometimes incorporated into the body of the structure as ribs. The typical *ghalibkari* design appears as a starburst. From the large star at the center, called a *shamsa* or solar motif, radiate the ribs, often in the form of intersecting helixes, curving down to the base of the dome. At the interstices or nodes are smaller stars, and the ribs now appear as rays emanating from the stars,

3 Mausoleum of Shah Rukn-i-Alam, Multan, 1334, main entrance façade.
Photo: Jacques Betant/ Aga Khan Award for Architecture

the whole ensemble making up a veritable galaxy, spiraling out of an exploding supernova. Once again, the basis of the design is a complex spherical geometry with an infinite variety of applications.

Geometry plays an integral part in the design of Sufi shrines, not only in determining the proportions of the building in plan, section, and elevation, but also in decorative details such as the curvilinear arabesques and polygonal *girih* patterns. This is not merely a mechanical tool but is profoundly connected with the metaphysics of the sacred sciences of number and geometry.[3] Thus every form, proportion and decorative scheme becomes a ground for contemplation of higher realities. Each design is contained by a frame that establishes a finite universe, reflecting a cosmos created in perfect balance, in perfect harmony, made up of a diversity of elements governed by symmetry and proportion, with a unique center, the origin, to which everything must return. On closer examination, each element turns out to be a microcosmic representation of the larger scheme, with its own frame containing a symmetrical arrangement of elements and a unique center.

The geometric patterns, called *girih* or knots, are made up of lines interwoven into nets or webs of constantly changing forms. The spaces between the lines appear now as pattern and now as ground, adding another layer of ambiguity and paradox in the relationship between the apparent, *zahir*, and the hidden, *batin,* between simplicity and complexity. This unveiling or unfolding of the same truth at each level is experienced as one moves towards and through the structures.

In the center of the wall facing towards the Kaaba, is often provided a prayer niche or *mihrab* which allows the individual to perform the ritual prayer in relative seclusion, undisturbed by the movement of other devotees circulating around the grave of the saint. The Quranic references to the niche make clear its symbolism as the innermost sanctuary, the heart, where one is in the presence of God. The niche is where the Virgin Mary spent her confinement in prayer. And in the chapter al-Nur, the Light of Allah, the light of the heavens and the earth, is "like unto a niche, within it a lamp: the lamp enclosed in glass: the glass as it were a brilliant star,

lit from a blessed tree, an olive, neither of the east nor of the west, whose oil is well-nigh luminous, though fire touches it not. Light upon light!" (Quran 24.35). Indeed it is here, in this innermost sanctuary, that "the eyes gain sight of the light of God." Yet another symbol associated with light is the minaret

4 Shrine at Okara, c. 1580, interior of the dome.
Photo: Yasmin Cheema

SUFI SHRINES IN PAKISTAN 403

or *minar*, literally a beacon of light that guides the traveler to his goal. In a Sufi tomb a pair of minarets will often flank the entrance, marking the way for the pilgrim, or in miniature form will mark the corners of the main chamber.

The Sufi shrine is also called a *maqam*, a station, or a *rawda* or *rauza*, a garden, and more specifically a garden of Paradise, based on a typically quadripartite design (Fig. 5). That signifies that the saint, having attained the station of unity with God, is already in Paradise. The paradise garden motif is found throughout the Islamic world, but placing the tomb inside such a garden is an extravagance usually only affordable under royal patronage. A more affordable solution is to place the tomb in a "virtual" paradise by decorating its surfaces with floral designs (Fig. 6).

Plants, flowers, trees, and fruits, are the most obvious allusion to the garden, and each species has its own symbolic meaning. The rose is the epitome of beauty, the sunflower is a solar motif, the grape vine evokes the states of ecstasy and intoxication. The cypress is a symbol of the perfect man, the

5 *Charh Bagh* or Paradise Garden carpet, eighteenth century.
Photo: Charles Correa courtesy *Mimar: Architecture in Development*, no. 27, 1988

6 Mausoleum, c. 1580, floral pattern tiles.
Photo: Yasmin Cheema

7 Tomb of Daata Ganj Bakhsh, Lahore, tomb interior in 2014.
Photo: ocoo Images, Lahore

8 Daata Ganj Bakhsh, Lahore, interior of the dome with twentieth-century calligraphy and tilework.
Photo: ocoo Images, Lahore

insan e kamil, but with its top bent, it becomes a symbol for the submission of the Muslim, and with an intertwining vine it represents the lover and the Beloved. Two cypresses in a flower bed symbolize lovers in Paradise, and alternating with blossoming fruit trees, it recalls the pairs of trees and fruits of every kind that shall be served in silver platters. The fruits of paradise are also shown in a dish, sometimes with a knife cutting into a melon, a reference to the ecstatic effect of the beauty of the prophet Joseph on the ladies of Egypt. The fruit dish is often shown flanked by a pair of wine decanters, a reference to the wine of the purest kind that the inmates of Paradise will be given to drink.

It is not uncommon to find, in the architecture of Sufi shrines, elements borrowed from non-Islamic sources. The basic form of the cube chamber topped by a hemispherical dome is the pre-Islamic *chahar taq* funerary structure found in Sasanian Iran and Baluchistan. Here the symbolism of the structure, with its high arched openings, oriented towards the four cardinal points or the direction of the four winds, and its decorations is connected with the four elements of nature: fire, water, air, and earth, that occupy a central place in the Zoroastrian tradition. In South Asia the dome is invariably topped by a *maujbah* and *kalas*, the inverted lotus and finial of the Hindu temple *shikara* spire. Other such borrowings from Hindu and Buddhist sources include solar symbols such as *swastika*s and sunflowers, and *yantra* geometric patterns, the *padma* lotus symbolizing wisdom and enlightenment, and the trefoil arched niche in which the figure of the deity is replaced by an Arabic inscription, usually the word Allah.

These borrowings from local non-Islamic sources, together with adaptations and modifications necessitated by the specifics of climate, materials and cultural norms, results in the characteristics that distinguish each regional expression. Yet there is a unifying thread, a subtle quality that infuses the diversity of Islamic arts and architectures.

This quality derives largely from the treatment of the form or object as signifier, in relation to the content or concept as the thing signified. Thus where other traditions may treat the object as allegory or metaphor, and "realize" or concretize the metaphysical content in the form of anthropomorphic and naturalistic representations, Islamic art and architecture treats the object as sign or symbol, and "idealizes" or abstracts the floral and other natural forms, so that together with proportion, number, and geometry, they become, according to the epistles of the *Ikhwan al-Safa* or Brethren of Purity (attributed to Abu Hassan Ali and his friends al-Maqdisi, al-Nahrajuri and al-Awfi from Basra), the "gates through which we move to the knowledge of the essence of the soul, ... the root of all knowledge".[4] But the most efficient vehicle for the communication of this knowledge is the word, spoken, as in the recitation of the Quran, or written, as in calligraphy.

Inscriptions may include Quranic texts, *Hadith* (sayings of the Prophet), and verses from the buried saint or other Sufi poets. These texts are carefully selected to convey particular meanings relevant to the saint in question, his character, spiritual station, and teachings. A typical example is the Persian inscription over the entrance of the shrine-tomb of Hazrat Abul Hassan Ali Hajveri (a.k.a. Daata Ganj Bakhsh) who lived from 990–1077, in Lahore (Figs. 1 and 7–8), that may be translated [5] as: "Bestower of treasures, of grace and munificence to the world, the manifestation of the Light of God: The perfect mentor to the less-than-perfect, a guide for the perfected ones."

KAMIL KHAN MUMTAZ As practicing architect, educator, author, and pioneer in the movement for conservation of architectural heritage Kamil Khan Mumtaz, has been a leading influence in raising standards of architectural design in general and in the search for a contemporary, appropriate architecture for Pakistan responsive to climate, economy and materials yet rooted in the indigenous culture.

SUGGESTIONS FOR FURTHER READING

Ardalan, Nader and Laleh Bakhtiar. *The Sense of Unity* (Chicago: University of Chicago Press, 1973).

Bakhtiar, Laleh. *Sufi: Expressions of the Mystic Quest* (New York: Avon Books, 1976).

Burckhardt, Titus. *Art of Islam, Language and Meaning* (Westerham: World of Islam Festival Publishing Company, 1976).

Michon, Jean-Louis. *Lights of Islam: Institutions, Cultures, Arts and Spirituality in the Islamic City* (Islamabad: Lok Virsa, 2000).

Quraeshi, Samina. *Sacred Spaces* (Cambridge, MA: Peabody Museum Press, 2009).

NOTES

[1] Mohammad Haidar, "Ahwal al Sheikh Dawood Jhunniwal," *Muqamaat i Dawoodi* (Sayyid Mohammed Mohsin, Lahore, undated), Appendix 2.

[2] Translated by the author.

[3] Keith Critchlow, *Islamic Patterns* (New York, Schocken Books, 1976), 7–8.

[4] Critchlow, *Islamic Patterns*, 7.

[5] Translated by the author.

Pre-Islamic and Vernacular Elements in the Southeast Asian Mosques of Nusantara

IMRAN BIN TAJUDEEN

1 Great Mosque, Rao-rao, West Sumatra, Indonesia, 1918, three-tier *tajug* roof with four-*gonjong* top tier pavilion and Dutch gables for masonry verandah additions.
Photo: Imran bin Tajudeen

Nusantara is a cultural region encompassing the homeland of Austronesian-speaking communities in Southeast Asia; its Muslim communities, the world's largest today, are found in the present-day nation states of Indonesia, Malaysia, and Brunei.[1] Substantial indigenous Muslim minorities are also found in Singapore, southern Philippines, southern Thailand, and the former Champa principalities in Vietnam. The term "Jawa" and its adjective "Jawi" are also used to refer to Nusantara and its Muslim communities.[2]

The region's earliest extant mosques were built by Islamic polities that emerged during the fifteenth-century decline of Majapahit (c. 1294–1527), an East Javanese kingdom that claimed suzerainty over almost the entire region in the preceding century and professed a syncretic Hindu-Buddhist creed.[3] Consequently the formative period of Nusantara's Islamic art and architecture is profoundly shaped by the synthesis of autochthonous and Indic-derived elements developed by Majapahit and other regional polities of similar religious persuasion. The manifold continuities of Nusantara's pre-Islamic art result from the employment of craftsmen and builders from pre-Islamic centers, and the long and formative history of local traditions of orthodox Islamic mysticism in several Sufi *tarīqa* (Malay and Javanese *tarekat*).[4] These played an important role in early conversions and in fostering an accommodative spirit between local, pre-Islamic traditions and Islam.[5]

Whereas brick or stone was commonly employed for Javanese and Sumatran *candi* or Hindu and Buddhist sanctuaries, the prayer halls of Nusantara mosques feature post-and-beam structures of teak, ironwood, or other local hardwoods supporting multi-tier roofs. These mosque halls are based on four vernacular structural-formal dwelling and hall types that are depicted on eight- and thirteenth-century temple reliefs from Java and several ninth- to fourteenth-century clay tablets from Sumatra (Fig. 2).[6]

2 Detail, narrative relief panels from Candi Prambanan illustrating hip and extended gable-and-hip roof building types, Central Java, Indonesia, ninth century.
Photo: Imran bin Tajudeen

3 Grand Mosque, Demak, Central Java, Indonesia, c. 1478, main hall with three-tier *tajug* roof, and front pavilion (*serambi*) to the right with hip or *limas* roof.
Photo: Imran bin Tajudeen

4 Kasepuhan Grand Mosque, Cirebon, West Java, Indonesia, 1480, main hall to the right with three-tier hip or *limas* roof, surrounded by ancillary pavilions (*serambi*), and brick gateway to the left with two-tier stylized pairs of wings.
Photo: Imran bin Tajudeen

EARLY *TAJUG* AND *LIMAS* MOSQUES: SACRED COLUMNS

Nearly all extant fifteenth- and sixteenth-century Grand Mosques, or Masjid Agung (royal mosques), and mosques built in mausoleum complexes in Nusantara are distinguished by multi-tier pyramidal-hip roofs, called *tajug* in Javanese, built over a square plan.[7] The *tajug* roof's uppermost tier (Javanese: *brunjung*) may be supported either by four principle columns (Javanese, *soko guru*), one central column (Javanese, *soko tunggal*), or one central column surrounded by four or eight secondary columns (Minangkabau, West Sumatra, *tonggak macu*).[8] Demak Grand Mosque (c. 1478) is widely considered the definitive example of the fifteenth-century *tajug* mosque (Fig. 3).[9] Meanwhile, two early Grand Mosques possess hip or *limas* roofs instead – Kasepuhan, Cirebon, West Java (1480) (Fig. 4), and Buton, Southeast Sulawesi (1538 or 1558).[10]

Both Demak and Kasepuhan Mosques were reputedly built by Raden Sepat, a Majapahit master builder, while Sunan Kalijaga, one of Java's fifteenth- and sixteenth-century Wali Songo or Sufi-type proselytizers, is reputedly behind the erection of their respective sacred "bundled column," or *soko tatal*.[11] These are traditionally considered the most ritually potent among their principal columns.[12] Both mosques retain their original roofs and teak structure today. The importance of Demak's *soko guru* is relayed not only through their size at 1.14m diameter and 22m height, but also through stories of their erection by four different Wali Songo.[13]

Tajug pavilions with five principal columns – a central one surrounded by four columns – were considered sacred in the Javanese Indic period.[14] They constitute the direct precedent for the Minangkabau *tonggak macu* model.[15] The *soko guru* of old Javanese *tajug* mosques and the *tonggak macu* of old Minangkabau ones are considered symbolically potent; oral histories recount the fortuitous and often miraculous circumstances surrounding the selection and felling of timber, and the communal effort in transporting these massive logs to the construction site. Reverence for principal columns similar to that found in Demak and Kasepuhan also obtains for the single *soko tunggal* of Palopo's Grand Mosque in South Sulawesi (1604). Another local expression of this notion

is seen in Lombok where, during Maulid Nabi celebrations, four functionaries are seated against the four principal columns of local *tajug* mosques according to their religious hierarchical rank.[16] The notion of sacred principal columns is linked to similar symbolic signification of core columns in the architecture of houses and communal and ritual halls in other Nusantara and Austronesian-speaking societies – in Malay, Javanese, Samoan, Tongan and Madagascar houses alike.[17]

Kasepuhan Cirebon, which receives inordinately less attention in studies of Javanese mosques than Demak, is enigmatic in two aspects. Whereas Demak's *soko guru* format is ubiquitous in *tajug* mosques, Kasepuhan's twelve principal columns (four by three) that support its uppermost *limas* roof tier, with a middle row of four columns supporting the top roof ridge directly, is unprecedented and has never been repeated.[18] Moreover, although both Kasepuhan and Buton Mosques possess *limas* roofs – in three and two tiers respectively – they differ in the orientation of their roofs and rectangular plans in relation to the *qibla*. Buton's *qibla* wall is on the short side of its rectangular plan, whereas Kasepuhan's rectangular plan and roofs stretch lengthwise in relation to the *qibla* wall. Kasepuhan's orientation remains exceptional, whereas Buton's plan is the standard among *limas* mosques.

MOUNTAIN SYMBOLISM

Multi-tier roofs, along with the raised terraces of some mosque foundations, signify the exalted status of the building and evoke the symbolism of mountains, which are regarded as the place of origin of ancestors and the abode of their deified spirits *hyang* in autochthonous belief systems in Nusantara. These notions are evocatively embodied in such highland toponyms as Pariangan (Minangkabau, West Sumatra), Parahyangan (West Java), and Dieng (Di-Hyang, Central Java). Mountain cults are particularly prevalent in Java, where mountains are honored as places of spiritual retreat and rejuvenation. This symbolism is most successfully conveyed by the *tajug* roof form.[19] In the Indic cultures of Java and Sumatra, this spiritual potency is further reinforced by its resonance with the Hindu-Buddhist Meru, mountain abode of the gods. Seen in combination with the notion of sacred columns, these factors explain the widespread adoption of the *tajug* pavilion/hall type mosque form above all other vernacular forms. There have been mistaken suggestions that the *tajug* mosque is derived from two multi-tier roof buildings from Java and Bali – the *meru* temple towers and the *wantilan* ritual cock-fighting halls[20] – or from Chinese timber pagodas and Kerala and Kahsmiri timber mosques, based on the superficial resemblance between their profiles.[21]

The cosmic mountain symbolism of the mosque hall is enhanced by its immediate juxtaposition with pools. This is especially seen in the shallow step-pools, sometimes in the form of moats, built for the Grand Mosques of Kasepuhan Cirebon, Banten (1552) (Fig. 5), Jepara, Kotagede (c. 1580s), Surakarta (1763–68), and Yogyakarta (1773). Demak's compound incorporates an old pool while a unique pool with a Greek cross plan is found in Banten's Kasunyatan Mosque (c. 1550s).[22] In Minangkabau pools or *taluk* are used for fish-breeding, the proceeds of which accrue to the mosque; this practice is exemplified by the three pools flanking Taluk Mosque in Agam (1860).[23]

Demak Grand Mosque features a three-tier roof, as do the vast majority of Javanese *tajug* mosques, containing true upper stories. However, two extant *tajug* mosques that predate Demak, Wapauwe (1414), and Ampel (c.1450), several mosques on the small isles of eastern Nusantara, and small community prayer halls possess two-tier *tajug* roofs instead.[24] Upper stories are absent in these mosques, and a high interior space is created, dominated by tall, slender columns and lit by clerestory windows. Two-tier roofs are counted as single-tier with verandah additions (*emperan*) in traditional typological reckoning – with the exception of Ampel where the uppermost roof tier is supported not only by the *soko guru* but also the next set of twelve columns (*soko rawa*).[25] In this sense they are closer to the numerous single-tier pyramidal-hip-roof pavilions depicted on the friezes of thirteenth- to fifteenth-century East Javanese *candi*, and similar sacred pavilions found in the Nusa Tenggara islands east of Java.

Conversely, several historic *tajug* mosques had five-tier roofs of two formal categories. In one type, the third roof layer, supported by the *soko guru*, is surmounted by two miniature roof tiers supported by a single central, branched kingpost-column, for example Banten Grand Mosque,[26] Aceh's seventeenth-century Bitay Old Mosque; and possibly Aceh's sixteenth-century Grand Mosque (c. 1520).[27] Second, tall five-tier *tajug* roofs were also built with full upper stories in the expunged sixteenth-century Jepara Grand Mosque,[28] and in several Minangkabau mosques such as the 55m tall Limo Kaum Mosque (1710) (Fig. 6).

EXTENDED-GABLE-ON-HIP AND MULTI-TIER GABLE ROOF MOSQUES

Early mosques in areas of western Nusantara that lay beyond Majapahit's advances were derived from two other vernacular building types. While buildings with gable roofs with extended ridges and outward-slanting gables atop lower hip roof tiers are depicted in ninth-century Javanese *candi*

5 Grand Mosque, Banten, West Java, Indonesia, 1552, main hall in the center with three-tier *tajug* roof topped by two miniature tiers, front pavilion (*serambi*) with two-tier *limas* roof, and brick minaret, 1560s.
Photo: Imran bin Tajudeen

6 Limo Kaum Great Mosque, West Sumatra, Indonesia, 1710, five-tier *tajug* roof with top lantern.
Photo: Imran bin Tajudeen

reliefs, they have no longer been built in Java since the tenth century. Today mosques featuring such roofs are found in Patani and Kelantan in northeastern Malayan Peninsula, and in Champa and Minangkabau. The oldest extant examples are two early seventeenth-century mosques: Teluk Manok (Wadi al-Hussein) in Patani (c. 1610) (Fig. 7), and Surau Syekh Burhanuddin, Minangkabau (c. 1630s).[29] Their roofs, originally of *ijuk*, have been replaced respectively by terracotta tiles and corrugated iron sheets.

Teluk Manok Mosque, built using Malabar ironwood, features carved wood panels, posts, and beams.[30] Its roof structure comprises an extended-gable roof atop two lower hip-roof tiers, separated by a plaster neck articulated by horizontal moldings. The former Great Mosque building (1867) in Kelantan's capital Kota Bahru assumed a similar form and was distinguished by crossed gable boards; unfortunately it was demolished in 1922 to make way for the current *limas*-roof, concrete Muhammadi Mosque.

The Minangkabau form of the extended-gable roof possesses a very pronounced curved ridge and dramatic upward-sweeping ridge ends. The roof thus appears to sag in the middle and soar

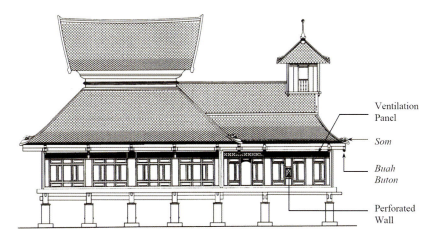

7 Teluk Manok Mosque, Narathiwat Province (Patani Malay cultural region), Thailand, c. 1610, extended gable-on-hip roof, and *mihrab* vestibule to the left with two-tier gable-roof and a *tajug*-roof tower.
Drawing: KALAM © 2011

8 Minangkabau *surau* (prayer hall), West Sumatra, Indonesia, with *gonjong*-roof tier atop a lower hip roof.
Photo: Imran bin Tajudeen

PRE-ISLAMIC AND VERNACULAR ELEMENTS IN NUSANTARA 413

at its ends, and is called *gonjong*. Surau Syekh Burhanuddin features the *gonjong* roof supported on four columns on a square plan surmounting two lower hip roof tiers.[31] Smaller Minangkabau *surau* or prayer halls such as the clan *surau*s surrounding the main mosque in the highland ancestral village of Pariangan possess this roof form and rectangular plans (Fig. 8).

Patani's Surau Aur presents an excellent example of the multi-tier gable roof mosque that retains full timber construction and symbolic details, including abstracted *kala-makara* and *naga* motifs in the Langkasuka style.[32] The design of the slender vase-shaped carved kingposts, *tunjuk langit*, in Surau Aur's roof structure is distinctly Malay and is also found in traditional Lampung houses of southern Sumatran; it differs from Thai architectural details, and may point to Surau Aur's basis in old Malay architectural forms that are possibly of Sumatran origin.[33] Late eighteenth- and nineteenth-century examples of this mosque form, rebuilt in brick and concrete, are found in Melakan *surau* such as Banda Hilir, Kampung Melayu Tengkera Pantai (Fig. 9), and Bukit Darat, Tanjung Keling. A timber *surau* is also found in Kelantan, converted from a former royal pavilion.[34]

ROOF ORNAMENTS AND THE STYLIZED *NAGA* MOTIF

The typological and symbolic importance of roof forms in Nusantara's vernacular mosques is augmented by the curved and foliated ornaments that often appear on the roof ridges of *tajug* and *limas* roofs, on the lower hip-roof tiers of extended-gable-on-hip roofs, and on the barge board of multi-tier gable roofs – called *pemeleh* in Patani and Kelantan. These ornaments represent *naga*s or serpents, a common motif in the Indo-Pacific world.

On Javanese *tajug* mosques the heads of the *naga*s, found at the ridge ends, are given either the elaborate *makuta* (Javanese, crown) ornament or the simpler *bungkak* upward curl. Terracotta antefixes also adorn roof ridges. These Javanese ornamental motifs have been simplified into repeated *tanduk* (horn) ornaments on the roof ridges of Palembang

9 Kampung Melayu Tengkera Pantai *surau* (prayer hall), Melaka, Malaysia, simple gable roof over prayer hall (*surau*) with verandah extensions, eighteenth century, renovated nineteenth century.
Photo: Imran bin Tajudeen

and Jambi mosques.[35] On Melaka mosques the ridge-end ornaments assume the Malay foliated motif called *sulur bayung*, initially of carved timber but also rendered in plaster and coral stone (Figs. 14 and 18). In Banjarmasin they are called *tatah hujung pilis* and are elaborately foliated.

On *tajug* roofs an Indic motif is additionally signified; the *naga* on the four ridges guard the elixir of life or *brahmāmūla* symbolized by carved roof finials, called *mustoko* or *memolo* in Java and Palembang, *kepala som* in Melaka, and *pataka* in Banjarmasin, which are of elaborate foliated or bulbous design. This motif also appears on the *tajug* roof sheltering one model of the *minbar*.[36] In Java and Palembang finials are of terracotta or copper, while in Melaka they are of coral stone, and in Banjarmasin ironwood. In Minangkabau stainless steel finials have been used at least since the early nineteenth century; tin, mined in Sumatra, was used originally.

The application of these motifs in Nusantara Islamic art illustrates the development of an autochthonous aesthetic for religious buildings that continued into the middle of the twentieth century, for instance in the mosques of Melaka, Palembang, and Batavia/Jakarta.[37] Sufist interpretations of layers of existence and of the manifestation of the divine have also been imposed upon the multi-tier roofs and *tajug* finials in an attempt to align them with Islamic mysticism.[38]

STONE AND BRICK WALLS IN EARLY MOSQUE HALLS AND THEIR ORNAMENTS

In Java the walls of some mosque halls are built of brick and decorated with carved stone or terracotta medallions and decorative tiles. The blue-and-white glazed ceramic tiles are specially made to order from Vietnamese kilns for various Majapahit and Javanese Islamic sites.[39] Their unique shapes sometimes resemble those of contemporary Seljuk tiles. The prominence of Kurdish *ulama* among the teachers of Nusantara religious students in the Hejaz may prove to be one link.[40] These tiles are found on Demak's *qibla* wall and the front wall that divides its inner prayer chamber from an outer pavilion, the *serambi*. Numerous stone medallions, featuring floral and knot motifs and depictions of mountainous landscapes with meditation pavilions or caves, are found on the *qibla* and threshold walls of Mantingan, and on the walls and the frame of the main doorway leading to the inner prayer chamber of Kasepuhan Cirebon. The Majapahit sunburst royal emblem is found above the *mihrab* in Demak and Kasepuhan Cirebon (Fig. 10), while Javanese epigraphic chronograms indicating the year of construction according to the Javanese or Hegira calendar are often incorporated into the ornamental motifs of *mihrab*s, *minbar*s, and *qibla* walls.[41]

The walls of exposed flat bricks in sixteenth-century Cirebon's Kasepuhan Grand Mosque and Panjunan Mosque, and plastered brick walls of Banten Grand Mosque and the mosques of Gala (c. 1500) and Giri (1544) in East Java, feature horizontal moldings and articulated frames for doorways and *mihrab* niches with stylized Javanese Indic motifs translated from the schema of Javanese *candi* façades and recreated in original abstracted forms.[42] The brick walls in the two Cirebon mosques stand separate from the last set of timber columns holding up the lowest roof tier, while the plastered brick walls of the latter examples support the lowest roof tier in place of columns.

Stone walls are also a feature of some early mosques. Melaka Sultanate's royal mosque, dismantled by the Portuguese upon their conquest of Melaka in 1511, had a square plan and thick walls built of "stone cubes," or laterite blocks, coated with lime plaster.[43] The seventeenth-century South Sulawesi *tajug* mosque of Palopo features unique 92cm thick walls of granite blocks, closely fitted without mortar and left un-plastered, in the manner of Javanese *candi*.[44] Melaka may indeed have had a stone *candi* tradition prior to its Islamization circa 1414, as a stone *makara* spout has been unearthed near the site of the Grand Mosque – its Islamic royal tombs, also dismantled by the Portuguese, were likewise built of stone. The plastered brick walls of seventeenth-century Katangka Mosque, South Sulawesi are also exceptionally thick. The late eighteenth-century Selo Mosque in Yogyakarta, Central Java is unique in being built entirely of stone, including its two-tier *tajug* roof and antechamber.[45] The thick walls on these mosques may have been intended to allow them to serve as fortifications of last resort –

10 Kasepuhan Grand Mosque, Cirebon, West Java, Indonesia, 1480, *mihrab* niche framed by pilasters with lotus bud capitals and stylized *kala-makara* motif crowned by the Majapahit sunburst royal emblem.
Photo: Imran bin Tajudeen

PRE-ISLAMIC AND VERNACULAR ELEMENTS IN NUSANTARA   415

11 Ampel Mosque and tomb complex, Surabaya, East Java, Indonesia, c.1450, one of five *paduraksa* gateways.
Photo: Imran bin Tajudeen

Melaka's Royal Mosque served such a purpose during the Portuguese siege in 1511.

The significance of thresholds is highlighted by the ornamentation of *minbar*s and *mihrab*s in Nusantara mosques. The design of *mihrab* niches and *minbar*s of carved timber ulitize geometricized or foliated pre-Islamic motifs. The *kala-makara* motif, which frames doorways and niches for statues in Javanese temples or *candi*s, frames the *mihrab* niches of Cirebon's Kasepuhan and Panjunan mosques, and are ubiquitously found on the gateway frames of Nusantara-style *minbar*s, as seen for example in Bali and Lombok,[46] and also in Melaka. In fact, the *minbar*s of Sendang Duwur, Ampel and Giri are akin to the "thrones" that are still used for autochthonous spirit-deities in Bali.[47]

**TOMB COMPLEXES:
WALLED COURTS, GATEWAYS AND TERRACES**

A distinct Javanese Islamic art attained its apogee in the proliferation of sixteenth-century mosque-and-tomb complexes that express not only the continuity of Javanese Indic motifs and forms, but also their innovative translation into new structures and layouts, and the invention of new forms. They form the loci of pilgrimage, *ziarah*, involving Javanese syncretic practices of Islamized meditation and the veneration of various Wali Songo proselytizers and deceased rulers who are regarded as spiritually potent.[48] The overall approach to the landscape in these complexes echo that of east Javanese *candi* complexes, older Javanese mountain shrines and terraced ancestral mounds or *punden*, and the Polynesian *marae* – ceremonial terraced stone courtyards – and terraced ancestral mound structures from Hawaii, Tonga, and French Polynesia. The mosque hall in these complexes is but one element within a much larger assemblage of buildings, various types of gateways, and walled courtyards, constructed in stone or brick and incorporating Javanese Indic stonework and architectonic forms.

The importance of thresholds is expressed in these complexes through elaborate split-gates *candi bentar*, and lintel-gates *paduraksa* or *kori agung*; courtyard walls are articulated by horizontal

12 Kudus Mosque, Central Java, Indonesia, 1549, three-tier *tajug* roof, original brick minaret, gateways and walls in the foreground, main hall in the centre background (rebuilt 1918) and new entrance gateway with stainless steel dome to the right (added 1933).
Photo: Imran bin Tajudeen

416 TAJUDEEN

moldings and geometric panel designs between pilasters topped by *candi laras*, miniature *candi*. In this respect, a progression from simpler early examples to more elaborate layouts can be discerned. In fifteenth-century Ampel five relatively plain *paduraksa* gateways mark the passage to the mosque and a series of three courts that culminates in a simple grave for Sunan Ampel (died 1471) (Fig. 11). Sixteenth-century complexes are more elaborate and lavishly decorated. Their series of courtyards may be aligned along an axis or follow a non-axial route; they may be built on flat or terraced hilly sites. The examples built on flat ground include Bonang (in Tuban, 1520s), Kadilangu (near Demak, 1532), Jipang (in Bojonegoro, 1540s), Kudus (1549), Mantingan (near Jepara, 1559), and Kotagede (c.1590s). Examples from hilly locations, where the mosque halls and main mausolea are located at the summit surrounded by walled courts containing other graves that descend the slopes, include Tembayat (c. 1512), Giri (1544), Sendang Duwur (1561), Gunung Sembung/Jati (near Cirebon, c.1570), Drajat (near Lamongan, late 1500s), and Imogiri (c.1640s).[49] The variety of expression in these gateways and remarkable sculpted landscapes is perhaps epitomized in the complexes of Kudus (Fig. 12) and of Sendang Suwur, the latter famous for its "winged gate" and to date the only complex for which a detailed monograph exists.[50]

The mausoleum buildings or *cungkup* are likewise richly ornamented. Carved stonework panels characterize the walls of the Kudus, Giri and Sendang Duwur mausolea. The stairway leading to Sunan Giri's hilltop *cungkup* is flanked by a pair of crowned *naga*s; this is an example of Javanese zoomorphic chronograms that give the Javanese Saka year of a building's completion.[51]

In contrast the Grand Mosques of Demak, Kasepuhan Cirebon, and Banten do not contain courtyard sequences, though the latter two mosques have walled compounds with several original brick lintel-gates. The compounds of Demak and Banten do however contain *cungkup* with two-tier *tajug* roofs built over the grave of important early rulers. Meanwhile Kotagede Grand Mosque is a modest two-tier *tajug* prayer hall set within the tomb complex for the founders of the powerful Islamic Mataram

kingdom (c.1584); the grave of the third ruler and subsequent kings of this dynasty, which continues through Yogyakarta and Surakarta today, are found in the lofty terraced sanctuary of Imogiri complex.

Unique tomb forms are also built by the Bugis and Makassarese of South Sulawesi and assume two forms: tall rectangular tombs of exposed brick whose molded profiles recall the bases of Javanese *candi*, and pyramid-domed masonry mausolea that typically incorporate simplified neoclassical moldings and ornament. The best examples are found near Makassar, in the sixteenth-century Tallo' royal cemetery and several seventeenth-century mausolea found next to Katangka Mosque.

ANCILLARY SPACES: THE *SERAMBI* ANNEX AND WOMEN'S PRAYER HALLS

Hip-roof annexes called *serambi* are a ubiquitous addition to the prayer hall of all four vernacular mosque types. The *serambi* is typically left unwalled, in contrast to the main prayer hall. The open nature of the *serambi* fits well with the various social functions it is meant to accommodate, which includes religious instruction; in the days of independent sultanates the *serambi* of royal mosques often functioned as the religious court of the *qadi*.

The *serambi* of the Great Mosque of Demak reputedly uses spoila columns taken from the *pendopo* or front pavilion of the Majapahit palace,[52] thus lending added legitimacy to the rulings of the upstart fifteenth-century coastal Islamic polity which had grown to become a regional power. Kasepuhan Cirebon meanwhile is distinguished by altogether seven *serambi* surrounding the core prayer chamber, including inner *serambi* beneath the lower hip roofs than lie outside the walls of the inner chamber; the eastern inner *serambi* has its own *soko tatal*.[53]

Women's prayer halls are built south of the main hall in some Javanese mosques. In Demak this hall, called the *pawestren*, is an original *limas* building of brick with white coral rock.[54] Yogyakarta's Grand Mosque likewise includes a *pawestren* in a *limas* hall built in 1839,[55] while Giri's *masjid wedok* or women's mosque is housed in a two-tier *tajug* building built in 1857.[56]

13 Grand Mosque, Palembang, South Sumatra, Indonesia, 1738–49, original hall with entrance portico, *mihrab* vestibule and old minaret (c.1753) to the right, and new hall and minaret (2003) to the left.
Photo: Imran bin Tajudeen

THE FIRST TWO MINARETS AT KUDUS AND BANTEN

The earliest known minaret in Nusantara is a tower in Kudus, Central Java (1549) built of exposed flat bricks that is modeled after the tall East Javanese *candi* with its high multi-level bases, with a wooden pavilion atop the tall brick structure bearing a chronogram giving the Javanese year equivalent to 1685; this is most likely the date of repair.[57] The brick tower is a unique geometricized version devoid of any of the figural representations that would typically adorn such structures. An inscription set into the wall above the *mihrab* provides the Arabic names al-Quds, Jerusalem (Kudus), though an initial reading of the term al-Manar, or "The Minaret," has been revised to al-Mubarak.[58] Subsequent minarets of old mosques tend to be later additions.

Banten Royal Mosque's unique minaret (1560s), often likened to a lighthouse, is a tapered hexagonal tower of brick and plaster.[59] It features an abstracted, geometricized *kori agung* gateway framing its doorway, and a *mustoko* finial.

TAJUG MOSQUES SINCE THE EIGHTEENTH CENTURY

The Dutch East Indies Company (VOC) initiated numerous wars in the region beginning in 1619 to pursue its goal of economic dominance, many of which utterly destroyed several pre-colonial Nusantara emporia and their Grand Mosques – among them Jayakarta (pre-colonial Batavia/Jakarta), Palembang, Banjarmasin, Makassar, Jepara, and Surabaya. One historian has dubbed these developments the region's "seventeenth-century crisis".[60] The dire consequences for Java in particular has had a visible effect on Javanese Islamic artistic developments from the eighteenth century.[61]

Eighteenth-century *tajug* Grand Mosques and *jami* mosques illustrate divergent trends in construction. While the lofty Grand Mosques of the Central Javanese kingdoms of Yogyakarta (1773) and Surakarta (1757),[62] and Banjarmasin's Jami Mosque, South Borneo (1777), retain full timber construction,[63] Sumenep Grand Mosque, Madura (1781) features thick masonry columns that support

14 Tengkera Mosque, Melaka, Malaysia, 1728, renovated 1890 and 1910, with brick minaret and gateway from 1910.
Photo: Ahmad bin Osman

15 Sawah Lio Mosque, Jakarta, Indonesia, 1717, four principal columns (*soko guru*) in masonry.
Photo: Imran bin Tajudeen

timber upper stories.[64] Conversely, Palembang Grand Mosque, South Sumatra (1738–49) (Fig. 13) features slender teak columns, masonry walls, distinctive horizontal plaster moldings that define a neck separating the top *tajug* tier from the lower roofs, and concrete roof ridges ornamented with repeated *tanduk* (horn) ornaments, giving these mosques a distinctive profile.[65] This set a precedent for other *tajug* mosques subsequently built in Palembang and the surrounding south Sumatran region.

Palembang and Melaka's urban neighborhood and suburban community mosques indicate that vernacular craft practice in the Nusantara continued up to the 1960s. Four eighteenth-century timber *tajug* mosques from Melaka were renovated in the late nineteenth and early twentieth centuries with masonry walls, tiled roofs, and concrete ridges while retaining their original four core columns made of *ulin* or *belian* ironwood, which were always specifically procured from Borneo. The *mustoko* finial ornaments in Melaka were built by craftsmen using coral stone collected by the local community. Meanwhile, the influence left by Chinese contractors employed for these renovations is evident in the hybrid roof ornamentation scheme in which the Chinese ridge form is combined with the Malayo-Javanese *mustoko* finial and *sulur bayung* ridge end ornaments. The four mosques are Peringgit (c. 1720, renovation date unknown), Kampung Keling (1728, renovation 1872), Melaka's former State Mosque at Tengkera (1728, renovated 1890, 1910) (Fig. 14), and Kampung Hulu (1728, renovated 1892).[66] Tengkera Mosque's timber *sulur bayung* ornaments are affixed to the end of the Chinese ridges. Interestingly, this is also the decorative detail of Batavia's (Jakarta) Angke Mosque (1761, renovation date unknown). The original timber mosque was built for a Muslim community from Bali.[67]

Early twentieth-century "Melaka-style" *tajug* mosques with masonry walls and timber columns are ubiquitous in Melaka State.[68] The last such mosque was built in 1964, and up to the 1930s the four principal columns of new mosques were always of imported Borneo ironwood.[69] This new hybrid-vernacular tradition also spread to neighboring areas, seen for example in two expunged *tajug* mosques

PRE-ISLAMIC AND VERNACULAR ELEMENTS IN NUSANTARA 419

from Singapore, Sultan Mosque (1824–1924) and Maarof Jeddah Street Mosque (1870–1980s).[70]

In contrast, many of the small *tajug* community mosques in colonial Batavia (Jakarta), such as the ones at Sawah Lio (1717) (Fig. 15), Tambora (1767), and eighteenth-century Kali Krukut and Mangga Dua, possessed masonry principal columns, while their tiled roofs were devoid of ridge end ornaments; the finials sometimes assumed the miniature false chimney form used for gable end summits on Dutch colonial buildings.[71]

Tajug-type Great Mosques (Masjid Raya) featuring neoclassical or Art Deco details were built in several towns under Dutch colonial rule – they include Makassar and Watampone in South Sulawesi, and Jember (c.1800s),[72] Sumedang (1850–54), Manonjaya (1873), and Carita Pandeglang (1889–95) in Java.[73] Examples from Java were typically commissioned by the local native governors and built by European firms.

REGIONAL MODEL VARIATIONS OF THE *TAJUG* MOSQUE

Wapauwe's modest timber structure, older than Demak's, is a square hall ten meters wide and a two-tier *tajug* roof of *rumbia* or sago thatch which retains its original form though it has been continually repaired.[74] It represents Maluku's vernacular construction – the timber structural members are tied together using *ijuk* cord – a feature of eastern Nusantara construction that is shared with Micronesia and Polynesia – and can be dismantled and reassembled at a different site.[75] Originally built on higher ground, Wapauwe Mosque has been relocated twice, reaching its present harbor town location in 1464.[76] Two comparable, well-preserved sixteenth-century thatched, two-tier *tajug* mosques also exist in Lombok, namely Bayan and Rambitan.[77] An expunged mosque at Lando Lake, Marawi in Mindanao, Philippines was also of this form.[78]

Other *tajug* mosques beyond Java likewise exhibit model variations based on local architectural practices. Javanese *tajug* mosques are built with stereobate floors directly on the ground; in Wapauwe and eastern Nusantara they are built with earth floors. In yet other areas *tajug* mosques were built with *panggung* or raised timber platform floors, and their roof profile and ornamentation are also executed in accordance with local practice. One example is Kampung Laut Mosque in Kelantan, northeastern Peninsular Malaysia,

built circa 1756 by Javanese migrants, with its bulbous *labu-labu* finial.[79]

The two earliest *tajug* mosques in the Banjarmasin cultural area of southern Borneo were reputedly built by proselytizers from Java – the sixteenth-century Pusaka Banua Lawas Mosque in Tabalong,[80] and the early seventeenth-century Kyai Gede Mosque in Kotawaringin-Pangkalan Bun.[81] The Banjarese *tajug* mosque is characterized by the use of ironwood (*belian*, *ulin*) and other hardwoods for columns and beams as well as for wood shingles and walls, and by a steep incline of the top roof tier, corresponding to the deliberately heightened pitch of the upper gable roof of the Banjarese vernacular house model, the *Rumah Bubungan Tinggi* (High Roof House). This characteristic high-peak roof form was reproduced by Banjarese migrants in Bagan Serai, Perak, Peninsular Malaysia when they built their congregational mosque Masjid Tinggi (Tall Mosque) in 1929.[82] In other Bornean Islamic polities beyond the Banjarese southern coast, royal or *jami* mosque of the *tajug* type built in ironwood adopted eclectic top-tier roof form. Examples include the royal mosques of Pontianak (1771) and Sambas (1885), and the *jami* mosque of Samarinda (1881) and Kutai (1930).[83]

The earliest extant examples of the Minangkabau variant of the *tajug* form are seen in the late sixteenth-century Old Wooden Mosque of Jao and the seventeenth-century Syekh Burhanuddin Mosque.[84] Unlike the previous examples, no direct Javanese links are discernable in their construction history. Moreover, etymological, structural, and formal features of Minangkabau pyramidal-hip-roof mosques suggest their independent development. Minangkabau mosques are called *surau* (small) and *surau gadang* (large); the term 'surau' has been compared to the root word in *pasuroan*, shrines for offerings to ancestral deities found in Batak communities living just north of the Minangkabau region.[85] The *surau* continued the function of pre-Islamic meeting halls and sleeping houses for male members of Minangkabau matrilineal clans.[86]

The Minangkabau *tajug* roof form tended to be steeper and had the distinction of curved roof ridges and eaves, and correspondingly curved wall plates and outward-slanting walls. This relates to the architecture of Minangkabau clan houses or *Rumah Gadang* with its saddle-back ridge profile and upturned gable ends with pinnacles made of tin, a characteristic repeated in *tajug* mosques in the form of elaborate finials. *Tajug* mosques built by Minangkabau migrants in eastern Sumatra and in Peninsular Malaysia's Negri Sembilan state reproduce the curved ridges and eaves that distinguish Minangkabau timber construction.[87]

Minangkabau *tajug* mosques are also distinguished by a central column, *tonggak macu* (Minangkabau, Malay/Indonesian *tiang mercu*). A distinct tower-pavilion form developed in nineteenth-century examples where a massive central trunk supports a pavilion or lantern at the pinnacle of the multi-tier roof. This lantern, typically octagonal, contains glass windows and an octagonal Mughal-style *chhatri* dome made of corrugated iron sheets – in this manner, a minaret is integrated with the apex of the pyramidal-hip roofs. This remarkable development is exemplified by the aforementioned Limo Kaum (Five Clans) Mosque, the *jami* mosque in Singkarak cooperatively built by five clans (c. 1750) and rebuilt in the course of the nineteenth century.[88]

The marketplace mosques of the coastal ports of Pariaman and Padang were also built in the form of pavilion-topped mosques. Their masonry walls and verandah additions incorporate European-style columns and moldings, and European patterned floor tiles. Padang's Ganting Mosque (c. 1876) has twenty-five pillars, and its central pillar supports a spiral staircase leading to its pavilion-tower.

Minangkabau influence or migration is reflected in the appearance of these mosque features outside West Sumatra. Palopo Mosque in South Sulawesi contains a single central column, and in fact three Minangkabau religious teachers are reputed to have been the agents of Islamization among the Makassarese and Bugis. One of these Minangkabau religious scholars had also been active at Pasir in southeast Borneo, and Pasir's royal mosque at Tanahgrogot possesses the *tonggak macu*.[89]

Some Minangkabau mosques have a top tier consisting of extended gable elevations on all four sides, an old Austronesian type that is also seen in the Karo Batak chiefs' *rumah anjung-anjung* and the ancestral skull house or *geriten*.[90] An example is the Lubuk Bauk mosque (1915–1920), which features a massive four-*gonjong* roof tier atop which sits a large octagonal pavilion. This model is adopted by the "Kotopiliang" *laras* (sections or moieties) which recognizes aristocracy, while the normal pyramidal-hip roof represents the more egalitarian "Bodi Caniago" *laras*.[91]

The adaptation and synthesis of simplified Corinthian columns and Dutch gables into mosques topped byeither four-*gonjong* tier topped or octagonal pavilion can be observed in three Minangkabau mosques: Rao-Rao Batusangkar (1918) (Fig.1); Gurun (Sa'adah) Batusangkar; and Muara Labuh, Solok Selatan. Their roofing material, originally in *ijuk* or areca palm thatch, has been replaced by corrugated iron sheets.

LIMAS MOSQUES
SINCE THE EIGHTEENTH CENTURY

Community mosques built through philanthropic *waqf* endowments (Malay/Indonesian *wakaf*) by Muslim merchants and philanthropists in colonial cities often feature one- or two-tier *limas* roofs. Some of these mosques were built or renovated by Hadhrami, Tamil, and southern Chinese Muslim communities and incorporate their distinctive motifs and architectural forms. Aspects of European neo-classicism are also integrated into their form and ornamentation. Examples with single-tier roofs include Penang's Lebuh Acheh Melayu Mosque (1808) and Batavia's Langgar Tinggi Pekojan (1829 or 1833). Singapore's Haji Muhammad Salleh Mosque (1909) and Khadijah Mosque (1920) (Fig. 16) and Batavia's Hidayatullah Mosque (1921) feature two-tier hip roofs.[92] Their roof ornaments and masonry columns and walls exhibit the synthesis of various combinations of Malay, Javanese, European neoclassical, and Tamil Muslim architectural motifs and forms, reflecting the taste of their patrons and the exigencies of construction practices and materials in the colonial

16 Khadijah Mosque, Singapore, 1920, two-tier *limas*-roof hall, gateway and compound wall.
Photo: Imran bin Tajudeen

17 Surau Tok Kerinchi, Kuala Terengganu, Malaysia, early 1900s, two-tier *limas* roof and timber construction.
Photo: Imran bin Tajudeen

milieu. Yet other examples attest to excellent indigenous timber craftsmanship, for instance the two-tier hip-roof Surau Tok Kerinchi in Kuala Terengganu (early 1900s) (Fig. 17).

Meanwhile, nineteenth-century royal mosques in the small kingdoms of Peninsular Malaysia and Riau-Lingga archipelagoes invariably feature simple hip roofs. Three large and opulent royal mosques in Johor Bahru (1892), Kuala Terengganu (mid-1800s) and Kota Bahru Kelantan (1922), and the *jami* mosque of Muar, a small Johor town, featured single-tier hip roofs and masonry walls augmented by small towers and elaborate neoclassical elements. Significantly, the examples from Johor were designed by Malay architects. Simple hip roofs also feature on the small royal mosques of Daik on Lingga Island (c.1803) and in Riau's famed Penyengat Island Royal Mosque (c.1760s) before the original hip roof was replaced by its distinctive multiple brick domes (1832).

NUSANTARA'S MINARETS SINCE THE EIGHTEENTH CENTURY

Minarets built since the eighteenth century in Nusantara were polygonal or circular tapered brick towers with plaster finish, and typically had one or two parapet levels or a top pavilion, and a tiled or concrete pitched roof capped by the *mustoko* ornament.[93] Palembang Grand Mosque's minaret (c. 1753) has an octagonal plan and a roof that was initially thatched before being replaced by terracotta tiles.

Several eighteenth- and nineteenth-century brick and plaster minarets were reminiscent of examples in the Hadhramaut, southern Yemen, with their characteristic tapered profiles, top pavilions and stucco ornaments; Hadhrami communities and leaders were dominant in the Muslim districts of colonial cities.[94] They were behind the construction of minarets in the mosques of Surabaya's Ampel District (c. 1746), Jakarta's An-Nawier Pekojan (Khwaja District) (1760), Penang's Acehnese Malay Quarter (1808), and Melaka's Kampung Hulu (1892).

Nineteenth-century Melaka and Minangkabau mosques featured free-standing minarets in masonry and plaster. Two early minarets in Melaka that were built by Chinese contractors resemble Chinese brick pagodas but are capped by *mustoko* finials and feature the Malay *sulur bayung* ridge end ornaments: Tengkera Mosque's octagonal minaret (1910), and Kampung Keling (Tamil Muslim) Mosque's square minaret (1872) – the Melaka minarets were meant to approximate the square and octagonal minarets of Tamil Nadu, India.[95] Later minarets in Melaka continued the tapered profile and steep roofs with *sulur bayung* ornament but displayed ornaments of European Classical derivation and were somewhat akin to cathedral spires – examples include the minarets at Duyong

422 TAJUDEEN

18 Minaret, Tanjung Keling Mosque, Melaka, Malaysia, 1930.
Photo: Imran bin Tajudeen

(1909) and Tanjung Keling (1930), Melaka (Fig. 18). Minangkabau minarets typically feature European moldings with local tendril motifs and European-style festoon ornaments, as seen in Jami Taluk's minaret (1860) and the twin minarets built for Syekh Burhanuddin Mosque from a nineteenth-century renovation.[96]

EPILOGUE: INDO-SARACENIC, MODERNIST, AND NEO-VERNACULAR MOSQUES

Developments since the turn of the twentieth century display three dominant trends. Aceh's seventeenth-century Grand Mosque was destroyed in 1879 by the invading Netherlands India colonial army; a military engineer designed and built the now famous replacement, Baiturrahman Mosque (1879–1881) in Mughal-Moorish eclectic style, including a shingle-roof central timber dome.[97] This eclectic domed form spread rapidly among new royal mosques in the northern Straits of Melaka region immediately around Aceh – in northern Sumatra's Serdang (1884), Tanjungpura Langkat (1899), Medan (1906–1909), and Labuhan Deli (1927),[98] and in northern Peninsular Malaysia at Kangar, Perlis (1910), Alor Setar, Kedah (1912), and Kuala Kangsar, Perak (1913–17).[99] This trend had become commonplace when British Indo-Saracenic imaginings also informed the design of the Jami Mosques built in Ipoh (1898), in colonial Malaya's capital Kuala Lumpur (1909), and in Singapore's Sultan Mosque, rebuilt in Indo-Saracenic style in 1924 to replace an old *tajug*-roof hall. This is the dramatic start of the Indo-Saracenic style mosques that broke with the vernacular type and is

dominant today, manifest in ever more exuberant creations throughout Nusantara.

The Istiqlal (Independence) Mosque of Indonesia (Istiqlal begun 1961, completed 1978) and Malaysia's Negara (National) Mosque (1965) meanwhile respectively feature a large hemispherical dome and a circular folded plate roof as their crowning features.[100] These forms demonstrate the attempt respectively to reject the *tajug* roof and appeal to the abstraction of the dome; and to re-interpret the *tajug* roof into an abstract form evoking an open royal umbrella alluding to the patronage of the Muslim community by Malaysia's traditional Sultanates.

Since the late twentieth century, the *tajug* type has been evoked in several neo-vernacular mosques exemplified by Melaka's Al-Azim State Mosque (1984–90) and numerous district mosques in Melaka State, Malaysia, as well as Darul Aman Mosque (1984) in Singapore. This trend has also been adopted for several early twenty-first-century Jami, Provincial or District Mosques in West Sumatra, Java and South Sulawesi, Indonesia.[101]

IMRAN BIN TAJUDEEN researches architectural encounters in maritime Southeast Asia across the longue durée. His research into mosque forms in transregional interactions and translations across vernacular and Indic architecture is published in *A Companion to Islamic Art and Architecture* (Wiley-Blackwell, 2017), and in *Journal18* (2017). He is a Visiting Fellow at the Oxford Centre for Islamic Studies and is writing a monograph on Southeast Asia's Islamic architecture. He is currently Visiting Senior Fellow at the Department of Malay Studies and the Department of Communications and New Media at the National University of Singapore.

SUGGESTIONS FOR FURTHER READING

Alam, Rudy Harisyah, ed. *Sejarah masjid-masjid kuno di Indonesia* (Jakarta: Badan Litbang Agama Departemen Agama RI, 1998).

Behrend, T. E. "Kraton, taman and mesjid: a brief survey and bibliographic review of Islamic antiquities in Java," *Indonesia Circle* 35 (November 1984), 29–55.

Budi, Bambang Setia. "A Study on the History and Development of the Javanese Mosque I: A Review of Theories on the Origin of the Javanese Mosque," *Journal of Asian Architecture and Building Engineering* 3,1 (2004), 189–195.

Nasir, Abdul Halim. *Mosque architecture in the Malay world*, trans. Omar Salahuddin Abdullah (Bangi: Penerbit Universiti Kebangsaan Malaysia, 2004).

O'Neill, Hugh. "South-East Asia," in *The Mosque: History, Architectural Development and Regional Diversity*, eds. Martin J. Frishman and Hasan Uddin Khan (London: Thames and Hudson, 1994), 225–240.

Zein, Abdul Baqir. *Masjid-masjid bersejarah di Indonesia* (Jakarta: Gema Insani, 1999).

NOTES

[1] Much of the original fieldwork outside Java upon which this chapter is based was conducted with the Asia Research Institute (ARI) Graduate Student Overseas Fieldwork Grant 2005, while extensive research was also conducted during the author's postdoctoral fellowship at two institutions: the Aga Khan Program for Islamic Architecture at MIT and at the International Institute of Asian Studies (IIAS), Leiden, the Netherlands, as well as with the National University of Singapore-MOE Tier 1 Grant (R–104-000-029-114).

[2] Michael Laffan, "Finding Java: Muslim nomenclature of insular Southeast Asia from Srivijaya to Snouck Hurgronje," in *Southeast Asia and the Middle East: Islam, movement, and the Longue Durée*, ed. Eric Tagliacozzo (Singapore: NUS Press, 2009), 17–64. The adjective *Jawi* also denotes the Malay *lingua franca* and the modified form of the Arabic script used to write the Malay language; a variant of this script called *Pegon* is used for Javanese.

[3] John N. Miksic and Endang Sri Hardiati Soekatno, *The Legacy of Trowulan* (Singapore: National Heritage Board, 1995).

[4] G. Drewes, "New light on the coming of Islam to Indonesia?" *Bijdragen tot de Taal-, Land- en Volkenkunde* 124, 4 (1968), 433–59; Martin van Bruinessen, "The origins and development of Sufi orders (tarekat) in Southeast Asia," *Studia Islamika – Indonesian Journal for Islamic Studies* 1.1 (1994), 1–23.

[5] A.H. Johns, "Modes of Islamization in Southeast Asia," in *Religious Change and Cultural Domination, 30th International Congress of Human Sciences in Asia and North Africa*, ed. David N. Lorenzen (Mexico City: El Colegio de México, 1981), 60–77; R. Jones, "Ten conversion myths from Indonesia," in *Conversion to Islam*, ed. Nehemia Levtzion (New York: Holmes & Meier, 1979), 129–58; L. F. Brakel, "Islam and local traditions: syncretic ideas and practices," *Indonesia and the Malay World* 32.92 (2004), 5–20; Rota Rose Di Meglio, "Arab Trade with Indonesia and the Malay Peninsula from the 8th to the 16th century," in *Islam and the trade of Asia: A Colloquium*, ed. Donald Sidney Richards (Philadelphia: University of Pennsylvania Press, 1970), 105–135.

[6] Parmono Atmadi, *Some Architectural Design Principles of Temples in Java: a Study Through the Buildings Projection on the Reliefs of Borobudur Temple* (Yogyakarta: Gadjah Mada University Press, 1988); Theodoor Paul Galestin, *Houtbouw Op Oost-Javaansche Tempelreliefs* ('s-Gravenhage: Proefschrift RU Leiden, 1936). On the Sumatran clay tablets see Mai-Lin Tjoa-Bonatz, J. David Neidel, and Agus Widiatmoko, "Early Architectural Images from Muara Jambi on Sumatra, Indonesia," *Asian Perspectives* 48, 1 (2009), 32–55; Jacques Dumarçay and Michael Smithies, *Cultural Sites of Malaysia, Singapore, and Indonesia* (New York and Kuala Lumpur: Oxford University Press), 31 and Fig. 8.

[7] Bambang Setia Budi, "A Study on the History and Development of the Javanese Mosque II: The Historical Setting and Role of the Javanese Mosque under the Sultanates," *Journal of Asian Architecture and Building Engineering* 4.1 (2005), 1–8; Bambang Setia Budi, "A Study on the History and Development of the Javanese Mosque III: Typology of the Plan and Structure of the Javanese Mosque and Its Distribution," *Journal of Asian Architecture and Building Engineering* 5, 2 (2006), 229–36.

[8] Yuwono Sudibyo, *Arsitektur Tradisional Mesjid Sumatera Barat: Pengamatan Sepintas* (Padang: Author, 1987).

[9] Sugeng Haryadi, *Sejarah berdirinya Masjid Agung Demak dan Grebeg Besar* (Godong: Mega Berlian, 2002), 19.

[10] Abdul Baqir Zein, *Masjid-masjid bersejarah di Indonesia* (Jakarta: Gema Insani, 1999), 170; Budi Cahyana, *Ziarah Masjid dan Makam* (Jakarta: Departemen Kebudayaan dan Pariwisata, 2006), 89; Yulianto Sumalyo, *Sejarah Arsitektur Masjid dan monument sejarah Muslim* (Yogyakarta: Gajah Mada University Press, 2000), 541; Hugh O'Neill, "South-East Asia," in *The Mosque History Architectural Development and Regional Diversity*, eds., Frisman, Martin J. and Hasan Uddin Khan (London: Thames and Hudson, 1994), 235 (225–240).

[11] Martin van Bruinessen. "Najmuddin al-Kubra, Jumadil Kubra and Jamaluddin al-Akbar: Traces of Kubrawiyya influence in early Indonesian Islam," *Bijdragen tot de Taal-, Land- en Volkenkunde* 150 (1994), 305–329; and section on "The 'Nine Saints' of Java" in Frederick M. Denny, "Islam and the Muslim Community," in *Religious Traditions of the world: A Journey through Africa, Mesoamerica, North America, Judaism, Christianity, Islam, Hinduism, Buddhism, China, and Japan*, ed. H Byron Earhart, (San Francisco: HarperSanFrancisco, 1993), 603–712.

[12] Peter Carey, "Civilisation on Loan: The Making of an Upstart Polity: Mataram and its Successors, 1600–1830," Special Issue: The Eurasian Contexts of the Early Modern History of Mainland Southeast Asia, 1400–1800 *Modern Asian Studies* 31, 3 (July 1997), 711–34. For a specific illustration of the art of Majapahit in the Pasisir cultural context, see Uka Tjandrasasmita, "Art de Mojopahit et art du Pasisir," *Archipel* 9 (1975), 93–8.

13 Junus Satrio Atmodjo, ed. *Masjid kuno Indonesia*. (Jakarta: Direktorat Perlindungan dan Pembinaan Peninggalan Sejarah dan Purbakala, Direktorat Jenderal Kebudayaan, Departemen Pendidikan dan Kebudayaan, 1999), 150; Haryadi, *Sejarah berdirinya Masjid Agung Demak*, 19-20.

14 Satyawati Suleiman, *The Pendopo Terrace of Panataran* (Jakarta: Proyek Pelita Pembinaan Kepurbakalaan dan Peninggalan Nasional, 1978), 39.

15 Yuwono Sudibyo, *Arsitektur Tradisional Mesjid Sumatera Barat* (Lampiran Gambar), Drawing Appendices 7a, 7b, 7c.

16 Galih Widjil Pangarsa, "Les mosquées de Lombok, évolution architecturale et diffusion de l'islam," *Archipel* 44 (1992), 75-93.

17 See Hugh O'Neill, "South-East Asia," on a comparison of the four principal posts in Javanese mosques with a similar structural type in Sumbanese houses.

18 T. D. Sudjana, *Masjid Agung Sang Ciptarasa dan muatan mistiknya* (Bandung: Humaniora Utama Press, 2003), 29.

19 M. Amin Nurdin and Jusna Joesoef Ahmad, "Islamic Influences in Javanese Court Art," *Kultur* 1 no. 2 (2001), 64-65.

20 Compare the structural features of these building forms as illustrated in R. K. Ismunandar, *Joglo: arsitektur rumah tradisional Jawa* (Semarang: Dahara Prize, 1986).

21 Bambang Setia Budi, "A Study on the History and Development of the Javanese Mosque I: A Review of Theories on the Origin of the Javanese Mosque," *Journal of Asian Architecture and Building Engineering* 3,1 (2004), 189-95. For a summary and discussion of the claims by the following Dutch scholars: G. F. Pijper, "The Minaret in Java," in *India Antiqua. A Volume of Oriental Studies Presented by his Friends and Pupils to Jean Philippe Vögel*, eds. F. D. K. Bosch et. al., 274-83 (Leiden: Brill, Kern Institute, 1947); W. F. Stutterheim, *Leerboek der indische cultuuregeschiedenis* vol. 3, De Islam en Ziijn komst in den archipel (Valenbreder: Antiquarian Bookseller, 1835); H. J. De Graaf, "The Origin of the Javanese Mosque," *Journal of Southeast Asian History* 4,1 (March, 1963), 1-5.

22 Atmodjo, *Masjid Kuno*, 152; Yulianto, *Sejarah Arsitektur Masjid*, 504.

23 Yulianto, *Sejarah Arsitektur Masjid*, 477.

24 Sri Sugiyanti, *Masjid kuno Indonesia* (Jakarta: Direktorat Perlindungan dan Pembinaan Peninggalan Sejarah dan Purbakala, Direktorat Jenderal Kebudayaan, Departemen Pendidikan dan Kebudayaan, 1999), 180, gives the date of mosque completion and the death of Sunan Ampel as 1450 and 1481, while M Habib Mustopo, *Kebudayaan Islam di Jawa Timur: kajian beberapa unsur budaya masa peralihan* (Yogyakarta: Jendela Grafika, 2001), 54, gives 1440 and 1468 respectively.

25 See building section in Zein M. Wiryoprawiro, *Perkembangan arsitektur masjid di Jawa Timur* (Surabaya: Bina Ilmu, 1986), 185.

26 Yulianto Sumalyo, *Sejarah Arsitektur Masjid*, 504.

27 Abdul Halim Nasir, *Mosque Architecture in the Malay world*, trans. Omar Salahuddin Abdullah (Bangi: Penerbit Universiti Kebangsaan Malaysia, 2004), 54.

28 See engraving in Wouter Schouten, *Oost-Indische Voyagie* (Amsterdam: J. Meurs, 1676), 39.

29 Mohammad Zamberi Abdul Malek, *Wadi al-Hussein: masjid kayu terindah* (Bangi: Penerbit Universiti Kebangsaan Malaysia, 2001); Atmodjo, *Masjid Kuno*, 41.

30 Suthep Sudwilai, ed., *Muslim Worship Sites in Thailand* (Bangkok: Middle East Division, Department of South Asian, Middle East, and African Affairs, Ministry of Foreign Affairs, 2001), 62.

31 Sudibyo, *Arsitektur Tradisional Mesjid Sumatera Barat* (Lampiran Foto), Photo Appendix 2.

32 Rosnawati Othman, "The Language of the Langkasukan Motif," *Indonesia and the Malay World*, 33, 96 (2005), 97-111.

33 Wayne Bougas, "Surau Aur : Patani Oldest Mosque,"*Archipel* 43 (1992), 89-112.

34 See image in Abdul Halim Nasir, *Panduan ke tempat-tempat bersejarah, Kelantan = Guide to Historical Sites, Kelantan* (Kuala Lumpur: Jabatan Muzium, 1979), 170-1.

35 Imran bin Tajudeen, "Mosques and Minarets: Transregional Connections in eighteenth-century Southeast Asia," *Journal*18 4 (2017).

36 For a detailed treatment of the design motifs on the ridge ends and finials of Melakan mosques, see Abdullah b. Mohammed (Nakula), *Bentuk-bentuk bangunan masjid: kunci memahami kebudayaan Melayu* (Kuala Lumpur: Kementerian Kebudayaan Belia dan Sukan, Malaysia, 1978).

37 Imran bin Tajudeen, "Mosques and Minarets".

38 Abdullah b. Mohammed, *Bentuk-bentuk bangunan masjid*, 24, 31; Hamka (Haji Abdul Malik Karim Amrullah), *1001 soal-soal hidup* (Jakarta: Penerbit Bulan Bintang, 1961).

39 Sakai Takashi, "Preliminary Study of Vietnamese Decorated Tiles Found in Java, Indonesia (1)," 美術史研究集刊 25, 国立台湾大学芸術史研究所 (*Journal of Art Historical Studies*, National Taiwan University Institute for Art History) 25 (2008), 131-66; Sakai Takashi, "Preliminary Study of Vietnamese Decorated Tile Found In Java, Indonesia (2)" 金沢大学考古学紀要 (*Kanazawa Bulletin of Archaeology*) 30 (March 2009), 28-41; John Guy, "The Vietnamese Wall Tiles of Majapahit," *Transactions of the Oriental Ceramics Society* 53 (1988-9), 27-46.

40 Martin van Bruinessen, "Kurdish 'Ulama and Their Indonesian Disciples," *Les Annales de l'autre Islam* 5 (1998), 83-106.

41 Atmodjo, *Masjid Kuno*, 183. On the Javanese inscriptional chronogram over the *mihrab* of Mantingan Mosque on a square terracotta medallion, see ibid., 160.

42 Zein M. Wiryoprawiro, *Perkembangan arsitektur masjid di Jawa Timur* (Surabaya: Bina Ilmu, 1986), 199, 208; Inayati Adrisiyanti Romli, *Masjid Gala, Bayat dan pemugarannya [Klaten]* (Semarang: Bagian Proyek Pelestarian/Pemanfaatan Peninggalan Sejarah dan Purbakala Jawa Tengah, Departemen Pendidikan dan Kebudayaan, 1993), 3; Atmodjo, *Masjid Kuno*, 164, 165, 183.

43 Manuel Joaquim Pintado, *Portuguese documents on Malacca* (Kuala Lumpur : National Archives of Malaysia, 1993), 243.

44 Yulianto, *Sejarah Arsitektur Masjid*, 538.

45 Marcel Bonneff. "La 'Mosquée de pierre' (Masjid Sélo) de Yogyakarta," *Archipel* 30 (1985), L'Islam en Indonésie II: 31-8.

46 Moh. Ali Fadillah, "L'art ancien des mimbar dans les mosquées de Bali," *Archipel* 44 (1992), 95-114; Pangarsa, "Les mosquées de Lombok".

47 Wiryoprawiro, *Perkembangan arsitektur*, 220.

48 M. Mufti Mubarok. *Kaji blangkon : hajinya orang Jawa* (Surabaya: Java Pustaka Media Utama, 2008). Nelly van Doorn-Harder and Kees de Jong, "The Pilgrimage to Tembayat: Tradition and Revival in Indonesian Islam," in *The Blackwell Companion to Contemporary Islamic Thought*, ed. Ibrahim M Abu-Rabi' (Oxford: Blackwell Pub., 2006), 483-505.

49 Inayati Adrisiyanti Romli, *Masjid Gala, Bayat dan pemugarannya [Klaten]* (Semarang: Bagian Proyek Pelestarian/Pemanfaatan Peninggalan Sejarah dan Purbakala Jawa Tengah, Departemen Pendidikan dan Kebudayaan, 1993), 3; Tjandrasasmita, "Art de Mojopahit"; Uka Tjandrasasmita, *Islamic Antiquities of Sendang Duwur*, trans. Satyawati Suleiman (Jakarta: Archaeological Foundation, 1975).

50 Tjandrasasmita, *Islamic Antiquities*.

51 Wiryoprawiro, *Perkembangan arsitektur*, 195, 210, 223-8.

52 Haryadi, *Sejarah berdirinya Masjid Agung Demak*, 33-4.

53 Atmodjo, *Masjid Kuno*, 103-4.

54 Tutin Aryanti, "The Center vs. The Periphery in Central-Javanese Mosque Architecture," *Dimensi Teknik Arsitektur* 34, 2 (December 2006), 73-80; Atmodjo, *Masjid Kuno*, 152.

55 Hasan Basri. "Masjid Besar Kauman Yogyakarta," in *Sejarah masjid-masjid kuno di Indonesia*, ed. Rudy Harisyah Alam. (Jakarta: Badan Litbang Agama Departemen Agama RI, 1998), 28.

56 Wiryoprawiro, *Perkembangan arsitektur*, 199.

57 Isman Pratama Nasution, "Menara masjid kuna Indonesia: suatu survei dan studi kepustakaan," *Wacana: jurnal ilmu pengetahuan budaya* 6, 1 (2004), 36.

58 Ludvik Kalus and Claude Guillot, "Kota Yerusalem di Jawa dan Mesjidnya Al-Aqsa: Piagam pembangunan Mesjid Kudus bertahun 956H/1549M," in *Inskripsi Islam tertua di Indonesia*, eds. Claude Guillot and Ludvik Kalus (Jakarta: Gramedia and EFEO, 2008), 101–32.

59 For alternative dating, see Nasution, "Menara masjid kuna," 32; Abdul Baqir Zein, *Masjid-masjid bersejarah*, 164a; Yulianto Sumalyo, *Sejarah Arsitektur Masjid*, 501.

60 Anthony Reid, "The 'Seventeenth Century Crisis' as an approach to Southeast Asian History," *Modern Asian Studies* 24, 4 (1990), 639–59.

61 Imran bin Tajudeen, "Mosques and Minarets".

62 Atmodjo, *Masjid Kuno*, 153.

63 Narliswandi, *Historic Mosque*, 83–4; Atmodjo, *Masjid Kuno*, 163; Taufiq Hidayat and Harry Widodo, eds., *Masjid-masjid bersejarah dan ternama Indonesia: direktori* (Jakarta: Permata Communications, 2005), 125.

64 Wiryoprawiro, *Perkembangan arsitektur*, 230

65 Djohan Hanafiah, *Masjid Agung Palembang : sejarah dan masa depannya* (Jakarta: Haji Masagung, 1988).

66 *Sejarah masjid-masjid dalam negeri Melaka*, 23, 24, 27.

67 Adolf Heuken, *Historical Sites of Jakarta* (Jakarta: Cipta Loka Caraka, 1982), 159.

68 *Sejarah masjid-masjid dalam negeri Melaka* (Malaysia : s.n., 1979); and Mohamed bin Hj Ahmad, Datuk Hj. *Sejarah ringkas masjid-masjid Negeri Melaka* (Kuala Lumpur: Majlis Agama Islam Melaka, 1989)

69 Abdul Halim Nasir, *Seni bina masjid di Dunia Melayu-Nusantara* (Bangi: Penerbit Universiti Kebangsaan Malaysia, 1995), 34, 35

70 Imran bin Tajudeen. "State Constructs of Ethnicity in the Reinvention of Malay-Indonesian Heritage in Singapore," *Traditional Dwellings and Settlements Review* 18, 2 (2007), 7–27.

71 See images in Philippus Samuel Van Ronkel, *Moskeeen van Batavia* (Amsterdam: Jan Luykenstr, 1916).

72 Image in H. Aboebakar, *Sedjarah mesdjid dan amal ibadah dalamnja* (Banjarmasin: Adil & Co., 1956), 200

73 Hidayat and Widodo, *Masjid-masjid bersejarah*, 82, 86, 87.

74 Moh. Zahid, "Masjid Mapauwe [sic] Kaitetu, Leihitu Maluku Tengah," in *Sejarah masjid-masjid kuno di Indonesia*, ed. Rudy Harisyah Alam (Jakarta: Badan Litbang Agama Departemen Agama RI, 1998), 123–32.

75 This construction technique, using lashings from vegetal cord, is a feature of eastern Nusantara that is shared with Micronesia and Polynesia.

76 Moh. Zahid, "Masjid Mapauwe [sic]', 123; M. Azis Tunny, "How old [is] Wapauwe Mosque?" The official site of Dinas Kebudayaan & Pariwisata Provinsi Maluku (Maluku Province Ministry of Culture and Tourism), last modified June 15, 2009, http://www.disbudparmaluku.org/index.php/component/content/article/36-study-case/202-how-old-wapauwe-mosque.html

77 Galih Widjil Pangarsa. "Les mosquées de Lombok, évolution architecturale et diffusion de l'islam," *Archipel* 44 (1992), 75–93; Atmodjo, *Masjid Kuno*, 201–5.

78 See Abdul Halim Nasir, *Mosque Architecture*, 75, for an old photograph of this Marawi mosque.

79 As recorded by Abdul Halim Nasir, *Panduan ke tempat-tempat bersejarah, Kelantan*, 139. See also Jacques Dumarçay, "La mosquée de Kampung Laut (Kelantan): étude architectural," *Archipel* 44 (1992), 115–22.

80 Atmodjo, *Masjid Kuno*, 90.

81 Narliswandi et.al., eds., *Historic Mosque in Indonesia – Masjid-Masjid Bersejarah di Indonesia* (Jakarta: Jayakarta Agung Offset, 1994), 52.

82 See drawing in Abdul Halim Nasir, *Mosque Architecture*, 70.

83 Ahmad Musthofa Hadna, "Masjid Jami' Sultan Abdurrahman Pontianak Kalimantan Barat," in *Sejarah masjid-masjid kuno di Indonesia*, ed. Rudy Harisyah Alam (Jakarta: Badan Litbang Agama Departemen Agama RI, 1998), 185–199; Atmodjo, *Masjid Kuno*, 86; Narliswandi, *Historic Mosque*, 45, 48–9, 54–5.

84 Usria Dhavida, ed., *Masjid dan surau tua di Sumatera Barat* (Padang: Museum Daerah Sumatera Barat Adityawarman, 2002), 59–64, 80; Atmodjo, *Masjid Kuno*, 41–2; Sugiyanti, *Masjid kuno*, 42.

85 Roxana Waterson, *The Living House: An Anthropology of Architecture in South-East Asia* (Singapore: Oxford University Press, 1990), 48.

86 Waitlem, *Surau* (Jakarta: Dian Ariesta, 2002), 2–4, 19, 20–5.

87 See Abdul Halim Nasir, *Mosque Architecture*, 71–2, for two examples of Minangkabau mosques in Negri Sembilan, Peninsular Malaysia.

88 Al Humam M. Z., *Benda-benda bersejarah sebagai khazanah kebudayaan Islam di Indonesia: Sejarah masjid raya/kuno lima kaum di Kabupaten Tanah Datar Batu Sangkar Propinsi Sumatera Barat*, ed. Musdah Mulia (Jakarta:Pusat Penelitian dan Pengembangan Lektur Agama, 1999), 18–19, 25.

89 Christian Pelras, "Religion, Tradition, and the Dynamics of Islamization in South Sulawesi," *Indonesia* 57 (April 1994), 133–54.

90 The latter comparison is also made by O'Neill, "South-East Asia," 238; a picture of a *geriten* is reproduced in Waterson, *The Living House*, 5.

91 Yuwono Sudibyo, *Arsitektur tradisional mesjid Sumatera Barat*, 43.

92 See also Henri Chambert-Loir and Jacques Dumarçay, "Le Langgar Tinggi de Pekojan, Jakarta," *Archipel* 30, L'Islam en Indonésie II (1985), 47–56.

93 For a typological discussion of early minarets from Indonesia, see Isman Pratama Nasution, "Menara masjid kuna Indonesia." A pictorial survey that includes examples from Malaysia is found in Abdul Halim Nasir, *Mosque Architecture*, 155–9.

94 Peter G. Riddell, "Arab Migrants and Islamization in the Malay World during the Colonial Period," *Indonesia and the Malay World* (2001) 29, 84, 113–28.

95 Imran bin Tajudeen, "Mosques and Minarets".

96 Yulianto, *Sejarah Arsitektur*, 477

97 O'Neill, "South-East Asia," 225; Bunyamin Yusuf, "Masjid Baiturrahman Banda Aceh," in *Sejarah masjid-masjid kuno di Indonesia*, ed. Rudy Harisyah Alam (Jakarta: Badan Litbang Agama Departemen Agama RI, 1998), 201 (201–218).

98 Puspa Dewi, *Exploring Old Mosques in North Sumatra* (Jakarta: Department of National Education, 2001), 12–19.

99 Nash Rahman, *Masjid: sejarah, ciri-ciri pembentukan dan pembinaan masjid-masjid dunia, Malaysia dan Kuala Lumpur* (Kuala Lumpur: Puncak Awal, 1998), 278, 282.

100 Solichin Salam, *Masjid Istiqlal : Sebuah monumen Kemerdekaan* (Jakarta : Pusat Studi dan Penelitian Islam, 1990); Yong, Long Lim and Nor Hayati Hussain, *Masjid Negara, The National Mosque.* (Kuala Lumpur: Creative Communications, 1990).

101 Imran bin Tajudeen, "Adaptation and Accentuation: Type Transformation in Vernacular Nusantarian Mosque Design and their Contemporary Signification in Melaka, Minangkabau and Singapore," *Pace or Speed? 4th International Seminar on Vernacular Settlement* (Ahmedabad: Print Vision, 2008), 158–62.

The Mosque in China   NANCY S. STEINHARDT

1 Minaret, Huaisheng Mosque, Guangzhou, Guangdong province, 1350 with later restoration.
Photo: Nancy Steinhardt

Islam is the unique monotheistic, aniconic religion that has maintained a significant presence in China for nearly 1400 years, almost as long as the history of the faith itself. In China as elsewhere, the mosque is the center of communal religious life, Muslim education, and socialization. One of the reasons mosques have survived and often flourished is because their architectural necessities can be accommodated by the Chinese building system. Mosques stand on the Chinese landscape alongside traditional Buddhist, Daoist, and Confucian religious architecture with few exterior features to indicate their purpose, much less their original building date. China's architectural tradition makes this possible. Approximately seventy Chinese mosques retain buildings or inscriptions of historic interest. They comprise a tiny fraction of the more than 39,000 mosques in China today.

CHINA'S FIRST MUSLIMS
AND EARLIEST WORSHIP SPACES

Chinese records inform us that an envoy from the region named Dashiguo (usually translated "Arab lands") paid respects to the Chinese emperor in the capital city Chang'an (today Xi'an) in 651, fewer than forty years after the rise of Islam on the Arabian Peninsula.[1] Ambassadors had been coming to China's capitals Luoyang and Jiankang (today Nanjing) from the Sasanian empire at least 200 years earlier.[2] Between 798 and 946, at least thirty-five Arab and twenty Persian envoys came to China.[3] If someone from Arab lands was in China in the seventh century, Chang'an is a likely place for him to have been. Capital of China's Tang dynasty (618–907), the city had a population of more than one million that included practitioners of Zoroastrianism, Manichaeism, and Church

of the East Christianity (Nestorianism), as well as Buddhism and Daoism. All five groups had religious institutions.[4] The Chinese names of all of them ended in the character *si*, a word borrowed from its original meaning of official institution to a suffix for a worship space. There is no physical evidence of a mosque in the Tang capital, although a line on a placard at a mosque today known as Daxuexixiang Mosque infers construction in the early eighth century.[5] If worship occurred in Chang'an, it probably took place in private houses. Such had been the case in the first decade of Islam in Arabia, and such was the practice for Buddhism in the early CE centuries when that religion entered China from the West and domiciles were converted into houses of worship.[6]

Perhaps the Muslims in Chang'an were neither numerous nor permanent enough to sustain a mosque. Travel to Chang'an from the West was almost exclusively by land routes along the Silk Roads. By the Tang dynasty, Arabs also were coming to China by boat. Sea routes circled southern India, with ships arriving at port cities along China's southeastern coast. Sometimes referred to as the Silk Road of the Sea,[7] entry into China by boat for mercantile purposes became even more frequent after the fall of the Tang dynasty when land travel across Central Asia became more dangerous. The earliest extant mosques in China are in the most important international southeastern entrepôts, Guangzhou (Canton), Quanzhou (Zayton), Hangzhou, and Yangzhou. By the year 900, there are said to have been 120,000 foreign merchants in Guangzhou.[8] There is no record what percent of them were Muslim.

Whenever and wherever Muslims first entered China, the architecture around them was already a coherent system with a multi-millennial history.

Any Muslim who had worshiped in a mosque in West, Central, or South Asia had prayed in spaces untouched by the Chinese architectural system. The convergence of the two building systems would require little accommodation of existing Chinese architecture. At the same time, the necessities of Muslim worship space would not be compromised.

CHINESE AND MOSQUE ARCHITECTURAL SPACE SUMMARIZED

The Chinese building system has been largely immune to innovation or change for the first nineteen centuries of the Common Era. The following features have governed Chinese buildings and the placement of buildings in relation to one another since that time: 1) Chinese buildings are not conceived in isolation – inherent to the concept of a building is that it is part of a group of structures. 2) Buildings form around four-sided, enclosed courtyards. 3) Space develops horizontally along major north-south and east-west axes. Spatial magnitude is expressed by longer and longer horizontal axes, not vertically. 4) Building complexes have focal structures along major axial lines, with balance achieved by a symmetrical disposition of buildings and space. 5) Formal gateways mark entries both to individual building complexes and to units of those complexes as large as cities. They are psychological as much as physical structures. Like the enclosing spaces to which they may join, gates mark the boundaries between more sanctified or imperial space behind them and the profane world in front or outside them. 6) The core of a Chinese building is the flexible timber frame, easily adaptable to increase, decrease, or movement of individual components. Replacement due to damage or movement of parts due to change of purpose is simple. A palace hall becomes a temple by moving interior pillars and replacing a throne with an altar; yet the decorative roof above it and courtyard that encloses it are unchanged. 7) Chinese architecture is modular. The measurement and proportions of the module indicate a building's eminence. 8) Eminence is indicated by the height of a platform, plinth, use of marble, balustrades,

number of pieces of a bracket set, and roof type, but none of these features indicates a building's purpose. 9) Chinese architecture is highly polychromed, with color integral to a decorative scheme. 10) Domes and other intricately constructed ceilings are standard in eminent buildings. 11) Behind the façade, courtyard, gate, and outer wall, interior space is totally private. The Forbidden City is a well-known complex where one can see all eleven features.

Evolution still occurs in Chinese architecture, particularly in bracket set formations. But the fundamental features – pillars that define a bay system, bracket sets, roof frame, and ceramic tile roof – are as immutable as the arrangement of buildings in space, no matter the specific components used to put them together.

The necessities of mosque construction are also few. Of the five architectural features associated with a mosque, only the *qibla*, the wall oriented in the direction of the Kaaba in Mecca, usually indicated by the *mihrab* niche, is necessary. Three others, a stepped pulpit (*minbar*), *maqsura* (enclosure for an important person such as the caliph), and courtyard (*sahn*), modeled after the Prophet Muhammad's house, are easily accommodated into Chinese construction, as is a pool for ablutions. The minaret is not essential. If mosques existed in the Tang period, it is unknown if they had minarets; by the Song dynasty (960–1279), the minaret was present at some Chinese mosques. Finally, Muslim prayer occurs in a large, open space, which was especially true in China where almost every mosque was congregational.

Like the Chinese palace or monastery, the mosque is a group of buildings. The Chinese word for mosque logically takes the suffix *si*, a character originally referring to an official institution that came to be used as the suffix for a Buddhist monastery. *Qingzhensi* (pure true worship complex), is also the Chinese word for synagogue; Bosisi (Persian *si*) is the Chinese word for a Zoroastrian religious complex. *Zhenjiaosi* (true religion *si*) is an alternate Chinese word for mosque. The prayer hall in a Chinese mosque is often called *libaitang*, the word for worship hall in a Buddhist monastery or Chinese church. Chinese names for minaret vary. They include *bangke lou*, *bangke* derived from *bang*, the Persian word for minaret, and *lou* meaning tower in Chinese; and *huanli lou* (call to prayer tower).

The buildings that are part of or adjacent to Chinese monasteries and mosques are similar. First are educational structures. Buddhist, Daoist, and Confucian complexes historically have included schools, a religious institutional setting often the only means of education for poor boys in premodern China. Similarly, *madrasa*, usually schools of higher learning, often are adjacent to or affiliated with mosques, and elementary education often is provided in a building within the mosque complex. Second, lecture halls for the education of clergy and sometimes for visitors to receive religious training also are part of monastery and mosque complexes. In both China and the Islamic world, dormitories for students and hostels for short-term visitors are often part of the religious complexes. Third, markets, often the unique open meeting area where someone from city or country can come to hear the news as well as shop often are located in the front courtyard of a mosque or monastery. Finally, a time-keeping structure usually exists at both mosques and monasteries. In a mosque, calls from the minaret remind worshipers of the five daily calls to prayer, and in addition, since the nineteenth century a clock has been present in the worship hall of a mosque.[9] In China the structure is either a bell or drum tower. Like a minaret, a tower is higher than the other buildings in its complex, and it includes a device that is rung or beaten to let monks know the time of day, including prayer times.

TWO EARLY MOSQUES

China's oldest mosques are in the southeastern port cities Guangzhou and Quanzhou. Both are among the most important mosques in China.

Legend says that Huaishengsi (Cherishing the Prophet Mosque; the Chinese word for sage [*sheng*] is translated as Prophet) in Guangzhou was founded by a relative of Muhammad in 627. The earliest date of any existing building is 1350. Huaishengsi was restored in 1695, 1935, and more recently. The prayer hall dates to 1935.[10]

The most unusual structure of Huaishengsi is the minaret, named Guangta (Tower of Light).[11] The syllable *ta* in its name is the Chinese character most often translated as pagoda, an example, like *si*, that indicates the incorporation of the mosque into the vocabulary of Chinese religious architecture. Guang, meaning light or brightness, is explained as a translation of the Arabic *manara*, meaning light, perhaps because it was a beacon for ships coming into the port or a tower from which the direction of the wind was determined; and as symbolic of the power (light) of Islam in Guangzhou.[12]

Elevated on a circular platform, Guangta is a brick building covered with white stucco that rises 35.75 meters at the southwest corner of the complex (Fig. 1). The structure has precedents in China. Brick walls of subterranean tombs were faced with white lime to provide a painting surface in the early CE centuries in China. The White Pagoda of Miaoying Monastery in Beijing, dated 1279, is a tall building with a brick circular drum covered by white plaster walls.

Although the mosque was larger in the past than today, the minaret always was visible from far beyond the mosque's exterior walls. Song literatus Yue Ke (1183–1234) wrote in *Tingshi* (Bedside-table history) that the building was like no tower he had ever seen.[13] Yue Ke further wrote that there were ten stairs on each level of the interior. One wonders if he had ascended, or if this statement is based on a verbal or written description; and if Yue ascended, if he was a Muslim or if non-Muslims were permitted entrance to the Guangta.

The ability to ascend inside raises the possibility that pagodas may have been precedents for the minaret's structure. A majority of pagodas in eleventh- and twelfth-century China were brick and octagonal, the octagon perhaps as close to a circle as a builder could accomplish using the straight sides of Chinese construction. The octagonal Liaodi Pagoda of Kaiyuan Monastery in Ding County, Hebei, dated 1055, was eleven stories and 84 meters high, with interior stairs that made it possible to ascend between an inner core and outer corridor. The 76-meter pagoda of Bao'en

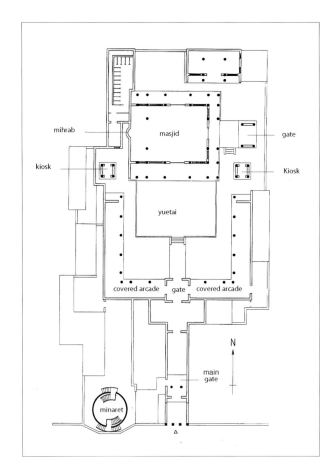

2 Plan of Huaishengsi, fourteenth century, probably retaining locations of architecture from earlier centuries.
After Liu, *Zhongguo Yiselanjiao jianzhu*, 11. Redrawn by author

Monastery, in Suzhou, constructed between 1131 and 1162, also has an inner core and outer corridor and can be ascended.

The other buildings of Huaishengsi date to the Qing dynasty (1644–1911) or later, but the ground plan is believed to be of the thirteenth century. It demonstrates how closely a mosque followed the arrangement of contemporary Buddhist monasteries (Fig. 2). The entrance to Huaishengsi is at the southern side, like the majority of Buddhist, Daoist, Confucian, and Chinese palatial complexes. Two gates lead from the stem of the T-shaped approach to a gate that is joined on its east and west sides by a covered arcade that encloses the prayer space. Inside the arcade, stairs provide access to a large, open platform at the back (north) of which is a covered corridor that encloses the worship hall. To enter for prayer, however, one must walk 90 degrees to the east. Like any standard mosque, the *mihrab* is on the western wall, in the direction of Mecca, here opposite the entry. This directional change is evident only after one has passed through the gates and ascended the platform or has walked through a courtyard to the east of the south-north central passageway through the monastery. To this point, the plan is that of a standard Buddhist or Daoist monastery: the main worship hall is in the same space as at the mosque. Although the entrance to the mosque prayer hall creates an alternate building axis, it is concealed behind arcades and walls so that the fact that this is a Muslim prayer space is apparent neither from the plan nor when standing in the first or second courtyard. A comparison between the plan of Huaishengsi and that of an eleventh- or twelfth-century Buddhist monastery such Shanhuasi in Datong, Shanxi province, shows a common front gate, hall with a large platform corresponding to the location of the second gate of Huaishengsi, and then the main hall with another platform in front, all along the main north-south axial line and all enclosed by arcades. Muslim worship thus occurred at Huaishengsi behind the façade of a thoroughly Chinese religious compound with the only alteration the orientation of the worship space. Yet the boldly rising minaret indicates that the Muslim community of Guangzhou was secure enough not to conceal its presence. The Chinese style of all other buildings was as intentional as the style of the minaret.

Shengyousi (Mosque of the Companions) in Quanzhou, Fujian Province, built in 1009–10, also proclaimed Islam from the street and also contains several unique features. The configuration of this mosque is believed to survive as it was in 1310. An inscription informs us that a man from Srivijaya established the mosque and that it was one of six or seven in the city.[14] Today Shengyousi is the only mosque in China proper with a stone, pointed-arched gateway (Fig. 3). The structure is the form of a Persian *pishtaq*; a three-part archway, the solid, upper portion of the first arch is decorated with four pointed arches of different patterns, one at the highest level and three at the second level. All three sides are ornamented with raised patterns that may be intended to imitate *muqarnas*. It is on the south side of the mosque. Pointed, or ogee-shaped, arches also are found along the interior walls of the courtyard, some of them open for access and others blind. All the arches are segmented. Many have passages from the Quran or Hadith inscribed on lintels or just beneath the arches.

Eight windows west of the *pishtaq* also are unique among mosque survivals in China. Today they allow a view into the main worship space (now destroyed). As in Buddhist and Daoist worship halls, side walls in mosque worship areas are usually solid. In a Chinese context, side walls often are the location of religious murals, and in all cases, they render worship private from the outside. Perhaps another courtyard separated the *pisthaq* and windows from the city, in which case the windows would have been a source of interior lighting. If the granite exterior walls and the *pishtaq* were apparent from the street, then as in Guangzhou, in Quanzhou the existence of a mosque was not concealed in the eleventh-fourteenth centuries.

The prayer space behind the wall and gate was supported by stone pillars arranged in hypostyle fashion in three rows of four. Nine of what are believed to have been an original twelve survive. This formation of columns recalls Abassid-period (758–1258) mosques such as the Samarra Mosque in Iraq or the Great Mosque in Qayrawan in northwestern Tunisia. The same construction was used in religious and palatial architecture in China, sometimes with central columns eliminated to make room for an altar or throne. Buildings of the Forbidden City and sacrificial halls at the Ming Tombs outside Beijing are Chinese examples.

If one mosque in China is likely to have most reflected the architecture of the land of origin of its congregation, Quanzhou is where one would expect to find it. In addition to the well-documented presence of Islam, the city preserves buildings, building pieces, and hundreds of stone inscriptions that document the Manichaean, Brahmanical, and Church of the East communities that co-existed with Chinese residents and their faiths in the Song (960–1279) and Yuan dynasties (1271–1368).[15] Today, Persian and Arabic inscriptions are gathered at the mosque, in Muslim cemeteries that formed in the Song dynasty and into the fourteenth century, and in Quanzhou's museums.

3 Gateway and wall of Shengyousi, Quanzhou, Fujian province, 1310 with later restoration.
Photo: Nancy Steinhardt

MOSQUES UNDER MONGOL RULE

In addition to the mosques in Guangzhou and Quanzhou, nine others are associated with the Tang or Song or a contemporary dynasty in north China: Zhuxian Mosque in a village of that name twenty-two kilometers south of Kaifeng, established between 976 and 983; Ox Street Mosque, established in 996 (of the Liao dynasty, 907–1125) in Beijing; Taiyuan (in Shanxi province) Old Mosque; Daxuexixiang Mosque in Xi'an; Huajuexiang Mosque in Xi'an; Fenghuang (Phoenix) Mosque in Hangzhou; Xianhe (Transcendant Crane) Mosque in Yangzhou; Jianzixiang Mosque in Zhenjiang, near Shanghai; and Datong Mosque (in Shanxi).[16] All these mosque and others, a total of about thirty that flourished during the period of Mongolian rule, retain buildings or have a documented history of construction at this time. During this pan-Asian empire, the circumstances of a Muslim presence in China were different from earlier times. Under the Mongol-ruled Yuan dynasty (1267–1368), not only was the ruling family non-

THE MOSQUE IN CHINA 433

4 Tomb of Tughluq Temür, Huocheng (Yili, Almaliq), Xinjiang Uyghur Autonomous Region, 1363.
Photo: From *Ancient Chinese Architecture*, uncopyrighted

Chinese, official policy actively encouraged the involvement of non-Chinese in the government and actively discouraged the involvement of the Chinese population. Muslims were part of the non-Mongol, non-Chinese group given privileges second only to those of Mongolian nativity, whose numbers were too small to fill the needs of the Mongol government. Already in China as successful merchants, opportunities for Muslims residents as well as émigrés increased in the Yuan period, such that imperial financiers and highly successful generals practiced Islam. The oldest Arabic Quran produced in China is from the Yuan dynasty. Mosques were built in any part of the empire where there were Muslims.

The most influential Muslim in China under Mongolian rule was Sayyid Ajjal Shams al-Din Omar al-Bukhari (1211–79), known in Chinese as Saidianchi Zhansiding and as his name indicates, a native of Bukhara. Said to be a twenty-sixth-generation descendant of the Prophet, after the fall of his region to the Mongols, Shams al-Din joined Chinggis Khan's forces in battle, became a military leader and government official under subsequent Khans, and rose to financial minister of the Yuan Empire. During the last five years of his life, Shams al-Din was governor of the Dali kingdom in Yunnan province to which he brought Islam while allowing for continued patronage of Confucian learning and Buddhist monasteries. Mosques in Kunming, the capital of Yunnan, are still associated with him.[17] Muslim tombs also were built under Mongolian rule, the most famous of which is the tomb of Tughluq Temür (c. 1330–63) in Huocheng, Xinjiang (Fig. 4).[18]

CHINA'S MOST FAMOUS MOSQUES

China's two most famous mosques trace their origins to the pre-Yuan period and are in two of China's most important capital cities, Xi'an and Beijing. Huajuexiangsi (Mosque on Huajue Lane), in Xi'an, is China's most popular mosque among tourists and is one of China's most complete premodern mosques. Huajuexiangsi is intimately associated with China's famous seafarer-eunuch-official, Zheng He (1371–1435), born a Muslim named Ma Sanbao in Yunnan province, who also was the patron of a mosque in Nanjing. The Xi'an mosque was restored four times during imperial renovations at religious complexes throughout China.

Huajuexiangsi consists of five courtyards along an extremely long, axial building line, oriented due west (Fig. 5). This east-west orientation is a departure from known mosques built before the Ming dynasty (1368–1644). The front gate leads directly to the front entrance of the prayer hall. Behind the front gate are screen walls; side gates; a ceremonial gate; a five-bay stone ceremonial gate; a second courtyard; another stone gate; an octagonal structure named Examining the Heart Tower; two more courtyards, one with a hall for ablutions; and then one comes to the main part of the mosque. The fourth courtyard begins with three parallel gates and includes lecture halls, a pair of octagonal pavilions, and a pair of four-sided stele pavilions, after which, finally, is the prayer hall, which leads from the fourth into the fifth courtyard. The main prayer hall and the adjoining *qibla/mihrab* are the only structures in the last courtyard, which terminates at a screen wall.

The remarkably Chinese architecture demonstrates a true convergence of Chinese and Islamic features, and even more impressive, the Chinese elements are those of China's most eminent architectural tradition. The wooden ceremonial gate and screen walls, for example, have their counterparts at the most important Confucian temple in China, in Qufu, Shandong province, the city of Confucius' birth, and at the Qing imperial tombs in Hebei province. The hexagonal pavilion has a counterpart in a Qing building at the Temple to the Northern Peak in

Quyang, Hebei province, where the emperor or his surrogate performed imperial rites. The plan recalls China's most distinguished religious complexes, from the long, narrow, tenth-twelfth-century Longxing Monastery in Zhengding, Hebei, to the nine-courtyard Confucian Temple in Qufu, built over ten centuries. All four Chinese complexes whose buildings and plans are logically compared with those at Huajuexiang Mosque are associated with the imperial family. As mentioned above, Chinese architecture is a ranked system. The fact that the architecture of Huajuexiang Mosque conforms to the building standards of imperial temples, mausolea, and monasteries is consistent with the fact that its buildings follow China's most eminent construction practices.

The second extremely famous Chinese mosque is Ox Street Mosque in Beijing, today the largest mosque with the longest history in the capital (Fig. 6).[19] The name and street name are references to the Muslim prohibition against eating pork and the ritual slaughter of oxen. The history of Ox Street Mosque traces to the year 960 when a Muslim seafarer and his son came to this district of Beijing, at that time the southern capital of the Liao dynasty, to teach Islam. The son Nasuluding (Nasr al-Din?) was presented an official title and

5 Courtyard of Huajuexiangsi, Xi'an, Shaanxi province, 1392 with later restoration.
Photo: Nancy Steinhardt

THE MOSQUE IN CHINA 435

6 Front entrance today, Ox Street Mosque, Beijing, founded 960, buildings c. 1496 with many later repairs.
Photo: Nancy Steinhardt

given permission to build a mosque. The mosque flourished under Mongolian rule. Cenotaphs for two Yuan-period imam are there today. They survive as new monuments. The earliest extant buildings are from the Ming period.

Like the mosque in Xi'an, Ox Street Mosque is oriented east-west. Today it begins at a screen wall. Directly behind it are a Chinese ceremonial gate and then a hexagonal pavilion known in Chinese as Wangyuelou (Tower for Viewing the Moon). The shape and position are suggestive of a minaret, but another multi-story structure that goes by the more standard Chinese name for a minaret, *bangkelou*, stands behind the prayer hall. *Bangkelou* was constructed in the Qing period. Towers for Viewing the Moon were sometimes ascended to watch for the full moon to known when to break the daily fast during Ramadan. Some mosques have both minarets and moon-viewing towers, some have one, and some mosques have neither.

MOSQUES ALONG THE GRAND CANAL

By the Ming dynasty, when the Mongols fled north and China returned to native rule, the majority of Muslims in China were Hui, Chinese-speaking Muslims who lived as Chinese. Following repairs of the Grand Canal between 1411 and 1415, commerce flourished between southeastern cities with large Muslim populations such as Yangzhou and northern cities in eastern China such as Tianjin. Muslims were active in this trade. Mosques rose and flourished along the canal.

The Great East Mosque (Dongdasi) in Jining, the first major city north of Yangzhou on the Canal, is the third largest mosque in China, superseded in size only by Xi'an and the original mosque built by Zheng He in Nanjing (Fig. 7).[20] Eight structures stand along the east-west axial line of the mosque, today all Qing-period buildings. Following two gates are a three-part, cruciform-shaped prayer complex. The form becomes increasingly common in the Ming period: a front porch functions as an antechamber, a wider prayer area behind it, and a narrower space behind it known as *yaodian* (literally "kiln or hole hall"). *Yaodian* is a unique feature of Chinese

THE MOSQUE IN CHINA 437

7 Great East Mosque, Jining, Shandong, founded 1454–64.
Photo: Nancy Steinhardt

8 Datong Mosque, Shanxi, renovated in the twenty-first century.
Photo: Nancy Steinhardt

mosques. It can serve as a place for a small group of worshipers with a *mihrab* at the very back. A moon-viewing tower and ceremonial gate are at the back of the mosque.

The mosque in Botou, Hebei province, also on the Canal, was founded in 1404 by Muslims who moved into the region from Nanjing. Like most Ming mosques, it faces east. It has a two-story minaret with an enormous prayer hall behind it. Cangzhou, farther north in Hebei, has seven old mosques. North Mosque, founded in 1402 is one of the oldest. Tianjin Great Mosque, founded in the late nineteenth century, replaced an earlier mosque on that site. It is oriented only roughly east-west, with a simple two-courtyard plan.

MOSQUES IN WESTERN HEBEI AND SHANXI

Three Hebei mosques with old architecture lie between 150 and 225 km southwest of Beijing. North Mosque in Baoding was established during the Yongle reign (1402–24). Baoding West Mosque was founded in 1616 and restored in 1906. Dingzhou Mosque was founded in 1348. Xuanhua North Mosque, closer to Beijing, was constructed in 1703. Its massive worship hall is an example of the cruciform arrangement used in other Chinese mosques, with a front porch, large open worship space, and narrow *yaodian* at the back.

According to inscriptions, two mosques in Shanxi were first built in the Tang dynasty. The current mosques are much newer. Datong Mosque's twenty-first-century façade opens onto a pedestrian plaza (Fig. 8). The 4000-sq.m site includes a three-part prayer hall that consists of front porch, prayer space, and *yaodian*. A four-sided moon-viewing tower and a hall with an octagonal dome with lattice ceiling are in the courtyard behind it. The Taiyuan Mosque may have been founded in the period 785–805. Inscriptions record repairs in the Song, Yuan, and Ming dynasties.

Kaifeng in Henan province has two important mosques. Great East Mosque was founded in the Ming dynasty and repaired many times after that. Zhuxian Mosque in Kaifeng is considered one of the four most famous old mosques in China.[21]

Begun between 976 and 983, Zhuxian Mosque was rebuilt in 1531 and again in 1744, and repaired in 2006. Like most other mosques with histories as long as its repair was in Chinese style. Occupying more than 9000 sq.m it has a standard arrangement of a front gate, pair of stele pavilions, one with a stele inscribed in Arabic and the other in Chinese behind it, a three-part prayer space, offices, residential space, lecture hall, a room for ablutions on either side, and a back gate. Great North Mosque in Henan's capital Zhengzhou also has a mosque from the Ming period.

MOSQUES IN JIANGSU AND ZHEJIANG

Two of China's oldest mosques, in Yangzhou and Hangzhou, are in Jiangsu and Zhejiang in southeastern China, respectively. Songjiang Mosque, located in what is now a suburb of Shanghai, is also in this region. Just as buildings in mosques from North China such as the mosque in Xi'an take on the features of northern Chinese religious construction in the North, the Songjiang Mosque is a complex of white-washed walls, grey tile roofs and wall-top decoration, and winding foliated paths with trees in courtyards of the kind one finds in gardens of Suzhou and greater Jiangsu (Fig. 9).

MOSQUES IN NORTHWESTERN CHINA

China's Northwest comprises the provinces of Gansu and Qinghai and the autonomous region Ningxia. In the seventeenth century, four Sufi orders became active in this region.[22] The majority of Muslims involved in these sects were China-born, Chinese-speaking Muslims. Two new building types occurred in their mosques: *daotang*, or instructional halls, in which the religious leader supervised religion and life more generally, and *gongbei*, the Chinese word for *qubba* (dome), referring to the mausoleum of a holy man. *Gongbei* always include a domed building in which the memorialized holy man is interred. There are nearly seventy *gongbei* in Ningxia.

Na Family Mosque in Yongning is one of the few mosques in Ningxia with a definite founding date and

9 Songjiang Mosque, fourteenth century and later.
Photo: Nancy Steinhardt

10 Entrance to Na Family Mosque, Yongning, Ningxia, 1524.
Photo: Nancy Steinhardt

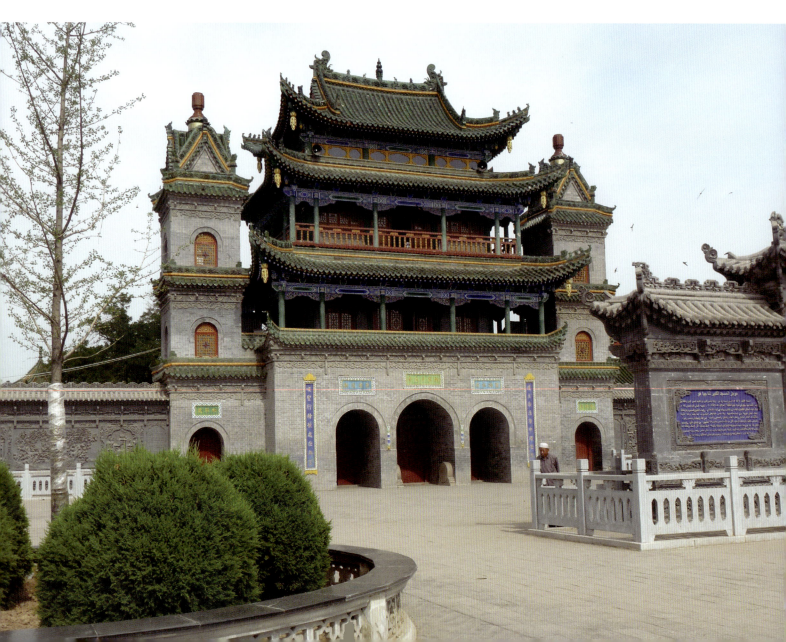

certainty about its patrons. It is also a rare Chinese mosque closely associated with one family. The mosque is dominated by two structures: a gate with side towers and the prayer complex behind it. The green roof tiles of the gate, reconstructed after 1982, present the image of a late Ming-early Qing tower (Fig. 10): central bays are the widest on each level; the uppermost story has a hip-gable roof; each story of each pavilion has two sets of rafters beneath the convex ceramic end tiles; the upper rafters are four-sided in section and the lower rafters are circular. The paired minarets are reminiscent of Iranian Islamic architecture as well as Chinese gate-towers. The lattice patterns in the windows of the towers are found in mosques in many parts of the world, but the highly stylized bracketing that appears like lotus petals on architraves that support lintels derive from Chinese buildings. The worship space, 1102 sq.m in extent, consists of the same three parts as define the majority of mosques in China. From the side, one observes six roofs that alternate between curved and overhanging gables above the front porch, nine-bay-deep (860 sq.m) prayer hall, and *yaodian* at the back. On the perimeter are the standard mosque spaces of lecture halls, educational rooms, dormitories, a guest hall for the imam, and an ablutions chamber.

The Tongxin Mosque, near the center of Ningxia, began as a Buddhist monastery in the Yuan period. It was converted to a mosque during the early Ming dynasty. This kind of transformation for use by

11 Entrance and minaret of Pingzhuang Mosque, Donxiang Autonomous Hui Hamlet, Gansu.
Photo: Nancy Steinhardt

THE MOSQUE IN CHINA   441

12 Aba Khoja mausoleum, Kashgar.
Photo: Christopher Little – Aga Khan Award for Architecture

another religion, or between secular and religious functions, is standard in China.

In 2008, Gansu had more than 2800 mosques, the earliest with histories dating to the Yuan dynasty.[23] Almost no pre-twentieth-century mosque architecture survives there. Thus as in Ningxia, the decision to construct with ceramic tile roofs, wooden pillars, and bracket sets or imitation-bracket sets is noteworthy. The mosques that do survive concentrate in Hui (Sinophone Muslim) autonomous regions of and around Linxia.

Laowang Mosque is one of the largest. Founded in 1377, the next date associated with the mosque is 1736 when a wealthy Muslim of the local community paid for repairs and expansion.[24] The most recent reconstruction took place between 1980 and 1983. Laohua Mosque was founded between 1465 and 1487 and rebuilt in 1981. Throughout Gansu, hexagonal minarets with sharply upturned eaves mark minarets that in a Buddhist context would be pagodas. Pingzhuang Mosque in Dongxiang Autonomous Hui County, contiguous to Linxia, exhibits a similar convergence of Chinese architecture and required mosque space (Fig. 11). Inverted-pyramidal-shaped bracket sets of the kind used on the Pingzhuang Mosque gate are employed at Hongshuiquan Mosque, about 30 kilometers from the center of Xining, in Qinghai. These bracket sets are used in mosques and Buddhist architecture in and around Xining.

MOSQUES IN XINJIANG

Finally are the mosques farthest west in China, in Xinjiang Uyghur Autonomous Region, sometimes known as Chinese Turkestan or Chinese Central Asia. According to tradition, a merchant named Satoq Bughra of Qarakhanid ancestry brought Islam to the city that is today Kashgar in the tenth century. Today Xinjiang has more than 25,000 mosques. Adjacent to Kyrgyzstan, Uzbekistan, Tajikistan, Afghanistan, and Pakistan, mosques and worshipers in western Xinjiang are structurally and ethnically linked to West Asia and its Muslim Uyghur population; they are not Hui mosques.

Two of Kashgar's monuments represent

premodern Islamic architecture in these western lands. The mosque of Id Kah (Aitige'er in Chinese) is Xinjiang's largest mosque. Its name combines Arabic and Persian words, giving it the name "place of worship on a festival day".[25] The current golden brick structure was begun in 1798 and enlarged in 1838. Entered via an eight-meter-high archway that is joined by walls to two distinctive eighteen-meter minarets at the corners of an enclosure, the prayer area is divided into two sectors, each with its own *mihrab*. The trapezoidal interior courtyard is enclosed by a gate and minarets at the front, and the enormous back section includes a pool for ablutions, lecture halls, and residences for the imam and students.

The mausoleum of Aba Khoja is the holiest Muslim building in Xinjiang. Built in about 1640 as the tomb of the Naqshbandiyya Sufi Muhammad Yusuf, the man sometimes credited with spreading Sufism in China, his son Aba Khoja and three more generations of the Khoja family are interred here, a total of seventy-two people. The mausoleum complex takes a standard form of *mazar* or shrine: a central dome rises seventeen meters over a nearly square space, surrounded by four corner minarets (Fig. 12). Originally most of the exterior was tiled. The complex includes a prayer hall, lecture hall, and large cemetery that are in use today. The buildings are distinguished by thin, wooden, fluted columns, brightly painted and with highly elaborated capitals.[26]

In the second half of the twentieth century, mosques in China were often indistinguishable from mosques in any other part of the world. Contemporary mosques may receive patronage from outside China, may use materials from the Islamic world, may employ craftsmen who have built mosques outside China, and bear external identifying evidence such as the crescent moon projecting atop a dome. Examples are found not only in China but also among populations of "overseas Chinese" in places like Malaya and Singapore. This kind of change toward global modernism has occurred much less frequently in contemporary Buddhist, Daoist, and Confucian architecture in China. The architecture of contemporary Islam in China is Muslim architecture, not Sino-Islamic.

NANCY S. STEINHARDT is Professor of East Asian Art and Curator of Chinese Art at the University of Pennsylvania. Steinhardt's most recent books are *Chinese Architecture in an Age of Turmoil* (2014); *China's Early Mosques* (2015); *Chinese Architecture: A History* (2019); and *The Borders of Chinese Architecture* (2022). In 2019 she received the Distinguished Teacher of Art History from the College Art Association and the Provost's Award for Distinguished PhD Teaching and Mentorship from the University of Pennsylvania. She does fieldwork in China, Korea, Japan, and Mongolia.

SUGGESTIONS FOR FURTHER READING

Chen Yuning and Tang Xiaofang. *Zhongguo Huizu wen* [Cultural relics of the Hui nationality] (Yinchuan: Ningxia People's Press, 2008).

Liang Xinli. *Beijing qingzhensi diaocha ji* [Digging into Beijing mosques] (Beijing: Guojia tushuguan chubanshe, 2013).

Liu Zhiping. *Zhongguo Yiselanjiao jianzhu* [Chinese Islamic Architecture] (Urumqi: Xinjiang People's Press, 1985).

Qiu Yulan. *Zhongguo Yiselanjiao jianzhu* [Chinese Islamic architecture] (Beijing: China Architecture and Building Press, 1993).

Steinhardt, Nancy S. *China's Earliest Mosques* (Edinburgh: Edinburgh University Press, 2015).

Wu Jianwei, ed. *Zhongguo qingzhensi zonglan* [Compendium of Chinese mosques] (Yinchuan: Ningxia Peoples Press, 1995).

NOTES

[1] Liu Xu (887–946), *Jiu Tangshu* [Standard history of the earlier part of the Tang dynasty] (Beijing: Zhongguo shuju, 1975), 5315.

[2] Donald Leslie, *Islam in Traditional China* (Belconnen: Canberra College of Advanced Education, 1986), 16.

[3] Qiu Yulan, *Zhongguo Yiselanjiao jianzhu* (Chinese Islamic architecture) (Beijing: China Architecture and Building Press, 1993), 116; Donald Leslie, *Islam in Traditional China*, 31.

[4] Victor Cunrui Xiong, *Sui-Tang Chang'an: a Study in the Urban History of Medieval China* (Ann Arbor: University of Michigan Center for Chinese Studies, 2000), 235–42.

[5] Chen Yuning and Tang Xiaofang, *Zhongguo Huizu wen* [Cultural relics of the Hui nationality] (Yinchuan: Ningxia People's Press, 2008), 71.

[6] Richard Ettinghausen, Oleg Grabar, and Marilyn Jenkins-Madina, *Islamic Art and Architecture 650–1250* (New Haven and London: Yale University Press, 2001), 5–6; W. Jenner, *Memories of Lo-yang: Yang Hsüan-chih and the Lost Capital, 493–534*. (Oxford: Oxford University Press, 1981), 68–69; Olivia Milburn, *Urbanization in Early and Medieval China* (Seattle: University of Washington Press, 2015): 138, 142, 143, 146, 147, 148,

[7] Angela Schottenhammer, *Trade and Transfer across the East Asian "Mediterranean"* (Wiesbaden: Harrassowitz, 2005).

[8] Qiu, *Zhongguo Yiselanjiao*, 116.

[9] See Muhammad al-Asad, "The Mosque of Muhammad 'Ali in Cairo," *Muqarnas* 9 (1992), 46 (39–55).

[10] Lu and Zhang, *Zhongguo Yiselanjiao jianzhu*, 38–40.

[11] Yue Ke (1183–1234), *Tingshi* [Bedside-table history], 1214 (Beijing: Zhonghua shuju, 1981), 125–27; and Fang Xinru (1177–1220), *Nanhai baiyong* [Chantings of the Southern Seas], *juan* 2.

[12] Liu, *Zhongguo Yiselanjiao jianzhu*, 13.

[13] Yue Ke, *Tingshi*, 126.

[14] For the inscription, see Chen Dasheng, *Quanzhou Yiselanjiao shike* [Stone-carved Islamic inscriptions of Quanzhou] (Yinchuan: Ningxia Peoples' Press, 1984), 6 and Lu and Zhang, *Zhongguo Yiselanjiaojianzhu*, 41.

[15] Angela Schottenhammer, ed. *Emporium of the World: Maritime Quanzhou 1000–1400* (Leiden: Brill, 2000); Schottenhammer, *Trade and Transfer*; Iain Gardner, Samuel Lieu, and Ken Parry, eds. *From Palmyra to Zayton: Epigraphy and Iconography* (Turnhout and New South Wales: Brepols, 2005).

[16] Lu and Zhang, *Zhongguo Yiselanjiao*; Chen and Tang, *Zhongguo Huizu wenwu*.

[17] Na Weixin, *Yuan Xianyang wang Saidianchi Shansiding shijia* [On the family of the Prince of Xianyang of the Yuan dynasty Saidianchi Shams al-Sin] (Beijing: China Today Press, 1994).

[18] Bernard O'Kane, "Chaghatai Architecture and the Tomb of Tughluq Temur at Alamliq," *Muqarnas* 21 (2004), 277–87

[19] Xie Tianli, ed. *Qingzhen guyun: Beijing Niujie libaisi* [Tones of an ancient mosque: Ox Street Mosque in Beijing] (Beijing: Wenwu chubanshe, 2009).

[20] Liu, *Zhongguo Yiselanjiao jianzhu*, 80.

[21] Lu and Zhang, *Zhongguo Yiselanjiao jianzhu*, 101.

[22] Khufiyya and Jahriyya, both Naqshbandiyya orders, in addition to Qadariyya and Kubrawiyya. See Michael Dillon, China's Muslims (Hong Kong and New York: Oxford University Press, 1996), 19–24 and Joseph Fletcher, Jr., "The Naqshbandiyya in Northwest China," in *Studies on Chinese and Islamic Inner Asia*, ed. Beatrice Manz, 2 vols. (Aldershot: Variorum, 1995), 2: 1–46.

[23] Chen and Tang, *Zhongguo Huizu wen*, 81.

[24] Ding Sijian, *Zhongguo Yisilan jianzhu yishu* [The Art of Islamic architecture in China] (Yinchuan: Ningxia Renmin chubanshe, 2013), 158 and Lu and Zhang, *Zhongguo Yiselanjiao jianzhu*, 123.

[25] Qiu Yulan and Yu Zhensheng, *Zhongguo Yiselanjiao jianzhu* [Chinese Islamic architecture] (Beijing: China Architecture and Building Press 1992), 194.

[26] Lu and Zhang, *Zhongguo Yiselanjiao*, 193–195.

The Great Mosque of Xi'an (Qing Zhen Si)   HASAN-UDDIN KHAN

1 Great Mosque of Xi'an, painted wood ceiling of the minaret.
Photo: C. Little / Aga Khan Award for Architecture

The city of Xi'an, the capital of Shaanxi Province in western China, is located in the south-central part of the province. Xi'an has been of importance through history, being the eastern terminus of the Silk Road that connected China with the Mediterranean. It was the capital of the western Han Dynasty (206 BCE – 25 CE), but continued to decline over the centuries after the downfall of the Tang though it remained as a center for Central Asian trade as noted by Marco Polo in the thirteenth century.[1] Muslims first came to China in 587 in a delegation led by Abi Waqqas, the Prophet Muhammad's maternal uncle. Arab mercenaries, sent by Emperor Su Tsang to quell a rebellion in the western provinces, never returned and formed the nucleus of Muslims in western China today. According to Tang Dynasty records the first Muslim embassy was established in Xi'an in 651.[2]

The name Xi'an (Western Peace) was adopted upon the establishment of the Ming Dynasty (1368–1644). In the twentieth century the city became a manufacturing, agricultural production and communications hub. It attracts significant tourism due to the presence of various historic pagodas, temples, three city gates, towers, and the Great Mosque of Xi'an, a.k.a. Mosque on Hua Jue Xi'an (Mosque on Hua Jue Lane) and Dong Da Mosque (Great Mosque in the East). Xi'an, now one of the most populous metropolitan areas in inland China with more than 8.5 million inhabitants (2020 estimate), is chiefly inhabited by Hui minority people, traditionally Chinese Muslims.

At the beginning of the Ming Dynasty, two well-known great mosques were built in China – in Nanjing and in Xi'an – the two most important cities at the beginning of the dynasty in the kingdom, both of which had major Muslim populations.

The mosque complex in China is often built on a long rectangular site on a symmetrical, linear plan, based on a traditional Chinese temple layout, and on the architectural design and construction of the period. Traditional Chinese Buddhist temples typically consist of a number of halls separated by courtyards. Gateways leading to courtyards are common as is the presence of different pavilions that house different functions. The pagoda form can often be seen in mosques, usually used as minarets

2 Great Mosque of Xi'an, 1392, birds-eye view.
Print: collection of Hasan-Uddin Khan

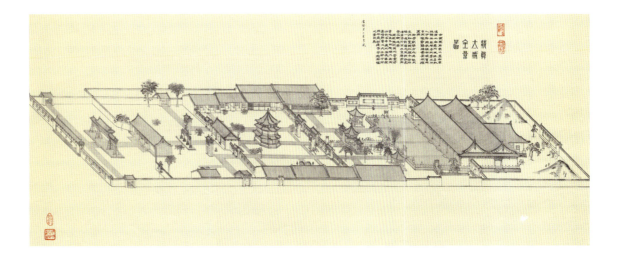

and markers in the landscape. Like other Chinese construction, the pavilions are usually single storey with timber frames, with the tiled roofs held up by a grid of columns of either wood or stone. A birds-eye view scroll drawing of the mosque is housed in the archives of the complex (Fig. 2).

THE ARCHITECTURE OF QING ZHEN SI

The Great Mosque of Xi'an (Qing Zhen Si) is the largest ancient and most important mosque in the country. It said to have been founded under the Tang Dynasty (618–907), probably by foreign mercenaries employed by the Han, in 742. An inscribed stone tablet in which it is stated that the mosque was built in that year has been proved to be a fake, but traditional sources describe the existence of a mosque on the site around that time. It is located along a quiet street, one block from the historic Drum Tower of 1380, in a densely populated residential area inhabited mainly by Muslims.

The present mosque was erected in 1392 during the reign of the Hongwu Emperor (given name, Zhu Yuan-Zhang), the founder of the Ming Dynasty (1368–98), who also ordered the construction of several mosques in Nanjing, Yunnan, Guangdong and Fujian, and had inscriptions praising the Prophet Muhammad placed in them. The Xi'an mosque was then partially rebuilt in 1413. According to a stone tablet in the mosque, the reconstruction is attributed to the Muslim eunuch diplomat and explorer Admiral Zheng He (1371–1435), known as Hajji Mahmud Shamsuddin, who also served a Commander of Nanjing. The mosque has since undergone several renovations in the fifteenth and sixteenth and early eighteenth centuries, with additions between 1662 and 1722, and major restoration work in the 1980s.

The Xi'an mosque is composed of five courtyards along the east-west axis on a site of 123,000 square feet (800 × 154 ft.) – the longest central axis of any Chinese mosque (Fig. 3). The complex's buildings cover some 40,000 square feet. Each courtyard is designed as an independent space with a central focal pavilion – currently, some of the courtyards are partially used for vegetable gardens. Usually, in the courtyards, is a *pailou* (a freestanding monument or memorial in the form of an arched gateway), separated from the others by screens, walls, and gateways (Fig. 4). Each of these structures are methodically planned and meticulously executed to complement the exterior spaces within which they are housed. The mosque rests on stone or brick foundations. Structural walls are of brick, while timber columns rest on stone bases. The typical hipped roofs are timber framed and tiled,

3 Great Mosque of Xi'an, plan. Drawing: courtesy Cheng Jing Qi

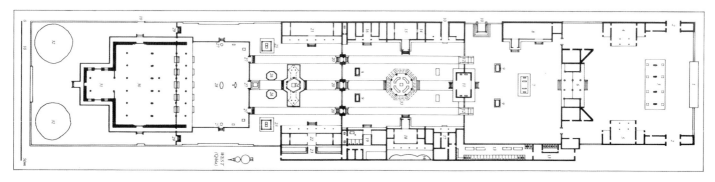

1	Wall of mirrors	10	Reception	19	Vistors' washroom	28	Platform
2	Main entrance	11	Three-arched gateway	20	Four-bay entrance gates	29	Moongate
3	Memorial archway	12	Floral gates	21	North Hall	30	Prayer hall
4	Visitors' room	13	Ablution rooms	22	South Hall	31	Mihrab
5	VIP room	14	Imam's room	23	Tablet gallery	32	Moon observation hills
6	Two-arched gateway	15	Library	24	Phoenix pavilion	33	Sheng Xin Lou Minaret
7	Stone gateway	16	Restrooms	25	Pavilion	34	Landscaped court
8	Reception	17	Washrooms	26	Pond		
9	Stone archways	18	Visitors' lounge	27	Stone gateways		

4 Great Mosque of Xi'an,
gateway in the first courtyard
of the mosque, 1392.
Photo: Hasan-Uddin Khan

5 Great Mosque of Xi'an,
octagonal minaret, probably 1413.
Photo: C. Little / Aga Khan Award
for Architecture

and edged with traditional Chinese auspicious figures, such as dragons.

The main entrance is on the north wall on the long side of the site, giving access to the first courtyard of the complex. There are also several other entrances on other sides that are used by the neighborhood residents. The entrances converge onto a central open-air pedestrian spine, which passes through a large tri-partite timber painted *pailou* dating from the Qing Dynasty (1644–1911), and an open building which acts as a reception area where visitors might wait. It is unclear whether the memorial arch was built during the reign of Emperor Chengua (1465–87) or Emperor Jiajing (1522–66).

The second court has a smaller *pailou* and two stone and wood gates that stand sentinel-like in the open space. There is also a smaller entrance from the street on the north wall. Smaller gateways give access to the third court. On either side of them are

THE GREAT MOSQUE OF XI'AN 449

two buildings: the northern one acts as a reception area and the rooms along the south edge are used as shops for foodstuff and goods such as prayer rugs, and contain the ablution rooms (literally "water rooms"). The space to the south of the courtyard was originally designated as a Hui cemetery but was never used for that purpose.

The third courtyard is accessed through a main gate raised on a platform flanked by two stone gateways. A major octagonal building in the center of the courtyard, Place of Introspection or Meditation (Qing Xin Dian), the minaret pavilion, dates from the Ming Dynasty (Fig. 5). The tallest structure in the complex, some 45 feet high, it measures approximately 48 feet across. This pagoda consists of three storeys with a movable staircase and balconies. The interior of the ground floor space is decorated with a magnificent painted ceiling, in which the timber beams that form a "dome" are ringed with red chrysanthemums, an emblem of the Chinese emperors (Fig. 1). It is crowned with three-

6 Great Mosque of Xi'an, front façade of the prayer hall.
Photo: Hasan-Uddin Khan

tiered roofs covered with traditional glazed tiles. According to the imam of the 1980s, it served as the mosque's minaret (Sheng Xin Lou), and continues to do so, except that the imam does not climb the stairs to call for prayer, which is broadcast from several loudspeakers in different parts of the complex.³

Within this court, to the east and west of the minaret, on either side if the central axis there are four tall stone archways topped by a traditional Chinese tiled roof. To the sides are two enclosed structures. In the north structure are the imam's chambers, the library, and bathrooms. The library annex contains Arabic manuscripts written in China, and some 30 books that date from the seventeenth century. An old painting on one wall shows a map of Mecca with the Kaaba at its center: it is used for instructional purposes. There are also a number of stone tablets of Arab and Persian origin. In the court's south annex there are several rooms for more distinguished visitors to stay. They are well-appointed with some marvelous traditional Chinese screens, vases, and furniture. To the side of these rooms, towards the external wall is an unexpected narrow 16-foot-wide landscaped court, which is more Buddhist in character than anything else. Also to the south are ablutions chambers.

The fourth courtyard, the main one of the complex, is entered through three gateways. On both side of the courtyard are halls, one of which is connected to the ablution facilities for women in the third court, and the other is used for smaller gatherings.

Within the last two courtyards is the principal building, the great prayer hall (Fig. 6), preceded by a large granite platform known as the Moon Platform, which is used as an overflow extension of the prayer space during festival days. It is enclosed by a low screen wall with carved railings and defined by five gateways – three in the front and one on each side of the platform. An exquisite and elaborate pavilion in the courtyard acts as the *dikka* (a platform raised upon columns), from which the prayers are conveyed to those who cannot see the imam in the prayer hall itself. As customary, it is aligned with the position of the *mihrab*. It is also used for recitations of the Quran at other times.

7 Great Mosque of Xi'an, *mihrab* wall.
Photo: Hasan-Uddin Khan

8 Great Mosque of Xi'an, one of the moon gates located between the fourth and fifth courtyards of the mosque complex.
Photo: C. Little / Aga Khan Award for Architecture

9 Great Mosque of Xi'an, wood brackets of the mosque's traditional structure revealed during the process of restoration.
Photo: Hasan-Uddin Khan

The orientation of the hall is to the west, roughly towards Mecca, but is as much in the traditional east-west orientation of temples. The hall itself is a seven bay rectangular space following the plan-type of the Central Asian regional mosque. The timber structure (108 × 125 ft.) is topped by an M-profile roof. The entrance to the main hall has a front porch colonnade made of wood and painted with Chinese motifs. To the right of the entrance stands the old imperial altar, formerly located in the center, which was used to render homage to the Emperor before praying to Allah. There is an almost square extension of the prayer hall at the rear. The paneled ceiling and supporting brackets of the main hall with polychromatic painting are traditional Chinese. The outstanding feature of the prayer hall is its interior carved and painted arched niche timber *mihrab* wall, with its calligraphy and arabesque decoration in dark red, brown, and gold (Fig. 7). The dimly lit space gives it a mysterious serenity.

In line with the entrance porch of the prayer hall, on either side are two Moon Gates (*yuemen*), a traditional architectural element in Chinese gardens (Fig. 8). Their circular openings act as a pedestrian passageway into the more informal rear garden, which contains small mounds. It was possibly a spiritual place for retreat and meditation, but in more recent times is unkempt and seems to be primarily used for storage.

Apart from the Arabic calligraphy and the influence of western Asia apparent in the floral designs, the mosque follows Chinese architecture, with its eaves decorated with dragons, bats, and unicorns of the local vernacular. The carvings in brick and wood, which are of excellent craftsmanship, are regarded as being the best surviving examples of their period.

THE MOSQUE TODAY

Over the years, especially in the twentieth century, new structures were haphazardly added to the complex. By the 1970s many of the structures were in need of repair and the mosque community was unable to maintain them. With the liberalization of the country and the influx of visitors to the city and the complex, city and government funds and expertise were made available to start repairs on the buildings.

The most recent conservation program, undertaken in the mid-1980s, began with the removal of structures that housed activities irrelevant to the functioning of the mosque complex and which obscured the courtyard organization. Structures were repaired by-and-large using internationally recognized conservation and restoration techniques (Fig. 9). New timber members matched the old ones, and repairs to the masonry work were carefully executed. In general, the work, which took some six years, was well conceived.[4]

As the mosque is part of a living community there were inevitable changes. The original function of some spaces was changed: classrooms, for example, have been transformed into the reception rooms for visitors. Toilets were updated. Some of the paint-work was restored but much of the interior of the main prayer hall was left untouched and intact – a situation that existed until the turn of this century.

The mosque is recognized as one of the most important architectural monuments in the region, continues to attract many visitors and tourists, and remains a center for Muslims in the country.

HASAN-UDDIN KHAN, Distinguished Professor Emeritus of Architecture and Historic Preservation at Roger Williams University, is an architect and critic who has worked all over the globe. He helped form the Aga Khan Award for Architecture in 1977, was its second Convenor, and coordinated H.H. the Aga Khan's worldwide architectural activities until 1994. He was Editor-in-Chief of the international journal *Mimar: Architecture in Development* and is editor/author of nine books, including two on mosques, and over seventy articles.

SUGGESTIONS FOR FURTHER READING

Liu Zhiping. *Zhongguo Yiselanjiao jianzhu* [Chinese Islamic Architecture] (Urumqi: Xinjiang People's Press, 1985).

Frishman, Martin and Hasan-Uddin Khan, eds. *The Mosque: History, Architectural Development & Regional Diversity* (London: Thames & Hudson, 1994).

Zhang Jing-qiu. "Mosques of Northern China," *Mimar: Architecture in Development* 3, ed. Hasan-Uddin Khan (Singapore: Concept Media Ltd., 1982), 58–73.

Steinhardt, Nancy. "China's Earliest Mosques," *Journal of Society of Architectural Historians* 67.3 (September 2008), 330–61.

NOTES

1. Sa'd ibn Abi Waqqas was one of the companions of the Prophet and reportedly the seventh person to embrace Islam. He is known for his conquest and governorship of Persia and his diplomatic sojourns to China.

2. See "Brief History of Muslims in China" by Brigadier Iqbal Shafi in an unpublished background paper prepared for the seminar *The Changing Rural Habitat*, Aga Khan Award for Architecture, held in Beijing, 1981.

3. Author's conversation with the imam of the mosque in March 1982.

4. The work was executed by the Chinese Department of Archaeology in conjunction with the local authorities, assisted by Paul Tsakok, a consultant to the Aga Khan Award for Architecture.

Australia

New Australian Mosques   TAMMY GABER

1 Punchbowl Mosque, Sydney suburb, street view. Photo: Tammy Gaber

Three centuries ago, Muslims from Makassar seasonally visited northern Australia for fishing, but did not form any settlements in the country. Over a century and a half ago, Muslims started to permanently settle in Australia, arriving from Afghanistan and North India on boats with camels and changed the landscape and accessibility of the desert, establishing routes, settlements, and mosques. The oldest extant mosque, still in use, in Adelaide is still referred to as the "Afghan chapel" and is part of a larger story that attests to the often forgotten presence and impact of Muslims in the country. Due to shifts in government policies the population of Muslims rose in the 1960s and 1970s and most mosques constructed during this time were neo-historicist. Two recent mosque constructions, the Punchbowl Mosque designed by Angelo Candalepas and the Newport Mosque designed by Glenn Murcutt and Hakan Elevi, are significant departures from the design of most of the mosques in the country. The contemporary architectural language and four key considerations set these two mosques apart: the expansion of mosque programming, the relationship of the space to cosmic order, accessibility of gendered spaces, and the external presence and transition to the interior. The presence and experience of the Muslim communities can be better understood in relation to the architecture of the mosque – a building type that vacillates between aesthetic objectification and vital community lifeline.

MUSLIMS IN AUSTRALIA

The first recorded Muslims in Australia, the Makassar from southern Sulawesi (modern day Indonesia) seasonally fished for trepang (sea slugs) and formed agreements with local Aboriginal populations for the regular bartering of services and goods from the seventeenth to the nineteenth centuries. The continued exchange of goods and services over the course of many years impacted the mortuary rituals of the Warrimi people on Elcho Island. As well, there are petroglyphs of their vessels in Aboriginal rock art.[1]

The first permanent communities of Muslims in Australia dates to the mid-1800s with the influx of camels brought in initially by British expeditions such as Horrock's and Burke and Wills Expeditions, who also brought in the camel drivers, "cameleers" from Afghanistan, North India (now Pakistan), and Baluchistan. Colloquially all of the cameleers were called "Afghans" or "Ghans".[2] By the 1890s the Muslim cameleers dominated the camel business and earned livelihoods as merchants and brokers and became a part of the communities in inland Australia. The Aboriginal Arrente created words for Muslim: "*apagana*" and "*matawalpala*" and a hand sign.[3] Between 1870 and 1920 over 2000 cameleers came into the country and 20,000 camels.

The discoveries of gold at Kalgoorlie and Coolgardie increased demand.[4] The establishment of trade routes and the trading hubs in various outback locations coincided with the construction of the earliest mosques in the late nineteenth century, in Maree (formerly Hergott Springs), Coolgardie, Alice Springs, Bourke, Broken Hill, and Adelaide.[5] Interestingly, the town of Marree had two small active mosques but not a church.[6] These early mosques were constructed from makeshift materials such as mud and tree trunk walls/columns, thatch, or iron sheet gable roofs. Most of these mosques are no longer extant in their original form save for the mosque constructed of bonded brick in Adelaide.[7]

Constructed in 1889, the Adelaide mosque, called the "Afghan Chapel" demonstrated important

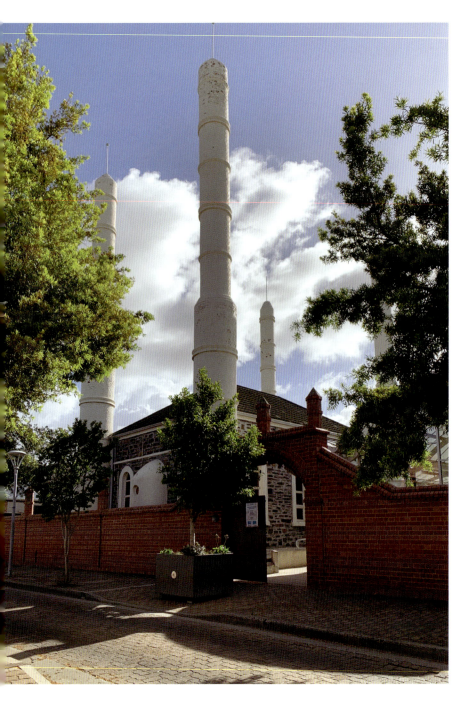

2 Adelaide Mosque, street view.
Photo: Tammy Gaber

pioneering efforts to cultivate a space for Muslims in the region – completely funded by local and regional cameleers.[8] The imposing minarets were added in 1903 and surrounding brick wall fence in 1908[9] (Fig. 2). Originally with a courtyard pool (for ablutions) and many fruit trees, the mosque has been since modified with the addition of an outdoor canopy and small buildings in the courtyard (Fig. 3). Situated in a dense, leafy, residential neighborhood the mosque was "rediscovered" in 1952 when several Bosnian Muslims, newly arrived, found the mosque in disrepair and several "ancient turbaned men" camped out within it.[10] The turbaned men were the last surviving Australian Muslim cameleers, who had sought this space as their last refuge. The following generations of newly arriving Muslims have since maintained the mosque which remains an active hub in the community.[11] The interior of the mosque was minimal with a contemporary wooden balcony added for women (Fig. 4).

The "Immigration Restriction Act of 1901" known as the "White Australian policy" was established to explicitly block the entry of non-White people into the country, and this significantly affected the numbers of Muslim cameleers. Many returned to their homeland and those who stayed formed families by marrying local Aboriginal or White women.[12] European Muslims were not banned and began to arrive in Australia after the end of the World Wars in 1918 and 1946, mostly from Albania and former Yugoslavia.[13] By the 1960s the only main mosques in use included Adelaide, Brisbane, and Perth (established by Afghan cameleers) and the Canberra mosque established by Muslim diplomats.[14]

The "White Australian policy" was abolished in 1966. The 1967 migration agreement, "Australian Government Assisted Passage Program," with Turkey allowed for thousands of Turkish people to come to Australia, mostly to work in factories. By 1971 there were twenty-two thousand Muslims in Australia. The brutal civil war in Lebanon in 1975 led to thousands migrating to Australia, including Muslims and Maronite Christians.[15] In the wake of this influx of Muslims the number of mosques – in converted and purpose-built spaces – increased in Australia, especially in Melbourne and Sydney. Almost all the

3 Adelaide Mosque, court view with contemporary canopy addition.
Photo: Tammy Gaber

4 Adelaide Mosque, interior view from women's balcony.
Photo: Tammy Gaber

5 Preston Mosque, Melbourne, street view.
Photo: Tammy Gaber

mosques were designed with neo-historicist styles, in relation to the ethnicity of the majority group users. Large mosques included the Preston Mosque (Umar bin Al Khattb) established by Bosnian and Arab Muslims in 1976 in Melbourne (Fig. 5). The Gallipoli Mosque was established in 1979 by the Turkish community in Sydney (Fig. 6). Both mosques utilized direct refences to Ottoman architecture. The Lakemba Mosque (Imam Ali bin Abi Taleb) established in Sydney by the Lebanese Muslim Association 1976 utilized an architectural style with adapted historical forms from historical Ummayyed mosque architecture (Fig. 7).

However, most recently, two newly constructed mosques signaled design approaches beyond historical references. The design processes for each mosque responded to issues of expanded program, cosmic orientation, gendered spaces as well as expressed external identity and approach to the mosque spaces. The Newport Islamic Society (NIS) in Newport (Melbourne) designed by Glenn Murcutt and Hakan Elevi and the Punchbowl Mosque (Sydney) designed by Angelo Candalepas have translated the community program requirements and ideas of identity into architectural form to express a presence of inclusivity – of diverse backgrounds and of permanent presence in the Australian built environment. The degree to which each mosque articulated forms for function, community, faith, and beauty is understood within the framework of "armor" and "adornment."

EXPANDED PROGRAMMING, COSMIC ORDER, GENDER AND IDENTITY IN NEW MOSQUES

Mosques in the diaspora function many ways for their communities. Serving as a primary hub to connect with other Muslims, the spaces of the mosque are for both religious gathering (prayer, celebration) and for social activities including education, fundraising, food, and clothing drives and open houses. These mosques serve in many ways as a community center and the programming of contemporary mosques, especially in the diaspora, has expanded to include a variety of specific and multi-use spaces. In both the Newport

7 Lakemba Mosque, Sydney, street view.
Photo: Tammy Gaber

6 Gallipoli mosque, street view.
Photo: Tammy Gaber

and the Punchbowl Mosques the limitations of funding meant that the construction of the mosque complexes was completed in phases, with the primary focus on the prayer hall and additional spaces in planning.

The location of mosques in the sub-tropic of Capricorn region, in particular Australia, has meant not only relative isolation with respect to how Muslim communities create spaces of gathering and identity but also isolation in reconciling the cosmic ordering of Mecca orientation and calculation of sacred time. The extreme southern latitudes effected the calculation of orientation and times which depend on both the cycles of the sun and the moon, not encountered in Tropic of Cancer and Tropic of Capricorn regions (but does parallel issues Muslim communities struggle with near the Arctic Circle region). Mecca orientation is reflected in architectural design and the calculation of sacred time directs prayer times and fasting times which impact when and how mosques are used. In addition to reconciling orientation within the design of the mosque, the experience of the cosmic connection through orientation has historically been manifested with the *mihrab* in a *qibla* wall facing Mecca. The niche form in historical mosques was often the only or main area of surface elaboration, filled with color, costly materials, patterns, and allusions to paradise with either vegetal motifs or text.[16] Thus the *mihrab* and *qibla* wall served in physical form as a virtual portal to both Mecca and paradise, which in Islam, is a verdant garden. Also, historically in Islam, the material arts (such as building decoration, prayer rugs etc.) expressed the gardens of paradise populated with local flora, making more connected the imagined and local natures. What that orientation is in these Australian cities, and how these two mosques include in the physical form the virtual portal to paradise, is opportunity for further grounding and connection of the mosque to their contexts.

The issue of gender accessibility is not addressed nearly enough when discussing the design of contemporary mosques, although there are some studies that are beginning to address this from an architectural approach.[17] It comes down to an issue of full accessibility to a space created in the name of a religion that fundamentally espouses human equality. A survey of the Quran, Hadith and the earliest mosques built underscore behavioral etiquette for communal worship and not architectural walls of division.[18] The shift to requiring women to only utilize a smaller, separated, space historically has its roots in building types that were either converted into mosques or influenced mosque design as the religion spread geographically, in particular the Ottoman adoption of the Byzantine *gynaeceum* and the regularized inclusion of a women's balcony in mosques across its vast empire. Inherited in many countries where Islam is the main religion, there is an assumption and association that separated women's spaces were somehow religiously sanctified and often this erroneous argument is supported with patriarchal notions of women's roles. It is important to understand this layered history and how it effects diasporic communities. The clash of inherited assumptions and contemporary secular understandings of full, unbarred, access for all people in public buildings comes to the fore when designing new mosques. Often considered "taboo" or argued as a religious norm, many contemporary mosques are designed with inherent biases that limit the participation of women in the Muslim community and clash with the norms of the rest of that society where women have otherwise full access to all public spaces. To some this is a debate, and for architects commissioned to design such important buildings that function as community space, these ideas need to be discussed – design decisions impact behavior, use and, ultimately, longevity of a space. In the two mosques in Newport and Punchbowl the requested program for a separated, balcony space for women was not questioned and for all the innovative notions of creating space and identity, the reality is that half of the community is reminded of their secondary status that is neither sanctioned by religion nor the norm in Australian society.

Finally, the exterior presence of the mosque, particularly purpose-built ones, communicate intentional statements of presence, arrival, and community identity. How people enter building, the balance of invitation and perceived inclusion as well as curated ritual transition into the worship space, begins to speak of the deeper, eternal qualities of a worship space. The movement and access from the street into the inner contemporary space of the mosque is traditionally the subject of choreographed design, to heighten the experience of the approaching contemplative worship space and provide transition. In mosques, often within this physical transition zone are the ritual ablution facilities which allow for metaphysical transition in the purification of the self through *wudu*. Historically mosques have included fountains either on the exterior of the mosque in the forecourt courtyards or in smaller adjacent buildings. The sensorial, or phenomenological, experience of a place of worship is key in the approach and transition into the main space.[19] This can either help to heighten the appreciation and prepare the worshiper for an inner transcendent experience or can simply leave all of that on the shoulders of user, as ritual becomes a series of motions rather than an internal contemplation.

These four issues work together to understand the impact and success of a mosque – analyzing only the materials or physical form leaves empty the real and lived qualities these spaces have – especially for minority Muslim communities that live in the diaspora, like Australia, and depend on the mosque for so many facets of their lives.

NEWPORT MOSQUE, MELBOURNE

By the late 1800s, approximately 400 Muslims were recorded to live in the Melbourne region and across Victoria state. There were several failed attempts to establish a mosque, especially in two neighborhoods where most of the Muslim community lived. By 1900 and 1901 two small prayer rooms were established and by 1930 and 1938 two small Muslim "chapels" were established.[20] The influx of Muslims after the abolition of the White Australia Policy, the agreement with Turkey and the civil war in Lebanon, signaled an increase in the Muslim population in Melbourne.

In the city of Melbourne, nearly 190 thousand Muslims utilize a number of mosques or prayer spaces scattered throughout the city and in various suburbs.[21] The growing Muslim community in the western suburb of Newport fundraised and envisioned a new kind of mosque – one that clearly signaled their identity in landmark form as "Australian." The Newport Islamic Society (NIS)

8 Newport Mosque, Melbourne suburb, exterior view
Photo: Tammy Gaber

was established in 1989 and by the mid-2000s the community had grown sufficiently with fundraising to seek out an architect to design a purpose-built mosque.[22] One member of the community, familiar with Murcutt's work with the Aga Khan Award for Architecture (AKAA) jury recommended him for the commission.[23] Murcutt considered this an "... opportunity of a lifetime to design new mosque".[24] As his first large-scale project he further researched into the typology, participated in community discussions regarding their aspirations, and requested collaboration with a local Muslim architect, for which the community recommended Hakan Elevi. Throughout the design process there were several meetings with the community to share the design proposal and gain feedback. The project manager Mohammed Haddara (who is both a member of the Muslim community and Director of Haddara constructions) was a part of the design consultation process from the beginning. The design and construction was prolonged over ten years due to funding. At times the architects were faced with questions and curiosity by the community who ultimately embraced the innovative qualities of the mosque when it was completed (Fig. 8). The high-profile nature of the mosque, further emphasized with publications and the production of a film documenting the process, underscored the celebration of the structure.[25]

Like almost all purpose-built mosques in the diaspora, the Newport community aspired for a diverse range of programmatic activities in the

NEW AUSTRALIAN MOSQUES 463

9 Newport Mosque, Melbourne suburb, *mihrab*.
Photo: Tammy Gaber

10 Newport Mosque, *mihrab* detail of calligraphy.
Photo: Tammy Gaber

▼ 13 Newport Mosque, *wudu* area outside of entrance.
Photo: Tammy Gaber

mosque complex that included various religious and social activities. As this was locally funded by the community, gathering the necessary resources took time and drew out the design and construction phase over a decade. At the time of the opening in 2018 the Newport mosque included two prayer areas (one for each gender), ritual washing areas, a library, basketball hall, reception area and public restaurant and a residence for the imam onsite. The masterplan accounts for the rest of the desired programming to be built with more funding, including the addition of educational facilities and further landscaping. In front of the mosque is a vacant site owned by the local council and Murcutt was consulted to suggest potential programming and design. Murcutt recommended a cultural contribution, with a community garden, based on other similar projects in Europe, including smaller plots rented out to individuals to grow what they want. According to Murcutt, "people can garden together, European and Islamic Australians, and create community." In tandem with this, Murcutt proposed a weekly farmers market be set up on the walkway leading to the mosque, before and after prayer (on Fridays and Saturdays), and he specified the waterline underground on this path based on the dimensions of stalls to integrate the

11 Newport Mosque, view of main space.
Photo: Tammy Gaber

12 Newport Mosque, view from women's balcony.
Photo: Tammy Gaber

pattern. The programming is not only inclusive of community social and religious activities, but is in a state of flux as changes in the user community continue and opportunities encourage further imaginative ways of use.

In Newport, the calculated *qibla* is N82W and the mosque was designed with this orientation accordingly. In Australia, the *qibla* is essentially western, facing the setting sun. There is a beautiful potential in this moment, for the *maghrib* (which exactly translates as "western") prayer at sunset, to face the sunset. In the design of the Newport mosque, instead of a niche in the wall decorated with abstract or imported images of paradise, the glass wall faces long narrow water-courtyards that are the exact length of the *qibla* wall. Filled with local water plants, the verdant growth makes local the allusions to paradise. However, behind the water-courtyard is a tall concrete wall blocking all potential view of a setting sun. Some light pours indirectly into the *qibla* wall in the afternoon until sunset and is caught on the gold leaf calligraphy in the concrete *mihrab* (Figs. 9–10).

According to Murcutt, his consideration of orientation was intertwined with his consideration of color and light: "Color is incredibly important, for example, yellow means paradise. Louis Barragan who

NEW AUSTRALIAN MOSQUES 465

I met, taught me you can connect color to orientation, so that for the morning, yellow is the east, for midday, green for north and for the afternoon red for the west. In the summer blue is the south". [26] The lanterns are the most impactful architectural gesture and Murcutt saw that the lanterns not only would indicate time (daily and seasonally) but would formally replace the idea of the dome.

Internally, the main worship space, two stories in height, is dedicated to men (Fig. 11). A concrete balcony, with a concrete half-wall acting as a railing, comprises approximately one third of the total prayer area and is the dedicated women's prayer space. The balcony is accessible by a concrete staircase (with high concrete railings – which were designed to be "protective") from the main space, or by way of the narrow concrete staircase from the exterior, near the exterior landmark wall. During the interview I discussed with him the critical theory regarding the accumulation of gendered spaces that were not a religious requirement of mosques to which he expressed surprise.

> It was very important for the whole building to be inclusive. Another threshold broken was women separated from men. In some mosques women [were located] in one space not in the front. I separated women, traditional women had veils, and [their spaces] had louvers so they could look out and see. I see the connection between traditional architecture and the veil. In my design I put the women's space to overlook the men's, and I put the staircase [which] connected women to men in the prayer hall. There will come a time in this country for the desire for equality and women can pray in the men's space. The possibility is there, well beyond my lifetime, there will be a great sense of equality between two and possibility for men and women to pray together. [27]

Despite this being the aspiration of the architect, the women's balcony space is still smaller and more compressed with the lower ceiling. In addition to this, with a solid concrete half-wall as a railing, the view to the main space or the *qibla* wall from the women's balcony is only possible if standing immediately next to it and leaning over, and not at all from the vantage of any of the women praying (Fig. 12). The women's balcony has a closer experience of the light changing from the lanterns,

but this does not compensate for the need to see the main space in order to follow prayer movements, adequately follow the *khutba* or public address, and to feel a part of the larger community.

Rather than within the bifurcated mosque prayer space, the place Murcutt felt there was a need for transparency was the exterior approach to the mosque. In conceptualizing the Newport mosque Murcutt began the design with the notion of a transparent transition into the mosque, so that the whole of the main prayer space (men's) interior was completely visible from the exterior with a series of transparent glass doors. Located in the open air, in front of the glass entry doors is the ablution area and an open space with picnic tables for communal eating (Fig. 13). In a purpose-built mosque this is rather irregular, and the temperatures in Newport meant that on certain cooler days, performing *wudu* outside, and walking on the concrete floor to approach the prayer hall was uncomfortable. In Murcutt's vision for the design he was motivated by his perception that it was necessary to mitigate potential politically and racially motivated hate crime with a transparent entry sequence.

> I made the most wonderful friendly collaboration with architects, foremen, clients and workers. One of the biggest issues the muslims face was mistrust. Looking at the threshold I realized mosques are in a sense, in the Arab world, exclusive because they do not have openness to public... I removed all the walls of the courtyard but landscaped the terrace with meaningful approach and it only has native deciduous trees... I created a courtyard, a prayer hall that was open to the street by being transparent and welcoming people. This is the first threshold. [28]

The prosaic and profound impacts of such design decisions are manifold. For the user, the ablution area is cold and uncomfortable and completely exposed.

> The ablution area, there is one upstairs for women, but most people do ablutions before they come to mosque so they can go right in. Men always washing in entry way seen from the street so that everything happening is clear for European Australian, and not some mystery. The cleanliness and respect for entry

and nothing is concealed and the processes are all there.[29]

Once inside, if there is direct sunlight the colored lanterns animate an otherwise cool interior rendered in grey concrete with grey rugs. On an overcast day, not much color comes into the space. To augment this, some members of the community started to bring in small decorative items to hang inside the building, which Murcutt noticed,

> I said the building is getting an international reputation and people need to learn how to use building. So the Mosque [governance] formed a committee for maintenance of the architecture of the building, so that people come for a spiritual experience.[30]

From this we can see that the "armor" of the building lies in its transparency for the outside to see in, so that the peaceful activities are amply revealed to the comfort of those not familiar with the religion, but that there is opacity for those praying facing the imagined virtual paradise beyond and further opacity for the women praying in the separated balcony. The entry sequence, rendered in complete transparency, is essentially collapsed and the shift from outside world to inside spiritual space does not have a transition allowing for adjustment of the body and mind. The "adornment" of the mosque relies solely on the exterior gestural large wall with the crescent and the color, mostly animate, light wells that fill the space.

PUNCHBOWL MOSQUE, SYDNEY

The population of Muslims in Sydney grew significantly with the influx of Turkish migrants and Lebanese refugees and several prayer spaces and mosques were established in the past fifty years. Three of the largest mosque projects in the city include the Lakemba and Gallipoli Mosques, and most recently the Punchbowl Mosque. The Lebanese Muslim Association (LMA) was founded 1962 and originally utilized a small house in the Lakemba neighborhood for gathering and worship.[31] The house was eventually demolished and one of the country's largest mosques constructed on the Lakemba site in 1976. The Turkish community grew in the city and by 1979 a house in Auburn was converted into their mosque and gathering space,

which was demolished in 1986 and the purpose-built Gallipoli Mosque competed in 1999.[32]

Similar to the communities in Lakemba and Auburn, the Muslim community in the Punchbowl suburb, south-west of Sydney, formed the Australian Islamic Mission (AIM) in 1973 and utilized several rented spaces, eventually purchasing one of them in 1996.[33] With fundraising the community purchased the four adjacent plots by 2007 and consolidated them in order to commission a purpose-built mosque celebrating their permanent presence. One of the community members was familiar with the work of local architect Angelo Candalepas' design for the All Saints Primary School in association with a church in the nearby city of Canterbury, and Candalepas was commissioned to design the AIM mosque complex in 2007.[34] Unlike the Newport community, the Punchbowl community expressly requested the symbolic elements of a dome and a minaret be included in addition to the programmatic requirements. Candalepas' accomplished attention to craft and design complemented his conceptual approach to the design of the space. Beginning with the interior alignment to Mecca, which on the lot was the western corner, he designed with repeated geometric proportions to create a sequence of spaces that curated the experiences of the spiritual.[35] In collaboration with members of the community, the architect published a monograph including essays, design, construction drawings, and construction photographs of the mosque.[36]

The Australian Islamic Mission (AIM) Punchbowl community has organized study circles in Arabic and English, youth activities, community outreach and interfaith events, and several youth clubs and sports as well as an Arabic language school on the weekends.[37]It was the aspiration of the Punchbowl community to have a complex to house a large number of these activities, in an expanded way. Currently, the completed portion of the Punchbowl Mosque includes the main prayer (for men) and two smaller prayer areas for women, gathering spaces, and the required 150-car garage under the site (Fig. 1). Plans are under way for a multi-story school and community hall in the future.[38]

Candalepas began with the orientation to Mecca in his deliberations designing the complex. The diagonal orientation, to the western corner of the site, inspired the geometric resolution of emphasizing two sides of the mosque with a series of ascending half domes – 102 in total – which

14 Punchbowl Mosque, Sydney suburb, *wudu* area in transition zone into mosque.
Photo: Tammy Gaber

culminated with one large, stepped dome. "I wanted a stone dome to last 300 years, I wanted to show I believed that a building can last thousands of years and that time has to be absent from the equation. So I designed the mosque to hold a stone dome, and the community could not afford one now, but one day it'll be fit in".[39] In contemplating the challenge of the orientation and of satisfying the clients wishes for including the recognizable form of the dome, Candalepas, a man of deeply professed faith, drew on ancient and timeless lessons of volume and geometry translated in a uniquely contemporary form. When asked about the importance of time in the design of this mosque, one that necessarily connects itself to a larger cosmic order, Candalepas responded:

> I don't believe time exists in a conventional sense in architecture [that] has to do with something that engages in the universal idea. Time has something to do with the building existing at all times. The most exciting moment is unveiling the scaffold holding up the board concrete, revealing the moment of disengagement of the building offered back to time…The best building has no tense, which is all of it at once, no present, no past. Walk into any great building and it touches us all, in its eternity. Imagining eternity exists in this way realizes an architectural engagement of human condition [that] takes away all doubt time exists. The efforts have tangibility if the efforts are sacred, the building is sacred. The building, icons, relics represent sacred and become sacred.[40]

By germinating the whole of the geometry of the design of mosque form the angle of orientation, the space became firmly rooted to the site, as if the *mihrab/qibla* wall were enlarged to become the entire focus of the mosque.

Candalepas discussed the difficulty of the conversation with the clients, the AIM board, and their unwavering desire for a separated space for women. He then chose to the place the women's space above, as a form of elevated vantage in the space. Candalepas considered references such as the *gynaeceum* at the Hagia Sophia, where the Empress had a privileged position. Candalepas conceded to the clients' wishes and wanted to at least create a beautiful space for women worshippers to see but not be seen. The two smaller balconies located facing the *qibla* are approached with a rising staircase which extends on the exterior to express the vertical signature of the building. Each balcony is ensconced with floor-to-ceiling narrow strips of wood with equal spaces between them. There is ample daylight from external walls and a view

15 Punchbowl Mosque, Sydney suburb, main prayer area.
Photo: Tammy Gaber

of the main (men's) space is possible if seated or standing in the front row. The approach to the women's space is separate from the men's and has a different processional experience that is well designed to allow for the sense of transition.[41]

The approach to the mosque includes two separate sequence of spaces that initially compress (in height and width), with carefully curated daylighting in an unfolding route. Both begin with ablution areas and end in a revelatory moment in the respective prayer halls. Drawing on more ancient concepts of initial compression in the threshold before release to the larger prayer hall, the ablution areas are housed in exquisitely detailed wood and smooth concrete spaces to the left (women) and right (men) of the main entrance (Fig. 14). Once completed, the male community members proceed to circle around and enter the main space (Fig. 15). The women are led up into two successive balcony spaces (Figs. 16–17). The entire material palette of the mosque is limited to smooth-form concrete, finely crafted wood details and the final elaborations of gold painted calligraphy on the half domes (Figs. 18–19). The red carpets are made of New Zealand wool and woven in Turkey. Candalepas acknowledges that "space is not sacred, but we curate movements. The entrance contracts and I see it as a processional propylaea entry, experiential constriction then explosion by contrast, intimate and personal building space. The public nature and the private dwelling [within it] and thus the private nature of the building."[42]

The "armor" of this mosque is the restrained exterior, with minimal clues of signage and a

NEW AUSTRALIAN MOSQUES 469

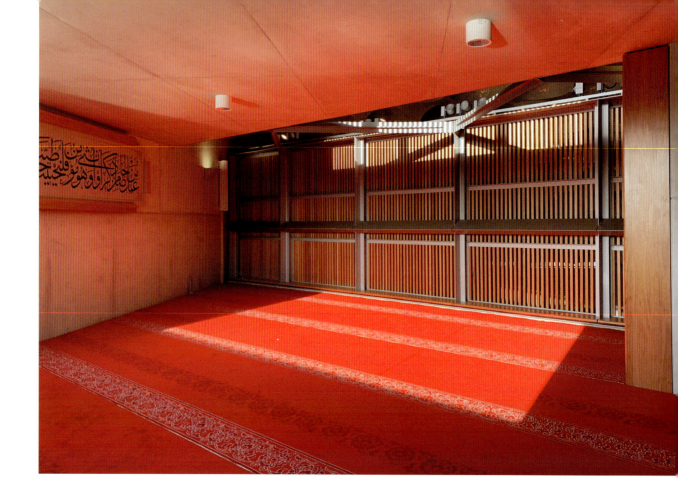

16 Punchbowl Mosque, Sydney suburb, view from women's prayer area.
Photo: Tammy Gaber

17 Punchbowl Mosque, view of two balconies (dedicated to women's prayer) from the main (men's) space.
Photo: Tammy Gaber

high degree of craftsmanship. It clearly stands in the neighborhood, which has a high population of Muslims, as mosque but does not reveal what lies within. To reach this, the visitor/user proceeds through narrow spaces of a slight circumambulatory nature, to purify themselves, leave behind their shoes and step into a space populated with half domes carved out from the pinholes of light coming through. The "adornment" of the light catches on the gold painted names of Allah and the deep red carpet (Figs. 11–15).

CONCLUSION – ARMOR AND ADORNMENT?

The population of Muslims settled in Australia, from the nineteenth century to the present, has multiplied and has contributed to the built environment in a number of ways including the construction of mosques.[43] The earliest mosques created by cameleers were mostly humble constructions with the exception of the still extant Adelaide Mosque. Shifts in national policies effecting migration paralleled the shifts in the numbers of Muslims in the country, as reflected in the numbers of mosques

constructed. In the past fifty years, as the population of Muslims steadily grew, so too did the mosques – the majority of which were neo-historicist. Exceptionally, two recent mosques constructed – the Newport and Punchbowl mosques – were constructed with the intent of creating a new, rooted, Australian mosque space for their respective communities.

Both mosques adorned their spaces with light, a commodity in this region which shifts dramatically throughout the day and the seasons. In both, light is brought in to animate the spaces which are both large, smooth form concrete, constructions. At Newport the light passes through colored glass to form moving patterns throughout the space on clear sunny days. At Punchbowl, the light entering through the 102 small windows and dome skylight, carve out from the shadows the unfolding curved surfaces that focus attention to the *qibla*. Problems of attempting to armor the spaces with transparent transition and/or segregated women's spaces are architectural issues that need continued examination within the community and with architects. However, the architectural identity of these mosques presents Muslim communities in the country that is committed to forging an identity which is uniquely Australian.

TAMMY GABER is Director and Associate Professor at the McEwen School of Architecture, Laurentian University in Canada. She has researched and published on contemporary mosques for two decades including her forthcoming book *Beyond the Divide: A Century of Canadian Mosque Design*. Dr. Gaber won the "Women Who Inspire" award from the Canadian Council of Muslim Women, was awarded Laurentian University's Teaching Excellence Award in 2020 and was an invited CTI scholar at Princeton University, 2020–2021.

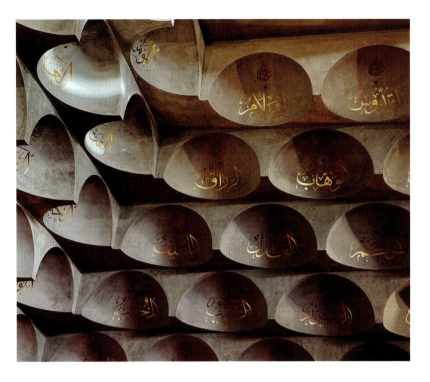

18 Punchbowl Mosque, domes detail.
Photo: Tammy Gaber

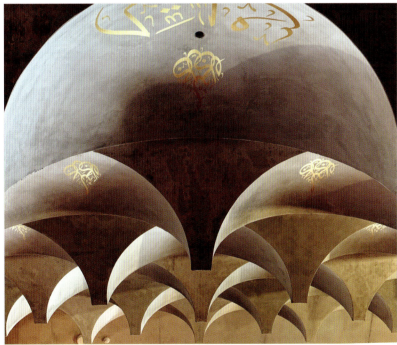

19 Punchbowl Mosque, domes detail with calligraphy.
Photo: Tammy Gaber

SUGGESTIONS FOR FURTHER READING

Curtin, Adrian. *Angelo Candalepas. Australian Islamic Mission* (Fitzroy: UroPublications, 2019).

Haveric, Dzavid. *History of Islam and Muslims in Australia: Early Encounters, Settlements and Communities Prior to the Mid-1940s* (Victoria: Lambert Academic Publishing, 2019).

Jones, Philip and Anna Kenny. *Australia's Muslim Cameleers Pioneers of the Inland 1860s-1930s* (Melbourne: South Australian Museum, 2010).

NOTES

1   Peta Stephenson, "The Makassans," *Boundless Plains The Australian Muslim Connection,* ed. Moustafa Fahour (Melbourne: Islamic Museum of Australia, 2019), 10.

2   Philip Jones and Anna Kenny, *Australia's Muslim Cameleers Pioneers of the Inland 1860s–1930s* (Melbourne: South Australian Museum, 2010), 9.

3   Ibid., 20-22.

4   Ibid., 37.

5   Hanifa Deen, "Doors Open – Doors Close," *Boundless Plains: The Australian Muslim Connection,* ed. Moustafa Fahour (Melbourne: Islamic Museum of Australia, 2019), 23 (22–63).

6   Dzavid Haveric, *History of Islam and Muslims in Australia: Early Encounters, Settlements and Communities Prior to the Mid-1940s* (Victoria: Lambert Academic Publishing, 2019), 140–141.

7   The mosque at Marree and in other places have been reconstructed based on historical images, and the towns all still bear witness to the Muslim presence with extant Muslim graveyards and local streets named after Muslim cameleers. See Fahour. *Boundless Plains,* 5.

8   Muslims from Adelaide, Oodnadatta, and Alice Springs contributed including sizable contributions and leadership from Haji Mullah Merban, Faiz Mahmoed, and Abdul Wahid. The total cost at the time was 450 pounds and a *waqf* (endowment) was created to maintain it. See Haveric, *History of Islam and Muslims in Australia,* 141–142.

9   The minarets cost 250 pounds. Afghan carrier Abdul Wade and local herbalist Mahomet Allum each contributed to the ongoing costs and debts of the mosque. See Haveric, *History of Islam and Muslims in Australia,* 143–146.

10 Shefik Talavanic and his friends found six or seven men, aged 87-111 who were camped out in the mosque, most of whom had contributed to the cost of mosque construction in the 1880s. Talavanic and his friends took care of the men until each passed away and was given a Muslim burial in the city's Muslim section of the West Terrace Cemetery. See Jones and Kenny, *Australia's Muslim Cameleers,* 9.

11 Historically it was documented that in the early 1900s approximately 20–40 people came for Friday prayers and that early 100 would participating in Islamic festivities. See Haveric, *History of Islam and Muslims in Australia,* 145. Today the additions of the external canopy (providing shade for extended prayer areas), the outdoor buildings with offices and washroom facilities and the internally constructed wooden balcony (for women) allow for many more to regularly attend. Observations from October 2019 visit.

12 Deen, "Doors Open – Doors Close," 23.

13 Ibid.

14 Alexandra Biggs, "Islam in the Antipodes: Australian Mosque-Building and the 'Muslim Migrant' 1967–1990," BA Thesis, (Australian National University. October 2016), 4–21.

15 Ibid.

16 Tammy Gaber, "Paradise Present – The imagined and manifested images of Paradise in Islam," *Faith and Form* 48.3 (2015), 10–16.

17 Tammy Gaber, "Gendered Mosque Spaces: Cultural, Religious, or Accessibility Issue?" *Faith and Form* 48.1 (2015), 10–13.

18 For the full survey of textual analysis of the Quran and Hadith, and architectural analysis of the earliest mosques, refer to: Tammy Gaber, "The Space and Place of Women in Mosque Architecture: Between Realities and Misconceptions." PhD diss. (Cairo University, 2007).

19 Lindsay Jones, *The Hermeneutics of Sacred Architecture: Experience, Interpretation, Comparison,* Volume 1. (Cambridge: Harvard University, 2000).

20 Haveric, *History of Islam and Muslims in Australia,* 162–163.

21 According to the 2016 Australian Census, 42% of the country's Muslims reside in Sydney, 31% in Melbourne and 8% in Perth. See "Religion in Australia, 2016 Data Summary," Australian Bureau of Statistics. https://www.abs.gov.au/ausstats/abs@. nsf/Lookup/by%20Subject/2071.0~2016~Main%20 Features~Religion%20Data%20Summary~70

22 According to Murcutt, the project was entirely funded by the local Muslim community who gave money and time (volunteering in construction process) and that there was not any government support or subsidies. See Catherine Hunter and Glenn Murcutt, *Glenn Murcutt: Spirit of Place,* directed by Catherine Hunter (Australia: Catherine Hunter Productions, 2016), film.

23 "Glenn Murcutt 1980–2012 Feathers of Metal" *ElCroquis* 163/164 (Madrid 2012), 409.

24 Hunter and Murcutt, *Glenn Murcutt: Spirit of Place*.

25 Ibid.

26 Glenn Murcutt (architect), in interview with author. Sydney, October 17, 2019.

27 Ibid.

28 Ibid.

29 Ibid.

30 Ibid.

31 Biggs, "Islam in the Antipodes," 30–31.

32 "Auburn Gallipoli Mosque." https://www.gallipolimosque.org.au/mosque accessed September 2020.

33 The AIM NSW Vice-President in 2018: Zachariah Matthews, "The history of the Australian Islamic Mission and design brief," *Angelo Candalepas Australian Islamic Mission. Architecture in Detail* No. 1. (Melbourne: Uro publications, 2018), 5.

34 Ibid.

35 Angelo Candalepas. (architect), in interview with author. Sydney, October 16, 2019.

36 Angelo Candalepas et al., *Angelo Candalepas Australian Islamic Mission. Architecture in Detail* No. 1. (Melbourne: Uro publications, 2018).

37 "About Us." Australian Islamic Mission. https://aim.org.au/about-us/ accessed September, 2020.

38 Angelo Candalepas, "Architect's statement," *Angelo Candalepas Australian Islamic Mission. Architecture in Detail* No. 1 (Melbourne: Uro publications, 2018), 11.

39 Angelo Candalepas. "Absence of Things,' Lecture at Western Sydney University. October 17, 2019 in the "Making the City Series – Identity."

40 Angelo Candalepas. (architect), in interview with author. Sydney, October 16, 2019.

41 Ibid.

42 Ibid.

43 By 1981 the number of Muslims in the country was 76 thousand, by 1994 there was 147 thousand Muslims in the country. The Muslim population rose from 2.2% in 2011 to 2.6% in 2016 - (608, 000 Muslims of Australia's 23,401,892). See "Religion in Australia, 2016 Data Summary," Australian Bureau of Statistics. https://www.abs.gov.au/ausstats/abs@.nsf/Lookup/by%20Subject/2071.0~2016~Main%20Features~Religion%20Data%20Summary~70 accessed September, 2020.

Glossary

Unless otherwise indicated, terms are from Arabic.

Ablaq striped or bicolor masonry

Abr (Persian) cloud bands (a motif of Chinese origin)

'Ahd, also **mīthāq** divine covenant

Ahi, ahis (Turkish) a brotherhood, fraternity, guild

'Ahl al-Kitāb People of the Book

'Alids, Alids the Prophet Muhammad's descendants through the lineage of his cousin and son-in-law, Ali ibn abi Talib

Amir lord or commander-in-chief

Anṣār Prophet Muhammad and followers, helpers in Medina

Apagana, also **matawalpala** Aboriginal Australian terms for Muslims

Ard al-muqaddasa Holy Land

'Ashura (literally, "Tenth") anniversary of Husayn's death, called after the tenth day of the month of Muharram on which he was killed

Athar vestiges or traces

Awqāf inalienable charitable endowment under Islamic law

Awliyā saint's tomb

Azzan, Adhan the call to prayer

———————

Bab gate or door (e.g., *Bab ar-Rahmah* or *Rahma* – Door of Mercy; *Bab al-Ziyada* – Door of the Addition)

Badroon curvilinear designs

Bagh (Persian) garden

Baghche (Urdu) usually, though not exclusively, smaller gardens or palace courtyards

Bahr (Persian) a body of water (such as a lake, river, or sea), also used to refer to the Nile

Bangke lou (Chinese) minaret (derived from *bang*, Persian, and *lou* meaning tower); also, *uanli lou*, call to prayer tower

Baoli (Hindi) stepwell

Baradari (Persian, Urdu) pavilion

Baraka (literally, "blessing") blessed emanations of a saint

Basilica (Latin) rectangular aisled building

Barzakh a place separating the living from the hereafter; a veil between the dead and their return to the world of the living, but also to a phase happening between death and resurrection

Bast (Persian) sanctuary

Bayt, Beit house

Beylerbeyi (Turkish) governor-generals (*akıncı beyleri*: raider-commanders)

Beylic (Turkish) territory under the jurisdiction of a Bey (lord)

Bhadraka (Hindi) multi-sectioned, square-order columns

———————

Bismallah in the name of Allah (invocation used by Muslims at the beginning of any undertaking)

Buq'a dwelling, plot of land, prominent place

Burj citadel

———————

Caliph, khalif title for any of the religious and civil rulers of the Islamic world, claiming succession from the prophet Muhammad

Candi (Indonesian) Hindu and Buddhist sanctuaries

Candi bentar split gates

Candrasala (Indonesian) dormer-window motif

Cardo (Latin) a north-south street

Cella (Latin) inner chamber of an ancient Greek or Roman temple

Chadar (Hindi, Persian) textured water-chute

Chahar bagh (Persian) a cross-axial garden layout with four parts

Chahar taq (Persian) four arched opening (domed)

Chajja (Hindi, Urdu) eaves

Chatri (Hindi, Urdu) (literally, "umbrella") rooftop pavilion

Chilla-nishini (Persian) a 40-day spiritual seclusion and meditation

Citrakhanda (Indonesian) multi-sectioned columns

Cubit (English) conventional measurement of length about 50 cm/20 inches or the length of the forearm (the cubit varied among builders in Arabia and from country to country)

Cungkup (Indonesian) mausoleum buildings

———————

Dāda nursemaid

Dalan (Hindi) cloister

Daotang (Chinese) instructional hall

Dar house, seat (*Dar al-Imara* – seat or palace of the governor or government)

Dargah (Persian, Hindi) shrine

Darussifa (Turkish) hospital

Dawlatkhana treasury

Decumanus (Latin) east-west street

Dhikr (literally, "remembrance") a form of Sufi prayer

Dhimmi, dhimma the people of the covenant (historical term for non-Muslims living in an Islamic state with legal protection)

Dikka a platform raised upon columns from which the Quran is recited and prayers are intoned by the imam

Do'a prayer or invocation

Duwar (Hindi) ruler, judge

———————

Emperan (Indonesian) veranda

———————

Fada'il praises

Fara'iz obligatory duties

Farman, firman order

Fatwā, fetva, futuwwa legal decision

Fayz grace

Fina lower level where funeral prayers may be offered

Firdaus (Persian) paradise, also the highest level of heaven

———————

Ghalib kari, Qalabkari (Hindi) patterns of interlocking rib

Ghazi Muslim soldier, an individual who participated in military expeditions or raiding; and later (Turkish) wars of conquest

Ghulam slave

Ghurfahā upper room, *ghurafat* – chamber

Girih (Persian) knotted

Gongbei (Chinese) domed space for the mausoleum of a holy man

Gonjong (Indonesian) extended-gable roof with a very pronounced curved ridge and dramatic upward-sweeping ridge ends

Gumbati (Hindi, Urdu) miniature solid domes

Gunbad (Hindi) dome chamber

Guldasta (Hindi, Urdu) bouquet

Gynaeceum (Greek) the part of a dwelling used by women

———————

Hadith a saying, or action traditionally attributed to the Prophet Muhammad

Hadra supererogatory ritual performance by Sufi orders

Hajj annual pilgrimage to Mecca

Haram sanctuary within a mosque, sacred enclosure in early Islam, (The Haram – religious and political center in Jerusalem), also forbidden

Hasht bihisht (Persian) eight Paradises

Hayat life

Hazār bāf (Persian) (literally, "thousand threads") decorated in a technique referring to a carpet-like effect formed

Hazira a tomb contained within an enclosure which often includes a mosque

Hierophany (English) a manifestation of the sacred

Hijra the migration of the Prophet Muhammad from Mecca to Medina in 622

Hujurat enclosure

Hukm-i şerif (Turkish) imperial decree

Hyang (Javanese, Balinese) unseen supernatural entity

Hypostyle (English) hall with a roof is supported by columns

'Idgah large, open-air prayer-space (for Eid)

Ijuk (Indonesian) dark fibrous feather palm bark or thatch

'Ilmiyye legal scholars

Imam the person who leads prayers in a mosque, title of various Muslim leaders, especially of Shiite Islam

'Imara, also **zawiya** lodge (**imaret**, in Turkish)

Insan e kamil, the perfect or complete man (reference to the Prophet Muhammad)

Islam submission (to the one God)

Islimi (Persian) split palmettes

Isnad transmission

'Isra Night Journey (by the Prophet Muhammad)

Iwan (Persian **ayvan**) rectangular hall or space, usually vaulted, walled on three sides, with one end entirely open

Iznik (Turkish) a decorated ceramic with a distinctive under-glaze blue color and design, produced from the fifteenth century to the seventeenth (named after the town of Iznik in western Anatolia where it was made)

———

Jalal majesty

Jali (Hindi, Urdu) screens

Jamal beauty

Jami congregational or Friday mosque

Jannat paradise

Jihad spiritual struggle within oneself against sin; struggle or fight against the enemies of Islam

———

Kaaba (literally, "cube") building at the center of Islam's most important mosque, the Masjid al-Haram in Mecca, Saudi Arabia

Kala (Persian) pinnacle

Kanisa church

Kapalıçarşı (Turkish) Grand Bazaar

Karamat miracles

al-Karma vine

Kathisma (Greek) seat

Kawthar the fountain in heaven

Khādim servant

Khan an inn for travelers, built around a central courtyard, also lord or prince

Khangah, khanqah (Persian) Sufi hospice or convent, hostel

khilāfa caliphate, form of government

Khutba Friday oration or sermon

Kiosk (Persian) a small garden pavilion open on some or all sides

Kiswa the traditional covering of black cloth, renewed annually, on the Kaaba, Mecca

Kitabkhana library

Kufic an early angular form of the Arabic alphabet, script

Külliye (Turkish) complex of buildings centered on a mosque and composed of a *madrasa*, clinic, soup kitchens, and other buildings for various charitable services

Kungra (Persian) a hook-shaped decorative element

Kutab a primary school where children were taught the fundamentals of religion

———

Labu-labu (Indonesian) bulbous finial

Laras (Indonesian) sections or moieties

Libaitang (Chinese) worship hall in a Buddhist monastery or Chinese church

Limas (Javanese) hip roof

Loca sancta (Latin) holy or sanctified place (*loca sancta* of Islam, includes the Masjid al-Haram in Mecca, the Haram al-Sharif in Jerusalem, and the Mosque of the Prophet in Medina)

———

Madhab, Madhhab, Madhdhab Sunni school of law or thought within *fiqh* (Islamic jurisprudence). The four major schools are Hanafi, Maliki, Shafi'i and Hanbali

Madrasa educational institution or legal college

Magaz an indirect entrance from the street

Maghrib (literally, "western") fourth mandatory prayer, *salat,* of five in Islam (also prayer facing the sunset)

mahfili (Hindi) the place where the *muezzin* performs his call for prayers

Majmū'ah albums, or *jung* (Persian)

Makruh (literally, "detestable") a disliked or discouraged offensive act

Maktab Quran school

Makuta (Javanese) crown ornament

Malkaf wind catch, or tower oriented toward the prevailing breeze

Mamlūk (literally, "owned") slave, especially used to refer to the Mamluk Sultanate of 1215–1517

Manara (literally, "light") beacon, minaret or tower

Maqad, **maqaad** seat, place of sitting, raised covered porch

Maqam place, location, or position

Maqamat stations, praying pavilions

Maqṣura enclosure screens to protect the caliph or governor

Marghola (Urdu) multi-foiled pointed arches, so called by local masons

Mashhad (literally, "place of witnessing") Shi'ite shrine, place of memorial

Mashrabiyya wooden or metal latticework, perforated screen

Masjid (pl. **masajid**) place of prostration; *masjid jami*, congregational mosque (Masjid al-Haram or Sacred Mosque)

Mathnawi a poem based on independent, internally rhyming lines

Maujpa (Persian) finial

Mawlawi, mawlana title given to Muslim religious scholars, or *ulama*, preceding their name

Mawlid observance of the birthday of the Prophet Muhammad (Mawlid al-Nabi al-Sharif)

Maydan (Persian, Urdu) open space or square

Mazar (literally, "place of visitation") shrine

Mehman khana (Persian) guest house

Mese (Greek) main thoroughfare

Meydan (Turkish) ritual hall (*kırklar meydanı*: Hall of the Forty)

Mihrab (plural **maḥārīb**) the recess or niche in a mosque indicating the direction of Mecca (*qibla*)

Minar minaret, tower

Minbar pulpit for the Friday oration or sermon

Mi'raj ascension; *al-Mi'raj* the ascension, referring to the Prophet Muhammad's journey into heaven

Misraka (Hindi) multi-sectioned columns

Mudakhat intervention or interference

Mudarris instructor

Muezzin a man who calls Muslims to prayer (usually from the minaret of a mosque)

Mufti Islamic legal authority or jurist

Muharram first month of the Islamic calendar

Muhiy' receiver

Muqarnas ornamental vaulting composed of small concave elements, often employed to fill the zone of transition between supporting walls and a dome

Muravvij (Persian) propagator

Musalla large outdoor prayer space, prayer matts, also *namazgah* (Persian)

Mustoko (Indonesian) carved roof finials (*memolo* in Java and Palembang, *kepala som* in Melaka, and *pataka* in Banjarmasin)

Muthannā mirrored script

———

Naga (Sanskrit) serpent

Namazgah (Persian) place of prayer

Naus (Greek) a large sailing vessel with a high forecastle and poop

Nazr votive offering

Nilufar (Persian) lotus

———

Oculus (Latin) a round or eye-like opening

Opus sectile (Latin) a kind of mosaic, composed of pieces of stone cut in different shapes and inlaid in walls or floors to form a larger design

———

Paduraksa, also **kori agung** (Javanese) lintel-gates

Pailou (Chinese) a freestanding monument or memorial in the form of an arched gateway

Panggung (Javanese) raised timber platform floors

Parvāna (Persian) minister or chancellor

Pas o pesh (Persian) recessed rectangular panels

Pietra dura (Latin) inlay technique of using cut and fitted, highly polished colored stones

Pir (Persian) spiritual leader

Pishtaq (Persian) tall raised arched entrance/portal

Porphyry (English) a hard igneous rock containing crystals

Prayers (English) the five daily prayers in Islam: *fajr* (dawn), *zuhr* (mid-day), *'asr* (afternoon), *magrib* (west), and *'isha* (night)

Punden (Javanese) terraced ancestral mounds

GLOSSARY 475

Qa'a reception room for male guests

Qadi a magistrate or judge of a Sharia court

Qalamdani (Urdu) domical vaults with concave margins

Qapuchi (Persian) palace complex

Qibla the direction of Muslim prayer towards Mecca, indicated by the presence of the *mihrab* set in the wall of a mosque or by the *qibla* wall

Qubbat, qubba dome or domed space

———

Rabb al-bayt eternal Lord

Rawda funerary enclosure

Rawshan, rowshan (Hindi) wood latticed windows (usually higher up), element that lets in light, bright light

Rawza a garden, specific to the funerary context

Ribat hospice, lodge, small fortification, Islamic monastery

Riwaq arcade or portico open on at least one side

Rumah (Indonesian, Malay) house

Rumbia (Indonesian) sago thatch

———

Sabil public fountain

Sahn courtyard

Sahib al-zaman lord of the age

Sa'i one of the integral rites of Hajj and Umrah, which refers to the ritual of walking back and forth can be performed

Sama listening; a Sufi ceremony performed as *dhikr*, listening to recitation

Sakhra rock, referring especially to that enshrined by the Dome of the Rock in Jerusalem

Serambi (Malay, Indonesian) outer pavilion (often an addition)

Shabistanat (Persian) prayer halls

Shadhrwan fountain, with the main purpose of providing water for drinking or ritual ablutions for several people

Shafa'a saint's mediating power

al-Sham Syria; (*Bilad al-Sham* – Greater Syria: today Israel, Palestine, Syria, and Jordan)

Shari'a Islamic canonical law based on the teachings of the Quran and the traditions of the Prophet (Hadith and Sunna)

Sharīfayn (Turkish) custodian (usually refers to the custodian of the two Holy Mosques)

Shabistan (Persian) enclosed hall for night-time or winter use

Shaykh, Sheikh Muslim religious scholar, or chief of a tribe or a royal family member

Shir (Persian) tiger (*sher* in Hindi or Urdu)

Shuksheika tower covering in a room

Siciller (Turkish) judges' registers

Sikhara (Sanskrit) (literally, "mountain peak") tower or spire of a medieval Indian temple

Soko guru (Javanese, Indonesian) four principal columns supporting a roof (*soko rawa* – twelve columns)

Spandrel (English) the space between the shoulders of adjoining arches and the ceiling or molding above

Spolia (Latin) repurposed building material

Suffah platform or bench, room with three walls

Sulh-i kull peace for all

Sulur bayung (Indonesian) ridge end ornaments

Sunna practice, custom, tradition, model, law, habit, convention, and personal mannerisms

Surahi, also **vangrhian wala** (Hindi) multi-cusped arch

Sura, Surah, Surat Quranic chapter

Surau (Malay) an Islamic assembly building used for worship and religious instruction

———

Tabhana hospice

Tadhkira remembrance

Tafsir Quranic exegesis

Taḥannuth secluded ritual prayer (from pre-Islam)

Tahlil invocation ("there is no god but God")

Tajug (Javanese) pyramidal-hip roofs

Ta'ifas independent Muslim principalities of al-Andalus

Takiyya (Turkish) Ottoman institution for distribution of food to the poor

Taktaboosh open breezeway

Tanduk (Indonesian) horn

Tanzimat reforms

Tāpū land surveys

Taqwa being conscious and cognizant of God, of truth, "piety, fear of God"

Tarīq, tariqa Sufi doctrine or path of spiritual learning (*tarekat* in Malay and Javanese)

Tawaf circumambulation (around the Kaaba as pilgrims do): Abrahamic ritual practice, the *jāhilī* practice of circumambulation of the shrine, *duwār*, later *tawafr*

Tawhid unification or oneness of God

Temenos (Greek) a piece of land cut off and assigned as an official domain, a sacred precinct

Templum Domini (Latin) Temple of the Lord

Templum or **Palatium Salomonis** (Latin) Temple of Solomon or Solomon's Palace (with reference to al-Aqsa Mosque)

Terminus ante quem (Latin) (literally, "end before which") latest possible date for something

Theotokos (Greek) Mary as the Mother of God (used in the Eastern orthodox church)

Tiraz (Persian) embroidery, or band of calligraphic inscription usually in the form of armbands sewn onto robes of honor (in architecture, as bands of calligraphy bordering arches or other elements)

Toldo (Spanish) sunshade (takes its name from the movable textile structures in the streets of Andalusia)

Tonggak macu, tiang mercu (Minangkabau, Malay, Indonesian) central column

Topoi (plural of *topos*) (Greek) basic theme or concept

Thuluth a proportional calligraphic script with curved and oblique lines

Trabeate (English) post-and-lintel building system

Turba, Turbah tomb (*turba azīma* – large tomb); also, *darih* – burial place

Tympanum (Latin) semi-circular or triangular decorative wall surface over an entrance, door or window, which is bounded by a lintel and an arch

———

'Ubbad residence of worshipers

Ulama Muslim scholars having specialist knowledge of Islamic sacred law and theology

Ulin, also **belian** (Indonesian) ironwood

Umra minor Hajj, the "lesser" pilgrimage to Mecca undertaken by the faithful outside the prescribed time of the Hajj (especially in the month of Ramadan)

'urs observances

———

Velayetnames (Turkish) wardship: holiness for piety, virtue

Verde antiqua (Latin) a veined light green marble

Vihara (Sanskrit) monastery

Vilayet guardianship (a key tenet of Shi'ism); also, district or dominion

———

Wali Friend (of God)

Wantilan (Indonesian) ritual cock-fighting halls

Waqf charitable endowment; *waqfiyya* – endowment deeds (*waqf ahli* – family endowment)

Wudu ablution or ritual purification

———

Yaodian (Chinese) (literally "kiln or hole hall") a narrow space behind the prayer hall, which can serve as a place for a small group of worshipers

Yatir (Turkish) tomb of a holy person

Yuemen (Chinese) Moon Gates

———

Zam zam (literally, "don't spread, don't go away") *Zamzam* spring, well

Zawiya (literally, "a corner"), a praying room, chapel or small mosque, a place of religious retreat, hospice

Zhenjiaosi (Chinese) true religion – an alternate Chinese word for mosque

Ziarah, ziyara visitation, pilgrimage, shrine visitation

Ziyadah surrounding precinct wall

Ziyaratkhana structure for pilgrims

Zuhhad residence of ascetics

Zullah shaded portico, covered colonnade

Index

Aba Khoja Mausoleum, Kashgar, *442, 444*

Abarqu, see Abarquh

Abarquh, 150, 239

Abarquh, Masjid-i Birun, 150

Abbasids, 27, 88, 90, 92, 98, 126, 145, 149, 161–70, 180–81, 204, 206, 210, 227, 347, 348

Abboud, Michel, 49

'Abd al-Hamid, 130

'Abd al-Latif, 134

Abd al-Majeed, 103

'Abd al-Malik, 109, 113–15, 119, 178, 180, 201

'Abd al-Mu'min ibn 'Abd Allah Khan, 254

'Abd al-Qadir al-Jilani, 209

'Abd al-Rahman al-Jami, 303

'Abd al-Rahman ibn Muhammad, 303

'Abd al-Samad, Tomb of, 237–38, *238*

Abd Allah Ansari, Shrine of, 246, 247

'Abd Allah ibn Iskandar Sultan, 252

'Abd ibn Hamdan, 204

Abdel-Aziz al-Sulaiman, 341, 344

Abdel Wahid El-Wakil, 29, 341–45, 347–48, 351–52

'Abdī Beg Shīrāzī, 63

Abdul Aziz al-Saud, 348

Abdul-Rahman Hussaini, 350

'Abdülhamid II, 300

Abdullah al-Sulaiman, 341

'Abdurrazzaq (b. Ulugh Beg), 387

Abi Waqqas, 447

Abraham, 20, 85–87, 90, 109–10, 144, 182, 200–2
Tomb of, 144

Abraj Mosque, Jeddah, 343–44

Abu 'Abd-Allah Muhammad ibn Musa al-Kazim, 166

Abu al-Fida, 142

Abu al-Hayja ibn Hamdan, 163

Abu al-Su'ud, 301

Abu Ayyub al-Ansari, 310

Abu Bakr, 102, 135

Abu Dhabi, Sheikh Zayed Grand Mosque, *350,* 352

Abu Hanifa, Tomb of, 163, 207

Abu Hassan Ali, 406

Abu Hatab, Babil Governate, *166, 167*

Abu Sa'id, 227, 234, 387

Abu'l Hayja 'Abdallah, 220

Abu'l-Walid Shrine, Azadan, *247, 247*

Abul Zafar Muhy-ud-Din, 393

Abyssinians, 101

Aceh
Bitay Mosque, 412
Grand Mosque, 412, 424

Achaemenids, 26, 151

Ad-Darriyah, 350

Adalaj Stepwell, *367*

Adam, 17, 85, 261

Adelaide, 457–58
Adelaide Mosque, 457–58, *459*

Adil-shahis, 368–69

Adina Mosque, Pandua, 363, *364*

'Adud al-Dawla, 220

Adzhina-Tepe, Buddhist monastery, 152

Afaq Khvaja, Tomb of, *252, 254*

Aflaki, 303

Afyon, 280, 319, *325*
Gedik Ahmet Pasha Mosque, 319, *325*

Aga Khan Award for Architecture, Geneva, 30, 72, 178, 340–42, 349–50, 356, 403, 442, 449, 451, 463

Aga Khan Development Network (AKDN), 72, 76

Aga Khan Documentation Center at MIT, 23, 30–31, 63, 67, 72–73, 75–76, 149–50, 153, 154, 157, 161, 164, 166, 168, 190, 207, 215, 219–20, 222, 269

Aga Khan Historic Cities Programme, 72, 76

Aga Khan Program for Islamic Architecture (AKPIA), Cambridge (MA), 73, 76

Aga Khan Trust for Culture (AKTC), Geneva, 30, 75–77

Aga Khan Visual Archive, Cambridge (MA), 73

Agam, Taluk Mosque, 412, 424

Agamy, 341
Halawa House, 341

Agnawi, Sami, 72

Agra, 35–36, 42–44, *45,* 46, 375–76, 379, 382, 393–94, 397,
Fort, 398
Friday Mosque, 375
Taj Mahal, 35, 36, 43–44, *46,* 68, 234, 367, 376, *382, 383,* 384, 386, 388–89, 393
Tomb of I'tmad ud-Dawla, *36,* 44, *45, 46, 385*

Ahlat, 41, 286, *286*
Cemetery, *40*

Ahmad al-Badawi, Shrine of, 209

Ahmad ibn Hanbal, 165

Ahmad ibn Hizr, 220

Ahmad Jami, 388

Ahmad Khvafi Madrasa, Khargird, 248

Ahmad Yasavi, 243–44, *244*

Ahmadabad, 367–68
Friday Mosque, 368

Ahmadnagar, 380

Ahmadshah, 289–90

Ahmed III, 42

Ain Shams Universiry, Cairo, 341

Aisha, 101, 218

Ajmer, 309, 361
Shrine of Muin al-din Chishti, 309

Akbar, 44, 373–74, 379, 381–82, 384, 386–89, 393
Tomb of, 44, *384*

Akin, Gunkut, 333

Akşehir, 303
Tomb of Sayyid Mahmud Khayrani, 303

al-Aqmar Mosque, Cairo, 27

al-Aqsa Mosque, Jerusalem, 20, 85, *111,* 115, *118,* 119, 125, *175,* 177, 179–84, *181,* 200

al-Ashraf Qaytbay, 103, 118, 193

al-Awfi, 406

al-Azhar Mosque, Cairo, 27

al-'Aziba, Babil Governate, *167,* 168

al-Azim State Mosque, Melaka, 424

al-Baqi Cemetery, Medina, 203

Al-Beeah Group, 350

al-Bukhari, 217

al-Ghazali, 199

al-Hakim, 116

al-Hakim Mosque, Cairo, 27

al-Harawi, 134, 145, 183, 189, 198, 200, 202, 204, 288

al-Harithy Mosque, Jeddah, 344

al-Hasan ibn 'Ali ibn Abi Talib, see Hasan ibn Ali ibn Abi Talib

al-Hujurat, 101

al-Husayn, see Husayn ibn Ali ibn Abi Talib

al-'Ilmawi, 134

al-Istakhri, 358

al-Jarrah Mosque, Damascus, 189, 191, 193, *194*

al-Kamil, 118, 208

al-Kazimiyya Shrine, Baghdad, *74,* 164–65

al-Khatib al-Baghdadi, 163

al-Khidr, 134, 202

al-Kindi Plaza, Riyadh, *350,* 351

al-Mahdi (twelfth Shi'i Imam), 203, 206

al-Mahdi al-Abbasi, 103

al-Malik al-Adil,194

al-Malik al-Ashraf Musa, 191–92

al-Malik al-Kamil, 208

al-Malik al-Zahir, 205–6

al-Ma'mun, 164

al-Mansur, 27, 88, 90, 92, 163

al-Maqdisi, 406

al-Maqrizi, 39

al-Mas'udi, 130, 359

al-Miqat Mosque, Dhul Hulayfa, 347

al-Muqaddasi, 131–32, 145, 163, 180, 182, 200, 204, 223

al-Mu'tamid, 165

al-Mutawakkil, 164

al-Nahrajuri, 406

al-Narshakhi, 154

al-Nasir li-Din Allah, 168–70, 206, 210

al-Nasir Muhammad, 201

al-Nawawi, 199

al-Qiblatain Masjid, Medina, *346,* 347

al-Radi, 162

al-Rusafa
Church of St. Sergius, 140–41, *143*
Great Mosque, 140, *142, 143*
Mosque, *344*

al-Samhudi, 101–2

al-Shafi Cenotaph, Cairo, *207,* 207, *208*

al-Shakhawi, 208

al-Tabari, 145

al-Tawba Mosque, Damascus, 191–194, *193*

al-'Uzza, 18

al-Walid, 26, 103, 115, 125, 128, 130–32, 135, 141, 145, 180, 347

al-Zahir, 181, 206

'Ala al-din 'Ali, 303

'Ala al-Din Kayqubad I, 277, 280, 281, 287, 290

Alaeddin Bey Mosque, Bursa, *325*

Alaeddin Bey Mosque, Larende, 293

Alaeddin Mosque, Konya, 276, 277–79, *278,* 284, 286, 288

Alaeddin Mosque, Niğde, 315, *316,* 317, 320, *325*

'Alam al-din Qaysar, 303

'Alam al-Din Sanjar al-Jawali, 201

'Alamgir, 373, 376, 381–82, 384, 393–94
Alamgiri Gate, Lahore, 394
Alanya, Citadel of, 277
Alawis, 68
Alawites, 68
Aleppo, 190, 201–2, 205, 206, 301
 Great Mosque, 125, *140*, 191
 Madrasa al-Firdaws, *190*, *191*, 194
 Madrasa al-Halawiyya, 140, *141*
 Shrine of Husayn ibn Ali ibn Abi Talib, *205*, *206*
Alhambra, Granada, 39
'Ali, see Ali ibn Abi Talib
Ali al-Hadi, 163
 Shrine of, 198
'Ali al-Harawi, 198
Ali Hajveri, 406
Ali ibn Abi Talib, 135, 162, 204, 228, 234, 258–59, 263, 333
 Shrine of, *203*, 220
'Ali ibn al-Harawi, 183
Ali ibn Hamzeh, Tomb of, *43*
'Ali ibn Shahsuwar, 308
Ali Qapu, Isfahan, *260*, *261*, 262–63, 265
Ali Riza Abbasi, 266–67
Ali Shuaibi, 350
'Ali Shah, 227–28, 234
'Ali Shah Mosque, Tabriz, 227, *227*–28
Alids, 203, 206–7, 216, 229, 231, 238
Allahabad 384
Allan, James, 162
Almoravids, 68
Alpay Ozdural, 341
Amasya, 285, 288, 315–21, 325
 Bayezid II Mosque, *319*, 325
 Bayezid Pasha Mosque, 325
 Burmalı Minare Mosque, *274*, 285, 288, 315, *316*, *325*
 Fethiye Mosque, 288
 Gök Madrasa Mosque, 315–21, *317*
Amber, 381
Amin Khvaja, 254
Amin Mosque, Turfan, *254*
Amirs of Sind, 360
Ampel Mosque, Surabaya, 412, *416*, 417, 422
Amphilochios, 277
'Amr Mosque, Cairo, 27, 38–39, 191
An-Nawier Mosque, Jakarta, 422
Anastasios, 133
Anastasis Rotunda, Jerusalem, 110, 113
Angke Mosque, Jakarta, 419
Anıtkabir, Atatürk's Mausoleum, 29
Ankara
 Arslanhane Mosque, 281, 288
 Kocatepe, Mosque, *328*, *329*–336, *330*, *331*, *336*, *337*
Anthemius and Isidorus, 321
Antioch, Church of St. Mary, 132
Apéry, Paul, 130
Aq Astana Baba, Surkhandariya Province, 152, 218–20
Aq Saray Palace, Shahr-i-Sabz, 243
Aqda, Friday Mosque, 150
Aqsa Mosque, Jerusalem, see Al-Aqsa
ar-Rahman Mosque, Baghdad, 55, *56*
Ar-Rahman Mosque, New York, 31
Arab Ata, Tim, 151, 218–22
Arculf, 131
Ardabil, 63, 228, 237, 257, 260–61, 263, 308–9, 380
 Friday Mosque, 228

Shrine of Shaykh Safi, 63, 66, 237, *260*, 261, 263, 300, 308–9, 380
 Tomb of Safi al-Din Ishaq, 309
Ardalan, Nader, 57, 59
Ardestan, 151, 158, 237
Ardistan, see Ardestan
Arghuns, 368
Arjun Dev, 394
Arslanhane Mosque, Ankara, 281, 288
Asaf Khan, 384, 386
'Ashiq-Pasha-zade, 299
Ashmolean Museum, Oxford, 70
Ashtarkhanids, 249
Ashtarjan, Friday Mosque, 227
Asnaq, Friday Mosque, 228
Atala Mosque, Jaunpur, *364*, *365*
Atatürk's Mausoleum, Anıtkabir, 29
'Atiqa Mosque, Kashgar, 254, *254*
Aurangabad, 381, 386
Aurangzeb, see 'Alamgir
Ayasuluk
 Church of St. John, 282
Ayasuluk, see also Ephesus
Ayazma Mosque, Istanbul, 326
Ayverdi, E. H, 320
Ayyubids, 118, 129, 184, 189–95, 199, 202, 205–6, 280, 286
Azadan, Abu'l-Walid Shrine, *247*
Azapkapı Sokollu Mosque, Istanbul, 323
Azezeyia Mosque, Jeddah, 345
Azhina-Tepe, Buddhist monastery, 217
Aziran, Friday Mosque, 228

———

Ba'th Party, 71
Bab al-Saghir, Damascus, 193, 203
Baba Qasim, 231
Babil Governate
 Abu Hatab, *166*, 167
 Al-'Aziba, *167*, 168
 Imam al-Najmi, 167, *168*
 Umm al-Awlad, *166*, 167
Babur, 42–43, 373, 381, 387–88
 Tomb of, *42*, *43*, 44, *387*
Badr al-din al-Tabrizi, 303
Badr al-Jamali, 201–2, 205
Badran, Rasem, 348–50
Badshahi Masjid, Lahore, 352–53, 376, *378*, 392–98, *394*, *395*, *396*, *397*
Bagan Serai, Masjid Tinggi (Tall Mosque), 420
Bagh-e Babur, Kabul, *43*
Baghdad, 27, 71, 152, 161–64, 168–70, 180, 207, 209–10, 227–28, 344, 357
 Abu Hanifa Tomb, 163, 207, 217
 Ahmad ibn Hanbal Tomb, 165
 al-Kazimiyya Shrine, *74*, 164–65
 Ar-Rahman Grand Mosque, 55–56
 Baghdad State Mosque, 348, *349*
 Baghdad University, 352
 Kazimiyya Shrine, *74*, 164, 165
 Khan Mirjan, 240
 Khulafa Mosque, *75*, 352
 Nizamiyya Madrasa, 170
 Shrine of Umar al-Suhrawardi, *169*, 170, 210
 Tomb of Abu Hanifa, 207
 Zumurrud Khatun Tomb, 168, *169*
Baha al-din Walad, 303

Baha' al-Din, al-'Amili, 267–68
Bahadur Shah I, 381–2
Bahmanis, 368
Bait Ur Rouf Mosque, Dhaka, *62*
Bakhtiar Kaki, 382
Bakhtiar, Laleh, 57, 59
Bala Hauz Mosque, Bukhara, 254
Bali, Malqoch-oghli, 308
Balis, 194–95, 204
Balım Sultan, see Khidr Bali
Balkh, 249, 317
 Masjid-i Nuh Gunbad, 152–55, 317
 Mausoleum, 254
Bam, 150
Banau Lawas, Pusaka Banua Lawas Mosque, 420
Banbhore, 358
 Friday Mosque, *358*
Banda Hilir, Melaka, 414
Banjarmasin, 414, 418, 420
 Friday Mosque, 418
Banna, Baqir 266–67
Banten, Grand Mosque, *412*
Bao'en Monastery, 431
Baoding Mosque, 439
Barid-shahis, 368
Barriere, Jacques, 56
Barsian, 152
 Mosque, *148*, 152
Bashan Mosque, 154
Basra, 27, 149, 406
 Mosque, 26
 Tomb of Rabi'a al-'Adawiyya, 207
Bavandids, 222–3, 285
Bayan Mosque, 420
Baybars, 118, 129–30, 145
 Tomb of, 129
Bayezid II Mosque, Amasya, *319*, 325
Bayezid II Mosque, Edirne, 320, 322, 325
Bayezid II Mosque, Istanbul, 320, 322, 323, 325
Bayezid II, 299–300, 303–5, 308
Bayezid Pasha Mosque, Amasya, 325
Bazid, Ustad, 401
Begley, Wayne E., 388
Beijing
 Ox Street Mosque, 433–37, *437*
 White Pagoda of Miaoying Monastery, 431
Beirut, 30, 74
Beit Gamal adin Dahabi, Cairo, 339
Beit Kathoda, Cairo, 339
Beit Souheimi, Cairo, 339
Bektashi, 307, 333, 334
Ben Ezra Synagogue, Cairo, 64
Berlin, Museum fur Islamische Kunst, 70
Besim Hakim, 73
Bethlehem, 112, 144, 202
Beylerbeyi Mosque, Istanbul 326
Beyşehir, 320
 Eşrefoğlu Mosque, *280*, 281, 288, 320
Bhadresevar, Chhoti Mosque, 360, *361*
Bhadreshvar (Kachh), 360, 367
Bibi Khanum Mosque, Samarqand, see Great Mosque of Samarqand
Bibi-ka Maqbara, Aurangabad, 382, 384, *386*, 387
Bijapur, 364–65, 369, 379–80
 Gol Gumbad, 369
 Tomb of Ibrahim II Adil Shah, *365*, *369*
Bilad Bani Bu Ali Mosque, Sharqiya, 352

Bilecik, Convent-Shrine of Ede Bali, 299, 300
Bīmāristān of Nūr al-Dīn, Damascus, 70
Binladin Construction, 344
Bistam, Shrine of Bayazid, 237
Bitay Mosque, Aceh, 412
Bitlis, 315
Black Stone, Mecca, 86–89, 87
Blair, Sheila, 65, 166,
Blue Mosque, Tabriz, 235, 264
Böhm, Paul, 31
Bonang Tomb Complex, Tuban, 417
Bonatz, Paul, 329
Bonner, Jay, 105
Bordeaux pilgrim, 175–6
Bosra, 144
Bostancı Mosque, Istanbul, 326
Botou Mosque, Cangzhou, 439
Brindavan, 381, 387
    Govind Deva Temple, 380, 381
Brunei, 409
Brunelleschi, Filippo, 232
Bsheer, Rosie, 72
Buddhists, 150, 152, 198, 217, 358, 360, 363, 406, 409,
    412, 429, 430–34, 441–44, 447, 451
Bukhara, 154, 220
    Bala Hauz Mosque, 254
    Char Bakr, 252
    Friday Mosque, 219
    Maghok-i Attari Mosque, 152
    Samanid Tomb, 214, 218, 220–21, 234
Bun, Kyai Gede Mosque, 420
Buraq, 231
    Tomb of, 231
Burhanuddin, 384
Burmalı Minare Mosque, Amasya, 274, 285, 288, 315,
    316, 325
Bursa, 235–36, 264, 292, 318–20, 325
    Alaeddin Bey Mosque, 325
    Great Mosque, 319, 320, 325
    Hüdavendigar Mosque, 318, 319, 325
    Muradiye Mosque, 325
    Tomb of Ottoman Princes, 303
    Yeşil Mosque, 319, 332, 333
    Yıldırım Mosque, 319
Burujird, 150
Buton Mosque, southeast Sulawesi, 411
Buyids, 156, 163–64, 204, 223, 251

Cadet, Auguste, 75
Cairo, 27, 30, 38–40, 64–66, 68, 71, 118, 189–90, 204–5,
    207–9, 216, 281, 303, 339
    al-Shafi Cenotaph, 207, 208
    Beit Gamal adin Dahabi, 339
    Beit Kathoda, 339
    Ben Ezra Synagogue, 64
    Church of al-Mu'allaqa, 145
    Complex of Sultan Hasan, 228, 345, 347
    Dār al-Maḥfūẓāt al-'Umūmiyya, 71
    French Institute for Oriental Archaeology, 339
    Mosque of 'Amr, 27, 38–39
    Mosque of al-Aqmar, 27
    Mosque of al-Azhar, 27
    Mosque of al-Hakim, 27
    Mosque of Ibn Tulun, 341, 347
    Qarafa al-Kubra' Cemetery, 203, 207–9

Shrine of Husayn ibn Ali ibn Abi Talib, 196, 197,
    202
Shrine of Zayn al-Din Yusuf, 209
Turbat al-Za'faran, 205
Cambay, see Khambhat
Cambridge (MA), Aga Khan Documentation Center
    at MIT, 72, 76
Cameleer, 456, 458, 471–72
Candalepas, Angelo, 457, 460, 467–70, 472–73
Candilis, Georges, 75
Cangzhou, North Mosque, 439
Cansever, Turgut, 332
Canton, see Guangzhou
Carita Pandeglang, Great Mosque, 420
Carmona, 38
Casablanca, 75
    Hassan II Mosque, 352
Cathedral of Florence, 232
Cathedral of St. John, Damascus, 26
Cave of the Patriarchs, Hebron, see Tomb of the
    Patriarchs, Hebron
Chahar Sutun Mosque, Termez, 152, 154
Chaldiran, 301
Champa, 409
Chandraprabha Temple, Jaiselmer, 368
Chang'an, 429
Char Bakr Complex, 252
Chatterjee, Nandini, 68
Chaulukya, 360
Chehel Dukhtaran, Damghan, 223
Chelebi Oghlu, 231
Chengua, 449
Chhoti Mosque, Bhadresevar, 360, 361
Chilburj Mosque, 154
Chingis Khan, 249, 434
Chivi-zade, 300
Chor Sutun, 317
Christ, see Jesus
Christianity, see Christians
Christians, 20, 26, 30, 109–21, 131, 134, 139–45, 150,
    175–84, 197–23, 227, 268, 275, 277, 282, 285, 299,
    358, 429, 458
Church of
    al-Mu'allaqa, Cairo, 145
    Hagia Sophia, Istanbul, 26, 30–2, 42, 178, 320, 321,
        323, 325, 342, 347
    John the Baptist, Damascus, 131, 141
    Sant'Apollinare Nuovo, Ravenna, 130
    St. Amphilochios, Konya, 277
    St. John, Ayasuluk, 282
    St. John, Hama, 142
    St. Sergius, al-Rusafa, 140–41, 143
    St. Stephen, Umm al-Rasas, 139
    the Ascension, Jerusalem, 110, 113, 114, 118, 176
    the Holy Sepulcher, Jerusalem, 20, 110, 113, 116–17,
        144, 176, 178, 182
    the Kathisma, 112, 144, 145
    the Tomb of Mary, Jerusalem, 112
Çifte Kümbet Tomb, Kayseri, 287
Cihangir Mosque, Istanbul, 326
Cirebon
    Grand Mosque, 410, 411, 415
    Panjunan Mosque, 415
Citadel Mosque, Divriği, 279, 80, 315, 317
Civil Courts of Justice, Madrid, 58
Clavijo, Ruy Gonzalez de, 244
Cologne, 31

Constantinople, 27, 116, 130, 178, 183, 299, 310, see also
    Istanbul
    Chalke Gate, 129
    Hagia Sophia, 26, 30–2, 42, 178, 320, 321, 323, 325,
        342, 347
Convent-Shrine of Ede Bali, Bilecik, 299–300
Cordoba, 27, 38–40, 43, 106
    Great Mosque, 12, 13, 26, 34, 38, 40, 43, 53, 54, 106,
        125, 151–52
Çorlulu Ali Pasha Mosque, Istanbul, 326
Corniche Mosque, Jedddah, 338, 343, 344
Costa, Paolo M., 167
Crac des Chevaliers, 189
Creswell, K.A.C., 27, 69–70, 120, 129, 164, 215
Ctesiphon, Palace, 228

D'Aranco, Raimondo, 326
Daata Ganj Bakhsh
    Shrine of (Lahore), 400, 406
    Tomb of (Okara), 405, 406
Dalokay, Vedat, 329–336
Damascus, 37, 40, 66, 140–2, 180, 189, 191, 197, 200–1,
    204–5, 208, 281, 287, 301–3, 310
    al-Jarrah Mosque, 189, 191, 193, 194
    al-Tawba Mosque, 191–194, 193
    Bab al-Faradis, 193
    Bab al-Saghir, 193, 203
    Bīmāristān of Nūr al-Dīn, 70
    Cathedral of St. John, 26
    Church of John the Baptist, 131, 141
    Great Mosque, 13, 16, 17, 26, 27, 37, 40, 73, 124,
        125–135, 125, 126, 127, 128, 131, 132, 133, 141, 145,
        149, 198, 202, 204, 281, 287, 347
    Jebel Jawshan, 205
    Madrasa al-Zahiriyya, 129
    Madrasa and Tomb Complex of Nur al-Din, 287
    Markaz al-Wathā'iq al-Tārīkhiyya, 66
    Mashhad al-Ra's Mosque, 189, 197, 203, 204
    Shrine of Husayn ibn Ali ibn Abi Talib, 204
    Shrine of Ibn al-'Arabi, 209, 298, 299–303, 300,
        301, 302
    Shrine of John the Baptist, 135
    Shrine of Shaykh Arslan, 209
    Tomb of Baybars, 129
    Tomb of Nur al-Din, 53, 54, 287
    Tomb of Rabi'a al- Shamiyya, 207
    Tomb of Salah al-Din, 129
Damat İbrahim Pasha Mosque, Nevşehir, 326
Damat İbrahim Pasha, Mosque, Istanbul, 326
Damghan, 151
    Chehel Dukhtaran, 223
    Tarik Khaneh Mosque, 150, 151, 153, 155
Daniel, 182
Danishmendids, 178
Dār al-Maḥfūẓāt al-'Umūmiyya, Cairo, 71
Dar al-Siyada, Mashhad, 247
Darb-i Imam Shrine, Isfahan, 51, 52, 54, 259
Darriyah Mosque, Wadi Hanifah, 350
Darul Aman Mosque, Singapore, 424
Dashiguo, 429
Dashti, Friday Mosque, 228
Datong Mosque, Shanxi, 438, 439
David, 18, 110, 113–14, 119, 178–80, 182, 201, 301
Daxuexiang Mosque, see Xi'an Mosque
Daybul, 358
Da'ud al-Qaysari, 302

INDEX 479

Deccani Sultanates, 357, 369

Dehistan
Shir Kabir Tomb and Mosque, 216–18, 220
Tomb of 'Ali ibn Sukhari, 217

Delhi, 36, 43–45, 71, 361–64, 366, 375–76, 381–82, 384
Divan-i- Khas, 398
Friday Mosque, 376, 377, 394
Hauz Khas, 43, 44
Jahannuma Masjid, 376, 379
Jami Masjid, 376, 377, 394
Moti Masjid, 379
Qutb Minar, 362, 363, 393
Qutb Mosque, 362
Tomb of Humayun, 36, 43–44, 45, 385

Demak
Grand Mosque, 410, 411
Tomb of Kadilangu 417

Deobandi, 373

Derbent, Great Mosque, 125

Develi Mosque, Kayseri, 315

Dhaka, Bait Ur Rouf Mosque, 62

Dhul Hulayfa, al-Miqat Mosque, 347

Digaran Mosque, Hazara, 152, 153, 154

Dingzhou Mosque, 439

Divriği
Citadel Mosque, 279, 80, 315, 317
Great Mosque, 279, 284, 286, 289–90, 315, 317, 320
Kale Mosque, 279, 280
Mosque and Hospital Complex of, 286, 289, 289–90

Diwan-i-Khas, Delhi, 398

Diyarbakır, 315
Great Mosque, 125, 315

Djenne, 105

Doha, Siddique Mosque, 352

Dome of the Ascension, Jerusalem, 114, 118, 174, 184

Dome of the Chain, Jerusalem, 114, 115, 117–19, 175, 179, 180, 182–83

Dome of the Rock, Jerusalem, 13, 16, 17, 20, 31, 32, 37, 108, 109, 109–21, 111, 112, 115, 119, 120, 125, 134, 144, 145, 175, 177, 178–184, 178, 179, 200, 201, 208, 217, 333

Donxiang Autonomous Hui Hamlet, Pingzhuang Mosque, 441, 443

Dougouba Mosque, 76

Drum Tower, Xi'an, 448

Dulqadirids, 308

Duyong Mosque, Melaka, 422

E.A. Juffali and Brothers, 344

Écochard, Michel, 73

Ede Bali, 299–300

Edirne, 292, 318, 320, 322, 323, 325
Bayezid II Mosque, 320, 322, 325
Eski Mosque, 320, 325
Üç Şerefeli Mosque, 320, 325
Selimiye Mosque, 54, 323, 325, 326, 329–33, 331, 334, 344

El-Wakil, see Abdel Wahid El-Wakil

Elevi, Hakan 457, 460, 463

Elijah, see al-Khidr

Ephesus, Temple of Artemis, 282

Ephesus, see also Ayasuluk

Eretna, 287

Erzincan, 286, 289–90

Erzurum, 286, 315
Great Mosque, 315

Eski Fatih Mosque, Istanbul, see Fatih Mosque, Istanbul

Eski Mosque, Edirne, 320, 325

Eşrefoğlu Mosque, Beyşehir, 280, 281, 288, 320

Ettinghausen, Richard, 57

Eusebius of Caesarea, 176

Eve, 261

Evrenos Ghazi, 308

Eyüp Sultan Mosque, Istanbul 326

Ezekiel, 197, 200

Fahad ibn Abd al-Aziz, 103, 342, 345

Fahd ibn Abdul-Aziz, see Fahad ibn Abd al-Aziz

Fahraj, 151

Fakhr al-Din 'Ali, 291

Faridal-Din 'Attar, Tomb of, 246

Fars, Gunbad-i 'Ali, 223

Faryumad, Friday Mosque, 227

Fatehpur Sikri, 374–75, 393
Friday Mosque, 372, 374, 375, 379, 395
Tomb of Salim Chisti, 374

Fathy, Hassan, 339–44, 348

Fatih Mosque, Istanbul, 27, 28, 325

Fatima, 203

Fatimids, 27, 64, 115–16, 144, 181–82, 201, 205, 207, 215

Fatmev, 154

Fenghuang (Phoenix) Mosque, Hangzhou, 433, 439

Fethiye Mosque, Amasya, 288

Fez, Qarawiyyīn Mosque, 68

Fidai Khan Koka, 393

Firoz Shah, see Firuz Shah

Firuz Shah III, 364

Firuz Shah, 43, 363
Tomb and Madrasa of, 363

Firuzanids, 223

Florence, S. Maria del Fiore, 232

Freer and Sackler Galleries, Washington, D.C., 70

Friday Mosque of
Agra, 375
Ahmadabad, 368
Aqda, 150
Ardabil, 228
Ashtarjan, 227
Asnaq, 228
Aziran, 228
Banbhore, 358
Bukhara, 219
Dashti, 228
Delhi, 376, 377, 394
Faryumad, 227
Fatehpur Sikri, 372, 374, 375, 379, 395
Herat, 246
Isfahan, see Great Mosque of Isfahan
Istakhr, 26
Jerusalem, see al-Aqsa, Jerusalem
Kaj, 228
Khiva, 154, 156, 280
Konya, 305
Kutai, 420
Lahore, 352–53, 376, 378, 392–98, 394, 395, 396, 397
Mashhad, 245Nayin, 152–53, 154, 156
Samarinda, 420

Samarqand, see Great Mosque of Samarqand
Sultaniyya, 24
Veramin, 227

Fustat, 'Amr Mosque, 27, 38–39, 191

Gabriel, 18, 101, 182, 201

Gabriel, Albert, 316–17, 319, 325

Gahadavalas, 359

Gala Mosque, 415

Gallica, 75

Gallipoli Mosque, Sydney, 460–61, 461, 467, 473

Gandhara, 360

Ganting Mosque, 421

Garlandan, Tomb, 235

Gate of David, Jerusalem, 182

Gate of Mercy, Jerusalem, 114, 180

Gate of Repentance, Jerusalem, 114, 180

Gawhar Shad, 245

Gawhar Shad Friday Mosque, Herat, 246

Gawhar Shad Madrasa, Herat, 248

Gazur Gah, Shrine of Abd Allah Ansari, 246, 247

Gedik Ahmet Pasha Mosque, Afyon, 319, 325

Gehbard, David, 330

George Town, Lebuh Aceh Mosque, 421–22

Ghazan, 227, 235

Ghazana, 362

Ghaznavids, 360, 362

Ghazni, Tomb of Ulugh Beg "Kabuli," 387

Ghiyath al-Din Kaykhusraw II, 285, 287–88, 290

Ghiyath al-Din Muhammad, 235

Ghiyath al-Din Tughluq, 363

Ghiyathiyya Madrasa, Khargid, 248

Ghurids, 361–63

Giri, 416

Giri Mosque, 415, 417

Godard, André, 151

Goitein, S.D., 65

Gök Madrasa Mosque, Amasya, 315–21, 317

Gök Medrese, Sivas, 291, 291-2

Gol Gumbad, Bijapur, 369

Golconda, 379–80

Golden Gate, Jerusalem, 179, 180, 182

Golombek, Lisa, 73, 237

Gopaksetra, 358

Govind Deva Temple, Brindavan, 380, 381

Grabar, Oleg, 39, 57, 149–50, 178, 215, 217

Granada, Alhambra, 39

Grand Mosque of
Banten, 412
Cirebon, 410–11
Demak, 410, 411
Jepara, 412
Kotagede, 412, 417
Palembang, 414, 418
Palopo, 411, 415, 421
Sultan Qaboos, Muscat, 352
Surakarta, 412, 418
Yogyakarta, 412, 417–18,

Great East Mosque, Jining, 437, 438

Great East Mosque, Kaifeng, 437, 438, 439

Great Mosque of
al-Rusafa, 140, 142
Aleppo, 125, 140, 191
Bursa, 319, 320, 325
Carita, Pandeglang, 420

Cordoba, *12*, 13, 26, *34*, 38, 40, 43, 53, *54*, 106, 125, 151–52

Damascus, 13, *16*, 17, *26*, 27, *37*, 40, 73, *124*, 125–135, *125*, *126*, *127*, *128*, *131*, *132*, *133*, 141, 145, 149, 198, 202, *204*, 281, 287, *347*

Derbent, 125

Divriği, 315, 320

Diyarbakir, 125, *315*

Erzurum, 315

Hama, 142, *143*

Harran, 125

Isfahan, *53*, 149, 151–52, 156–57, *157*, 167, 228, 228–30, 244, 320

Jember, 420

Kalan, 248–49

Kayseri, 288, 290–1, 315, *316*, 320

Kelantan, Kota Bahru, 413

Kufa, 26

Limo Kaum, 412, *413*

Makassar, 420

Malatya, 280

Manisa, 281, 320, *325*

Manonjaya, 420

Rao-rao, *408*, 409, 421

Samarqand, 149, 151, 243, 244, *245*, 250

Samarra, 155, 433

Silvan, 316, 320, *325*

Siraf, 149, 151, 154

Sivas 315

Sumedang, 420

Watampone, 420

Xi'an, 433–34, *435*, 439, *446*, 447–52, *447*, *448*, *449*, *450*, *451*, *452*

Yazd, *236*, 236–37

Great North Mosque, Zhengzhou, 439

Guadix, 38

Guangta, *428*, 431

Guangzhou, 429, 431–33, 448

Huaisheng Mosque, *428*

Gujarat Sultanate, 368

Gujarat, 360, 364, 367–68, 373, 375

Gülnüş Emetullah Mosque in Üsküdar (Yeni Valide), Istanbul, 41, *42*, 324, 326

Gulpaygan, 158

Gunbad-i 'Ali, Fars, 223

Gunbad-i Qabus, Maragha, 284, 215–16, 220, 223

Gur-i Mir, Samarqand 234, 243, *242*, 244

Gurji Khatun, 303

Gurun Mosque, 421

Gwalior, 358–59, 360

Madhya Pradesh, *359*

————

Habsburgs, 299

Hacı Beşir Ağa Mosque, Istanbul, 326

Hacı Kılıç Mosque, Kayseri 315,

Hacı Paşa, 285

Hacıbektaş, Shrine of Haji Bektash, 299, 301, 307–10, *308*, *309*

Hadid, Zaha, 49, 56, 58

Hadith, 17, 102, 134, 177, 199, 217, 219, 233, 261, 267, 271, 292, 333, 406, 433, 462

Hadrian, 175–6

Hafeyer Mosque, Mecca, 348

Hāfız li-Din Allah, 64

Hagia Sophia, Istanbul, 26, 30–2, 42, 178, 320, *321*, 323, *325*, 342, 347

Haji Bektash al-Khurasani, 299, 301, 307–8, 310

Shrine of, 299, 301, 307–10, *308*, *309*

Haji Muhammad Salleh Mosque, Singapore, 421

Haji Piyada (Noh Gumbad) Mosque, 317

Hajj, 20, 85–86, 88, 103, 105, 163, 198, 344, 103

Hakim al-Termezi, Tomb of, 153, *219*, 220

Hakim Sulayman, 254

Halawa House, Agamy, 341

Hama, 142

Church of St. John, 142

Great Mosque, 142, *143*

Hamdanids, 164, 204, 220

Han Dynasty, 447–48

Hanafis, 93, 134, 246, 307, 373

Hanbalis, 93, 134, 301–3

Hangzhou, 429

Hangzhou, Fenghuang (Phoenix) Mosque, 433, 439

Haram al-Ibrahimi Mosque, Hebron, 200–3, *201*, *202*

Haram al-Sharif, Jerusalem, 13, *14*, 15, 18, 20, 110, *111*, *112*, 114–19, 121, 142, 175–184, *175*, *178*, 200

Haram Museum, Jerusalem, 117

Harand, 150

Harb ibn Khalid ibn Yazid ibn Mu'awiya, 132

Haroon Sugich, 342

Harput, 315

Harran, Great Mosque, 125

Harun al-Rashid, 164, 168, 204

Harun-i Vilayat, Isfahan, *259*, 258–59, 260–61, 270

Hasan al-Askari, 163

Shrine of, Samarra, 203

Hasan ibn Ali ibn Abi Talib, 203–4

Shrine of, 203

Hasan ibn 'Ali ibn Babawayh, 237

Hasan ibn 'Ali ibn Muhammad, 234

Hasan Pasha, 307

Hasan, Tomb of, 228

Hassan II Mosque, Casablanca, 352

Hassan II, 71

Hatice Turhan Sultan, 41–42

Hauz Khas, Delhi, 43, 44

Hauz Khas, Tomb and Madrasa of Firuz Shah, 363

Hayreddin, 321–23

Hazara, 317

Digaran Mosque, 152, *153*, 154, 317

Hazrat Abul Hassan Ali Hajveri, see Daata Ganj Bakhsh

Hazrat Dawood Bundi, Tomb of, 401, *402*, *404*

Hebron, 201

Haram al-Ibrahimi Mosque, 200–3, *201*, *202*

Tomb of Abraham, 144

Tomb of Isaac, 144, 202

Tomb of Jacob, 144

Tomb of Leah, 144

Tomb of Rebecca, 144

Tomb of Sarah, 144

Tomb of the Patriarchs, 144, 201–2

Hekimoğlu Ali Pasha Mosque, Istanbul, 326

Heraclius, 182–3

Herat, 235, 245, 303, 387

Gawhar Shad Friday Mosque, 246

Gawhar Shad Madrasa, 248

Herodian Temple, Jerusalem, 175–76, 201

Herzfeld, Ernst, 70, 165, 167–68, 190, 193–94, 206

Hidayatullah Mosque, Jakarta, 421

Hidayet Mosque, Istanbul, 326

Hilal al-Sabi, 162

Hillenbrand, Robert, 152

Hırka-i Şerif Mosque, Istanbul, 326

Hindus, 26, 29, 42–43, 198, 357–60, 364, 369, 373, 381, 387, 393, 406, 409, 412

Hoca Hasan Mosque, Konya, 325

Holy Mosque of Mecca, see Masjid al-Haram, Mecca

Holy Sepulcher, see Tomb of Christ; Church of the Holy Sepulcher

Hongwu, 448

Huaisheng Mosque, Guangzhou, *428*

Huaishengsi, *428*, 431–432, *432*

Huajuexiangsi, Xi'an, *435*

Huand Hatun Complex, Kayseri, 287, *290*, 290–1

Hud, 134

Hüdavendigar Mosque, Bursa, *318*, 319, 325

Hui, 443

Hulagu, 227

Humayun, 43–44, 373, 375, 381–82, 384, 386–88

Tomb of, *36*, 43–44, *45*, *385*

Hunat Mosque, Kayseri, 316, *317*

Huocheng, Tomb of Tughluq Temür, *434*

Hurrem, 41

Tomb of, *41*

Husam Hussein Khasoggi, 342–43

Husayn ibn Ali ibn Abi Talib, 135, 162–3, 189, 197, 203–5, 206, 234

Shrine of (Aleppo), *205*, 206

Shrine of (Cairo), *196*, 197, 202

Shrine of (Damascus), *204*

Tomb of, 164, 203, 220, 234, 270

Hushang Shah Ghuri, 366

Tomb of, *366*, 367, *368*

Hussein, Saddam, 71

Huzuri Bagh, 394, 396

————

I'tmad ud-Dawla, 44, 384, 386, 393

Tomb of, *36*, 44, *45*, *46*, *385*

I'timaduddawla, see I'tmad ud-Dawla

Ibn 'Asakir, 129, 131, 189

Ibn al-'Arabi, 209, 388–89

Shrine of, 209, *298*, 299–303, *300*, *301*, *302*

Ibn al-Jawzi, 163

Ibn al-Shihna, 140

Ibn al-Zaki, 117

Ibn al-Zayyat, 208

Ibn Arabi, see Ibn al-'Arabi

Ibn Battuta, 208, 276, 285, 289, 308

Ibn Hauqal, 359

Ibn Hawkal, 204

Ibn Jubayr, 38, 126, 135, 189

Ibn Kamal, 300, 303

Ibn Khurdadbih, 359

Ibn Qudama, 199

Ibn Shaddad, 189

Ibn Shakir, 131

Ibn Shuhayd, 40

Ibn Taymiyya, 199, 302

Ibn Tulun, 302

Ibn Tulun Mosque, Cairo, 341, 347

Ibn 'Abdun, 40

Ibrahim Bey, 292–93

Ibrahim II Adil Shah, Tomb of, *365*, 369

Ibrahim Rauza Tomb and Mosque, Bijapur, *365*, 369

Ibrahim, see Abraham

Id Kah Mosque, Kashgar, 443–44

Ilkhanids, 157, 224, 227–39, 244, 270

Imad-shahis, 368

Imam al-Najmi, Babil Governate, 167, *168*
Imam al-Shafi'i, Tomb of, *207, 208*
Imam Dur Tomb, Samarra, *160*, 166–68, 170
Imam Husayn Shrine, Karbala, see Husayn ibn Ali ibn Abi Talib, Tomb of
Imām Riżā Shrine, Mashhad, 66, *67*
Ince Minareli Madrasa, Konya, 54, *55*
Independence Mosque, Jakarta, 29
İplikçi Mosque, Konya, 280
'Isa, see Jesus
'Isa Bey, 281, 282, 285
Isa Bey Mosque, Selçuk, 281–82, *282*
Isaac, 110, 202
    Tomb of, 144, 202
Isfahan, 157, 227–29, 231, 237, 239, 257–63, 265–67, 269, 320
    Ali Qapu, *260, 261*, 262–63, 265
    Darb-i Imam Shrine, *51*, *52*, 54, 259
    Great Mosque, *53*, 149, 151–52, 156–57, *157*, 167, 228, *228*–30, 244, 320
    Harun-i Vilayat, *258*, 258–59, 260–61, 270
    Imamzada Baba Qasim, 231
    Imamzada Ja'far, 231
    Jurjir Mosque, *155*
    Madrasa Imami, *226*, 227, *229*
    Shah Mosque, *268*, 268–71, *269, 270, 271*
    Shaykh Lutfullah Mosque, *256*, *258*, 261, 263–71, *264, 265, 266, 267*
    Tawhidkhana, *260*, 260–65, *261*
Isho'yahb III, 144
Iskhak Ata, Tomb of, 218–20
Iskodar, 154
Islamabad, King Faisal Mosque, *24, 25*, 29, 329
Islamic Society of Boston Cultural Center (ISBCC), 72, 74
Island Mosque, Jeddah, *30, 343*
Isma'il (son of Abraham), 85–87, 257–63
Isma'il Safavi, 257, 301, 380
Isma'ilis, 27, 205, 207
Ismail (Samanid ruler), 220, 221
İsmail Efendi Mosque, Istanbul 326
Ismaili, see Isma'ilis
Istakhr, Friday Mosque, 26
Istanbul, 30, 41–42, 49, 54, 66, 119, 292, 306, 320–25, 329
    Archaeology Museum, 292
    Ayazma Mosque, 326
    Azapkapı Sokollu Mosque, 323
    Bayezid II Mosque, 320, 322, 323, *325*
    Beylerbeyi Mosque, 326
    Bostancı Mosque, 326
    Cihangir Mosque, 326
    Çorlulu Ali Pasha Mosque, 326
    Damat İbrahim Pasha Mosque, 326
    Edirnekapı Mihrimah Sultan Mosque, *314*, 322, *325*
    Eyüp Sultan Mosque, 326
    Fatih Mosque, *27, 28, 325*
    Gülnüş Emetullah Mosque in Üsküdar (Yeni Valide), 326
    Hacı Beşir Ağa Mosque, 326
    Hagia Sophia Church, 26, 30–2, 42, 178, 320, *321*, 323, *325*, 342, 347
    Hekimoğlu Ali Pasha Mosque, 326
    Hidayet Mosque, 326
    Hırka-i Şerif Mosque, 326
    İsmail Efendi Mosque, 326

Kadırga Sokollu Mosque, 323
Kağıthana Mosque, 326
Kamer Hatun Mosque, 326
Karaköy Mosque, 326
Kilic Ali Pasa Mosque, 54, *55*
Laleli Mosque, 326
Mahmud Pasha Mosque, 320, *325*
Mecidiye Mosque, 326
Nişancı Mehmed Pasha Mosque, 323
Nuruosmâniye Mosque, 326
Nusretiye Mosque, 326
Ortaköy Mosque, 326
Pertevniyal Valide Sultan Mosque, 326
Rüstem Pasha Mosque, 323
Sakirin Mosque, 30
Şehzade Mosque, 322, 323–24, *325*
Shrine of Abu Ayyub al-Ansari, 310
Sokullu Mehmet Pasha Mosque, 342
Suleymaniye Mosque, *27, 28, 41*, 54, 323–25, *324*, *325*, 329, 332–33
Sultan Selim I Mosque, 320, 322
Sultanahmad Mosque, 324
Tomb of Hurrem, *41*
Tomb of Selim II, *42*
Topkapı Palace, 27, 66, 308
Üsküdar Mihrimah Sultan Mosque, 323, *325*
Üsküdar Selimiye Mosque, 326
Yavuz Selim Mosque, 325
Yeni Valide Mosque, *41, 42*, 324, 326
Yıldız Mosque, 326
Zal Mahmud Pasha Mosque, 323
Zeynep Sultan Mosque, 326
Istiqlal (Independence) Mosque, Jakarta, 424
Iznik, 302, 345
    Yeşil Mosque, *325*
'Izz al-Din Kaykawus I, 277
'Izz al-Din Saltuk II, 286

———————

Jacob, 182–3
    Tomb of, 144
Jahanara, 375–76, 379, 384
Jahangir, 44, 373, 376, 379, 381–82, 386–87, 393
    Tomb of, *384*, 386–87
Jahannuma Masjid, Delhi, 376, 379
Jahanpanah, 363
Jahanshah, 235, 259
Jai Singh, 68
Jaiselmer, Chandraprabha Temple, 368
Jakarta, 414, 418
    An-Nawier Mosque Pekojan, 422
    Angke Mosque, 419
    Hidayatullah Mosque, 421
    Istiqlal (Independence) Mosque, 424
    Independence Mosque, 29
    Kali Krukut Mosque, 420
    Langgar Tinggi Mosque, 421
    Mangga Dua Mosque, 420
    Sawah Lio Mosque, 419–20
    Tambora Mosque, 420
Jalal al-Din al-Rumi, see Jalal al-Din Rumi
Jalal al-Din Qaratay, 291
Jalal al-Din Rumi, 283, 299–301, 303–7
    Tomb of, 299–301, *304, 305*, 303–307
Jami Masjid, Delhi, *376, 377*, 394
Jami Masjid, Lahore, see Badshahi Masjid, Lahore

Jami Mosque, Kutai, 420
Jami Mosque, Samarinda, 420
Jami Mosque, see also Friday Mosque
Jamshid al-Kashi, 52
Jamshids, 52
Janids, 249
Jao Old Mosque, 420
Jaunpur, 364, 365, 366, 367
    Atala Mosque, 364, *365*
Java, 409–412, 414–420, 424
Jawi, 409
Jebel Jawshan, Damascus, 205
Jeddah, 29, 105, 339, 341–48, 420
    al-Harithy Mosque, 344
    Abraj Mosque, 343–44
    Azezeyia Mosque, 345
    Corniche Mosque, *338*, 343, 344
    Island Mosque, *30, 343*
    Juffali Mosque, 344
    King Saud Mosque, 344–45 *345*, 347
    Ruwais Mosque, *344*
    Sulaiman Mosque, *344*
Jember, Great Mosque, 420
Jepara, 412, 418
    Grand Mosque, 412
Jerusalem, 13–16, 18–20, 26–27, 31, 65, 101, 109–21, 125, 142, 144, 175–184, 197–202, 301, 347, 418
    Anastasis Rotunda, 110, *113*, *144*
    al-Aqsa Mosque, 20, 85, *111*, 115, *118*, 119, 125, 175, 177, 179–184, *181*, 200
    Bab al-Silsila, 182
    Church of the Ascension, 110, *113*, 114, 118, 176
    Church of the Holy Sepulcher, 20, 110, *113*, 116–17, 144, 176, 178, 182
    Church of the Tomb of Mary, 112
    Dome of the Rock, 13, 16, *17*, 20, *31*, 32, 37, *108, 109*, 109–21, *111, 112*, 115, *119*, 120, 125, *134, 144, 145, 175, 177*, 178–184, *178, 179*, 200, 201, 208, 217, 333
    Dome of the Ascension, *114*, 118, *174*, 184
    Dome of the Chain, 114, *115*, 117–19, *175, 179*, 180, 182–83
    Gate of David, 182
    Gate of Mercy, 114, 180
    Gate of Repentance, 114, 180
    Golden Gate, *179*, 180, 182
    Haram al-Sharif, 13, *14*, 15, 18, 20, 110, *111, 112*, 114–19, 121, 142, 175–184, *175, 178*, 200
    Haram Museum, 117
    Herodian Temple, 175–76, 201
    Jewish Temple, 13, 18, 20, 109–10, 113–14, 116–17, 119, 121, 175, 177
Jerusalem (*contined*)
    Madrasa al-Ashrafiyya, 118
    Madrasa al-Salahiyya, 190
    Temple of Solomon, 109–10, 113–14, 116, 176, 178, 200
    Templum Domini, 116–17, 182
    Templum Salamonis, 117
    Tomb of Christ, *113*, 176
Jesus, 110, 112–13, 118, 130, 144, 176, 178, 182–83, 200-2
    Tomb of, *113*, see also Jerusalem, Church of the Holy Sepulcher
Jewish Temple, Jerusalem, 13, 18, 20, 109–10, 113–14, 116–17, 119, 121, 175, 177
Jews, 13, 18–20, 109–17, 119, 121, 144, 175–77, 180, 182, 197–203

482 INDEX

Jiajing, 449
Jining, Great East Mosque, 437, *438*
Jipang Mosque, 417
John of Würzburg, 117, 183
John the Baptist, 131, 134-34 144, 200, 202
    Shrine of, 135
Jonah, 201
Joseph, 117, 201-2, 406
Joshua Shrine, near Tiberias, 200
Judaism, see Jews
Juffali Mosque, Jeddah, 344
Julian, 176
Jurjir Mosque, Isfahan, *155*
Justinian, 116, 178, 183, 197
Jutai, Jami Mosque, 420

———

Ka'ba, see Kaaba
Kaaba, Mecca, 15, 19, 20, 26-27, 27, 37, *84, 85*, 85-97, *91, 92, 93, 96, 97*, 109, 115, 233, 348, 403, 430, 451
Kabul, 42-43, 77, 373, 387
    Bagh-e Babur, *43*
    Tomb of Babur, 42, *43, 44*, 387
Kachh, see Bhadreshvar
Kachwaha Raja, 375
Kadırga Sokollu Mosque, Istanbul 323
Kağithana Mosque, Istanbul 326
Kaifeng, Great East Mosque, 437, *438*, 439
Kairouan, see Qayrawan
Kaiyuan Monastery, 431
Kaj, Congregational Mosque, 228
Kalan, Great Mosque, 248-49
Kale Mosque, Divriği, 279, 280
Kali Krukut Mosque, Jakarta 420
Kamal Ismail, 348
Kamer Hatun Mosque, Istanbul 326
Kampong Laut Mosque, Kota Bahru 420
Kampung Hulu Mosque, Melaka, 419, 422
Kampung Keling Mosque, Melaka 419
Kampung Melayu Tengkera, Pantai, 414
Kamran, 373, 387
Kanauj, 359
Kara, Hanif, 56
Karaköy Mosque, Istanbul 326
Karaman, see Larende
Karamanids, 282, 292
Karatay Madrasa, Konya, 320
Karbala, 161, 163, 164, 170, 203-5, 217, 234, 270
    Tomb of Husayn ibn Ali ibn Abi Talib, 164, 203, 220, 234, 270
Kasepuhan, 411, 412, 415
Kasepuhan Grand Mosque, Cirebon, *410*, 411, *415*
Kashan, 237
    'Atiqa Mosque, 254, *254*
    Tomb of Afaq Khvaja, *252, 254*
Kashgar, 254
    'Atiqa Mosque, *254*
    Aba Khoja Mausoleum, *442, 444*
    Afaq Khvaja, *252, 254*
    Id Kah Mosque, 443-44
    Tomb of Afaq Khvaja, *252, 254*
Kastamonu, 280
Kasunyatan Mosque, Banten, 412
Katangka Mosque, 415
Kathisma Church, 112, 144, *145*

Kayseri, 283, 287-88, 290, 315-17, *316, 317*, 320
    Çifte Kümbet Tomb, 287
    Develi Mosque, 315
    Great Mosque, 288, 290-1, 315, *316*, 320
    Hacı Kılıç Mosque, 315
    Huand Hatun Complex, 287, 290, 290-1
    Hunat Mosque, 316, *317*
    Köşk Medrese, 286-87
Kazimayn, 203
Kazimiyya Shrine, Baghdad, see al-Kazimiyya Shrine, Baghdad
Keder, 154
Kelantan Mosque, Kota Bahru, 413
Kemah, 284-85, 290
    Tomb of Sultan Melik, *283*, 285
Kemal-Pashazade, see Ibn Kamal
Kemalettin Bey, 326
Kerala, 412
Khadijah, 291
Khadijah Mosque, Singapore, *421*
Khaja Bulkhak, 217-18
Khaja Mashhad, 216-18, 222
    Tomb of, 216-18, 222
Khalid ibn al-Walid, 135
Khalifa Rajab, Tomb of, 218-20
Khaljis, 361, 363
Khalwatis, 303, 307
Khambhat (Cambay), 360
Khan Mirjan, Baghdad, 240
Khargird, Pir Ahmad Khvafi, 248
Kharraqan, 224
Khayzuran Cemetery, Baghdad, 162
Khidr Bali, 308
Khiva, 254
    Friday Mosque, 154, 156, 280
Khmel'nitskii, Sergei, 152, 154, 216
Khoja Roshan, Surkhandariya Province, 218
Khorasan, see Khurasan
Khulafa Mosque, Baghdad, 75, 352
Khuldabad 384
Khurasan, 364, 366, 387
Khurram Pasha, 307
Khusrau Bagh, 384
Khvaja Ahmad Yasavi, 243
Kilic Ali Pasa Mosque, Istanbul, 54, 55
King Faisal Mosque, Islamabad, *24, 25*, 29, 329
King Khaled Airport Mosque, Riyadh, 29
King Saud Mosque, Jeddah, 344-45, *345*, 347
King, Geoffrey, 152
Kirkuk, 202
Kiz Bibi, Tomb of, 216, 218-19
Kızıltepe, 315
Kocatepe Mosque, Ankara, *328*, 329-336, *330, 331, 336, 337*
Koch, Ebba, 388
Konya, 277, 280, 283-84, 286-87, 291, 320, 325
    Alaeddin Mosque, *276*, 277-79, *278*, 284, 286, 288
    Church of St. Amphilochios, 277
    Friday Mosque, *305*
    Hoca Hasan Mosque, 325
    Ince Minareli Madrasa, 54, 55
    İplikçi Mosque, 280
    Karatay Madrasa, 320
    Sahib 'Ata Complex, 291

Tomb of Jalal al-Din Rumi, 299-301, *304, 305*, 303-307
    Tomb of Kılıç Arslan, *284*
    Tomb of Shams al-Tabrizi, 307
Köşk Medrese, Kayseri, 286-87
Kota Bahru, Great Mosque Kelantan, 413
Kota Bahru, Kampong Laut Mosque, 420
Kotagede, Grand Mosque and Tomb Complex, 412, 417
Kuala Lumpur
    Negara (National) Mosque, 424
Kudus Mosque, *416*, 417
Kufa, 27, 149, 323
    Great Mosque, 13, 26, 145
Kuhpaya, 150
Kuhsan, Madrasa of Tuman Agha, 247
Kuran, Aptullah, 318, 320, 322, *325*
Kushmelkhan, 154
Kutahye, 345
Kutai, Jami Mosque, 420
Kuwait State Mosque, Kuwait City, *351*, 352
Kuyuji Murad Pasha, 307
Kyai Gede Mosque, Bun 420

———

Lahore, 375-76, 379, 381-82, 384, 386, 401, 406
    Alamgari Gate, 394
    Badshahi Masjid, 352-53, 376, *378*, 392-98, *394, 395, 396, 397*
    Maryam al-Zamani Mosque, *378*, 379
    Roshnai Gate, 394
    Shrine of Daata Ganj Bakhsh, *400*, 406
    Tomb of Jahangir, *384*
Lajim, 223
Lakemba Mosque, Sydney, 460-61, *461*, 467
Lala Mustafa Pasha, 306
Laleli Mosque, Istanbul, 326
Langar, Tomb of Qasim-i Anvar 246
Langgar Tinggi Mosque, Jakarta, 421
Laowang Mosque, 443
Larende, 292-3
    Mosque of Alaeddin Bey, 293
Leah, Tomb of, 144
Lesser Qiz Qala, Tomb of, 216
Liaodi Pagoda, 431
Library of Congress, Washington D.C., 71, 76
Limo Kaum Great Mosque, 412, *413*
Linxia, 443
Little, Donald, 65
Lodis, 361
Lombok, Rambitan Mosque, 420
London Central Mosque, Rifat Chadirji Project, 75
Loos, Adolf, 58
Losch, Flora, 74
Lubuk Bauk Mosque, 421
Lutfullah al-Maysi al-'Amili, 263-64, 267
Luxor, 342
    Temple of Karnak, 209

———

Ma Sanbao, see Zheng He
Maarof Jeddah Street Mosque, Singapore, 420
Madhya Pradesh, Gwalior, 359

Madrasa
    al-Ashrafiyya, Jerusalem, 118
    al-Firdaws, Aleppo, *190, 191*, 194
    al-Salahiyya, Jerusalem, 190
    al-Zahiriyya, Damascus, *129*
    Imami, Isfahan, 226, 227, *229*
    of al-Halawiyya, Aleppo, 140, *141*
    of Gawhar Shad, Herat, 248
    of Mir-i 'Arab, Bukhara, *249*, 250
    of Nur al-Din, Damascus, 287
    of Pir Ahmad Khvafi, Khargird, 248
    of Shir Dar, Samarqand, *251*
    of Tila-Kari, Samarqand, *250*, 251, *252*
    of Ulugh Beg, Samarqand, *250*
    Ghiyathiyya, Khargid, *248*
    Gök, Sivas 291–2
    Ince Minareli, Konya, 54, *55*
    Karatay, Konya, 320
    Köşk, Kayseri, 286–7
    Nizamiyya, Baghdad, 170
Madrid, Civil Courts of Justice, *58*
Madura, Sumenep Grand Mosque, 418
Magaz, 339
Maghok-i Attari Mosque, Bukhara, 152
Maharashtra, Bibi-ka Maqbara, 382, 384, *386, 387*
Maḥkama li'l-Aḥwāl al-Shakhṣiyya, Cairo, 66
Mahmoud Bodo Rasch, 348
Mahmud (Mawlawi dervish), 305–6
Mahmud I, 42, 326
Mahmud Pasha Mosque, Istanbul 320, *325*
Mahmud Pasha, 307
Mahpari Khatun, 287, 290–1
Mainstone, Rowland, *325*
Majapahit, 409, 415
Makassar, 418, 420
    Great Mosque, 420
Makiya, Mohammad Saleh, 352
Makrana, 375
Malatya, 280
    Great Mosque, 280
Malatya Ulu Cami, see Malatya, Great Mosque
Malaysia National Mosque, Kuala Lumpur, 29
Malda, 381
Malik Muhammad, 288
Malikis, 93,
Malik-Shah, 130
Malqoch Ghazi, 308
Mama Khatun, 286
    Tomb, 286–87
Mamluks, 64–65, 71, 73, 93, 103, 117–19, 129–30, 134, 139–40, 190, 199, 201–2, 208–9, 228, 281, 282, 301–3, 345, 347
Man Singh, 381
Manama, Mosque of Yateem, 348
Mandu, 362, 364, 366, 367
    Tomb of Hushang Shah Ghuri, *366, 367, 368*
Mangga Dua Mosque, Jakarta, 420
Manisa, 281, 285, 320, *325*
    Great Mosque, 281, 320, *325*
Manonjaya, Great Mosque, 420
Mansura, 357, 358
Mantingan Mosque, 415, 417
Maqaad, 339
Mar Gabriel in the Tur 'Abdin, 133
Mar Musa al-Habashi, near Damascus, 203
Maragha, 279, 284
    Gunbad-i Qabus, 284, 215, 216, 220, 223
Marathas, 373

Marawi, Mosque at Lake Lando, 420
Marçais, Georges, 70
Mardin, 315
Marjdabiq, Shrine of Prophet David, 301
Markaz al-Wathā'iq al-Tārīkhiyya, Damascus, 66
Marwani Musalla, 177, 182
Mary, 18, 110, 112, 117, 144, 182–3, 202, 403
    Tomb of, 112
Maryam al-Zamani Mosque, Lahore, *378, 379*
Maryam, see Mary
Mashhad, 373
    Dar al-Siyada, 247
    Friday Mosque, 245
    Imām Riżā Shrine, 66, *67*
Mashhad al-Ra's Mosque, Damascus, 189, 197, 203, 204
Mashour al-Harithy, 344
Masjid al-Aqsa, see al-Aqsa Mosque, Jerusalem
Masjid al-Haram, Mecca, 13, 15, 19, 20, 26, *84*, 85–98, *88, 89, 91, 92, 93, 94, 95, 96*, 115, 181
Masjid al-Nabawi, see Mosque of the Prophet, Medina
Masjid Tinggi (Tall Mosque), Bagan Serai, 420
Masjid-e Jameh, Isfahan, see Great Mosque of Isfahan
Masjid-i Diggaran, Hazara, 317
Masjid-i Kirmani, Turbat-i Shaykh Jam, 237
Masjid-i Nuh Gunbad, Balkh, 152–55, 317
Masjid-i Shah, Isfahan, see Shah Mosque, Isfahan
Mauryas, 358, 359
Mawlawis, 304–7
Mawlay Rashid, 68
Maydani Mosque, Riyadh, 348
Mecca, 13, 15, 20, 27, 27, 32, 37, 42, 85–98, 101, 110, 115, 119, 125, 129, 177, 179–80, 198, 200, 204, 233–34, 299, 301–2, 339, 344, 347–48, 393, 432, 461, 467–68
    al-Mas'a, 88–90, 92, 98
    al-Mataf, 85–86, 88–94, 98
    al-Multazam, 87
    Hafeyer Mosque, 348
    Hijr Isma'il, 86–92
    Kaaba, 15, 19, 20, 26–27, *27*, 37, *84*, 85, 85–97, *91, 92, 93, 96, 97*, 109, 115, 233, 348, 403, 430, 451
    Maqam Ibrahim, 87–89, 92–94
    Masjid al-Haram, 13, 15, 19, 20, 26, *84*, 85–98, *88, 89, 91, 92, 93, 94, 95, 96*, 115, 181
    The Black Stone, 86–89
    The Holy Mosque, see Masjid al-Haram, Mecca
    Zamzam Well, 87–89, 92, 94
Mecidiye Mosque, Istanbul, 326
Medina, 13, 15, 27, 38, 85, 101–5, 115, 119, 125, 177, 200, 204, 217, 234, 299, 301–2, 339, 344–8
    al-Baqi Cemetery, 203
    Bab al-Nisa, 101
    Bab al-Rahmah, 101
    Bab Gibreel, 101
    Bodo Rasch, 105
    Mosque of the Prophet, 13, 15, 38, *100*, 101–6, *102, 103, 104, 105, 106*, 129, 145, 149–50, 216, 347, *348*
    Qiblatain Mosque, *346*, 347
    Quba Mosque, *346*, 347
    Shrine of Hasan ibn Ali ibn Abi Talib, 203
Mehmed II, 27, 292, 299–300, 310
Mehmed IV, 42
Melaka, 414–16, 419, 422
    al-Azim State Mosque, 424
    Duyong Mosque, 422
    Kampung Hulu Mosque, 419, 422
    Kampung Keling Mosque, 419
    Melaka Sultanate Royal Mosque, 414–16
    Peringgit Mosque, 419

    Tanjung Keling Mosque, 422–24
    Tengkera Mosque, *419*
Melbourne, 458, 460, 462, 472
    Newport Mosque, 462–65, *463, 464, 465*
    Preston Mosque, *460*
Melik, Tomb of, *283, 285*
Mengujekids, 275, 279, 283, 286, 289–90
Merinids, 41
Merv, 149, 154, 216–17, 224, 234
    Tomb of Sultan Sanjar, 224
Mestorian, 155
Metropolitan Museum of Art, New York, 38, 70, 73, 77, 190, 193, 194, 206, 228, 237
Miaoying Monastery, 431
Mihrimah Sultan Edirnekapı Mosque, Istanbul, *314*, 322, *325*
Mihrimah Sultan Mosque, Üsküdar, 323, *325*
Mikhal Ghazi, 308
Mil-i Radkan, Radkan, *221*, 223
Mimar Sinan, see Sinan
Ming Dynasty, 434, 437, 439, 441, 447–48, 450
Mir Sayyid Bahram, 221
Mir-i 'Arab Madrasa, Bukhara, *249*, 250
Mirza Shah Husayn, 258
Mizdakhan, Tomb of Khalifa Rajab, 218–20
Mohamed Makiya, 73
Mohammed, see Muhammad
Mohammed Ali al-Ameri, 350, 352
Monastery of
    Bao'en, 431
    Kaiyuan, 431
    Miaoying, 431
    Shanhuasi, 432
Mongols, 65, 161, 168, 227–28, 234–35, 238, 275, 281, 285, 288, 290–91
Mopti, 105
Moses, 18, 198, 200, 202
Mosques, see under specific mosque, masjid, or city names
Mosque of the Prophet, Medina, 13, 15, 38, *100*, 101–6, *102, 103, 104, 105, 106*, 129, 145, 149–50, 216, 347, *348*
Mosque of Walid I, Medina, 216
Mosul, 72, 140, 201–2, 204
Moti Masjid, Delhi, 379
Mount Meru, 389
Mount Moriah, Jerusalem, 13, 182
Mount of Olives, Jerusalem, 110, 112, 114, 116, 176, 180
Mu'in al-Din Sulayman, 291
Mu'awiya, 15, 177
Mua'izz al-Daula 'Abbas, 222
Muara Labuh Mosque, Solok Selatan, 421
Mughals, 35, 42–44, 68, 234, 243, 252, 300, 309, 310, 357, 369, 373–89, 393, 397–98, 421, 424
Muhamad Adil Shah, 369
Muhamadiyya, Sar-i Kucheh Mosque, 152
Muhammad, 13, 15, 17–20, 25, 85, 87–91, 109–110, 114–17, 129, 135, 177–178, 180–182, 184, 199, 200–4, 228, 263, 267, 270, 291, 303, 310, 430, 447, 448
Muhammad al-Jawad, 163
Muhammad al-Taqi (Imam) Shrine, Najaf, 203
Muhammad Alamgir, 393
Muhammad ibn Nasser, Tomb of, 222
Muhammad Riza, 263, 266
Muhammed Said al-Farsi, 341–42
Muhammad Sultan, 244
Muharram, 204
Muhy al-din Ibn al-'Arabi, see Ibn al-'Arabi

Mujahid al-Din Muhammad Qilij, 193
Multan, 357-58, 363, 402
Tomb of Shaikh Rukn-i Din Rukn-i Alam, 357, 363, 403
Mumina Khatun, Tomb of, 284-85
Mumtaz Mahal, 43-44, 382
Munir, Hisham, 73
Muqaddasi, see al-Muqaddasi
Murad II, 302
Murad III, 306
Murad IV, 90
Muradiye Mosque, Bursa, *325*
Murcutt, Glenn, 457, 460, 463-67, 471
Musa al-Kazim, 163, 166, 203
Muscat, Sultan Qaboos Grand Mosque, 352
Museum für Islamische Kunst, Berlin, 70
Mustafa II, 42
Mustafa 'Ali, 307
Mutazilites, 156
Muwaffaq Mohammed Al-Harithy, 344
Muzaffarid, 157, 227, 229, 231, 237
Mu'in al-din Sulayman, 303

Na Family Mosque, Yongning, 439-41, *440*
Nadir Shah, 373
Najaf, 161, 170, 203, 217, 234
Shrine of Ali ibn Abi Talib, 162, *203*, 203-4, 220
Najdi, 351
Najm al-Din al-Khabushani, 208
Nakhchevan, 284-85
Tomb of Mumina Khatun, 284-85
Nasir-i Khusrau, 181-82
Nasr ibn Ahmad, 221
Nasuh Matrakçi, 235, 306
Natanz, Tomb of 'Abd al-Samad, 237-38, *238*
Nayin, 152-56
Friday Mosque, 152-53, *154*, 156
Necipoğlu, Gülru, 49, 175, 334
Necropolis of Shah-i-Zinda, Samarqand, 42, *243*
Negara (National) Mosque, Kuala Lumpur, 424
Nevşehir, 326
Damat İbrahim Pasha Mosque, 326
New Gourna, 339-41
New Gourna Mosque, *340*
Newport Mosque, Melbourne, 462-65, *463, 464, 465*
New York
Ar-Rahman Mosque, 31
Metropolitan Museum of Art, 38, 70, 73, 77, 190, 193, 194, 206, 228, 237
Park51, *48*
Niğde, 315-17, 320
Alaeddin Mosque, 315, *316*, 317, 320, *325*
Nişancı Mehmed Pasha Mosque, Istanbul, 323
Nisibin, 204
Nizam-shahis, 368
Nizamiyya Madrasa, Baghdad, 170
Nizamuddin, 382
North Mosque, Xuanhua, 439
Nuh Gunbad Mosque, Balkh, 152-55, 317
Nur al-Din, 53-54, 129, 184, 207, 287
Tomb of, 43, *54*, 287
Nur Jahan, 382, 384, 386
Nuruosmânîye Mosque, Istanbul, 326
Nusretiye Mosque, Istanbul, 326
Nysa, 317
Parthian Temple, 317

Okara, 401
Tomb of Hazrat Dawood Bundi, 401, *402, 404*
Omar, see 'Umar ibn al-Khattab
Orhan, 300
Ortaköy Mosque, Istanbul, 326
Osman III, 42, 326
'Osman Ghazi, 299
Othman, see Uthman ibn Affan
Ottomans, 26, 28-29, 31-32, 38, 41-42, 54, 64-66, 68, 85, 90, 932, 98, 102, 113, 119-20, 128, 210, 235-36, 243, 263-64, 275, 282, 286-88, 292-93, 299-310, 315-26, 329-36, 345, 348, 380, 460, 462
Oudh Nawab, 373
Ox Street Mosque, Beijing, 433-37, *437*
Oxford, Ashmolean Museum, 70

Pahlavan Mahmud, 254
Palace of
Aq Saray, Shahr-i-Sabz, 243
Ctesiphon, 228
the Bukhar Khodahs, Varakhsha, 155
Theodoric, Ravenna, 130
Palembang, Grand Mosque, 414, *418*
Palmyra, Temple of Bel, *19*
Palopo, Grand Mosque, 411, 415, 421
Pandua, 363
Panjab, 360
Panjunan Mosque, Cirebon, 415
Pantai, Kampung Melayu Tengkera, 414
Paradise, 35-40, 44-46, 109, 114, 119, 132, 178, 229, 233, 260-1, 269, 303, 333-34, 336, 382, 388-89, 404, 406, 461, 465-67
Paramaras, 358
Pariaman Mosque, 421
Pariangan, Mosque, *413*, 414
Park51, New York City, *48*
Parsa, Khvaja, 254
Parthian Temple at Nysa, 317
Parwana Mu'in al-Din Sulayman, 291
Pasargadae, 70
Pasir Royal Mosque, Tanahgrogot, 421
Patani
Surau Aur, 414
Teluk Manok Mosque, *413*
Patriarchs Tomb, Hebron, 144, *201*, 201-2, 202
Pawestren, Yogyakarta Grand Mosque, 412, 417-18
Peringgit Mosque, Melaka, 419
Persepolis, 70
Pertevniyal Valide Sultan Mosque, Istanbul, 326
Petra, 202
Petruccioli, Attilio, 70
Philip II, 68
Pingzhuang Mosque, Donxiang Autonomous Hui Hamlet, *441*, 443
Pir Ahmad Khvafi Madrasa, Khargird, 248
Pir-i 'Alamdar, 223
Pir-i Bakran, 237
Piyale Pasha, 41
Plato, 277
Pontianak Royal Mosque, 420
Preston Mosque, Melbourne, *460*
Prophet Muhammad, see Muhammad
Pugachenkova, Galina, 216
Punchbowl Mosque, Sydney, *456*, 460-62, 467-71
Pusaka Banua Lawas Mosque, Banau Lawas, 420

Qaboos bin Saud, 352
Qabus ibn Vushmgir, 223
Qadariyya, 209
Qajars, 228
Qal'at Sem'an, 197
Qara, 142
Qarafa al-Kubra' Cemetery, Cairo, 203, 207, 208, 209
Qarakhanids, 218, 220-22
Qaramanid, see Karamanid
Qaraqoyunlu, see Qaraquyunlu
Qaraquyunlu, 259, 235
Qarawiyyīn Mosque, Fez, 68
Qarshi, 152, 218
Qarshi, Mosque at the Shrine of Khusam Ata, 152
Qasim-i Anvar, Tomb of, 246
Qasr al-'Ashiq, Samarra, 165
Qasr al-Hayr al-Gharbi, *140*
Qasr al-Hokm Mosque and Justice Palace Complex, Riyad, 348-51
Qavam al-Din Shirazi, 246
Qayrawan, 105, 433
Qazvin, 264-65
Qiblatain Mosque, Medina, *346*, 347
Qing Dynasty, 432, 434, 437, 439, 441, 449
Qing Zhen Si, see Xi'an Great Mosque
Qılıch Arslan II, 277, 284
Tomb of, 277, *284*, 284-5
Quanzhou, 429, 431, 433
Shengyousi, 432-433, *433*
Quba Mosque, Medina, *346*, 347
Qubbat al-Miraj, Jerusalem, see Dome of the Ascension
Qubbat al-Sakhra, see Dome of the Rock, Jerusalem
Qubbat al-Silsila, see Dome of the Chain
Qubbat al-Sulaibiyya at Samarra, *164*, 165-66, 215-17
Quraman, 307
Quran, 14-16, 18-20, 35-36, 41, 44, 46, 85, 86, 101, 110-11, 115-16, 119, 134, 156, 175, 177-78, 182-84, 200, 215-16, 223, 233-34, 267-68, 284, 286, 292, 302, 307, 334, 373, 388, 401, 403, 406, 433-34, 452, 462
Qurva, 150
Qusam ibn 'Abbas, 243
Quşayr (Red Sea), 64
Qutaiba ibn Muslim, 150
Qutb al-Din Mubarak Shah I, 363
Qutb Minar, Delhi, *362*, 363, 393
Qutb Mosque, Delhi, see Qutb Minar, Delhi
Qutb-shahis, 369
Qutham ibn Abbas, 42, 243

Rabat, 41, 68
Chella Funerary Complex, 41
Rabi'a al- Shamiyya, Tomb of, 207
Rabi'a Dawrani, 382
Rab'-i Rashidi, Tabriz, 235-36
Radkan, Mil-i Radkan, *221*, 223
Raghib, Yusuf, 216-17
Raja Man Singh, 381
Rajab Abdel Aziz, 344
Rajmahal, 381
Rambitan Mosque, Lombok, 420
Ranjit Singh, 393-94
Rao-rao, Great Mosque, *408*, 409, 421
Rarz, 154
Rashid al-Din, 235-36

INDEX 485

Ravenna
    Church of Sant'Apollinare Nuovo, *130*
    Palace of Theodoric, 130
Rayy, 223, 227
Rebecca, Tomb of, 144
Regisistan Square, Samarqand, *450–451*
Resget, Tomb Tower, 222, 223
Ridaniyya, 301
Riegl, Alois, 57
Rifat Chadirji, 73
Riyadh, 339, 348–50
    al-Kindi Plaza, *350*, 351
    King Khaled Airport Mosque, 29
    Maydani Mosque, 348
    Qasr al-Hokm Mosque and Justice Palace
        Complex, 348–51
Roshan, Khoja, 219–20
Roshanara, 384
Roshnai Gate, Lahore, 394
Royal Mosque, Pontianak, 420
Royal Mosque, Sambas 420
Rukn al-din, 236
Rukn-i Alam, see Rukn-i Din Rukn-i Alam
Rukn-i Din Rukn-i Alam, 355, 357, 363, 402
    Tomb of, *356*, 363, *403*
Rukniyya, Yazd, 236
Rumi, see Jalal al-Din Rumi
Rusafa, 197, 202, 210
Rustam Pasha, 307
Rüstem Pasha Mosque, Istanbul, 323
Rustow, Marina, 64–5
Ruwais Mosque, Jeddah, *344*

———————

Sa'd al-Din, Khvaja, 252
Saewulf, 182–83
Safavids, 63, 66–67, 204, 237, 243, 251, 257–71,
    299–303, 306–9, 380–82, 388
Safi al-Din Ishaq, 257, 261, 309
    Tomb of, 309
Safid Buland, Shah Fazl, 222
Safiye Sultan, 41
Sahib 'Ata Fakhr al-Din 'Ali, 291–2
Sahib Ismail ibn Abbad, 156
Sakirin Mosque, Istanbul, 30
Saladin, see Salah al-Din
Salah al-Din, 117–18, 129, 134, 175, 183–4, 189, 191,
    201, 207
    Tomb of, *129*
Salim Chishti, 374, 375
    Tomb of, *374*
Saltukids, 275, 286
Samadi, 394
Samanids, 150, 154, 215–22, 224, 234, 317
Samarinda, Jami Mosque, 420
Samarkand, see Samarqand
Samarqand, 149–50, 154, 243, 249–50, 387
    Friday Mosque, 149, 154, 243, 244, 250
    Gur-i Mir, 243, *242*, 244,
    Regisistan Square, *450–451*
    Shah-i Zinda, 42, *243*
    Shir Dar Madrasa, *251*
    Shrine of Qusam ibn 'Abbas (Shah-i Zinda), 152
    Tila-Kari Madrasa, *250*, 251, *252*
    Ulugh Beg Madrasa, 250
    Zoroastrian Temple, 149

Samarra, 70, 155–56, 161–64, 166, 170, 203, 206, 215–16
    Great Mosque, 155, 433
    Hasan al-Askari Shrine, 203
    Imam Dur Tomb, *160*, 166–68, 170
    Qasr al-'Ashiq, 165
    Qubbat al-Sulaibiyya, *164*, 165–66, 215–17
    Shrine of 'Ali al-Hadi, 203
Sambas Royal Mosque, 420
Sanjar al-Jawali, 201
Sanjar, Tomb of, 234
Sar-i Kucheh Mosque, Muhamadiyya, 152
Sarah, Tomb of, 144
Sarandib, 358
Sasanians, 149–52, 161, 221–23, 228, 260, 285, 360,
    406, 429
Sasaram, 387
Sassanian, see Sasanian
Sauvaget, Jean 151
Saveh, 150
Sawah Lio Mosque, Jakarta, 419–20
Saydnaya, 197
Sayyid Ahmad Khan, 71
Sayyid Ajjal Shams al-Din Omar al-Bukhari, 434
Sayyid Battal Ghazi, 307
Sayyid Mahmud Khayrani, 303
Sayyid Mir 'Abd Allah Yamani, 250
Sayyida Nafisa, 207
Sayyids, 361
Şehzade Mosque, Istanbul 322, 323–24, 325
Selçuk, Isa Bey Mosque, 281–82, *282*
Selim II, 41–42, 307
    Tomb of, *42*
Selimiye Mosque, Edirne, 54, 323, *325*, 326, 329–33,
    331, *334*, 344
Seljuks, 51, 125, 130, 156–58, 223–24, 234, 243, 275, 277,
    279–81, 284–92, 303, 315–23, 325, 329, 332, 336
Selo Mosque, Yogyakarta, 415
Sendang Duwur, Mosque and Tomb Complex, 416–17
Seyitgazi, Shrine of Sayyid Battal Ghazi, 307
Seyyid Hossein Nasr, 57, 59
Shafi'is, 93, 134, 208, 210, 235
Shah 'Abbas, 234, 244, 249, 261–64
Shah Begum, 384, 386
Shah Fazl, Safid Buland, 222
Shah Jahan, 42–44, 234, 393, 398 , 373, 376, 379, 380,
    381, 384, 388
Shah Mosque, Isfahan, *268*, 268–71, *269*, *270*, *271*
Shahdara, 386, 393
Shah-i Zinda, Samarqand 42, *243*
Shah-i Zindeh, see Shah-i Zinda
Shahjahan Mosque, Delhi, *376*, 376, 379
Shahjahan, see Shah Jahan
Shahr-i-Sabz, Aq Saray Palace, 243
Shams al-din al-Fanari, 302–303
Shams al-din, 236
Shams al-Tabrizi, 307
Shamsiyya, Yazd, 236
Shanhuasi, Monastery, 432
Shanxi, Datong Mosque, *438*, 439
Sharaf al-Dawla Muslim ibn Quraysh, 166
Sharaf al-Din 'Ali Yazdi, 243
Sharaf al-Mulk al-Khwarizmi, 162
Sharqiya, Bilad Bani Bu Ali Mosque, 352
Shaybanids, 300, 373, 380
Shaykh Arslan, Shrine of, 209
Shaykh Lutfullah Mosque, Isfahan, *256*, *258*, 261,
    263–71, *264*, *265*, *266*, *267*

Shaykh Safi al-Din Shrine, Ardabil, 63, 66, 237, *260*,
    261, *263*, 300, 308–9, 380
Sheikh Zayed Grand Mosque, Abu Dhabi, *350*, 352
Shengyousi, Quanzhou, 432–433, *433*
Sher Shah Sur, 387
Shia, see Shi'ites
Shib 'Ata, 291
Shibanids, 249–50, 300, 380, 388
Shihab al-Din Umar al-Suhrawardi, 169
Shihab Hakim, 366
Shiis, see Shi'ites
Shikari, 303
Shir Dar Madrasa, Samarqand, *251*
Shir Kabir Tomb and Mosque, Dehistan, 216–18, 220
Shiraz, 43
Shiraz, Tomb of Ali ibn Hamzeh, *43*
Shi'ism, see Shi'ites; Twelver Shi'ism
Shi'ites, 197–200, 203–7, 229, 234, 257–60, 261,
    263, 268
Shrine of
    'Ali al-Hadi, Samarra, 203
    Abd Allah Ansari, Gazur Gah, 246, 247
    Abu Ayyub al-Ansari, Istanbul, 310
    Ahmad al-Badawi, Tanta, 209
    Ali ibn Abi Talib, Najaf, 162, 203, 203–4, 220
    Astana Baba, 152, 219, 220
    Bayazid, Bistam, 237
    Daata Ganj Bakhsh, Lahore, *400*, 406
    Darb-i Imam, Isfahan, 51, *52*, 54, 259
    Haji Bektash, Hacıbektaş, 299, 301, 307–10,
        308, *309*
    Hakim al-Termezi, Termez, 150, 152, 218, *219*, 220
    Harun-i Vilayat, Isfahan, *259*, 258–59, 260–61, 270
    Hasan ibn Ali ibn Abi Talib, Medina, 203
    Husayn ibn Ali ibn Abi Talib, Aleppo, *205*, 206
    Husayn ibn Ali ibn Abi Talib, Cairo, *196*, 197, 202
    Husayn ibn Ali ibn Abi Talib, Damascus, *204*
    Ibn al-'Arabi, Damascus, 209, *298*, 299–303, *300*,
        301, *302*
    Jalal al-Din Rumi, Konya, 299–301, *304*, *305*,
        303–307
    John the Baptist, Damascus, 135
    Khusam Ata, Qarshi, 152
    Muin al-din Chishti, Ajmer, 309
    Prophet David, Marjdabiq, 301
    Qusam ibn 'Abbas (Shah-i Zinda), Samarqand, 152
    Sayyid Battal Ghazi, Seyitgazi, 307
    Shaykh Ahmad, Turbat-i Shaykh Jam, 237
    Shaykh Arslan, Damascus, 209
    Shaykh Safi, Ardabil, 63, 66, 237, *260*, *261*, *263*,
        300, 308–9, 380
    Shaykh Yusuf Abu'l Hajjaj, Luxor, 209
    Umar al-Suhrawardi, Baghdad, *169*, 170, 210
    Zayn al-Din Yusuf, Cairo, *209*
Siddique Mosque, Doha, 352
Siirt, 315
Sikandara, see Sikandra
Sikandra
    Tomb of Akbar, 44, *384*
Silsila Abdullah, 344
Silvan, 315–16, 320, 325
    Great Mosque, 316, 320, 325
Simyon (Simeon) Kalfa, 326
Sinan Pasha, 307
Sinan, 28, 54, 66, 322–26, 329, 331, 342, 344
Sindh, 357–58, 360, 364, 368; see also Amirs of Sindh

Singapore, 409, 420–24
  Darul Aman Mosque, 424
  Haji Muhammad Salleh Mosque, 421
  Khadijah Mosque, *421*
  Maarof Jeddah Street Mosque, 420
  Sultan Mosque, 420, 424
Siraf, 360
  Great Mosque, 149, 151, 154
Siroux, Maxime, 237
Sitt Zubayda, 168
Sivas, 283, 291–92, 315
  Gök Medrese, *291*, 291–2
  Great Mosque, 315
Sivrihisar, 280
Sogdians, 149–50, 155, 217
Sokullu Mehmet Pasha Mosque, Istanbul, 342
Solok Selatan, Muara Labuh Mosque, 421
Solomon, 109–10, 113–14, 119, 175–6, 178, 180, 182, 200–1
Sonderkonsruktionen und Leichtbau, 348
Song Dynasty, 430, 433
Songjiang Mosque, 439, *440*
Sophronius, 176
Soqollu Hasan Pasha, 307
Soqollu Mehmed Pasha, 307
St. George, 144
St. James the Less, 117
St. Sergius, 144
Steffian Bradley Associates, 72
Su Tsang, 447
Sufis, 57, 69, 163, 169–70, 182, 189, 200, 207–10, 227, 231, 237–39, 243, 247, 257, 261–65, 268, 275–76, 287–88, 291–92, 299–310, 332–34, 366, 373, 380, 382, 388, 401–6, 409, 411, 414, 439, 444
Sufism, see Sufis
Sulaiman Mosque, Jeddah, *344*
Sulawesi (southeast), Buton Mosque, 411
Suleyman Bey, 281, 288
Suleyman, 41, 113, 119, 235, 299, 301–2, 305
Suleymaniye Mosque, Istanbul, 27, *28*, *41*, 54, 323–25, *324*, *325*, 329, 332–33
Suli Pasha, 287
Sultan bin Salman, 342
Sultan Hasan Mosque, Cairo, 345, 347
Sultan Mas'ud III, 362
Sultan Mosque, Singapore, 420, 424
Sultan Qaboos Grand Mosque, Muscat, 352
Sultan Saodat complex, Termez, 218, 222
Sultan Saodat, Tomb of, 222
Sultan-Abu Sa'id, 387
Sultan-Nisar, Begum, 384
Sultanahmad Mosque, Istanbul, 324
Sultanate Royal Mosque, Melaka, 414–16
Sultaniyya
  Friday Mosque, 24
  Tomb of Sheikh Buraq, *231*
  Tomb of Uljaytu, 157, 232–35, *232*, *233*
Sumedang, Great Mosque, 420
Sumenep Grand Mosque, Madura, 418
Sunnis, 27, 162–65, 170, 189, 198–200, 203–7, 215, 227, 229, 231, 246, 250, 300, 307, 332, 334, 363, 373, 379, 380–81
Sunnism, see Sunnis
Surabaya, 418, 422
  Ampel Mosque, 412, *416*, 417, 422
  Grand Mosque, 412, 418
Surau Aur, Patani, 414

Surau Syekh Burhanuddin Mosque, Nagari Ulakan, 413–14, 420, 424
Surau, 413, 420
Surau Tok Kerinchi, Kuala Terengganu, *422*
Surkhandariya Province
  Aq Astana Baba, 152, 218–20
  Khoja Roshan, 218
  Tomb of Ataulla Said Vakkos, 219–20
Swat, 360
Sydney, 458, 460, 467
  Gallipoli Mosque, 460–61, *461*, 467, 473
  Lakemba Mosque, 460–61, *461*, 467
  Punchbowl Mosque, *456*, 460–62, 467–71, *468*, *469*, *470*, *471*
Syekh Burhanuddin Mosque, 420, 424

———————

Tabbaa, Yasser, 73, 167
Tabriz, 227, 236, 264, 286, 292, 303, 363
  Blue Mosque, 235, 264
  Ghazaniyya, 235
  Mosque of 'Ali Shah, 227, 227–28
  Rab'-i Rashidi, 235–36
  Sham (Shemb), 235
Tahmasp, 63, 264–65, 380
Taiyuan Mosque, 433, 439
Taj al-Mulk, 157
Taj Mahal, Agra, 35, 36, 43–44, *46*, 68, 234, 367, 376, *382*, *383*, 384, 386, 388–89, 393
Taj Sultana, 369
Taluk Mosque, Agam, 412, 424
Taluk Mosque, Minangkabau, 412, 424
Tambora Mosque, Jakarta, 420
Tanahgrogot, Pasir Royal Mosque, 421
Tancred of Antioch, 182
Tang Dynasty, 429, 439, 447–48
Tangier, 76
Tanjung Keling Mosque, Melaka 422–24
Tankiz al-Nasiri, 201
Tanta, Shrine of Ahmad al-Badawi, 209
Taraz, 150, 219
Tarik Khaneh Mosque, Damghan, 150, *151*, 153, 155
Tashkent, 249, 352, 387
  Tomb of Yunus Khan, 387
Tawhidkhana, Isfahan, *260*, 260–65, *261*
Tayla, Hüsrev, 29–30
Tekelioglu, Nejat, 29
Teluk Manok Mosque, Patani, *413*
Temple Mount, Jerusalem, see Haram al-Sharif, Jerusalem
Temple of
  Artemis, Ephesus, 282
  Bel, Palmyra, *19*
  Karnak, Luxor, 209
  Solomon, Jerusalem, 109–10, 113–14, 116, 176, 178, 200
Templum Domini, Jerusalem, 116–17, 182
Templum Salamonis, Jerusalem, 117
Tengkera Mosque, Melaka, *419*
Tercan, 286
  Tomb and Complex of Mama Khatun, 286–87
Kuala Terengganu, Surau Tok Kerinchi, *422*
Termez, 150, 155, 218, 222, 317
  Chahar Sutun Mosque, 152, 154
  Shrine of Hakim al-Termezi, 150, 152, 218, 219, 220
  Sultan Saodat Complex, 218, 222
Thamanin, 202

Tianjin, 437
Tianjin Mosque, 439
Tila-Kari Madrasa, Samarqand, *250*, *251*, 252
Tilla Halaji Tomb, 216, 218
Tim, Tomb of Arab Ata, 151, 218, *219*, 220–22
Timur, 234, 243–44, 349, 364, 366, 373
Timurids, 42, 49, 65, 224, 237, 239, 243–51, 257–58, 303, 309, 364, 366, 373–74, 384, 386–89
Tomb at Garlandan, 235
Tomb of
  'Ali ibn Sukhari, Dehistan, 217
  'Ali, Najaf, 162, 203–4, 220
  'Abd al-Samad, Natanz, 237–38, *238*
  Abraham, Hebron, 144
  Abu Hanifa, Baghdad, 163, 207, 217
  Afaq Khvaja, Kashgar, 252, *254*
  Ahmad ibn Hanbal, Baghdad, 165
  Akbar, Sikandra, 44, *384*
  Ali ibn Hamzeh, Shiraz, *43*
  Arab Ata, Tim, 151, 218, *219*, 220–22
  Atatürk, Anıtkabir, 29
  Ataulla Said Vakkos, Surkhandariya Province, 219–20
  Babur, Kabul, 42, *43*, 44, 387
  Baybars, Damascus, 129
  Bibi-ka Maqbara, Aurangabad, *382*, 384, 386, 387
  Bonang, Tuban, 417
  Christ, Jerusalem, 113, 176
  Daata Ganj Bakhsh, Okara, *405*, 406
  Faridal-Din 'Attar, Nishapur, 246
  Firuz Shah, Hauz Khas, *363*
  Hakim al-Termezi, Termez, 153, *219*, 220
  Hazrat Dawood Bundi, Okara, 401, *402*, 404
  Humayun, Delhi, *36*, 43–44, *45*, 385
  Hurrem, Istanbul, 303
  Husayn ibn Ali ibn Abi Talib, Karbala, 164, 203, 220, 234, 270
  Hushang Shah Ghuri, Mandu, *366*, 367, *368*
  I'tmad ud-Dawla, Agra, 44, *45*, *46*, 385
  Ibrahim II Adil Shah, Bijapur, *365*, 369
  Imam al-Shafi'i, Cairo, *207*, *208*
  Imam Dur, Samarra, *160*, 166–68, 170
  Isaac, Hebron, 144, 202
  Iskhak Ata, 218–20
  Jacob, Hebron, 144
  Jahangir, Lahore, *384*
  Jalal al-Din Rumi, Konya, 299–301, *304*, *305*, 303–307
  Jesus, Jerusalem, 113, 176
  Kadilangu, Demak, 417
  Khaja Bulkhak, 217–18
  Khaja Mashhad, 216–18, 222
  Khalifa Rajab, Mizdakhan, 218–20
  Kılıç Arslan, Konya, *284*
  Kiz Bibi, Taraz, 216, 218–19
  Leah, Hebron, 144
  Lesser Qiz Qala, 216
  Mama Khatun, Tercan, 286–87
  Mary, Jerusalem, 112
  Melik, Kemah, 283, *285*
  Muhammad ibn Nasser, Safid Buland, 222
  Mumina Khatun, Nakhchevan, 284–85
  Nur al-Din, Damascus, 53, *54*, 287
  Ottoman Princes, Bursa, 303
  Qasim-i Anvar, Langar, 246
  Rabi'a al- Shamiyya, Damascus, 207
  Rabi'a al-'Adawiyya, Basra, 207
  Rebecca, Hebron, 144

Rukn-i Din Rukn-i Alam, Multan, *357, 363, 403*
Safi al-Din Ishaq, Aradabil, 309
Salah al-Din, Damascus, *129*
Salim Chisti, Agra *374*
Sarah, Hebron, 144
Sayyid Mahmud Khayrani, Akşehir, 303
Selim II, Istanbul, 42
Shams al-Tabrizi, Konya, 307
Sheikh Buraq, Sultaniyya, *231*
Shir Kabir, Dehistan, 216–18, 220
Sultan Hasan, Cairo, 228
Sultan Melik, Kemah, *283, 285*
Sultan Sanjar, Merv, 224
Sultan Saodat, Termez, 222
the Patriarchs, Hebron, 144, 201–2
Tughluq Temür, Huocheng, *434*
Uljaytu, Sultaniyya, 157, 232–35, *232, 233*
Ulugh Beg "Kabuli," Ghazni, 387
Yunus Khan, Tashkent, 387
Zumurrud Khatun, Baghdad, 168, *169*
Tomb Tower near Resget, 222, 223
Tongxin Mosque, 441
Topkapı Palace, Istanbul, 27, 49, 66
Topkapı Scroll, 49, 51–52
Toqay Timurids, see Janids
Tughluq Temür, Tomb of, *434*
Tughluqs, 361–64, 366, 368
Tuman Agha, 243
Tuman Agha Madrasa, Kuhsan, 247
Turan Malik, 286, 289–90
Turbat al-Za'faran, Cairo, 205
Turbat-i Shaykh Jam, 237
Shrine of Shaykh Ahmad, 237
Turfan, 254
Amin Mosque, *254*
Turushkadanda, 359
Twelver Shi'ia, see Twelver Shi'ism
Twelver Shi'ism, 204, 257–58, 268

'Ubaydallah Khan, 250
Üç Şerefeli Mosque, Edirne, *320, 325*
Udegram, 360
Mosque, *360*
Uljaytu, 157, 228–35, 363
Tomb of, 157, 232–35, *232, 233*
Ulu Cami, see Great Mosque
Uluengin, Fatin, 29
Ulugh Beg, 249
Ulugh Beg "Kabuli," Tomb of, 387
Ulugh Beg Madrasa, Samarqand, *250*
Umar, see 'Umar ibn al-Khattab
'Umar ibn al-Khattab, 103, 135, 176–77, 180
Umar Suhrawardi Tomb, Baghdad, *169*, 170, 210

Umayyads, 13, 15, 20, 25–26, 63, 90, 92, 103, 109–19, 125–33, 139, 142–43, 145, 149, 178–80, 182–83, 189, 191, 193, 198, 201–2, 204–5, 217, 307, 347, 358
Umm al-Awlad, Babil Governate, *166, 167*
Umm al-Rasas, Church of St. Stephen, *139*
Unicorns, 452
Uqbah ibn Nafi, 105
Urfa, 140, 315
Üsküdar, 323
Mihrimah Mosque, 323, *325*
Selimiye Mosque, 326
Uthman ibn Affan, 91, 102–3, 347
Uyghurs, 443
Uzgend, 222
Three Tombs, 222

Varakhsha, Palace of the Bukhar Khodahs, 155
Veramin, Friday Mosque, 227
Victoria and Albert Museum, London, 70, 202, 209, 237
Vienna, 299
Vijayanagara, 368, 369
Viollet-le-Duc, Eugène, 57
Virgin Mary, see Mary

Wadi Hanifah, Darriyah Mosque, 350
Walsham, Alexandra, 68
Wangyuelou, 437
Wapauwe Mosque, 412, 420
Washington D.C.
Freer and Sackler Galleries, 70
Washington Mosque, 71
Washington Mosque, Washington D.C., 71
Watampone, Great Mosque, 420
Wazir Khan, 376
White Pagoda of Miaoying Monastery, Beijing, 431

Xi'an Mosque, see Xi'an, Great Mosque
Xi'an, 447
Drum Tower, 448
Great Mosque, 433–34, *435*, 439, *446*, 447–52, *447, 448, 449, 450, 451, 452*
Huajuexiangsi, *435*
Xianhe Mosque, Yangzhou, 433
Xuanhua North Mosque, 439

Yakubşah bin Sultanşah, see Hayreddin
Yalangtush Bahadur, 251
Yangzhou, 429
Xianhe Mosque, 433

Yaqt, 198
Yaqat al-Hamawi, 162
Yaqut, 198, 200,
Yateem Mosque, Manama, 348
Yavuz Selim Mosque, Istanbul, 325
Yazd-i Khvast, 149, 151
Yazd, 236–37, 239, 246
Great Mosque, 236, *236–37*
Rukniyya, 236
Shamsiyya, 236
Yazdgerd III, 149
Yazid, 204
Yazid ibn Muawiya, 310
Yeni Valide Mosque, Istanbul, 41, *42*, 324, 326
Yeşil Mosque, Bursa, 319, *332, 333*
Yeşil Mosque, Iznik, 325
Yıldırım Mosque, Bursa, 319
Yıldız Mosque, Istanbul, 326
Yogyakarta Grand Mosque, Pawestren, 412, 417–18
Yogyakarta, Selo Mosque, 415
Yongning, Na Family Mosque, 439–41, *440*
Yuan Dynasty, 433–34, 437, 439, 441, 443
Yunus Khan, 387
Yusuf Abu'l Hajjaj, Shrine of, 209

Zacharias, see Zechariah
Zahmatabad, 154
Zal Mahmud Pasha Mosque, Istanbul, 323
Zamzam Well, Mecca, 87–89, 92, 94
Zangids, 191
Zavareh, 151–52, 158
Mosque, 152
Zayed bin Sultan Al-Nahyan, 352
Zayn al-'Abidin, 135
Zayn al-Din al-Mastari, 237
Zayn al-Din Yusuf, Shrine of, *209*
Zayton, see Quanzhou
Zechariah, 18, 176, 182
Zeynep Sultan Mosque, Istanbul, 326
Zheng He, 434
Zheng, Haji Mohammad Shamsuddin, 448
Zhengzhou, Great North Mosque, 439
Zhu Yuan Zhang, 448
Zhuxian Mosque, 433, 439
Ziyarids, 222–23, 285
Zoroastrian Temple, Samarqand, 149
Zoroastrians, 149, 216–18, 227, 358, 406, 429–30
Zumurrud Khatun, 168
Tomb of, Baghdad, 168, *169*